SECOND EDITION

the Modern Guide to Golf Clubmaking

The Principles and Techniques of Building Golf Clubs From Component Parts

BY
Tom W. Wishon

WITH TECHNICAL ASSISTANCE PROVIDED BY
Jeff Summitt

PHOTOGRAPHY BY   ART & DESIGN
Greg A. Brown   **Kirk E. Homrighouse**
Bob Andersen

PUBLISHED BY
DYNACRAFT GOLF PRODUCTS, INC.
71 Maholm Street
Newark, Ohio USA 43055

Published by:
Dynacraft Golf Products, Inc.
71 Maholm Street
Newark, Ohio USA 43055
1-800-321-4833

Manufactured in the United States of America

Printed by ProGraphics, Inc.
Columbus, Ohio

Distributed by Dynacraft Golf Products, Inc.

ISBN - 0-9619413-3-2

ACKNOWLEDGMENTS

Dynacraft Golf Products, Inc. was founded in 1981 by Joseph Altomonte Sr. for the purpose of bringing the great business of golf clubmaking to the shops of golfers everywhere. When I joined Dynacraft in 1986, the custom clubmaking industry was meager in comparison to its standing today. What began as a cottage industry with a handful of suppliers and clubmakers back in the late 1970s and early '80s has boomed into a viable force in the golf industry that supplies millions of golfers with the equipment they need. So significant is this growth that custom clubmakers now utilize an estimated 20% of all the shafts and grips produced today!

As the world's largest supplier of golf clubheads for custom clubmaking, Dynacraft and Joe Sr., as he is known, have given me a tremendous opportunity to try out many of my ideas and concepts of club design. This is a freedom that I could not have had with any other company and for which I am very thankful. My thanks to Mr. Chinneng Lin, Miss Peggy Chia and Mr. Paul Liu and the staff of Dynamic Precision Casting Company, as well as the staffs of several other production foundries, for their help in allowing these club design ideas and concepts to "come to life." I also would like to thank Mr. Bob Kuntz of Dayton, Ohio, who I truly believe is the most knowledgeable man in the entire field of golf history. His assistance in research and his warm friendship are both priceless. In addition, I would like to thank each of the golf industry component suppliers for their assistance in providing information about their products for this book, and for recognizing the growing importance of the craft of custom clubmaking within the golf industry.

In the First Edition of *The Modern Guide to Golf Clubmaking*, I used this space to thank all of my friends and co-workers at Dynacraft for their input and support in the production of this book. That was four years ago, however, when our staff was much smaller. At the risk of leaving someone's name out, let me just say "Thank you" to everyone who has worked so hard to make Dynacraft what it is today. I firmly believe clubmaking would not be where it is today without your efforts!

This book is dedicated to two very special people, my wife, Mary-Ellen, and my son, Kyle. I thank them for their love, support and patience, not just in this project but in my life as well.

I also want to thank my parents, Winston and Jan Wishon, for instilling in me the enthusiasm to never stop trying to learn, and for signing me up for a series of indoor lessons back in the winter of '61.

In addition, my sincere thanks and respect continue to go to Mr. Joseph Altomonte Sr. for giving me the opportunity and freedom to discover what a great pleasure it really is to work in this greatest of all games!

The Second Edition of *The Modern Guide to Golf Clubmaking* is the fourth book in a series dealing with the assembly and technical understanding of modern golf equipment. Preceded by the First Edition of *The Modern Guide to Golf Clubmaking* and two editions of *The Graphite Shaft Addendum*, this Second Edition of the *Modern Guide* serves as the most up-to-date reference manual on clubmaking available today - at least until we publish the Third Edition!

TABLE OF CONTENTS

Continued on next page

A NOTE TO CLUBMAKERS

In today's era of high technology, keeping tabs on the latest trends in any field is a difficult pursuit. What is "in" one day may be "out" the next. What qualified as a technological breakthrough a year ago may be viewed as a dinosaur today. Think about it. Remember 20 years ago when we all marveled at the abilities of a small handheld calculator? Or when we scoffed at the idea that someday almost everyone would utilize computers at home, at school or in the office? Change, like death and taxes, certainly *is* inevitable - as we have seen in no uncertain terms over the last few decades.

As you are probably all too well aware, the golf industry has been no stranger to the influx of high technology. Some 15 years ago, to the horror of many traditionalists, the metal wood was introduced. Since then we have seen aluminum, graphite, ceramics, compression-molded and injection-molded plastics and a host of other materials utilized in the design and manufacture of clubheads, grips and shafts with varying degrees of success. To the golfing public, these new designs represent an attractive alternative as they seek the model (or models) that will help them manage a seemingly unmanageable game. To the clubmaker, however, the new era represents more in the form of both a challenge and an opportunity - a challenge to keep abreast of the latest technological advances that seem to pop up nearly every day, and an opportunity to learn about the innovations and become recognized in your community as an "expert" on the latest equipment trends.

Over the last several years, it is the component "clubmakers" that have taken the lead to become the true experts on golf equipment "in the field." Traditionally, golf professionals have been regarded as the best source for information about golf equipment, but except for a small percentage who have strived to stay abreast of the tremendous changes in golf equipment, their expertise has dwindled through the years with an increase in responsibility regarding the day-to-day operation of the golf course. While some PGA pros do practice the craft of clubmaking and do it well, the reality of the 1990s is that most pros prefer to simply buy pre-assembled clubs from major assembled club manu-facturers and suffer with the low margins that now accompany those sets. Another potential source for equipment information is the off-course golf store, but again profit looms as the driving force at many of these establishments. Given the option of selling a set of irons perfectly matched to a player's game at $250 or pushing a set that is poorly made but carries a higher profit margin, the volume off-course store will invariably choose the latter. Thus, for true information about golf equip-ment, custom fitting and game improvement technology, today's clubmakers stand as the golfer's best source. Like you, most club builders have gotten involved in the craft because of their fascination with golf equipment. Certainly there is substantial profit to be earned if a clubmaker does his work well, but your first commitment has to be to quality and the thrill of making sure that a player is fit with a set of clubs that are perfectly suited to his needs. In today's golf market, you will find clubs that are cheaper than yours, and clubs that carry more recognized "brand" names than those you stock; therefore, your goal must be to guarantee that no clubs are built better or backed by better service.

To use the title "clubmaker" today means much more than simply having the ability to epoxy a wood or ironhead, a shaft and a grip together. "Clubmaking" means having the ability to assemble golf clubs to standard lengths, lofts and lies, as well as non-standard measures. Clubmaking means being able to perform alterations to assembled clubs so they "feel right" to the player. Clubmaking means having the ability to know which type of clubhead, shaft or grip is best suited to player's game, and furthermore, being able to explain why to the golfer. Clubmaking means having the capability to take all of the confusing marketing terminology used today and simplify it so the customer knows what he needs. That said, it is obvious that being a clubmaker today means doing your homework. Keeping tabs on all the latest technical information about various components and recognizing which are best suited for the players who frequent your shop. Learning all you can about the "hot" models being used on Tour and explaining why such a component will or won't work for your customers.

There is no doubt that today's clubmakers are a viable force in the golf industry. In 1990, True Temper Corp. and Eaton Golf Pride, the two largest manufacturers of shafts and grips respectively, reported that nearly 20% of their products were sold through component supply companies to custom clubmakers like yourself! Component manufacturers are quickly recognizing the market share custom clubmaking has gained and are actively seeking your business. Never has the opportunity for you to enjoy and succeed at custom clubmaking been better - but that opportunity comes with a price. You must dedicate yourself to learning all you can about the components you use and make absolutely certain that you assemble those components in the manner which they were designed. You've already taken a step in that direction by purchasing the Second Edition of this book.

My purpose in revising *The Modern Guide to Golf Clubmaking* was not only to provide the most up-to-date, step-by-step procedures for professionally assembling golf clubs, but to offer the most thorough look at the technical side of golf equipment as well (which is why you will find more than 120 pages dedicated to shafts alone). I have attempted to organize the book to allow you to read from start to finish or to jump from section to section and still improve your clubmaking ability. Even though many of the club assembly procedures feature identical steps, I have taken the time and space to show these procedures in each section. Where necessary within the step-by-step assembly sequences, I have interjected notations to allow you to refer to more extensive coverage of the procedure else-where in the book.

Whether your dedication to the craft of clubmaking is on a part-time or full-time basis, I challenge you to adopt a commitment to become the best clubmaker you can be. Poor workmanship and misinfor-mation have no place in clubmaking and are a detriment to you, your customers, fellow clubmakers and the game of golf itself. There is an old adage in clubmaking that I would like to offer: *Good work, like cream, rises to the top.* Learn, practice and strive always to improve your skills and knowledge and you will earn the well-deserved respect of golfers in your area as a "clubmaker."

Tom W. Wishon

CHAPTER 1 - The Evolution of Clubmaking

A History of Clubmaking
The Development of Golf Clubmaking Companies
The Technical Revolution in Golf Equipment
The Modern Resurgence of Clubmaking

The Early Beginnings

One of the most interesting facts about this great game we all enjoy is that no one is really sure just when golf originated. Only through painstaking research have students of golf have been able to piece together bits of information gleaned from medieval town records that recount brief references of a number of games that in one way or another may be related to golf.

Historians have found that in ancient times the Romans played a game called *paganica* which involved striking a leather covered ball around open fields. Yet another early stick and ball game which closely resembled golf was *Pall Mall* or *Jeu de Mail*, which was originally played in Italy and later adopted by the French and the English.

Steven J. H. van Hengel, the late Dutch historian of golf, from research conducted for his book, *Early Golf,* unearthed documents that trace the playing of a game called *colf* on Boxing Day, December 26, in the year 1297. Along with the written reference to the game of colf, van Hengel also found a map of North Holland depicting the

"course" with its four "holes" measuring some 4,500 meters!

As a rule and quite curiously so, each of the various games that are awarded some credit as being among the first versions of golf did *not* involve striking a ball toward a target hole in the ground. While not fully substantiated,

credit for this addition to the game has been given to the Scots, with best estimations of this alteration occurring in the mid-1400s.

Yet regardless of whether it were the Dutch, the Romans, the Italians, French, English or the Scots who were responsible for creating the game of golf, the fact remains that clubs and balls were required for participation. While it is thought that Roman *paganica* players often used just common sticks or even shepherd's crooks as their "clubs," each of the ensuing games that resembled golf called for a striking implement specially fashioned by skilled individuals for the purpose of playing the game.

As a result, golf clubmaking has to be considered as old as the game itself. Ian Henderson and David Stirk, in their 1981 historical treatise, *Golf in the Making,* stated that the first written account of golf clubmaking could be traced to a record of purchase of golf clubs for King James IV of Scotland in the year 1502.

In their research the British authors found that many of the early clubmakers were, in fact, bowmakers. The writers felt that since the earliest records of clubmaking date back to the same approximate era that gunpowder and firearms displaced the bow and arrow as the weapon of choice, it was the bowmakers who first likely diversified into golf clubmaking — probably out of vocational necessity! Because of that, golf clubmaking in the 16th century was somewhat fragmented, and may have been best classified as a "sideline" business for the individuals who plied the craft.

As golf evolved and more and more people began to participate in the game, the role of full-time clubmakers soon became established. Henderson and Stirk found references to individuals in the early 1600s who were appointed as official clubmakers to members of the royal family, and their research also showed that a number of full-time clubmakers became established throughout the latter half of the 17th century in the Scottish towns near Edinburgh such as Leith, Musselburgh and St. Andrews, where the game enjoyed exceptional popularity.

Part of the reason precise details of the earliest (16th and 17th century) clubmakers are sketchy at best is that none of the clubs they built remain in existence today. However, thanks to the efforts of golf historians and international members of the Golf Collectors Society, a significant number of the old clubs of the late18th and early 19th centuries have been recovered. The oldest set of golf clubs in existence today date to the late 1600s, a set accidentally discovered behind a wall during the rennovation of an old Scottish house. This set has since been preserved and is now on display in the clubhouse of the Royal Troon G.C. affording us a glimpse of early clubmaking design and workmanship. As these and other antique clubs are retrieved, there comes a clearer picture of not only who the first full-time professional clubmakers were, but how their clubs and skills changed and evolved over the years.

To some, the names Cossack, Philp, Forgan, McEwan, Morris, Dunn, Park and Patrick are recognizable as a few

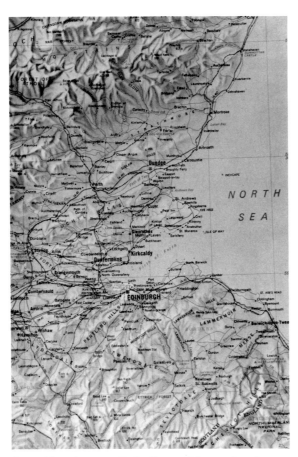

Some historians credit the Scots with creating the "modern" game of golf.

of the "fathers of clubmaking." While part of the reason this "title" may be ordained is due to the tremendous prices the few existing examples of their work may command at auction today, their real contribution to clubmaking can be seen in the clubs they made and the professional nature of the businesses they established. For it was from the clubmaking shops of these and others of their time that the business of clubmaking truly began to flourish.

Prior to the late 1700s, most clubmakers operated as one-man or small family businesses, deriving their income from producing clubs to individual order and depending strictly upon "word-of-mouth" advertising to perpetuate their craft. But in the hands of these men and their families, clubmaking began to become more business oriented. Apprenticeships were granted to train young men in the art of making golf clubs, and several of the firms grew quite large, often employing as many as 50 workers. Local golf clubs and membership societies granted contracts for clubmaking services and competition was keen among the clubmakers, especially for the coveted title of Royal Clubmaker to the King. Possession of the Royal Crest (which certainly can be thought of as the first "staff promotional contract!") often carried with it an instant guarantee of success for the firm, and once awarded, the crest was displayed prominently by the company on their shop premises.

As the family clubmaking firms expanded, so did the paths of distribution of the clubs they produced. At first, clubmakers supplied only the residents of their respective towns, but in the late 1800s some of the firms began to branch out and deliver orders for clubs to other communities. Eventually, some of the more enterprising early clubmakers began to actually set up what could best be classified as "retail outlets" for their clubs, and began to place advertising in the local newspapers to solicit business.

Because many early clubmaking firms were headed and staffed by golf professionals, many new designs and models began to appear. The clubmaking professionals of the time would utilize their playing ability and golfing imagination to come up with new ideas for clubs in an attempt to develop better equipment and establish superiority over the other practitioners of the trade. In fact, so creative were some of their designs that many of the clubmaking innovations of the1800s have been "reintroduced" by modern club manufacturers in the second half of the 20th century! As an example of this practice of reintroduction, the Stan Thompson Company's runner sole Ginty wood, thought by most upon its introduction in the 1970s to be a completely new design, in fact owes its origin to a runner sole wood called the Tom Ball Altus Spoon…made in the late 1890s!

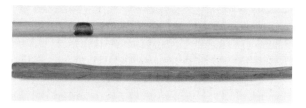

Early Clubmaking Materials

The clubmakers of the early days of golf in Britain were entirely self-sufficient, producing each of the individual components needed to make golf clubs. Since a network of suppliers did not exist, clubmakers became very skilled in being able to shape all of the parts of a club from raw materials. From their research for *Golf in the Making*, Henderson and Stirk found written reference to shaftmaking as early as 1687, from an entry in the diary of one Thomas Kincaid of Edinburgh that noted hazelwood was used by clubmakers to produce shafts. Another common hardwood used for producing early wood shafts was ash. Readily available in England and Scotland, ash had been used for centuries for making drawbows. In addition, some clubmakers used lemonwood and lancewood for shaftmaking, but while able to resist warping better than ash, these hardwoods were higher in density and tended to result in shafts that were much stiffer and heavier than what was considered standard at the time.

In the mid-1800s America began to export hickory to Britain for use as handles for axes and other various hand tools. Hickory was not native to England and Scotland, and when clubmakers experimented with the wood, they found that the strength and flexibility characteristics of hickory were better suited for making shafts than hazel or ash. So superior were the new shafts that by 1860, hickory had been adopted by clubmakers as their primary shaft making material. In forming the shafts, clubmakers soon found that splitting the hickory from the logs prior to the hand shaving process produced shafts of higher quality and durability than those made from sawn blanks. Sawing the blanks out of the logs tended to cut across grain layers, making the shafts much

more susceptible to warping in wet weather.

The British clubmakers' demand for hickory shafts increased heavily over the late 1800s and it was not long before the exporting American firms began to switch from simply shipping the logs and pre-cut billets to taking over the entire process of manufacture of the finished shafts. Splitting and sawing were both used to produce hickory blanks, but the tedious hand process of shaft shaping was performed on lathes. In the process, one worker on a lathe could produce hundreds more shafts in a week than what could be done by hand. This was a significant step in the evolution of clubmaking for it not only took the time consuming step of actual shaft making out of the hands of the clubmakers, but it established an important domestic supply source for America's later entry into the golf club manufacturing industry.

Clubhead Materials, Woods

The predominant set makeup in the 17th, 18th and early 19th centuries consisted almost entirely of wooden-headed clubs. The hand stitched "featherie" was the predominant ball of the time, but was fragile and tended to break apart when struck by a heavy headed iron club.

As a result, very few irons were produced and early clubmakers developed and practiced the skills of woodmaking only. The technique of producing duplicated heads through the use of a copying lathe did not come about until the late 1800s, so clubmakers had to cut their own hardwoods and make each individual head by hand. Hand shaping the curve of the hosel into the head and still achieving adequate strength in the neck was a very difficult procedure. If not performed with great care this hand operation would result in a head that would break or crack after a few rounds of use. Therefore, to develop heads with consistent strength in the hosel, clubmakers of the 17th and 18th century began to intentionally plant thorncuts on sides of sloping banks. The thorncuts would take root on the slope, first growing horizontally out of the bank. Then the thorncuts would grow vertically, and in the process of growth create the necessary curve between what was to be the hosel and the head. This practice yielded heads with stronger natural grain in the hosel which could stand up to the stress of play. Other hardwoods used by the early clubmakers for making their woodheads were apple and pear, which also produced heads that performed adequately when used with the feather golf ball.

When balls made from gutta percha displaced "the featherie" in the middle 1800s, new clubhead materials had to be found. The "gutty" was more durable and performed better than the feather ball, but it was much harder and had a tendency to chip and crack clubheads made from thorn, apple or pear. As a result, clubmakers began using beech, a wood that was in plentiful supply in Britain. Beech became popular for clubmaking because it was less brittle than previously used woodhead materials and possessed a natural resilience that could better withstand the stress of impact with the harder gutta percha ball. Even after the change to beech, tedious hand-making techniques were still used by clubmakers through most of the 1800s to make their woodheads. However, in the latter part of the century, the increased demand for more clubs led a few progressive clubmakers to bypass much of the hand labor and rely on a machine called a copying lathe to rough shape their heads. The copy lathe was invented by an American from Massachusetts named Thomas Blanchard and variations of his original machine were already being used in Britain to produce duplicated wood parts such as gun stocks and furniture parts. Many protests were issued by clubmakers who felt that hand making was the only way to produce a quality golf club, and as a result a wholesale conversion on behalf of all clubmakers to use the copy lathe for mass producing rough shaped woodheads did not occur. This disdain for progressive change among many British clubmakers is important to note, for this decision not to upgrade methods of manufacture was destined to have a negative effect on the future of clubmaking in Britain.

The Advent of Ironheaded Clubs

As mentioned earlier, because of the adverse effect they had on the leather covered feather ball, very few iron-headed golf clubs were produced by clubmakers. The life expectancy of the featherie was short enough as it was, and just one blow from an iron could easily burst a feather ball. Therefore, the few iron-headed clubs that were produced were used only in special situations when a wooden head club would not fit the need. Small headed "rut irons" were carried by some golfers to extricate a ball from a wagon wheel track, and a number of other assorted irons existed for general play when there was a question on a particular shot whether the wooden head would be damaged if used.

Because working with metal was not one of the skills possessed by early clubmakers, early ironheads were hand forged by local blacksmiths and then dispatched to the clubmaker for assembly with the shaft and grip. Because the term "clubmaker" applied to the craftsman who produced only woods, the ironhead makers became a separate entity known as *cleekmakers*. Because of the low demand for iron clubs, early cleekmakers still derived most of their income from their regular blacksmithing tasks. However, when the gutta percha ball replaced the featherie, irons began to gain in popularity. Unlike the

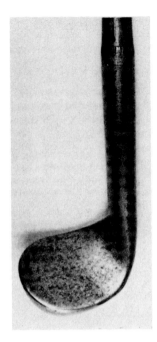

featherie, the harder guttie ball could easily withstand the force of impact with an ironhead. After this change, cleekmakers recognized the opportunity for increasing their trade and soon began to take over the entire process of making and shafting the irons. Full time cleekmaking shops opened and golfers soon became used to frequenting both the clubmaker's and the cleekmaker's establishments to acquire their full set of clubs.

Making an ironhead was a very labor intensive and time consuming task. Each head was painstakingly hand-made from a flat bar of steel which after heating, was first hammered around a tapered mandrel to form the circular hosel. Great care was taken to form the round hosel so that no outer seam line was visible when completed. Then through successive steps of heating and then hammering on huge anvils, the shape of the blade along with its lie and loft angles were established. After the hand-forging process, a great amount of filing was then necessary to produce the head's final shape. The cleekmaker then completed his job by punching rivet holes and hammering nicks on the top rim of the hosel. When the

iron shaft was made, one end was formed to a taper to fit into the hosel. During assembly, the shaft was driven into the hosel so that the nicking marks would lock the head to the shaft. After the rivet was installed, the installation was complete and the shaft would remain fixed to the head.

In the late 1800s some clubmakers began to expand to include cleekmaking along with their woodmaking business. While crude grinding wheels began to replace hand filing for the final shaping procedures, the hand hammering, punching and stamping operations remained the same. This type of expansion on behalf of the clubmakers to include iron making was rare because of the capital expense involved, so most production of woods and irons in the 19th century was separated between the clubmakers and the cleekmakers.

Origin of the Grip

In the very early days of clubmaking, golf clubs were not made with a grip. Since shafts were all hand made, 17th century clubmakers would simply shape the butt end of the shaft larger in diameter to accommodate a golfer's hands. However, because the game was often played under wet conditions, and because of the uncomfortable vibration felt in the hands from the shock of impact, clubmakers began the practice of wrapping strips of leather and sheepskin on the end of the shaft to solve the problems. The first grips were very large in diameter, which coincided with the accepted instructional technique of the time to grip the club more in the palms than in the fingers. To produce larger diameter grips, strips of wool or linen were wrapped under the leather or sheepskin grip. The wool strips often came from the ends of bolts of wool, called the rind of the fabric, while the linen strips became known as "listings." Because these strips were used under the leather, the term underlisting was adopted and is still used today to refer to the foundation of leather grips. Apprentice clubmakers often started their training as leather grip makers for the shop, and hours were spent first cutting the leather and then hand-skiving (thinning the edges) the edges with a knife or chisel.

Through the era of the gutta percha golf ball, grips remained large to help absorb what was an even more harsh vibration that was felt from impact with this very hard ball. However, with the introduction at the beginning of the 20th century of the more resilient rubber core ball, vibration was no longer considered a problem and grip sizes began to decrease. This required thinner underlistings and as shaft making turned from wood to steel in the 1920s, paper replaced fabric for the purpose of creating the foundation for leather grips. In addition, the introduction of steel shafts meant that clubmakers now had to cover the end of the hollow tube, so tapered end plugs made of wood were created to fill this requirement.

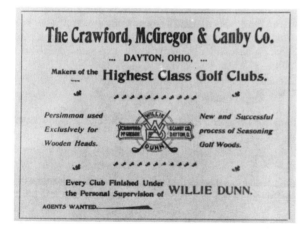

Clubmaking Moves Abroad

At the same time that clubmaking in Britain was progressing by leaps and bounds, America was just beginning to discover the game of golf. Commercial travel across the Atlantic Ocean was becoming more commonplace, and some American businessmen traveling abroad had the opportunity to become introduced to the game. Upon their return to the States, the newfound interest they had acquired in golf coupled with the previous golfing experience of British emmigres introduced golf to America. What started in New York with "The Apple Tree Gang" in 1888 soon began to boom and by 1900 there were an estimated 1,000 golf courses in the United States! Along with increased participation came a growing demand for instruction and equipment, so the first American clubmakers were actually English and Scottish professionals who had chosen to move abroad to take advantage of the new boom in U.S. golf.

Literally within just a few years after golf took root, full-scale golf club manufacturing began in earnest in America, and with it came the demise of the British as the leaders in clubmaking. As mentioned, American companies had already been supplying all of the hickory shafts to British clubmakers for several decades. With such an important domestic supply in place, the transition into manufacturing in America was quite natural. The A.G. Spalding and Brothers Company was founded in 1876 and was a large sporting goods manufacturing company with modern mass-production machinery already in place in their factory. In 1892, due to the efforts of one of Spalding's officers, the company began importing a very small number of golf clubs from Britain for distribution to golfers in America.

Finally, seeing that the game indeed had a future in the States, Spalding first began producing golf clubs in 1894. Key to their entry into the clubmaking business was their ability to incorporate existing modern industrial methods into producing clubheads. With the shoe making industry heavily represented in the New England area, copy lathes were already in use for the manufacture of wooden shoe lasts. Therefore, Spalding was able to incorporate copy lathes in their facility for rough turning woodheads. In addition, Spalding is credited with being the first manufacturer to use large, drop forging hammers for the purpose of mass-producing raw iron heads. Instead of

hand hammering each ironhead over an anvil, these huge machines could literally pound out a raw forging from heated steel billets in a matter of seconds. Utilizing this technique, which was not yet being used in Britain, Spalding soon began to export great numbers of ironheads and later, sell thousands of completed golf clubs abroad, thus establishing a great degree of control over the total British golf club industry. With this advance in the field of club manufacture, Spalding soon positioned itself as one of the largest manufacturers of golf clubs in the world.

Equally important was the contribution of the other major American manufacturing concern that made an early entry into the clubmaking business, the Crawford McGregor & Canby Company of Dayton, Ohio. Although different versions of the story are in existence, its introduction of an all-new woodhead material further contributed to establishing American control of golf clubmaking. In a story that certainly must go down in the annals of golf, one day company head W.H. Crawford cracked the head of one of his woods and turned to his firm to correct the situation. Crawford's company was a large and well established manufacturer of wooden shoe lasts, and was large enough to control their own raw material supply through ownership of forests and saw-mills. Not wanting to wait for a replacement head to be shipped from Scotland, Crawford prevailed on company engineer George Mattern to fashion a replacement. At the time, the company used a hardwood called persimmon to make their smaller size shoe lasts. Noting that the size of the cracked woodhead roughly corresponded to the size of the persimmon blocks used in the factory, Mattern chose this type of wood to produce his employer's new woodhead. Persimmon was even tougher than the beech being used in existing clubheads, and in Mattern's opinion would make a superior head for overcoming the stress of impact between clubhead and ball.

Since copying lathes were already in use in the factory for mass producing shoe lasts, Crawford saw that an opportunity existed to export woodheads to Britain. The year 1896 brought with it a depression in the shoe last business, and after listening to advice from Cincinnati C.C. professional Robert White, Crawford ordered a division of his company to begin production of the new persimmon rough turned heads. In that first year of the new venture, Crawford, McGregor and Canby "turned" and exported over 28,000 heads abroad to British club-makers. Realizing that they were able to acquire hickory shafts from local sources, Crawford, McGregor and Canby soon began to manufacture completed golf clubs, and by 1900, the firm was exporting over 100,000 completed clubs per year to Britain. In a very short period of time through the efforts of Spalding and McGregor (later the company changed the spelling to MacGregor), America had become entrenched as the world's supplier of golf equipment and clubmaking supplies.

The Development of the Clubmaking Companies

With the introduction of mass-production machinery and factory manufacturing techniques, the face of club-making began to change rapidly. However, one other major factor was beginning to take place at the turn of the century that also contributed to the rise of large clubmaking factories. The rate at which golf was gaining followers in America was absolutely astounding and the only way new golfers' demands for equipment could be filled was through large factory participation in the clubmaking industry. Just 12 years after the game was introduced, America had 1,000 golf courses. By 1910, there were 1,400 golf courses, and by 1931 the number of golf facilities had swelled to nearly 5,000! Unbelievably, between 1910 and 1930 the number of American golfers literally exploded, growing from 350,000 to 2,000,000! Golf was *the* sport of the day and there was just no way

the clubmaking industry's pre-1900 way of conducting business could survive in the face of such increases. The early American manufacturers' risky decision to enter clubmaking without a domestic market was paying off. With American golf becoming well established, the focus of sales soon switched away from export to concentrate more heavily on domestic needs. In the early 1900s, several more American companies entered the clubmaking buisness to take advantage of the opportunity afforded by the boom in golf. In 1910 in Newark, Ohio, the Burke Golf Shaft Company decided to expand its production and began to produce complete golf clubs to complement its already existing hickory shaft making venture. The Thomas E. Wilson Company of Chicago, through an existing sporting goods manufacturing divi-

sion, expanded into clubmaking in 1914, and in 1916, The Hillerich and Bradsby Company branched out from the baseball bat business to go into clubmaking. Because many club professionals in America had developed club repair and assembly skills from their British roots, each of the American clubmaking companies continued to sell clubheads and component parts in addition to their fully-manufactured clubs. With so many supply sources manufacturing and selling finished component parts, the professionals no longer needed to practice their full clubmaking skills, but could still "custom assemble" golf clubs made from component parts for their golfing members. Thus, the foundation for the practice of today's custom clubmakers to custom build golf clubs from component parts was established many years ago.

Golf's Technical Revolution

When golfers today sit down to read one of the many available golfing publications, they are immediately confronted with a barrage of information in the form of articles and advertisements that seemingly require the background of an engineer for full understanding. Technology is in full bloom in the golf industry today, and most current clubmaking firms are relying on technical data in one form or another to offer proof of the quality of their equipment to the public. But this approach to golf clubs and their manufacture is not new to our age, only the *degree* to which it has been carried. Debates concerning the technical merits of golf clubs have raged on for as long as clubmaking has been in existence. The main difference is that in the days of early clubmaking, no accurate testing methods of proving or disproving technical claims were in existence. Therefore, golfers relied on the opinions of the golf professionals, clubmakers and better players to determine if one type of design was superior to another. With possible financial gain hanging in the balance, often these professional opinions were less than accurate. Therefore, with no way of proving the validity of one claim or another, a great deal of misinformation persisted concerning the technical excellence of golf clubs and their component parts.

Golf's earliest "technical" debates occurred as a result of the different raw materials that were used to produce shafts and clubheads. From old golf books and magazines we can tell that whenever a clubmaker made a switch to another type of hardwood, there was a fair amount of speculation issued on behalf of other clubmakers doubting the quality of the new materials. Some of the dissenting opinions were no doubt pure speculation, but in other cases real changes could be recorded in the performance of the clubs. For example, clubmakers and players who made and used shafts from lancewood soon found that while the wood had a tendency to resist warping (a problem with ash) it resulted in shafts that were much heavier and stiffer than what was acceptable. Such observations can be considered empirical in nature and do offer proof that clubmakers did have rudimentary standards and means of making some comparative measurements to those norms.

Another of the clubmaking industry's true technical debates came about when machine-oriented techniques for producing clubheads and shafts began to replace hand-shaping methods. Some traditionalists offered the opinion that rough turning woodheads on a copy lathe produced a poor club when compared to hand making the head from a block of wood. So fierce were their feelings and their effect on the golfing consumers of the day, that many clubmakers who had changed to the machine-oriented methods were compelled to refute the dissenting claims through advertising. Because no scientific method for judging the quality of either production method existed, golfers could only rely on heresay evidence, with the weightier points being established by those players and clubmakers with greater reputations.

Perhaps the greatest clubmaking controversy of the early 20th century concerned the golf industry's switch from hickory to steel shafts. Hickory shaft suppliers and the clubmakers who were faithful to the wooden shafts seized on the poor quality of the first metal shafts to convince golfers that steel shafts were not only deficient to wood in performance, but were bad for the game itself. So furious did the controversy rage that many English and Scottish golf clubs and organizations actually banned the use of steel shafts out of fear that they would provide an unfair edge to golfers who used them in competition. American clubmaking companies, more concerned with improving the quality of equipment than preserving the traditional nature of the game, moved much faster than their British counterparts to accept the shafts, but it was still years before their use was fully accepted. In fact, to aid their campaign for acceptance, steel shaftmaking firms and the clubmaking companies that had decided to convert, used the theme in their advertising statements that the new steel shafts could deliver *the same feel as hickory*. The controversy started with a little known patent for a steel shaft design in 1894 did not end until 1931, when Billy Burke won the U.S. Open and became the last player to win a major championship using hickory shafts.

As with any manufacturing oriented field, the technical advances of component parts and clubmaking techniques are what has been responsible for the constant improvement of the quality of golf clubs. The list of technical achievements in clubmaking is almost endless. When the hard gutta percha ball replaced the featherie, iron clubs came into more predominant use and woodhead materials had to be changed. When machinery entered the clubmaking shop, more clubs could be produced and done so at lower prices; therefore, more golfers could in turn gain access to the game. As drop forging replaced hand forging of ironheads, more precise shapes and designs could be produced, thus improving playability characteristics of irons. To combat the wear on the faces and bottom of woods from constant impact with the ground during use, metal soleplates were introduced.

After steel shafts had replaced hickory, golfers no longer had to worry about shaft durability, inconsistency or poor shot results due to excess torsion. Step tapering of shafts allowed more precise playability differences from shaft-to-shaft, and when cold drawing as a method of tube forming was perfected, shaft consistency was even further established. As mentioned, a list of technical achievements in golf clubmaking could go on and on. However, if such a list were studied, it would become apparent that achievements in manufacturing techniques were established by technical engineering analysis, while many of the advancements concerning the playability or design of clubheads and components were either accidental or the result of trial and error. For example, the move to using copy lathes for rough turning woodheads was an example of a change borne out of engineering analysis. Clubmakers with a machine tool background were already aware of the copy lathe being used in non-golf related businesses and made their decision to switch purely from a production and numbers basis. On the other hand, the addition of a soleplate was first done to prevent wear and tear on the bottom of the head. Entirely by accident, the clubhead's performance was improved due to the fact that the center of gravity of the head was lowered in the process. The effect such a change could have on shot performance was not understood by club-makers or golfers for years after the alteration; all they knew at the time was that for some reason, the "Brassies" (as they were first popularly known) could produce more successful shots from slightly questionable lie conditions than clubs without metal on the sole.

Through the middle of the 1900s clubmaking companies gradually began to become more aware of their ability to make technical design changes on the different parts of golf clubs that would definitely improve shot performance. As these realizations began to take place, the clubmakers then attempted to pass on the explanations to golfing consumers through advertising. While the intent of the advertising was shifted to make golfers more technically aware, consumers still tended to make their choices based on what the great players of the time used, rather than through any thought of just how a technical change could make a difference for *their* game. As a result, a golfer would choose a design that was identical to that used by a professional, unaware that the design characteristics of that club were often not well suited to his/her game.

Technical Revolution Moves into High Gear

During World War II, most of America's golf club manufacturing facilities were converted into war material production plants. Whether it was gas masks, airplane parts or shovels, the golf clubmakers all did their part to contribute to the Allies' victory. After the war, when life returned to normal and people began to participate more in recreational activities, the golf clubmaking companies went back to the business of making clubs. However, what was left as a legacy of frenzied war-time production were some all-new methods of manufacturing. America's victory in the war had been in no small part due to the tremendous breakthroughs in machinery and production practices that had allowed factories to produce needed items more quickly and efficiently than ever before. As a result, after the war every manufacturing-oriented business benefited from an infusion of new engineering technologies. Relying on heavy machinery for producing many of its parts, the clubmaking industry began to put this technology to work to develop new and bigger machinery to make better golf clubs even faster. Giant milling machines that could produce more intricate shapes into the back of irons were developed, allowing club designers the ability to "re-distribute" weight on the back of the head. The techniques of the automatic drilling machines that had accurately bored thousands of gun barrels were adopted into new machinery for drilling iron hosels, and some of the concepts of rubber molding that kept tires on our troop transports were refocused into new processes for making all new rubber grips.

As golf moved into its next great boom period, "The Palmer Era," the technology of the industry was well established but the technological awareness of the golfing public was not. Golfers still selected clubs on the basis of what the current stars of the day used and not with regard for what might be best suited to them. Then, in what could arguably be termed the most significant clubmaking breakthrough in the history of golf, the public began to achieve an awareness of equipment technology that began to force golf club manufacturers to offer more scientifically-proven game improvement designs.

That breakthrough was the advent of investment casting as a method of producing wood and iron clubheads. In the early 1960s a limited number of putter heads were investment cast, but it was not until ironheads began to be produced by the process that the real benefit of this space-age method of production was realized. Through the age-old process of forging ironheads, designers were limited in their ability to distribute weight about the ironhead's surfaces. The cost and time involved to machine recesses or cavities on the back of an ironhead were too great, and as a result, all of the forged irons produced by manufacturers were just variations of previously seen designs.

However, with investment casting, foundries could supply manufacturers with an entirely new array of design shapes. Deep back cavities were now possible and the look of an ironhead was only limited by the imagination of the designers. With the ability to now move the mass virtually anywhere on the head, club makers began to learn what the effect of changing weight distribution and clubhead center of gravity could have on the playability of the club. The terms *perimeter weighting* and *center of gravity* became household words for golfers and brought to the clubhead a degree of "forgiveness" never before seen in golf equipment. By moving the mass or weight *around* the perimeter of the head, golfers soon found that better shot results would occur from a shot hit off the center of the face. And in lowering the head's center of gravity (or sweet spot as it used to be called) much more success could be achieved in consistently striking the hard-to-hit, less-lofted long irons. Additionally, investment casting radically changed woodhead manufacture when metal woods were introduced in the 1970s. While woodheads made from aluminum had been offered as early as the 1890s, aluminum afforded no real design

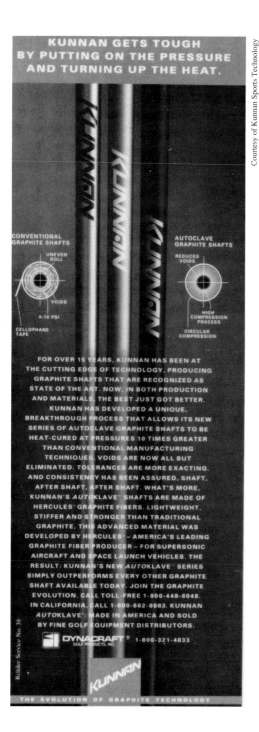

benefits over wood other than durability. Casting the new generation metal woods from stainless steel had the similar iron design effect of creating perimeter weighting and lower center of gravity, features which made the new woods easier to hit than any club previously conceived. Golf club manufacturers began to refer to these corrective clubhead designs as *game improvement* models and it wasn't long before the public accepted the fact that the same clubs used by professionals were not necessarily the best for them. Thus for the first time in clubmaking history the public began to recognize what technological advances could do for them. Seeing that scientifically explained differences in design could result in clubs that were easier to hit, golfers began to demand new golf club models with proven game improvement benefits matched to their needs.

In addition to the advancements allowed in design, investment casting also brought with it a shift in the way the golf industry conducted business. When forged irons and wooden woods were the only available clubhead designs, companies wishing to begin making clubs had to absorb a tremendous investment in machinery to turn the raw forgings and wood blocks into finished heads. But with the advent of investment casting, new golf clubmaking companies sprung up almost overnight. A small group of foundries took on the task of supplying totally finished iron and metal woodheads, and new clubmaking companies had only to equip themselves for the procedures of assembly. This had the result of shifting the golf club manufacturers' primary focus from production to marketing and sales distribution, and competition between the older and new-line companies increased heavily. With technological improvements in golf club design now on the minds of golfers, the long established manufacturers found they could no longer simply rely on their past reputations for success, and were forced to change to the modern techniques to keep up.

The Modern Clubmaking Resurgence

Just as the modernization of manufacturing techniques

brought protests from experienced clubmakers in the 1800s, so did the move to investment casting in the '70s. Cries were heard from the traditionalists that forged clubs "felt" better than cast clubs, and many players were less than pleased with the sound at impact with metal woods. Perhaps in response to the latest step forward in manufacturing technology, a move on behalf of golfers to seek out older golf clubs and completely restore them with modern shafts and grips began to gain popularity. Tournament professionals were often seen in competition with complete sets of fully restored 20-year old golf clubs, refitted with components and built to specifications that were tailor-made to their abilties. Interested golfers attending tournaments quickly began to notice and before long the "classic club" phenomenon was born. Because skill was required to refit older clubs with new parts, the "classic club" movement brought about the need for a new type of clubmaker, one well-schooled in the skills of restoration and golf club repair with a technical knowledge of club fitting. In the 1970s, club repair and classic club restoration became very popular, though not as a full-time venture, but as a serious part-time hobby. Because the cost of the necessary tools and machinery was very low and the work was enjoyable and satisfying, many golfers became interested in part-time repair. A few repair tool and supply companies opened to meet the needs of the new repairmen and in an effort to build their own businesses, spread the movement into garages and basements all over the country. So great was the interest in working on golf clubs that by the early 1980s, almost every town of 10,000 population or more could boast several club repair shops.

As the repairmen practiced their restoration skills, some of the component supply companies began to realize the potential for distributing clubhead designs for custom club building. After all, the same skills that were used to repair clubs could also assemble golf clubs, providing the small shops could gain access to clubheads. With an array of different shaft and grip types now available to them, the repair shops began to offer custom made and fitted golf clubs to individuals. As repairmen soon learned that custom club assembly required less work and could bring more profit than straight repair work, the business of assembling golf clubs from components began to grow.

The new breed of modern clubmakers quickly began to gain a place in the golf club industry because a number of other factors were also playing a part. In 1965, the retail price of a professional line set of irons was $200. By 1975, the price for a set of irons averaged $300, by 1980 it was $400. In 1982 $500 bought the same irons, and in 1984 the price went to $600! In addition, golfers were becoming more aware of what custom-made golf clubs could do for their games. With their primary focus being large-scale production of standard specification clubs, the major manufacturers of golf clubs were not in a position to quickly fill the requests for specially-altered sets. With most companies, three to four months was the average time required to fill an order for custom clubs and anxious golfers were not willing to wait that long. With the market demand for reasonably-priced, custom-made golf clubs beginning to grow, small-scale custom club assembly shops found themselves in the position of being the only clubmakers able to meet these increasing requests.

Major manufacturing companies at first ignored the efforts of this army of small club assemblers, playing on their established reputations to exercise their market superiority in clubmaking. However, as the quality and selection of available component clubheads increased, so too did the amount of business the collective group of custom club builders were beginning to acquire. In addition, many of the new club assemblers were building a storehouse of technical knowledge about the various components and transmitting that information on to their customers. This education of the consumer on behalf of the club builder began to gain more credibility and respect for the small club assembler to the point that by 1986, it was estimated that over 25% of the sales of golf clubs in the US came from custom club assemblers!

Is the custom assembly market here to stay? No one can predict the future with any degree of certainty, but if we

L.A. Kelly Photography

can use the teachings of the past to learn for the future, one major point stands out. Most of the successful clubmakers of any era have been individuals or companies who were able to offer up-to-date, playable designs that are built to the highest quality standards, priced in accordance with their position in the industry and delivered to customers on time. Whether it is an individual or a major manufacturer is of little significance. If the points that brought success to Philp and McEwan in the 1800s, or fame to MacGregor and Ping in the 1900s, are followed by clubmakers in the future, success will be theirs'.

CHAPTER 2 - Getting Started in Clubmaking

The Required Tools and Machinery for Clubmaking
The Necessary Supplies and Small Parts for Clubmaking
The Major Components of Clubmaking
Setting Up the Clubmaking Shop
The Industry of Clubmaking

What You Need to Know to Get Started

"**W**ithout a doubt the fastest growing segment of the golf equipment industry involves the custom building of golf clubs from component clubheads, shafts and grips," is a statement that is even more true today than when it was made in the first edition of *The Modern Guide to Golf Clubmaking*.

During the 1980s the game of golf experienced its greatest period of growth, with the number of golfers climbing from 11 million in 1980 to just over 25 million in 1990. At the same time, the golf equipment industry also achieved tremendous growth in the 1980s, not simply in the number of companies and their sales, but in the technology of the equipment they produce. Metal woods came and dominated, graphite shafts experienced a fantastic rebirth, exotic metals and space-age composites found their way into clubheads, and 21st century designs became the norm.

Along with the advent of high tech in design also came high prices for the high tech equipment - $1,500 sets of irons, $400 drivers and $150 putters all made their debut,

pushed into the hands of golfers by multi-million dollar advertising and marketing campaigns. Every company seemingly had the latest and greatest design, all promising to deliver greater distance, pinpoint accuracy and solid feel.

Confused by the vast selection in equipment, golfers searched for answers to their questions about the new age of club design. But they weren't the only ones confused by the rising wave of high tech - so too were the golf professionals. Once the premier source for equipment information, golf professionals saddled with responsibilities of running their shops and golf courses just didn't have the time to study and absorb all the information required to answer the equipment questions of golfers.

Rising out of the confusion with the ability to translate equipment high-tech into understandable answers has come the component clubmaker. Whether operating a cottage business or a full-scale factory, the rising number of individuals who have become clubmakers have just begun to come to the forefront in equipment knowledge.

Having the time, the energy and the devotion to equipment, clubmakers have now established a strong niche within the golf equipment industry. When the reasons for this success are analyzed, it is becoming evident that the position of the clubmaker will likely rise to an even greater level in the near future.

Entering the field of clubmaking affords golfers the opportunity to try many types of equipment for themselves, to begin a satisfying and enjoyable hobby, or to even change careers by becoming a full-time golf club builder. With the availability of a wide variety of clubhead models, a tremendous assortment of shaft patterns and grip types, plus the tools and supplies necessary for assembly, clubmakers now have the opportunity to experiment, play with, and fit themselves and their customers with virtually any conceivable type of **professional quality** golf club - and do so all for a very economical price.

Perhaps the greatest aspect of becoming a clubmaker lies in the fact that you can select the level of involvement you

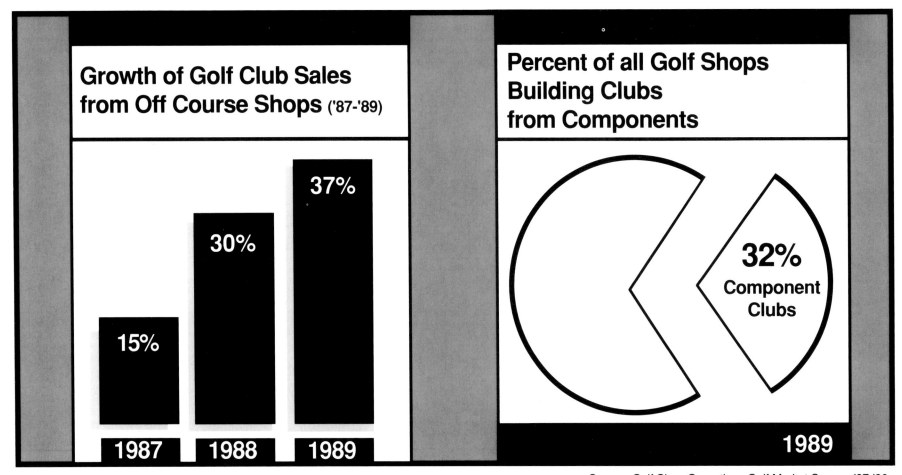

Growth of Golf Club Sales from Off Course Shops ('87-'89)

37%

30%

15%

1987   1988   1989

Percent of all Golf Shops Building Clubs from Components

32% Component Clubs

1989

Source: Golf Shop Operations Golf Market Survey '87-'90

want. There are very few vocations that offer what clubmaking can - relatively low start-up costs, the ability to work from your home or a commercial shop as you choose, to be able to operate with or without advertising and promotional expenditures, to be able to offer professionally made equipment for a better price than the traditional outlets, make a fair profit from your investment, and be able to work in a field that you really like, dealing with people who share your love for golf.

Underneath all of these positive aspects of clubmaking though, is one very serious point. While the game golf is a recreational activity, make no mistake that the business of golf is in fact, a business. All of the major manufacturers of golf equipment take their business very seriously, so if you are already a clubmaker or are just beginning to take the steps to become one, then regardless of what level of involvement you pursue, you must take the work seriously too.

Four years ago it was estimated that some 15% of total golf club unit sales came from component clubmakers. While the field of assembling golf clubs from component parts is still relatively new, it has continued to grow dramatically to the point that custom builders now account for an estimated 20% - 25% of total golf club unit sales.

Unofficial figures released by the two largest manufacturers of grip and shafts show that over 25% of their total units are redistributed to clubmakers by component supply companies. With such figures, proof exists that club builders **are** seriously involved in the business and thus, are in active competition with each of the major golf club manufacturers.

Because of that, custom golf club assemblers must make a commitment to produce golf clubs that are built to only the highest standards of clubmaking. From choosing the highest quality component parts to developing and using the most professional equipment knowledge and skills, today's new breed of clubmakers must take their work seriously. If you enter the field of clubmaking without these all-important skills, you will be doing an injustice to yourself, your customers, the industry and the game.

This obligation to high quality clubmaking begins by first setting up, stocking and equipping your shop with the necessary tools and supplies to properly handle all of the clubmaking tasks you will face. To effectively plan your operation you will need to acquire the right tools and machinery, an inventory of supplies and components, and set up a work shop that is well thought out and efficient in its layout.

Purchasing the Necessary Products for Clubmaking

In setting up and stocking a shop for clubmaking, small parts and components such as clubheads, shafts and grips will need to be purchased on an ongoing reorder type basis. As you enter the field of clubmaking you will gradually gain the knowledge of each of the items that are required and with it, an awareness of the sources for each of the products.

In the golf equipment industry, there are currently some 50 manufacturers of clubheads, 25 shaft producers and 10 makers of grips. However, these companies are full scale manufacturing firms that are not set up to distribute their products in the small quantities that clubmakers will buy. These clubhead, shaft and grip factories are set up to cater to major manufacturers and distributors who are able to purchase the components they produce in very large quantities. As a result, the clubmakers who buy in small quantities rely on some 50 component supply companies in the country who not only stock clubheads, shafts and grips, but who may offer the necessary small parts, tools and even machinery used for making golf clubs.

At first glance, it might seem with the component supplier set up as a middle man, clubmakers will pay substantially more for the products than if they were able to deal direct with the actual manufacturer. In most cases

this is not true due to the lower price the distributors pay the manufacturers in return for very large order commitments. For example, to be able to do business direct with one of the reputable clubhead investment casting foundries, a clubmaker or golf company would have to be able to order a minimum of 200 sets at a time, be able to place the order 4 - 9 months in advance of delivery and pay for the goods 30 days before they are received. For all but a few clubmakers, such minimum quantities and lead times are just not compatible with the type of business the clubmaker will conduct. However, should you become very successful in clubmaking, should you be able to satisfy the requirements of the head, shaft and

grip makers, by all means it would be wise to structure your advance planning to do business direct.

In dealing with the various component supply companies, you will find a vast array of company types from very large to very small, with services and products to match. As with any golf company, the quality of the clubheads being offered will be directly proportional to the knowledge of the company's technical staff and the expertise of the head manufacturer with whom they are contracting their business. While you as a clubmaker will not likely ever know the experience of the original head manufacturer, you can evaluate the abilities of the component supplier to provide quality clubheads. By teaching yourself how to accurately measure clubhead specifications you can police the quality of any supplier's heads, and thus assure your customers of receiving only the best in the golf clubs you build.

For shaft and grip purchases, you will not have to teach yourself the skills of measuring specifications to make buying decisions. Because shafts and grips are branded by the original manufacturer, each of the component companies will be offering the same popular models and styles. For example, the Black and Green Golf Pride Victory grip from one supplier will be the same as it is from any other supplier. As a result, clubmakers should price shafts and grips from one supplier to the next and buy at the best price. A word of caution - because of the range in size of component supply firms, many times the one with the lowest price will not always have the item you need in stock. In addition, not all companies are able to ship in-stock orders in the same amount of time. Therefore, a grip that cost $.10 less but took two weeks to arrive might not result in worthwhile savings to the clubmaker.

Because the field of clubmaking does involve fitting golfers to a vast array of technically made components, you are bound to have numerous questions about the products you buy. What shaft is the best for this type of golfer? How do I trim this shaft? What is the difference between this specification on this head and that specification on the other head? Get into clubmaking and the questions about the technology of golf equipment just seem to flow. Because you need answers to your technical questions, some of the component supply companies are set up with technical service departments staffed by knowledgable clubmakers or technicians to answer your questions while some are not.

Fortunately the manner in which most of the component suppliers conduct business has made the task of keeping a clubmaking shop well stocked a simple proposition. Because the golf club component supply companies are set up to do business by catalog mail order, your order may be placed by telephone or by mail. With some

companies, the efficiency is great enough that your orders can be handled and shipped within 24-48 hours. With others, one week may be the norm. To increase your efficiency, get in the habit of placing your orders by telephone and if possible, use your VISA, Master Card or Discovery card as the method of payment. By using a credit card to pay for orders, the company is able to ship your order immediately and you in essence, will receive an open account type of payment terms, since your bill will not be due to the charge card company for 30 days. Providing you use the credit card wisely and pay the balance each month, you will not be paying excess interest on the goods you buy. The result will be both you and your supplier will have achieved what you both want from the transaction.

However, while some component suppliers are able to ship orders within 48 hours, you must realize that each of these suppliers are occasionally subjected to factors outside their control that affect how fast or how complete your orders are sent. Since there are so many different items a component supplier is expected to stock and since the component supply business is subject to varying seasonal demands, your suppliers cannot be expected to constantly be able to keep every supply item in stock at the same time. Suppliers are dependent upon the actual component part manufacturer for delivery as well as the market's demand for particular items. Therefore, some delays in delivery often cannot be anticipated. As a result, you will occasionally encounter back orders for products that you have requested. When you receive a back order for an item, it means that the supply company does not have that item in stock at the time of your order, but that it has been noted and will be shipped as soon as their inventory has been replenished.

The busy season for the component suppliers runs from February through August. During this time of the year, try to anticipate your needs slightly more in advance to avoid any delay in receiving the parts you need to finish a job. Because back orders in the golf club assembly business are a fact of life that club assemblers occasionally will have to deal with, here are a few tips to help keep those out-of-stock notices at a minimum:

* Try to anticipate your supply needs 1-2 weeks in advance. Never allow yourself to get into the habit of ordering after you run out of an item. In the case of small, inexpensive parts that are used in every club-making job, such as ferrules, epoxy or grip tape, keep at least a 1-2 month supply on-hand at all times.

* Shop around between your suppliers. Often if one is out-of-stock another may be in-stock with the same item at the time of your request.

* Be sure to keep track of your orders and any back ordered items. Too many times clubmakers are guilty of keeping poor business records and lose track of what should have been shipped or what may be outstanding on order.

* Note the market demands for particular items before the supplies become critical. If one type of clubhead design, shaft or grip is becoming very popular, either with your customers or with the entire country in general, act before that demand increases, and increase your inventory level accordingly.

* Don't hesitate to order comparable types of an item when available. For example, many of the steel shaft makers produce the same shaft patterns, marketed under their own product name. Learn the comparable products and be prepared with adequate technical information to present to your customers to explain the alternative.

* Large clubmaking shops should get in the habit of analyzing their upcoming year's needs in the fall of the previous year. If you have had a problem with keeping items in stock during most of one playing season, look at your needs and carefully increase your supply orders for next year in the fall. Autumn brings a reduced demand upon the suppliers and a careful analysis on your part may allow you to lift your inventory at a time when it is easier to secure items.

Tool & Machinery Requirements

The cost of equipping a clubmaking workshop with the tools and machinery necessary to assemble golf clubs is relatively low. Depending upon the level of involvement you choose, the workshop can be equipped with just a small array of hand tools and gauges or set up with everything from power tools to sophisticated machinery. While any decision about shop equipment must be based on the amount of work you are going to perform, even beginning or part-time club builders must realize that there has to be a minimum commitment to properly equip the shop before you build the first club. Later, as the business grows and the need for different types of tools and machinery is discovered, the income generated by your clubmaking can be used to pay for equipment upgrades.

To begin your tool and machinery purchases, list the services in clubmaking you plan to offer. Then set an initial dollar amount you are comfortable with spending for equipping your shop. Use the catalogs from the various clubmaking supply companies to make a list of the tools you need to perform each of the clubmaking services you wish to offer. Upon completion of the list of tools, add up the total cost. If this figure is less than your proposed tool and machinery investment, take time to go over the list once more to make sure you have not forgotten anything you'll need. If the total is still less than your initial tool investment figure, then think about adding a time-saving piece of power machinery or a specialized club fitting gauge or machine.

On the other hand, if the total cost of your preliminary list of tools is greater than your anticipated investment figure, take a moment to see if you have underestimated what it takes to begin assembling golf clubs. As a clubmaker, you have a commitment to perform high quality work and that will require the proper tools to do the job. To assist the set up of the workshop and plan your clubmaking investment, on the following pages are offered three different tool and machinery lists.

If you are interested in getting started in clubmaking to be able to assemble golf clubs from fully finished components only, with no capability to perform small repairs or custom alterations, Tool and Machinery List #I will equip your shop with everything you need. Purchased from a component supply company, these items represent the minimum complement of tools required to assemble golf clubs.

TOOL and MACHINERY LIST - Option I
Assembling Golf Clubs Using Finished Components Only

Qty	Item / *Use*	Qty	Item / *Use*
1	**Bench Vise** / *Holding clubs*	1 set	**Metric Hex Head Screw Wrenches** / *Removing weight port screws*
1	**Shaft Vise Clamp** / *Securing club in vise*	1	**Ball Peen Hammer** / *Miscellaneous*
1	**Swingweight Scale**[1] / *Weight measurement*	1	**Awl or Sharpened 3/32" Pin Punch**[2] / *Backscrew installation*
1	**48" Ruler (Wood or Metal)** / *Measuring club, shaft lengths*	1	**3/8" Variable Speed, Reversable Drill** / *Changing bore size and installing backscrews*
1	**48" Ram Rod** / *Swingweighting*	1 ea.	**Assorted Drill Bits** / **(R letter bit and 3/8", 11/32", 1/8" bits)**[2] / *Changing Bore Size and Installing Backscrews*
1	**Shaft Tubing Cutter** / *Cutting steel shafts*	1	**General Purpose Knife** / *Miscellaneous*
6	**Shaft Cutter Wheels** / *(They wear out fast!!)*		
1	**Hacksaw and Metal Cutting Blade** / *Cutting graphite shafts*		
1 set	**Standard Size Hex Head Screw Wrenches** / *Removing weight port screws*		

[1] Swingweight scales can be purchased for as little as $45 or as much as $1,200. For a professional quality scale, plan on a cost of @ $125. Be sure you purchase a swingweight scale that has a 14" fulcrum and can measure swingweight as well as total weight.

[2] Extras of these tool items will be handy to keep around your shop as they can break or wear out quickly.

Tool List Option I should be considered the minimum investment to equip the workshop and will carry a total approximate cost of $175 to $200. With the tools mentioned, you will be able to fully assemble any type of metal wood, wooden wood, graphite wood, iron or putter pre-finished clubheads. Should you decide that you would like to equip your shop to be able to fully assemble golf clubs using both finished and unfinished component heads, as well as perform a number of custom alterations for personalized fitting purposes, the items listed in Tool List - Option II should be acquired.

TOOL and MACHINERY LIST - Option II
Assembling Golf Clubs Using Finished and Unfinished Component Heads

First compile the Option I tools as listed below

The additional tools and machinery required is as follows:

Qty	Item *Use*
1	**Bench Vise** *Holding clubs*
1	**Shaft Vise Clamp** *Securing club in vise*
1	**Swingweight Scale**[1] *Weight measurement*
1	**48" Ruler (Wood or Metal)** *Measuring club, shaft lengths*
1	**48" Ram Rod** *Swingweighting*
1	**Shaft Tubing Cutter** *Cutting steel shafts*
6	**Shaft Cutter Wheels** *(They wear out fast!!)*
1	**Hacksaw and Metal Cutting Blade** *Cutting graphite shafts*
1 set	**Standard Size Hex Head Screw Wrenches** *Removing weight port screws*
1 set	**Metric Hex Head Screw Wrenches** *Removing weight port screws*
1	**Ball Peen Hammer** *Miscellaneous*
1	**Awl or Sharpened 3/32" Pin Punch**[2] *Backscrew installation*
1	**1/8" Pin Punch**[2] *Backscrew installation*
1	**3/8" Variable Speed, Reversable Drill** *Changing bore size and installing backscrews*
1 ea.	**Assorted Drill Bits** **(R letter bit and 3/8", 11/32", 1/8" bits)**[2] *Changing bore size and installing backscrews*
1	**General Purpose Knife** *Miscellaneous*

Qty	Item *Use*
1	**Reed & Prince Screwdriver** *Insert, soleplate screws*
1	**Phillips Screwdriver** *Insert, soleplate screws*
1 set	**Woodhead Vise Pads** *Holding woodheads*
1 set	**Brass or Aluminum Vise Pads** *Holding ironheads, putters*
1 pr	**Safety Glasses** *Eye protection*
1	**Propane Torch** *Melting lead, shaft and soleplate removal*
1 ea	**Assorted Drill Bits (O, P, Q, 5/16")**[2] *Changing bore size*
1	**Face Radius Gauge (8,10,12,14 type)**[3] *Custom fitting loft*
1	**Grip and Shaft Butt Gauge** *Custom fitting grips*
1	**Machinist's Protractor** *Custom fitting loft*
1	**Shaft Bending Block** *Custom fitting face angle*
1	**Medium Cut File** *Ferrules, custom fitting*
1	**Fine Cut File** *Ferrules, custom fitting*
1	**File Cleaner** *Cleaning files*
1	**Scriber** *Screw removal*
1	**Screw Heater** *Screw removal*

[1] Swingweight scales can be purchased for as little as $45 or as much as $1,200. For a professional quality scale, plan on a cost of @ $125. Be sure you purchase a swingweight scale that has a 14" fulcrum and can measure swingweight as well as total weight.

[2] Extras of these tool items will be handy to keep around your shop as they can break or wear out quickly.

[3] While face radius gauges are available for every dimension from 7" up to 22", the 8", 10", 12", 14" gauge is the one used most often.

Including the fundamental items from Tool Option List I, equipping your shop with the items comprising Option II will require a total investment of approximately $250 to $275. There is one main difference in the clubmaking services you can offer when you equip your shop with the Option II tool inventory. With custom fitting an important part of clubmaking in the 1990s, you will be able to perform additional customizing services such as altering loft, bulge, roll, face angle and under-the-plate swingweight changes to wooden and graphite woodheads.

If your desire is to participate in golf club assembly on a limited or part-time basis, the tool inventory outlined in Options I and II will equip your shop properly. However, if your goal is to offer a full clubmaking service, or even build a full-time clubmaking business, then the following Option III list of clubmaking tools and machinery will be necessary.

TOOL and MACHINERY LIST - Option III
For Complete Mechanized Clubmaking Including Custom Fitting Alterations

First compile the tools as listed in Options I and II

Qty	Item / *Use*	Qty	Item / *Use*	Qty	Item / *Use*
1	**Bench Vise** *Holding clubs*	1	**Phillips Screwdriver** *Insert, soleplate screws*	1	**Bench Grinder, 1/2 HP/3,450 RPM** *Shaft cutting, miscellaneous*
1	**Shaft Vise Clamp** *Securing club in vise*	1 set	**Woodhead Vise Pads** *Holding woodheads*	1	**Shaft Cut-off Wheel for Grinder** *Shaft cutting*
1	**Swingweight Scale**[1] *Weight Measurement*	1 set	**Brass or Aluminum Vise Pads** *Holding ironheads, putters*	1	**Loft and Lie Machine**[5] *Loft/lie changes on irons*
1	**48" Ruler (Wood or Metal)** *Measuring club, shaft lengths*	1 pr	**Safety Glasses** *Eye protection*	1	**Golf Club Specs Measuring Gauge**[6] *Checking specifications of heads*
1	**48" Ram Rod** *Swingweighting*	1	**Propane Torch** *Melting lead, shaft and soleplate removal*	1	**Gram Weight Scale** *Checking headweights*
1	**Shaft Tubing Cutter** *Cutting steel shafts*	1 ea	**Assorted Drill Bits (O, P, Q, 5/16")**[2] *Changing bore size*	1	**Drill Press, 1/2 - 3/4 HP, Multi-Speed**[7] *Changing bore size on irons & metal woods*
6	**Shaft Cutter Wheels** *(They wear out fast!!)*	1	**Face Radius Gauge (8,10,12,14 type)**[3] *Custom fitting loft*		
1	**Hacksaw and Grit Edge Blade** *Cutting graphite shafts*	1	**Grip & Shaft Butt Gauge** *Custom fitting grips*		
1 set	**Standard Size Hex Head Screw Wrenches** *Removing weight port screws*	1	**Machinist's Protractor** *Custom fitting loft*		
1 set	**Metric Hex Head Screw Wrenches** *Removing weight port screws*	1	**Shaft Bending Block** *Custom fitting face angle*		
1	**Ball Peen Hammer** *Miscellaneous*	1	**Medium Cut File** *Ferrules, custom fitting*		
1	**Awl or Sharpened 3/32" Pin Punch**[2] *Backscrew installation*	1	**Fine Cut File** *Ferrules, custom fitting*		
1	**1/8" Pin Punch**[2] *Backscrew installation*	1	**File Cleaner** *Cleaning files*		
1	**3/8" Variable Speed, Reversible Drill** *Changing bore size and installing backscrews*	1	**Scriber** *Screw removal*		
1 ea.	**Assorted Drill Bits (R letter bit and 3/8", 11/32", 1/8" bits)**[2] *Changing bore size and installing backscrews*	1	**Screw Heater** *Screw removal*		
1	**General Purpose Knife** *Miscellaneous*		**The additional tools and machines required are as follows:**		
1	**Reed & Prince Screwdriver** *Insert, soleplate screws*	1	**Belt Sanding Machine; 1" x 42"**[4] *Ferrule dressing, shaft tip preparation, resurfacing soleplates, etc.*		

[1] Swingweight scales can be purchased for as little as $45 or as much as $1,200. For a professional quality scale, plan on a cost of @ $125. Be sure you purchase a swingweight scale that has a 14" Fulcrum and can measure swingweight as well as total weight.

[2] Extras of these tool items will be handy to keep around your shop as they can break or wear out quickly.

[3] While face radius gauges are available for every dimension from 7" up to 22", the 8", 10", 12", 14" gauge is the one used most often.

[4] It will be handy to make or purchase a fixture to attach to the belt sander for holding clubs while turing ferrules.

[5] An assortment of types are available ranging in price from $200 to $4,000.

[6] A limited selection of specification measuring gauges are available. A good gauge should be able to assist your measurement of face angle (woods), loft, lie, face progression, hosel offset, and sole angle (irons).

[7] May not be necessary if you choose to assemble clubs only from parallel bore head models.

Equipping your workshop with the total complement of tool and machinery items from List III will require an investment of approximately $1,500. Since this represents a substantial increase over the cost of tool Lists I and II, you must seriously evaluate your commitment to determine if such an expenditure is in line with your goals. Investing in the extra machinery outlined in the Option III tool list will enable you to speed up your procedures of clubmaking and complete more work in the process. In addition such an investment will open up your clubmaking offerings to include every conceivable type of custom clubfitting option.

Most clubmakers who currently own a fully equipped workshop have followed the course of starting with the complement of tools and machines outlined in List II. Then as the profits from small volume clubmaking begin to come in, they have chosen to add on the additional machinery pieces.

To Finish Or Not Finish Wooden Heads
The tool and machinery lists that have been offered in this chapter are all set up with one common point in mind - that any wooden woodheads the clubmaker assembles into finished clubs will arrive at the clubmaker's workshop in pre-finished form. Some 10-15 years ago, when wooden woods controlled the woodhead market no clubmaker would set up a workshop without investing in the machinery required to apply a factory quality finish to woodheads. Today, with metal woods accounting for 75% of the wood market, many successful custom clubmakers not only have not included woodhead finishing as part of their shop services, but have never chosen to learn the procedures of applying a quality woodhead finish!

Despite the fact metal woods comprise such a large portion of the total woodhead market, laminated maple and persimmon woodheads do still have loyal followers among the 25 million golfers in the U.S. Therefore, depending on the particular market area, adding on the machinery required to finish woodheads may be a good business decision for the shop. By setting up to finish

wooden heads, clubmakers will have the ability to offer their customers a choice of finish colors to suit their tastes. And, if performing full custom fitting is a major commitment, clubmakers will find it far easier to perform loft or roll/bulge changes on an unfinished woodhead than on a pre-finished head.

To be able to apply a factory quality finish to component woodheads that are purchased in unfinished or what is called pro-sanded form, some of the small tools that were included in Tool List II and III, such as files, scriber, belt sander, vise, vise clamp, vise pads and face gauges will also be used for finish application procedures. To equip the shop for finishing, the following additional tools and machinery will be required. To additionally equip the workshop with this finish equipment will call for an additional investment of approximately $150 to $500 depending upon the type of sanding machine that is selected.

ADDITIONAL EQUIPMENT REQUIRED FOR FINISH APPLICATION	
Qty	Item *Use*
1	**Motorized Woodhead Sanding Machine**[1] *Final sanding woodheads*
1	**Face Line Scoring Saw** *Rescoring wood face lines*
1	**1/2" x 82° Countersink** *Reinstalling face screws*
1	**Golf Club Drying Rack** *Finish Curing*
1	**Bristle Brush** *Face clean up for finishing*
1	**Scraper** *Face lean up for finishing*

[1]While final sanding of pro-sanded woodheads can easily be performed by hand, clubmakers find it much more efficient to use one of the variety of special woodhead sanding machines that are available.

Small Parts & Necessary Supplies

In the process of planning your clubmaking workshop, treat the tools and machinery you buy as a one-time investment. If you take care of your equipment it will last a lifetime and aside from parts such as cutting wheels or blades, will likely never have to be replaced. Once the shop has been equipped, the next step is to learn the numerous clubmaking supplies and small parts that must be kept on hand to assemble and make golf clubs. While a golfer may think it is only a grip, a shaft and a clubhead that go into the assembly of a golf club, clubmakers know there is a vast array of small parts and supplies that are used in the production of clubs, that include such items as string whipping, plastic ferrules, epoxy, solvents and tape, just to name a few. While a golf club cannot be built without a grip, shaft or head, neither can it be completed without all the necessary parts and supplies as well.

Unlike the tools, your parts and supply inventory represents items that you will purchase, use and then reorder. Therefore, in the efficient operation of your clubmaking business it will be necessary to always monitor the small parts and supplies inventory in the shop. To prevent running out of supplies in the middle of a clubmaking job, first take the time to learn just what is needed to make each type of club. Study the procedures for assembling all types of golf clubs that are outlined in Chapters 5-10 of this book. Step by step make notes of the various small parts and supplies that are used in each type of assembly.

After gaining a better understanding of what parts and supplies are required, next take time to set up a system for tracking the use of these supplies so that reorders can be made in plenty of time. For most shops such a system may simply consist of a weekly mental or visual inspection of your supply inventory while making notes of which items are running low. Once you have determined what you need to reorder, get in the habit of contacting your suppliers to immediately place your restocking requests.

In the case of larger clubmaking shops, a little more organization may be necessary to manage the supply inventory. Larger shops will usually have the benefit of experience in golf club assembly, so levels of use for each item will be known to the clubmaker. If you are aware at what rate you use each of the supply items, prepare lists that include the minimum amount of each item you need to keep on hand. Then as you perform your weekly inventory check, note which products are close to the minimum level and place your reorders accordingly. It is a good idea for clubmakers to order and stock larger quantities of minor supply items to avoid the frustration of running out, and having to constantly take the time to review the inventory for reordering purposes. Following is a list of all of the necessary small parts and supply items, plus a recommendation of inventory levels for each item. This list is divided into three parts :

A. Small Parts and Supply Item-
   Minimum Inventory

   The minimum inventory of small parts and supply items to stock to get started in clubmaking.

B. Small Parts and Supply Item-
   Complete Inventory

   A complete list of small parts and supply items necessary for completing all aspects of building golf clubs from components

C. Required Supplies for Finishing
   Wooden Heads

   The additional supplies that are necessary for finishing wooden clubheads, should you choose to offer the clubmaking option of making woods from unfinished woodheads.

Small Parts and Supply Item Inventory
MINIMUM INVENTORY for CLUBMAKING
Approximate Cost - $90-$100

Qty.	Item *Use*	Qty.	Item *Use*
1 pt.	Shafting Epoxy *Shaft installation*[1]	1 lb.	Lead Powder *Swingweighting*
2 pkg.	5-Minute Epoxy *Small fix-ups*	100	Corks *Swingweighting*
2 shts.	80 grit sand paper *Shaft abrasion/installation*	200 yd.	Whipping *Wooden and graphite woods*
1	Felt Tip Marker *Shaft marking for trimming*	6 doz.	Ferrules for Irons *Iron club assembly*[4]
1 roll	Masking Tape 2" x 36 yd *Grip buildup tape*[2]	3 doz.	Standard Ferrules for Woods *Wooden/graphite wood assembly*[4]
1 roll	2" x 36 yd 2-Way Tape *Grip installation*	3 doz.	Short Ferrules for Woods *Metal wood assembly*[5]
1 qt.	Grip Solvent *Grip installation*[3]	25	#5 x 1 1/8" Steel Backscrews *Backscrew installation woods*
1 pt.	Acetone *Ferrule clean-up*	12	Wood Plugs *Through-bore wood shafting*
2 rolls	Paper Towels *General clean-up*		

[1] A variety of shafting epoxies are available, most of which are two-part in nature. Check with your supplier for information about the shear strength rating of the epoxy. As a rule shafting epoxies must have a minimum shear strength rating of 2,000 psi.

[2] Masking tape for built-up grips must have thickness of .005" to ensure correct oversizing of grips.

[3] Use a lower flash point grip solvent such as Perchlorethylene or Naphtha for grip installation. Avoid using very flammable solvents such as gasoline or lighter fluid. With any grip solvent care should still be taken to avoid fumes and prolonged skin contact.

[4] Ferrules should be ordered to match the tip diameters of wood and iron shafts you are using. In addition, a variety of ferrules are available with/without shank for woods, with/without attached color rings for cosmetic appeal.

[5] Metal woodheads that are designed with a square top hosel require a special short (1/2") ferrule.

Small Parts and Supply Item Inventory
COMPLETE INVENTORY for ALL PROCEDURES of CLUBMAKING
Approximate Cost - $485-$500

Qty	Item / Use	Qty	Item / Use	Qty	Item / Use
1 pt.	Shafting Epoxy / *Shaft installation*[1]	24 doz.	Ferrules for Irons / *Iron club assembly*[5]	100	#4 x 5/8" Brass Screws / *Insert screw replacement*
10 pkg.	5-Minute Epoxy / *Small fix-ups*	12 doz.	Standard Ferrules for Woods / *Wooden/graphite wood assembly*[5]	100	#5 x 3/4" Brass Screws / *Insert screw replacement*
5 shts.	80 Grit Sand Paper / *Shaft abrasion/installation*	8 doz.	Short Ferrules for Woods / *Metal wood assembly*[6]	200	#5 x 1 1/8" Steel Backscrews / *Backscrew installation woods*
1	Felt Tip Marker / *Shaft marking for trimming*	12 doz.	Assorted Color Rings / *Optional ferrule assembly*	100	Wood Plugs / *Through-bore wood shafting*
1 roll	1/2" x 36 yd Masking Tape / *Head/shaft protection*[2]	6 doz.	Plastic Grip Collars (.600") / *Leather grip installation*[7]	50	Assorted Shims / *Shaft installation*
2 rolls	Masking Tape 2" x 36 yd / *Grip Buildup Tape*[3]	6 doz.	Plastic Grip Collars (.620") / *Leather grip installation*[7]	1 roll	1/2" x 36 yd Lead Tape / *Temporary swingweighting*
3 rolls	2" x 36 yd 2-Way Tape / *Grip installation*	2 doz.	Plastic End Caps (.580") / *Slip-on leather grip installation*[8]	1 roll	Thin Masking Tape / *Securing plastic bags*
2 qt.	Grip Solvent / *Grip installation*[4]	2 doz.	Plastic End Caps (.600") / *Slip-on leather grip installation*[8]	500	Plastic Woodhead Bags / *Completed clubs*
1 pt.	Acetone / *Ferrule clean-up*	3 doz.	Iron Rivets (3/32") / *Ironhead pinning*[9]	500	Plastic Ironhead Bags / *Completed clubs*
3 rolls	Paper Towels / *General clean-up*	2 doz.	Metal Shaft Extenders (.580") / *Lengthening steel shafted clubs*	500	Plastic Grip Bags / *Completed clubs*
2 lb.	Lead Powder / *Swingweighting*	2 doz.	Metal Shaft Extenders (.600") / *Lengthening steel shafted clubs*	100	Knit Cloth Head Bags / *Optional for completed clubs*
100	Corks / *Swingweighting*	2 doz.	Metal Shaft Extenders (.620") / *Lengthening steel shafted clubs*	2 doz. ea.	Extra Shaft Labels / *Replacements for damaged labels*
2 lb.	Lead (rod form for melting) / *Permanent wood swing-weighting*	1 doz.	5/8" Hardwood Dowels / *Lengthening composite shafts*[10]		
1 pt.	Cutting Oil / *Reboring metal hosels*	4 doz.	Set Screws / *Weight ports for woods*[11]		
2,000 yd.	Whipping / *Wooden and graphite woods*	100	#8 x 5/8" Brass Screws / *Soleplate screw replacement*		
		100	#7 x 3/4" Brass Screws / *Soleplate screw replacement*		

[1] A variety of shafting epoxies are available, most of which are two-part in nature. Check with your supplier for information about the shear strength rating of the epoxy. As a rule shafting epoxies must have a minimum shear strength rating of 2,000 psi.

[2] General purpose masking tape to cover the sharp edges on the butt end of shafts after trimming for safety and securing the plastic bags that are placed over the heads and grips after the club is built.

[3] Masking tape for built-up grips must have thickness of .005" to ensure correct oversizing of grips

[4] Use a lower flash point grip solvent such as Perchlorethylene or Naphtha for grip installation. Avoid using very flammable solvents such as gasoline or lighter fluid. With any grip solvent care should still be taken to avoid fumes and prolonged skin contact

[5] Ferrules should be ordered to match the tip diameters of wood and iron shafts you are using. In addition, a variety of ferrules are available with/without shank for woods, with/without attached color rings for cosmetic appeal.

[6] Metal woodheads that are designed with a square top hosel require a special short (1/2") ferrule.

[7] To make grip collar installation easier, use .600" size on .580" shafts and use .620" collars on .600 and .620" shafts. If you anticipate making underlistings for .560" ladies shafts (none exist today) then add .580" grip collars to your list.

[8] End caps will be used primarily for slip-on leather grip installation. Although the end cap assembly is included with shipment of the grip, suppliers usually send the .580" end cap size, so you will need a few .600" size to complete your stock. Because it is not recommended to install slip-on leather grips on .620" shafts, no .620" end caps are needed in your inventory

[9] Very few component ironheads require a rivet, but if you wish to custom install them through the hosel, 3/32" size are more cosmetically pleasing than the 1/8" variety.

[10] Because of the inside diameter difference between steel and composite shafts, metal extenders cannot be used for lengthening graphite/composite shafts A few component supply companies now provide plastic extenders for use as an alternative to wooden dowels.

[11] Set screw sizes in your inventory should correspond to the size already in heads you order, or to the size you wish to use, should you decide to custom install your own weight ports in woodheads. Size 10-32 is the most common for wooden heads, while 1/4" x 28 threads per inch is common for metal woods.

Required Supplies for Finishing Wooden Heads
Approximate Cost - $140-$150

Qty	Item / Use	Qty	Item / Use
5 qt.	**Water Base Stains** *Staining woodheads*[1]	1 pt.	**Alcohol (Denatured)** *Head degreasing*[2]
1 qt.	**Natural Filler** *Fill sealing woodheads*	2	**Beeswax Tackrags** *Head clean-up*
1 qt.	**Less Intense Black Filler** *Fill sealing woodheads*	1 roll	**2" Wide Masking Tape** *Head masking for color cote*[3]
1 can	**Aerosol Black Color Cote** *Opaque painting woodheads*	1 roll	**Cellophane Tape (1/2")** *Masking top of insert*
2 qt.	**Oil Modified Polyurethane** *Finish coats for woodheads*	10 shts.	**400 Grit Wet/Dry Sandpaper** *Sanding between finish coats*
10 shts.	**180 (Fine) Grit Sandpaper** *Final sanding woodheads*	2 lbs.	**3/0 or 4/0 Steel Wool** *Smoothing finish coats*[4]
5	**Small Artist Brushes** *Face masking urethane*	3 half pt.	**Scoreline, Engraving Paint** *Paint filling woodheads*[5]
10	**Burlap or Terry Rags** *Filler wiping*	Assorted	**Decals** *Woodhead cosmetics*[6]

[1] Variety of colors is up to the individual, but should at least include Black, Walnut, Burgundy and Light Brown. If stain containers are not shipped with the water base stain powder, they should be purchased and used

[2] Acetone can also be used to degrease soleplates prior to primer sealer application and to wipe the wood surface after the filler is dry. Never use acetone on the color coted (painted) part of woodheads as it will remove the paint

[3] Wide cellophane or thin masking tape can be used, with preference up to the individual. Be cautioned that some cellophane tapes will leave an adhesive residue upon removal that can be time consuming to remove

[4] 3/0 and 4/0 grade steel wools are considered very fine in abrasive. However, shop carefully to buy steel wool with a very low percentage of oil to prevent finish adhesion problems

[5] Fast dry, latex enamel paint in colors of your choice for filling engravings and stampings on woodheads

[6] If desired, personalized decals or an assortment of alignment decals can be used on custom finished woodheads

As in the case of all of the example inventory lists in this book, the exact quantity of any item must be based on individual shop volume of usage. Still, it is recommended that clubmakers try to keep a higher level of small parts and supplies in stock at all times to prevent the frustrating problem of running out of a necessary item in the middle of a job. The cost of delaying a job due to running out of a supply item in terms of service and reputation is far greater than the monetary cost of keeping an adequate inventory of these items. In addition, the finishing supplies that have been recommended are based on current popularity among clubmakers and ease of use. Individual clubmaking shops may wish to use other finishing stains, fillers, color cotes and dipping or spraying polyurethanes with which they have had experience. This is entirely acceptable providing interproduct compatability and proper curing techniques of the alternative finishing materials are always observed.

Major Component Supply Considerations

With the equipment and the small parts and supplies necessary to build clubs taken into account, it is time to begin your education on what are referred to as the major component supply items - the clubheads, shafts and grips you will use to build the clubs you play and sell. The tools and machinery as well as the small parts and supplies used to build clubs are items that have not changed for years. But the major components? In the last 10 years, and in particular the last five, the number of clubhead, shaft and grip options from which a clubmaker can choose is staggering. In just one example, in the four years since the first edition of *The Modern Guide to Golf Clubmaking* was published, nearly 20 new shaft manufacturers have become a part of the industry! Add to that the sheer increase in, and the annual changes of, new clubhead, shaft and grip designs among existing manufacturers and it is very easy to see just how confusing choosing components can be.

To be able to successfully sell assembled golf clubs, whether built to standard or custom specifications, is first and foremost going to require that you possess a solid level of information about the clubheads, shafts and grips within the industry. If you have not yet been subjected

to them, as a clubmaker you will undoubtedly be barraged with a host of questions from your customers about every aspect of component performance and quality. "What's the difference between this head with offset and this one without?" "Why does this shaft have boron and this one does not?" "What is this grip made from?" As the word spreads in your area that you are a clubmaker, the technical questions about components will come in a flood. Without a doubt, clubmakers who study and stay current on their level of component knowledge will be far more successful than those who simply assemble components. The following information will prove helpful in making decisions about the clubheads, shafts and grips that you will use in clubmaking.

Clubhead Purchasing and Stocking Needs

Clubheads are among the most important supply items that you will need to purchase or keep in stock. With the variety of designs and models that are available, coupled with the buying tastes of your golfing customers, you will need to carefully analyze several points before you make your clubhead selections. Before you buy, conduct an informal survey of clubhead design popularity within your local area and compare the results to what is popular with the overall golfing market, nationwide. Gaining an awareness of what sells and what doesn't is helpful because the golf industry has been known for decades to run "hot and cold" in its clubhead likes and dislikes - what was "in" last year might lose favor and be "out" the next. In addition, to help estimate what clubhead designs are popular with your local market, take a look what the local pro shops are selling and keeping in stock. When you visit the courses and driving ranges in your area, spend time looking in players' golf bags. Above all, never base your clubhead buying analysis simply on what *you* personally would use. While your opinion is helpful, it should never be the only basis for selecting playable clubhead designs for your customers.

Once you have analyzed what clubhead model styles are likely to be popular in your area, you need to make some decisions on just how many clubheads you should keep in stock. Since just a few sets of clubheads can add up to a lot of money, you must first estimate your shop's sales

potential. If your venture into golf club assembly is part-time, keep a few single head models to show to customers. By relying on the fast shipping services of experienced component supply companies, you can avoid the cost of carrying an inventory and still deliver the sale in a reasonable period of time.

On the other hand, if your commitment to clubmaking is much larger or full-time in nature, you must keep at least a minor inventory of clubheads in stock to avoid missing a sale. Use your experience in clubmaking to make the selections of potentially good selling models to keep on hand. Full-time or larger volume clubmakers should always take advantage of normal quantity price discounts that are offered by all clubhead suppliers. Being able to purchase 5-10 sets or more at a time will enable you to reduce the per head cost of your inventory and gain more profit from the sale in the process.

In today's competitive component market, suppliers will frequently offer particular models at a reduction in price or as a close-out special. Because the supplier is trying to reduce its inventory or sell out a particular model, stock may be limited. This means sales such as these usually don't last long, so you must plan to take advantage of them when they are for a particular model that you can sell to your market. Cultivating wise buying habits, gauging your local market and letting the component companies carry the inventory for you whenever possible are very important to your success in clubmaking.

Component Head Quality

A major point that you must not compromise in sourcing and buying clubheads is the quality of the heads and their accuracy with regard to specifications. To ensure quality, buy from established component head suppliers and teach yourself to perform your own control checks to verify the quality of what you buy. Above all, practice and learn to be able to **accurately** measure all specifications on a clubhead. A good component supplier should always be willing to replace any clubhead that has been proven to be defective or outside of stated specifications. Some of the points for which you should inspect your clubhead purchases are:

Clubhead Cosmetic Checks

- Is the appearance and quality of the finish consistent from head to head through the set?
- Do all engravings or stampings appear to be the same depth, thus showing good workmanship in production?
- On wooden woods, does the face area have a professional appearance, with a consistent smooth line between the stained and unstained portions of the head?
- Are all the paint fillings consistent on the face, sole and back?
- Does the head have a professional, high quality "look," free of scratches or dents?
- Are the sandblasted portions of the head consistent or does the sandblasting fade out on its edges or extend over into an area of the head on which it should not be?

Specification Checks

- Are the loft, lie and face angles for each head within the tolerances stated by your supplier?
- Regardless what the actual bulge radius may be, is the radius consistent across the face of the woodhead?
- Is the weight for each clubhead within the tolerance as stated by your supplier?
- Is the hosel bore diameter for each head within the tolerance as stated by your supplier?
- Is the bottom of hosel bore to back edge of heel dimension consistent within the same set design? Or is the bore depth the same for each head within a set? (This design specification may be different in one set design versus another, but within the #1 - 9 in the same model, hosel length should remain consistent. From tradition within the golf equipment industry, it is allowable for a PW and SW to vary in these dimensions for individual design purposes, but if in doubt, check with your supplier for more information.)
- Is the hosel and its bore, whether for wood or for iron, consistent and straight in its alignment with the shaft? In other words, upon shaft insertion, the shaft and hosel should appear to be in line and not crooked.
- If weight ports are present, are they sufficient in capacity to allow for normal final swingweighting needs?

Which Bore to Select, Taper or Parallel?

In purchasing clubheads for assembly, you will be faced with a decision whether to buy clubheads with tapered or parallel bore diameters. The differences between tapered and parallel tip shafts will be discussed in a succeeding chapter, but with respect to the clubheads, there are a few points you must consider before deciding which bore sizes you plan to use. In 1971, when True Temper® Corp. introduced the parallel tip design for steel shafts, it did so primarily with the major golf club manufacturers in mind. Using taper tip shafts to build a full set requires the clubmaker to stock as many as 13 different raw lengths of shaft per flex, thus creating an inventory number that multiplies when additional shaft patterns are added. To help manufacturers keep their inventory stock keeping units (SKUs) more manageable, True Temper began to produce shafts with two flexes contained within the one shaft and a constant diameter from the tip to the first step down. Such parallel tip, combination flex shafts were not offered as a replacement, but rather as an alternative for most of their popular taper tip patterns. With the parallel tip type of design, manufacturers have the benefit of only having to order two different shaft SKUs to complete a full set, compared to the 26 SKUs that are required when using the taper tip version of a shaft.

Most of today's clubhead component suppliers produce their wood and ironhead designs with a parallel hosel bore, .335" for woodheads and .370" for irons. However, since there are a few component clubhead companies that provide models with tapered hosel bores, you will have some decisions to make whether to order the parallel or the taper type. If your shop is equipped with the necessary tools and machinery to rebore the diameter of the hosel, then stocking a few models with tapered bores will be OK. However, realize that should you have to enlarge the bore of an entire set, the procedure will take time that you will probably not be able to recoup in the cost of the set. Therefore, because virtually all shafts are available in parallel tip form, it is recommended that you plan the majority of your clubhead purchases to include models with parallel bores. By doing this, you will avoid

having to inventory a larger number of tapered shafts, and avoid the possibility of back orders that is a far greater risk with taper tip shafts than with the parallel tip variety. As time continues to pass in the modern golf equipment industry, very few golfers cling to the once held myth that better players need to use tapered shafts. Plan most of your purchases for parallel bore heads, but be prepared to call on a supplier for an occasional tapered bore head, should the need arise.

Wooden heads, Pre-Finished or Pro-Sanded?

Whether you purchase the wooden heads for clubmaking in fully finished or unfinished form corresponds directly to your level of involvement in clubmaking. If your work shop is set up to be able to apply finishes to wooden heads, then purchasing all of your laminated maple and persimmon heads in pro-sanded form will allow you to offer custom finish colors and a wide variety of clubhead custom alterations to your customers. However, if you have not included woodhead finishing in your shop set-up, then you should restrict your wooden head purchases to pre-finished heads only. The current difference in cost among component suppliers between the a model in pre-finished compared to pro-sanded form is approximately $5.00. Given the cost of your time and labor rates in general, most clubmakers will find that they just cannot apply a factory quality finish for $5.00. Still, so much of clubmaking can be classified as a "labor of love," so if you have the desire to be full service, there is a lot to be said about the pride that can come from producing a beautiful, factory quality custom finished wood.

As already mentioned, the variety of clubhead model types from which you can choose to assemble your golf clubs is quite large. To give you an idea of the selection, following is a list of the current woodhead, ironhead and putter head options available from component supply companies as well as some helpful information to assist in making your purchasing decisions.

■ WOODHEADS

Persimmon

The oldest material still being used for making woodheads is persimmon. Because the predominant source for persimmon trees is the United States, almost all of the persimmon heads you will choose to purchase are domestically made. Noted for its beautiful grain structure, persimmon underwent a tremendous resurgence in popularity in the 1970s, when major manufacturers attempted to recreate the look of many of the "classic" persimmon woods that had been produced in the 1950s and '60s. Despite the fact that persimmon woodheads have decreased in their percentage of woodhead market share, they are still a favorite of many low handicap players as well as equipment traditionalists. Today, component clubhead suppliers offer persimmon heads in a variety of styles and shapes, but tend to opt more toward full-sized head shapes with medium-deep to deep face heights.

Persimmon Woods

Today, most of the component suppliers that produce persimmon models offer the woodheads in pre-finished form, made only to standard specifications. By offering the heads produced to standard specifications, suppliers are better able to keep models in stock and thus ensure faster delivery. Despite the proliferation of metal wood designs today, clubmakers should be aware that all wooden heads such as persimmon can be made to a far

greater variety of custom specifications than the metal woods. Metal woods are made from molds through a process that is impossible to make custom changes on individual heads without changing the mold. On the other hand, wooden heads are individually made, with each head having to be routed, bored, sanded and finished. This manufacturing process, while somewhat slow, does allow the customization of heads for golfers to be done.

A few of the component supply companies that do offer persimmon also offer the service of manufacturing the wooden heads to custom specifications of loft, lie, face angle, weight, bore size and cosmetics. Because each custom-made head has to be made up after the clubmaker's order is placed, more time must be allowed for delivery. When custom head specifications are desired by your customer, having the manufacturer make the head from "scratch" is the best decision to make. Still, if the customer is unwilling to wait the 6-10 weeks for delivery, and if you have developed the skills to make custom alterations, it will be faster for you to order standard specification heads in unfinished form and perform the required changes in your shop.

An interesting point about wooden woods that is just beginning to surface is their versatility in weight distribution when compared to metal woods. In the late 1970s when metal woods were introduced, it was immediately believed they possessed a lower center of gravity and had superior weight distribution to wooden heads. Assumed to be so because of their hollow shell construction, research has now proven between a metal wood and a wooden wood of *equal face height*, the wooden wood will have the lower center of gravity. If the two types of identical size heads are cut in half horizontally, the two halves of the metal wood will possess 50% each of the head's weight while for the wooden wood, some 65% of the head's weight is located in the bottom half. The nod goes to the wooden wood because it has an attached metal soleplate which has a greater density than the wood itself. In addition, wooden head manufacturers have also discovered by inserting lead or metal weight plugs in different areas of the head they can begin to duplicate the

perimeter weighting aspect so favorably awarded to the metal woods.

Does this mean a comeback for persimmon in the 1990s? Golfer perceptions combined with equipment marketing techniques have in large part been responsible for driving the metal wood to the status it enjoys today. Whether scientific data can overcome the 10 years of perception built up in favor of metal woods will remain to be seen. Suffice to say, for clubmakers who may be in search of a wood that is easy for their customers to get up into the air, there is no better choice than a heavy soled wooden wood.

Persimmon woodheads rank as one of the most expensive of all the types of component woodheads, with costs ranging from $25 up to $60 per head. The high cost of the raw persimmon turning combined with the tremendous number of production steps and labor required in manufacture results in higher costs for the clubmaker. If sophisticated drying techniques are used on the head, or if strict grading procedures on the wood turnings are used, the cost of the persimmon heads can be even higher. Should custom specifications be desired, the cost of individually making the head to precise parameters will drive the price even higher yet.

As an alternative, some persimmon suppliers offer a choice of different priced persimmon woodheads, using what is known in the industry as "UR" Grade turnings. To contrast, an "A" Grade turning is a persimmon wood that comes out of the turning process with a U-shaped grain pattern and no cosmetic flaws. A "UR" turning (Useable Reject) is a persimmon wood that has a minor surface or cosmetic defect such as a black mineral spot or a slight grain discoloration. Because the market prefers the more perfect persimmon woods, when URs occur in production, the manufacturer is faced with reducing their price to make them sell. Contrary to the myth, such UR flaws do not have any adverse effect on the playability or durability of the club.

Exotic Hardwoods

A creation of a very limited number of skilled manufacturers, woodheads produced from such exotic hardwoods as Dogwood, Bois d'Arc, Osage and a few others

Dogwood Wood

are available to clubmakers to offer their very upscale, discerning customers. Exotic hardwood heads have never been a mainstay of the golf equipment industry because of the scarcity of the raw material and the extreme care and time that often must be taken to properly dry the wood prior to woodhead production. Because of their very high prices, in excess of $100 per woodhead, exotic hardwood woodheads represent a limited, but potentially lucrative alternative for clubmakers who may have developed a clientiele that includes a number of upper income golfers.

Laminated Maple

Pioneered by the Wilson Sporting Goods Co. in the early 1940s, laminated maple woodheads rank as the most durable of the wooden heads. Recognizable by their distinctive "striped" pattern, these veneered maple heads have decreased rapidly in popularity over the last 10 years. Currently there are two types of laminated maple woodheads (layups, as they are called) that are available to club assemblers. The oldest and most common layup is made of alternating strips of one layer of the darker end grain and two layers of the lighter colored side grain of

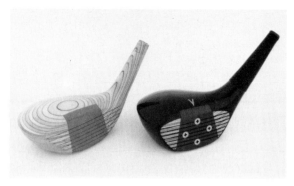

Laminated Maple Woods

the maple. In its unfinished form as viewed from the top, this type of layup is recognized by reddish-brown rings that occur from the use of dark colored glue that bonds the layers of maple together.

The other type of laminated layup consists of all side grain strips of maple bonded together by a light colored glue. These heads, which were first introduced by Birchwood Manufacturing for use by the MacGregor Golf Co. in 1972, bear a look similar to persimmon since only the light colored side grain layers are used and the dark rings of the lamination are not present. The result is a much lighter colored wood which some clubmakers feel is more attractive than the conventional type of laminated layup.

Laminated maple heads undergo the same individual manufacturing processes of routing and boring as the persimmon and exotic woodheads. However, due to the lower cost of the blocks, laminated maple heads are sold for a much lower price than persimmon woodheads. Golf clubs built from laminated maple are a good choice for economy-minded beginners or experienced players who prefer a wooden head, but need the added durability offered by the lamination process. Laminated heads resist moisture damage and cracking much better than persimmon, thus making them a good choice for golfers who do not take care of their equipment or golfers who play with two-piece golf balls and suffer from hitting repeated shots off the toe or the heel of the clubface.

Graphite - Injection and Compression Molded

A relatively modern entry in the clubhead design market are woodheads made from graphite. Currently two distinctly different types of graphite woodheads are available, one made through the compression-molding process and the other produced by injection molding. Compression-molded graphite heads are made from long fibers or sheets of graphite material that are pressed around a foam core and characteristically possess a very high percentage of graphite (50-75%). Recognized by their striated look or woven fibrous type of surface pattern, compression-molded graphite woodheads are much more expensive than the injection-molded versions, averaging between $30 and $50 per finished head. This higher cost is due to the greater percentage of graphite used in the head, the fact that long fiber graphite is used in its manufacture, and the fact that compression molding is itself an expensive process of production.

Injection-molded graphite heads consist of a small percentage of chopped or mashed graphite fibers (10-15%) that are mixed with a material such as ABS or Cycolac® plastic with an epoxy binding resin. Binders and additives such as those mentioned are blended with the graphite to facilitate the melting and then an injection of the material is shot through a small nozzle into a steel mold. Because they contain a much lower percentage of graphite than compression molded heads, and because the molding process is faster than compression-molding, injection-molded graphite woodheads are priced much lower, in the range of $20-30 per finished head. Unlike the heavily striated look seen on the surface of the compression-molded heads, injection-molded graphite heads have a smooth, plain opaque surface appearance with very little striation and are often color coted with paint as part of their finishing process.

Playability-wise there is no difference between graphite woodheads produced by the injection or compression-molding methods. The claims by many graphite woodhead manufacturers of increased playability due to perimeter weighting (supposedly due to the foam filled or hollow core inside the heads) is true but not to the extent

Compression-Molded Graphite Wood

Injection-Molded Graphite Wood

that this weight distribution principle is present in the stainless steel woods, for example. Therefore, graphite woodheads exist as a high-tech clubmaking contribution of the '80s, with the primary differences when compared to other wood materials being outstanding durability and a slightly different feel at impact.

Of the two types of graphite woodheads, compression-molded woods are said by some manufacturers to be superior in playability to the injection-molded heads because they are stronger. Because compression-molded heads are made from long fiber graphite, they are stronger than the injection-molded heads. However, this is a fact that makes absolutely no difference. Golf clubheads are simply not subjected to high levels of stress in which

the strength difference of the two types of heads would play an important role. While an injection-molded aircraft part may not hold up to the stress placed on it, an injection-molded golf clubhead will easily withstand the rigors of play. This strength factor is a point that compression-molded graphite woodhead manufacturers have played upon in an attempt to compete with the lower cost per unit of the injection-molded heads.

Because of the very light weight of the composite material, graphite woodheads can be molded to sizes that are significantly larger than conventional wooden or metal woodheads and still achieve the proper weight specifications for building golf clubs to a normal range of swingweight. While there has been some recent belief that the oversize graphite woodhead improves distance and playability because its center of gravity is farther from the shaft's axis, outright proof of this fact has not yet come to the forefront. Still, as designers search for lighter and lighter materials with which to offer oversize heads or improved weight distribution, graphite is a viable contender. As more research continues to be done, if designers are able to prove that substantially larger head shapes do improve playability, graphite will find a permanent place in the world of clubmaking. Because the graphite woodhead market has remained stable through the 1980s and '90s with an estimated 8% total wood market share, and because the oversize graphite woodheads have begun to carve their own niche in the equipment industry, as a clubmaker you cannot afford to ignore the potential in sales these heads may represent.

Stainless Steel Metal Woods

One of the most famous clubmaking developments that came about as a result of the introduction of the investment casting process into golf has been the development of stainless steel metal woods. First seen in 1975, but refined into their current shape in 1979, stainless woodheads now account for over 75% of all wood sales, giving them by far the largest market share of all the woodhead types. So great has been their rise in popularity, at the time of publication of the first edition of *The Modern Guide to Golf Clubmaking* in 1987 stainless metal woods held a 40% market share!

Stainless Steel Metal Wood

For clubmakers, stainless steel woods represent the easiest of all woodheads to assemble. Far less labor is required to assemble stainless wood clubs, since no whipping or backscrew installation is required. Because of their ease of assembly, and the incredible popularity they enjoy among golfers, club assemblers must view stainless woodheads as a major part of their business in making woods.

Also because of their popularity, a wide variety of stainless steel woodhead models and designs are available to clubmakers. Stainless woodheads can be offered in what is referred to as the original "pencil hosel" version (hosel shape reminiscent of the shape of a pencil), in designs with a tapered outside hosel shape, with different face heights that in some cases approach the size of deep-face wooden heads, with runner sole construction and even in styles that mimic a traditional wood with imitation face inserts, imitation soleplates and plastic whipping covers. In addition, metal woodheads are available in a variety of surface finishes from paints to chemical darkening to offer even more variety of selection.

Stainless metal woods are produced by first investment casting two separate parts, a top shell and a soleplate. During the manufacturing process the soleplate is welded to the top shell, subjected to grinding, polishing and painting processes, and then filled with polyurethane foam to deaden the sound created at impact by their hollow construction. Because stainless woods are produced with extremely thin walls to facilitate headweight requirements, only 17-4 grade stainless steel should be used in their manufacture. Of the various grades of stainless steel used to investment cast woodheads and ironheads, 17-4 is capable of being made the strongest. Unless major technical breakthroughs are made in the future in current heat treatment and hardening processes, clubmakers are advised only to use 17-4 stainless steel metal woods in their work. Woods made from 4-31 stainless steel may be less expensive than those produced from 17-4, but are susceptible to face crushing at clubhead speeds in excess of 100 mph.

Current industry prices for 17-4 grade stainless steel woodheads average between $17 and $30 per finished head, depending upon the supplier, the head quality and design characteristics. Many models are being designed with weight ports to allow the clubmakers to make their final swingweight adjustments in the head. Building metal woods to custom specifications will usually require purchasing the head with those specifications already cast into the head. Due to their thin wall construction stainless woods cannot be refaced for loft or roll/ bulge changes. While clubmakers are just discovering it is possible to bend the hosel of stainless woods to achieve custom lie and face angle requirements, such alterations do require the use of bending machines that are only cost effective for large clubmaking shops. Fortunately, the popularity of stainless woods has allowed some component suppliers to expand their model offerings to include metal woods cast to a variety of custom specifications. Whenever possible clubmakers are advised to purchase the metal woodheads with the required custom specifications cast into the head.

Aluminum Metal Woods

An important point for clubmakers to realize is that the 75%+ market share awarded to metal woods in 1991 is primarily made up by the stainless steel version. When the metal wood boom first hit in the mid-1970s, the first metal heads were not made from stainless steel, but were

Aluminum Metal Wood

in fact die cast from aluminum with a wooden or plastic block inlaid into a cavity in the back of the head. While some of these combination heads still exist, most aluminum woodhead makers dropped the wood/plastic inlay and evolved the design into an all-aluminum die cast woodhead. When the stainless wood was refined into its present form in 1979, most of the aluminum woodheads were relegated to the lowest status in the golf industry and used as the woodhead of choice for starter sets and junior sets. Yet thanks to very recent technological and design advances, aluminum woods appear on the verge of a comeback, though not as a starter set entry but rather as a high-end wood.

The type of low-priced aluminum woodheads used in starter sets are produced through low pressure die casting, a process in which the molten metal itself is injected into a steel mold. Separate die cast molds are made for the soleplate and for the top shell (the top of the woodhead with neck and open bottom). After production of each piece, the soleplate is actually hammered or screwed onto the bottom of the top shell, positioned in place by four aluminum posts protruding out from the cavity of the top shell that meet with four holes in the plate. After the posts of the top shell fit through the holes in the soleplate, the protruding top of the posts and the edge of the top shell around the plate are peened with a hammer to hold the two parts together. The simplicity of the

production and the nature of the die casting process combine to create the low cost ($9-$12 per head) of the two-piece aluminum woodheads.

In the late 1980s, aluminum woodheads began to make a transition from low end to high end as more sophisticated die casting processes found their way into golf equipment production. Through such processes as one-piece high pressure die casting and even forging, a new generation of aluminum woodheads were introduced to golfers. Now as component heads being offered to clubmakers with large capacity or multiple weight ports and designed in many cases to oversize head shapes, these aluminum woodheads are far more sophisticated than their low-end forerunners and are sold in a range from $18-30 per head. Because the lightweight nature of aluminum allows designers to create large, oversize head shapes, because the heads still possess a degree of perimeter weighting and can eliminate the hollow sound of stainless woods, the modern high-end die cast aluminum woods may represent a new direction in clubmaking for the future that clubmakers should not ignore.

Fiber Reinforced Plastic, Thermoplastic Woodheads

Very much a product of the high-tech influence in golf equipment design, woodheads injection-molded from a variety of space age plastics began to appear in the late 1980s. In both shaft and in clubhead design, manufactur-

High-Strength Plastic Compound Wood

ers are constantly on the lookout for new very light weight materials that possess very high strength. For clubheads the introduction of what are referred to as space age plastics is just beginning to allow designers to work on making improvements in woodhead weight distribution characteristics. By using a lightweight, high strength plastic material for the head combined with a heavier metal for the soleplate, manufacturers can move another step forward in their attempt to offer clubheads with a low center of gravity.

While some manufacturers are touting greater impact velocity as an additional benefit of the space age plastics material, initial research is showing that such claims are not realistic. Therefore, clubmakers should look to the introduction of the new plastic woodheads for weight distribution advantages rather than outright material created shot improvement. Available to clubmakers from a limited number of component supply companies, fiber reinforced or thermoplastic woodheads carry a cost between $22-28 per finished head.

■ MISCELLANEOUS WOODHEADS

Ash Woodheads
While clubmakers will note that the vast majority of woodhead choices come from the previous types, there are a limited number of other woodhead types that are occasionally seen in the golf industry. Very few of these

Ash Wood

other woodheads are available on a component assembly basis, but it will be helpful for you to know a little bit more about them should your golfing customers make inquiry. One little known type that is available to club builders are woodheads that are made from ash. Ash woodheads are often mistaken for persimmon by less experienced golfers, because both are made from solid wood blocks and exhibit a somewhat similar grain pattern. However, upon close comparison, it is easy to see the color and slight grain difference between the two wood types, with ash darker in color and showing slightly less pronounced grain lines than persimmon. Most ash woodheads originate in the Far East where persimmon is not available, and are sold primarily in Japan, Australia and Europe as an alternative for persimmon.

ABS/Cycolac® Woodheads
Another type of head that is available to clubmakers are woodheads injection molded from ABS plastic. Not a new introduction, ABS woodheads, or low-end plastic as they are often referred to, were heralded as a revolutionary new design as early as 1962. Not to be confused with

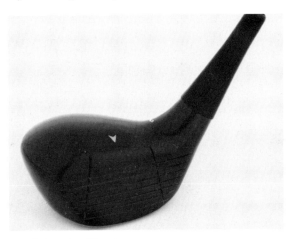

ABS®/Cycolac Wood

woodheads made from the new generation of fiber reinforced or thermoplastic materials, ABS plastic head woods have been relegated to "low-end" status in clubmaking. As such, the ABS woodheads do offer a good alternative for junior or beginners' sets. Because they both possess a smooth black surface, ABS plastic wood-

heads can be confused with injection-molded graphite heads. For clubmakers to avoid mistaking injection-molded ABS and graphite heads, most of the ABS heads are made with conventional face inserts to keep costs a low as possible, while the injection molded graphite heads are produced primarily with all-graphite inserts. This, plus the fact that ABS heads are much lower in price, will help clubmakers identify the difference between the two types of heads.

Ceramic Woodheads
The American golf industry's move to exotic materials for clubhead making has brought about a great variety of woodhead types. Heads now are being made from ceramic materials and other composites on a very limited basis, but as of yet very few of these types of woodheads have been made available for use by golf club assemblers.

Major Component Supply Items

■ IRONHEADS and WEDGES
Although the clubmaker's selection of ironhead and wedge material types is not nearly as vast as that with woodheads, the variety of component ironhead and wedge design types from which clubmakers may choose seems infinite. From cavity back to muscleback to flanged sole to hollow iron to wide sole and more, wedge and ironhead designers seem to have no limit to the variations they can conceive. Yet before clubmakers can focus on the model type of ironhead or wedge, it is important to understand the four major processes of production that are employed to create the various designs.

One of the greatest areas of misinformation within clubmaking concerns the manufacturing processes and materials used to make ironheads and wedges. Currently, four manufacturing processes - investment casting, forging, die casting and compression molding - are used in conjunction with a variety of materials to produce all the ironheads and wedges used by clubmakers in their work. To begin your understanding, die casting as an ironhead and wedge production process is usually employed with zinc while compression molding is always used with graphite.

Keeping those points in mind it is within the processes of investment casting and forging that clubmakers experience the most confusion. Too often clubmakers hear the term investment casting and assume that all ironheads and wedges produced by this process are made of hard stainless steel. In turn, the assumption is also made that all ironheads and wedges manufactured through forging are made from soft carbon steel. With these assumptions, clubmakers then are all too often of the belief that all investment cast heads exhibit a higher level of hardness than heads produced by the forging method of manufacture.

The terms investment casting and forging refer only to processes of manufacturing. In and of themselves, they have nothing to do with the material from which a clubhead is made. They simply represent two different ways to form the shape of a clubhead. Whether an ironhead or wedge is hard or soft has nothing to do with the process of investment casting or forging.

In investment casting, molten steel is poured into shells

For example, in the history of golf equipment, ironheads and wedges have been forged from several different types of carbon steel as well as from a number of types of stainless steel. In turn, ironheads and wedges have been investment cast from many types of stainless steel as well as carbon steel. In other words, ironhead hardness is a product of the material and its post-forming heat treatment, not the manufacturing process used to form the head.

Many golfers mistakenly associate shotmaking feel or performance with ironhead hardness, with the most common myth being the softer the metal, the softer the feel at impact with the ball. Whether soft or hard, feel at impact is not a product of the metal hardness of the ironhead. If a golfer is able to perceive any differences in feel between soft and hard metal ironheads at impact, it will be created by weight distribution differences in the clubhead design, difference in golf ball construction (two-piece vs wound) and differences in shaft material, flex and bend point. In blind tests using identical irons with the only difference being metal hardness, touring professionals could not tell any difference in feel at impact (see *GOLF Magazine*, "Test Case," March 1983).

Most clubmakers mistakenly associate an ironhead's bendability for loft and lie adjustments with its manufacturing process, instead of the head's metal hardness or design characteristics. The assumption that all investment cast ironheads cannot be bent is simply not true. For example, ironheads investment cast from 18-8 (304) grade stainless steel actually can be bent for loft and lie adjustment easier than most forged carbon steel irons. While it is true that ironheads made from the 17-4 and 4-31 type stainless steels are harder to bend than most forged carbon steel ironheads, recent advancements in bending machine design and bending techniques have now made it possible to alter these harder steel heads for loft and lie (see Chapter 10, Loft and Lie Alteration).

When you select ironheads and wedges for your clubmaking, a high priority should be placed on choosing the styles and designs that will appeal to the majority of golfers within your local market. If you plan to accent fitting and wish to offer custom loft and lie alterations as a part of your clubmaking service, you should also take into account the bendability of the heads as well as your ability and experience in being able to make the alterations. Following is an overview of each of the types of ironheads that are available to clubmakers on a component basis.

Investment Cast Stainless Steel
By far the ironhead type that commands the greatest segment of sales in the golf industry are the designs investment cast from one of the various types of stainless steel. Because of the nature of investment casting, virtually any conceivable design can be produced, and done so with a high degree of accuracy from head to head. Investment cast stainless steel ironheads can be made in any form of head design, in steel hardness variation from soft to hard, and will cost the clubmaker approximately $7-12 per finished head, depending on the quality and the intricacy of the design. Therefore, it will be possible to fit the entire spectrum of golfer types into the differenct varieties of ironheads and wedges. As such, investment cast stainless designs will likely make up the majority of the ironheads and wedges you will select for your clubmaking business.

The process of investment casting begins with the making of a complete set of master model heads. Usually machined, filed and ground from a soft metal such as brass or aluminum, the masters must be made as accurately as possible to each specification, and must include every single feature that is intended to be on the finished head, including the scorelines, names and logos. Calculations of the volume area of the masters are made and multiplied times the density of the stainless steel to determine what the expected finished head weights will be.

After fine tuning and final specifications checking of the masters, a mold for each ironhead must be made. Large blocks of aluminum are halved with recesses carved into each half of the mold. The master is coated with a release agent and is floated in one side of the mold in plaster. After the plaster hardens the other half of the mold is closed over the plaster suspended master. A soft, work-

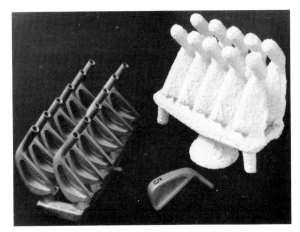

Shells or molding trees produce the raw clubheads

able amalgam such as tin/bismuth, antimony/lead or a special type of epoxy is then injected under pressure into the open cavity of the empty mold half to form tightly around one side of the master. After hardening of the amalgam, the mold is opened and the master is carefully removed. After cleaning out all the plaster from the other half of the mold, the master is mounted back into the completed half of the mold. The mold is clamped back together and the amalgam is shot into the half of the mold once filled with plaster, thus completing the making of the mold. After intensive fine tuning, the molds are checked, tested and ready for wax injection.

The procedure of investment casting begins with the injecting of a special wax into the molds. Extreme care must be taken to prevent changing loft and lie specifications when withdrawing the wax heads from the mold. One after another, perfect wax replicas of each head come out of the mold which are then melt sealed to wax frames. The wax frames with like numbered heads, or "trees," are then dipped several times into successively changing viscosities of ceramic slurry mixtures to form a shell around the entire "tree of waxes."

After proper cooling and hardening under controlled temperature and humidity, the shells are placed inside a large autoclave where, under heat and pressure the wax is melted and forced out, leaving an empty ceramic shell.

The hollow ceramic shells are then placed into ovens to bring their temperature up high enough to receive the molten metal. After metal pouring, the shells are "fluxed" to stabilize the gas emissions of the molten steel and set aside to cool and harden. The shells are then broken away from the heads, the frames are cut away and what remains are unfinished ("as cast") duplicates of each ironhead, complete with score lines and all design features and engravings. Depending upon the individual foundry, the hosel bore may be cast into the head or drilled after casting. In the final steps of investment casting, the heads are checked for loft and lie angle accuracy, heat treated to harden the metal, ground to final weight and then finished to the desired surface appearance.

Investment casting has taken over as the primary method of golf clubhead production because it eliminates all of the machining steps that are synonomous with forging. If the masters and molds are accurately made, each head that comes out of the shell is virtually a duplicate to each other of the same number. The only way that inaccuracy can occur on investment cast heads is - 1. If the masters or molds are incorrect, in which case all of the heads made from that incorrect mold or master will show the discrepancy; 2. If the waxes are carelessly removed from the mold, thus causing the soft wax hosel to bend; 3. If the heads are not individually checked for loft and lie and adjusted accordingly; 4. If the heads are improperly ground for final weight, in which case the gram weights will vary by more than the stated ± tolerance for the design. Despite these possible areas for error, the investment casting process is accepted as being a more accurate means of producing ironheads than forging.

Investment Cast Carbon Steel
In the middle 1960s, some of the problems that had to be overcome before investment casting could become a viable method for manufacturing ironheads were to determine ways of preventing high reject rates due to porosity, and face sinking. Different adjustments in the technique of building the molds and forming the ceramic shells solved most of these problems, but still, foundries discovered that only certain grades of metal lent them-

selves to high quality ironhead investment casting. The metals that performed the best and delivered lower reject rates were certain grades of stainless steel, since it was found that most carbon steels (the predominant metal types used in forging) would not fill out the shells properly when poured and thus resulted in poor quality castings.

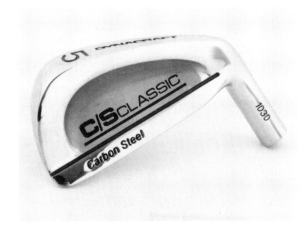

Investment Cast Carbon Steel Iron

After some experimentation, in the middle 1970s it was found that some carbon steel varieties could be used to produce investment cast ironheads. Such an attempt was made because it was felt such a combination would deliver the best of both worlds - the repetitive accuracy of the investment cast process plus the attractive chrome plated finish and loft and lie alterability of carbon steel. Even though the breakthrough has been made to allow its introduction, investment cast carbon steel reject rates are still much higher than what is experienced with stainless steel. In addition, carbon steel clubheads are more expensive to produce into a finished head since the additional step of chrome plating is required to prevent corrosion. As a result, very few manufacturers chose to offer investment cast carbon steel ironheads.

However, in the late 1980s, a slight resurgence of popularity in carbon steel ironheads has triggered a new wave of carbon steel designs utilizing cavity backed styling. While first produced through forging, some manufacturers found that producing a deep cavity back carbon steel ironhead could be done more accurately through investment casting. This, coupled with the fact that 1980s labor costs had drastically driven up the cost of forged ironheads, made casting carbon steel a much more viable proposition. As a result, more and more investment cast carbon steel models, of all types of designs, began to make a comeback in the late 1980s.

From the basis of selecting heads for component assembly, clubmakers should view the available models of investment cast carbon steel ironheads in much the same way as forged carbon steel heads. With cast carbon steel, alteration for loft and lie is easier than with 4-31 and 17-4 stainless heads as long as caution is used to avoid cracking the plating. Still, whether forged or investment cast, carbon steel ironheads and wedges are much more expensive than their stainless steel counterparts, costing clubmakers in the range of $15-20 per finished head.

Investment Cast Ironheads From Special Metals

Once the method of producing heads by investment casting was perfected, some foundries began to experiment with using the process to fashion ironheads and wedges from several other types of metals. However, before choosing another metal for investment casting, very precise requirements had to be met. Because individual ironhead sizes and weights in clubmaking have to be controlled within narrow ranges, any new materials from which heads are made must exhibit the same approximate density as previously used metals. Otherwise, ironheads that are produced from the different metals will end up too heavy or too light to achieve the normal range of playing swingweight.

In addition, the process of investment casting requires metals that possess very specific "flow" characteristics. In other words, when melted and poured the metals used must flow properly into each area of the ceramic shell and exhibit metallurgical stability during the cooling process or else high reject rates will occur from pitting, scaling or lack of homogeneity (uniform hardness over the entire head).

Therefore, the number of different metals that can successfully be investment cast into an ironhead or wedge are limited. In the 1970s and 1980s a number of foundries were able to successfully cast ironheads from such exotic metals as Aluminum Bronze and Beryllium Copper, and putters from Manganese Bronze. Examples of all types have been made available to club builders for custom club assembly. These types of ironheads are expensive by virtue of the cost of the raw material ($15-20 per finished head) and do not offer any distinct playability advantages over heads made from stainless or carbon steels. However, from a cosmetic standpoint, heads cast from exotic metals are eye-catching to a number of golfers and as such, can represent a potential for sales for club assemblers.

Forged Carbon Steel

The oldest style of ironhead and wedge manufacture still in existence is forging. Although forging underwent

Forged Carbon Steel Irons

many machinery changes through the first half of the 1900s that streamlined and speeded up the process, it still remains as the most labor intensive form of ironhead manufacture. Because so many machining and hand operation steps are required, and because the cost of labor has risen drastically, forged ironheads and wedges have become far more expensive than investment cast heads. In addition, the amount of labor required to produce forged ironheads makes them more susceptible to errors

in specifications. Quality control grading does reduce this potential for error but in turn further contributes to forging's higher cost.

To produce a forged ironhead, most manufacturers with the in-house capability of finishing forgings will contract with a supplier for a raw forging with the design characterisitics they wish to offer. A raw forging comes to the manufacturer without the bore drilled and with no detail completed other than the basic head shape. The raw forging may possess a plain, flat back to allow the manufacturer to machine out the desired back design, or can be supplied with the basic ridges or levels already formed on the head.

From the raw forging, the first steps to finish the ironhead are to saw or grind the top of the hosel square and centerless grind the outside of the hosel perfectly round. Large drilling machines index the round hosel and bore the hosel square in alignment to the hosel's outside diameter. The face of the raw forging is not perfectly flat so heavy duty grinding or milling machines are then used to resurface the face.

If a different back design is required other than what is already on the raw forging, the back is machined to create the different levels of ironhead weight distribution. Preliminary loft and lie corrections are made through bending, after which the heads are rough ground to prepare for the roll die stamping of the score lines, clubhead logos and numbers. Each of the required head stamps are pressed or rolled deep into the head to allow for material removal during the head's final grinding procedures. A substantial amount of material is removed from the head to achieve final shape and style features, to soften all sharp edges created through machining, and to prepare the head's surface for electroplating.

Because the raw head is produced by large drop forge hammers that literally pound a heated rod of metal into the ironhead's rough shape, the forging of golf clubheads is generally restricted to the use of softer metals such as carbon steel. Clubmakers who cling to the cast vs. forged hardness myths will be interested to know that it is possible to forge even 17-4 stainless steel. However, such a process does require special machinery and techniques that would make such an endeavor far too expensive for use in making such an item as an ironhead.

Soft carbon steel is most often employed for ironhead forging because it will conform to the desired raw forging shape with a minimum of work. Once again, clubmakers should be aware that first in the 1920s, and then again later in the 1950s and 1960s, a number of golf club manufacturers did produce ironheads that were forged from soft stainless steel. Because of the higher cost of stainless steel and the fact that the market found no real playability benefits from using stainless steel, the predominant material for forged ironheads and wedges has remained carbon steel.

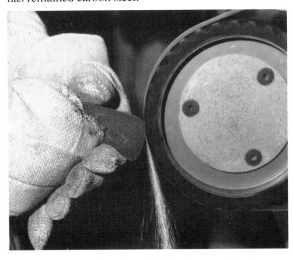

Forged irons are hand sanded during production

To the untrained eye, recognizing the difference between forged carbon steel and investment cast stainless steel ironheads can be difficult. Since cavity back and muscleback designs can be produced through both processes, clubmakers can often be fooled in their effort to tell one from the other. To separate a forged ironhead from an investment cast head, first inspect the head's finish and inside of the hosel bore. Tumble or dull finished ironheads are virtually all made through invest-

ment casting because such a finish is virtually impossible to create and make corrosion resistant on carbon steel. Stainless heads that have been mirror polished or satin finished upon close inspection just do not have the look, or "color," as bright chrome or satin chrome plated finishes on carbon steel heads. Inspecting the hosel bore is another way to tell forged carbon steel heads from the investment cast stainless ironheads. On a carbon steel head, the inside of the bore will show signs of corrosion, a condition that will not be present on a stainless steel head.

Because the forging primarily represents the traditional side of golf equipment, because there are still a number of traditional-minded golfers and because the myth of forging being superior to casting still remains in the minds of many golfers, forged ironheads and wedges could be an important part of your clubmaking business. From the clubmaker's standpoint, forged carbon steel irons are likely to be more popular with lower handicap golfers. In addition, the generally softer nature of the heads will make them easier to bend for loft and lie fitting purposes than the majority of stainless ironheads. Still, caution in bending must be observed to prevent the chrome plating from cracking.

Forged Stainless Steel

It was mentioned through the first half of the 20th century a few golf club manufacturers did produce forged stainless steel ironheads, but halted the practice when the golfing market found no playability advantage inherent in the design. Very few forged stainless ironheads exist today, with virtually none in the component clubhead industry because of the high cost of the metal compared to carbon steel and the high cost of the forging process. However, should component head companies offer such a model, clubmakers may be interested in buying an occasional set. Among the reasons for using forged stainless ironheads would be: 1. As a forging, the stainless would be soft enough to allow easy alteration of loft and lie for fitting purposes, and 2. Being stainless, the heads in all likelihood would not be plated and therefore, not susceptible to chrome plating failure.

Graphite Ironheads

Modern materials and forming technology advancements in the 1980s have made it possible to produce ironheads from graphite. Not a complete all-graphite head, these models are rather a combination of graphite

Graphite Ironhead

that is compression molded over a stainless steel sole, hosel and face plate to form the design. If the entire head were made from graphite, headweights would be too light, so manufacturers must introduce a metal core into the design to increase the head's weight and absorb the stress of impact with the ground. Because of the combination graphite/metal design, these heads can have the ability to keep the center of gravity low on the head while still exhibiting any conceivable shape and style features across the back of the blade. While graphite ironheads do represent a breakthrough in design that can improve weight distribution and club playability over stainless or carbon steel designs, other less favorable aspects inherent to the design have so far prevented graphite ironheads from achieving a great degree of popularity in the game.

Some of the factors limiting the success of graphite ironheads are - 1. Cost - Being made from compression-molded graphite and including an investment cast stainless core, graphite ironheads are very expensive to make. The few designs that have been made available to component assemblers sell for $24-30 per finished ironhead. 2. Lack of Alterability - With the composite material molded over a steel hosel, it is impossible to alter the loft or lie of a graphite ironhead. Loft and lie alterability is becoming an important factor of ironhead selection to both golfers and club builders, and is a situation that cannot be remedied other than through the manufacturer constructing multiple numbers of very expensive molds, an offering that is not likely to happen; 3. Cosmetic appearance - While the stainless sole of the graphite ironheads will stand up well to normal wear and tear, the sole, along with the graphite covered face, back and hosel of the heads are coated with polyurethane. When subjected to play from sand bunkers, shots hit from wet grass with the usual amount of soil residue between the face and the ball, or clubs knocking against each other in the bag, it isn't long before these expensive heads begin lose their original appearance and look pitted and "shop-worn."

Die Cast Ironheads

Once thought of as the lowest in quality of all ironhead types, in the late 1980s die cast ironheads underwent a transformation that has had the effect of increasing their

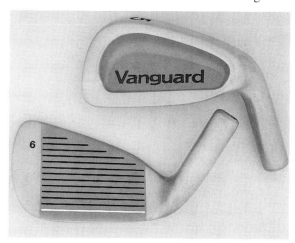

Die Cast Irons

popularity as an economical choice for starter sets and beginners. As a result of their increased popularity, more and more designs of die cast ironheads are becoming available to clubmakers.

Usually made from a soft metal such as Zinc, die cast irons are coming of age in clubmaking as foundries

discover new techniques for the design and finishing of these low priced heads. Still, because the soft metal used in die casting is not as strong as stainless or carbon steel, assemblers should exercise judgment with regard to the types of golfers (i.e. golfer strength) for whom the set is to be made.

In die casting as opposed to investment casting, the molten metal is introduced directly into the mold, after which the heads are subjected to grinding and finishing. Far fewer steps are required to make a die cast ironhead than an investment cast head, one of the main reasons for the die cast ironhead's lower cost ($4-5 per finished head). Unlike an investment cast mold, a die cast mold is made from hard steel to be able to withstand the temperature of the molten zinc or composite metal. As a result, the cost of a die cast mold is much higher than an investment cast mold, thus making die casting cost effective to a manufacturer only if a very large number of pieces are going to be produced.

Almost unbelievably, die casting is a more accurate process for achieving the specifications of the head than is investment casting. Providing the molds are properly made, loft, lie, headweight and even the integrity of logos and artwork in die casting are far less subject to errors because of the fact the metals used have far lower melting temperatures (@ 900° for die casting vs. @ 2,700° for investment casting) and are introduced directly into the mold itself.

Recent changes in the finishing of die cast ironheads has been the major reason for the heads' increase in popularity. Previously, all die cast ironheads were bright chrome electroplated, a finish which gave the heads a very cheap appearance. Now with the ability to perform tumble or vibratory finishing and satin chrome plating, die cast ironheads have taken on a much finer look, almost to the point that golfers cannot tell the difference between a die cast and an investment cast head.

The untrained eye will have a difficult time identifying die cast ironheads, but upon close inspection a few points of difference can be noted: 1. The outside diameter of the

hosel on a die cast ironhead will always be larger than the hosel of forged or investment cast models. This increase in hosel diameter is necessary to give the soft metal the ability to withstand the normal wear and tear of use; 2. Die cast irons may be tumble finished, satin or bright chrome plated, but in many cases will also be covered by a laquer or polyurethane coating. This glossy finish on the head is another indication of die casting; 3. Because of the composition of the metals used, die cast clubs cannot be bent for loft and lie alteration purposes. The grain structure of the soft metals used in die casting is very granulated and can break when just a small amount of pressure is applied to the hosel. In addition, some die cast irons that are made from metal composites can actually melt when subjected to heating, such as is done during the procedure of shaft removal.

Clubmakers should also be aware that using die cast ironheads does present a very good way to offer low priced golf clubs to juniors. With more and more die cast ironheads offering the weight distribution designs needed by beginners, this is a very good way to attract parents or schools to invest in equipment for the purpose of promoting junior play.

Major Component Supply Items

■ PUTTER HEADS

When club builders take note of the variety of putter heads that are available for custom assembly, the first thing that may come to mind is "so what, putters are putters." Before you overlook putters as being insignifi-

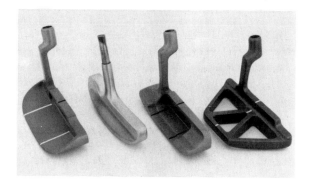

cant when compared to sets of woods or irons, first realize that putters are used to execute approximately half of the shots a player will make in a round of golf.

Such an important club does deserve attention from clubmakers, not just because of the putter's importance in a round, but because of the sales potential they represent. More than woods or irons, putters represent almost an impulse buy on behalf of golfers. The average golfer owns 3-4 putters and, owing to the frustration involved with this part of the game, will be a candidate for purchasing even more.

As in the case of the different forms of manufacture that exist for wood and ironheads, club builders will be faced with selecting putter heads that are produced in a variety of ways, from an assortment of different materials. Within each of the methods of putter head manufacture, similar designs do exist, so the following is a brief description of the methods of putter head manufacture that are available to clubmakers.

Investment Cast Putter Heads
Using this more modern head making technique, foundries have been able to offer manufacturers and clubmakers putter heads of literally any shape and style, made

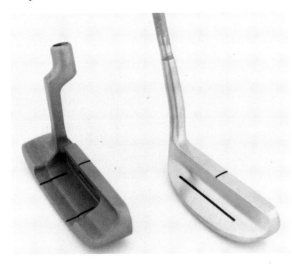

Investment Cast Putters

from quite a variety of metals. Manganese bronze, aluminum bronze, silicon bronze and several varieties of stainless steel are just a few of the metals that have been used to fashion a virtual encyclopedia of putter head designs through investment casting. Because of the cost of the process compared to other methods of putter head making, the investment cast types will usually be found by clubmakers to be a little higher in price than the other types of putter heads, ranging from $7-15 per head, depending upon the type of finish and the intricacy of the design.

Die Cast Putter Heads
While it was mentioned that die casting is used to produce ironheads for starter sets, putter heads made by the same process are not restricted to use by beginners.

Die Cast Putters

The lower strength inherent with die cast ironheads is not a problem with die cast putter heads. Since a putter is not swung at the same clubhead speed as an iron, there is virtually no chance that a die cast putter head will break during the normal course of play. Because the stress factors are so much less on a putter than an ironhead, very soft metals such as aluminum and brass (that would ordinarily be too weak to be used for an ironhead) can be used in addition to the slightly stronger zinc and composite metals for putter head manufacture. Using an assort-

ment of creative finishing methods, die cast putter head makers can offer clubmakers a high quality look that gives the heads a very high-end appearance. However, club builders who insist on heads that will give them the capability of altering loft and lie must be aware that bendability will vary with the material used. Brass and aluminum die cast putter heads will be very easy to bend, while extreme care must be taken before attempting to bend the zinc or zinc composite heads.

Sand Cast Putter Heads
The lowest quality production means of making putter heads involves the use of the sand casting process. A very soft metal such as brass is gravity poured into molds

Sand Cast Putter

made from firm sand. As can be expected, the surface of the metal comes out very rough and pitted from the gravity sand casting, so for a high quality appearance to be achieved on the finished part, quite a lot of grinding and polishing is required. Since sand casting is used to keep tooling and mold costs low, foundries usually opt for leaving the head somewhat rough in the finished state or choose to use a polished or laquered finish to achieve more of a quality look. As long as care is taken to create an accurate master, sand casting can yield putter heads of adequate quality, so club builders should not shy away from these types of putter heads as a potential item to stock.

Forged Carbon Steel Putter Heads

Once the method of manufacture for all ironheads, wedges and putters, forging is used very little today as a process of manufacturing putter heads. Aside from the

Forged Carbon Steel Putter

higher cost of forging today, the reason forged putter heads have all but disappeared is because of the change in putter head design over the last 20 years.

Some 20 years ago, puttter head design moved away from the plain blade or flange type styles into intricate and elaborate heel/toe types of designs with thin stemmed hosels. Such intricate shape and style features are difficult to forge, so when that drawback is coupled with the types of designs that sell well in today's market, it is apparent why each of the other forms of putter head manufacture are more widely used today. Because the costs of labor involved in producing a forging are high, even the traditional weight distribution designs that used to be synonomous only with forging are made in one of the other forms of manufacture. As a result, practically no forged putter heads are offered by component supply companies.

Injection-Molded Putter Heads

Rarely seen in the past in clubhead manufacturing, injection-molded putter heads are now being offered to clubmakers in limited design styles as an adjunct of the injection-molded woodhead business. Because injection molding is perfomed with lightweight materials, putter

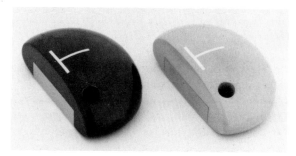

Injection-Molded Putters

heads made through the process must have added weighting to be able to achieve standard putter head weights. As a result, virtually all injection-molded putter heads are modeled in a mallet style, a design which allows the manufacturer to add the necessary weight. Though limited in styles, injection-molded putter heads will allow the clubmaker to offer one more option to golfers.

Major Component Supply Items

■ SHAFTS

In no part of clubmaking has the variety of options available for use in building golf clubs increased as it has within the shaft making industry. Once only a slightly confusing part of a golf club, triggered by the tremendous advancements in graphite shaft technology, clubmakers now have literally thousands of shafts from which to choose.

In Chapter 3, the entire spectrum of shaft information and technology will be covered to help clubmakers gain the technical background necessary for accurately building golf clubs. In this section, the shaft needs of the clubmaking shop will be addressed in an effort to help you set up an adequate inventory.

There is a very competent clubmaker/golf professional in the Chicago area who once made the statement that he carried $20,000 worth of golf shafts in inventory at all times and often found that he *still* didn't have the shafts

he really needed! Rather than make you panic and feel that you have to mortgage the house to finance a shaft inventory, that statement needs a little qualification for full understanding. This particular clubmaker is a head golf professional at a large club where custom fitting of golf clubs is stressed very highly. In his business, shaft fitting is awarded a very high priority and a lot of effort is made to discover the exact shaft for each of the golfers who come in to be fit. Therefore, he and his staff are constantly fitting golfers to a tremendous variety of shafts: taper tip, parallel tip, standard weight shafts, light weights, very light weights, graphites, composites, titaniums, low bend points, mid bend points, variable bend points, high bend points, frequency matched ... in other words, this clubmaker has committed to being able to satisfy almost every possible shaft fitting option available.

Such a shaft commitment is a priority that does not come in a clubmaker's first year of work, but rather may come after years of education, training and experience in the business. Until such experience is gained, what clubmakers need is a guideline to help them be efficient and economical in their selection of shafts for their inventory. If the total number of shaft units available from the world's shaft manufacturers were compiled by pattern, flex, length, etc., the number would reach well over 2,000! Fortunately, most clubmakers will never have to worry about even a fraction of that total, but that number may impress upon you the importance of careful shaft buying and shaft inventory management.

How to Plan your Shaft Needs

When you plan the shaft buying needs of your shop, allowing for an adequate inventory can be a very tricky venture. With all the designs available today, not to mention flexes, lengths and tip diameters, it would be very easy to misjudge your needs and spend hundreds of dollars on shafts that do no good for your shop. Before you plan your shaft needs and orders, take time to think about a few of the following questions:

Q. **What are the predominant bore sizes of the clubheads I plan to use?**

A. A major priority in managing the inventory of your total shop needs is to plan your clubhead purchases. If you are going to work primarily with heads that have tapered hosel bores, then you must obviously plan your shaft inventory to reflect that; if parallel bores are going to be predominant on the heads you buy, then lean heavily toward parallel tip shafts. If you plan to build clubs from components only and expect to perform no re-shafting of other manufacturer's golf clubs, restrict your shaft purchases to the parallel tip varieties only.

Q. **What are the most popular shaft patterns used in golf clubs?**

A. Currently, the most popular shaft patterns in club-making are:

STEEL SHAFTS
1. True Temper Dynamic/Dynamic Gold
2. True Temper TT Lite
3. Apollo Shadow

GRAPHITE SHAFTS
1. Aldila Low Torque (scheduled for a 1992 redesign)
2. Aldila HM-40
3. Aldila HM-30

Since so many golf clubs are made with these shafts both by clubmakers and major manufacturers alike, it is only natural to lean toward these popular patterns as a way to please your customers. Most of these popular patterns are manufactured in tapered and parallel form, so select the version depending upon the predominant hosel bore size you use. Again, whenever possible, choose the parallel version of a shaft to reduce your inventory units.

If you plan to offer custom fitting, be aware that the shaft patterns that are most popular are not necessarily what most of your golfers *should* be playing with. For example, while the Dynamic/Dynamic Gold is the most popular shaft pattern used by major manufacturers, its playing characteristics are not well suited for the majority of average golfers.

Q. **Why should I care about stocking any shafts other than the most popular ones?**

A. If building golf clubs that are primarily made to standard specifications is your goal, then you will probably stick to these more popular patterns. However, two factors will affect that: 1. Shaft availability - Since the above shafts are more popular there will be times your suppliers may be out of stock and unable to fill your orders in the quantities you need or within the time you desire; 2. Custom fitting - Since individually fitting golfers can be a valuable part of your business, you should strive to educate yourself about all of the other shaft patterns and be able to match their benefits to the golfers you service. As mentioned, what major manufacturers choose for standard shaft patterns is not necessarily what the average golfer should use.

Q. **What do I do when I am back ordered and cannot receive these popular shaft patterns?**

A. Each of the major steel shaft manufacturers produce patterns that are virtually identical to each other. For example, the AP44 from Apollo and the ProPel II from Brunswick are equivalent in all playing characteristics to the Dynamic from True Temper. In Chapter 3 equivalent shaft patterns will be discussed in detail, but for stocking purposes, if your first choices are not available when you order, always look for the comparable patterns that exist.

Q. **How many shafts should I plan to carry in inventory?**

A. If you had an unlimited bank account, it would be nice to order a year's supply and then just sit back and make clubs without worrying about reordering. However, this is never the case, so you have to plan your shaft purchases carefully. If you do not include reshafting or repair as a major part of your services, then most of the shafts you stock will be used for clubmaking. If so, it is an easy formula to figure on having at least a 1-2 month supply of shafts on hand at any time. To some individuals this may be as few as 50-100 shafts, but to larger club assembly shops it may mean an inventory of at least 500 or more. Add to that the needs created by any accent you may make toward custom fitting and these numbers may double. If you carry a small stock of shafts, be sure to issue back up orders to your suppliers as the shafts are used to replenish the inventory.

In addition, the industry's overall demand for shafts and the lead time for shipments will have a great bearing on the size of on-hand inventory you may keep. For example, in 1987-88 demand for shafts exceeded the shaft manufacturers' and distributors' ability to supply. Backorders were the norm for even common shaft patterns. Therefore, clubmakers had to carry a far larger inventory of shafts than they did in 1990, when the supply caught up with the demand.

A cardinal rule to follow in planning your shaft needs is to **avoid quoting delivery of a set of clubs before you have the shafts in your possession.** While it is best for clubmakers to try and let their suppliers carry the inventory, it will not be helpful to the reputation of your business if you miss a promise for delivery because you did not check the availability of the shafts. If you sell a set of golf clubs for which you do not yet have the shafts, check with your supplier before quoting a delivery date to the customer.

Q. **How should I store the shafts that I buy?**

A. Organization is one of the greatest virtues of a clubmaker, so take time to plan a good system for storing and organizing the shafts you have in inventory. If your inventory is small and you do not carry a wide variety of patterns, clean cardboard boxes with the appropriate shaft code marked plainly on the outside will suffice. However, as your inventory needs increase you will have to put more effort into planning your methods of storing shafts. The best idea is to add up the number of different shafts you plan to stock by pattern, by flex and by raw shaft length to come up with a final figure of storage compartments that will be required. Build an open rack from wood with a lattice of compartment openings, about 6" x 6" in size, to store the shafts in a horizontal position. Such a rack can be placed in a corner of your shop and take up a little as 16 square feet, yet can hold as many as 1,000 shafts or more.

Since shaft storage methods are only limited by your imagination, there are several other options you may wish to explore. However, a couple of guidelines are to always keep your steel shafts away from moisture (to prevent rusting and pitting over long term storage) and **never** allow different shaft flexes, lengths or patterns to get mixed together.

Q. What other tips will help in planning shaft purchases?

A. If you plan to purchase taper tip shafts either for reshafting or new club assembly, you will need to stock different raw uncut lengths within the same flex and pattern to be able to assemble full sets. Try to avoid "breaking" full sets of taper tip shafts. Failure to do so will mean that when an order for a full set comes along you might not be able to complete all the clubs within the set. The most commonly used raw lengths of tapered shafts are 44" (for Drivers) and 35" (for wedges and putters). Therefore, keep more of these in stock but also keep the rest of the lengths in full set increments.

When working with parallel tip shafts, always use the combination flex form (i.e. the UDWC Dynamic R & S flex for woods as opposed to the separately made UDWR and UDWS) of a shaft to keep the number of inventory units down.

Because of their higher cost, restrict your in-house inventory of graphite shafts to parallel tip versions for woods. Clubmakers will sell far more graphite shafted Drivers and woods than irons, so having graphite-iron shafts in stock can be a waste of inventory dollars. Try to use the suppliers' inventory of graphite shafts whenever possible.

While most component supply companies have different clubhead models, the shaft patterns that they supply will be the same. In other words the Aldila HM-40 that one company has will be the same as the HM-40 from another. Since the product is the same, be sure to shop competitively with two major points in mind: 1. Price - There is no need to pay more for the same product; 2. Delivery - While one company may advertise a lower price for a shaft, that price is of no use if they do not ship

in a timely manner. Become aware of the time required by each supplier to ship your orders.

Sample Shaft Inventories
Obviously, the number of shafts you buy will be dependent upon several factors: whether you perform reshafting for repair purposes and therefore will not be using your inventory strictly for club assembly, the amount of business you do, and whether you wish to order a lot of different shaft patterns and types for fitting purposes. The following lists are simply to be taken as examples of sample shaft inventories for different business sizes. These lists are examples only but may be helpful in planning your individual requirements.

SMALL SHAFT INVENTORY
Approximate Cost - $330

Qty	Code *Flex*	Shaft Pattern *Woods/Irons*
15	UDIC *R/S Combination*	Dynamic Steel[1] *Irons*
10	UDWC *R/S Combination*	Dynamic Steel *Woods*
15	UTTLIC *R/S Combination*	TT Lite Steel[2] *Irons*
10	UTTLWC *R/S Combination*	TT Lite Steel *Woods*
10	U2LIAL *A/L Combination*	TT Lite Steel *Irons*
8	U2LWAL *A/L Combination*	TT Lite Steel *Woods*
3	ALWRS *R/S Combination*	Low Torque Graphite *Woods*

[1] Comparable patterns to the True Temper Dynamic® are the Pro Pel II® from Brunswick and the AP44 from Apollo Shaft Corp. Clubmakers should always rely on comparable patterns as needs dictate. Depending upon the individual market demand, the Dynamic Gold may be substituted for the standard Dynamic.

[2] Comparable patterns to the True Temper TT Lite® are the Phoenix® from Brunswick and the Spectre® from Apollo Shaft Corp. Clubmakers should always rely on comparable patterns as needs dictate.

The above sample inventory is considered a very small stock of shafts but, taking combination flex characteristics into account, will allow you to assemble a possible total of more than 20 sets of woods and irons over four different flexes. In addition, such a list assumes that your entire inventory of clubheads are of the parallel bore variety and that very few shafts will be used for repair purposes. Since standard issue parallel tip steel shafts can be used in metal woods with extra trimming allowances, no tip reinforced shafts will be necessary. Also, as long as parallel bore putter heads are stocked, any of the above iron shafts can be used for their assembly.

MEDIUM SHAFT INVENTORY
Approximate Cost - $1,100

Qty	Code *Flex*	Shaft Pattern *Woods/Irons*	Qty	Code *Flex*	Shaft Pattern *Woods/Irons*
10	UDIX *X*	Dynamic Steel *Irons*	10	SHIRS *R/S Combination*	Shadow Steel[4] *Irons*
5	UDWX *X*	Dynamic Steel *Woods*	5	SHWRS *R/S Combination*	Shadow Steel *Woods*
25	UDIC *R/S Combination*	Dynamic Steel[1] *Irons*	10	SHIL *L*	Shadow Steel *Irons*
15	UDWC *R/S Combination*	Dynamic Steel *Woods*	5	SHWL *L*	Shadow Steel *Woods*
25	UTTLIC *R/S Combination*	TT Lite Steel[2] *Irons*	10	AP46IR *R*	AP 46 Steel[5] *Irons*
15	UTTLWC *R/S Combination*	TT Lite Steel *Woods*	5	AP46WR *R*	AP 46 Steel *Woods*
10	UDGIS *S-200, 300 or 400*[3]	Dynamic Gold Steel *Irons*	2	9063P *Putter*	Putter Steel *Putter*
5	UDGWS *S-200, 300 or 400*[3]	Dynamic Gold Steel *Woods*	4	ALWRS *R/S Combination*	Low Torque Graphite *Woods*
10	UGPIR *S-300*[3]	Gold Plus Steel *Irons*	2	HM40WS *S*	HM-40 Graphite *Woods*
5	UGPWR *S-300*[3]	Gold Plus Steel *Woods*	1	TIWR *R*	Titanium *Woods*
			1	TIWS *S*	Titanium *Woods*

[1] Comparable patterns to the True Temper Dynamic® are the Pro Pel II® from Brunswick and the AP44 from Apollo Shaft Corp. Clubmakers should always rely on comparable patterns as needs dictate.
[2] Comparable patterns to the True Temper TT Lite® are the Phoenix® from Brunswick and the Spectre® from Apollo Shaft Corp. Clubmakers should always rely on comparable patterns as needs dictate.
[3] Which of the precise sub-flexes of Dynamic Gold or Gold Plus is selected is an individual decision
[4] Comparable pattern to the Apollo Shadow is the Brunswick Microtaper.
[5] Economically priced steel shaft for use in starter sets.

The above sample inventory is considered a medium, but well rounded stock of shafts and will allow you to satisfy quite a few clubmaking options for your customers. In standard weight and lightweight patterns you will have most of the flexes for each shaft type, plus you have the ability to offer different bend point options in lightweight shafts through a choice between TT Lite style and the Shadow pattern shafts. Graphite shafts for different player types for woods are also included in the list to allow you to capitalize on this market. In addition, included are special putter shafts as well as low priced steel shafts for use in starter sets. As before, such a list assumes that your entire inventory of clubheads are of the parallel bore variety, but the difference is that the inventory is large enough to allow some shafts to also be used for repair purposes.

LARGE SHAFT INVENTORY
Approximate Cost - $2,700

Qty	Code / Flex	Shaft Pattern / Woods/Irons
STEEL SHAFTS		
10	UDIX / *X*	Dynamic[1] / *Irons*
5	UDWX / *X*	Dynamic / *Woods*
40	UDIC / *R/S Combination*	Dynamic / *Irons*
25	UDWC / *R/S Combination*	Dynamic / *Woods*
40	UTTLIC / *R/S Combination*	TT Lite[2] / *Irons*
25	UTTLWC / *R/S Combination*	TT Lite / *Woods*
20	U2LIAL / *A/L Combination*	TT Lite / *Irons*
10	U2LWAL / *A/L Combination*	TT Lite / *Woods*
15	UDGIR / *R-200, 300 or 400[3]*	Dynamic Gold / *Irons*
8	UDGWR / *R-200, 300 or 400[3]*	Dynamic Gold / *Woods*
25	UDGIS / *S-200, 300 or 400[3]*	Dynamic Gold / *Irons*
12	UDGWS / *S-200, 300 or 400[3]*	Dynamic Gold / *Woods*
10	UGPIR / *S-300[3]*	Gold Plus / *Irons*
5	UGPWR / *S-300[3]*	Gold Plus / *Woods*
20	SHIRS / *R/S Combination*	Shadow[4] / *Irons*
10	SHWRS / *R/S Combination*	Shadow / *Woods*
10	SHIA / *A*	Shadow / *Irons*
5	SHWA / *A*	Shadow / *Woods*
10	SHIL / *L*	Shadow / *Irons*
5	SHWL / *L*	Shadow / *Woods*

Qty	Code / Flex	Shaft Pattern / Woods/Irons
2	2LWR-44 / *R*	TT Lite Taper / *#1 Woods*
2	2LIR-39 / *R*	TT Lite Taper / *#1, 2-Irons*
2	2LIR-38 / *R*	TT Lite Taper / *#3, 4-Irons*
2	2LIR-37 / *R*	TT Lite Taper / *#5, 6-Irons*
2	2LIR-36 / *R*	TT Lite Taper / *#7, 8-Irons*
4	2LIR-35 / *R*	TT Lite Taper / *#9-iron, PW*
2	2LWS-44 / *S*	TT Lite Taper / *#1 Woods*
2	2LIS-39 / *S*	TT Lite Taper / *#1, 2-Irons*
2	2LIS-38 / *S*	TT Lite Taper / *#3, 4-Irons*
2	2LIS-37 / *S*	TT Lite Taper / *#5, 6-Irons*
2	2LIS-36 / *S*	TT Lite Taper / *#7, 8-Irons*
4	2LIS-35 / *S*	TT Lite Taper / *#9, PW Irons*
2	DWS-44 / *S*	Dynamic Taper / *#1 Woods*
2	DIS-38 / *S*	Dynamic Taper / *#3, 4-Irons*
2	DIS-37 / *S*	Dynamic Taper / *#5, 6-Irons*
2	DIS-36 / *S*	Dynamic Taper / *#7, 8-Irons*
4	DIS-35 / *S*	Dynamic Taper / *#9,-iron, PW*
10	AP46IR / *R*	AP 46[5] / *Irons*
5	AP46WR / *R*	AP 46 / *Woods*
5	9063P / *Putter*	Putter / *Putter*
8	APJI / *Juniors*	Apollo Jr / *Irons*
4	APJW / *Juniors*	Apollo Jr / *Woods*

Qty	Code / Flex	Shaft Pattern / Woods/Irons
GRAPHITE/COMPOSITE SHAFTS		
8	ALWRS / *R/S Combination*	Aldila Low Torque / *Woods*
2	ALWL / *L*	Aldila Low Torque / *Woods*
10	ALIRS / *R/S Combination*	Aldila Low Torque / *Irons*
1	T50WX / *X*	Unifiber / *Woods*
2	HM40WS / *S*	Aldila HM-40 / *Woods*
2	HM30WR / *R*	Aldila HM-30 / *Woods*
2	FS100 / *Flexible*	FiberSpeed / *Woods*
2	TIWR / *R*	Ti Shaft Titanium / *Woods*
2	TIWS / *S*	Ti Shaft Titanium / *Woods*
1 set	FMI 6.5 / *S*	Precision FM[6] / *Irons*
5	FMW 6.5 / *S*	Precision FM / *Woods*

[1] Comparable patterns to the True Temper Dynamic® are the Pro Pel II® from Brunswick and the AP44 from Apollo Shaft Corp. Clubmakers should always rely on comparable patterns as needs dictate.

[2] Comparable patterns to the True Temper TT Lite® are the Phoenix® from Brunswick and the Spectre® from Apollo Shaft Corp. Clubmakers should always rely on comparable patterns as needs dictate.

[3] Which of the precise sub-flexes of Dynamic Gold or Gold Plus is selected is an individual decision

[4] Comparable pattern to the Shadow from Apollo Shaft Ltd.is the Brunswick Microtaper.

[5] Economically priced steel shafts for use in starter sets.

[6] Precision FM Shafts for irons are sold in pre-packaged sets, set make-up to be the discretion of the distributor. Because these shafts are more likely to be a choice of better players, set make-up should be to cover the #2 - PW, or at least nine shafts.

The preceding list is considered an extensive inventory of shafts and will allow you to satisfy virtually all possible clubmaking options for your customers. In standard weight and lightweight patterns you can offer all of the possible flexes, plus you have the ability to vary the bend point offered in both standard and lightweight shafts through a variety of choices. Graphite shafts for woods and irons, as well as Titanium wood shafts are listed in the most popular flexes and are included to allow you to further capitalize on these specialty markets. A sampling of three different frequency matched patterns, Dynamic Gold, Gold Plus lightweight and Precision FM are included for custom fitting needs. As before, such a list assumes that your entire inventory of clubheads are of the parallel bore variety, but the difference is that the inventory is large enough to allow shafts to be used for many different repairs as well as custom fitting purposes. Also, taper tip shafts in TT Lite for average players and Dynamic for better players are included for replacement reshaft work. Such an extensive shaft inventory will cost approximately $2,700, based on average 1991 industry distributor prices.

Taper Tip Shafts - A Word About Stocking

When the statement was made that more than 2,000 different shafts are available from all of the shaft manufacturers, it must be understood a large percentage of that number is taken up by the taper tip version of different patterns of shafts. In 1971, True Temper introduced the concept of the parallel tip, unitized, combination flex steel shaft. This change in shaft tip design allowed manufacturers to reduce the stock units in their shaft inventories. In the world of taper tip shafts, a different shaft must be ordered and used for each wood or iron in a set. For a set of four woods (#1, 3, 4, 5) and 10 irons (1 - 9 plus PW) the clubmaker has to order 13 different raw uncut lengths to complete the set - and that is just for one flex! Compare that to the fact that to cover the same set but in two different flexes, only two unitized, combination flex, parallel tip shafts need to be ordered.

With the increasing demands that have been placed upon the shaft manufacturers due to the growth of golf, the chances of any of the necessary taper tip shafts being out of stock are much greater than the same chances for only two parallel tip shafts not being available for shipment at the time of order. If you receive a back order from your supplier for even one of the taper tip shaft lengths you cannot properly complete the set. In addition, shaft distributors will often not carry all of the necessary taper tip raw shaft lengths in each of the various patterns. They too have inventory decisions to make to keep their inventory at manageable levels. Such supplier decisions mean you might be faced with having to trim the tip of certain tapered shafts and then rebore the hosels on some of the heads in the set to achieve the correct mounting of the shafts throughout the set.

If you decide that taper tip shafts must be a part of your inventory, realize that in stocking taper tip shafts, your inventory needs are going to increase and your needs for more shaft storage bins to organize the greater number of shafts will increase too. To aid your planning should you decide to stock taper tip shafts, the most widely used patterns in taper version are the same as for the parallel variety. However, remember that in placing your orders you will be asked to specify the raw length in addition to the pattern and flex. See Chapter 3 for more shaft information about tapered vs. parallel tip shafts.

Major Component Supply Items

■ GRIPS

Because their individual cost is low, grips might seem to qualify more as a small part item rather than a major component supply item. Yet, because there are so many varieties to choose from, because golfers have so many different tastes, and because most club builders can't help but attract additional business in the form of regripping existing sets of clubs, the total cost of an adequate grip inventory can add up to be a major workshop expense. Therefore, clubmakers would be wise to carefully plan their grip stocking needs to be sure of handling all of the necessary types, styles and core sizes.

Rubber Composition Grips

Ever since the introduction of the first slip-on grips some 40 years ago, the variety of rubber grips from which a clubmaker can compile an inventory is quite large.

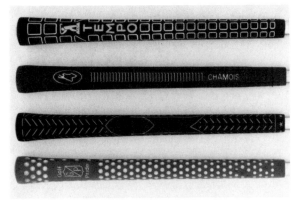

Rubber Composition Grips

Foremost among the types of grips used in clubmaking today is the slip-on style grip that is injection molded or compression molded from a rubber and cork composition material. Cork is mixed with the blended rubber compound to act as a filler and somewhat as a moisture retardant for the grip. While at first glance it would seem one grip maker's rubber compound is the same as all others, in fact this is not true. Each manufacturer formulates its own rubber compounds for grip making. As a result, rubber grips are offered with varying degrees of tackiness, color and durability. Once manufactured only by compression molding, most grip makers today are slowly converting over to the use of injection molding as the process of choice for rubber grip production.

To start the production of the grip, multi-cavity molds ensuring the outside diameter size and surface design are tooled by engineers to precise tolerances along the entire length of the grip. Steel mandrels, called core bars, are made to the same dimensions as the various shaft butt sections and are inserted into each grip mold cavity to form the inner hole, or the core for each grip. After a pre-made end cap of a harder rubber compound is placed into the end of each mold cavity the molds are closed and joined with the injection nozzle. The injection molding machine then forces the rubber composition material under great heat and pressure into the mold cavities, thus forming the grips. After blowing the grips off the core bars to withdraw them from the molds, the rubber grips are sanded to remove the excess flashing of rubber on the mold seam lines. Then through successive painting steps the color fill of each grip is established. Conventional rubber/cork composition slip-on grips are made in a wide variety of shapes, patterns, colors, core sizes, lengths, outside diameters and inside rib designs, so that all golfers can have a choice to suit their needs.

Rubber/Cord Grips

The other popular style of slip-on grip used in clubmaking is the rubber and cord composition grip. These grips, recognized by the cloth fibers that protrude through the

Rubber/Cord Grips

rubber are manufactured through the compression molding process. Separate strips of rubber and cotton fiber material are laid into each mold cavity and through compression molding, the fibers are literally squeezed into the rubber until they protrude through the surface of the grip. As extensions of the process, rubber/cord grips with the fibers located around the entire circumference, in half circumference sections or even quarter sections are all available for use in clubmaking. Because rubber/cord grips are made through the more expensive compression molding form of manufacture, and because there exists a greater chance for reject rates due to inconsistent positioning of the fiber cord material, cord

grips sell for far higher prices than rubber grips.

Synthetic Grips

Another popular slip-on grip that is a product of modern molding technology are grips made from a variety of synthetic rubbers or pliable plastics. Kraton®, a thermoplastic material invented by Shell Oil is used to

Synthetic Grips

manufacture most of the Tacki-Mac and Poulin companies' grips, while Silplus®, a silicone rubber from G.E., is used to make the Tac-Flo brand grips. Using a process similar to injection molding, grips made from Kraton® or Silplus® are known for their high durability and slightly tacky feel.

Leather Grips

Leather wrap-on grips, once the only grip used in clubmaking, are still popular with a certain segment of golfers despite their higher price. Improved tanning and finishing techniques have given the golf industry leather straps that are available in several colors, in varying degrees of

Leather Grips

tackiness, and are already "skived" on the edges for overlap wrapping purposes. Once a time consuming and difficult procedure because of the skill required to hand-wrap the paper underlisting, leather grips are now much easier to install thanks to the introduction of slip-on rubber underlistings. Recently, further developments in grip manufacturing technology have made leather grip installation even easier through the introduction of slip-on leather grips. In these designs, the leather strap is already attached to the rubber underlisting, thus making installation almost as easy as with normal rubber grips.

Since the 1983 grip revisions in the Rules of Golf, a much wider variety of grip shapes are allowed for use on putters than on woods and irons. As a result, clubmakers can choose from several varieties of putter grip shapes and styles in slip-on rubber, slip-on leather and in shaped underlistings for leather wrapped putter grips. Certainly a variety of grips for all grip installation needs have been provided by the various manufacturers; now what you need are some guidelines to help you select your inventory. When you plan the grip buying needs of your shop, again, take time to think about a few of the following details:

How to Plan your Grip Needs

Q. How do I know what to buy?

A. Just as in the case of clubheads and shafts, the grips you stock in your shop should reflect what is currently popular both in your local area and in the golf industry. It is no secret that the number one selling grip in the industry has been the men's black/green Victory grip, manufactured by Eaton Golf Pride. A tremendous number of major manufacturers use this model as their standard issue grip, so you will need to feature this grip in your inventory. After the standard Victory, some of the other very popular grip styles are Golf Pride's Victory made in a number of other paint fill colors, the Golf Pride Dimple grip with gold fill, the Golf Pride

Victory Velvet or Half Cord for men and the jumbo oversize Victory grip.

From the Lamkin Grip Co. the black and green Conquest and Ultra Tac models are a popular choice among golfers. The British grip makers, Avon, produce the Chamois slip-on grip for men and women, an ultra-soft rubber grip that has moved into second place among all grips of choice. Kraton® grip molders, Tacki-mac, claim a large number of followers with their black knurl pattern grip known for its high durability and tacky feel. In addition, if you have developed the skill to wrap leather, you should stock a number of rubber underlistings (from either Golf Pride or Lamkin) and leather straps. Currently, the most popular leather straps are manufactured by the R. Neumann company.

To determine what other grips to stock, you should also take the demands of your local players into account. Take a look at golfers' clubs when you visit the golf course. In addition, take note of your climate; traditionally, in hot and humid areas, tacky compound rubber grips as well as leather and cord styles might be a little more popular than in cool, dry climates. This can be attributed to the fact that cord and leather grip styles are able to resist slipping from hand perspiration better than the all-rubber or rubber/cork composition grips while tacky grips are able to hold up to moisture without slipping.

Finally, recent golfer trends have just begun to show a slight move from the older traditional grip designs to the very new wave of high-tech grips. Called high-tech for the graphically bold geometric surface designs and exotic colors, this new generation of grips is fast gaining a following that as a clubmaker you can't afford to ignore.

Q. What about the different grip core sizes? Or ribbed vs. non-ribbed types of grips? Or all the other unconventional shapes and styles of grips that are on the market?

A. There is little doubt that the imaginations of golf equipment designers are very fertile, and the number of different shapes, styles and cosmetic designs of grips that are available today are a good example. The first consideration you will have to make concerns the fact that most slip-on grips and underlistings are manufactured in different core sizes. The core size dictates the size of the hole inside the grip, and is important because it determines what the size of the grip will be after it has been installed on the shaft (see Chapter 4 for complete details on grip sizing and installation).

Ideally, you would want to have all the different core sizes available to match up with the different shaft butt diameters you will encounter in clubmaking. However, such a selection would require clubmakers to carry extremely large grip inventories. Therefore, when choosing grip core sizes for the models you order, think about three things: 1. What are the predominant shaft butt diameters with which you will work? 2. Do you think you will field a number of requests for oversized grip installation? 3. Do your suppliers carry adequate inventories of the different core sizes to meet your needs? While most suppliers stock a predominance of .580" (men) and .560" (ladies) core grips, from the popularity of custom grip fitting many now offer a good assortment of popular styles in the .600" and .620" core sizes as well.

Perhaps one of the most illogical points in clubmaking is that more shafts are used in clubmaking that have .600" butt diameter, yet the most widely sold grip core size is the 58, or .580" dimension. When a 58 core size grip is installed on a .600" shaft butt with one wrap of 2-way tape, the installed grip will be + 1/64" over standard size. Therefore, it might be safe to assume that a lot of golf clubs are being made today with oversized grips. With the recent popularity increase in graphite shafts, it will be wise to stock a few men's grips in .620" core size and ladies grips in .600" core size. As a rule, graphite shafts are made with larger butt diameters than steel shafts of the same flexes, so the larger core sizes will help you avoid accidentally installing grips to an oversize condition. Still, from an inventory standpoint it is better to stock 58 and 60 core sizes in men's grips and 56 core sizes in ladies slip-on grips.

The terms "ribbed" or "round" refer to the shape that a conventional grip or underlisting assumes once it has been installed on the shaft. During the grip making process, the mandrel that is inserted into the mold to create the core can be completely round, or have a flat section machined down one side. If the core is made from a mandrel with a flat side, the core will be formed with an ridge of rubber on the bottom side of the grip. Therefore, when the grip is installed, the shaft pushes against this inner section of rubber to create a slight protrusion on the bottom of the grip, hence the "rib" that is felt in the hands by players when they use the grip.

A "round" grip is formed when the mandrel inserted into the mold is round, therefore leaving the core of the grip completely smooth and round, without a rib. Upon installation of this style of grip, the golfer will feel no protrusion in the hands, since the grip assumes a round shape on the shaft. In the industry, ribbed grips are more widely used, but you may wish to stock a few round varieties to satisfy the preference of some better players who do not like the feel of a ribbed grip in their hands.

There is no doubt you will be faced with a number of requests for some of the odd-shaped or "different feel" grips. After all, two of the most popular grips in the game today have been the hourglass-shaped Silhouette (now deemed as a non-conforming grip shape by the USGA) and the air cushioned Chamois. Each of the grip makers have one or more versions of specialty grips from which you can choose. In addition, abnormally large grips are offered by manufacturers, so you will want to stock some of the Jumbo Victory or Tacki-mac oversize grips to help players looking for a very large grip or to help those suffering from hand disorders such as arthritis gain comfort when they play.

Q. How many grips should I plan to carry?

A. As in the case of shafts, the size of your grip inventory will depend upon the size of your business, as well as how many of your grips are used for clubmaking as opposed to regripping existing sets. Generally, if your business is small and is more of a hobby than a career, you may be able to get by with five basic types of men's grips and two styles of ladies grips covering as few as 100 grips total. On the other hand, if your clubmaking is a serious side line or a even a full-time venture, you may wish to stock 10-15 men's models, four or five ladies styles, different putter grips, plus an assortment of leather grips. With such an extensive selection, an inventory for a large shop may easily exceed 500 or more total grips. Regardless of the level of your business, if you work with a supplying company that can ship your orders within days of your request, the smart and efficient thing to do is to try to keep only a two week to one month supply on-hand.

Q. **What are the best ways to store grips? Do grips have a "shelf life?"**

A. As long as rubber and leather grips are kept away from dust, bright light and wide changes in room temperature, they will remain fresh almost indefinitely. However, too many times clubmakers store grips in open "cubbyholes" under their main work bench where they can quickly become shopworn before they are used. The result are grips that have a "dingy" appearance and wear out sooner than normal (although the latter is probably good for your business!).

If you do not carry a large inventory of grips, old shoeboxes may not be very classy, but will make a great way to organize and store your supply. If your grip usage dictates that you can order in case quantities (usually 150 pieces for most grip companies, 200 for Tacki-mac) you will not only save money, but you will receive a good heavy box for storage purposes. Stacking grip case boxes on durable shelving with one end of the box cut open for easy access is a tried and true system used by many clubmakers and manufacturers alike. Finally, if you choose to build a special rack with multiple cubicles, make sure that the open sections are large enough to allow for an adequate number of grips per style. Also, to keep dust out of the grip storage bin openings, it will be wise to devise a curtain to cover the front of the rack.

SMALL GRIP INVENTORY
Approximate Cost - $265

Qty	Grip Style	Core Size
36	Men's Black/Green Victory	M58 (.580")
18	Men's Black/White/Gold Crown	M58 (.580")
24	Men's Chamois	M58 (.580")
12	Men's Velvet Victory Cord	M60 (.600")[1]
12	Men's Victory Half Cord	M60 (.600")
12	Men's Black Knurl Tacki-mac	M58 (.580")
12	Men's Jumbo Victory	M44 (.600")[2]
18	Ladies Blue/White Victory	L56 (.560")
18	Ladies Chamois	L56 (.560")
6	Pro Only Putter	M58 (.580")
6	Grip Rite Paddle Putter	M58 (.580")

[1] The M60 core size is recommended for all men's cord grip purchases due to the predominance of larger shaft butt diameters seen on clubs used by players preferring cord style grips.
[2] The M44 core size code is given to Golf Pride grips that have a special shape as part of their design and does not correspond to an actual diameter size.

The small clubmaking grip inventory above is suggested as a minimum on-hand supply of the most popular grips that you will encounter in your clubmaking and regripping work. The quantity of each grip model to be ordered will depend upon restocking lead times from your suppliers as well as how many of the grips are going to be used for making new clubs as opposed to regripping older sets. If regripping older sets is a major focus of your business, stocking levels should be adjusted higher.

The medium size grip inventory at right is offered for clubmaking shops who do not wish to reorder as often and who wish to be able to offer a slightly greater assortment of grip styles to their customers. While the styles listed are not advised to be stocked in large numbers, the actual quantities of each grip is entirely up to the clubmaker. For example, medium size clubmaking shops usually have a good feel for what grip styles sell well to their local market. If one particular grip style is

MEDIUM GRIP INVENTORY
Approximate Cost - $725

Qty	Grip Style	Core Size
60	Men's Black/Green Victory	M58 (.580")
24	Men's Black/Green Victory	M60 (.600")
18	Men's Black/White/Gold Crown	M58 (.580")
18	Men's Black/Gold Dimple	M58 (.580")
36	Men's Chamois	M58 (.580")
18	Men's Velvet Victory Cord	M60 (.600")[1]
18	Men's Victory Half Cord	M60 (.600")
18	Men's Black Knurl Tacki-mac	M58 (.580")
12	Men's Jumbo Victory	M44 (.600")[2]
24	Ladies Blue/White Victory	L56 (.560")
24	Ladies Chamois	L56 (.560")
12	Junior Victory	50 (.500")[3]
12	Pro Only Putter	M58 (.580")
12	Grip Rite Paddle Putter	M58 (.580")
18	Men's Leather Underlisting	RM60[4] (.600")
6	Putter Underlisting	58 (.580")
24	Leather Straps[5]	—

[1] The M60 core size is recommended for all men's cord grip purchases due to the predominance of larger shaft butt diameters seen on clubs used by players preferring cord style grips.
[2] The M44 core size code is given to Golf Pride grips that have a special shape as part of their design and does not correspond to an actual diameter size.
[3] If most of the shafts you use in building junior sets have a .500" butt diameter, purchase the 50 (.500") core size in junior grips. If you use conventional parallel tip steel shafts in regular flexes for use in junior clubs, the 58 (.580") core junior grips will be a better choice.
[4] The RM code designates an underlisting that is ribbed. If the round version is desired, the core size code would be SM followed by the numbers indicating core size.
[5] To be your choice of color, leather quality and manufacturer.

far more popular than another, it might be wise for the medium shop owner to purchase that grip in full case quantity to secure a better price per grip. The primary purpose of advising this medium size grip inventory is to make the point that as the shop grows in size, so too must the variety and quantity of grips that are offered as well.

LARGE GRIP INVENTORY
Approximate Cost - $1,600

Qty	Grip Style	Core Size	Qty	Grip Style	Core Size
150	Men's Black/Green Victory	M58 (.580")	36	Men's Victory Half Cord	M60 (.600")
60	Men's Black/Green Victory	M60 (.600")	36	Men's Black Knurl Tacki-mac	M58 (.580")
24	Men's Black/Green Victory	M62 (.620")	18	Men's Grey Knurl Tacki-mac	M58 (.580")
48	Men's Black/White/Gold Crown	M58 (.580")	12	Men's Arthritic	M58 (.580")
24	Men's Black/White Victory	M60 (.600")	24	Men's Tempo Standard	58 (.580")
18	Men's White/Gold Victory	M60 (.600")	24	Men's Royal Grip	60 (.600")
24	Men's Black/Gold Dimple	M58 (.580")	18	Men's Silhouette	59 (.590")[4]
18	Men's Air Cushion	M44 (.580")[1]	24	Ladies Chamois	L56 (.560")
24	Men's Hi-Tack	M59 (.590")	18	Junior Victory	50 (.500")[5]
24	Men's Jumbo Victory	M44 (.600")[1]	12	Pro Only Putter	M58 (.580")
24	Ladies Blue/White Victory	L56 (.560")	12	Grip Rite Paddle Putter	M58 (.580")
18	Ladies Black/Green Victory	L56 (.560")	6	Classic Putter	M58 (.580")
12	Ladies Black/Green Victory	L60 (.600")[2]	4	Chamois Putter	M58 (.580")
18	Ladies Air Cushion	L44 (.560")[1]	3	Men's Tiger Shark	M58 (.580")
60	Men's Chamois	M58 (.580")	24	Men's Leather Underlisting	RM60 (.600")[6]
18	Men's Grey/Black Charger	M58 (.580")	6	Putter Underlisting	58 (.580")
36	Men's Velvet Victory Cord	M60 (.600")[3]	30	Leather Straps[7]	—

[1] The M44 core size code is given to Golf Pride grips that have a special shape as part of their design and does not correspond to an actual diameter size.

[2] The L60 ladies core grips are for use on graphite shafts, many which are made with a .600" butt diameter on the L-flex versions.

[3] The M60 core size is recommended for all men's cord grip purchases due to the predominance of larger shaft butt diameters seen on clubs used by players preferring cord style grips.

[4] The Silhouette grip from Lamkin Grip Co. has been ruled as non-conforming to the USGA Rules of Golf. Such rules pertain to use in USGA sponsored tournaments, so it is your choice whether you want to offer non-conforming components to golfers.

[5] If most of the shafts you use in building junior sets have a .500" butt diameter, purchase the 50 (.500") core size in junior grips. If you use conventional parallel tip steel shafts in regular flexes for use in junior clubs, the 58 (.580") core junior grips will be a better choice.

[6] The RM code designates an underlisting that is ribbed. If the round version is desired, the core size code would be SM followed by the numbers indicating core size.

[7] To be your choice of color, leather quality and manufacturer.

The primary purpose in offering this example of a large inventory of grips is to primarily illustrate the variety of grip styles that are necessary for a large shop to carry. Of course, the quantity of any individual grip model must be dependent upon individual shop size. Many large clubmaking shops are already in the practice of ordering full case quantities of several of their styles. By ordering in full case amounts, shops can avoid having to reorder as often and will receive approximately a 10% grip savings in price. Therefore, if you can afford to order in case quantities, it is a wise idea to do so. This example of a large grip inventory will cost approximately $1,600 based upon averages of 1991 golf industry component supplier prices.

Setting Up the Clubmaking Shop

■ PLANNING THE LAYOUT OF THE WORKSHOP

Tremendous differences exist in the level of involvement between clubmakers. As a result, the workshops in which clubmakers ply their trade or dabble in their hobby are quite varied. From spare bedrooms, basements, garages and back rooms of pro shops to shopping center rentals, warehouses and factories, the location of clubmaking facilities can vary almost as much as the components that go into the making of a golf club. Obviously, the shop location and amount of space that is right for your clubmaking is primarily dependent upon the volume of work to be performed, the clubmaking services to be offered and the amount of machinery and inventory that is required to do the work.

Regardless of the size of your shop, there are certain points that must be taken into account before you begin to move in and set up shop. As with any light manufacturing business, the shop set up must include these major considerations: 1. Adequate storage for the inventory and supplies; 2. Enough space to perform the work, set up the required machinery and house the clubs during their assembly; 3. A "flow" that corresponds to the clubmaking procedures to be performed that is condusive to overall shop efficiency.

How to plan your workshop  **Q&A**

The first step in planning your shop layout is to list all of the procedures of clubmaking that you intend to perform. To help you define such a list of your services, take time to answer the following questions:

Q. How can I best set up a woodhead refinishing center?

A. To offer wooden head finishing as a service of your clubmaking business will require an area to sand the clubheads, an area for finish application and storage of finishing supplies, and an area for properly drying the finish coats. The actual procedures for finishing as well as the type of finishing materials that are used can vary and with them, so too will the shop layout requirements. Because the sanding machine(s) will put out dust that can play havoc with keeping new golf club components clean, a dust collection system may be required or a separate sanding area that is well away from the rest of the clubmaking flow.

If the finishing materials are applied by dipping, a separate workbench just for these procedures will be necessary. On the other hand, if spray type finishing materials are used, a separate spraying area with spray booth and exhaust system will be a must. While some finishing materials require only room temperature for proper curing, some require separate drying areas or space in which the temperature and humidity can be controlled. While many clubmakers devise a drying cabinet with light bulbs for heat, some have converted closets or small rooms for the purpose. Suffice to say any drying area must be free from dust that is generated in other clubmaking operations.

Q. **What do I need to know before setting up the necessary machinery?**

A. Larger pieces of machinery such as belt sanders, head sanders, grinders, cut-off saws, loft and lie machines, etc., take up space, so more room will be necessary to fit them into the flow of your production. Be aware of the motor sizes and the amperage requirements of your machines. While most clubmaking machines are set up to run from a single phase, 110V power supply, larger motors (1/2 hp and up) will sometimes draw more amperage than a standard household current can supply, particularly when they are switched on. To avoid tripping circuit breakers or dimming the lights every time you turn on a machine, note the amperage loads of your motors and check with an electrician before you set up the shop.

Q. **What should I keep in mind for the custom fitting part of my business?**

A. Conducting a professional clubfitting session involves working with customers, showing them club component options and allowing them to hit shots as you lead them through the session. If a professional approach to clubfitting is going to be a part of your business, adequate space for a showroom and/or hitting area with net must be included in the layout.

Q. **I anticipate stocking a wide variety or large quantity of different clubheads, shafts and grips. What about storage space?**

A. The more variety in the inventory, the more storage space will be required to organize the different products. Therefore, if you plan an extensive on-hand supply of components, adequate room for storage for each type of component will be necessary. Also, be sure to remember the small parts and supplies that are so much a part of every clubmaking job. Because ferrules, tape, epoxy, etc. should be close at hand when you are performing the procedures of clubmaking, be sure to plan for small parts storage near the main workbench.

Q. **I intend to do a lot of sanding and grinding in my business. Is dust a concern?**

A. The accumulation of dust from sanding wooden heads can be a real problem for not only the clubs in process, but for your inventory of components as well. If sanding and grinding procedures are going to be a part of your clubmaking, installing a type of dust control vacuum system may be wise. If so, plans for ducting the system must be an early part of your shop planning.

Q. **I anticipate excellent growth in my business. How can I best plan ahead?**

A. If you have little competition in your area, or if you have the goal of continuing to build and expand your business, making early plans for anticipated future space

increases might be wise. Trying to expand and move while a business is growing is always more difficult that anticipating for more space in advance.

Taking the time to answer questions such as these will give you a good idea of just how much room you will need and help discover what kind of built-in shop facilities will be necessary. Once you have acquired a general idea of what your shop layout needs are going to be, the next step is to begin to set up the workshop to establish an efficient "flow."

When the term "flow" is used with regard to clubmaking, it means planning the proper direction of movement for the golf clubs as they move through the shop, with all of the necessary tools, machinery and supplies set up to be "in the right place at the right time" for each successive operation, thus making your work as efficient as possible. Regardless of how small or how large your shop area may be, there is still a definite need to follow a comfortable direction of flow for your work. Keeping different shop size needs and requirements in mind, following are a list of general guidelines for setting up your clubmaking shop.

Setting Up the Clubmaking Shop

■ THE SMALL SHOP
(@ 200 Square Feet or Less)

Home is a Great Place to Start
For clubmakers interested in assembling golf clubs as a sideline or hobby, a spare room, the garage or the basement in your home will work fine. By working out of your place of residence, shop overhead and expenses will remain very low, plus you will have the added advantage of being able to start and stop your workshop sessions at your own convenience. While conducting business from your home is not very professional in its appeal, many "part-timers" discover that most of the people for whom they will build golf clubs are likely to be friends or associates. If so, your "customers" will

usually not have second thoughts about coming to your house to transact business.

Establishing the Flow

If your shop is small, or located in a single room of @ 200 square feet or less, the work should flow in a simple circular direction around the room. Obviously, such a small shop prevents using benches in the center of the room, so all of your work stations should be arranged against the walls. Start with a main 6-foot long workbench with a wall mounted pegboard for tools to perform most of your basic shaft installation and gripping procedures. In a small workshop, all of the assembly steps from shafting to ferrule dressing to gripping must be performed at this main workbench.

Storage and Work in Progress

If desired, you can set up a separate space next to the bench to keep such steps as swingweighting and woodhead whipping separate from the other operations. Storage for grips, heads, shafts and supplies can be accommodated by using a closet or the wall opposite to the main workbench. In such a small shop, wooden head finishing will not be afforded a lot of separate room, so it is recommended that shops of 200 square feet or less use pre-finished woodheads exclusively for clubmaking.

In addition, because floor space is at a minimum, the type of club racks that are going to be used to hold the golf clubs while they are being built must be carefully planned. Normal stacking type club racks, built on wood frames with casters, may require too much space. In that case, the best way to arrange the clubs while they are awaiting work is to lean them against a wall mounted rack. To avoid the frustrating problem of clubs continually falling down, it is recommended that you install small dowel pegs on the front of the bench, against which the clubs may lean. This way the routine amount of bench vibration that occurs from normal work procedures will not result in a pile of clubs on the floor.

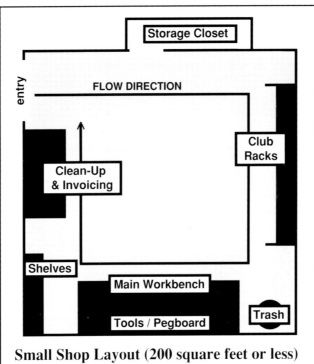

Small Shop Layout (200 square feet or less)

Clean-up and Organization

In the planning of a small workshop it is important to devote an amount of space to handle clean-up, bagging and paperwork procedures. Build a small table at the end of your circular production flow that is stocked with plastic bags, rubber bands, tape, cleaning solvents and rags, and invoice forms so you can professionally "finish" each clubmaking job. This way your clubs will take on more of a business-like look before they are presented to your customers. The above drawing illustrates a sample floor plan for a small single room workshop.

Setting Up the Clubmaking Shop

■ THE MEDIUM SHOP
(200 - 500 Square Feet)
Adjusting to the Room Dimensions

The most ideal in-house area that will lend itself well to a medium size shop layout is the garage or basement. Depending upon the actual length and width dimensions in an area of 200-500 square feet, decisions can now be made whether the center part of the room can be utilized for work, or whether the flow will still be restricted in a circular fashion to move along the wall areas. In medium size areas that take on more of a square shape (e.g. 20' x 20' as opposed to 10' x 40') not using the center of the room will mean that you are wasting a valuable part of the floor area. When bringing the center part of your shop space into the workshop procedures, remember that the direction of flow will change from a circular mode to take on more of a "zig-zag" form. This will be of particular importance should wooden head finishing be incorporated into the business, because in such a medium size shop, space will be available to separate finish application from the rest of the clubmaking procedures.

Help in Your Business

With more space available, thought should be given to whether you will be working alone or employing others in your business. If additional people are going to be a part of the general assembly operations, another main assembly workbench must be incorporated into the early part of the flow. If your shop planning allows for duplicate tools for both workers, then the tool pegboards should be separated so that the people are not reaching over each other during the course of the workday. However, if your budget dictates that a single inventory of tools is all that can be allowed, make sure a main tool board is located within easy reach of both workers. Should any additional personnel be employed for the purpose of woodhead finishing, their work station will more than likely be on the opposite side of the shop, meaning that a second assembly bench would not likely be needed in the layout.

Setting Up Machinery

Having a medium size area in which to work will allow you to incorporate larger clubmaking machinery such as a belt sander, shaft cut-off machine (grinder with shaft cut-off wheel), drill press, loft and lie machine or wood-head sander into the shop set up. These types of machines should be located at a point along the shop's flow where they will be most efficient. For example, if the grinder is utilized primarily for shaft trimming, keep it positioned early in the flow since shaft trimming is one of the early procedures of clubmaking. On the other hand, since a belt sander can be used for steps that are not always successive in the assembly process (shaft tip abrading as opposed to turning ferrules), its location should be as close as possible to the places where it will be used the most.

Because a head sanding machine will create dust, it should be positioned far away from the finish application and drying areas. Another consideration to plan for in locating your machinery is to try to group each of the dust creating machines close enough together to allow them to be served by the shortest possible length of dust control vacuum ducting or single shop vacuum. This will make even a small shop vacuum draw dust more efficiently, do a better job of keeping your area dust free and reduce the cost of installing such a system.

Electrical Needs

Another point to think about when incorporating machinery into your operation is your shop's electrical circuit capacity. Household circuits are rated by total ampere loads. If you inspect the electrical panel in the house or building, on top of each breaker switch will be a number which indicates the maximum amp load for the circuit. Most common 110 volt household circuits are wired with 15 or 20 amp circuit breakers. If the total ampere requirement of electrical tools plugged into a single circuit exceeds 15 or 20 amps, the circuit will be overloaded and will trip, or switch off, as a safety procedure to prevent overheating the wire.

To avoid electrical overload problems in your shop simply add up the ampere ratings found on the motor plate of each of your electrical tools and make sure that the total of all machines on the same circuit does not

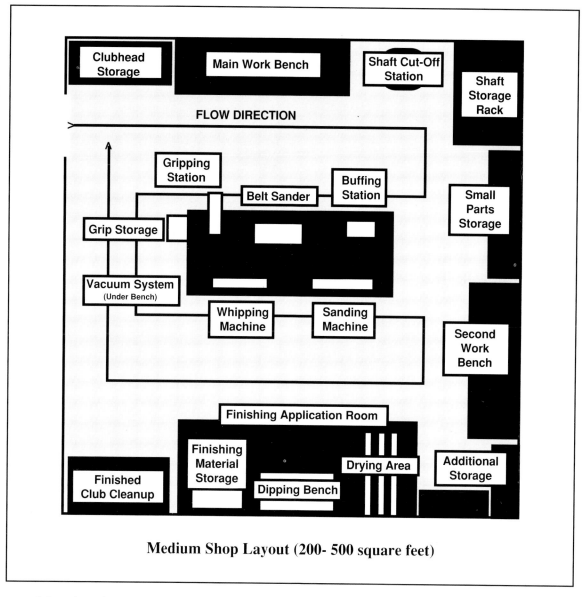

Medium Shop Layout (200- 500 square feet)

exceed the rating of the circuit. In most one-man shops this will not be a problem, since it is unlikely that more than one machine will be operating at the same time. Running your machines on two or more different circuits would be advised if you have an employee and foresee multiple machine usage at the same time. Don't forget to check whether the lights and electrical devices that are going to be continually in use in your shop are on the same circuit as your machines. In some cases several overhead lights, a radio and one clubmaking machine operating at the same time could overload the circuit and trip the breaker.

Always be aware that the initial start-up ampere draw for most machines is usually three times the machine's operating amperage. While this quick surge lasts only for a split second before the machine settles down to its normal requirement, it could be enough to trip a breaker when a near overloaded circuit condition already exists. If you need to rearrange some circuits to accommodate your shop, contact a qualified electrician to have the work performed.

Setting Up for Finishing Woodheads
If you decide to incorporate wooden head finishing into a medium size shop, plan to install the area on the side of the shop that is opposite from the main assembly workbench. If you care to make the extra effort, an idea that will pay off in efficiency is to build a separate room inside your shop for applying and drying the various finishing materials. By enclosing this area, you can prevent the dust from the sanding and grinding operations from settling on clubs that have just been set up to dry. Should the finishing materials require controlled temperature conditions for proper curing, you will be able to heat a small drying room more efficiently than an entire shop. Such a partitioned finishing area need not be bigger than 30-40 square feet but should include a small bench for applying the finishing materials and a drying rack for setting clubs aside to cure. If you decide to apply finishing coats by spray gun instead of by dipping, the finishing area will have to be larger and include an adequate spray booth in its design.

Component and Small Parts Storage
Since medium size shops usually require larger inventories of components and clubmaking supplies, a larger and more organized storage area will have to be set up. For medium size shops, a "cubbyhole" rack for shaft and grip storage should definitely be used. In addition, shelves with multiple storage boxes or bins will be needed to store all of the small parts that are so necessary for clubmaking. All of the constantly used supplies should be in the same general area of your shop, within easy access to all who may be using them. Because so many of the parts and components are used in the early

stages of the assembly procedures, the main storage area should be located as close to the main assembly workbench as possible. One major exception to this will be in the storage and handling of finishing materials and solvents. To satisfy insurance requirements and keep your shop safe, combustible materials such as these should be stored in a metal cabinet, away from excessive heat (furnace or space heaters for example) sources or other combustible objects. The drawing on the preceding page is an example of a medium size shop layout.

Setting Up the Clubmaking Shop

■ THE LARGE SHOP
(over 500 Square Feet)

A Small Factory - Or a Large Workshop
If your goal is to turn a part-time hobby into a full-time clubmaking business, a greater commitment on behalf of the workshop and your time will be necessary. Not only will more space be required to handle a larger volume of work, but an adequate area for a showroom or fitting area will need to be taken into account. To operate the business in a professional manner space must be allowed for handling paperwork and taking care of all the administrative needs of the business. A business phone should be installed with a Yellow Pages listing and all other utilities should be contracted for in the name of the business. In addition, you need to check with local, state and federal agencies to apply for and receive each of the necessary business licenses and permits. In most cases, clubmakers actively pursuing the business of making clubs will have to look for shop space in properly zoned areas of the community. Most residential areas are not zoned for walk-in business trade, and the professional image you will want to project to customers may not be possible when the shop is located in your place of residence.

Remember that a clubmaking business outside the home means overhead. All too often clubmakers who start their business in the home forget to plan adequately for

the increased overhead that accompanies a move to a store or warehouse, and as a result end up closing the doors with a bad taste in their mouth about a hobby that got out of hand. If your current clubmaking shop is located in your home and you have dreams of expanding or turning the hobby into a business, the first step should be to write up a business proposal. If you are not fully aware of all the expenses that go along with operating a real business, talk to an accountant or visit other clubmakers who have made the jump to an outside shop.

While competition says that clubmakers in your immediate area are not likely to offer help, visit a clubmaker outside your area when you take a vacation to ask questions. Joining the Professional Clubmakers' Society will give you access to hundreds of clubmakers all over the country from whom you can obtain advice. Above all, be honest and search inside yourself to determine if your 10 hour/week hobby is still going to be enjoyable if you jump to 40 hours/week. Finding out that you preferred the lighter work load after the fact is a lesson better off not learned.

Renting Workshop Space
When you begin to search for commercial rental space, you will be faced with a tough decision. Commercial space located in the small strip-type shopping centers that are so prevalent today will bring a volume of "foot traffic," but will also bring more costly rental rates. On the other hand, industrial parks filled with thousands of feet of warehouse space have sprung up all over the country, and have attracted many businesses because of their lower lease prices. Most industrial parks charge lower rent because they are most often located away from the heavy traffic flow of retail shopping areas, or because their total layout involves a larger number of spacious buildings for rent.

So, here is the dilemma - do you pay more for less space and hope the foot traffic will make your business successful, or do you locate in a more economical warehouse area and hope you can get the people to come to you?

Certainly there is no one answer for every aspiring clubmaker, for experience has proven golf club assemblers have been successful in both environments. Rather, the answer for each club builder will lie in an analysis of the financial commitment you can afford to make in the business. If you have the capital to spare, a move into the more costly but greater traffic space location might be the way to start. But, if you are working on a tighter budget, the industrial park must be your choice.

In either case, there are a few points that you must be aware of before you sign a commercial lease for your business. Foremost among these is checking the zoning restrictions for the location you have in mind. Not all commercial space will allow manufacturing, particularly if your business will include machinery that creates dust and noise, so be sure to ask the leasing agent or local officials to be sure of this point. If you are considering retail space that might not allow manufacturing be sure to consider whether you really wish to include wooden head finishing in your business. Often this one operation of clubmaking, due to the solvents, spraying or sanding operations is enough to cause the leasing agent to say no. Many clubmakers have found that once the agent understands heavy manufacturing steps are not a part of the assembly of golf clubs from finished components, they can gain approval for the retail type footage.

When you move into a commercial shop for the purpose of assembling golf clubs, there will certainly be a lot of interior changes that will have to be performed before you can "open the doors." In many light manufacturing rentals or warehouses, all you receive when you sign the lease are four walls, some overhead lights, a lavatory, an existing number of electrical outlets and the keys to the door. Therefore, before you sign a lease, you must have a plan for the shop layout already in mind so you can determine if the space will accommodate your needs. If partitions, extra heat or air conditioning, more electrical outlets or circuits or other built-in services are needed, this must be discussed well in advance with the agent or owner. Such a discussion must leave you with no doubt as to who pays for and owns any of the improvements that have to be made.

Planning the Large Workshop
Once you have finished the groundwork for commer-

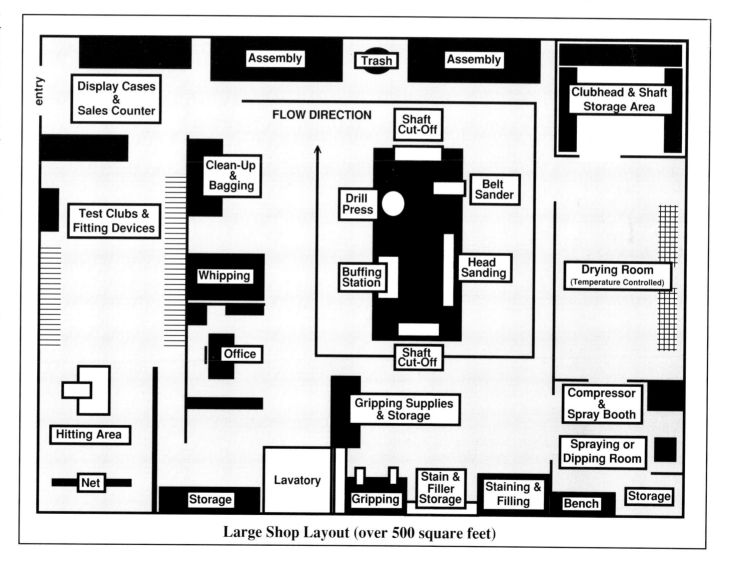

Large Shop Layout (over 500 square feet)

cially locating your shop, the workshop flow and layout decisions can be made. To deal with the public and fully capitalize on the business of club assembly, a large clubmaking shop should include a showroom or fitting area. With such an area, customers will feel more like they are in the hands of a professional and will naturally have more confidence in your abilities. The showroom should be large enough to display the various head designs you offer plus assembled versions of at least one head in each model so they can see what the club will actually look like in the "playing position." If you are trained and qualified to offer custom clubfitting, the shop should include a hitting net with sample or fitting test clubs for the customers to try out. There are hundreds of options for setting up a fitting center, so the depth of involvement in this area will depend upon how deeply your business is committed to servicing each individual golfer's needs.

The actual manufacturing layout of the large shop has to be set up in the same manner as the small and medium size shops. Determine all of the services you plan to offer, whether you will be hiring employees, the anticipated volume of work and the approximate size of the total inventory of components and supplies before you begin to move in the workbenches. Just as in the smaller shops, a large shop must have an efficient flow incorporated into the plan.

Before the benches are moved in, spend time just standing in the middle of the empty shop while you mentally envision clubs being made. The best way to do this is to actually build one golf club "in your mind" while you look at all of the empty space in the shop. As you think of and "see" every single step that has to be performed in the procedure of making a club you can get an idea of just where the various production areas might best be located. Once you have a general idea of the layout with respect to the flow around the larger shop, then take time in your mind to think of how much space 20, 30 or even 50 golf clubs being built at the same time will occupy. Perhaps the best way to put this point into perspective is to understand these points:

1. **It takes the same number of steps to build 100 clubs as it does one club.**
2. **Regardless of whether you have one or 100 clubs to build, you can only work on one at a time.**
3. **100 clubs take up a hundred times more space than does one club.**

Therefore, in a large shop, more of the space should be allowed **between** the stations of each production step instead of **for** the actual production steps. Another great way to plan the shop layout is to draw the shop floor to scale and cut out shapes of your shop fixtures, also made to scale. Moving pieces of cardboard around a square to layout and conceive your workshop is a lot easier than moving the actual fixtures all over in a search for the "right layout."

The Industry of Clubmaking

■ PERIODICALS

One of the points that has been stressed about clubmaking is that anyone who decides to learn how to build golf clubs can choose their level of involvement to match the commitment they wish to make in the field. If you want to build golf clubs just for yourself, your family or a few of your golfing associates, you can do so. If you want to make a few more sets to offer for sale to members of your golf league, people you may work with, friends of friends and the like, and make a few profit dollars in the process, you can do that too. Or if you want to jump headlong into developing a thriving business in clubmaking, that is an option within the field as well.

Regardless of your level of involvement in clubmaking, knowledge of current trends in the golf equipment industry, knowledge of the technical aspects of golf clubs and an awareness of clubmaking in general should be a part of your commitment. To increase your market awareness, begin your education by subscribing to the various golf industry and clubmaking publications. By using magazines and newsletters to stay abreast of the latest happenings in clubmaking and in golf, you can also gain valuable information that will assist your business planning and increase your technical equipment awareness. Some of the publications and newsletters that will enhance your overall market awareness include the following:

Golf Shop Operations Magazine
5520 Park Avenue
PO Box 395
Trumbull, CT 06611
Published nine times per year, "GSO" as it is called, covers the entire golf retailing industry from the pro shop or off-course golf store's point of view. The largest of the golf industry trade publications in number of pages per issue, GSO is a good source of information about all product areas related to golf retailing. GSO publishes the results of surveys the magazine conducts covering many aspects of golf product sales analysis by product area and type of golf shop. Not much information is covered relating directly to clubmaking from components, however, GSO in conjunction with the Professional Clubmakers' Society sponsors the annual Clubfitter of the Year Award.

Clubmakers' Digest Magazine
71 Maholm Street
Newark, OH 43055

The only "trade" publication dedicated strictly to clubmaking from components, Clubmakers' Digest is a magazine published by Dynacraft Golf Products, Inc. Despite the tie in with component supplier Dynacraft, CD magazine covers all the technical aspects of clubmaking from

an "open minded"'approach in an effort to keep clubmakers abreast of all the technical aspects in head, shaft and grip design. In addition, CD offers "how-to" articles covering different procedures of clubmaking in an effort to help clubmakers improve their skills.

The PCS Journal
18403 Aiken Road
Anchorage, KY 40233

The official publication of the independent Professional Clubmakers' Society, the PCS Journal newsletter is mailed four times per year to members and covers the ongoing activities of the Society's effort to promote and upgrade the image of clubmaking as a

business. Included in each issue are technical articles written by members covering all aspects of clubmaking.

Golf Industry Magazine
1545 NE 123rd Street
North Miami, FL 33161

Also published nine times per year, Golf Industry magazine parallels the information and analysis contained in GSO. Accenting retail advice more to golf professionals, GI is known for its dedication to surveys with a heavy emphasis toward ana-

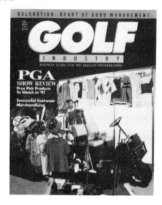

lyzing business trends as they occur within the golf industry. A regular column feature in GI magazine is Clubmakers' Workbench, in which a guest clubmaker/club repair person is asked to offer information relating to different aspects of repair or clubmaking.

The Golf Clubmaker
2053 Harvard Avenue
Dunedin, FL 34698

The Golf Clubmaker is the official publication of The Professional Golf Club Repairmen's Association. Published in newsletter form and mailed approximately 3-4 times per year to PGCRA members, the publication covers many of the technical aspects of golf club re-

pair and fitting through articles written both by members and PGCRA staff.

The Industry of Clubmaking

■ ORGANIZATIONS

Since clubmaking from components is a relatively new part of the golf industry, an established organization on behalf of clubmaking that functions in the same manner as the PGA of America for the nation's golf professionals has not completely come forth as of yet. However, within the field of clubmaking three organizations do exist, two of which are tied directly to component supply companies and one which is attempting to evolve as an independent association for clubmakers.

The Professional Golf Club Repairmen's Association
2053 Harvard Avenue
Dunedin, FL 34698

The oldest of the organizations formed to advance the trade of clubmaking and club repair, the PCGRA was founded in 1978 by the late golf professional/clubmaker Irv Schloss. Managed today by the Schloss family and associates, the PGCRA was formed to offer club repair training as well as component supplies to members. The PGCRA conducts a number of four-day training seminars each year at its south Florida location in which staff members teach the skills of club repair to association members. In addition, 3-4 times per year the organization publishes its own newsletter, the Golf Clubmaker, to keep members abreast of the latest in club repair techniques and to offer pricing on the component supplies they sell. Funded by the members' annual $25 dues along with the profits from the sale of component supplies, the PGCRA has approximately 1,200 members.

West Coast PGA Show in Long Beach, California

The Golf Clubmakers' Association
10206 North IH-35
Austin, TX 78753

Another organization tied to a supplier, the Golf Clubmakers' Association is primarily operated as a promotional arm of the component supply company, Custom Golf Inc. of Austin, Texas. The GCA publishes a quarterly newsletter offering information to members that is both business and technically related to clubmaking and repair. In addition, the publication highlights a number of Custom Golf's items for sale or promotion. Each year the GCA also hosts a three-day seminar encouraging members to travel to Austin to attend workshops and lectures from technical representatives of the GCA as well as from selected shaft and grip manufacturers.

The Professional Clubmakers' Society
18403 Aiken Road
Anchorage, KY 40233

Formed in 1989 by clubmakers as an alternative to a company promotional organization, the Professional Clubmakers' Society is an independent association attempting to promote the business of clubmaking and set quality standards for the skills of clubmaking. The PCS conducts marketing campaigns in national golf publications to inform the public about clubmaking and offers accreditation testing services to verify the clubmaking skill level of members.

The PCS publishes a newsletter four times per year to keep members not only updated on technical information related to clubmaking, but also to report on society news and member services. Member services offered or planned in the future, in addition to the existing promotional campaigns and accreditation testing, are health and liability insurance programs as well as seminars and workshops.

The Industry of Clubmaking

■ TRADE SHOWS

To remain current on what's going on within the field of golf equipment, you might find it helpful to attend one of the PGA of America's annual golf industry trade shows. Currently, two national golf trade shows are conducted each year. The largest of the two, the PGA Merchandise Show, is a four-day exhibition staged over the fourth weekend of January in Orlando, FLA. Virtually every company engaged in the business of supplying products to the golf industry is in attendance to introduce new products, book new orders and enhance their relationships with their wholesale buying customers.

Now serving as the show when golf club manufacturers first unveil their new designs to the industry, the West Coast PGA Merchandise Show is held in Long Beach, Calif. each August. Once a local show only, due to its August show dates coordinating with the time when many club manufacturers finish their new model designs, the West Coast Show has now grown into a widely attended national exhibition.

Primarily open to PGA members and their apprentices, the PGA's merchandise trade shows do allow admittance to non-PGA participants in the golf industry who are actively engaged in the business of golf. Though geared primarily toward the pro shop or golf shop retailer, clubmakers can also find the shows worth attending. At the shows, most of the grip and shaft manufacturers exhibit their latest designs and staff their booths with personnel who can answer questions about the various products. In addition, most of the clubmaking industry's suppliers are also in attendance exhibiting their latest clubhead designs. Admission to non-PGA personnel is granted by presenting business credentials at the show and paying the buyer admission fee. If you are serious about finding out what is going to be popular in golf each year, you might be well advised to attend. For information on the shows, contact:

The Orlando PGA Merchandise Show
The PGA Merchandise Show
PGA of America Headquarters
100 Avenue of the Champions
Palm Beach Gardens, FL 33410

The West Coast PGA Show
West Coast PGA Golf Show
2323 W. Lincoln Ave
Suite 229
Anaheim, CA 92801

Additional golf equipment trade shows are conducted by the PGA of America's regional sections in virtually every state. For information on these regional trade shows contact the PGA's local section in your area. To find the PGA section office in your area, ask your local PGA professional or write to the PGA headquarters in Palm Beach Gardens, Fla.

CHAPTER 3 - A Technical Discussion of Shafts

The Principles of Shaft Design
Shaft Design Characteristics
Graphite and Composite Shaft Design
The Principles of Shaft Construction
A Complete Guide to Shaft Trimming and Installation
The Proper Techniques For Installing Shafts
Golf Shaft Manufacturers and Their Available Patterns

Shafts - The Mysterious Component of Clubmaking

Without a doubt the one component of clubmaking that creates the most confusion among clubmakers and golfers is the shaft. In the four years since the first edition of *The Modern Guide to Golf Clubmaking* was published, the shaft manufacturing industry has experienced a boom never before seen in shaft design; currently, some 20 shaft making firms produce no less than 2,000 different shafts for use in building golf clubs!

Never before in the golf equipment industry have there been so many new shafts and shaft developments unleashed on the golfing public. Yet with all the new shaft making companies and the abundance of new shaft designs, so little in the way of meaningful information is actually known about them.

While each of the various shaft producers have flooded the market with information to help "explain" their latest shaft designs, the data is usually offered with a tinge of marketing, with general claims of greater distance or straighter shots being the theme of virtually all. Compounding the problem is the fact that even when information is offered by a manufacturer to establish a technical understanding for the shaft, it is difficult to use that information to compare with another manufacturer's shaft. The reason? Despite the 70 years since shafts first

moved to high tech in the change from hickory to steel, there has never been a standard benchmark for defining such shaft design characteristics as flex, bend point or torque, three of the most important design parameters of any shaft. For example, one manufacturer's R-flex shaft may not carry the same bending characteristics as another manufacturer's R-flex shaft. When a golfer makes a new shaft choice and selects an R-flex because he has been comfortably using an R-flex for years, often he experiences a totally different feeling of stiffness, and the result is confusion and often a lack of confidence in the clubmaker or company who made the clubs.

Or the low bend point of one shaft might not be low at all when compared to another company's low bend point shaft. Currently bend point is only defined in such terms as low, mid and high, general descriptions that have no relevance from one manufacturer to another.

Or, using the example of another recently discovered point of shaft design, because of different methods for obtaining shaft torque measurements, the 2° torque of one shaft might not be the same as the 2° reading obtained by another manufacturer for its shaft. Apples to apples comparisons in the shaft industry? It has never been so, and as a result golfers and more importantly, clubmakers live in a world of shaft confusion.

To further express how confusing shafts have become, think about this point: The effect various clubhead design specifications have on the flight of the ball is very easy to demonstrate. For example, in almost every case, if you fit a golfer who slices the ball with a set of woods that are made with a closed (hook) face angle, a definite change in shot direction will be noticed. Or, if a golfer uses two similarly designed #5-irons that are made with different degrees of loft angle, a difference in distance and height will likely be seen between the clubs. These are given facts; change most clubhead specifications and a predictable shotmaking outcome will result. But give a golfer two clubs with different shafts and the chances of realizing an immediate difference in shot performance are less likely. Not to negate the performance of shafts, there is no doubt certain shaft changes *are* noticed by golfers, but it is a fact that alterations in clubhead specifications are far more predictable in their results than are changes in shafts.

But if the differences between shafts are so often subtle, why is so much emphasis placed on shafts? Perhaps it has to do with the fact that a primary role of the shaft is to transfer the energy of the golfer's swing to the ball. If a golfer uses a Driver with a different shaft and all of a sudden hits the ball 25 yards farther you can bet the emphasis of excitement will be directed toward the shaft.

For golfers, the need for greater awareness of shafts has to be in the form of answers to their questions about what a particular shaft will do for their game. But for clubmakers, the requirement for shaft understanding is much greater. Because clubmakers work with shafts on a daily basis, and because the number of new shaft designs has increased at a fantastic pace, clubmakers **must** learn as much as possible about all aspects of shafts - from what they are, how they work, how they compare to each other and how they should be installed to achieve their stated performance.

The Principles of Shaft Design

■ THE PARTS OF A SHAFT

To begin a technical discussion about shafts, it is important to learn the terminology used to describe the physical parts of a shaft. Not only will this begin to help develop an understanding of the information to be discussed in this chapter, but it will be vital to assist in identifying one particular shaft from another. Refer to the accompanying drawings for the location and designation of each of the physical parts of a shaft.

Shaft Tip (all shafts)
The tip is the small end of the shaft, and is always the portion of the shaft to be attached to the hosel of the clubhead. One of the major design principles that controls the overall flex of a shaft is the diameter. Therefore the size of the tip is one of the factors that can contribute to determining what flex a particular shaft may be. The tip is always referred to in a measurement of diameter, expressed in decimal equivalent of inches, so refer to the following chart for a list of the various tip diameters that are seen in shafts today.

Tip Diameter Variation in Shafts

Tip Diameter	Tapered or Parallel Construction	For Use in Wood or Iron
.277"	Taper Tip	Wood
.286"	Taper Tip	Wood
.294"	Taper Tip	Wood
.300"	Both[1]	Wood & Iron[1]
.320"	Both[1]	Wood & Iron[1]
.335"	Parallel Tip	Wood
.355"	Taper Tip	Iron
.370"	Parallel Tip	Iron
.382"	Flared Tip	Putter
.395"	Parallel Tip	Iron[2]

[1] Check the manufacturers' shaft tables in this chapter for which .300" and .320" tip diameter shafts are tapered or parallel and which are for use in woods or in irons.
[2] .395" tip diameter shafts are only used for installation on irons or putters that require an over the hosel (overfit) mounting of shaft to head.

The previous chart lists all of the shaft tip diameters that are currently exhibited in the design of shafts by major shaft manufacturers. While other shaft tip diameters

SHAFT TIP

have been utilized in shaft designs, those were usually manufactured by the shaft company expressly for use by a particular golf club manufacturing company (a proprietary, or private brand shaft pattern) and are no longer in current production. Where the chart indicates a shaft tip diameter in tapered only, or parallel construction only, or for use in a wood, iron, or putter, understand that there are no exceptions. This information is very important because it will aid you in the task of identifying one shaft from another.

Tip Section (steel or stepped shafts only)
The tip section of the shaft is defined as the portion of the shaft from the tip to the first step, or to the first diameter change on the shaft. Because virtually all graphite shafts are manufactured without step downs, only steel shafts

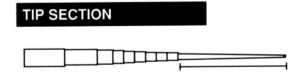

TIP SECTION

are defined as possessing a tip section. By measuring the diameter of the tip section, it is possible to determine if a shaft is designed in taper tip or parallel tip form. If the shaft tip section gradually becomes larger from the tip up to the first step it is a taper tip construction, while if the tip section remains one constant diameter up to the first step, it is considered to be a parallel tip shaft. The differences between taper tip and parallel tip shafts will be covered later in this chapter.

The length of the tip section is very important because it is a major factor in controlling how stiff or flexible a particular shaft will play once it has been installed into the clubhead. In other words, within a single steel shaft design, the shorter the tip section the stiffer the shaft will play. And conversely, for any particular steel shaft, the longer the tip section, the more flexible the shaft will be.

It is very important to qualify such a statement about tip section length, "within the same shaft design, the shorter the tip section the stiffer the shaft will be." When comparing tip section length between different shaft designs, this statement is not always true. For example, the parallel tip Dynamic R flex shaft for woods (UDWR), has a tip section length of 12 1/2", the parallel tip Dynamic S flex shaft for woods (UDWS) has a tip section length of 10 1/2" and the parallel tip Dynamic X flex for woods has a tip section length of 8 1/2". Because all three shafts are of the same design (Dynamic) and have the same .335" tip diameter and .600 butt diameter, it is true that the shorter tip section length in the UDWX makes it play stiffer than the UDWS shaft and then accordingly, makes the UDWS stiffer than the UDWR. To contrast, the parallel tip Gold Plus pattern is a different shaft design from the Dynamic. The tip section length of the Gold Plus R-flex is 10 1/8", which might foster the belief that it is stiffer than the Dynamic R or even the Dynamic S. Because it is a different shaft design, factors other than the tip section length have been employed by the manufacturer to establish the flex. Remember, within the **same shaft design,** the shorter the tip section, the stiffer the shaft will be.

Yet within the same shaft design, there still could be situations when a shorter tip section does not make the shaft stiffer. Beyond tip section length, the overall diameters of the shaft are very important in establishing flex. To illustrate how shaft diameters have an effect on tip section length and flex, the parallel tip Dynamic A

flex shaft (UDWA) has a tip section length of 11 7/8". Comparing that measurement to the 12 1/2" tip section of the UDWR might make it seem the Dynamic A is stiffer than the Dynamic R. However, while both shafts have a .335" tip diameter, the UDWA has a .560" butt diameter while the UDWR has a .600" butt diameter. Since shaft diameter is a major determinant of overall stiffness, the UDWA's smaller butt diameter explains how it becomes more flexible than the UDWR, despite the fact the tip section is shorter.

Tip Parallel Section (all types of shafts)

The tip parallel section is the portion of the tip section that exhibits one constant diameter. In the case of the .320" parallel, .335" parallel and .370" parallel tip diameter

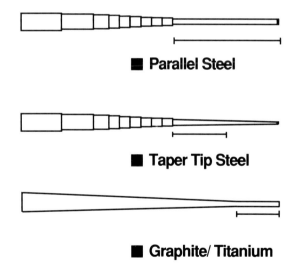

TIP PARALLEL SECTION

■ **Parallel Steel**

■ **Taper Tip Steel**

■ **Graphite/ Titanium**

Tip parallel section differences between different shaft types

steel shafts, the tip parallel section is by definition to be the same as the tip section and will always extend

entirely from the tip to the first step. But in the case of .335" and .370" parallel tip graphite or titanium shafts, tip section is defined differently.

Graphite, titanium and shafts such as the Alloy 2000 are manufactured without step downs using a type of construction called a straight taper tube. For straight taper tube construction shafts, the tip parallel section is defined only as the portion of the shaft tip that possesses one constant diameter. At some point on a straight taper tube type shaft, the shaft has to begin to taper larger in diameter toward the butt end. Therefore, on straight taper tube construction designs, the shaft remains parallel for a set distance and then tapers larger toward the butt end. A tip parallel section is created on straight taper tube type shafts to allow clubmakers to install the shafts into parallel bore clubheads or to allow for the trimming of successive amounts from the tip, should the shaft design call for such a trimming formula.

In the case of the taper tip steel shafts for woods and irons, the tip parallel section is defined as the portion of the tip section where the tapering ceases and the tip section assumes one constant diameter up to the first step. To fully understand this concept in taper tip shafts, first realize that taper tip shafts do not taper the entire way from the tip up to the first step. In their manufacturing process, taper tip steel shafts are initially produced with a fully parallel diameter tip section. Then, a predetermined length of that tip section is "swaged" (squeezed) into the tapered configuration that is called for in the design of the shaft.

With a micrometer or caliper, it is easy to find where the tip parallel section of a taper tip steel shaft begins. Starting at the tip, by taking measurements every 1/2" up the shaft, soon the point on the tip section can be found where the tapering ceases and the shaft becomes parallel the rest of the way up to the first step. For example, a .294" taper tip Dynamic S flex shaft for a Driver tapers up to a point 6" from the tip end, after which it ceases to taper and becomes a parallel .350" in diameter the rest of the way up to the first step.

Note in the shaft manufacturers' tables of shaft specifications found later in this chapter there is a column entry under taper tip steel shafts for the tip parallel section diameter. The purpose of listing this dimension within the taper tip steel shafts is to assist in identifying one shaft from another. For example, if two different taper tip shafts are shipped to you unlabeled it can be difficult to separate one from the other. The tip parallel section diameter thus is another piece of information about shafts that can help determine their identity.

Step (steel shafts only)

A step is the small "knurl" that is formed on a steel shaft in the manufacturing process to allow the shaft to become larger in diameter as it progresses from the tip up to the

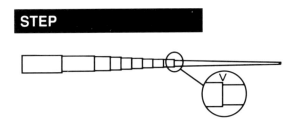

butt. As of this writing, there have existed two models of graphite shafts, one from the Wilson Company in the 1970s, and one from the Slazenger Company in the late 1980s that were made with step downs. The exception rather than the rule, graphite shafts are not ordinarily made with step downs so this discussion on steps will be taken to relate to steel shafts only. The process of forming a series of steps on the steel shaft to facilitate the change of the shaft from small to large in diameter is called step tapering. In the early days of steel shaft manufacture, step tapering did not exist so the only way manufacturers could produce a shaft from steel was to create a straight taper tube, just as the shape of today's graphite and titanium shafts are manufactured.

Straight tapering a steel shaft proved to be a very costly and inefficient manner of production, and was one of the problems that prevented steel shafts from overtaking hickory when steel shafts were first introduced. However, it was in 1927 that the American Fork and Hoe Company (today known as True Temper Corp.) achieved a major breakthrough in technology and was awarded a patent for the step tapering process. This development of a way to create steps on a shaft immediately established the steel shaft's domination and positioned True Temper as the pre-eminent manufacturer in the shaft industry.

Step tapering describes the process of squeezing a single diameter steel tube into progressively smaller and smaller sections from the butt down to the tip. Using specialized swaging machinery, all steel shaft manufacturers use this same basic process to form the required changes in diameter that are called for on all of the steel shafts they produce. Again, a step is simply the actual point on the shaft where a change in diameter occurs and is easily recognized by the "knurl" created by the step tapering machine. Therefore, a step should not be confused with the next two parts of a shaft, the step length and the step pattern.

Step Length (steel shafts only)

Step length is defined as the distance between any two steps on a steel shaft, and is one of the factors that begins to determine a shaft's "personality," or playability char-

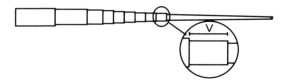

acteristics. In addition, the step length can be very important with regard to identifying one shaft pattern from another. For example, the True Temper Dynamic parallel tip shafts for woods and irons have a step length of 1 7/8", the Apollo Spectre in both parallel and taper tip form have a step length of 1 1/2", Brunswick's Microtaper has a step length of 3/4", and so on. By varying the length

and arrangement of the steps on the shaft, differences in bend point, flex and playability can be established.

Through differences in step length, shaft manufacturers are also able to control the shaft's cost of production. For example, a shaft producer's catalog may refer to certain shafts they make as being First Grade, Second Grade or Commercial Grade. First Grade shafts are more expensive than Second Grade or Commercial Grade shafts because they undergo many more time consuming and quality control procedures. Among the processes that contribute to the cost of a shaft is step forming. It is more costly to produce shorter step lengths on a steel shaft because of the greater number of swaging operations required, so shafts with step lengths of 2" or less cost more to produce than shafts with a step length of 3" or more. Shorter step length shafts usually end up as First Grade shafts while the shafts with longer step lengths that are less costly to make are usually sold as Commercial Grade shafts for starter sets.

Step Pattern (steel shafts only)

The step pattern of a steel shaft is a description of the arrangement of the steps and step lengths over the entire shaft. In the manufacture of steel shafts, the step pattern

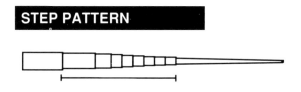

may either be described as being constant or variable. In a constant step pattern, virtually all of the steps will be the same distance apart, while on a variable step pattern shaft the arrangement of step lengths will be spaced differently.

For example, the Dynamic, TT Lite, AP44, Spectre, Pro Pel II, and Phoenix shaft designs all have constant step patterns because the distance between steps remains the same. By comparison, because the distances between steps are not constant, the FM Precision, UCV-304, and ExtraLite are examples of shafts that have variable step patterns. Through the step pattern configuration, steel shaft manufacturers are able to control such playability features of the shaft as bend point and flex.

Recessed Section (steel shafts only)
In the manufacturing history of steel shafts, there have been certain patterns which have been designed with a recessed section located at a specified position on the

RECESSED SECTION

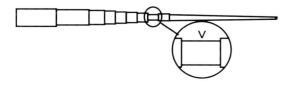

shaft. In the normal procedures of step forming, a shaft becomes progressively smaller from the butt down to the tip. However, there have been particular shafts that have been manufactured in such a way that the step tapering process reverses itself over a short section so that the shaft becomes larger, then smaller, then larger again in diameter.

Through the positioning of a recessed section on the shaft, the manufacturer is able to more precisely create a desired bending effect for the shaft and thus offer a particular feature of shaft bending performance.

Butt Section (all shafts)
The butt section is the portion of the shaft from the last step to the large end (butt) of the shaft. The butt section is important because it has a direct influence on what size

BUTT SECTION

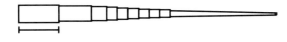

the grip will be after installation. When grip manufacturers design the inside core diameter of their models, attention and detail must be given to the butt section length of all the various shafts. By calculating an average of all of the common butt section lengths on shafts, grip makers are able to decide on a rate of taper for the core of their grips that will ensure the correct installed grip size.

For example, when a men's 58 core size grip is installed on any .580" butt diameter shaft with one wrap of 2-way grip installation tape, the grip will become standard men's size. However, if the butt section is shorter than normal, or if the shaft has been trimmed incorrectly during installation so that the butt section is shortened too much by the clubmaker, the grip will not achieve its proper size along the entire length of the grip. Therefore, clubmakers should always learn and employ the correct shaft trimming procedures, not simply to ensure the right flex, but to achieve consistency in grip size as well.

Shaft Butt (all shafts)
The large end of a shaft is called the butt and is important in clubmaking with regard not only to grip sizing but shaft flexibility as well. It was mentioned that one of the ways shaft manufacturers are able to control the flexibility of their shafts is through the various diameters up and down the shaft. The larger the diameter of the butt, the stiffer the shaft will be. Consequently, it is logical to observe that most of the industry's L and A- flex

SHAFT BUTT

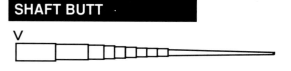

patterns have a .560" or .580" butt diameter, while most of the S and X flex shafts have butt diameters of .600" or .620". While no longer in production, it is interesting to note the .700" butt diameter shafts of the late 1970s were not designed for overall stiffness but rather to add the necessary strength to make up for very thin shaft wall thickness employed in the design. Hence the increase in butt diameter was used to add strength to the shaft to make up for the decrease in strength that came from the shaft wall thickness reduction. Currently, the most common shaft butt diameters seen in the manufacture of shafts are the .560", .580", .600" and .620" sizes.

Shaft Design Characteristics

■ THE ROLE OF THE SHAFT IN THE GOLF CLUB
Proof of just how mysterious the world of shafts has become is evidenced by the tremendous number of questions that are posed to component distributors by clubmakers who are unsure of just how a particular shaft should be installed or how certain shafts compare. To better understand shafts and their installation, it is helpful for clubmakers to first be aware of how the shaft is supposed to perform in a set of clubs.

The primary role of the shaft is to transfer as much energy as possible from the golfer's swing to the clubhead, to deliver the clubface to the ball in a position consistent with the golfer's swing, and to deliver a comfortable "feel" or response of impact back to the golfer. To breed consistency in golfers, the shaft must perform this task consistently, shot after shot through the entire set of clubs.

The golf swing is the human element in the game. Golfers know all too well the tendency of the swing to break down and not consistently repeat itself. Therefore, it is the responsibility of the shafts to be consistent and similar in feel and not create any more mistakes for the golfer other than what were generated by the swing.

Producing shafts that will not multiply the mistakes already generated by a golfer's swing has not always been easy for shaft manufacturers to do. In the days of the hickory shaft, serious golfers often kept two sets of clubs; a favorite set to use in good weather and another set to use when the weather turned damp or wet. Wooden shafts were extremely susceptible to change with the weather. On wet days the hickory would absorb a great deal of moisture, thus causing the shafts to warp and contribute to an increase in the total weight of the clubs. For other than fair weather golfers, such changes in hickory shafts could not be avoided. As a result, golfers in the hickory shaft era were often forced to adjust their swing to match the day-to-day changes that occurred in the shafts.

The shaft must provide consistent performance from shot to shot and club to club.

When the steel shaft was introduced in the 1920s, its success was ensured by the fact that it brought with it a level of consistency not previously possible with hickory.

However, even though steel was much more durable and consistent when compared to hickory, the change to steel shafts did not occur overnight. While steel did not warp and eliminated the shaft induced errors that had been attributable to hickory, early steel shafts were heavier than the wood shafts they replaced and did not deliver the same "feel" back to the golfer that hickory could. Remember once more the role of the shaft - to consistently transmit the golfer's swing energy to the ball and the feel of the swing and impact back to the golfer. Steel shafts did reduce the number of poor shots in comparison to the hickory shaft, but until they had been subjected to many refinements in their production, golfers resisted their use because of that all-important factor of feel.

The ability of a shaft to perform consistently, to transmit the energy of the swing to the ball and in return convey a comfortable feel of impact back to the golfer, is a function of the shaft's material and design characteristics. Over the decades of shaft development, shaft manufacturers have acquired more and more of an understanding of just what has to be implemented in each design to enhance consistency, performance and feel. As a result, from a simple beginning with only flex as a means to delineate one shaft from another, shafts now are designed with multiple design characteristics, each one with its own contribution to give to the overall playability of the shaft.

Where once there was only flex (stiffness) to define one shaft from another, today there are no less than seven different design parameters that combine to give each shaft its own unique personality. Change just one of the seven design factors and the shaft can perform and feel differently. Because fitting the correct shaft to the individual is a vital part of the clubmaker's abilities, it is important to understand each of the different design principles of golf shafts.

The vast majority of golf club manufacturers are in agreement that all the woods and all the irons should demonstrate similar feel throughout the set. One way this is achieved is by building each of the clubs (except the wedges) within a set to have the same swingweight and

shaft flex (stiffness). In addition, to ensure each of the clubs will propel the ball a different distance, the loft angle and playing length of each club is varied in a proportionate manner through the set. If each golf club must be made to a different length, yet still have the same swingweight, the weight of each clubhead in the set must be different. As a result, in a standard set of golf clubs, normal golf club design guidelines dictate that the clubheads must increase proportionately in weight as the clubs decrease in length.

At first thought, it would seem logical that installing the same shaft in the same manner into each clubhead would give each club in the set the same feel. However, remember that each club is supposed to be made to a different length and that each head is produced to a different weight. Club length and headweight are two factors that have a great influence upon the feel and performance of a shaft. To illustrate, the shorter the shaft, the stiffer it will be, and the more weight that is placed on the end of a shaft, the more flexible it will be.

Therefore, to create a matched feel of similar flexibility within a set of clubs, the shafts within a set have to become progressively stiffer as they become shorter in length. Described in other terms, within a properly matched set of standard golf clubs, the shaft in the #5-wood will be stiffer than the shaft in the #4-wood, the shaft in the #4-wood will be stiffer than the shaft in the #3-wood, and so forth through the rest of the woods. Within the set of irons the same progression of stiffness must also exist. If each shaft does not increase in stiffness as playing length becomes shorter through the set, the progressively heavier headweights would make each shaft feel successively more and more flexible from the long to the short clubs, and thus the shafts would not feel as though they were matched in stiffness.

As a result, this progressive increase in stiffness is a standard factor that occurs within almost every set of golf clubs. In steel shafts, this mandatory stiffness increase is controlled by a gradual shortening of the distance from the tip end to the first step down of the shaft (tip section length) in each club. Therefore, in virtually all conventionally made sets of steel-shafted golf clubs, if each of the woods and then each of the irons are lined up side by side, the position of the last step down on the shaft will gradually move closer to the clubhead as the clubs get shorter in playing length. Thus, a matched set of shafts do not exhibit the same stiffness after all.

Understanding this beginning function of shafts is fundamental to a discussion of each of the various factors that determine how a shaft is to play. There are, in fact, seven separate shaft design parameters that must be understood:

1. **Shaft Flex (Relative Stiffness)**
2. **Shaft Frequency**
3. **Shaft Type (Weight)**
4. **Shaft Pattern (Bend or Kick Point)**
5. **Shaft Torque**
6. **Shaft Weight Distribution**
7. **Shaft Mounting (Installation)**

■ SHAFT FLEX (RELATIVE STIFFNESS)

In the discussion of the relationship of each of the shafts within a set of golf clubs, it is very important to understand that while the set does increase in stiffness as the

clubs become shorter in length, the shafts in the set are in fact all exhibiting the same playing flex, or **relative stiffness.** In other words, while manufacturers do offer different flexes within any particular shaft design, when a single flex is chosen for a golfer and installed in a set,

that particular flex must increase progressively in stiffness to be able to transmit the same feel from club to club.

In basic shaft design, five primary flexes exist to make golf clubs. Those five flexes in order from stiffest to most flexible are:

X	**Extra Stiff**
S	**Stiff**
R	**Regular**
A	**Amateur or Flexible**
L	**Ladies**

Over the years, shaft makers have occasionally deviated from this basic group of flexes by creating "in-between" versions of flex, but by and large this group of five flexes describes the variations in flex that are offered today. Described more often by their letter codes, occasionally the shaft flex codes have been altered by different manufacturers of golf clubs to fit into their scheme of product marketing. For example, the Ben Hogan Company has used the numbers 1, 2, 3, 4, 5 to denote the L, A, R, S and X flexes, in ascending order of stiffness.

In designing a golf shaft there are two primary ways in which the shaft manufacturer can control flexibility:

- **Shaft Diameter**
- **Shaft Wall Thickness (Shaft Weight)**

By varying the outside diameter of the shaft and by changing the thickness of the walls of the shaft, shaft makers are able to exert their greatest influence on shaft stiffness. The larger the diameter of a shaft, the stiffer it will be, and the thicker the walls of the shaft, the stiffer it will be. By studying a list of shaft diameter specifications, it becomes apparent that the X and S flexes of most designs possess the largest tip and butt diameters, while the R, A and L flexes have smaller tip and butt dimensions.

A specification that is never listed for shafts, wall thickness also has a major effect on stiffness. Evidence of this fact was seen in the early versions of lightweight steel shafts. The first versions of lightweight steel shafts seen in the early 1970s were created by reducing the wall thickness of existing standard weight steel designs. By reducing the wall thickness, shaft makers were able to reduce the weight of a shaft, but at the same time the very early lightweight shafts' flexibility decreased with the decrease in the wall thickness. Reacting to the early lightweight designs shaft manufacturers soon learned that if wall thickness was reduced, the overall diameter of the shaft (primarily the butt section), had to be increased to offset the flexibility decrease.

Best described as a product of the wall thickness, once the outside diameter and wall thickness have been established in a particular shaft, changing the shaft's weight will affect the flexibility as well. Within the same shaft design, the heavier the shaft, the stiffer it will be. Therefore, if you inspect the shaft specification tables included in this chapter, an example of this principle can be seen in the Dynamic Gold design from True Temper, in which the higher numbered sub-flexes of each major flex are the heaviest, with the lower numbered versions of each major flex being lighter, and in turn more flexible. The logic of this explanation can be seen in that for a single, particular shaft to be lighter, it has to be made with thinner walls than the heavier versions of the same shaft. Hence, if the walls are thinner, it would stand to reason that the shaft could not be as stiff as the same shaft design made with thicker walls.

Shaft flex, or relative stiffness as it is also referred, is the one shaft design factor that receives the most attention from golfers and clubmakers. Simply stated, relative stiffness is an expression of how the shaft reacts in overall bending properties when compared to other shafts. Traditionally, relative stiffness is measured by shaft manufacturers on a device called a shaft deflection board. To measure shaft relative stiffness, the operator securely clamps the butt of the shaft and hangs a known weight (usually 7 lb.) from the tip of the shaft.

Measurements of how far the shaft bends from the effect of the weight suspended from the tip (deflection) are

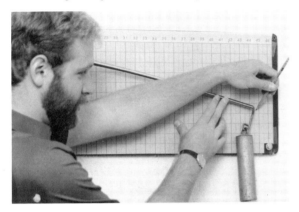

A deflection board measures relative stiffness.

taken at several points along the curve that is created in the shaft. Each position reading along the shaft can then be compared to similar position measurements recorded from other shafts. By comparing the results of the readings at identical locations along the lengths of the shafts, a comparison of relative stiffness can be made between any number of shafts.

Shaft flex has always been used to fit golfers with a level of shaft strength that would most closely match the clubhead speed they could generate. In this, the conventional form of shaft flex fitting, it is felt by many that a golfer with a slower swing should be matched to the more flexible shafts so the shaft will bend in approximately the same manner as will the extra stiff shaft in the hands of the player with very high clubhead speed.

An important point to note about shaft deflection board measurements is that the results obtained can be very confusing when trying to visualize playability differences between shafts. It is very common to compare two different shafts designed to be the same flex and notice that the point to which the tip end hangs is not the same for both shafts. Likewise, it is very common to observe from deflection board readings that an R-flex version of one shaft could actually deflect to a point higher on the board (and thus seemingly be stiffer) than another shaft

of an S flex. Such readings result in great confusion to clubmakers, since it would be logical to assume that all shafts of an identical stated flex should hang to the same point on the board, or that shafts should always deflect in order of their stiffness.

This lack of uniformity between shafts of the same flex and the absence of an even progression between the different flexes of different shaft designs are two of the many points that make fitting a player with the proper shaft so difficult. From research recently conducted it is becoming evident that a stiff flex in one shaft design will not always exhibit the same level of flexibility as a stiff flex of another design.

Why? Currently, no actual standards exist among shaft manufacturers for closely defining flex. Furthermore, there are no published or unanimously agreed upon quantitative measurements to define the stiffness of the L, A, R, S or X flex shafts. Does this sound ridiculous, given the modern age of high-tech shaft design? Rather than condemn the shaft makers, this situation bears a little more explanation.

Over the years of shaft development through today, the makers of shafts have discovered more and more factors that affect the performance of their products. As shaft manufacturers began to design shafts with different flexes, then different points of maximum bending, then different weight, different twisting properties and different balance points, each factor was in essence designed separately into the shaft. What is only now being realized is that each of these shaft design characteristics have an effect on each other which all combine to have an effect on the overall flex of the shaft.

As a result, an R-flex, lightweight, frequency-matched, low bend point, high degree torque, butt heavy shaft will likely not exhibit the same level of overall flex as an R-flex, standard weight, non-frequency-matched, high bend point, low degree torque, tip heavy shaft. Why? Despite the fact both are called R-flex shafts, the difference in the other design factors causes the shafts to exhibit a different overall flex from each other.

Rather than throw up your hands and admit confusion so early in this discussion on shafts, be aware that research is being conducted to discover the effect each shaft design parameter has on each other and on flex. Because such research is ongoing, as a clubmaker in today's golf equipment industry, you would be well advised to study all new information as it becomes available to continue to increase your understanding.

Shaft Flex Coding and Identification

Currently, most premium grade steel shafts as well as virtually all graphite shafts are produced and shipped to the clubmaker with the shaft name and flex either silk screened or pre-labeled on the shaft. However, most common pattern steel shafts are shipped without the name or flex on the shaft. For shafts that are not pre-labeled or named, clubmakers need to learn and be aware of the shafts' different identification codes to prevent mix-ups in their inventory.

During the discussion on shaft flex, the identity of a number of different shaft flex codes were revealed. While flex codes are likely the first of the shaft nomenclatures that any golfer or clubmaker will become aware of, there are variations in flex codes or symbols that can make identifying a particular shaft flex somewhat confusing. The following array of flex symbols are all used within the shaft industry by different manufacturers and can be found silk screened on the shaft itself or displayed on the shaft's label.

Flex	Various Flex Codes/Symbols			
Ladies	L	1		
Amateur/Senior	A	2		
Regular	R	3	B	T
Stiff	S	4	C	
Extra Stiff	X	5	D	
Extra Extra Stiff	XX			

In addition to these "discrete flexes," there also exist shafts that are either made to possess two separate flexes within one single shaft, or shafts that are produced to be in between two particular established flexes. Combination flex and in between flex shafts have their own distinct codes and nomenclature as well.

Flex	Flex Codes
L and A combination flex	A & L or A/L
R and S combination flex	R & S or R/S
A and R combination flex	A & R or A/R
S and X combination flex	S & X or S/X
In between A and R	AR
In between R and S	RS
In between S and X	TS

In addition to using codes/symbols on the shaft or its label, the flex of most shafts is also marked on the last 1-2" of the butt using a color code system. The color code system of flex identification is used by most shaft manufacturers to assist the clubmaker or clubmaking company in separating one flex from another.

Knowing the various manufacturers' color codes for flex is absolutely vital for accurate shaft identification and installation. Listed at the bottom of this page are the various flex/color codes that clubmakers will most often encounter.

Steel combination flex shafts are not color coded. Identification of these shafts will have to be performed by recognizing the step pattern, raw length and tip and butt diameters of the shaft.

In addition to the codes for flex, the shaft manufacturers also have individual product code designations that are used when placing orders for the various shafts. Currently, some of the component suppliers use the same shaft product codes that the manufacturers create for their shafts, while many others do not. As a clubmaker, get used to learning each of the shaft makers' shaft name codes when placing your orders. A list of shaft product codes is included in the listing of shaft manufacturer's available shaft patterns, found at the end of this chapter.

■ SHAFT FREQUENCY

Shaft frequency is a measurement of the rate of vibration of a shaft as expressed over a known unit of time. In the late 1970s, machines were developed to enable

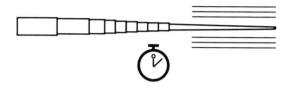

SHAFT FREQUENCY

clubmakers to measure the vibrational frequency of shafts. By clamping the butt of the shaft and oscillating the tip, a shaft's frequency of vibration can be recorded, and thus enable clubmakers to more clearly define flex and compare the flex of one shaft to another.

If the deflection board is considered to be a static measurement of shaft flex, frequency is considered to be its dynamic measurement. In comparative terms, the faster the rate of vibration of a shaft, the stiffer the flex, and the lower the frequency reading, the more flexible the shaft is considered to be. The reason shaft frequency is considered to be a dynamic measurement of flex, and therefore a more accurate way to actually identify and compare the flex of different shafts, is because the frequency recording machine takes the following factors into account:

• **Shaft Flex (Relative Stiffness)**
  The greater the stiffness within a particular shaft design, the higher the frequency; the more flexible the shaft within a particular shaft design, the lower the frequency.

• **Shaft Length (Club Length)**
  The longer the shaft in the club, the lower the frequency and the shorter the club, the higher the frequency. Hence the longer the club, the more flexible will be the shaft, and the shorter the club the stiffer it will be.

FLEX COLOR CODING
By Shaft Manufacturers

Flex	True Temper	Aldila	Kunnan	Carbon Fiber Products
L	Blue	Red	Blue	Yellow
A	Yellow	———[1]	Blue	———[1]
R	Black	Yellow	Orange	Green
S	Red	Green	Yellow	Blue
X	Green	Orange	———[1]	Red

[1] Denotes flex not offered by manufacturer

Note: Carbon Fiber Products uses orange and a double orange code to denote its very flexible series shafts. For steel shafts all color codes will be applied in the form of a marking pen or paint, while for the composite shaft companies the color is applied in the form of a colored strip of tape for shafts that are produced without a pre-attached label or without the flex silk screened on the shaft.

COMPARISON OF SHAFT FREQUENCY

NOTE: All shafts tested were for Drivers only, parallel tip versions. All A, R, S and X-flex Drivers were standard metal wood design with 43" playing length and D-1 swingweight. All L-flex Drivers were standard metal wood design with 42" playing length and C-7 swingweight.

Company	Shaft (Flex)	Driver Frequency	Company	Shaft (Flex)	Driver Frequency	Company	Shaft (Flex)	Driver Frequency
ACT	ACTivator R	242	Brunswick	FM Graphite 5.5	257		TI Low Flex S	254
	ACTivator S	248		FM Graphite 6.5	265		TI Low Flex X	259
Aldila	HM-30 L	235		FM Graphite 7.5	276	True Temper	Black Gold R300	258
	HM-30 A	245		FM Steel 5.5	256		Black Gold S300	255
	HM-30 R	247		FM Steel 6.5	264		Command R	248
	HM-30 S	264		Microtaper L	240		Command S	255
	HM-40 R	252		Microtaper A	238		Dynamic L	234
	HM-40 S	271		Microtaper R	251		Dynamic A	233
	HM-40 Lo R	265		Microtaper S	259		Dynamic R	249
	HM-40 Lo S	278	Dynacraft	Dyna Tech Std R	259		Dynamic S	260
	HM-55 R	258		Dyna Tech Std S	268		Dynamic X	272
	HM-55 S	269		Dyna Tech Classic R	265		Dynamic Gold R200	245
	Low Torque L	256		Dyna Tech Classic S	267		Dynamic Gold R300	245
	Low Torque R[1]	277	Fenwick	World Class R	255		Dynamic Gold R400	246
	Low Torque S[1]	290		World Class S	267		Dynamic Gold S200	258
	Low Torque X	306	FiberSpeed[2]	FS100	180		Dynamic Gold S300	258
	Questar R	262		FS200	197		Dynamic Gold S400	258
	Questar S	280		FS300	214		EV40 R	248
Alloy 2000	A2000 R	240	Grafalloy	M29 R	248		EV40 S	252
	A2000 S	250		M29 S	254		Gold Plus R300	252
	A2000 X	255		M60 R	245		Gold Plus S300	260
Apollo	AP44 R	248		M60 S	256		Jet Step R	251
	AP44 S	260		Senior Classic	245		Jet Step S	263
	Boron Tourline R	252		Lady Classic	235		TT Lite L	239
	Boron Tourline S	265	Kunnan	Comp50 R	253		TT Lite A	236
	Boron Tourline X	274		Comp50 S	273		TT Lite R	248
	G100 L	249		1460TFB R	247		TT Lite S	260
	G100 R	248		1460TFB S	268	Unifiber	T50 S	265
	G100 S	265		1400TFB L	243		T50 X	269
	MasterFlex R	251		1400TFB R	260			
	MasterFlex S	264		1400TFB S	272			
	MatchFlex 1	235		1400LFB A	250			
	MatchFlex 2	235		Autoclave 30 R	245			
	MatchFlex 3	240		Autoclave 30 S	260			
	MatchFlex 4	250		Autoclave 40 R	245			
	Shadow L	235		Autoclave 40 S	260			
	Shadow A	238		Autoclave 50 R	245			
	Shadow R	246		Autoclave 50 S	260			
	Shadow S	258	TI Shaft	TI Standard R	244			
	Spectre L	242		TI Standard S	254			
	Spectre A	242		TI Standard X	261			
	Spectre R	252		TI Low Flex A	234			
	Spectre S	262		TI Low Flex R	241			

[1]R and S flex tests on the Aldila Low Torque were performed on the R & S combination flex version of the shaft. Due to the special tip construction of the combination flex version, the frequency readings were unusually high for the respective R and S flexes. The R and S flex versions of the non-combination flex Low Torque would yield lower frequency measurements due to the different tip construction.

[2]FiberSpeed test Drivers were built to 43.5" playing length with C-5 swingweight as per manufacturer's recommended playing specifications.

- **Clubhead Weight**

    The greater the mass of the head on the end of the shaft, the lower the frequency, and the less the clubhead weight, the higher the frequency. Hence the greater the clubhead weight the more flexible the shaft will be and the lighter the headweight the stiffer the shaft will be.

- **Shaft Weight**

    The heavier a shaft within the same pattern, the higher will be the frequency; the lighter a shaft within the same pattern, the lower the frequency. Hence the heavier the shaft within the same design, the more flexible it will be and the lighter the shaft within the same design, the stiffer it will be.

While raw shafts can be tested for frequency, it is far more meaningful to perform frequency tests on shafts that have been installed in finished golf clubs. With a shaft properly installed into a finished club that has been assembled to a standard length and built to a standard swingweight, a frequency measurement can be obtained for that shaft. By then recording the frequency measurement of other shafts installed into golf clubs, it is possible to make a meaningful comparison between different shafts.

For example, if two different R-flex shafts are mounted in identical clubheads and compared by frequency it is possible to determine if the two shafts of the same flex really do exhibit the same relative stiffness. To illustrate an example of how flex variance exists in the shaft industry, the R-flex version of the Alloy 2000 shaft has a frequency of 240 cpm while the R-flex from the combination flex version of the Aldila Low Torque graphite shaft has a frequency reading of 277 cpm[1]. To qualify this information, approximately a 10 cpm change in frequency is considered to represent a change of one full flex in the average shaft design. Therefore, from high

---

[1]Frequency readings were for standard metal wood Drivers built to D-1 swingweight at 43" playing length with shaft installation performed as per the manufacturer's recommended trimming instructions.

to low in the shaft industry today there exists a range of nearly four flexes just within the R-flex!

As more and more information concerning the actual frequency readings of shafts becomes available, clubmakers will be able to become more proficient in advising golfers about flex. For example, without such information, a golfer playing a certain R-flex shaft who wishes to change to another type of R-flex shaft would have no idea whether the new shaft has the same flex as the old shaft or not. As this discussion develops to include the other aspects of shaft design, be aware that the proper fitting of shafts definitely must involve looking at more factors than just frequency. Many of the other shaft design parameters such as torque and bend point have a compound effect on overall flex feel that will have to be taken into account as well.

The facing chart is a list of Driver shaft frequency for many of the popular shafts of today. To standardize the readings and allow you to use the data to make meaningful shaft-to-shaft comparisons, all shafts have been installed as per their individual manufacturer's installation instructions. The A, R, S and X flex shafts have all been tested as installed in a standard metal Driver built to 43" length with D-1 swingweight. The L-flex shafts have all been tested as installed in a standard metal Driver built to 42" length with C-7 swingweight.

Another purpose of recording shaft frequency is to refine shaft-to-shaft matching within any chosen flex, pattern and type, to result in a more precisely made set of golf clubs. In defining shaft flex, it was stated that one of the factors that influences shaft flexibility is weight. Within the same shaft design, the heavier the shaft, the stiffer the shaft, and the lighter the weight, the more flexible will be the shaft. For example, between two True Temper Dynamic shafts, the heavier one will be stiffer than the lighter one.

Most common steel shafts are manufactured with a weight tolerance of approximately ±3/16 oz, an allowance that can be enough to create an overlapping of

adjacent flexes. In other words, if the designed weight of a particular shaft is 4.37 oz, due to its allowable weight tolerance, that shaft can weigh as much as 4.56 oz and as light as 4.19 oz. When tested for relative stiffness, the heavier shafts will be stiffer than the designated norm, so much that in some cases the shaft on the heavy end of the ± tolerance could actually read one full flex stiffer than the shaft on the low side of the weight tolerance.

Through frequency measurements, this high to low weight tolerance difference can show up as a deviation from the normal progression of stiffness through a set. To contrast, if a set of shafts produced with very tight weight tolerances is tested for frequency and charted, a line drawn through each shaft's frequency measurement will show up as a straight line on the graph. When such results are plotted on a graph, a straight line of frequency through all the clubs in the set means the differences in cycles per minute between each shaft (club) in the set have the same exact incremental change. When an even progressional change in frequency readings occurs within a set, the shafts are said to be frequency matched.

If the shafts within a set of golf clubs are not close in weight progression from shaft to shaft, or in ± tolerance to the shafts' designed weight specification, a graph of the set's frequency will reveal an uneven incremental change from club to club in frequency readings. The first example graph on page 66 shows a comparison between a form of frequency matching within a set and wide variations in frequency through a set. The set of shafts represented by the straight line drawn through the readings is considered to be frequency matched, and thus show an even incremental change in vibration rate from one club to the next. Contrasting that is the more "jagged line" on the graph which illustrates an example of how wide ranges in shaft weight (or other shaft design factors, too) can affect the even progression of frequency.

Slope of Frequency

The angle of the line on the graph connecting each of the clubs' frequency readings is called the Slope of the Frequency. Charting the slope of the frequency mea-

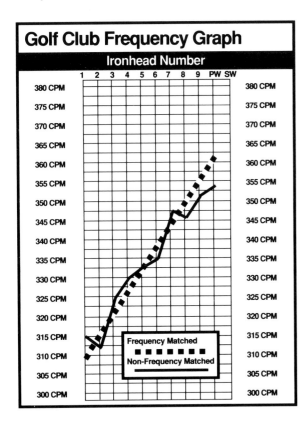

Golf Club Frequency Graph

Ironhead Number

Frequency Matched

Non-Frequency Matched

surements of a set of shafts is one way to express the relative change in flexibility from one shaft to another in the set. As the slope of frequency becomes more vertical on the chart, the shafts within the set become progressively more firm in their relative stiffness to each other. Conversely, as the slope created by frequency readings within a full set becomes more horizontal on the graph, the shafts do not exhibit as much of an increase in stiffness from one club to the next. Therefore, the slope of frequency can be said to show the relationship of the relative stiffness of the shafts within a set.

To better understand this principle, remember the point made earlier in this chapter. In a conventionally made set of woods or irons, from the long clubs to the short clubs the shafts are intended to increase in stiffness to offset the mandatory changes in headweight and length that are standard within sets in the golf industry. Therefore, if a

set demonstrates a straight horizontal slope of frequency, each shaft in the set would have exactly the same stiffness, but due to the effect of increased headweight through the set, the shafts would play and feel progressively more flexible from the long to the short clubs.

There is no one slope of shaft frequency that can be considered as being correct for every golfer. Different ball striking abilities, different perceptions of "feel" among golfers and other human swing factors all mean that pinpointing the correct slope for a golfer is more a requirement of individual clubfitting. However, what slope **can** do for the clubmaker is to reveal yet another way to relate the performance and feel of one particular shaft design to another. For example, the two most popular frequency-matched shaft patterns in the golf industry today are True Temper's Dynamic Gold and Brunswick Corp.'s FM Precision shaft patterns. When comparable flexes of both are mounted in identical sets of clubheads and built to standard length and similar swingweight, the two shaft designs will exhibit different slopes when charted for frequency on a graph (see chart at right).

Note that the slope of the FM Precision is steeper than the slope of the comparable Dynamic Gold. What this means to the clubmaker is that the Dynamic Gold shafts will make the longer clubs in the set feel firmer than the long clubs that are shafted with the FM Precision. But, as the set decreases in length through the fairway woods and short irons, the FM Precision shafts will gradually begin to play stiffer than the comparable Dynamic Golds.

NON-FREQUENCY MATCHED SHAFTS
While most common pattern steel shafts, (Dynamic, TT Lite, Shadow, etc.) are not expressly designed to be frequency matched, a form of frequency matching can be achieved within these types of shafts if time is taken to select shafts that are very close in ± tolerance to the shafts' designed weight. While it was mentioned that the ± 3/16 oz shaft weight tolerances that are normal with common pattern shafts do not allow for true frequency matching within a set, hand-picking shafts from any

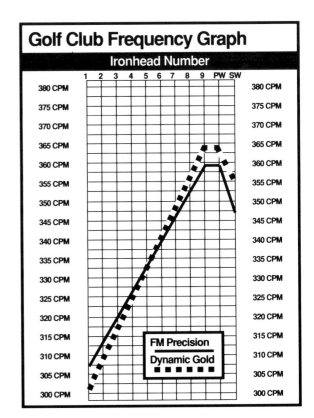

Golf Club Frequency Graph

Ironhead Number

FM Precision

Dynamic Gold

shaft design to be of similar weight will have the result of creating a type of frequency-matched set. Therefore, if all the shafts in a set are hand-picked to be the same weight, (or in the case of some taper tip shaft patterns, have the same incremental weight difference from one to the other) providing the clubs are built with identical weight grips and assembled to perfect incremental changes in playing length with the same swingweights, the clubs will achieve a weight-selected status of frequency matching.

Hand selecting identical weight shafts can be time consuming and is not always possible, given the number of shafts that would have to be weighed before coming up with a perfect set. However, recently shaft manufacturers have begun to recognize the need for tighter weight tolerances in their shafts. For example, the MatchFlex and the MasterFlex shafts from Apollo Shaft

Corp., are patterns that are designed and produced to weight tolerances of ± 1/15 oz and ±1/30 oz respectively. Much tighter weight controls such as these are enough to prevent shaft flex overlapping within the design and result in frequency-matched set of clubs.

The other form of frequency matching within a particular shaft design does not center around weight selection, but rather around the actual vibrational frequency of the shafts. While the Dynamic Gold from True Temper is frequency matched by virtue of weight selection, the FM Precision by Brunswick is matched by vibrational frequency. At the Brunswick factory, long, untrimmed shaft "blanks" are individually vibrated for frequency after which they are trimmed and matched into similar frequency groups.

Whether frequency matching is the ultimate method of shaft installation is still pretty much a discussion for the future. There exist today golfers who play well with common pattern shafts mounted to standard guidelines, just as there are golfers who play well with the available frequency-matched shaft patterns. What must be understood is that on its own, frequency matching is definitely not the only shaft fitting factor to consider.

For example, a high handicap golfer interested in a frequency-matched set comes to a clubmaker who fits him with Dynamic Gold or FM Precision shafts. After several rounds of golf with the new clubs, the high handicapper finds that he is still struggling to hit the ball. By focusing only on frequency matching in prescribing shafts for this player, the clubfitter has forgotten the importance of the other factors of shaft classification, among them the torque, weight and bend point.

In the above example, the reason the high handicapper experienced poor results from the frequency-matched set is that the Dynamic Gold and the FM Precision designs are best suited for players with good swing fundamentals; i.e. both shafts are tip firm with a high bend point. Had the clubmaker first selected a shaft for this less able golfer with torque, weight and bend point characteristics that would enhance his game, he then could take the time to weight select the shafts of choice and accurately assemble the set so that frequency-matching properties could be achieved. Not to be overstated, the frequency matching of shafts is but one of several shaft design parameters, all of which must be taken into account to fit the golfer with the proper shaft.

In the 1990s frequency measuring is going far beyond the simple checking of proper stiffness progression within a set. It is on the verge of being recognized as the best way to compare the flex of one type of shaft to another, thus setting the stage for a uniformity of flex dimensions within the golf shaft industry. While it will always be the choice of a shaft designer just how stiff their S-flex or R-flex should be, with the ability to record shaft frequency, the clubmaker and golfer will have a true means of comparison to help make more educated choices in the shafts they use and play.

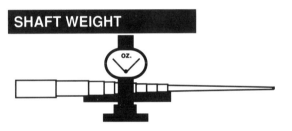

SHAFT WEIGHT

■ SHAFT TYPE (WEIGHT)

Shaft weight, or shaft type, as it is also known, is another very important design classification for a golf shaft. Currently, shafts are grouped into these basic weight (type) classifications:

Shaft Weight Classifications

Type	Material	Weight Range
Standard Weight	(Steel)	4.25oz to 4.62oz
Light Weight	(Steel or Alloy)	3.80oz to 4.24oz
Very Light Weight	(Steel or Alloy)	3.40oz to 3.79oz
Light Weight	(Composite)	3.20oz to 3.60oz
Very Light Weight	(Composite)	2.00oz to 3.19oz.

The above weights represent raw weights for shafts that are intended for installation in wood club

Prior to the early 1970s all shafts were made from steel and possessed a narrow range of weight from one design to another. Shaft design and forming technology had not advanced beyond the use of grades of carbon steel that all resulted in standard weight type shafts. With the introduction of the lightweight steel shaft, clubmaking companies gained the ability to affect a change in the total weight of a golf club, thus adding a new dimension to clubfitting. By lowering the weight of the shaft and in turn, decreasing the total weight of the golf club, players were given the opportunity to increase their clubhead speed without having to swing harder at the ball. This possible result of greater distance due to increased clubhead speed from the lighter shafts started a rush among shaft manufacturers to develop lighter and lighter shafts in the hope of delivering greater distance on shots to golfers. From lightweight steel, manufacturers have been able to decrease shaft weight even more through the use of lighter steel alloys and modern fiber composites.

Shaft weight (type) is a very important design factor because it can illicit a significant effect on the swingweight and the total weight of the finished golf club. Previously it was established that one of the ways manufacturers control shaft flexibility is through weight; once a particular design for a shaft has been conceived, the heavier versions of that design will be stiffer than the lighter versions. The reason this is true is that within the same particular shaft design, the heavier versions have greater shaft wall thickness to account for the weight difference.

In addition to creating lighter shafts by reducing wall thickness, shaft manufacturers can also use different raw materials to achieve a decrease in weight. Currently among metal shafts a number of lightweight and very lightweight shafts exist that are made from such alloys as titanium, chrome vanadium steel or nickel steel. By using lighter weight materials, metal shaft manufacturers are able to either retain normal wall thickness and still achieve the lighter weight, or through the increased strength of the alloy, thin down the wall to create even lighter shafts without fear of breakage.

Within the modern golf shaft industry, materials of choice that can produce the lightest of all shafts is graphite or a blend of ultra light fiber composites. With its high strength to weight ratio, shafts are now produced from graphite that weigh as little as 2 oz! However, because of the diversity of composite materials that shaft makers have at their disposal, not all graphite shafts can be classified as very light in weight. Materials used in the manufacture of graphite and composite shafts do vary in weight, sometimes to the point that certain graphite shafts can weigh as much as the lightest alloy shafts. Therefore, the weight classifications of shafts today now have been broadened as indicated in the chart on page 67.

Clubmakers soon discover another golf club specifications that is affected by shaft weight is swingweight. Often less experienced clubmakers are amazed what happens to the swingweight of a golf club when using different weight shafts in their work. To see the effect that shaft weight can have on the swingweight of an assembled golf club, study the following chart:

Effect of Shaft Weight on Swingweight

Club Head	Head Weight	Shaft Weight	Swingweight at Std. Length[1]
#2 iron	236g	4.375 oz	D-0
#2 iron	236g	4.000 oz	C-8.5
#2 iron	236g	2.750 oz	C-2

[1] Standard Length defined as 39" for the #2 iron

This chart illustrating the relationship of shaft weight to swingweight shows what can happen to swingweight when three identical weight ironheads are installed with different weight shafts and built to the same playing length with identical grips. As seen from the information in the chart, **the lighter the shaft, the lighter will be the swingweight.[1]**

---

[1]Not in all cases will a decrease in shaft weight bring a decrease in swingweight. In the rare case of very light shafts designed with more weight in the tip half, the swingweight will not decrease as much as with very light shafts designed with normal weight distribution.

The reason this loss of swingweight can occur is that on a Lorythmic swingweight scale (the scale with 14" fulcrum that reads in A, B, C, D increments) all weight lying on the clubhead side of the fulcrum has the effect of increasing swingweight, while all weight lying on the grip side of the fulcrum has the effect of decreasing swingweight. Since the majority of the shaft in any club in the set lies on the forward side of the scale fulcrum, a decrease in shaft weight will be reflected more on the head end than it will on the grip end of the scale's fulcrum point. Therefore, with a drop of 1 5/8 oz in shaft weight (such as in a change from standard weight to a very light weight shaft) more of that weight loss will be recorded in front of the fulcrum, thus resulting in a lower swingweight reading for the club.

Clubmakers will notice the greatest decrease in swingweight when very light weight graphite shafts are assembled with standard weight component clubheads. Since the majority of all golf clubs are assembled with standard weight or light weight steel shafts, component clubhead weights are usually designed to accommodate a range of standard swingweight when installed on these types of shafts. Therefore, since most graphite shafts are very light, the swingweight will drop substantially when the shafts are installed into standard weight clubheads. This is very important for clubmakers to understand because all too often when clubmakers notice the low C-range swingweight that occurs from installation on a very light shaft, they make the mistake of accusing the head manufacturer of producing a clubhead that is deficient in weight, when it is the effect of the shaft that has caused the swingweight decrease.

As a result, when building sets of golf clubs with very light weight shafts, it is important to select clubheads with suitable weight ports or heads that have been designed to heavier weights. Because of the recent increase in the popularity of very lightweight shafts, a number of clubmaking supply companies have begun to produce and stock an assortment of heavier weight clubheads.

Not only does shaft weight have an effect on swingweight but it is the primary determinant of total weight in a golf club as well. To understand this relationship, it is best to illustrate an example of two golf clubs built with different weight shafts.

Club #1 - Driver - Dynamic S-flex shaft, D-1 swingweight, 43" playing length, M60 rubber grip standard size.

Grip	51 grams	(1.80 oz)
Shaft	115.8 grams	(4.085 oz)
Head	206.7 grams	(7.29 oz)
Total	373.5 grams	(13.175 oz)

Club #2 - Driver - Aldila Low Torque graphite S-flex shaft, D-1 swingweight, 43" playing length, M60 rubber grip standard size.

Grip	51 grams	(1.80 oz)
Shaft	75 grams	(2.65 oz)
Head	216.4 grams	(7.63 oz)
Total	342.4 grams	(12.08 oz)

The only difference between the two assembled Drivers in this example is the weight of the shaft and headweight increase required to achieve the same D-1 swingweight, yet between the two Drivers there is a difference of more than a full ounce of total weight.

Another vital principle of shaft weight that clubmakers must understand is what happens to the weight of a shaft before and after it has been installed into a golf club. When a shaft manufacturer designs a new shaft, the published weight specification for the design is what is called the raw weight, or the weight of the shaft in its uncut, uninstalled form. For example, the raw weight of the UDWC shaft from True Temper is 4.625 oz, a weight that applies only to the shaft in its 47" long, uncut form. However, once the UDWC shaft is trimmed and installed in one of the various styles of available woodhead designs, it will be considerably different in weight (see the chart on page 69).

RAW SHAFT WEIGHT VS. CUT SHAFT WEIGHT

Raw Shaft	Raw Shaft Length/Wt.	Head Type	Cut Shaft Length	Cut Shaft Weight[1]
UDWC	47"/4.625oz	Thru-Bore	43"	4.250oz Driver
UDWC	47"/4.625oz	Blind Bore	42 1/2"	4.182oz Driver
UDWC	47"/4.625oz	Metal Wood	41 1/4"	4.085oz Driver[2]

[1] Based on 43" playing length for Driver, installed to S flex
[2] Based on bottom of bore to back of heel dimension of 1 1/4"

In studying the data from the chart, a number of important concepts are illustrated that clubmakers must understand. The term "cut shaft length" describes the length of the shaft after it has been trimmed and installed into each of the three different types of woodheads. The term "cut shaft weight" indicates the weight of the shaft after it has been trimmed and installed into each type of woodhead. To understand the information in the chart, realize that the same UDWC raw shaft will end up being three different cut shaft lengths and three different cut shaft weights when installed into the three different woodhead styles that are commonly seen in clubmaking today.

■ SHAFT PATTERN (SHAFT BEND POINT)

The term shaft pattern is sometimes referred to as the design or "brand name" of the shaft. However, clubmak-

ers must be aware of the true definition of shaft pattern is the distribution of the shaft's flexibility about the three major areas of the shaft; tip, butt and mid-section. To clarify, within the L, A, R, S or X flexes, a shaft can be manufactured so that one end of the shaft is firmer than the other, or so both halves of the shaft are equal in flexibility. Therefore, a shaft's pattern, or distribution of flexibility, is designed in one of three ways:

1. **Tip firm and butt flexible**
2. **Tip flexible and butt firm**
3. **Tip medium and butt medium.**

Slight variations between these basic descriptions of patterns are possible, but primarily, all of the shafts that are produced will fall into one of these three groups. Again, it is very important to understand that shaft pattern does not refer to the L, A, R, S or X flex of the shaft; it refers to the distribution of flexibility about the entire length of the shaft.

When the pattern of a shaft is determined by the manufacturer, the distribution of flexibility about the shaft determines another important shaft design specification called the bend point or kick point. When the distribution of a shaft's flexibility is established, the shaft will have one point where it will exhibit its greatest amount of bending. For example, shafts with a tip firm and butt flexible pattern will have a high bend point. Those shafts that are tip flexible and butt firm will possess a low bend point and the tip and butt medium pattern shafts will have a mid-shaft bend point.

The reason this shaft design specification is important is that bend point and pattern have a major effect on the "feel" of the shaft and a minor effect on the trajectory of the shot. From a feel standpoint, for those golfers who have developed a finite sense of detecting the movement of the shaft during the swing, the high bend point shaft will feel slightly more firm at impact than the mid-bend and low bend point shafts respectively. Conversely, the low bend point shafts will transmit more of a feel of the shaft having a definite kick just prior to impact.

To illustrate the effect of shaft bend point on trajectory, of three identical golf clubs yet with three different shaft patterns in the hands of the same golfer, the shaft with the high bend point will result in a lower trajectory, the mid-bend point shaft will show a medium height shot and the low bend point shaft will hit the ball with the highest trajectory. However, from a shaft fitting standpoint, modern research has shown that bend point does not have as pronounced of an effect on shot trajectory as was once believed. From the research being accumulated, such new thought is substantiated by a number of facts:

1. **A significant difference between high and low bend point location does not exist in shafts produced today.**

2. **Uniformity in bend point location varies from shaft manufacturer to shaft manufacturer.**

3. **Modern methods of measuring bend point are revealing that some shafts thought to possess a low bend point actually have a higher bend point than some shafts said to have a high bend point**

Therefore the guarantee that a player will be able to alter shot trajectory through a change in bend point just does not exist today. Dramatic trajectory changes in ball flight are much more affected through a change in clubhead center of gravity or loft angle than through shaft bend point. Part of the reason the shaft's bend point has only a minor effect on shot height is that steel shaft makers are limited in their ability to establish the bend point location on the shaft. Current steel shaft forming technology only allows a difference of less than 3" from low to high bend point on shafts for wood clubs, and less than 2" on shafts that are made for use in irons.

Perhaps then the greatest contribution of bend point in shaft fitting today lies in the differences the shaft pattern and bend point can contribute to the "feel "of the shot at impact. The lower the bend point, the more solid the shot will feel, especially to a golfer with a low clubhead speed.

SHAFT PATTERN (Bend Point)

This increase in clubhead feel due to a lower bend point occurs because the closer to the head that the shaft "bends," the greater the distance that the shock of impact is transmitted up the remainder of the shaft to the player's hands. Too often, clubmakers think only of the trajectory benefits that can come with different patterns when they advise their customers. Because pattern (bend point) does exert an influence on the feel of the club, this factor should be taken into account when fitting golfers with the proper shaft.

Recently it has been determined that graphite/composite shafts have the ability to exhibit a greater range in bend point location than steel shafts. Because the majority of graphite shafts are produced through a process that involves rolling individual sheets of graphite fiber around a forming mandrel, a graphite shaft maker can mix and match different types of graphite to achieve different performance properties. By intermingling sheets of graphite material with different strengths, it is possible to create graphite shafts with a much greater separation in bend point location than steel. Compared to the steel shaft's maximum high to low bend point separation of less than 3", a wider range of feel and trajectory influences could result from graphite than from steel. Much of this graphite advantage is still in theory, since from recent shaft research, while the high to low range in actual bend point locations of graphite shafts is greater than steel, the composite shafts' bend points are not separated by as much as what clubmakers have been led to believe by some of the manufacturers.

Because there are limits to the ways a manufacturer can create a steel shaft pattern, each of the companies that produce steel shafts manufacture similar patterns to each other. When fitting golfers with a particular pattern it is not always possible to obtain that particular shaft due to back orders or varying demands for the shaft. When a particular shaft is not available it will be necessary for clubmakers to know what shafts are similar in pattern to be able to make a substitution. At right is a chart of each of the shaft manufacturers comparable steel shaft patterns to help you learn this information.

Comparable Steel Shaft Patterns

Pattern Description (Type)	True Temper	Brunswick	Apollo
Tip Firm/Butt Flexible High Bend Point (Standard Weight)	Dynamic, Dynamic Gold, NDWS, NDIS	Pro Pel II	AP44, AP44 Elite, Torsion Matched, Torsion Matched II, MasterFlex (S, TS, X Flex), MatchFlex (S Flex)
Tip Firm/Butt Flexible High-Bend Point (Light Weight)	Dynamic Lite[1]	FM Precision	MasterFlex (R, RS Flex)
Tip Medium/Butt Medium Mid-Shaft Bend Point (Standard Weight)	Pro Fit, Comet	Champion	AP46
Tip Medium/Butt Medium Mid-Shaft Bend Point (Light Weight)	TT Lite	Phoenix	Spectre, MatchFlex (R, RS Flex)
Tip Medium/Butt Medium Mid-Shaft Bend Point (Very Light Weight)	Gold Plus	UCV-304 FM Lite	AccuLite
Tip Flexible/Butt Firm Low Bend Point (Standard Weight)	Jet Step, Century	Super Champion	AP83
Tip Flexible/Butt Firm Low Bend Point (Light Weight)	Flex Flow[2]	Microtaper	MatchFlex (AR Flex), Shadow, Lady Shadow, Senior Shadow

1 Available only on special order basis from True Temper
2 Variable bend point through each flex, low in the long irons, mid-shaft in the middle irons and high in the short irons

This chart of manufacturers' comparable steel shaft patterns and types will not only provide the necessary information to allow you to become familiar with shaft pattern and shaft type classification, but it can be used as a reference for ordering shafts, should a particular shaft you desire be out of stock with your supplier. For example, if a Dynamic pattern shaft is temporarily unavailable from your supplier, do not hesitate to substitute the Pro Pel II or the AP44 as equivalent patterns to achieve the same performance results.

■ SHAFT TORQUE

A shaft's resistance to torque is the measurement of its ability to resist the natural and unnatural twisting forces placed upon it. During the motion of the swing, the

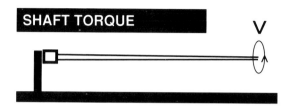

clubhead automatically begins to exert a twisting influence on the shaft. This natural twisting force is created because the shaft is attached to the heel area of the clubhead. Since the center of gravity of the clubhead is in the middle of the head and therefore is not in line with the shaft, under the force of the swing the head has a tendency to rotate about its own center of gravity and thus try to twist the shaft. In addition, an unnatural twisting force may be applied to the shaft as a result of any off-center impact of the clubhead with the golf ball. Shots struck on the toe or heel also have the effect of making the clubhead rotate about its own center of gravity, which applies another type of twisting force to the shaft. If the shaft cannot resist the twisting forces placed upon it, the result will be sidespin on the golf ball and misdirected shots that are hit off the intended target line.

Prior to the advent of the steel shaft, hitting accurate shots with hickory shafts was very difficult due to the fact that the wooden shafts could not resist the tendency of the clubhead to twist open or closed both during the swing and during impact with the ball. Therefore, when the steel shaft was introduced, its natural ability to exhibit rotational strength over hickory was one of the major reasons it was able to overtake hickory and become the pre-eminent shaft in the game.

After steel shafts replaced those made from hickory, shaft manufacturers and clubmakers paid little attention to the torque resistance characteristics of a shaft. After all, with steel or metal alloys, resistance to torque is a property that is virtually "built-in" to the shaft. When a shaft is produced from metal, once the weight, flex and bend point are all designed, the torque properties are set and cannot be altered. Given the type of metal from which a shaft is made and the fact that the shaft consists of the same metal throughout, torque was thought of as a factor that was not designed into a shaft, but rather a design parameter that "came with it," so to speak.

When graphite shafts first appeared in the early 1970s, lack of adequate raw material strength and the manufacturers' inability to design any change in resistance to twisting caused the first graphite shafts to have very little ability to resist torque. As a result not only did the shafts magnify misdirectional problems, they transmitted a very flexible feel to the golfer as well. Golfers who used the early graphite shafts reacted to the more flexible feel by selecting a shaft that was one or more levels of flex stiffer than what they had been playing with steel shafts.

Today, while there is still no way to effectively alter the torque of metal shafts, composite shaft manufacturers have developed the ability to affect torque by wrapping some of the sheets of graphite with the composite fibers aligned at an angle to the shaft. Being able to vary the angle of the fibers to the shaft and increase the strength of the graphite fibers used in the wrapping have allowed the manufacturers to very precisely control the modern shafts' resistance to torque. As a result, composite shafts now exist with torque measurements from as little as 1.6° to as much as 8°. This contrasts with the torque variation available with metal (steel, steel alloys, titanium) which exhibits a maximum high to low range of less than 1°.

Shaft torque is measured by clamping a specified length of the butt and applying a known force to twist the tip. Currently there is no set standard within the industry for measuring torque, although many shaft manufacturers are beginning to agree on the use of a twisting test force of one foot/pound. During the test, as the force is applied to the tip, the shaft begins to twist in relationship to its

ability to resist that twisting force. Through special measuring devices, the amount of twisting is measured in degrees of rotation. The higher the degree reading of the twisting, the lower is the shaft's ability to resist torque and the lower the reading in degrees, the greater is the shaft's resistance to torque.

Recently, shaft manufacturers and clubmakers have begun to realize that torque interacts with flex to give the golf shaft its true flex feel. Before graphite shafts made their big comeback in the 1980s, the very narrow range of torque exhibited by steel shafts meant that a shaft's overall stiffness feel was entirely a product of its flex. But with graphite shafts that range in torque by over 6° from high to low, one version of an R-flex shaft could be completely different in flex feel from another type of R-flex shaft.

For example, if a manufacturer makes two R-flex shafts that are identical in flex characteristics, the one with a low degree of torque will feel much stiffer in play than the one with the higher degree of torque. So significant is the effect of torque on shaft flex performance, that clubmakers must study the torque of a shaft and compare that design parameter to the shaft's flex to be able to advise golfers of the proper shaft choice.

■ SHAFT BALANCE POINT

A shaft's balance point is the expression of how the weight within the shaft is distributed over its length. In the past, despite the fact that a shaft was always designed to be small in diameter at the tip and large in diameter at the butt, manufacturers always designed their shafts to have equal weight distribution through the length of the shaft by making the shaft wall thicker at the tip and thinner at the butt. As a result, virtually all steel shafts in the past exhibited a balance point that was directly in the center of the shaft.

In the 1970s and later in the 1980s, two developments by shaft manufacturers opened the door toward research into the effect of altering balance point as a way to

change the performance of a shaft. In 1971, True Temper developed the concept of the combination flex, parallel tip shaft. With this type of shaft construction, golf club manufacturers could use one shaft type for woods and one for irons to assemble all the clubs in a set to a choice of two different flexes simply by successively trimming more from the same shaft. This was a contrast from the alternative method in which a separately-made taper tip shaft was created for each different clubhead in the set.

As the parallel tip, combination flex shafts were used and put into play, companies began to hear reports from golfers that the shafts played and felt a little different than the same version in taper tip form. While the weights of the two types of shafts were a little different after installation, golfers were also noticing the effect of a slight change in the parallel version's balance point. This was due to the fact that for the parallel tip version, more and more of the shaft was trimmed from the tip end to allow for installation through the set. For example, the same shaft might be tip trimmed 0" for the #1-iron and 4" for the #9-iron within the same flex. Since more and more of the tip end was being trimmed in the same set, more weight was being removed from the tip than from the butt and the balance point was shifted toward the butt.

The other revelation about shaft balance point came as a result of a special shaft design that was made in the early 1980s expressly for use in metal woods. When metal woods became popular, special tip-reinforced shafts were produced to afford more protection against bending from the stress of a short metal hosel. To produce such a design, shaft manufacturers thickened the tip end of the shaft, a practice that had the effect of shifting the shaft's balance point toward the tip. When golfers used the tip-reinforced version of a shaft design, they soon noticed

that it actually felt stiffer than the same flex of the same shaft made without tip reinforcement.

In the late 1980s, shaft manufacturers began to experiment with intentionally shifting the balance point away from the center of the shaft. Such shafts as the True Temper Gold Plus and the Tour Flex version of Apollo's MasterFlex pattern were designed with different balance point locations in an effort to improve shaft performance. While more research will be done to assess the effect of altering shaft weight distribution, as of this writing it is felt that moving the balance point of the shaft toward the butt could have the effect of improving the accuracy of shots hit with this type of shaft.

■ SHAFT MOUNTING

How a shaft is actually mounted into the clubhead can have a tremendous effect on its performance and playability. Each of the previous areas of shaft design- Flex,

Frequency, Type (Weight), Pattern (Bend Point), Torque and Balance Point, are all set and determined by the manufacturer before the shaft is installed into the club. However, once the shaft is produced, whether the shaft will exhibit those characteristics or not is controlled by the way the shaft is trimmed and installed.

When a shaft is produced the designer must also determine how the shaft is to be trimmed for installation into each of the heads in a set. To make a shaft perform to its designed parameters, the shaft designer may decide the shaft needs to be trimmed all from the tip, trimmed from the tip and the butt, or trimmed only from the butt. If a golf clubmaker happens to make a mistake and incorrectly trim the shafts during installation, the shafts will not play

to their designed characteristics.

There are two primary reasons why mistakes in shaft mounting occur in the clubmaking industry. As mentioned, not every shaft pattern is intended to be trimmed and installed in the same manner. Some shafts are both tip and butt trimmed, some tip trimmed only and some butt trimmed only. Lack of understanding on behalf of clubmakers and lack of proper communication from the manufacturers about the proper installation of each different shaft design can cause mistakes in installation and create differences in the playability of the shafts once they are installed into sets of heads.

Second, each clubhead manufacturer is free to design its heads in virtually any manner it desires, while still working within the dictates of the USGA's Rules of Golf. In the production of woodheads, there commonly exist what are called through-bore, blind bore and short bore designs for the hosel of the head. In a through-bore woodhead, the bore hole penetrates all the way through the head and out the bottom of the sole. The blind bore design allows for the bore to stop at a point 1/2" short of penetrating through the sole. Short bore designs are the norm on stainless metal woods, in which a small ledge is cast into the bore to stop the shaft tip usually 2" short of penetrating through the sole of the club.

For a shaft to be installed to perform the same, different trimming procedures have to be performed to allow for the hosel bore differences between each of the three varieties of woodhead designs. While many experienced clubmakers and manufacturers are aware of this need, there exists a lack of understanding in this area among beginning clubmakers. In addition, because there are also differences in iron hosel bore design from one clubhead maker to another, the same chances for inconsistency in shaft mounting for irons also exist.

Later in this chapter we will cover the procedures of proper shaft trimming for installation. In that section we will reveal exactly what trimming alterations must be made to standardize shaft mounting and allow for differences in hosel bore design for woods and ironheads.

Graphite/Composite Shaft Design

Why Graphite?

As long as the game has been played, golfers have searched for a shaft that would allow them to hit the ball longer and straighter. Using methods of trial and error through the 18th and early 19th centuries, clubmakers experimented with a number of different hardwoods to make shafts. As a result of one such experiment in the mid-1800s, hickory proved to possess the desired characteristics and became the first predominant material for making shafts. Of all the hardwoods used in the production of shafts, hickory's exceptional qualities of resilience made it superior to any hardwood previously used.

While virtually every golf club made between 1850 and 1920 featured a hickory shaft, one thing that history has proven is that golfers are never satisfied with what they have. While hickory exhibited superior playability features to other hardwoods, it still had a number of drawbacks that golfers soon began to notice. Due to changes in weather, hickory had a tendency to warp. For one, a golfer's favorite set could be rendered unplayable as a result of getting caught in a rainstorm during the course of a round. In addition, hickory was a hardwood that was not indigenous to Great Britain and was not a material that was easily accessible to all clubmakers. But most of all, hickory had very little ability to prevent the clubhead from twisting during the swing and thus magnifying the ill effects of a poor shot. This lack of resistance to torque became the major factor that caused clubmakers to continue their search for a better material from which to make shafts.

Late in the 1800s, clubmakers dreamed of finding a material that would address the shortcomings of hickory, but as it was, manufacturing techniques had not yet caught up with the clubmakers' imaginations. If hickory warped and twisted, what about steel? While the theory was sound, methods for forming the metal did not bring the steel shaft into reality until the 1920s. However, once manufacturing techniques advanced to a point that allowed shafts to be made from steel, hickory soon disappeared,

a victim of the steel shafts' superior durability, consistency and ability to hit the ball straighter.

While continual refinements in the manufacturing process through the first half of the 20th century brought about better and more consistent steel shafts, it wasn't until shaft makers began to better understand the components of shot distance that the next wave of shaft development began. In the early 1970s a number of companies reasoned if the shaft could be made lighter, greater distance could be realized. With such a shaft, more weight could be put into the clubhead with the net result being more mass behind the ball at impact, delivered by a lighter overall club that could be swung faster with the same effort.

But how to lighten the shaft? At first, shaft makers turned to aluminum, a light and reasonably strong material. For a few years shafts were produced from aluminum but soon fell by the wayside as low handicappers and professionals rejected the soft feel the thick-walled shafts transmitted at impact. Turning back to steel, shaft companies began to make attempts to thin the walls of the shaft to reduce weight, at the same time making up for the decrease in shaft strength by increasing the butt diameter.

Due to the thin shaft wall and thin grips that were required to accommodate the design, golfers soon rejected these overly large butt diameter shafts for the harsh, unresponsive feel they transmitted at impact. Realizing that a raw material change was the only realistic way to reduce the weight of the shaft, manufacturers turned to combinations of steel with other metals to create lightweight steel alloys. By using steel alloys, shaft companies could return to normal shaft diameter and wall thickness dimensions and reduce the weight of the shaft in the process. While reductions in shaft weight could be made through the use of new steel alloys, the amount of weight loss was not significant enough to yield the distance increases that had been originally conceived.

Within this same period of time, another group of innovative developers were working on the use of a completely different lightweight raw material for shaft form-

ing. Steel alloys, while exhibiting a high level of material consistency, had posed limitations on how light the shaft could be made. But graphite, a synthetic, high-strength fiber-based material, showed the ability to go well beyond steel alloys in creating lightweight shafts that still possessed the necessary performance features.

Today the problems with poor torque resistance that plagued the early composite shafts have been solved and graphite stands as the shaft forming material of the future. Because different strength fibers can be used within the same shaft, and because manufacturers can vary the positions of the fibers on the shaft, the potential for shaft design variability with graphite is almost limitless when compared to steel.

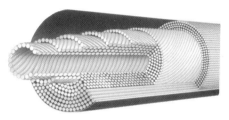

Courtesy Apollo, Ltd.

Composite shaft makers have hundreds of different fiber type materials from which to choose when creating a shaft. These fiber materials can be intermixed within the shaft and combined in a "sandwich" type of construction such that each individual shaft design parameter can be addressed on its own. This varying of materials within the same shaft is a characteristic that steel just cannot exhibit. Because its form of manufacture is so different from graphite, steel cannot be intermixed for the purpose of say, isolating one type of steel for the tip section of the shaft and another type of steel for the butt.

With graphite, the stacking of layers of composite sheets with different strengths in the same shaft allows the manufacturer to create performance differences from one shaft design to another. In addition, also because of the layering or wrapping form of manufacture, graphite shaft makers can vary the alignment of the fibers to the shaft, thus creating more ways to intentionally alter the performance of the shaft.

Quite different than with steel shaft manufacture, creating a graphite shaft is really somewhat like making a sandwich. Want increased stiffness? Add a layer or two of high modulus graphite with fibers aligned up and down to the shaft. Want a little less stiffness? Cut back on the modulus rating of the graphite being used. Want increased resistance to torque along with stiffness? Add a layer of high strength graphite followed by a layer with the fibers wrapped at a 45° angle to the shaft. Want just a little bit less resistance to torque than that? Back off a little and apply the radial wrap at a 30° angle to the shaft instead. Want to make changes in bend point? Apply layers of graphite with different strengths at different positions along the shaft. The graphite shaft designer's ability to individually adjust such shaft design parameters as flex, bend point, torque, weight and balance point is far, far greater than with steel.

Graphite As a Material

First and foremost, the key to composite shafts is the vast array of materials from which they are made. To begin understanding just what makes up a graphite shaft, it is important to first realize that graphite shafts are not made completely from graphite. Within the construction of the average graphite shaft are of course graphite fibers, but along with the fibers is also a very high percentage of epoxy and other non-graphite fiber materials as well.

Because graphite is a thin fiber, epoxy resins must be employed to hold the fibers together and allow the forming of the thin sheets (pre-preg) or yarn that are to be layered, wrapped or wound to make the shafts. The amount of resin binder that might be in a shaft depends upon the strength of the type of graphite fibers being used. Sheets of pre-preg made with ultra high strength graphite fibers contain a much higher percentage of binder than pre-preg made with lower strength fibers. This is because fewer high strength fibers will be needed in a sheet to reach a set pre-preg strength requirement than with the use of lower strength fibers. Hence when fewer fibers are required to achieve a set sheet strength, more epoxy will be needed to make the pre-preg.

As a result, the old adage "strength in numbers" does not

apply to graphite; rather "strength within fiber" is the real key to graphite's design variability. While the strength of any material can be measured in a number of different ways, a key strength specification for a shaft is the material's ability to resist stretching or bending. This specification, called the modulus of the material, can be compared for a variety of different shaft materials. For example, aluminum has a 10 million modulus rating and steel has a 30 million modulus rating. To contrast, the various types of graphite fibers available for use in shaft forming can range from 30 million all the way up to 110 million for a few of the newest ultra high strength fibers.

The higher the modulus rating of a fiber, the stronger and stiffer the fiber will be. In the average graphite shaft, a combination of fibers with different modulus ratings will be used. Some levels of modulus strength are better suited for controlling flex, some for resisting torque and still others for adding strength to the tip section to prevent breaking. So specialized are the various fibers and their uses within the shaft that no graphite shaft is made from the same fiber material throughout.

In addition to the graphite fibers, a number of other synthetic fibers can also be used to bring special features to the shaft. Kevlar, fiberglass and Boron are just a few of the special materials that have been employed in composite shaft designs to bring about differences in performance. Each type of fiber or material that may be used in a shaft is selected on the basis of its own unique characteristics. Kevlar is often used to change or enhance the impact shock absorption, or the feel characteristics of a shaft. Fiberglass can be used as a lightweight "filler" in the production of pre-preg sheet as a way to reduce resin content and slightly enhance strength.

Boron is a very specialized material that has probably received more attention in composite shafts than graphite itself. Not a fiber or naturally-occurring material, Boron finds its way into a shaft as a coating on a Tungsten wire filament. Through a chemical reaction, Boron is deposited on the surface of the Tungsten wire, in the process changing the characteristics of the filament. From the reaction, the Boron Tungsten filament becomes

Courtesy Kunnan

Boron fibers surrounded by graphite

very rigid, exhibiting a tremendously high modulus rating. As a result, when a shaft has a need for extremely high strength in a certain area, Boron can be used.

Traditionally, Boron is used for two primary reasons in a composite shaft. When introduced in the tip section, Boron will greatly increase the strength of the shaft and help prevent the shaft from fracturing due to the stresses imparted at impact from the top edge of the clubhead's hosel. When aligned up and down around the entire shaft, Boron can increase the shaft's overall strength and stiffness and allow more of the graphite layers to be used for altering torque or bringing other special bending characteristics to the design.

For Boron to deliver its full benefit to the design of a shaft, the filaments must be arranged consistently in an up and down fashion, around the full circumference of the shaft. Because some Boron graphite shafts are made with as few as three or four Boron filaments, Textron Corporation, the world's only commercial supplier of Boron, stepped forward and initiated a quality control program to back the credibility of the properly-made Boron added shafts. Through a label awarded to shafts that pass Textron's quality program, clubmakers can be assured the Boron is used properly in the shaft.

During the late 1980s so much was said about Boron's use in graphite shafts that it was thought any shaft made without Boron was severely deficient to those made with the special filaments. As fiber technology has advanced into the 1990s, higher modulus fibers have become available so that boron is not as necessary as it once was to give the shaft enough strength in the tip to resist breaking. In addition, because some shaft advertisements have been responsible for coining the term "Boron shaft," many golfers have the mistaken belief that the shafts are made entirely from Boron. Not the situation at all, Boron is simply a small part of certain graphite shaft designs.

Graphite Shaft Production

Graphite shafts are manufactured by layering several plies of graphite composite sheets or filaments, with the direction of the individual fibers within groups of layers oriented at various predetermined angles to the shaft. Currently, two different methods, sheet wrapping and filament winding are used to make graphite shafts.

In sheet wrapping, the predominant method of composite shaft manufacture, pennant-shaped sheets of pre-preg graphite called flags are wrapped around a forming mandrel. The various flags of pre-preg can be wrapped one by one around the mandrel or can be compressed together on the forming table and then wrapped all in one procedure around the mandrel. After wrapping, the layers are then compressed tight around the mandrel to squeeze out and eliminate as many air pockets or voids between layers as possible.

Courtesy Aldila, Inc.

Depending upon the individual design, up to 16 layers of composite material may be used in the manufacture of a shaft. In the procedure, layers which are applied with the fibers aligned up and down to the shaft control stiffness, while the layers that are wrapped with the fibers at an angle to the forming mandrel play the major role in determining the torque value of the shaft.

After the wrapping of the layers is complete, a cover of clear polypropylene shrink wrap is placed over the shaft. Each shaft is heat cured to compress the shrink wrap and meld the composite layers together, after which the shaft is sanded to its final outside diameter specifications. After sanding, each shaft is inspected and tested for its particular design parameters after which it is painted and finished with specially-formulated coatings.

Within the sheet-wrapping process, research continues to develop better ways to control shaft-to-shaft consistency. The major focus in improving the sheet wrapping process centers behind efforts to make the shaft wall thickness more consistent by developing new methods of wrapping and compressing the layers. As of the early 1990s, the only drawback to sheet-wrapped composite shafts is their more-than-occasional tendency to exhibit flex inconsistency from shaft to shaft and wall thickness inconsistency within the shaft. Because of this, when some sheet-wrapped shafts are measured for vibrational frequency in a series of radial positions around the shaft, it is not uncommon to observe a 7-10 cpm range in frequency within the same shaft.

The other method for manufacturing graphite shafts utilizes a process called filament winding. Through filament winding, a multiple series of continuous strands of blended graphite material are wetted with binding resin and machine wound around a rotating forming mandrel to produce the shaft. Because of the continuous winding process, filament wound shafts do not have a start and stop point for layers as do the sheet wrapped type of shafts. As such, filament wound shafts are said to possess a higher level of wall thickness consistency from shaft to shaft.

Making pre-preg from graphite fibers.

The reason wall thickness consistency is shaping up as the great graphite shaft debate of the '90s is because of the effect variances in the wall thickness within the shaft have on the flex. If a shaft exhibits a distinct variation in wall thickness, when the shaft is frequency tested at different points around its circumference, variations in the frequency will be seen. From high to low it was mentioned before that such a variation can be as much as 7-10 cpm in frequency within the same shaft. If 10 cpm can be accepted as approximating a full flex of variation, it could then be said that depending upon how the shaft is installed in the clubhead, the golfer might experience as much as a full flex of variation off from what the shaft's flex was designed to be. Thus the golfer would never know if the shaft being used was the right one for him or not.

While filament winding does deliver shafts with a narrow range in 360° radial frequency and therefore more consistency in flex, there are slight differences in the process when compared to the sheet wrapping method. While some variation in fiber strength is possible, it is not possible for filament winding to offer as wide of a variation in fiber design as sheet wrapping. Still, since flex consistency is a vital part of any shaft, until wall thickness in sheet wrapping is better controlled it appears that filament winding does stand as the most accurate way to currently manufacture a graphite shaft.

The Principles of Shaft Construction

■ TAPER TIP SHAFTS

Within some of the discussions that have ensued in this chapter the fact has been established that certain shaft designs are produced in both taper tip and parallel tip versions. While some of the differences between the two types of shaft construction have been mentioned, it is important to complete this discussion as a step toward greater shaft understanding.

From the earliest days of golf, shafts were designed with a tapered shape at the tip end. In 1971, True Temper Corp. devised the parallel tip shape as an alternative to the taper tip construction in an effort to help golf club manufacturers reduce the level of their shaft inventories. Building sets of golf clubs with taper tip shafts requires that a different raw shaft length be used for each head in the set. Therefore, to ensure the proper progression of stiffness through a set, using the taper tip shafts meant that a manufacturer had to keep large numbers of different raw length shafts in their on-hand inventory.

For example, if a clubmaker wished to offer sets of four woods and nine irons (#1, 3, 4, 5-woods and #2 - 9-irons plus PW) in both the R and S flexes, to build the sets using taper tip shafts, a total of 24 different raw length shafts would have to be stocked (the #9-iron and PW use the same raw length taper tip shaft). With the parallel tip shaft, a clubmaker can assemble the same set makeups to the same flexes while using only two raw length shafts. By doing so, the inventory requirement can be reduced from 24 shafts down to just two (one for woods, one for irons).

To fully understand how two shafts can function for 24 requires that clubmakers have a full level of understanding of how shafts are designed to play within a full set of golf clubs. Earlier in this chapter it was explained that a matched set of shafts actually increases in stiffness through the set as the clubs become shorter in playing length. A practice that is unilaterally accepted today, this progression of stiffness did not always exist. Prior to the

1960s, shaft manufacturers would provide only one taper tip shaft for each flex for woods and only one taper tip shaft for each flex for irons. After installation with no tip trimming for any club in the set, the golf clubmaking company would trim only from the butt end to achieve the playing length for each club in the set.

From research performed in the 1960s by the Wilson Sporting Goods Company, it was found that this practice would yield golf clubs that felt like they became more flexible as the clubs got shorter in playing length. Because golf clubs change in playing length but at the same time remain the same swingweight, the weight of each head increases from Driver to #7-wood and from #1-iron to #9-iron. In fact, within a standard set of clubheads, the #7-wood will weigh some 30 grams more than the Driver and the #9-iron will weigh approximately 56 grams more than the #1-iron. Unless the shafts through the set are made progressively stiffer, this increase in head weight will make the shafts feel to the golfer as if they are becoming more and more flexible.

From Wilson's research, True Temper developed a set of shafts with this required stiffness increase already designed into each shaft. To accomplish this, True Temper made the shafts with progressively shorter tip sections for the woods and for the irons. Thus when such a set of shafts was installed in a set, the position of the first step down moved closer to the clubhead from the Driver through the fairway woods and from the #1-iron through the #9-iron. In the 1960s, because shafts were all made with a taper tip, this new shaft design concept required a differently made shaft for each clubhead in the set. Hence the situation of needing 12 different raw length taper tip shafts to build a single flex set of golf clubs was born.

The increase in stiffness through the set was created by developing a

series of shafts that successively became shorter in the tip section. The photo below shows a full set of tapered shafts that have been lined up in order by raw length from longest to shortest. As you can see, the difference in raw length and the increase in stiffness from shaft to shaft is accomplished by a successive shortening of the tip section.

If this same set of taper tip shafts is installed in a set of clubheads (as depicted by the photo on page 77) it is possible to see how the the position of the first step down descends from the long irons to the short irons. In such a correct mounting, the taper tip shaft in the Driver and the #1-iron have the longest tip section length. Successively through the #7 wood (woods) and the #9, PW, SW (irons), the position of the first step down on each shaft descends in half-inch increments as shown in the photo.

Of course taper tip shafts do exist today, so to properly use this variety of shaft construction, clubmakers must understand which raw length is to be matched with which clubhead. The chart on page 77 lists the industry's accepted proper raw shaft lengths per each head to guide your taper tip shaft installation:

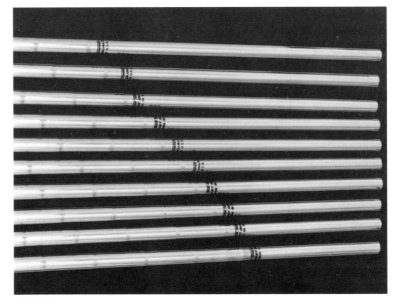

Taper tip shafts have a shorter first step length as the set progresses.

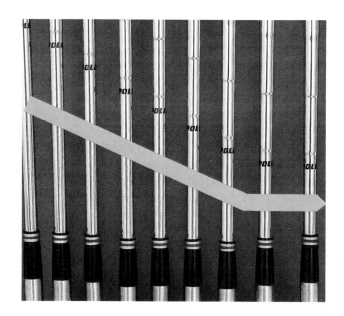

Correct taper tip steel shaft installation does require that the listed raw shaft lengths are used for each clubhead as depicted. However, because shaft suppliers themselves have inventory constraints and cannot stock all the raw lengths for each shaft pattern, there will be times that you cannot acquire all of the necessary raw lengths to as-semble a full set of golf clubs. Therefore, if you do not have all of the correct raw taper tip shaft lengths you will have to use the same length shaft for more than one clubhead. For such cases, the following chart of Limited Shaft Availability for Taper Tip Assembly should be used to guide your installation.

Raw Taper Tip Shaft Selection by Head Number

Head Number	Taper Tip Raw Shaft Length	Head Number	Taper Tip Raw Shaft Length
1-iron	39"	1-wood	44"
2-iron	38 1/2"	2-wood	43 1/2"
3-iron	38"	3-wood	43"
4-iron	37 1/2"	4-wood	42 1/2"
5-iron	37"	5-wood	42"
6-iron	36 1/2"	6-wood	42"
7-iron	36"	7-wood	42"
8-iron	35 1/2"		
9,PW,SW	35"		

Remember: Taper tip shafts for woods are made in half-inch incremental raw lengths from 42" to 45". In some cases, manufacturers have chosen to use tapered raw lengths for woods that are 1" greater than the above listed standards.

One exception exists to this chart. True Temper's current taper tip graphite shafts deviate from this standard raw shaft length selection chart in that a different raw length is required for each ironhead. See shaft trimming Chart SS in this chapter for a full explanation.

LIMITED SHAFT AVAILABILITY FOR TAPER TIP SHAFT SELECTION

Head Number	If 1 Length is Available (44")	If 2 Lengths are Available (44",43")	If 3 Lengths are Available (44",43", 42")	If 3 Lengths are Available (39", 37", 35")	If 5 Lengths are Available (39",38",37",36",35")
1-wood	44"	44"	44"	—	—
2-wood	44"	44"	44"	—	—
3-wood	44" [1]	43"	43"	—	—
4-wood	44" [1]	43"	43"	—	—
5-wood	44" [1]	43" [1]	42"	—	—
1-iron	—	—	—	39"	39"
2-iron	—	—	—	39"	39"
3-iron	—	—	—	39" [2]	38"
4-iron	—	—	—	37" [3]	38"
5-iron	—	—	—	37	37"
6-iron	—	—	—	37"	37"
7-iron	—	—	—	37" [2]	36"
8-iron	—	—	—	35" [3]	36"
9,PW,SW	—	—	35"	35"	

[1] Additional successive trimming from the tip end and subsequent reboring of the hosel can be performed to prevent the finished fairway woods from playing too flexible compared to the rest of the set of woods.

[2] Additional trimming from the tip end and subsequent reboring of the hosel should be performed to prevent these particular irons from playing too flexible compared to the rest of the set of irons.

[3] Other previously published raw shaft selection tables have recommended different raw lengths for the #4-iron and 8-iron when only three raw tapered lengths are available. However, the above recommendation is better to ensure that these clubs end up playing closer in feel to the rest of the set.

The major reason using the full number of raw length taper tip shafts is preferred is to ensure that the proper change in flexibility from shaft to shaft within a full set is as even and accurate as possible. Keeping the information in mind that was revealed in the previous photos about the change in position of the first step down through the set, you can now visualize what will happen to the progression of the first step down should fewer than the required raw tapered lengths be used.

If only five raw lengths of taper tip shafts are used in a set of irons, the #1 and 2-irons will have the same tip section length, instead of being separated by the 1/2" incremental change that is desired. Between the #2 and #3 irons there would be a full 1" change in first step location, after which the #3 and 4-irons would have the same tip section length. This practice of two clubs having the same tip section followed by a 1" drop to the next two clubs would proceed through the rest of the set. What such a procedure of installation means is that the first step down location on the even numbered irons (#2, 4, 6, 8) would be too far up the shaft, and thus those clubs would play slightly more flexible than normal.

In the case of using only three different raw tapered lengths to build a set of irons, the first step down separation from club to club and resulting difference in flex feel between each head in the set would be even greater, unless additional shaft tip trimming and successive reboring of the tapered clubhead hosels is performed. Obviously, the amount of time and energy required to rebore tapered hosels to fit taper tip shafts that have been additionally tip trimmed may be enough of a reason to consider using the parallel tip variety shafts for ease of installation.

■ PARALLEL TIP SHAFTS

Since their introduction in 1971, parallel tip construction shafts have grown in popularity to the point that some 60+% of all shafts produced are made with this type of tip design. Today virtually all new shaft designs, whether metal or composite, are offered in the parallel tip type of construction. As was mentioned, the primary reason the

parallel type of tip construction was conceived was to assist clubmakers and manufacturers in keeping their shaft inventories at reasonable levels. Using the same shaft pattern in parallel tip form, a clubmaker can get by with stocking only two shaft units where with the taper tip version, 24 different shaft units would be needed.

With taper tip shafts, the different tip section lengths through a set are designed into each different raw length shaft; with the parallel tip version, the progression in tip section length is established by successively trimming more and more from the tip. But not only can clubmakers enjoy the benefit of being able to use one shaft for all woods and one shaft for all the irons, the parallel tip construction also allows consolidating different flexes within the same construction as well.

Most of the major steel shaft makers and a few of the composite shaft producers offer a number of their parallel tip designs in what are called **combination flex** form and some in **discrete flex** form. Combination flex shafts are those parallel tip varieties which can become one of two specified flexes depending upon how they are trimmed. Currently the two most popular types of parallel tip combination flex shafts offered for clubmaking are the R & S combination (R and S flexes within one shaft) and the A & L combination (A and L flexes within one shaft). In the late 1980s, Sandvik Corp., makers of the TI Shaft brand of titanium shafts, began to offer two new version of combination flex shafts, one which combined the X and S flexes and the other which put the R and A flexes together in one raw uncut shaft.

In addition to the types of combination flex, parallel tip shafts, the shaft makers also produce what are called discrete flex parallel tip shafts. A discrete flex shaft is a parallel tip shaft that is manufactured to one single flex and therefore does **not** contain two flexes in one shaft. For example, True Temper's 47" UDWC contains both the R and S flexes of their Dynamic pattern for woods. To contrast, also available from True Temper are the two separate flexes of the UDWR and the UDWS, which are both 45" in raw length. It is important to understand that

discrete flex shafts are the same as the combination flex form but with a part of the shaft, in essence, "already trimmed" to determine the final flex. Below is another way to view this example:

UDWR = UDWC minus 2" cut from butt end
UDWS = UDWC minus 2" cut from tip end

This relationship explains why the combination R & S flex steel shafts are always 2" longer than their discrete flex versions. Therefore, clubmakers should not hesitate to order an discrete flex version when available, as it is simply the same shaft as the combination variety but with the flex already established.

As mentioned, the reason the parallel tip shafts have gained in popularity is because of the fewer inventory units required to assemble full sets of woods and irons. Because the parallel shafts have one constant diameter from tip to first step, the tip can be progressively trimmed without having to rebore and enlarge the hosel. This is unlike the tapered tip shafts, where any removal of the tip end leaves you with a tip diameter larger than what the shaft originally had. Therefore, when using parallel tip shafts, no further reboring of the hosel is required to achieve a perfect incremental positioning of the first step through the set of woods or irons.

Parallel tip graphite shafts are quite different than their parallel tip steel counterparts. Because there are no step downs on a composite shaft, the tip remains one constant diameter for only a limited distance. Depending upon the particular design of the shaft, the parallel tip section length of a composite shaft may be as short as 4" or as long as 10". The longer the parallel portion of a composite shaft's tip section, the more likely it is a shaft designed to be successively trimmed from the tip for installation.

When the constant tip diameter steel shaft was introduced, it was officially called a Unitized Parallel Tip Shaft. What clubmakers have to be aware of is that the terms **unitized** and **parallel tip** actually refer to different characteristics in the construction of a shaft. Parallel is the term used to describe the fact that the shaft has one constant diameter from the tip to the first step. Unitized means that one shaft can be used to build an entire set of woods and one shaft can be used to assemble a full set of irons.

To fully understand the difference between parallel tip and unitized, consider the following statement:

All unitized steel shafts are parallel, but not all parallel tip steel shafts are unitized.

To explain the statement, realize that shafts such as Brunswick's FM Precision steel iron shafts and True Temper's former Flex Flow pattern are parallel tip in construction but **not** unitized in nature. In these designs even though the shaft has a parallel tip, a different raw uncut shaft length is still required to complete the assembly of a full set of woods and irons.

To explain some of the playability differences between taper tip and parallel tip shafts, first consider what happens to the weight of a shaft upon installation. Unitized parallel shafts are designed so that only two different shafts are required to assemble a full set of golf clubs, one for all of the woods and one for all the irons. With the tapered version of the same shaft pattern, as many as 12 different raw lengths of shafts are required to build a full set of clubs. In the taper tip version of the True Temper Dynamic, each of the different raw length shafts for the woods and irons are designed to weigh exactly the same, 4.50oz for the X-flex, 4.375oz for the S-flex and 4.250oz for the R-flex. Because there is a different raw length taper tip shaft for each of the heads in the set, for a standard 1/2" incremental change in playing length between clubs, each shaft will have the same amount trimmed during the installation process. Therefore, in the finished full set, all of the taper tip shafts in the set will all weigh the same.

Using the parallel version of the same shaft, all of the woods will be built with a 47" raw length shaft and all of the irons will be assembled with a 41" raw length shaft.

During the installation procedures, the least amount will be trimmed from the driver and #1-iron, while the most will be trimmed from the #7-wood, and the wedges. What this means is that of all the shafts in the woods, the shaft in the Driver will be the heaviest, with each other shaft in the woods in order having a slightly lighter shaft weight. In the irons, the #1-iron shaft will be the heaviest, decreasing proportionately in each of the other iron club shafts through the #9-iron and wedges. For more clarification of this comparison, study the following chart:

The purpose of the chart below is to show how the actual weight of shafts after installation is different for the taper tip and parallel tip types of shaft construction. Notice that the weight of the parallel tip version after it is trimmed and installed decreases in a proportional manner through the woods and through the irons.

As the playing length of the clubs gets successively shorter, more trimming is performed on the parallel tip version and the shafts get lighter. Contrast that with the

DIFFERENCES IN CUT SHAFT WEIGHT FOR PARALLEL AND TAPER TIP SHAFTS

CLUB HEAD	PARALLEL		TAPERED		CUT SHAFT		
	Raw Shaft[1] Weight	Raw Shaft[1] Length	Raw Shaft Weight	Raw Shaft[2] Length	Installed Length[3]	Parallel Shaft	Tapered Shaft
1-wood	4.625oz	47"	4.375oz	44"	43"	4.25oz	4.27oz
3-wood	4.625oz	47"	4.375oz	43"	42"	4.13oz	4.27oz
4-wood	4.625oz	47"	4.375oz	42.5"	41.5"	4.08oz	4.27oz
5-wood	4.625oz	47"	4.375oz	42"	41"	4.03oz	4.27oz
1-iron	4.56oz	41"	4.375oz	39"	38.5	4.16oz	4.32oz
2-iron	4.56oz	41"	4.375oz	38.5"	38"	4.11oz	4.32oz
3-iron	4.56oz	41"	4.375oz	38	37.5"	4.06oz	4.32oz
4-iron	4.56oz	41"	4.375oz	37.5"	37"	4.01oz	4.32oz
5-iron	4.56oz	41"	4.375oz	37	36.5"	3.96oz	4.32oz
6-iron	4.56oz	41"	4.375oz	36.5"	36"	3.91oz	4.32oz
7-iron	4.56oz	41"	4.375oz	36"	35.5"	3.86oz	4.32oz
8-iron	4.56oz	41"	4.375oz	35.5"	35	3.81oz	4.32oz
9,PW,SW	4.56oz	41"	4.375oz	35"	34.5"	3.76oz	4.32oz

[1] Example is based on using the DIS for the tapered shafts and the UDWC cut to an S-flex for the parallel shafts, with all clubs built to D-1 swingweight with standard size rubber grips.

[2] Manufacturers' recommendation for raw shaft length selection per clubhead number.

[3] Installed shaft length is based on a through-bore style woodhead and an ironhead with a standard bottom of bore to heel dimension of 1", and is the same for both tapered and parallel versions in this example.

taper tip version, in which a different raw length shaft is used for each wood and iron. In this case, the same amount is trimmed from each shaft to achieve the proper playing length, so therefore every shaft in the set of woods and then in the set of irons will weigh the same.

For clubmakers who are curious about measurable differences that exist between tapered and parallel versions of the same pattern, the preceding chart illustrates one of those factors. However, understand that not all taper tip shafts are designed to be the same weight regardless of raw length. In many of the taper tip versions of lightweight shafts, the raw shaft weight does decrease as the shaft gets shorter. In such cases, the parallel tip version can then be considered to be very similar in playing characteristics to its taper tip counterpart.

A Complete Guide to Shaft Trimming and Installation

■ THE PRINCIPLES OF SHAFT MOUNTING IN CLUBHEADS

During the discussion of the design parameters of shafts, it was mentioned that shaft mounting is the one design factor that is totally dependent on the clubmaker. If mistakes are made in the trimming and the installation of the shaft into the clubhead, a shaft cannot perform in the manner to which it has been designed. Before covering the various trimming formulas for all the types of shafts, it is very important to first understand the principles that guide the correct mounting of shafts.

When a shaft company manufactures a new shaft, a major part of the project involves determining how the shaft will be trimmed and installed into each clubhead in order for the shaft to perform as designed. Also in designing a shaft, it is the manufacturer's goal for the shaft to play the same regardless of the type of clubhead into which it may be installed. While there are some shafts that are expressly designed for one particular type of clubhead only, in general, most shafts are designed for use in any type of clubhead so clubmakers will be faced with installing a variety of different shafts into an assort-

ment of different clubhead types and trying to make the shaft play the same regardless of clubhead type.

To be sure that any particular shaft will perform the same in all types of clubheads, a standard for trimming and installing shafts must be established and understood. Therefore, the principle of **Uniform Shaft Mounting** is set up to allow clubmakers to achieve a standard for shaft performance regardless of the differences that are seen from one clubhead design to the next.

Uniform Shaft Mounting in Woodheads

The key difference between clubheads that has a bearing on shaft mounting is how the hosel bore is designed; in other words, where the tip of the shaft stops inside the hosel or neck of the clubhead. Within woodheads, there are three basic hosel bore designs, the Through-Bore, the Blind Bore and the Short-Bore. In through-bore woodheads, the hole for the shaft (bore) is designed to completely penetrate through the sole. In blind bore woodheads, the bore for the shaft stops approximately 1/2" short of where it does on the through-bore woodheads, on the average at a point in line with the bottom back edge of the heel of the woodhead. The short-bore is the hosel design seen on most stainless steel metal woods. On short-bore woodheads, the bore for the shaft stops approximately 1 1/2" short of where it does on the blind bore and 2" short of the through-bore.

Blind Bore Woodhead

Short-Bore Woodhead

If three identical shafts are prepared for installation using the same amount of tip trimming, once they are installed into a through-bore, a blind bore and a short-bore woodhead, the shafts cannot be expected to play the same in each type of head. The best way for clubmakers to understand this point is through an example using a parallel tip steel shaft. True Temper calls for 0" to be tip trimmed from the UDWR steel shaft (Dynamic R-flex parallel tip) before installation into a through-bore type Driver head. If three UDWR shafts are each 0" tip trimmed and installed into each of the three different woodhead hosel types, the position of the first step down on the shaft with respect to the clubhead will be different

Through-Bore Woodhead

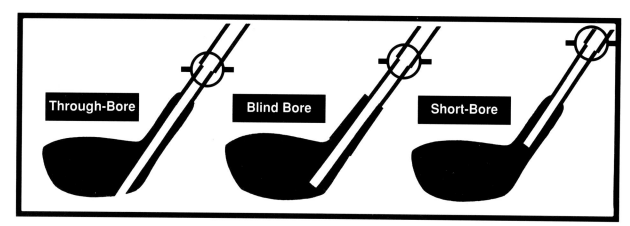

The first step down location is determined by the depth of penetration allowed by each clubhead type (through-bore, blind bore and short-bore).

On the through-bore Driver, the distance from the back edge of the heel of the Driver to the first step down on the UDWR shaft will be 12", on the blind bore Driver it will be 12 1/2" and on the short-bore Driver it will be 14". Since the length of the tip section within a shaft design controls its flexibility, it is evident that the UDWR will play much more flexible in the short-bore Driver than in the through-bore Driver, despite the fact all three shafts were trimmed the same way (0" tip trim).

Therefore, to achieve uniform shaft mounting in clubmaking, adjustments in shaft tip trimming must often be made to allow for the differences from the bottom of the hosel bore to the sole between different types of woodheads.

There are no rules in clubhead design which limit or dictate the distance from the bottom of the hosel bore to the sole of the woodhead. In addition, a shaft manufacturer is free to design a shaft so that its standard trimming may be set up for a through-bore, a blind bore, a short-bore or any type of bore they wish. As a result it is very important that clubmakers learn what bore type each shaft is designed for, and then learn how to adjust shaft trimming for differences in the bottom of the hosel bore hole to the sole dimension of the clubhead.

If the standard trimming for a shaft is set up for installation in a through-bore woodhead, those trimming guidelines can be adjusted to accommodate any of the other woodhead types by successively increasing the tip trimming. In the shaft industry, most but not all steel shafts are designed to accommodate normal through-bore clubhead installation. For shafts such as these, to achieve uniform shaft mounting for any other type of woodhead the clubmaker need only increase the standard through-bore tip trimming by the amount equal to the distance from the bottom of the bore to the sole. For example, if the UDWR shaft was to have 0" trimmed from the tip for installation into a through-bore Driver, when a metal Driver with a 2" distance from the bottom of the hosel bore to the sole of the clubhead is used, then 2" will be trimmed from the UDWR shaft tip to allow for the difference between the shaft's through-bore trimming and the short-bore into which the shaft is being installed. With this additional tip trimming the UDWR will play the same in the short-bore woodhead as it does in the through-bore woodhead.

In the early 1980s, when through-bore woodheads began to disappear, shaft manufacturers began to design the trimming of their new shaft patterns primarily for blind bore or even short-bore metal woods only. If a shaft is designed for blind bore woodheads, additional trimming can be performed to use them in short-bore woods, but if this blind bore designed shaft is used in a through-bore woodhead the shaft will not play as designed. For new shafts designed for installation only in short-bore woodheads, installation into a through-bore or blind bore woodhead will make the shaft play stiffer than it was designed. Therefore, clubmakers are urged to note which shafts can be used in all types of clubheads and which cannot. In the wood shaft trimming charts that accompany this chapter, reference is made for which of the woodhead types the shaft is designed to assist your work.

Uniform Shaft Mounting in Ironheads
In ironhead design, there also exist a number of different hosel bore depth options for which clubmakers will have to make allowances during the trimming and installation of the shafts. In a situation that is quite the reverse of how

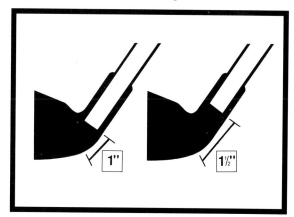

Ironhead Hosel Design

shafts for woods are designed, most iron shafts are set up for standard trimming and installation into ironheads with a bottom of bore to back edge of heel distance of 1". For example, the UDIR steel shaft from True Temper (parallel tip Dynamic R flex) is to be tip trimmed 0" before installation into a #1-iron with a bottom of bore to back edge of heel distance of 1". To show how adjustments can be made to conform to the principle of uniform shaft mounting, if the UDIR shaft is to be installed into a #1-iron with a bottom of bore to back edge of heel distance of 1 1/2", the amount to tip trim will be the difference between the 1 1/2" and the accepted standard of 1", which in this case will be 1/2". When such a trimming adjustment is done, the UDIR shaft will play the same in the ironhead with the 1" bottom of bore to heel dimension as it will in the ironhead with the 1 1/2" bottom of bore to heel dimension.

These examples for achieving the principle of uniform shaft mounting were illustrated only with a Driver and a #1-iron. Applying the principle to all other heads in the set is done the same way as it is in the Driver and #1-iron. Measure the distance between the bottom of the bore and the sole for each of the woods, then measure the distance between the bottom of the bore and the heel for each of the irons. Compare this dimension to the 0" standard for woods (if the wood shaft is designed for through-bore trimming) and 1" standard for irons, then add that difference to the normal amount to tip trim for each shaft.

Following is a step-by-step example of how the uniform shaft mounting principle is used for normal shaft installation.

WOODS
Example:
The woodheads are measured and are found to all have a bottom of bore to sole dimension of 2". The shaft is a UDWR to be installed to standard playing length for each woodhead.

Uniform Shaft Mounting for Woods

Normal Amount To Tip Trim for Through-Bore	Woodhead Number	Actual Amount to Tip Trim In This Example
0"	#1 wood	2"
1"	#3 wood	3"
1 1/2"	#4 wood	3 1/2"
2"	#5 wood	4"
3"	#7 wood	5"

Note: For all woodheads, the actual amount to tip trim is more than the standard trimming by the amount equal to the distance from the bottom of the bore to the sole.

IRON
Example:
The ironheads are measured and are found to all have a bottom of bore to heel dimension of 1 1/2". The shaft is a UDIR to be installed to standard playing lengths for each ironhead.

Uniform Shaft Mounting for Irons

Normal Amount To Tip Trim for Through-Bore	Ironhead Number	Actual Amount to Tip Trim In This Example
0"	#1 iron	1/2"
1/2"	#2 iron	1"
1"	#3 iron	1 1/2"
1 1/2"	#4 iron	2"
2"	#5 iron	2 1/2"
2 1/2"	#6 iron	3"
3"	#7 iron	3 1/2"
3 1/2"	#8 iron	4"
4"	#9 iron	4 1/2"
4 1/2"	Wedges	5"

Note: For all ironheads, the actual amount to tip trim is more than the standard trimming by the amount equal to the distance from the bottom of the bore to the heel.

The previous examples of adjusting for differences in the hosel bore design are illustrated using a common steel shaft. In the clubmaking industry most common steel shafts are designed to be tip trimmed in an increasing half-inch progression from the Driver through all the fairway woods and from the #1-iron through the wedges. However, not all shafts that are used in clubmaking are designed to be successively tip trimmed in half-inch increments through the set. In addition to successive half-inch tip trim shafts, there exist shafts that are designed to be trimmed all from the butt end, shafts that are designed to be trimmed all from the tip end and shafts that are to be trimmed in variable ways.

At first, shaft trimming can be confusing. However, understand that trimming instructions are all carefully planned by the shaft manufacturers to make their particular designs play as intended. To help make shaft installation less confusing, trimming instructions for hundreds of different shafts are included in the trimming and installation charts in this chapter.

If a shaft is designed to be trimmed completely from the tip end, do not worry about allowing for different bottom of bore to sole or heel dimensions. The all tip trim type of shaft installation has the ability built in to take differences in hosel bore into account to ensure uniform shaft mounting. But if the shaft is designed to be trimmed all from the butt end, or designed to be successively trimmed from the tip followed by some trimming from the butt, differences in the clubheads' bottom of bore to sole (woods) and bottom of bore to heel (irons) will need to be applied to the tip trimming to ensure uniform shaft mounting.

To apply the principle of uniform shaft mounting for accurate shaft installation regardless of clubhead type, study the procedures on the following page.

WOODS

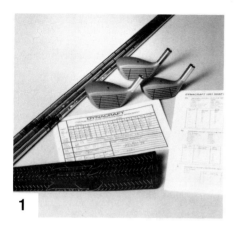

1

STEP 1: Find the standard tip trimming chart for the shaft to be installed. Be sure to note the type of woodhead that the trimming for the wood shaft being used is to be based upon (through-bore, blind bore or short-bore)

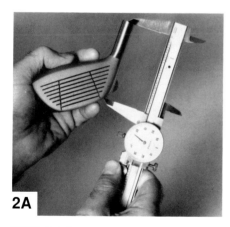

2A

STEP 2: Find the bottom of bore to sole dimension for the woodheads being assembled. To do this, measure the full length of the hosel from its top to the point on the sole directly under the bore (2A). Subtract the bore depth from this measurement to achieve the bottom of bore to sole dimension (2B).

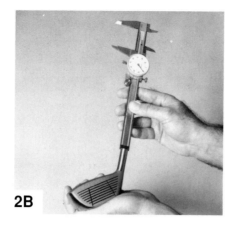

2B

STEP 3: If the woodheads are through-bore, follow the trimming indicated for the through-bore column. If the woodheads are blind bore with a 1/2" bottom of bore to sole dimension, follow the trimming indicated for the blind bore column. If the woodheads are short-bore (metal woods) with a 2" bottom of bore to sole (or 1 1/2" bottom of bore to heel) dimension, follow the trimming indicated for the short-bore (metal woods) column. If the blind bore woodheads have a different bottom of bore to sole dimension than 1/2", or if the short-bore (metal woods) woodheads have a different bottom of bore to sole dimension than 2" (or 1 1/2" bottom of bore to heel), adjustments to those trimming amounts would need to be made to ensure uniform shaft mounting.

Refer to the trimming chart in this chapter for the shaft being used. If the woods are a blind bore type, but the bottom of bore to sole dimension is *greater* than 1/2", subtract the 1/2" from your bottom of bore to sole measurement to find the amount to add to the blind bore tip trimming for each woodhead in the set. If your wood is a short-bore type (metal wood) but the bottom of bore to sole dimension is *greater* than 2", subtract the 2" from your bottom of bore to sole measurement to find the amount to add to the short-bore (metal wood) tip trimming for each woodhead in the set.

If your wood is a blind bore type but the bottom of bore to sole dimension is *less* than 1/2", subtract 0" from your

bottom of bore to sole measurement to find the amount to add to the through-bore tip trimming for each woodhead in the set. If your wood is a short-bore type (metal wood) but the bottom of bore to sole dimension is *less* than 2", subtract 0" from your bottom of bore to sole measurement to find the amount to add to the through-bore tip trimming for each woodhead in the set.

IRONS

STEP 1: Find the standard tip trimming chart for the shaft to be installed. The manufacturers' trimming for irons is almost always based on the 1" standard bottom of bore to heel dimension.

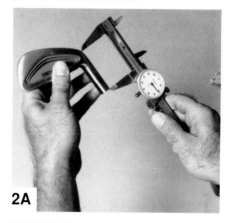

2A

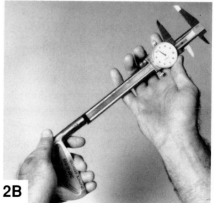

2B

STEP 2: Find the bottom of bore to heel dimension for the ironheads being assembled. To record this distance on irons, measure the full length of the hosel from its top to the back edge of the heel (2A). Subtract the bore depth from this measurement to achieve the bottom of bore to heel dimension (2B).

STEP 3: If the ironheads have a 1" bottom of bore to heel dimension, follow the standard tip trimming indicated for the irons column. If the ironheads have a different bottom of bore to sole dimension than 1", adjustments to the tip trimming amounts would need to be made to ensure uniform shaft mounting.

If the ironhead bottom of bore to heel dimension is greater than 1", subtract that amount from the 1" standard. This difference is the amount to add to the standard tip trimming for each ironhead in the set.

If the ironhead bottom of bore to heel dimension is less than 1", the head will have to be handled as if it were a through-bore or semi through-bore. Since this requires detailed understanding of shaft installation, a separate section is devoted to this type of ironhead shaft assembly. Refer to the section entitled Special Shaft Trimming found in this chapter.

■ SHAFT TRIMMING CHARTS FOR WOODS

Unitized Parallel Tip Shafts

Shaft charts A through 0 cover the proper trimming and installation procedures for all types of shafts that are designed for installation into woodheads. Each chart lists the shafts that are covered in the trimming formula by manufacturer and name. When searching for the trimming and installation procedures for a particular brand/name of a shaft look up "shaft trimming" in the index in the back of the book. The shaft trimming index will locate the proper trimming chart for each shaft along with its appropriate page number.

Charts A through F outline the standard trimming and installation for all unitized parallel tip shafts for woods.

To use the wood shaft trimming charts note the procedures that follow:

STEP 1: Check the shaft pattern listings to be sure the chart includes the particular shaft you wish to install.

STEP 2: Look for the column in the chart that refers to the woodhead hosel design type that is being assembled.

STEP 3: If the shaft is a combination flex type, pick the column that refers to the shaft flex to be achieved in the installation.

STEP 4: Reference the trimming chart to show the amount to tip trim for each clubhead. If adjustments to the trimming need to be made to ensure Uniform Mounting due to a different bottom of bore to sole dimension in the woodhead, make those calculations and apply them to the trimming amounts for each head. Look under the chart to note if further trimming from the butt end is required.

IMPORTANT NOTE REGARDING SHAFT TRIMMING TABLES FOR WOODHEADS: For all the shaft trimming charts for woodheads, the blind bore column entries are based on the standard blind bore bottom of bore to sole dimension of 1/2" and the metal wood (short-bore) column entries are based on the standard metalwood bottom of bore to sole dimension of 2".

CHART A

Parallel Tip Combination R/S Flex Steel Shafts For Woods

Apollo Shafts

1083	AP44 R/S
1513	Spectre R/S
1588	Torsion Matched Mk II R/S
1498	Shadow R/S

Brunswick Shafts

8076WRS	Precision Propel II R/S
7576WRS	Precision Phoenix R/S
8676WRS	Precision Microtaper R/S

True Temper Shafts

UDWC	Dynamic R/S
UPWC	Pro Fit R/S
UJWC	Jet Step R/S
UTTLWC	TT Lite R/S

All the above shafts are acceptable for use in metal woods

Tip Trim	Through-Bore		Blind Bore		Metal Woods	
	R	S	R	S	R	S
0"	1w					
1/2"	2w		1w			
1"	3w		2w			
1 1/2"	4w		3w			
2"	5w	1w	4w		1w	
2 1/2"	6w	2w	5w	1w	2w	
3"	7w	3w	6w	2w	3w	
3 1/2"		4w	7w	3w	4w	
4"		5w		4w	5w	1w
4 1/2"		6w		5w	6w	2w
5"		7w		6w	7w	3w
5 1/2"				7w		4w
6"						5w
6 1/2"						6w
7"						7w

Note: After tip trimming and installation of the shaft, measure and cut for the desired playing length of the woods from the butt end of the shaft.

CHART B

Parallel Tip Combination A/L Flex Steel Shafts For Woods

Apollo Shafts

1369   Spectre A/L

Brunswick Shafts

8056WAL   Precision Propel II A/L
7556WAL   Precision Phoenix A/L
8656WAL   Precision Microtaper A/L

True Temper Shafts

UDWAL   Dynamic A/L
U2LWAL   TT Lite A/L

**All the above shafts are acceptable
for use in metal woods**

Tip Trim	Through-Bore		Blind Bore		Metal Wood	
	L	A	L	A	L	A
0"	1w					
1/2"	2w		1w			
1"	3w	1w	2w			
1 1/2"	4w	2w	3w	1w		
2"	5w	3w	4w	2w	1w	
2 1/2"	6w	4w	5w	3w	2w	
3"	7w	5w	6w	4w	3w	1w
3 1/2"		6w	7w	5w	4w	2w
4"		7w		6w	5w	3w
4 1/2"				7w	6w	4w
5"					7w	5w
5 1/2"						6w
6"						7w

Note: After tip trimming and installation of the shaft, measure and cut for the desired playing length of the wood from the butt end of the shaft.

CHART C

Parallel Tip Combination R/S Flex Tip Reinforced Steel Shafts For Metal Woods

Apollo Shafts
TR1537   AP44 R/S Metal Wood
TR1522   Spectre R/S Metal Wood

Brunswick Shafts
8976WRS   Precision Microtaper R/S Metal Wood
7596WRS   Precision Phoenix R/S Metal Wood

True Temper Shafts
UDWCH   Dynamic R/S Metal Wood
UTTLWCH   TT Lite R/S Metal Wood

Tip Trim	Metal Woodhead	
	R	S
0"	1w	
1/2"	2w	
1"	3w	
1 1/2"	4w	
2"	5w	1w
2 1/2"	6w	2w
3"	7w	3w
3 1/2"		4w
4"		5w
4 1/2"		6w
5"		7w

Note: After tip trimming and installation of the shaft, measure and cut for the desired playing length of the wood from the butt end of the shaft. Tip reinforced shafts are designed expressly for metal woods with a short-bore (2" bottom of bore to bottom of sole) and should not be used in through-bore or blind bore woodheads. For those woodhead types, a non-tip reinforced version is manufactured.

CHART D

Parallel Tip Combination A/L Flex Tip Reinforced Steel Shafts For Metal Woods

Apollo Shafts
None

Brunswick Shafts
8956WAL   Precision Microtaper A/L Metal Wood

True Temper Shafts
None

Tip Trim	Metal Woodheads	
	L	A
0"	1w	
1/2"	2w	
1"	3w	1w
1 1/2"	4w	2w
2"	5w	3w
2 1/2"	6w	4w
3"	7w	5w
3 1/2"		6w
4"		7w

Note: After tip trimming and installation, measure and cut for the desired playing length of the wood from the butt end of the shaft. Tip reinforced shafts are designed expressly for metal woods with a short-bore (2" bottom of bore to bottom of sole) and should not be used in through-bore or blind bore woodheads. For those woodhead types, a non-tip reinforced version is manufactured.

CHART E

Parallel Tip Discrete Flex Steel And Graphite Shafts For Woods (Through-Bore, Blind Bore and Metal Wood Construction)

Apollo Shafts

1890	AP44 Elite R
1892	AP44 Elite S
1785	Lady Shadow
1584	Senior Shadow
1760	MatchFlex 1 AR
1762	MatchFlex 2 R
1764	MatchFlex 3 RS
1766	MatchFlex 4 S
1497	AP46 L
1153	AP46 R
1499	AP83 L
1075	AP83 R

Brunswick Shafts

UCV-304WR	UCV-304 R
UCV-304WS	UCV-304 S
3523WL	Super Champion L
2863WR	Super Champion R
2223WL	Champion L
2263WR	Champion R

Tip Trim	Through-Bore	Blind Bore	Metal Wood
0"	1w		
1/2"	2w	1w	
1"	3w	2w	
1 1/2"	4w	3w	
2"	5w	4w	1w
2 1/2"	6w	5w	2w
3"	7w	6w	3w
3 1/2"		7w	4w
4"			5w
4 1/2"			6w
5"			7w

Note: After tip trimming and installation of each shaft, measure and cut for the desired playing length from the butt end of the shaft.

True Temper Shafts

UDGWR	Dynamic Gold (all sub flexes of R-200-R-400)
UDGWS	Dynamic Gold (all sub flexes of S-200-S-400)
UDGWX	Dynamic Gold (all sub flexes of X-100-X-300)
UDWR	Dynamic R
UDWS	Dynamic S
UDWX	Dynamic X
URWLM	Comet L
URWR	Comet R
U3WL	Century L
U3W	Century R
UBGTWXH	Black Gold Tour Flex High Flex X (both sub flexes of X-100, X-400)
UBGTWXL	Black Gold Tour Flex Low Flex X (both sub flexes of X-100, X-400)
UGBTWSH	Black Gold Tour Flex High Flex S (sub flex of S-400)
UGBTWSL	Black Gold Tour Flex Low Flex S (sub flex of S-400)

UCBHWX	Black Gold X (all sub flexes of X-100-X-300)
UCBHWS	Black Gold S (all sub flexes of S-200-S-400)
UCBHWR	Black Gold R (all sub flexes of R-200-R-400)
UCBHWL	Black Gold L (all sub flexes of L-200-L-400)
UEI7WS	EI-70 S
UEI7WR	EI-70 R
UEI7WL	EI-70 L
UCMHWX	Modulus EV40 X
UCMHWS	Modulus EV40 S
UCMHWR	Modulus EV40 R
UCMHWL	Modulus EV40 L
UVWS	Command S
UVWR	Command R
UVWL	Command L

All the above shafts are acceptable for use in metal woods

CHART F

Dynacraft Dyna-Tech Standard And Dyna-Tech Classic Parallel Tip Wood Shafts

USWRS   Dyna-Tech Standard R/S   **Both of these shafts are acceptable for use in metal woods**
UCWRS   Dyna-Tech Classic R/S

| Wood | Tip Trim | | | | | |
	Through-Bore R	Through-Bore S	Blind Bore R	Blind Bore S	Metal Wood R	Metal Wood S
1w	0"	1"	1/2"	1 1/2"	2"	3"
2w	1/2"	1 1/2"	1"	2"	2 1/2"	3 1/2"
3w	1"	2"	1 1/2"	2 1/2"	3"	4"
4w	1 1/2"	2 1/2"	2"	3"	3 1/2"	4 1/2"
5w	2"	3"	2 1/2"	3 1/2"	4"	5"
6w	2 1/2"	3 1/2"	3"	4"	4 1/2"	5 1/2"
7w	3"	4"	3 1/2"	4 1/2"	5"	6"

Note: After tip trimming and installation of shaft, measure and cut for the desired playing length from the butt end of the shaft.

CHART G

Parallel Tip Established Flex Steel And Graphite Shafts For Woods (Blind Bore and Metal Wood Type Construction)

Apollo Shafts
G100WL   G100 L
G100WR   G100 R
G100WS   G100 S
HMFWR   HMF Lo Torque R
HMFWS   HMF Lo Torque S
BTWR   Boron Tourline R
BTWS   Boron Tourline S
BTWX   Boron Tourline X

Brunswick Shafts
None

True Temper Shafts
UGPWXH   Gold Plus X (all sub flexes)
UGPWSH   Gold Plus S (all sub flexes)
UGPWRH   Gold Plus R (all sub flexes)
UGPWLH   Gold Plus L (all sub flexes)

Note: After tip trimming and installation of shaft, measure and cut for the desired playing length from the butt end of the shaft.

Tip Trim	Blind Bore	Metal Wood
0"	1w	
1/2"	2w	
1"	3w	1w
1 1/2"	4w	2w
2"	5w	3w
2 1/2"	6w	4w
3"	7w	5w
3 1/2"		6w
4"		7w

All the above shafts are acceptable for use in metal woods

CHART H

Apollo MasterFlex Parallel Tip Steel Shafts For Woods

The Apollo MasterFlex steel shaft in parallel tip form is designed to enable clubmakers to achieve the standard range of flexes as well as flexes that are in-between the normal stiffnesses. Note the flex that is desired in the assembly, then check for the desired flex in the chart at right to determine what shaft is to be selected to achieve that flex and what trimming formula is to be used. For example, if the woods are to be assembled to the A/R flex (in between the normal A and normal R flexes), choose the MasterFlex II R-flex raw shaft and follow the trimming instructions as outlined in chart H1. If the woods are to be assembled to the S-flex, choose the MasterFlex IV S-flex raw shaft and follow the trimming instructions as outlined in chart H2.

Apollo Shafts

1720	MasterFlex II R
1722	MasterFlex IV S
1724	MasterFlex VI X

Desired Flex	Shaft to Use	Chart
AR (between A & R)	MasterFlex II R	H1
R	MasterFlex II R	H2
RS (between R & S)	MasterFlex IV S	H1
S	MasterFlex IV S	H2
SX (between S & X)	MasterFlex VI X	H1
X	MasterFlex VI X	H2

Chart H1

Tip Trim	Through-Bore	Blind Bore	Metal Woods
1w	0"	1/2"	2"
2w	1/2"	1"	2 1/2"
3w	1"	1 1/2"	3"
4w	1 1/2"	2"	3 1/2"
5w	2"	2 1/2"	4"
6w	2 1/2"	3"	4 1/2"
7w	2 1/2"	3"	4 1/2"

Chart H2

Tip Trim	Through-Bore	Blind Bore	Metal Wood
1w	1"	1 1/2"	3"
2w	1 1/2"	2"	3 1/2"
3w	2"	2 1/2"	4"
4w	2 1/2"	3"	4 1/2"
5w	3"	3 1/2"	5"
6w	3 1/2"	4"	5 1/2"
7w	3 1/2"	4"	5 1/2"

CHART I

Apollo Acculite Parallel Tip Wood Shafts

Apollo Shafts

1700   Acculite R
1702   Acculite S

Due the unique nature of the shaft and dimensionally enhanced double formed step pattern, the Apollo Acculite shaft is to be trimmed **all from the tip end** to the desired playing length. All tip trimming as a method of shaft installation takes into account any deviations in bottom of bore to sole measurements. Therefore, regardless of whether the woods are through-bore, blind bore or short-bore metal woods, no adjustments to the trimming will be necessary to achieve uniform shaft mounting.

To perform the all tip trimming installation, follow these steps:

STEP 1: Insert an Acculite raw shaft into each woodhead to the bottom of the bore without epoxy.

STEP 2: Place each club on the floor in the playing position. Slide a 48" ruler behind the shaft and note the difference between the uncut length of each wood and the desired playing length for each wood, (e.g. since the raw shaft length of the Acculite is 45", in a blind bore Driver the uncut length of the wood will be approximately 45 1/2". If the desired playing length of this Driver were 43", the difference would be 2 1/2".

STEP 3: Remove the shaft and trim the difference between the uncut length of each wood and the desired playing length from the tip (from the example in Step 2 this would be 2 1/2"). Perform the same procedures for each woodhead in the set, realizing that as playing length decreases through the fairway woods, the amount to be tip trimmed will increase.

■ **SHAFT TRIMMING CHARTS FOR WOODS**

Non-Unitized Parallel Tip Shafts for Woods

The previous charts cover the trimming and installation procedures for Unitized Parallel Tip Shafts for all types of woodhead designs. As mentioned, the term Unitized refers to parallel tip shafts that are designed so the shaft installation needs of all heads in the set of woods can be met using one raw length shaft. There does exist one shaft pattern, the **Flex Flow from True Temper**, that is a parallel tip shaft but is not unitized in design. Therefore, a different raw length shaft is required for each head

in a set of woods. This deviation from the normal parallel tip shaft installation principles is necessary to ensure that the special recessed section on the Flex Flow shaft remains in the correct position with respect to each clubhead.

Even though a different Flex Flow raw shaft length is required for each head in a set, the different woodhead design styles will dictate that some additional tip trim-

ming prior to installation may be necessary to ensure uniform shaft mounting due to differences in bottom of bore to sole dimension. Use the following chart to guide your installation of the Flex Flow parallel tip steel shaft.

NOTE: The parallel tip versions of the FM Precision steel shafts from Brunswick Shaft Corp. are non-unitized. Due to their unique design FM steel shaft trimming and installation is covered separately in Chart II.

CHART J

True Temper Flex Flow Parallel Tip Steel Shaft

Wood	Required Raw Shaft Length	Tip Trim		
		Through-Bore	**Blind Bore**	**Metal Wood**
1w	44"	0"	1/2"	2"
2w	43 1/2"	0"	1/2"	2"
3w	43"	0"	1/2"	2"
4w	42 1/2"	0"	1/2"	2"
5w	42"	0"	1/2"	2"
6w	41 1/2"	0"	1/2"	2"
7w	41 1/2"	0"	1/2"	2"

Note: After tip trimming and shaft installation, measure and cut from the butt end to the desired playing length. Even though a tip-reinforced version of the Flex Flow is produced, the above non-tip reinforced version can be used in metal wood assembly.

The above trimming procedures are correct for the industry standard A, R and S flexes based on standard playing lengths for men. Those lengths are as follows: 1-wood - 43", 2-wood - 42 1/2", 3-wood - 42", 4-wood - 41 1/2", 5-wood - 41", 6-wood - 40 1/2", 7-wood - 40".

The above trimming procedures are correct for industry standard L-flex feel based on standard playing lengths for ladies. Those lengths are as follows: 1-wood - 42", 2-wood - 41 1/2", 3-wood - 41", 4-wood - 401/2", 5-wood - 40", 6-wood - 39 1/2", 7-wood - 39". If

following petite ladies length (1/2" shorter than ladies standard length) use the same tip trimming procedures as above for normal L-flex.

CHART K

True Temper Flex Flow Parallel Tip-Reinforced Steel Shafts For Metal Woods

Wood	Raw Shaft Length	Metal Wood Tip Trimming
1w	43"	0"
2w	42 1/2"	0"
3w	42"	0"
4w	41 1/2"	0"
5w	41"	0"
6w	40 1/2"	0"
7w	40 1/2"	0"

Note: After tip trimming and shaft installation, measure and cut from the butt end to the desired playing length.

The above trimming procedures are correct for the industry standard A, R and S flexes based on standard playing lengths for men. Those lengths are as follows: 1-wood - 43", 2-wood - 42 1/2", 3-wood - 42", 4- wood - 41 1/2", 5-wood - 41", 6-wood - 40 1/2", 7-wood - 40".

The above trimming procedures are correct for industry standard L-flex feel based on standard playing lengths for ladies. Those lengths are as follows: 1-wood - 42", 2-wood - 41 1/2", 3-wood - 41", 4-wood - 401/2", 5-wood - 40", 6-wood - 39 1/2", 7-wood - 39". If following petite ladies length (1/2" shorter than ladies standard length) use the same tip trimming procedures as above for normal L-flex.

■ SHAFT TRIMMING CHARTS FOR WOODS

Taper Tip Shafts

The key to accuracy in the installation of tapered tip steel shafts is to have the proper raw shaft length for each clubhead to be assembled. Below is a chart that lists the proper uncut taper tip shaft length to be used for installation into each woodhead.

Wood	Required Taper Tip Raw Length Shaft
1 w	44"
2 w	43 1/2"
3 w	43"
4 w	42 1/2"
5 w	42"
6 w	42"*
7 w	42"*

* With True Temper's taper tip version of the Flex Flow shaft, a 41 1/2" raw length taper tip shaft is available and recommended for use in the #6 and 7-woods.

If all the necessary raw tapered tip shaft lengths to complete the job cannot be purchased, an assembly decision must be made between the following options:

1. The set can be built using only the lengths that are available, in which case the industry's standard uniform mounting through the set will not be fully achieved.

2. The proper raw shaft lengths can be "created" by tip trimming the shafts that are available to the required pre-installation lengths needed. For example, if the 44" length is only available, extra 44" taper tip shafts can be tip trimmed 1", 1 1/2" and 2" respectively to "create" the 43", 42 1/2" and 42" raw length shafts.

In working with taper tip shafts, if option #1 is followed it must be realized that the shafts in the finished set will not possess the necessary increase in stiffness that is called for under standard shaft installation principles. However, if the second option is followed, a little more work will be required to complete the assembly process. Creating the necessary raw shaft lengths by tip trimming longer taper tip shafts will have the effect of successively enlarging the tip diameter of each shaft. This tip trimming to "create" the proper raw shaft length will require the hosel diameter of the #3, 4 and 5 woodheads to be re-bored larger to fit the shaft, a procedure that is time consuming but necessary to ensure uniform, accurate mounting of the shafts throughout the set (see Chapter 10 for instruction in reboring hosels)

One important rule to follow is to never install taper tip shafts into metal woods with short-bore depths. All short-bore metal woods are now produced with a .335" parallel bore into which the smaller diameter taper tip shafts will not properly fit. Even though all taper tip shaft installation is to be restricted to the conventional through-bore and blind bore design woodheads, an additional 1/2" in tip trimming still must be performed to the blind bore models to follow the principle of uniform shaft mounting between the two types of woodheads.

When using the proper uncut taper tip shaft lengths for each head in a set of woods, follow Chart L on the next page for proper shaft tip trimming and installation:

CHART L

All Taper Tip Steel Shafts
(When Proper Raw Length Shafts Are Used)

Wood	Required Taper Tip Raw Shaft Length	Through-Bore	Blind Bore
1w	44"	0"	1/2'
2w	43 1/2"	0"	1/2"
3w	43"	0"	1/2"
4w	42 1/2"	0"	1/2"
5w	42"	0"	1/2"
7w	42"	0" (1")[1]	1/2" (1 1/2")[1]

[1] Golf industry standards for taper tip shaft installation into a #7-wood do not call for tip trimming, except for the case of a blind bore woodhead. However, if a decrease of first step position is desired for even more precise mounting, the amount indicated in the parentheses may be tip trimmed.

After tip trimming (if required) and shaft installation, measure and cut for the desired playing length from the butt end. If additional 1/2" tip trimming is performed for blind bore woodhead assembly, understand the bore may have to be enlarged to accommodate fitting the shaft into the hosel. For reboring woodheads, see Chapter 10.

Being able to purchase all of the required taper tip raw length shafts necessary to assemble full sets of woods and irons will not always be possible. Some shaft patterns are less popular than others and suppliers will not stock all of the necessary raw taper tip shaft lengths. When it is not possible to purchase each of the proper lengths for completing a full set of woods, refer to Chart M for assembling through-bore woods and Chart N for blind bore woodheads. Always remember that tip trimming taper tip shafts to "create" the proper raw lengths will in turn require enlarging the woodhead bore to make the shaft fit. Again, clubhead reboring techniques are covered in Chapter 10.

CHART M

Taper Tip Steel Shafts For Through-Bore Woods
(When Proper Raw Shaft Lengths Are Not Available)

Chart M shows how different raw length taper tip shafts can be used to assemble sets of through-bore woods. Note the fact in many cases a particular raw length of taper tip shaft is definitely not recommended for use in a particular clubhead. For example, the chart shows how a 45", 44 1/2" or a 44" raw length taper tip shaft are the only shafts that should be used for a through-bore Driver. Use of any taper tip raw length shaft shorter than 44" for the Driver will result in the shaft playing progressively stiffer than intended.

The most common situation of assembly without the proper raw length taper tip shafts is for the clubmaker to only have the 44" long shaft. In this case the chart shows how through successive tip trimming and hosel bore enlarging, the set can be built correctly. Chart M is valid for all patterns of taper tip steel shafts.

Chart M	**THROUGH-BORE WOODHEADS**

Tip Trimming Required For Through-Bore Wood Assembly

Taper Tip Raw Length	1w	2w	3w	4w	5w	6w	7w[1]
45"	1"	1 1/2"	2"	2 1/2"	3"	3"	(4")
44 1/2"	1/2"	1"	1 1/2"	2"	2 1/2"	2 1/2"	(3 1/2")
44"	**0"**	1/2"	1"	1 1/2"	2"	2"	(3")
43 1/2"	No[2]	**0"**	1/2"	1"	1 1/2"	1 1/2"	(2 1/2")
43"	No[3]	No[2]	**0"**	1/2"	1"	1"	(2")
42 1/2"	No[4]	No[3]	No[2]	**0"**	1/2"	1/2"	(1 1/2")
42"	No[5]	No[4]	No[3]	No[2]	**0"**	**0"**	(1")

Please note the location of the tip trimming entries of 0". These 0" tip trimming entries indicate that the raw lengths are the industry's recommended lengths for the woodheads heading their column.

[1] Golf industry standards for taper tip shaft installation into the #7-wood does not call for tip trimming, except in the case of the blind bore woodhead design. However, if a decrease of the first step position is desired for even more precise mounting, the amount indicated in the parentheses may be tip trimmed.

[2] Installation of this raw length shaft into this head will result in a shaft flex that is approximately 1/4 flex more tip stiff than standard for the flex being used.

[3] Installation of this raw length shaft into this head will result in a shaft flex that is approximately 1/2 flex more tip stiff than standard for the flex being used.

[4] Installation of this raw length shaft into this head will result in a shaft flex that is approximately 3/4 flex more tip stiff than standard for the flex being used.

[5] Installation of this raw length shaft into this head will result in a shaft flex that is approximately 1 full flex more tip stiff than standard for the flex being used.

CHART N

Taper Tip Steel Shafts For Blind Bore Woods
(When Proper Raw Shaft Lengths Are Not Available)

Chart N shows how different raw length taper tip shafts can be used to assemble sets of blind bore woods. Please note that in many cases a particular raw length of taper tip shaft is definitely not recommended for use in a particular clubhead. For example, the chart shows how a 45", 44 1/2", 44" or 43 1/2" raw length taper tip shaft are the only shafts that should be used for a blind bore Driver. Use of shorter raw lengths for the Driver will result in the shaft playing progressively stiffer than intended.

The most common situation of assembly without the proper raw length taper tip shafts is for the clubmaker to only have the 44" long shaft. In this case the chart shows how through successive tip trimming and hosel bore enlarging, the set can be built correctly. Chart N, located on the following page, is valid for all patterns of taper tip steel shafts.

Please note the location of the tip trimming entries of 0". While these raw lengths are 1/2" shorter than the industry's recommended length, understand that by using these you can have the proper step location, achieve uniform mounting of the shafts, and avoid the 1/2" tip trimming and reboring of the hosels that would be necessary for blind bore woodheads when using the proper lengths.

See page 96 for trimming instructions.

Chart N	BLIND BORE WOODHEAD

Tip Trimming Required For Proper Blind Bore Assembly

Taper Tip Raw Length	1w	2w	3w	4w	5w	7w	7w[1]
45"	1 1/2"	2"	2 1/2"	3"	3 1/2"	3 1/2"	(4 1/2")
44 1/2"	1"	1 1/2"	2"	2 1/2"	3"	3"	(4")
44"	1/2"	1"	1 1/2'	2"	2 1/2"	2 1/2"	(3 1/2")
43 1/2"	0"	1/2"	1"	1 1/2"	2"	2"	(3")
43"	No[2]	0"	1/2"	1"	1 1/2"	1 1/2"	(2 1/2")
42 1/2"	No[3]	No[2]	0"	1/2"	1"	1"	(2")
42"	No[4]	No[3]	No[2]	0"	1/2"	1/2"	(1 1/2")

[1] Golf industry standards for tapered tip shaft installation into #7-woods do not call for tip trimming, except in the case of the blind bore woodhead design. However, if a decrease of the first step position is desired for even more precise mounting, the amount indicated in the parentheses may be tip trimmed.

[2] Installation of this raw shaft length into this head will result in a shaft flex that is approximately 1/4 flex more tip stiff than standard for the flex being used.

[3] Installation of this raw shaft length into this head will result in a shaft flex that is approximately 1/2 flex more tip stiff than standard for the flex being used.

[4] Installation of this raw shaft length into this head will result in a shaft flex that is approximately 3/4 flex more tip stiff than standard for the flex being used.

CHART O

Taper Tip Graphite Wood Shafts
(For Shafts Available In Only One Raw Length)

While clubmakers rarely encounter taper tip graphite shafts in their work, many manufacturers do produce taper tip versions of certain graphite shaft designs primarily for use by major golf club manufacturers. When installing taper tip graphite shafts for woods, the procedure for trimming and installation is completely different than with taper tip steel shafts. When a taper tip graphite shaft is available in only a 44" or 45" raw length, the shaft should not be successively tip trimmed for each wood through the set in the same manner as taper tip steel shafts. Instead, for proper assembly of taper tip graphite shafts into blind bore woodheads using only one raw length, install the shafts all the way to the bottom of the bore with no tip trimming and trim to the desired playing length from the butt.

For through-bore assembly, insert the shafts with no tip trimming to a point adjacent to the back edge of the heel, approximately 1/2" short of penetrating through the sole. Fill the open hole through the sole with epoxy.

Industry Clubhead Standards For Iron Shaft Installation

Ironheads

During the discussion on uniform shaft mounting for irons, it was established that the golf industry's standard for shaft installation into ironheads is based on an ironhead with a bottom of bore to back edge of heel dimension of 1", regardless of hosel length and bore depth.

Having just explained the correct installation of shafts into all types of woodheads, understand that in the case of ironhead design, far more variations of hosel design can exist. The through-bore, blind bore and the short-bore designs cover the basic hosel designs that exist in woodheads. However, with ironheads, clubhead designers have used many different combinations of hosel length and bore depth, sometimes even within the same set. Therefore, sets of ironheads do exist within clubmaking that exhibit quite a variety of bottom of bore to back edge of heel dimensions. For uniform shaft mounting to exist between different sets of ironheads, this dimension should to be taken into account before arriving on the final correct trimming amounts for each shaft.

When assembling irons, it is very important for clubmakers to measure and calculate the bottom of bore to heel dimension **before** shaft tip trimming is performed. To review the proper sequence for correct shaft tip trimming and shaft installation into ironheads:

STEP 1: Measure the full hosel length of each of the ironheads from the top of the hosel to the back edge of the heel. Measure the bore depth by inserting a thin ruler into the bore. Subtract the bore depth from the hosel length to determine the bottom of bore to heel dimension.

STEP 2: If the bottom of bore to heel dimension is 1", no additional adjustments in the trimming will be necessary for any shafts listed in the iron shaft trimming charts that follow.

STEP 2A: If the bottom of bore to heel dimension is greater than 1", the amount over 1" must be added to the standard tip trimming for each shaft through the full set of irons.

STEP 3: Use the shaft index on Pages 172-177 to determine the proper chart to use for the shafts being installed.

STEP 4: If the shaft is a combination flex type, pick the column that refers to the shaft flex to be achieved in the installation.

STEP 5: Reference the trimming chart to show the amount to tip trim for each clubhead. If the ironheads being assembled have a bottom of bore to back edge of heel dimension greater than 1", add the amount over the 1" standard to the tip trimming for each clubhead. Look under the chart to note if further trimming from the butt end is required.

Before continuing on to the shaft trimming charts for iron club assembly, be sure to review your understanding of why the measurement of the bottom of bore to back edge of heel of the clubhead is so important. Remember, two identical shafts could be tip trimmed exactly the same way prior to assembly, but if they are installed into two similar numbered ironheads with different bottom of bore to heel designs, the shafts will not mount nor play the same in the finished club. Allowing for differences in the bottom of bore to back edge of heel between ironhead designs is the correct way to achieve uniform shaft mounting.

The shaft trimming charts for irons list the correct shaft trimming procedures for ironhead assembly, based on ironheads all with a bottom of bore to back edge of heel dimension of 1". If the heads being assembled have a bottom of bore to heel dimension greater than 1", the amount over 1" represents the additional tip trimming

that must be performed **in addition to the amount specified in each of the charts**. For example, if you are building a #2-iron with a bottom of bore to back edge of heel dimension of 1 1/4", and the trimming for the shaft requires 1/2" to be cut from the tip, then the total amount to be tip trimmed for the purpose of achieving uniform shaft mounting will be 1/2" (from the chart) + 1/4" (the amount over the 1" standard), or a total of 3/4" for that particular #2-iron.

1/2"	(From the chart)
+ 1/4"	(Amount greater than 1" standard)
3/4"	(Total to tip trim)

Remember, any additional trimming due to the bottom of bore to back edge of heel dimension being greater than 1" must be added to the standard tip trimming for all the shafts in the set.

■ SHAFT TRIMMING CHARTS FOR IRONS

Unitized Parallel Tip Shafts

Shaft charts P through U cover the proper trimming and installation procedures into ironheads for shafts that are unitized and parallel tip in design. Each chart lists the shafts that are covered in the trimming formula by manufacturer and name. When searching for the trimming and installation procedures for a particular brand/name of a shaft reference, use the shaft index on Pages 172-177. The shaft trimming index can be used to locate the proper trimming chart for each shaft along with its appropriate page number.

CHART P

Parallel Tip Combination R/S Flex Steel Shafts For Irons

Apollo Shafts

1085	AP44 R/S
1084	AP44 R/S Overfit
1514	Spectre R/S
1589	Torsion Matched Mark II R/S
1469	Shadow R/S

Brunswick Shafts

7876IRS	Precision Propel II R/S
7576IRS	Precision Phoenix R/S
8676IRS	Precision Microtaper R/S

True Temper Shafts

UDIC	Dynamic R/S
UDICO	Dynamic Overfit R/S
UPIC	Pro Fit R/S
UPICO	Pro Fit Overfit R/S
UJIC	Jet Step R/S
UJICO	Jet Step Overfit R/S
UTTLIC	TT Lite R/S

Tip Trim	R-Flex	S-Flex
0"	1i	
1/2"	2i	
1"	3i	
1 1/2"	4i	
2"	5i	1i
2 1/2"	6i	2i
3"	7i	3i
3 1/2"	8i	4i
4"	9i	5i
4 1/2"	wedges[1]	6i
5"		7i
5 1/2"		8i
6"		9i
6 1/2"		wedges[1]

[1] The practice of tip trimming all wedges 1/2" more than the #9-iron is a recent change. Clubmakers should be advised that this additional 1/2" tip trimming is recommended by the manufacturers of shafts to accommodate the heavier headweight of wedges.

Note: After tip trimming and installation of each shaft, measure and cut for the desired playing length of the irons from the butt end of the shaft.

CHART Q

Parallel Tip Combination A/L Flex Steel Shafts For Irons

Apollo Shafts

1382	Spectre A/L

Brunswick Shafts

7856IAL	Precision Propel II A/L
7556IAL	Precision Phoenix A/L
8656IAL	Precision Microtaper A/L

True Temper Shafts

UDIAL	Dynamic A/L
U2LIAL	TT Lite A/L

Tip Trim	L-Flex	A-Flex
0"	1i	
1/2"	2i	
1"	3i	1i
1 1/2"	4i	2i
2"	5i	3i
2 1/2"	6i	4i
3"	7i	5i
3 1/2"	8i	6i
4"	9i	7i
4 1/2"	wedges[1]	8i
5"		9i
5 1/2"		wedges[1]

[1] The practice of tip trimming all wedges 1/2" more than the #9-iron is a recent change from the old practice of trimming the #9 and wedges the same. Clubmakers should be advised that this additional 1/2" tip trimming is recommended by the manufacturers of shafts to accommodate the heavier headweight of wedges.

Note: After tip trimming and installation of each shaft, measure and cut for the desired playing length of the iron from the butt end of the shaft.

CHART R

Parallel Tip Discrete Flex Steel And Graphite Shafts For Irons

Apollo Shafts

1891	AP44 Elite R
1893	AP44 Elite S
1786	Lady Shadow
1585	Senior Shadow
1761	MatchFlex 1 AR
1763	MatchFlex 2 R
1765	MatchFlex 3 RS
1767	MatchFlex 4 S
1306	AP46 L
1305	AP46 R
1500	AP83 L
1077	AP83 R
G100IL	G100 L Graphite
G100IR	G100 R Graphite
G100IS	G100 S Graphite
HMFIR	HMF Lo Torque R Graphite
HMFIS	HMF Lo Torque S Graphite
BTIR	Boron Tourline R Graphite
BTIS	Boron Tourline S Graphite
BTIX	Boron Tourline X Graphite

Tip Trim	Ironhead
0"	1i
1/2"	2i
1"	3i
1 1/2"	4i
2"	5i
2 1/2"	6i
3"	7i
3 1/2"	8i
4"	9i
4 1/2"	wedges[1]

[1] The practice of tip trimming all wedges 1/2" more than the #9-iron is a recent change from the old practice of trimming the #9 and wedges the same. Clubmakers should be advised that this additional 1/2" tip trimming is recommended by the manufacturers of shafts to accommodate the heavier headweight of wedges.

Brunswick Shafts

UCV-304IR	UCV-304 R
UCV-304IS	UCV-304 S
3523IL	Super Champion L
2663IR	Super Champion R
3923IL	Champion L
2263IR	Champion R

True Temper Shafts

UDGIR	Dynamic Gold R (all sub flexes of R-200 - R-400)
UDGIS	Dynamic Gold S (all sub flexes of S-200 - S-400)
UDGIX	Dynamic Gold X (all sub flexes of X-100 - X-300)
UDIR	Dynamic R

True Temper Shafts (cont'd.)

UDIS	Dynamic S
UDIX	Dynamic X
UGPIL	Gold Plus L (all sub flexes of L-200 - L-400)
UGPIR	Gold Plus R (all sub flexes of R-200 - R-400)
UGPIS	Gold Plus S (all sub flexes of S-200 - S-400)
UGPIX	Gold Plus X (all sub flexes of X-100 - X-300)
URLIM	Comet L
URIR	Comet R
U3IL	Century L
U3I	Century R
UCBHIL	Black Gold L Graphite (all sub flexes of L-200 - L-400)

True Temper Shafts (cont'd.)

UCBHIR	Black Gold R Graphite (all sub flexes of R-200 - R-400)
UCBHIS	Black Gold S Graphite (all sub flexes of S-200 - S-400)
UCBHIX	Black Gold X Graphite (all sub flexes of X-100 - X-400)
UEI7L	EI-70 L Graphite
UEI7R	EI-70 R Graphite
UEI7S	EI-70 S Graphite
UCMHIL	Modulus EV40 L Graphite
UCMHIR	Modulus EV40 R Graphite
UCMHIS	Modulus EV40 S Graphite
UCMHIX	Modulus EV40 X Graphite
UVIL	Command L Graphite
UVIR	Command R Graphite
UVIS	Command S Graphite

CHART S

Dynacraft Dyna-Tech Standard And Classic Parallel Tip Iron Shafts

USIRS   Dyna-Tech Standard R/S
UCIRS   Dyna-Tech Classic R/S

Iron	Tip Trim	
	R-Flex	**S-Flex**
1i	1/2"	1 1/2"
2i	1"	2"
3i	1 1/2"	2 1/2"
4i	2"	3"
5i	2 1/2"	3 1/2"
6i	3"	4"
7i	3 1/2"	4 1/2"
8i	4"	5"
9, PW, SW	4 1/2"	5 1/2"

CHART T

Apollo MasterFlex Parallel Tip Steel Shafts For Irons

The Apollo MasterFlex steel shaft in parallel tip form is designed to enable clubmakers to achieve through special trimming the standard flexes as well as flexes that are in-between the normal stiffnesses. Note the flex that is desired in the assembly, then check the desired flex in the chart at right to determine what shaft is to be selected to achieve that flex and what trimming formula is to be used. For example, if the irons are to be assembled to the AR flex (in between the normal A and normal R flexes), choose the MasterFlex II R-flex raw shaft and follow the trimming instructions as outlined in chart T1. If the irons are to be assembled to the S-flex , choose the MasterFlex IV S-flex raw shaft and follow the trimming instructions for the appropriate ironhead as outlined in chart T2.

Apollo Shafts

1721	MasterFlex II R
1723	MasterFlex IV S
1726	MasterFlex VI X

Desired Flex	Shaft to Use	Chart
AR	MASTERIR	T1
R	MASTERIR	T2
RS	MASTERIS	T1
S	MASTERIS	T2
SX	MASTERIX	T1
X	MASTERIX	T2

Chart T1

Tip Trim	Ironhead
0"	1i
1/2"	2i
1"	3i
1 1/2"	4i
2"	5i
2 1/2"	6i
3"	7i
3 1/2"	8i
4"	9i
4 1/2"	wedges[1]

[1] The practice of tip trimming all wedges 1/2" more than the #9-iron is a recent change from the old practice of trimming the #9 and wedges the same. Clubmakers should be advised this additional 1/2" tip trimming is recommended by the manufacturers of shafts to accommodate the heavier headweight of wedges.

Chart T2

Tip Trim	Ironhead
1"	1i
1 1/2"	2i
2"	3i
2 1/2"	4i
3"	5i
3 1/2"	6i
4"	7i
4 1/2"	8i
5"	9i
5 1/2"	wedges[1]

[1] The practice of tip trimming all wedges 1/2" more than the #9-iron is a recent change from the old practice of trimming the #9 and wedges the same. Clubmakers should be advised this additional 1/2" tip trimming is recommended by the manufacturers of shafts to accommodate the heavier headweight of wedges.

CHART U

Apollo Acculite Parallel Tip Iron Shafts

1701   Acculite R
1703   Acculite S

Due the unique nature of the shaft and its dimensionally-enhanced, double-formed step pattern, the Apollo Acculite shaft is to be trimmed **all from the tip end** to the desired playing length. All tip trimming as a method of shaft installation already takes into account any deviations in bottom of bore to heel measurements.

To perform the all tip trimming installation, follow these steps:

STEP 1: Insert an Acculite raw shaft into each ironhead to the bottom of the bore without epoxy.

STEP 2: Place each club on the floor in the playing position. Slide a 48" ruler behind the shaft and note the difference between the uncut length of each iron and

the desired playing length for each iron (e.g. since the raw shaft length of the Acculite iron shaft is 39", in a #3-iron with a 1" bottom of bore to heel measurement, the initial uncut length of the club would be @40". If the desired playing length of this #3-iron is 38 1/2", the difference would be 1 1/2".

STEP 3: Remove the shaft and trim the difference between the uncut length of each iron and the desired playing length from the tip (in this example in Step 2 the tip trim would be 1 1/2"). Perform the same procedures for each ironhead in the set, realizing that as playing length decreases through the wedges, the amount to be tip trimmed will increase.

■ **SHAFT TRIMMING PROCEDURES FOR IRONS**

Non-Unitized Parallel Tip Shafts for Irons
The previous charts covered the trimming procedures for unitized parallel tip shafts for all types of ironhead designs. As mentioned, the term unitized refers to parallel tip shafts that are designed so the shaft installation needs of all heads in the set of irons can be met using one raw length shaft. There does exist one shaft pattern, the **Flex Flow from True Temper**, that is a parallel tip shaft but is not unitized in design. Therefore, a different raw length shaft is required for each head in a set of irons. This deviation from the normal parallel tip shaft installation principles is necessary to ensure that the special recessed section on the Flex Flow shaft remains in the correct position with respect to each clubhead.

Even though a different Flex Flow raw shaft length is required for each ironhead in the set, differences in ironhead hosel design (bottom of bore to back edge of heel) might dictate that some additional tip trimming prior to installation may be necessary to ensure uniform mounting from set to set. Use the following chart to guide your installation of the Flex Flow parallel tip steel shaft.

NOTE: The parallel tip versions of the FM Precision steel shafts from Brunswick Shaft Corp. are non-unitized. Due to their very unique design FM steel shaft trimming and installation is covered separately in Charts Z1 and Z2.

CHART V

True Temper Flex Flow Parallel Tip Steel Shafts for Irons

Clubhead	Required Raw Length	Tip Trim [1]
1 iron	39" [2]	0"
2 iron	39"	0"
3 iron	38 1/2"	0"
4 iron	38"	0"
5 iron	37 1/2"	0"
6 iron	37"	0"
7 iron	36 1/2"	0"
8 iron	36"	0"
9 iron	35 1/2"	0"
wedges	35"	0"

[1] Based on ironhead designs with a bottom of bore to heel dimension of 1". For irons with this dimension greater than than 1", the amount over the 1" standard will be the additional amount to tip trim from each shaft prior to installation.

[2] A 39 1/2" raw length Flex Flow shaft is not offered, so the 39" raw shaft will be used in both the #1 and 2 ironheads. As a result, the mounting will be the same for the #1 and 2-irons.

■ SHAFT TRIMMING PROCEDURES FOR IRONS

Taper Tip Shafts

Just as in the case of the woodheads, the key to accuracy in the installation of taper tip steel shafts is to have the proper raw shaft length for each clubhead to be assembled. To the right is a chart that outlines the proper raw taper tip shaft length to be used for installation into each ironhead. Note that unlike for taper tip woods, a different set of raw shaft lengths are used to assemble L-flex sets of irons.

If all the necessary raw tapered tip shaft lengths to complete the job cannot be purchased, an assembly decision must be made between the following options:

> 1. The set can be assembled using only the lengths that are available, in which case the golf industry's standard uniform mounting through the set will not be fully achieved.

> 2. The proper raw shaft lengths can be "created" by tip trimming the available shafts to the required pre-installation lengths needed. For example, if only the 39", 38", 37" and 36" lengths are available, additional 39", 38", 37" and 36" taper tip shafts can each be tip trimmed 1/2" to "create" the 38 1/2", 37 1/2", 36 1/2" and 35 1/2" raw length shafts.

In working with taper tip shafts, if option #1 is followed it must be realized that the shafts in the finished set will not possess the necessary increase in stiffness that is called for under standard taper tip shaft installation principles. However, if the second option is followed, a little more work will be required to complete the assembly process. Creating the necessary raw shaft lengths by tip trimming longer taper tip shafts will have the effect of increasing the tip diameter of each shaft. This tip trimming to "create" the proper raw shaft length will require the hosel diameter of the #2, 4, 6 and 8 ironheads to be rebored larger to fit the shaft, a

Iron Head	Taper Tip Raw Shaft Length A,R,S,X Flexes	L-Flex
1 i	39"	38"
2 i	38 1/2"	37 1/2"
3 i	38"	37"
4 i	37 1/2"	36 1/2"
5 i	37"	36"
6 i	36 1/2"	35 1/2"
7 i	36"	35"
8 i	35 1/2"	34 1/2"
9 i	35"	34"
PW , SW	35"	34"

procedure that is time consuming but necessary to ensure uniform, accurate mounting of the shafts throughout the set.

Even having the proper raw taper tip shaft lengths to assemble full sets of irons, it may still be necessary to tip trim an additional amount from each shaft to allow for differences in the bottom of bore to back edge of heel dimension of from the 1" standard for ironheads. Therefore, remember to take this factor into account when using the following charts for installation of taper tip shafts into ironheads.

When using the proper uncut taper tip shaft lengths for each head in a set of irons, follow Chart W on the next page for proper shaft tip trimming and installation.

CHART W

All Taper Tip Steel Shafts for Irons
(When Proper Raw Length Shafts Are Used)

Iron Head	Taper Tip Raw Shaft Length		
	A,R,S,X flexes	L-flex	Amount to Tip Trim[1]
1 i	39"	38"	0"
2 i	38 1/2"	37 1/2"	0"
3 i	38"	37"	0"
4 i	37 1/2"	36 1/2"	0"
5 i	37"	36"	0"
6 i	36 1/2"	35 1/2"	0"
7 i	36"	35"	0"
8 i	35 1/2"	34 1/2"	0"
9 i	35"	34"	0"
wedges[2]	35"	34"	0"

After tip trimming (if required) and shaft installation, measure and cut for the desired playing length from the butt end of the shaft.

[1] The 0" tip trimming for each shaft is based on installation into ironheads with a bottom of bore to heel measurement of 1". If the bottom of bore to heel dimension is greater than 1", the amount over 1" is the additional amount that must be tip trimmed from each shaft prior to installation to assure uniform industry mounting. If additional tip trimming is performed, it will be necessary to rebore the hosel to accept the larger tip diameter of each shaft.

[2] Sometimes the matching wedges do not have the same bottom of bore to heel dimension as the #1 - #9 irons in the same set. Be sure to check this measurement and adjust the tip trimming accordingly before installation, if uniform mounting is desired. It will be necessary to rebore the hosel if tip trimming is required.

CHART X

Taper Tip Steel Shafts for Irons
(When The Proper Raw Shaft Lengths Are Not Available)

Chart X shows how sets of irons can be assembled with taper tip shafts when all the proper raw lengths are not available. Please note that in many cases a particular raw length of taper tip shaft is definitely not recommended for use in a particular ironhead. For example, the chart shows how a 39" raw length taper tip shaft is the only shaft that should be used for a #1-iron. Use of shorter raw lengths for the #1-iron will result in the shaft playing progressively stiffer than intended.

The most common situations of assembly without the proper raw length taper tip shafts is for the clubmaker to only have the 39", 38", 37", 36" and 35" shafts, or the 39", 37" and 35" shafts to build the set. In these cases the chart shows how through successive tip trimming and hosel bore enlarging, the set can be built correctly. Chart X is valid for all patterns of taper tip steel shafts.

CHART X

Taper Tip Raw Length	Ironhead[1] Amount to Tip Trim								
	1i	2i	3i	4i	5i	6i	7i	8i	9i, Wedges
39"	**0**	1/2	1	NR	NR	NR	NR	NR	NR
38 1/2"	0^2	**0**	1/2	1	NR	NR	NR	NR	NR
38"	0^3	0^2	**0**	1/2	1	NR	NR	NR	NR
37 1/2"	0^4	0^3	0^2	**0**	1/2	1	NR	NR	NR
37"	0^5	0^4	0^3	0^2	**0**	1/2	1	NR	NR
36 1/2"	NR	0^5	0^4	0^3	0^2	**0**	1/2	1	NR
36"	NR	NR	0^5	0^4	0^3	0^2	**0**	1/2	1
35 1/2"	NR	NR	NR	0^5	0^4	0^3	0^2	**0**	1/2
35"	NR	NR	NR	NR	0^5	0^4	0^3	0^2	**0**

Note: After tip trimming (if necessary) and shaft installation, measure and cut for the desired length from the butt end of the shaft.

NR = Not recommended

[1] Based on bottom of bore to heel dimension of 1". If bottom of bore to heel dimension is greater than 1", add the amount greater than 1" to each tip trimming entry in the chart.

[2] If this raw length (at left) is installed into this ironhead with a bottom of bore to heel dimension of 1", it will yield a flex that is 1/4 flex FIRMER than the stated flex of the shaft.

[3] If this raw length (at left) is installed into this ironhead with a bottom of bore to heel dimension of 1", it will yield a flex that is 1/2 flex FIRMER than the stated flex of the shaft.

[4] If this raw length (at left) is installed into this ironhead with a bottom of bore to heel dimension of 1", it will yield a flex that is 3/4 flex FIRMER than the stated flex of the shaft.

[5] If this raw length (at left) is installed into this ironhead with a bottom of bore to heel dimension of 1", it will yield a flex that is 1 full flex FIRMER than the stated flex of the shaft.

Additional Valuable Information Contained in

CHART X

1. Notice the diagonal positioning of the 0" tip trimming entries. This is highlighted to show clubmakers the proper raw uncut taper tip shaft length for each ironhead.

2. The **NR** entries in the chart express the fact that under no circumstances should this shaft length be used for the clubhead number indicated. Use of these raw lengths for the clubhead indicated will result in the iron playing more stiff than intended.

3. The chart does not advise removing any more than 1" from the tip of a taper tip shaft. Tip trimming more than 1" from a taper tip shaft begins to change the playing characteristics of the shaft too much and therefore is not recommended.

4. Study the footnoted references of 0^2, 0^3, 0^4, and 0^5 in the chart. When using this raw shaft length for the indicated ironhead, you will achieve flexes stronger by progressive amounts than what is standard for the shaft being used. Think of this as a very handy way to satisfy requests from golfers for a flex that is **in between** two

standard flexes without actually having to cut off part of the tip end of the shaft. This practice, which is nothing more than using a different raw shaft length for each head, is entirely acceptable and is preferred over tipping because no reboring of the hosel is required.

For example: A clubmaker wishes to assemble a set of irons to a flex that is in between the R and S normal flexes for a golfer. Using one ironhead (#5) as the example, the 37" raw length R-flex shaft is intended to be used in a #5-iron to achieve a standard R-flex mounting. If a 36 1/2" raw length R-flex shaft is used in the #5-iron, the flex will be 1/4 stiffer than standard R because the tip section length will be 1/2" shorter than what would be standard when using the 37" raw length R-flex shaft.

Continuing, if a 36" raw length R-flex shaft is used in the #5 ironhead, the tip section length would now be 1" shorter than the #5-iron standard, which equates to a feel that is approximately 1/2 flex stiffer than the standard R. Understand that this example uses only the R-flex in a #5-iron as an illustration of how to achieve an in-between flex. In-between flexes can be achieved for all ironheads in the set and for any in between flex from L to X just by using different raw lengths.

In referring to the chart listings of 0^4 and 0^5, you can see as the raw shaft length is shortened further for any clubhead, the relative stiffness will increase up to a point that if a raw shaft length is used that is 2" shorter than what is proper, the stiffness will have increased by one full flex. This sets up a principle in shaft design that for most steel shaft patterns and types, **2" of tip section is equivalent to one full flex.**

In other words, if you shorten the tip section by 2" over the standard for that clubhead, either by cutting or by use of a shorter raw length shaft, the flex will be increased by one full level. This principle is true for all taper tip common pattern steel shafts, but is not always true for parallel tip construction shafts or for graphite shafts (for example the difference between L and A flexes in parallel shafts is usually 1". Information to assist installing parallel tip shafts to in-between flexes is offered later in this chapter in the section entitled, "Special Shaft Installation Principles."

Conversely, if you increase the tip section length for any clubhead over its standard for the shaft being used, the shaft will begin to play more flexible than its standard mounting. In other words, if you install a raw shaft length that is longer than what is called for, you can achieve an in-between flex that is softer than standard. For example, if you use a 37" taper tip raw length R-flex shaft in a #9 ironhead (when a 35" is the proper length) the shaft will play equivalent to an A-flex, one full flex softer than the standard for that shaft.

5. When interchanging raw shaft lengths to achieve in between flexes, realize if a raw shaft length is used for any head that is 1" shorter than the proper length, as in the example of a 36" shaft being installed into a #5 ironhead, standard men's playing length cannot be achieved without the use of a shaft extender. Again, this would be true for ironheads with a bottom of bore to heel dimension of 1".

Therefore, the principles of raw shaft length selection by clubhead used as shown in CHART X can be summed up:

In an Ironhead with a bottom of bore to heel dimension of 1"…

a. Use of raw shaft lengths SHORTER than the standard will result in relative playing flexes that are STIFFER than the standard for the flex being used.

b. Use of raw shaft lengths LONGER than the standard will result in relative playing flexes that are MORE FLEXIBLE than the standard for the flex being used.

c. Raw shaft length will affect the possible playing length of the club. Use of a raw shaft length that is 1" SHORTER than the standard for the clubhead will mean that an extender must be used to achieve standard playing lengths.

■ **TRIMMING AND INSTALLATION CHARTS FOR SPECIAL SHAFT TYPES & PATTERNS**

To this point, Chapter 3 has dealt exclusively with the shaft trimming and installation principles of common parallel tip and taper tip steel and graphite shafts. Such shafts may be considered to be "common" by clubmak-ers because they follow basic, common mounting procedures to achieve their standard playing character-istics. However, in addition to the large number of common parallel and taper tip shafts, there exist sev-eral other shaft types and patterns that are designed to incorporate special or unusual trimming principles. Because of their existence and special natures, each shaft type and pattern will be covered separately.

CHART Y

Advanced Composite Technologies
Parallel Tip Graphite Shafts for Woods

Introduced in 1990, the ACTivator and Tour Stik graphite shafts from ACT are two of the few composite shafts that are manufactured through the filament winding process. To accommodate successive tip trimming during installation, ACT shafts are designed with a long parallel tip section.

Trimming and installation for the ACTivator and the Tour Stik:

Wood	Through-Bore	Blind Bore[1]	Metal Wood[2]
1w	0"	1/2"	1 1/2"
2w	1/2"	1"	2"
3w	1"	1 1/2"	2 1/2"
4w	1 1/2"	2"	3"
5w	2"	2 1/2"	3 1/2"
6w	2 1/2"	3"	4"
7w	3"	3 1/2"	4 1/2"

After tip trimming and installation, mea-sure and cut from the butt end to the desired playing length.

[1]Assumes a bottom of bore to sole dimen-sion of 1/2".

[2]Assumes a bottom of bore to sole dimen-sion of 2".

CHART Z

Aldila Parallel Tip Discrete Flex Graphite Shafts For Metal Woods

The world's largest manufacturer of graphite shafts, Aldila offers a greater variety of composite shaft designs than any other composite shaft making company. To assist clubmakers in identifying Aldila flexes, the company uses the following color codes on the butt of their shafts to denote the various flexes: Red=L (light) flex; Yellow=R (regular) flex; Green=S (firm) flex; Orange=X (strong) flex.

Chart Z covers the proper trimming and installation of the following Aldila graphite shafts:

HM-55 parallel tip woods and irons	**All flexes**
HM-40 parallel tip woods	**All flexes**
HM-30 parallel tip woods and irons	**All flexes**
HM-30 Superlite parallel tip woods and irons	**All flexes**
Alda VIII parallel tip woods	**All flexes**
GLT parallel tip woods	**All flexes**
Receptor parallel tip woods	**All flexes**

Wood	Metal Wood	Blind[1] Bore
1w	0"	0" (-1 flex)
2w	0"	0" (-1 flex)
3w	0"	0" (-1 flex)
4w	0"	0" (-1 flex)
5w	0"	0" (-1 flex)
6w	0"	0" (-1 flex)
7w	0"	0" (-1 flex)

[1] For blind bore installation drop back one full flex softer than what is desired in the finished golf club, then tip trim as per the above column for blind bore woodheads.

CHART AA

Aldila Parallel Tip Discrete Flex Graphite Shafts For All Woods

Chart AA covers the proper trimming and installation of the following Aldila graphite shafts:

HM-40 Low Flex for woods   all flexes
Questar for woods   all flexes
44" Low Torque for woods   all flexes

Tip Trim	Through-Bore Blind Bore	Metal Woods
0"	—— 1w ——	
1/2"	—— 2w ——	
1"	—— 3w ——	—— 1w ——
1 1/2"	—— 4w ——	—— 2w ——
2"	—— 5w ——	—— 3w ——
2 1/2"	—— 6w ——	—— 4w ——
3"	—— 7w ——	—— 5w ——
3 1/2"		—— 6w ——
4"		—— 7w ——

After initial tip trimming and installation, measure and cut from the butt end to the desired playing length.

CHART BB

Aldila Parallel Tip HM-40 Graphite Shafts for Irons

Iron	Tip Trim
1i	0"
2i	0"
3i	1/4"
4i	1/2"
5i	3/4"
6i	1"
7i	1 1/4"
8i	1 1/2"
9i	1 3/4"
Wedges	1 3/4"

Chart BB covers the proper trimming and installation of the Aldila HM-40 graphite iron shafts only.

After tip trimming and installation, measure and cut from the butt end to the desired playing length.

CHART CC

Aldila Parallel Tip Discrete Flex Graphite Shafts For Irons

Chart CC covers the proper trimming and installation of the following Aldila graphite shafts:

HM40 Low Flex   all flexes
Questar   all flexes
39" Low Torque   all flexes

Iron	Tip Trim
1i	0"
2i	1/2"
3i	1"
4i	1 1/2"
5i	2"
6i	2 1/2"
7i	3"
8i	3 1/2"
9i	4"
PW, SW	4"

After tip trimming and installation, measure and cut from the butt end to the desired playing length.

CHART DD

Aldila Low Torque 39" Combination Flex Parallel Tip Shafts for Irons

Chart DD covers the proper trimming and installation of the following Aldila graphite shafts:

39" raw length Low Torque A&L
39" raw length Low Torque R&S

Iron	Tip Trim	
	For L or R	For A or S
1i	0"	0"
2i	0"	1/2"
3i	0"	1"
4i	1/2"	1 1/2"
5i	1"	2"
6i	1 1/2"	2 1/2"
7i	2"	3"
8i	2 1/2"	3 1/2"
9i	3"	4"
PW, SW	3"	4"

After tip trimming and installation, measure and cut from the butt end to the desired playing length.

CHART EE

Aldila Low Torque 41" Combination Flex Parallel Tip Shafts For Irons

Chart EE covers the proper trimming and installation of the following Aldila graphite iron shafts:

41" raw length Low Torque A&L
41" raw length Low Torque R&S

After tip trimming and installation, measure and cut from the butt end to the desired playing length.

Iron	Tip Trim	
	For L or R	For A or S
1i	0"	2"
2i	1/2"	2 1/2"
3i	1"	3"
4i	1 1/2"	3 1/2"
5i	2"	4"
6i	2 1/2"	4 1/2"
7i	3"	5"
8i	3 1/2"	5 1/2"
9i	4"	6"
PW, SW	4"	6"

CHART FF

Aldila Low Torque 45" Combination Flex Parallel Tip Shafts For All Woods

Chart FF covers the proper trimming and installation of the following Aldila graphite iron shafts:

45" raw length Low Torque A&L
45" raw length Low Torque R&S

After tip trimming procedure, measure and cut the butt end to the desired playing length.

[1] For through-bore assembly, insert the shaft to a point adjacent to the back edge of the heel @ 1/2" short of penetrating the sole. Fill the hole in the sole with epoxy.

Wood	Tip Trim			
	Through-Bore[1], Blind Bore		Metal Wood	
	For L or R	For A or S	For L or R	For A or S
1w	0"	1 1/2"	1"	2 1/2"
2w	1/4"	2"	1 1/4"	3"
3w	1/2"	2 1/2"	1 1/2"	3 1/2"
4w	1"	3"	2"	4"
5w	1 1/2"	3 1/2"	2 1/2"	4 1/2"
6w	1 3/4"	3 3/4"	2 3/4"	4 3/4"
7w	2"	4"	3"	5"

CHART GG

Alloy 2000 Composite Metal Shafts

Manufactured from eleven different metals blended together into a lightweight alloy, the Alloy 2000 shaft has a lower kick point in comparison to its bend point to provide increased trajectory. Manufactured in parallel tip form for woods, the Alloy 2000 is designed primarily for installation into metal woods.

Wood	Metal Wood	Blind Bore[1]
1w	0" (same flex)	1" (-1 flex)
2w	1/2" (same flex)	1 1/2" (-1 flex)
3w	1" (same flex)	2" (-1 flex)
4w	1 1/2" (same flex)	2 1/2" (-1 flex)
5w	2" (same flex)	3" (-1 flex)
6w	2 1/2" (same flex)	3 1/2" (-1 flex)
7w	3" (same flex)	4" (-1 flex)

[1] To retain the same flex when installing into a blind bore woodhead, drop down one full flex and trim an additional 1" from the tip over what is listed in the chart for the numbered club. If installation into through-bore woods is desired, select one full flex less than desired in the finished woods and perform the same tip trimming as for blind bore woods. Insert the shafts so that the tip stops @ 1/2" up from the sole. Fill the open hole up from the sole with epoxy.

After tip trimming and installation, measure and cut the butt end to the desired playing length. Each Alloy 2000 flex can be customized by trimming additional amounts from the tip; each additional 1/2" of tip trimming will make the shaft 1/4 flex stiffer. Using the above tip trimming amounts when installing the Alloy 2000 into a blind bore woodhead will increase the stiffness 1/2 flex stronger.

CHART HH

Carbon Fiber Products

Novus II parallel tip for woods and irons	all flexes
Novus CFP50 parallel tip for woods and irons	all flexes
Novus AC parallel tip for woods and irons	all flexes

The graphite shafts manufactured by Carbon Fiber Products are known for their unusual assortment of multi-color shaft cosmetics. In addition the company pursues the unique production technique of not sanding off the outer layers of the shaft's covering wrap after forming. This gives the Carbon Fiber shafts their unusual spiral wrapped look and feel. Currently, the company produces a number of different graphite shaft designs, all of which follow the trimming and installation instructions in the paragraph below.

> For all Carbon Fiber Products shafts, for both woods and irons, tip trim 0" before installation. Then measure and cut from the butt end to the desired playing length.

Brunswick FM Precision Steel and Graphite Shafts

Brunswick Shaft Co.'s FM Precision steel and graphite shafts are true frequency-matched designs that are produced in both taper tip and parallel tip form for the steel patterns and parallel tip form only in the graphite pattern. In the FM taper tip steel shafts, a different raw length is required for each wood and each iron. In the FM parallel tip steel shaft, one length of shaft is used to assemble each wood, but an entire set of different raw lengths are still required for proper assembly of the irons. For the parallel tip FiberMatch graphite pattern, one raw length for each frequency level is used to assemble all woods and one raw length for each frequency level is used to assemble all the irons.

Instead of categorizing the shaft by common industry flex designations, Brunswick produces the FM Precision steel and graphite shafts in a variety of frequency levels, each identified by a number code. These frequency levels are equivalent to the last two digits of the Driver frequency and represent a successive ranking of flex in that the lower the number, the more flexible the shaft.

FM Precision Frequency Level	Approximate Flex Equivalent
FM 3.5 (235 cpm)	L (Ladies)
FM 4.5 (245 cpm)	A (Flexible)
FM 5.5 (255 cpm)	R (Regular)
FM 6.5 (265 cpm)	S (Stiff)
FM 7.5 (275 cpm)	X (Extra Stiff)

The frequency of the FM Precision shafts are controlled by club length, swingweight and the clubhead's bottom of bore to heel dimension. For each FM Precision steel shaft to play to its designated frequency, each wood and iron must be built to standard length (43" Driver and 39" #2-Iron, with all other clubs to decrease in 1/2" incremental changes of length) with a D3 swingweight. In addition, for FM steel woods, the frequency is based on a through-bore design, while for irons, achieving the designated frequency is based on installation into ironheads with a bottom of bore to heel dimension of 1 1/4".

For each FM FiberMatch graphite shaft to play to its designated frequency, each wood and iron must be built to standard length (43" Driver and 39" #2-Iron, with all other clubs to decrease in 1/2" incremental changes of length). For FM FiberMatch graphite woods, the frequency is based on installation into a short-bore metal wood design, while for irons, achieving the designated frequency is based on mounting into ironheads with a bottom of bore to heel dimension of 1 1/4". Unlike the steel FM Precision swingweight standard of D3, each FM FiberMatch graphite frequency level has its own swingweight standard for the shaft to play at its designated frequency. Those FM graphite swingweight standards are as follows:

Standard Swingweights for FM Graphite	
FiberMatch Frequency Level	Standard Swingweight
FM 3.5	C-9
FM 4.5	C-8
FM 5.5	C-9
FM 6.5	D-0
FM 7.0	D-1
FM 7.5	D-2

In other words, if golf clubs assembled with the FM Precision steel and FiberMatch graphite shafts are built to playing lengths and swingweights different than the above standards, or installed into hosel bore designs different than the prescribed standards, the shafts will not play to their stated frequency level. By using frequency as a form of describing relative stiffness, it is possible to determine how much the shaft flex of the FM shafts change when specifications other than standard are used. In addition, using the frequency as a guide to expressing flex, it is also easy to make adjustments in the trimming to restore the FM shafts to their assigned frequency.

Following is an explanation of what varying the length, swingweight and hosel bore will do to the frequency. Included are how alterations in trimming can be made to readjust the frequency to the desired level.

1. For every 1/2" trimmed from the tip in excess of the standard installation procedures, the FM Precision frequency level will INCREASE BY 0.3.

EXAMPLE: An FM5.5 shaft with an additional 1/2" cut from the tip end will become FM5.8, and thus play slightly stiffer.

2. For every 1/4" that the bottom of bore to heel dimension of the ironhead is less than the FM Precision standard of 1 1/4", the FM frequency level will INCREASE BY 0.15.

EXAMPLE: Standard installation of an FM6.5 shaft into an ironhead with a bottom of bore to heel dimension of 1" will make the frequency FM6.65, and thus play slightly more stiff.

3. In woodheads, for every 1/2" that the tip of the shaft bottom out above the FM standard of a through-bore design, the FM frequency level will DECREASE BY 0.3.

EXAMPLE: Standard installation of an FM7.5 shaft into an average blind bore woodhead (1/2" above through-bore) will make the frequency FM7.2, and thus play slightly more flexible. Standard installation of an FM7.5 shaft into an average short-bore metal woodhead (2" above through-bore) will make the frequency FM6.3, and thus play much more flexible. Also, because the FiberMatch graphite shaft for woods is designed for installation into short-bore metal woods, installation of a FiberMatch graphite 6.5 into a blind bore wood will make the frequency FM7.4. Again, this is due to the fact the FiberMatch graphite shaft is designed primarily for metal wood installation.

4. For every 1 point the swingweight of the as-

sembled club is increased over the various FM steel and graphite standards, the FM frequency will **DECREASE BY 0.1.**

EXAMPLE: Any wood or iron installed with an FM5.5 steel shaft that is built to D4 swingweight will become an FM5.4, and thus play slightly more flexible. Installation of a FiberMatch graphite 5.5 into a golf club that is swingweighted to D-2 will make the shaft play at FiberMatch frequency level 5.2 (remember, the FiberMatch swingweight standards are different than those set up for the FM steel shafts, see page 115).

5. For every 1 point that the swingweight of the assembled club is decreased from the various FM steel and graphite standards, the FM frequency will INCREASE BY 0.1.

EXAMPLE: Any wood or iron installed with an FM5.5 steel shaft that is built to D2 swingweight will become an FM5.6, and thus play slightly stiffer. Installation of a FiberMatch 5.5 graphite into a golf club that is swingweighted to C-7 will make the shaft play at FiberMatch frequency level 5.7 (remember, the FiberMatch swingweight standards are different than those set up for the FM steel shafts).

6. For every 1/2" the playing length of an FM standard assembled club is increased over the FM first standards, the FM frequency will DECREASE BY 0.3.

EXAMPLE: Any standard specification FM6.5 shafted club that is lengthened by 1/2" over the FM standards for wood and iron length will become FM6.2, and thus play slightly more flexible.

7. For every 1/2" the playing length of an FM standard assembled club is shortened from the FM standards, the FM frequency will INCREASE BY 0.3.

EXAMPLE: Any standard specification FM6.5 shafted club that is shortened by 1/2" over the FM standards for wood and iron length will become FM6.8, and thus play slightly stiffer.

Each of the effects of altering the FM assembled club specifications or shaft tip trimming are cumulative; in other words, if you install an FM Precision steel or FiberMatch graphite shaft and build the club to a different length *and* different swingweight, both effects must be taken into account when calculating what

the new FM frequency will be. Therefore, the best way to organize your FM shaft installation is to first calculate in your mind what will happen to the FM frequency of the shaft you intend to use, once it is built to the specifications you desire. Calculating the effects of the length, bore depth and swingweight on the frequency before assembly will enable you to use the additional shaft tip trimming or switch to another FM shaft frequency to achieve your final frequency.

For standard installation of the FM Precision standard steel and light weight steel shafts in woods and irons, refer to trimming Charts II and JJ. The parallel tip FM Precision Steel shaft for woods is acceptable for use in both conventional and metal woodheads, providing the necessary additional amount is tip trimmed for the metal wood to allow for uniform shaft mounting. Do NOT use the tapered tip version of the FM shafts in metal wood assembly. For standard installation of the FM FiberMatch graphite shafts in woods and irons, refer to Chart KK. Be aware the parallel tip FiberMatch graphite shaft for woods is designed for use in metal woodheads. Therefore, installation of this shaft into through-bore or blind bore woods will result in a much stiffer (higher frequency) feel than what the shaft was designed.

CHART II

Brunswick FM Precision and FM Precision Lite Steel Shafts
Parallel Tip Steel Shafts for Woods And Irons

Wood[1]	Through-Bore	Blind Bore	Metal Wood
1w	0"	1/2"	2"
2w	11/16"	13/16"	2 11/16"
3w	1 3/8"	1 7/8"	3 3/8"
4w	2 1/16"	2 9/16"	4 1/16"
5w	2 3/4"	3 1/4"	4 3/4"
7w	4 1/8"	4 5/8"	6 1/8"

Note: After tip trimming and installation, measure and cut for the desired playing length from the butt end of the shaft.

[1] The parallel tip version of the Brunswick FM Precision steel shafts for woods is Unitized while the parallel tip version for the irons is not. Therefore, trimming for the parallel tip FM Precision iron shafts is based on using proper raw length shafts for each head. In addition, the correct installation of the parallel tip FM Precision steel shafts for irons is based on ironhead design with a bottom of bore to heel dimension of 1 1/4", not the 1" that virtually all other iron shafts ascribe to.

Chart II

Iron[1]	Tip Trim
1i	0"
2i	0"
3i	0"
4i	0"
5i	0"
6i	0"
7i	0"
8i	0"
9, Wedges	0"

Note: After tip trimming and installation, measure and cut for the desired playing length from the butt end of the shaft.

[1] The parallel tip version of the Brunswick FM Precision steel shafts for irons is not unitized. Therefore, trimming for the parallel tip FM Precision iron shafts is based on using proper raw length shafts for each head. Each FM Precision Steel iron shaft is marked for which ironhead it is intended. Therefore, clubmakers do not have to specify raw length when placing orders for the FM Steel iron shafts. In addition, the correct installation of the parallel tip FM Precision steel shafts for irons is based on ironhead design with a bottom of bore to heel dimension of 1 1/4", not the 1" that virtually all other iron shafts ascribe to.

CHART JJ

Brunswick FM Precision and FM Precision Lite Taper Tip Steel Shafts
Taper Tip Steel Shafts for Woods And Irons

Wood[1]	Through-Bore	Blind Bore
1w	0"	1/2"
2w	0"	1/2"
3w	0"	1/2"
4w	0"	1/2"
5w	0"	1/2"
7w	0"	1/2"

Iron[1]	Tip Trim
1i	0"
2i	0"
3i	0"
4i	0"
5i	0"
6i	0"
7i	0"
8i	0"
9, Wedges	0"

Note: After tip trimming (if necessary) and installation, measure and cut the desired playing length from the butt end of the shaft. FM Precision taper tip shafts are not to be installed in short bore metal woods.

[1] Trimming for the taper tip FM Precision iron shafts is based on using proper raw length shafts for each head. Each FM Precision Steel iron shaft is marked for which ironhead it is intended. Therefore, clubmakers do not have to specify raw length when placing orders for the FM Steel iron shafts. In addition, the correct installation of the taper tip FM Precision steel shaft for irons is based on ironhead design with a bottom of bore to heel dimension of 1 1/4", not the 1" that virtually all other iron shafts ascribe to.

CHART KK

Brunswick FiberMatch Graphite Shafts
Parallel Tip Graphite Shafts for Woods And Irons

Metal Wood	Tip Trim
1w	0"
2w	11/16"
3w	1 3/8"
4w	2 1/16"
5w	2 3/4"
6w	3 7/16"
7w	3 7/16"

Note: After tip trimming, trim the butt end to playing length. Trimming is the same for all frequency levels to retain the specific frequency. FiberMatch graphite shafts were designed for metal woods, so insertion into a blind bore wood head will increase the frequency by 9 cycles per minute. Insertion of FiberMatch graphite shafts into a through-bore woodhead will increase the frequency by 12 cycles per minute. For example, a FiberMatch 6.5 graphite shaft installed into a through-bore will result in the shaft playing at the 7.4 level.

Iron	Playing Length	Tip Trim
1i	39 1/2"	0"
2i	39"	9/16"
3i	38 1/2"	1 1/8"
4i	38"	1 11/16"
5i	37 1/2"	2 1/4"
6i	37"	2 13/16"
7i	36 1/2"	3 3/8"
8i	36"	3 15/16"
9i	35 1/2"	4 1/2"
Wedges	35"	5 1/16"

Note: After tip trimming procedure, measure and cut the butt end to the desired playing length.

The FiberMatch frequency level indicated on the shaft will be obtained at the following swingweights for both graphite wood and iron shafts. Deviation from the swingweight guidelines is certainly allowed, but will have the effect of changing the shaft's designed frequency. Again, refer to the information in this section to learn how to adjust frequency to any desired level through length, trimming and swingweight changes.

FM Level	Swingweight
3.5	C9
4.5	C8
5.5	C9
6.5	D0
7.0	D1
7.5	D2

CHART LL

Easton Aluminum/Graphite Parallel Tip Composite Shafts
Parallel Tip Composite Aluminum And Graphite Shafts For Woods

First introduced to the clubmaking industry in late 1990, the sports equipment manufacturer Easton Corp. manufactures a unique composite shaft made from an aluminum core overwrapped with graphite composite material. As of this writing Easton produces three different varieties of its graphite over aluminum design, the HP100, the MP200 and the MP300, each of which is available in various flexes for different player types.

All varieties of the Easton shafts for woods are designed to be installed with no tip trimming. After installation, measure for playing length and trim from the butt end. Easton shafts are acceptable for use in all types of woodheads.

CHART MM

Fenwick Graphite Shafts For Metal Woods And Irons

Fenwick World Class parallel and taper tip woods and irons
Fenwick Bioline parallel and taper tip woods and irons

One of the world's leading manufacturers of fishing rods, Fenwick began producing high quality graphite shafts for golf clubs in the late 1980s. Currently the company manufactures the World Class graphite shafts and the unique BioLine graphite series. The Bioline is characterized by a series of longitudinal lines placed on the tip section of the shaft to help the golfer square the clubface at address. Chart MM covers the trimming and installation of all Fenwick parallel and taper tip graphite shafts. Note the use of different raw lengths for correct iron installation.

Wood	Tip Trim	Iron	Raw Shaft Length	Tip Trim
1w	0"	1i	40"	0"
2w	0"	2i	40"	0"
3w	0"	3i	40"	0"
4w	0"	4i	40"	0"
5w	0"	5i	40"	0"
6w	0"	6i	37"	0"
7w	0"	7i	37"	0"
		8i	37"	0"
		9i	37"	0"
		Wedges	37"	0"

After installation, measure and cut from the butt end to the desired playing length.

CHART NN

Fiber Speed FS Series Composite Shafts
Parallel Tip Composite Shafts for Woods

Manufactured from specialized fiberglass composite, the Fiber Speed shafts are designed to significantly limber flexes in an effort to help players with lower clubhead speed generate more distance. Fiber Speed shafts are produced with a unique fiber arrangement that despite their extreme flexibility, allows the shafts to generate adequate resistance to torque from centrifugal force created during the swing.

Fiber Speed shafts are made from high-strength fiberglass bonded with resins and formed in a straight taper tube construction with an extra long parallel tip section. The long parallel portion of the tip area allows each of the three basic Fiber Speed flexes, FS-100, FS-200 and FS-300, to be trimmed and installed to achieve additional flexes that are "in-between" the established flex levels. The FS-100 is the most flexible of the series, the FS-200 is slightly stiffer than the FS-100, and the FS-300 is the firmest of the group. For all woods within a set, tip trimming is the same. For example, if the firmest mounting of the FS-300 shaft is desired, tip trim all shafts for the set of woods 1 1/2". All versions of the Fiber Speed shafts for woods are acceptable for use in short-bore metal woods. Color coding on the butt of the FS series shafts is as follows: FS-100 - Blue, FS-200 - Red, FS-300 - Green.

Shaft	Tip Trim	Achieved Flex
FS-100	0"	Flexible
FS-100	1/2"	Flexible +
FS-100	1"	Flexible ++
FS-100	1 1/2"	Flexible +++
FS-200	0"	Medium
FS-200	1/2"	Medium +
FS-200	1"	Medium ++
FS-200	1 1/2"	Medium +++
FS-300	0"	Firm
FS-300	1/2"	Firm +
FS-300	1"	Firm ++
FS-300	1 1/2"	Firm +++

The + marks indicated after the flex refer to gradually increased levels of stiffness for each shaft. After initial tip trimming (if applicable), mark and cut the butt end to the desired playing length.

Other Fiber Speed Shaft Patterns
TP-4000 Woods and irons
TP-4000 Plus Woods
Fiber Speed Putter Shaft

For each of the Fiber Speed shaft patterns at left, perform no tip trimming. Simply install the shafts into each clubhead and trim from the butt end to achieve the proper mounting and the desired playing length.

CHART OO

Grafalloy Graphite Shafts for Metal Woods & Irons

Lady Classic parallel tip woods and irons
Senior Classic parallel tip woods and irons
M14/I14 parallel tip woods and irons
M29/I29 parallel tip woods and irons
M54/I54 parallel tip woods and irons
M60/I60 parallel tip woods and irons
M66 parallel tip woods
M79/I79 parallel tip woods and irons

One of the oldest and most experienced manufacturers of graphite shafts, Grafalloy offers a wide selection of graphite shafts for all types of players. Grafalloy wood shafts are primarily manufactured for use in metal woods. Installation into through-bore or blind bore woods will cause each shaft to play stiffer than its marked flex. Chart OO covers the proper trimming and installation of all Grafalloy parallel tip graphite shafts for metal woods and irons.

Wood	Tip Trim	Iron	Tip Trim
1w	0"	1i	0"
2w	0"	2i	0"
3w	0"	3i	0"
4w	0"	4i	0"
5w	0"	5i	0"
6w	0"	6i	0"
7w	0"	7i	0"
		8i	0"
		9i	0"
		Wedges	0"

After installation, measure and cut from the butt end for the desired playing length.

CHART PP

Kunnan Parallel Tip Graphite Shafts For Woods And Irons

Autoclave Series 50 parallel tip woods and irons
Autoclave Series 40 parallel tip woods and irons
Autoclave Series 30 parallel tip woods and irons
Comp 50 FCB parallel tip woods and irons
1460 TFB parallel tip woods and irons
1400 TFB parallel tip woods and irons
1400 LFB parallel tip woods and irons

The second largest producer of graphite shafts, Taiwan-based Kunnan made a strong entry into the golf industry in the mid 1980s behind a series of sheet-wrapped graphite and graphite/boron shafts which soon gained a strong following. Currently Kunnan offers a wide array of shaft patterns including the unique compression-cured Autoclave series. The flex of all Kunnan graphite shafts may be identified by the following color code system found on the butt end of the shafts: Blue - L- flex and the A-flex only in the 1400 LFB pattern; Orange - R-flex; Yellow - S-flex. Trimming for all parallel tip Kunnan graphite shafts is outlined in trimming Chart PP.

Metal Woods	Tip Trim
1w	0"
2w	1/4"
3w	1/2"
4w	3/4"
5w	1"

Irons	Tip Trim
1i	0"
2i	0"
3i	1/4"
4i	1/2"
5i	3/4"
6i	1"
7i	1 1/4"
8i	1 1/2"
9i, Wedges	1 3/4"

After tip trimming and installation, measure and cut from the butt end to the desired playing length.

CHART QQ

TI Standard Bend Point Titanium Shafts
Parallel Tip Titanium Shafts for Woods and Irons

Sandvik Corp. TI Titanium shafts for woods and irons are manufactured as a non-step down shaft with a .335" parallel tip for woods and .370" parallel tip for irons. Produced in standard and low bend point designs, the TI standard bend point shafts are manufactured and distributed in the five basic flexes of L, A, R, S and X, while the low bend point version of the shaft is made in combination flex form. Characterized as lightweight in type, the TI shafts feature increased resistance to torque as a result of the titanium material from which they are produced.

For the woods, the length of the parallel portion of the tip will vary slightly from 4 1/2" on the X-flex design to 5 1/2" on the L-flex shaft. TI parallel tip shafts for woods are unitized in nature; one raw length shaft is to be used for each of the woods in a set. However, TI parallel tip shafts for irons are not unitized because a different raw length shaft is to be purchased for each of the ironheads in a set. Sandvik offers the TI parallel and taper tip shafts for irons in 1/2" incremental raw lengths. The proper raw length Titanium shaft for each ironhead is listed in the chart at the bottom of this page. In addition, TI Titanium shafts for woods are suitable for installation into both conventional and metal woodheads, with additional trimming to be performed for installation into metal woodheads to equalize the flex feel between the woodhead types.

TI Standard Bend Point Wood Shafts

Suggested Playing Length[1]	Amount to Tip Trim		
	Through-Bore[2]	Blind Bore[2]	Metal Wood[3]
43 1/2"	1/2" (-1 flex)	1" (-1 flex)	1/2" (same flex)
43"	1" (-1 flex)	1 1/2" (-1 flex)	1" (same flex)
42 1/2"	1 1/2" (-1 flex)	2" (-1 flex)	1 1/2" (same flex)
42"	2" (-1 flex)	2 1/2" (-1 flex)	2" (same flex)
41 1/2"	2 1/2" (-1 flex)	3" (-1 flex)	2 1/2" (same flex)
41"	3" (-1 flex)	3 1/2" (-1 flex)	3" (same flex)
40 1/2"	3 1/2" (-1 flex)	4" (-1 flex)	3 1/2" (same flex)

[1] TI trimming is set up by playing length rather than clubhead number. For example, for any 43 1/2" wood, whether it be a +1/2" overlength Driver, a +1 1/2" overlength #3-wood, etc., trim as per the chart indicates for that length. Thus the chart takes into account any overlength or underlength installation considerations.

[2] For through-bore and blind bore wood assembly, purchase 1 full flex softer than desired in the finished wood and trim as per the chart for each hosel type. For example, to end up with an S-flex blind bore 43" Driver, choose the R-flex and tip trim 1 1/2".

[3] For metal wood assembly, purchase the same flex as desired in the finished wood and tip trim as per the chart for the metal wood. For example, to end up with an R-flex metal wood 43" Driver, choose the R-flex and tip 1".

TI Standard Bend Point Iron Shafts
Parallel tip Titanium shafts for irons

TI standard bend point iron shafts are manufactured in different raw lengths just like taper tip shafts. For proper assembly choose the raw lengths for each ironhead as indicated in the chart. TI standard bend point iron shafts are designed to be installed in all ironheads with no tip trimming.

After installation, measure for playing length and trim from the butt end.

Iron	Raw Shaft Length	Tip Trim
1i	40"	0"
2i	39 1/2"	0"
3i	39"	0"
4i	38 1/2"	0"
5i	38"	0"
6i	37 1/2"	0"
7i	37"	0"
8i	36 1/2"	0"
9i	36"	0"
Wedges	36"	0"

CHART RR

TI Low Bend Point Titanium Shafts
Parallel Tip Titanium Shafts For Woods And Irons

Unlike the TI standard bend point shaft, the TI low bend point shaft for woods is manufactured in two combination flex varieties, the A & R and the S & X. Because of the various woodhead hosel types, there are precise formulations for the use of these combination flex shafts to achieve the desired final flex in the assembled golf club. Installation of the TI low bend point shaft for woods is outlined in this Chart RR. In the chart, the proper combination flex shaft to use is included with the amount to tip trim from that particular shaft for the woodhead type listed.

For example, to assemble a 43" metal wood driver to an R-flex, start with the A&R combination flex shaft and tip trim 3". The N/A designation in the chart means that a wood of that length and that flex cannot be achieved.

Wood Playing Length[1]	THROUGH-BORE				BLIND BORE				METAL WOOD			
	A-flex	R-flex	S-flex	X-flex	A-flex	R-flex	S-flex	X-flex	A-flex	R-flex	S-flex	X-flex
43.5"	N/A	AR 1"	AR 3"	SX 1"	N/A	AR 1.5"	AR 3.5"	SX 1.5"	AR 0.5"	AR 2.5"	SX 0.5"	SX 2.5"
43"	N/A	AR 1.5"	AR 3.5"	SX 1.5"	AR 0"	AR 2"	SX 0"	SX 2"	AR 1"	AR 3"	SX 1"	SX 3"
42.5"	AR 0"	AR 2"	SX 0"	SX 2"	AR 0.5"	AR 2.5"	SX 0.5"	SX 2.5"	AR 1.5"	AR 3.5"	SX 1.5"	SX 3.5"
42"	AR 0.5"	AR 2.5"	SX 0.5"	SX 2.5"	AR 1"	AR 3"	SX 1"	SX 3"	AR 2"	AR 4"	SX 2"	SX 4"
41.5"	AR 1"	AR 3"	SX 1"	SX 3"	AR 1.5"	AR 3.5"	SX 1.5"	SX 3.5"	AR 2.5"	AR 4.5"	SX 2.5"	SX 4.5"

[1] After tip trimming and installation, measure and then trim from the butt end for the desired playing length. TI trimming is set up by playing length rather than clubhead number. For example, for any 43 1/2" wood, whether it be a +1/2" overlength Driver, a +1 1/2" overlength #3-wood, etc., trim as per the chart indicates for that length. Thus the chart takes into account any overlength or underlength installation considerations.

CHART SS

True Temper Taper Tip Graphite Shafts For Woods And Irons

Command taper tip shafts for woods and irons
EV40 taper tip shafts for woods and irons
EI70 taper tip shafts for woods and irons
Black Gold taper tip shafts for woods and irons
Black Gold tour taper tip shafts for woods and irons

True Temper manufactures each of its graphite shafts in taper tip form as well as in the parallel tip variety. Because proper shaft installation requires that a different raw length be used than what is customary for all other True Temper taper tip shafts, Chart SS outlines this type of installation. Correct trimming and installation for the following True Temper taper tip graphite shafts is outlined in the charts at right.

True Temper Taper Tip Graphite Wood Shafts

Wood	Required Raw Length	Tip Trim
1w	45"	0"
2w	44"	0"
3w	44"	0"
4w	43 1/2"	0"
5w	43"	0"
6w	43"	0"
7w	43"	0"

After installation, measure and cut from the butt end of the shaft to the desired playing length. For through-bore assembly, insert the shaft only to a point adjacent to the back edge of the heel 1/2" short of penetrating through the sole. After installation of the shaft fill the open hole up from the sole with epoxy.

Iron	Required Raw Length	Tip Trim
1i	40"	0"
2i	39 1/2"	0"
3i	39"	0"
4i	38 1/2"	0"
5i	38"	0"
6i	37 1/2"	0"
7i	37"	0"
8i	36 1/2"	0"
9i	36"	0"
PW, SW	35 1/2"	0"

After installation, measure and cut from the butt end of the shaft to the desired playing length.

CHART TT

Unifiber Parallel Tip Graphite Shafts for Metal Woods And Irons

MasterStroke parallel tip woods and irons
PowerStroke parallel tip woods and irons
B7 parallel tip woods and irons
T50 parallel tip woods
ProStroke parallel tip woods
UFX parallel tip woods
SilverStroke parallel tip woods
Big Red parallel tip woods
Progressive Power parallel tip irons
MSII parallel tip irons

Unifiber offers a complete line of composite designs for all player types, including the unique 60" raw length Big Red composite shaft for extreme playing length requirements. Unifiber graphite wood shafts are designed primarily for use in metal woods only. Installation into through-bore or blind bore woods will make the Unifiber wood shafts play substantially stiffer than intended. Therefore, when installing Unifiber wood shafts into these traditional woodhead types, drop down one flex from what is desired in the finished club.

For all shafts except the Progressive Power iron shafts and the Unifiber MSII iron shafts, perform no tip trimming. After installation, measure and cut from the butt end to the desired playing length. When using the Unifiber Progressive Power iron shafts, use the 39" raw length for the #1, 2, 3, 4 ironheads, use the 37" raw length for the #5, 6, 7, 8 ironheads and the 35" raw length for the #9 and all wedges. When using the Unifiber MSII iron shafts, use the 39" raw length for the #1, 2, 3, 4 and 5 ironheads, and the 35" raw length for the #6, 7, 8, 9 and all wedges. For all other Unifiber iron shafts, only one raw length is made for all heads.

Special Shaft Trimming and Installation Situations

■ PUTTER SHAFT TRIMMING AND INSTALLATION

One of the most interesting paradoxes of clubmaking is how much emphasis is placed on wood and iron shaft installation while so little care is taken in the choice of installation of shafts into putters. It is very common for a clubmaker to take great pains to ensure the correct installation of shafts into woods and irons only to "throw just any shaft" into the putter.

Not to make a mountain out of a molehill, taking more time to ensure correct shaft mounting in woods and irons *is* more important than for a putter. Due to the fact that woods and irons are swung at much greater clubhead speed than a putter, an incorrect mounting of a shaft into a wood or iron can be noticed in the form of errant or poor feeling shots. Still, there are important considerations to be made in the selection and mounting of putter shafts that quality oriented clubmakers must pursue.

The key points to shaft installation in putters center around these basic points:

1. Whenever possible, select a shaft that is specifically made for a putter instead of a shaft that has been designed for use in an iron.

2. Learn the proper trimming of putter shafts to standardize the manufacturers' intended flex and feel.

3. Follow proper shaft to head bonding procedures to ensure permanent adhesion of the shaft to the putter head.

Shaft Selection for Putters

Currently each of the major manufacturers of steel and graphite shafts offer an assortment of putter shafts. While very little if anything is said by the manufacturers about the flex of putter shafts, there are distinct differences in their appearance and tip design.

Among all the styles of putter heads there are two basic hosel designs. The most widely seen type of putter hosel is the shaft-inside mounting which can vary in bore depth from 2" down to as little as 1/2". Less widely seen but still a popular design style is the shaft overfit type of hosel, in which the shaft is mounted over a thin, solid post that extends up from the putter head.

For the shaft-inside type of mounting, putter shafts are made in a variety of tip diameters from .300" taper to .355" taper to .370" parallel tip to satisfy the variation in putter bore diameter. Among putters designed with a shaft overfit hosel, matching shafts are now predominantly made with a .370" parallel tip, although a few special flared tip overfit shafts are made for special putter designs with a flared overfit hosel post. In addition, any .370" parallel tip putter shaft can be used with a shaft-inside or a shaft overfit type of hosel.

As with ironheads, putter heads do vary from company to company in hosel length, hosel depth and the resulting bottom of bore to sole (it is more correct for putters to refer to bottom of bore to sole) dimension. Just as it is important to adjust tip trimming to accommodate different bottom of bore to heel distances in ironheads, it is also important to make the same type of adjustments in putter shaft trimming when necessary.

The recognized industry standard for the bottom of bore to heel dimension for ironheads is 1", but for putters this same standard upon which shaft trimming is based is different. For shaft-inside hosel type putters, the most widely seen bottom of bore to sole dimension is 2 1/2" while on shaft overfit type putters, the standard bottom of bore (the ledge against which the shaft tip stops) to sole dimension is 2 1/4".

For installation of shafts made expressly for use in putters, there will be 0" tip trimming when the shaft is installed into a putter head with the respective 2 1/2" and 2 1/4" standard bottom of bore to sole dimensions. However, if the putter head has a bottom of bore to sole dimension that is greater than either of the two putter head standards, tip trimming adjustments will have to be made. For putter heads with a bottom of bore to sole dimension that is greater than 2 1/2" (for a shaft-inside type) or 2 1/4" (for a shaft overfit type), the amount to tip trim from the putter shaft will be the standard dimension subtracted from the putter's actual bottom of bore to sole dimension.

Hence if a shaft-inside type putter with a bottom of bore to sole dimension of 3" is being assembled, 1/2" will be trimmed from the tip of the putter shaft. After any tip trimming is performed and the shaft is installed, trimming to establish the playing length will be made from the butt end of the shaft. Remember such tipping adjustments are only for shafts made expressly for use in putters.

If the putter head being assembled has a bottom of bore to sole dimension that is less than the stated standards for each putter type, no adjustments can be made. Therefore, 0" will be trimmed from the tip, with the trimming to establish the desired playing length to come from the butt of the shaft.

If a putter must be assembled with a normal iron shaft, clubmakers are advised to trim the shaft for an R-flex with the same tip trimming as would be performed for a #9-iron. Then after such tip trimming and installation of the shaft, trimming for the desired putter playing length would be made from the butt end.

When tip trimming is performed for a shaft overfit type putter, extreme care must be taken to make the cut as square as possible. Overfit shafts must fit perfectly against the ledge of the hosel when they are installed. If the shaft tip is not cut perfectly square, unsightly gaps between the shaft tip and the hosel ledge will occur.

When installing a shaft into a very short (1/2") bore depth, care must also be taken to ensure that the tip is adequately abraded with rough sandpaper. The epoxy used to secure the shaft to the head will not adhere properly to a smooth chrome (steel shafts) or a urethane coated (graphite shafts) surface. Because so many putter heads have a short bore depth every effort to ensure the proper epoxy adhesion must be made. Therefore, the portion of the shaft tip to be inserted inside the hosel must be heavily abraded to give the epoxy more chance to bond the shaft to the head.

When installing overfit putter shafts it is not realistically possible to adequately abrade the inside of the shaft tip. Therefore, all abrasion for the purpose of increasing the holding power of the epoxy must be performed on the outside of the hosel post of the putter head. When sanding the hosel post on overfit type putters, take care not to sand the ledge against which the tip of the shaft will fit. Because the overfit hosel ledge is visible to the golfer, any mistakes in abrading

that carry over to the hosel ledge will show up as an unprofessional job of clubmaking.

■ SHAFT INSTALLATION FOR HIGH-LOFTED WOODS

The shaft trimming and installation tables for woods that have been presented in Chapter 3 cover normal procedures for assembling woodheads up to a #7-wood. While not as predominant as the Driver through #7-woods, there do exist #8 through #15 high-lofted woods that require proper understanding for the purpose of performing correct shaft installation.

Over the years that high lofted woods have been available, two basic sets of men's playing length specifications have evolved.

Woodhead	Men's Length 1	Men's Length 2
8 Wood	39 1/2"	39 3/4"
9 Wood	39"	39 1/2"
10 Wood	38 1/2"	39 1/4"
11 Wood	38 1/2"	39"
12 Wood	38"	38 3/4"
13 Wood	38"	38 1/2"
14 Wood	37 1/2"	38 1/4"
15 Wood	37 1/2"	38"

Note: Ladies length specifications for each option are accepted to be 1" shorter than each entry in the above columns.

The reason it is important to start the discussion on shaft trimming for high-lofted woods by referring to playing length is that shaft trimming and installation principles are very closely tied to playing length specifications. In all of the previous shaft trimming charts in this chapter for the Driver through #7-wood, the trimming amounts are based on building clubs to standard industry lengths. The current golf equipment standards for playing length call for a 1/2" decrease in length from club to club through the set. In terms of common steel shafts, this 1/2" decrease in playing length is usually accompanied by a 1/2" decrease in shaft tip section length.

Therefore, depending upon which set of length specifications is used to assemble the high lofted woods, the trimming of the shafts should also correspond to a comparable decrease in tip section length.

Parallel Tip Steel Shaft Trimming for High-Lofted Woods

Amount to tip trim in addition to #7-wood tip trimming for each shaft

Wood	Tip Trim In Addition to the #7-Wood Trimming*	
	For Option 1 Lengths	**For Option 2 Lengths**
8w	1/2"	1/4"
9w	1"	1/2"
10w	1 1/2"	3/4"
11w	1 1/2"	1"
12w	2"	1 1/4"
13w	2"	1 1/2"
14w	2 1/2"	1 3/4"
15w	2 1/2"	2"

Ladies tip trimming procedures when using L-flex shafts for high-lofted woods will be the same as above, based on assembly to standard ladies playing lengths.

* The tip trimming amounts listed in this chart are to be made in addition to the amount prescribed for each parallel tip steel shaft #7-wood.

Do not perform additional tip trimming for high-lofted woods when using any of the special steel tip-rein-forced (e.g. UDWSH, etc.) metal wood shafts. The tip section of the special tip-reinforced steel shafts is so short that any additional tip trimming will prevent the shaft from being installed in the hosel.

For standard shaft installation into high-lofted woods, because the playing length will be achieved by trimming from the butt after tip trimming and installation, it is possible that so much of the butt section will be trimmed that the butt will be reduced in diameter from its original size. Reduction in the butt diameter will affect grip sizing so when assembling high-lofted woods be sure to measure the butt diameter after all trimming is complete to be able to select the proper core size and thus ensure the proper grip sizing and installation.

Taper Tip Steel Shaft Trimming for High-Lofted Woods

The shortest taper tip raw length shaft for woods is the 42" version, the shaft that would normally be chosen for use in the #5-wood. Most of the taper tip shaft trimming charts for #1-7 woodheads have given clubmakers the option for #7-wood installation of installing the 42" raw length shaft with either 0" or 1" additional tip trimming over the #5-wood. For the assembly of high-lofted #8-15 woods with taper tip shafts, it is simply recommended to install the shafts with the same tip trimming that was performed for the #7-wood. After installation, the playing length of the woods will be achieved by trimming from the butt.

Parallel Tip Graphite Shaft Trimming for High-Lofted Woods

Because of the limited parallel tip section length on graphite and composite shafts, regardless of the playing lengths used for the #8-15 woods, no further tip trimming is advised in addition to what was performed for the #7-wood. Because the butt end of the shaft will be successively trimmed to achieve the various high lofted wood playing lengths, it is accepted that this butt trimming will stiffen the shaft sufficiently.

■ SHAFT INSTALLATION PRINCIPLES FOR THROUGH-BORE IRONS

All shaft installation and trimming guidelines for ironheads are based upon the standard bottom of bore to back edge of heel dimension of 1". While allowances have been discussed for ironhead hosel designs that have a bottom of bore to heel dimension greater than 1"(uniform shaft mounting), no guidelines have been set for proper shaft installation when the bottom of bore to heel distance is less than the 1" standard.

In the late 1980s, a number of through-bore and very deep hosel bore ironhead designs began to appear, all with the similarity that the bottom of bore to heel dimension was much less than the existing 1" standard upon which standard shaft tip trimming is based. Because using normal shaft installation principles with through-bore and deep bore ironheads will result in the shafts all playing much stiffer than designed, clubmakers must learn how to make trimming and installation adjustments when assembling these types of ironheads.

The key to proper deep bore ironhead installation will be to know when it will be necessary to select a flex that is one flex level softer in stiffness than what is desired in the finished golf club, and then how to perform modified tip trimming to bring the flex back to the desired level. For example, if the deep bore irons include a full set of #1-iron through the wedges and are to be built to play to an R-flex, the clubmaker will have to start with an A-flex and perform tip trimming so that the finished clubs will end up as an R-flex. However, if the deep bore set does not include a #1 or 2-iron, the irons can be built with an R-flex shaft and still end up as an R-flex in the finished clubs. For ease of explanation, when assembling parallel tip through-bore or deep bore irons, use the procedures outlined in the following charts. Please note the charts are set up to guide installation of common steel shafts into deep bore type ironheads. For a full through-bore iron design, in which the shaft actually penetrates through the sole, 1/2" may be subtracted from each tip trimming entry to standardize the flex feel.

■ DEEP BORE IRON SHAFT INSTALLATION

Using an A & L Combination Flex Steel Shaft

Iron	To Achieve R-Flex Deep Bore Tip Trim	To Achieve A-Flex Deep Bore Tip Trim	To Achieve R-Flex Through-Bore Tip Trim	To Achieve A-Flex Through-Bore Tip Trim
1i	2"	0"	1 1/2"	0"
2i	2 1/2"	1/2"	2"	0"
3i	3"	1"	2 1/2"	1/2"
4i	3 1/2"	1 1/2"	3"	1"
5i	4"	2"	3 1/2"	1 1/2"
6i	4 1/2"	2 1/2"	4"	2"
7i	5"	3"	4 1/2"	2 1/2"
8i	5 1/2"	3 1/2"	5"	3"
9i	6"	4"	5 1/2"	3 1/2"
Wedges	6 1/2"	4 1/2"	6"	4"

After tip trimming and installation, measure and trim from the butt end for the desired playing length. For full through-bore ironheads, the shaft tip will have to be ground, sanded or filed flush to the sole and filled with a rubber or wooden plug.

Using an R & S Combination Flex Steel Shaft

Iron	To Achieve R-Flex Deep Bore Tip Trim	To Achieve S-Flex Deep Bore Tip Trim	To Achieve R-Flex Through-Bore Tip Trim	To Achieve S-Flex Through-Bore Tip Trim
1i	N/A[1]	1"	N/A[1]	1/2"
2i	N/A[1]	1 1/2"	N/A[1]	1"
3i	0"	2"	0"	1 1/2"
4i	1/2"	2 1/2"	0"	2"
5i	1"	3"	1/2"	2 1/2"
6i	2 1/2"	3 1/2"	1"	3"
7i	3"	4"	1 1/2"	3 1/2"
8i	3 1/2"	4 1/2"	2"	4"
9i	4"	5"	2 1/2"	4 1/2"
Wedges	4 1/2"	5 1/2"	3"	5"
			3 1/2"	
			4"	

[1] Using an R&S Combination Flex Steel Shaft in deep bore #1 and 2-irons will result in a flex much stiffer than an R-Flex and is not recommended.

After tip trimming and installation, measure and trim from the butt end for the desired playing length. For full through-bore ironheads, the shaft tip will have to be ground flush to the sole and filled with a rubber or wooden plug.

■ SHAFT PLAYING LENGTHS FOR LONGER OR SHORTER THAN STANDARD

In the course of building custom-made sets of golf clubs, there may be times a player will issue a request for clubs that are built to playing lengths longer or shorter than standard. All of the shaft trimming and installation charts contained in Chapter 3 outline the recommended trimming procedures based on assembling golf clubs to men's standard as well as ladies standard and petite playing lengths. For full understanding, the accepted standard playing lengths for golf clubs are defined as follows:

MEN'S Modern Standard Playing Lengths

Wood	Standard Length	Iron	Standard Length
1w	43"	1i	39 1/2"
2w	42 1/2"	2i	39"
3w	42"	3i	38 1/2"
4w	41 1/2"	4i	38"
5w	41"	5i	37 1/2"
6w	40 1/2"	6i	37"
7w	40"	7i	36 1/2"
		8i	36"
		9i	35 1/2"
		Wedges[1]	35 1/2"

LADIES Standard Playing Lengths

Wood	Standard Length	Iron	Standard Length
1w	42"	1i	38 1/2"
2w	41 1/2"	2i	38"
3w	41"	3i	37 1/2"
4w	40 1/2"	4i	37"
5w	40"	5i	36 1/2"
6w	39 1/2"	6i	36"
7w	39"	7i	35 1/2"
		8i	35"
		9i	34 1/2"
		Wedges[1]	34 1/2"

LADIES Petite Lengths (5'3" or less in height)

Wood	Petite Length	Iron	Petite Length
1w	41 1/2"	1i	38"
2w	41"	2i	37 1/2"
3w	40 1/2"	3i	37"
4w	40"	4i	36 1/2"
5w	39 1/2"	5i	36"
6w	39"	6i	35 1/2"
7w	38 1/2"	7i	35"
		8i	34 1/2"
		9i	34"
		Wedges[1]	34"

[1] Wedges may vary slightly in length as per the custom of the player or the clubmaking company. For example, while the length of most pitching wedges is 35 1/2", some sand wedges and utility wedges (high loft) are made to 35 1/4" or 35".

Recent studies of shaft flexibility as expressed through shaft vibrational frequency measurements have shown that the previous practice of trimming extra amounts from the tip for playing lengths longer than standard is wrong. To illustrate why increased tip trimming for playing lengths greater than standard is not to be done, first study Graph 1 at right, illustrating shaft frequency within a set of woods and irons.

On the graph it can be seen within a matched set of woods and irons, as length increases the shaft frequency decreases. This is the normal situation in a set and illustrates the shaft-to-shaft progression of flex that all golfers have used within their sets for years. While the graphs of the woods and irons stop at 43" and 39" respectively, it can be seen that the 43" #1-wood has the lowest frequency of all the woods and the

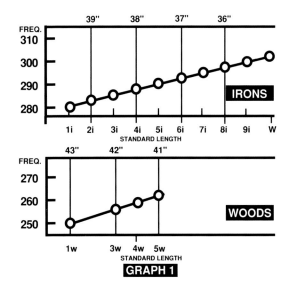

GRAPH 1

39 1/2" #`1-iron has the lowest frequency of all the irons. To illustrate the point to be made about shaft installation for longer golf clubs, study the extensions that have been added to Graph 2 on page 127.

The same graph of frequency for the woods and irons that was shown before has been extended to illustrate a set assembled to +1/2" longer playing length. Notice the points that represent the frequency of a 43 1/2" #1-wood and a 40" #1-iron on the graph. For the woods and for the irons, these two points represent a Driver and #1-iron that have been built 1/2" longer than men's standard length. As illustrated by the dotted straight line drawn through all the points on both graphs, the +1/2" longer Driver and #1-iron are a match in the sequence of frequency to all the other clubs in the set, yet they have a lower frequency than the 43" #1-wood

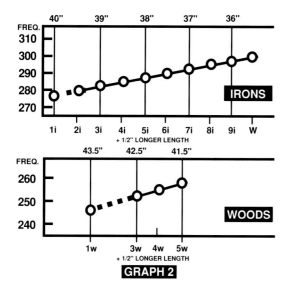

GRAPH 2

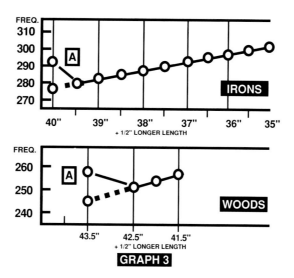

GRAPH 3

and the 39 1/2" #1-iron from Graph 1.

Note the position of the points marked with the letter A on Graph 3 for the set of woods and set of irons. The two points marked by the letter A represent a Driver and #1-iron that were also built 1/2" longer in playing length, **but with the shaft additionally tip trimmed by 1/2" over what was the standard tip trimming for the standard length Driver and #1-iron.** As the graph shows, this 1/2" longer Driver and #1-iron do not match the frequency slope of the rest of the clubs. In fact, by tip trimming the additional 1/2" the clubs have been made stiffer than what they should be in relation to the rest of the woods and irons. Therefore, the old practice of increasing the tip trimming by the amount equal to the length increase is not the proper way to install shafts when longer clubs are desired.

Instead, to retain the closest flex feel and shaft playability when building golf clubs to playing lengths that are longer or shorter than standard length, do not think of trimming in terms of the clubhead's number, but rather think of the trimming in terms of the length. To clarify, look again at Graph 3. The graph has been reproduced but without the clubhead numbers listed beside the playing lengths.

In the first graph, the 43" length and corresponding frequency were assigned to the Driver, because standard length for the Driver is 43". But if a clubmaker wished to assemble a #3-wood for a player to be 1" longer, that #3-wood would be 43" as well. At that 1" longer length the #3-wood should then have the same frequency as a standard length Driver. Therefore, the tip trimming for a +1" overlength men's #3-wood should be the same as the that for a standard 43" Driver.

Another way to express this comparison of frequency and trimming to length can be seen by studying the shaft trimming chart QQ for the Sandvik TI Titanium shafts for woods. In the trimming chart, Sandvik has not indicated the proper trimming by clubhead, but rather has indicated what the trimming should be for a particular length. Therefore regardless whether the Driver is being built to be 43 1/2", 43", 42 1/2" or whatever length, the chart indicates the amount to trim for the desired length, not the amount to trim for a Driver.

To apply this principle to all shafts, simply turn to the chart for the shaft being installed and apply the standard length dimensions to the entries for #1-wood, 2-wood, 3-wood and so on for all the woods and then for all the irons. Turning the chart into trimming by length instead of by clubhead number will then allow you to understand the trimming for any particular combination of playing length. For example, on the following page is the standard shaft trimming and installation for R&S Combination flex shafts for woods, altered to replace the clubhead numbers with lengths.

■ OVERLENGTH/UNDERLENGTH SHAFT TRIMMING FOR R & S COMBINATION FLEX STEEL SHAFTS FOR WOODS

Tip Trim	Golf Club Playing Length					
	Through-Bore		Blind Bore		Metal Woods	
	R	S	R	S	R	S
0"	43"	**45"**	**43.5"**	**45.5"**	**45"**	47"
1/2"	42.5"	**44.5"**	43"	**45"**	**44.5"**	46.5"
1"	42"	**44"**	42.5"	**44.5"**	**44"**	46"
1 1/2"	41.5"	**43.5"**	42"	**44"**	**43.5"**	45.5"
2"	41"	43"	41.5"	**43.5"**	43"	**45"**
2 1/2"	40.5"	42.5"	41"	43"	42.5"	**44.5"**
3"	40"	42"	40.5"	42.5"	42"	**44"**
3 1/2"		41.5"	40"	42"	41.5"	**43.5"**
4"		41"		41.5"	41"	43"
4 1/2"		40.5"		41"	40.5"	42.5"
5"		40"		40.5"	40"	42"
5 1/2"				40"		41.5"
6"						41"
6 1/2"						40.5"
7"						40"

Note: After tip trimming and installation of the shaft, measure and cut for the desired playing length of the woods from the butt end of the shaft. Also note the bold face length entires in the chart. These entires represent the tip trimming from R & S combination flex parallel tip steel shafts for the lengths indicated (e.g. for the S-flex in a through-bore wood, tip trim 1" to make a 44" wood).

The installation of parallel tip combination R & S flex steel shafts for woods and irons for over/under standard lengths should be thought of as a product of length and not the clubhead number. For example, a wood with a playing length of 43" is most often a standard length Driver; however, it could also be a 1" longer #3-wood, a 1 1/2" longer #4-wood, a 2" longer #5-wood, etc. For all those example cases the tip trimming would be the same. Therefore, regardless of the number on the woodhead, follow the tip trimming indicated in the chart for the length of wood desired.

To apply the same principle for longer or shorter length assembly for irons requires only that the same shift from clubhead number to length be done in the trimming charts. Just as the head number entries were shifted to lengths in the above chart for woodheads, so to would the same change be made for the irons. Therefore, the trimming chart for iron playing lengths longer or shorter than standard for R & S combination flex parallel tip steel shafts would appear as follows on Page 129:

■ OVERLENGTH/UNDERLENGTH SHAFT TRIMMING FOR R & S COMBINATION FLEX STEEL SHAFTS FOR IRONS

Tip Trim	Golf Club Playing Length	
	R-flex	S-flex
0"	39.5"	
1/2"	39"	
1"	38.5"	
1 1/2"	38"	
2"	37.5"	39.5"
2 1/2"	37"	39"
3"	36.5"	38.5"
3 1/2"	36"	38"
4"	35.5"	37.5"
4 1/2"	35"	37"
5"		36.5"
5 1/2"		36"
6"		35.5"
6 1/2"		35"

After tip trimming and installation, measure and cut from the butt end for the playing length.

Again, the same logic used in the overlength/underlength wood trimming chart can be used to clarify the trimming for over/underlength iron clubs. For example, regardless of club number, any iron club that is to be made 39" long with an R & S combination flex parallel tip steel iron shaft would be tip trimmed 1/2" for the R-flex and 2 1/2" for the S-flex. So whether that 39" club was a -1/2" underlength #1-iron, a standard length #2-iron, a +1/2" overlength #3-iron, a +1" overlength #4-iron, a +1 1/2" overlength #5-iron, etc., the tip trim for the R-flex of any R & S combination flex parallel tip steel iron shaft would be 1/2".

When the situation arises that the length is longer than the first 0" tip trim entry on the trimming chart (i.e. on the above chart a 40" R-flex iron) all that can be done when playing the R&S Combination flex type shafts is to keep the tip trim at 0". For example, consider what the full set trimming would be for a golfer who wishes to have a set that starts with a 40" #1-iron, with all other irons made to the customary 1/2" progression of playing length. The tip trim for the R-flex of any R & S combination flex parallel tip steel iron shaft would be 0" for the #1 and the #2-iron. While the frequency

progression will not be perfect between the #1 and #2-irons, when compared to the other clubs in the set, the frequency of the #1-iron would still be lower than the frequency of the #2-iron because the #1-iron is longer by 1/2".

Before continuing the discussion of other special shaft trimming situations, be sure to understand that over/underlength shaft trimming needs to be first referenced to the length and not the clubhead's number.

Shaft Installation to "In-Between" Flexes

Each of the shaft manufacturers produce their common pattern steel shafts in the five basic flexes of L, A, R, S and X. In addition, a few shafts are manufactured to what are called, "in-between" flexes. For example, the Apollo MatchFlex pattern is offered in the normal flexes of R and S as well as two "in-between" flexes. The MatchFlex A/R is halfway between the normal A and normal R in stiffness and the MatchFlex R/S represents a flex that is in-between the standard R and standard S.

While the five basic shaft flex levels are sufficient for satisfying the relative stiffness needs of the vast majority of golfers, clubmakers will occasionally be faced with having to install shafts for some customers to achieve a flex that is in-between two adjacent flex levels. To be able to accurately install shafts to levels of stiffness that are "in-between" adjacent flexes requires a full understanding of the principles of standard shaft flex installation, the effect of different hosel bore designs on shaft flex, and the difference between two flexes within different shaft designs.

In this chapter information has been provided to teach standard shaft trimming and installation, including a discussion on how adjustments must be made in shaft trimming due to the differences in bottom of bore to sole/heel dimensions of woods and ironheads. The third requirement for understanding how to accurately install shafts to "in-between" flex levels is knowing the difference between two flexes in a shaft. Such knowledge of how close any two adjacent flexes may be in stiffness to each other is very important because of differences in the actual design and manufacture of shafts.

The exact difference between any two flexes varies for the different types and patterns of shafts. In approximate terms, for most common pattern steel shafts, a change in tip section length of 2" will be equivalent to

one full flex; in other words, trimming an additional 2" from the tip of most common pattern steel shafts over the normal trimming will cause the shaft to become one full flex stiffer.

For example, the UDWX, UDWS, and UDWR shafts are all 45" in raw length, with 1 7/8" long steps, produced with a .335" parallel tip and a .600" butt diameter. The tip section of the UDWX is 8 1/2", the UDWS is 10 1/2" and the UDWR is 12 1/2". Therefore, if you tip trim 4" from the UDWR, it will have approximately the same flex as the UDWX. If you tip trim 2" from the UDWR it will closely approximate the flex of the UDWS, to complete the example.

However, this 2" rule is not true for all shafts. For example, in the case of the UDWAL, (Combination A & L flex Dynamic pattern from True Temper), the difference in one full flex is only 1". In other words, if a 46" raw length UDWAL is tip trimmed 1", it will become a 45" raw length UDWA shaft. Hence if the UDWR is tip trimmed 1", or accordingly if the UDWAL is tip trimmed 1/2", both shafts will end up in raw form to be halfway between R and S, and then A and L respectively.

Noting the actual difference in flex between one shaft and another is important because it will determine the effect additional tip trimming will have on shaft flex and feel. Tip trimming an additional 1" from the UDWR will effectively make the shaft play halfway between a normal R and S flex. However, a 1" extra tip trim will not achieve an in-between flex for all shafts. If it were incorrectly assumed that the difference between any two flexes in all shafts was 2", serious mistakes in mounting would occur. For example, tip trimming an additional 1" from a parallel tip L-flex shaft to achieve a flex halfway between L and A would not deliver the expected result, since in the case of A/L combination flex shafts, a 1" tip trim would make the L-flex increase in stiffness all the way up to an A-flex.

Clubmakers can determine the difference between two

flexes within a combination flex pattern by studying a listing of the tip section length of various shafts. By noting the difference in tip section length between any two flexes in each shaft design, it will be possible to gauge the amount of tip trimming to achieve different versions in-between two flexes. Pages 131-132 feature a chart of the raw tip section length of many of the current popular shafts. The third column shows the shaft flex from which to tip trim the extra amount to achieve the in-between flex. The fourth column indicates the amount to tip trim extra for each clubhead in addition to the normal tip trimming. The last column indicates the in-between flex that will be achieved through the procedure.

Shaft Installation To "In-Between" Flexes

Shaft Pattern	Tip Section Length	Use This Shaft With	Tip Trim This Much Extra*	To Achieve This In-Between Flex
True Temper				
Dynamic Gold R woods (all sub flexes)	12 1/2"	DGWR	1"	R/S
Dynamic Gold S woods (all sub flexes)	10 1/2"	DGWS	1"	S/X
Dynamic Gold R irons (all sub flexes)	12 1/4"	DGIR	1"	R/S
Dynamic Gold S irons (all sub flexes)	10 1/4"	DGIS	1"	S/X
Dynamic L woods	13 1/4"	UDWAL	1/2"	L/A
Dynamic A woods	12 1/4"	UDWAL	1/2"	A/R
Dynamic R woods	12 1/2"	UDWC	1"	R/S
Dynamic S woods	10 1/2"	UDWC	1"	S/X
Dynamic X woods	8 1/2"	UDWX	1"	X/XX
Dynamic L irons	14 7/8"	UDIAL	1/2"	L/A
Dynamic A irons	13 7/8"	UDIAL	1/2"	A/R
Dynamic R irons	12 1/4"	UDIC	1"	R/S
Dynamic S irons	10 1/4"	UDIC	1"	S/X
Dynamic X irons	8 1/4"	UDIX	1"	X/XX
TT Lite L flex woods	13 1/2"	UTTLWAL	1/2"	L/A
TT Lite A flex woods	12 1/2"	UTTLWAL	1/2"	A/R
TT Lite R flex woods	12 1/2"	UTTLWC	1"	R/S
TT Lite S flex woods	10 1/2"	UTTLWC	1"	S/X
TT Lite L flex irons	11 1/2"	UTTLIAL	1/2"	L/A
TT Lite A flex irons	10 1/2"	UTTLIAL	1/2"	A/R
TT Lite R flex irons	11"	UTTLIC	1"	R/S
TT Lite S flex irons	9"	UTTLIC	1"	S/X
Brunswick Shaft				
Microtaper L flex woods	15 1/2"	8656WAL	1/2"	L/A
Microtaper A flex woods	14 1/2"	8656WAL	1/2"	A/R
Microtaper R flex woods	14 1/4"	8676WRS	1"	R/S
Microtaper S flex woods	12 1/4"	8676WRS	1"	S/X

*Column indicates additional tip trimming, added to the normal amount to trim for each clubhead. E.G. If a UDIC is to be tip trimmed 4" for an S-flex #5-iron, for the flex in between R and S, trim 1" more for a total of 5".

Shaft Installation To "In-Between" Flexes (cont'd.)

Shaft Pattern	Tip Section Length	Use This Shaft With	Tip Trim This Much Extra*	To Achieve This In-Between Flex
Apollo Shaft				
AP44 R woods	12 1/2"	AP44WRS	1"	R/S
AP44 S woods	10 1/2"	AP44WRS	1"	S/X
AP44 R irons	12 1/4"	AP44IRS	1"	R/S
AP44 S irons	10 1/4"	AP44IRS	1"	S/X
Spectre L woods	11"	SPWAL	1/2"	L/A
Spectre A woods	10"	SPWAL	1/2"	A/R
Spectre R woods	12 1/2"	SPWRS	1"	R/S
Spectre S woods	10 1/2"	SPWRS	1"	S/X
Spectre L irons	11 1/2"	SPIAL	1/2"	L/A
Spectre A irons	10 1/2"	SPIAL	1/2"	A/R
Spectre R irons	13 1/2"	SPIRS	1"	R/S
Spectre S irons	11 1/2"	SPIRS	1"	S/X

*Column indicates additional tip trimming, added to the normal amount to trim for each clubhead. E.G. If a UDIC is to be tip trimmed 4" for an S-flex #5-iron, for the flex in between R and S, trim 1" more for a total of 5".

Rules For Tip Trimming to Achieve "In-Between" Flexes

1. For common pattern steel shafts where the difference between two flexes is 2", an additional tip trim of 1/2" = 1/4 flex stiffer; additional tip trim of 1"= 1/2 flex stiffer; additional tip trim of 1 1/2"=3/4 flex stiffer; additional tip trim of 2"=1 flex stiffer.

NOTE: Again, this is in reference to **additional** tip trimming in excess of what is necessary to achieve standard mounting for each clubhead.

2. For common pattern steel shafts where the difference between two flexes is 1", an additional tip trim of 1/4"=1/4 flex stiffer; additional tip trim of 1/2"=1/2 flex stiffer; additional tip trim of 3/4"=3/4 flex stiffer; additional tip trim of 1"=1 flex stiffer.

NOTE: Again, this is in reference to **additional** tip trimming in excess of what is necessary to achieve standard mounting for each clubhead.

The Principles Of Shaft Installation

The preceding portion of Chapter 3 has dealt with the technical side of shafts, imparting the information that is necessary to ensure a full understanding of shafts and the proper trimming of shafts as a part of clubmaking. While this information is of great importance, it is of no use if the proper techniques for physically installing the shafts into clubheads are not employed. For clubmakers, having a head come loose from the shaft is not only embarrassing, but is as close to an unforgivable sin as exists in clubmaking. Therefore, the final section of this chapter will deal with the proper techniques to ensure adequate bonding of the clubhead to the shaft. In the upcoming chapters dealing with the step-by-step procedures of assembly, when in doubt of the detailed steps for actually securing the shaft to the clubhead, refer back to this section.

The first task of installing the shaft into the clubhead is to determine the correct procedures of trimming for each shaft in the set of clubs. Since this is obviously a step that requires understanding the trimming procedures for a great number of shaft patterns, a large portion of this chapter has been devoted to how all the different kinds of shafts are trimmed. Once the trimming is known and the shafts are ready to be trimmed and installed into the clubheads, the installation procedures revert to the actual physical techniques of securing the shafts to the clubheads. This procedure of attaching the head to the shaft involves the following steps:

1. Cutting the shafts
2. Abrading or crimping the portion of the shaft tip that will be inserted in the hosel
3. Installing the proper size and type of ferrule (if a ferrule is required in the assembly)
4. Selecting and properly mixing the shafting epoxy
5. Inserting and seating the shaft in the head
6. Cleaning up and double checking the shaft installation

■ METHODS OF SHAFT CUTTING

In the assembly of golf clubs, clubmakers will install shafts made from a variety of different materials; carbon steel, steel alloys, titanium, graphite and other composite materials. Standard weight carbon steel, lightweight steel alloy and titanium shafts can be cut with a variety of tools, from a simple tubing cutter to a more sophisticated abrasive cut-off saw. In contrast, graphite and composite-type shafts are best cut by abrasive cutting devices to prevent splintering the shafts. Which tool or method is used will be dependent on what level of tool investment has been made in the shop, as well as what shaft materials are going to be cut.

Manual methods of cutting shafts such as tubing cutters or hacksaws are the slowest and most tedious ways to cut shafts. Using a tube cutter to trim steel shafts will require repeated steps of tightening and turning the tool, with another drawback being the fact the small cutter wheels have a tendency to wear out quickly. Tube cutters should never be used to cut graphite, fiberglass composite or graphite over steel shafts or splintering of the shaft can occur. While using a hacksaw is a good method to cut graphite and composite shafts, it is not recommended for cutting steel shafts because it is very time consuming and tiring. Therefore, it is recommended that all clubmakers invest in some type of motor driven method for cutting shafts.

1. Tube Cutter, Hacksaw
When using a tube cutter, care must be taken not to over tighten the cutter or longitudinal cracking of the shaft can result.

2. Bench Grinder with Friction Wheel
Bench grinders are relatively inexpensive, but for friction shaft cutting purposes a 3450 RPM machine of at least 1/2 horsepower is needed to prevent stalling of the motor during the cutting operation. A friction cut-off wheel is a non-abrasive steel disc that requires the clubmaker to apply the force to push the shaft through the wheel. The friction created by physically pushing the shaft through the rapidly rotating steel wheel is what cuts the shaft, with the advantage being that the wheel lasts for a very long time before wearing out. The only disadvantages of a friction cut-off wheel are that it leaves a substantial metal burr on the shaft that must be

METHODS OF SHAFT CUTTING	
Shaft Material	**Acceptable Methods of Cutting**
Standard Weight Carbon Steel	Tube cutter, friction cut-off wheel, abrasive cut-off wheel
Lightweight Steel	Tube cutter, friction cut-off wheel, abrasive cut-off wheel
Very Lightweight Steel	Friction cut-off wheel, abrasive cut-off wheel, tubing cutter
Titanium	Tube cutter, friction cut-off wheel, abrasive cut-off wheel
Graphite, Composites	Hacksaw, abrasive cut-off wheel

removed in a separate operation, and the force required to push the shaft through the wheel can stall even some 1/2 HP size grinders. In addition, friction cut-off wheels are not acceptable for cutting non-steel shafts as graphite or fiberglass composites.

2. Bench Grinder with Abrasive Cut-Off Wheel

One of the best methods of cutting shafts for small and medium size shops is to use an abrasive type metal cutting wheel attached to your bench grinder. As with the friction cut-off wheel, it is still recommended to use a 3,450 RPM, 1/2 HP grinder to keep the quality of the cut with the abrasive cutting wheel smooth and clean. When selecting an abrasive wheel, choose one that is rated for Ferrous metal cutting, as this type of cut-off wheel is designed to last longer when cutting any type of steel shaft. With an abrasive cut-off wheel, very little force is required to cut through the shaft, since the grit of the wheel supplies the cutting action. Abrasive wheels can be used to cut all types of shafts, from steel to titanium to graphite and composites.

4. Cut-Off Power Saw or Radial Arm Saw with Abrasive Wheel

Larger clubmaking shops should use a lever-arm cut-off saw or radial arm saw mounted with an abrasive cutting wheel to cut shafts. With the abrasive wheel replacing the saw blade, these machines can provide the fastest, most efficient way to cut all types of shafts. One additional plus in favor of the radial arm saw method of shaft cutting is that you can set up a special shaft positioning jig under the saw to enable cutting entire sets of shafts with one pass of the saw. This is the method used by many large manufacturers, so if you already own such a saw this is definitely the procedure to use.

When using any type of power driven shaft cutting device, <u>always</u> wear safety goggles or glasses with side eye protection flaps.

Regardless of which method for cutting shafts is used, there are a few techniques that must be observed to ensure professional quality.

1. Cut shafts as straight and accurately as possible

After marking each shaft for trimming, care must be taken to cut the shaft as straight and as close as possible to the exact length desired. With a tubing cutter, avoid overtightening the wheel on the shaft, as this can make the cutter "walk up the shaft" and miss the exact mark for cutting. In addition, overtightening the tubing cutter can place undue stress on the shaft, thus resulting in a longitudinal cracking of the shaft. On very light steel shafts such as Gold Plus, UCV-304 or Acculite, overtightening the tube cutter can crack the shaft due to the slightly more brittle nature of the alloys from which the shafts are made, or the fact that these types of shafts often have thinner walls as a part of their design. When using motorized cutting devices, ensure a straight cut by always keeping the shaft perpendicular to the cutting wheel. Failure to do so will result in shafts that are cut with a jagged end which eventually could cut through the end cap of the grip.

2. Deburr all shafts after cutting

Most methods of motorized shaft cutting will leave some type of metal burr around the edge of the cut. As a rule, shafts cut with the friction cut-off wheel will have more pronounced burrs than shafts cut with an abrasive cutting wheel. Either by turning the cut ends of the shaft against a sanding belt, grinder stone or wire brush wheel, or by manually scraping the inside edges of the shaft, these metal particles must be removed before installing the shafts. Not removing all of the burrs from the edges of the cut can result in the metal particles breaking loose and causing rattles inside the shaft after the club goes into play.

3. Avoid leaving sharp edges on the shafts

The thin wall nature of steel shafts coupled with the procedures of cutting and deburring can leave the cut ends of the shaft razor sharp. Before installing the tip end in the hosel and the grip over the butt end, get in the

habit of blunting off all cut edges of the shaft. Blunting the tip end can prevent hand injuries should you accidentally jam your hand against one of the cut ends during installation. Blunting off the butt end will prevent the shaft from cutting through a rubber grip cap. Blunting off the ends of the shaft after cutting is performed by filing across the ends of the shaft or by pushing the cut ends of the shaft flat against a belt sander, thus flattening off the cut (the only time a sharp edge on the butt end can help during clubmaking is when installing a plastic grip cap, since a sharp edge can actually help secure the cap by "digging" into its under side).

■ ABRADING THE SHAFT TIP FOR INSTALLATION

High-strength epoxies that are used to bond the shaft and clubhead together do not have the ability to adhere properly to smooth, polished surfaces. Therefore, for the epoxy to secure the shaft to the clubhead, the chrome plating (steel shafts) or urethane-type coating (graphite and composite shafts) of the tip portion must be adequately scratched or abraded. The degree

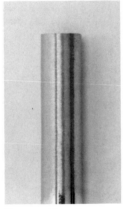

Proper Abrasion   *Improper Abrasion*

of shaft tip abrasion that is necessary for proper adhesion is a point that is often underestimated by many inexperienced clubmakers. Too many times the epoxy bond between the shaft and the head fails because of inadequate abrasion of the shaft tip on the part of the clubmaker. The following photos illustrate the difference between what is and what is not considered adequate shaft tip abrasion.

As in the case of cutting shafts, there are several methods that can be used to abrade the tip of the shaft prior to assembly. While tip abrasion can be performed by hand sanding or filing, it is highly recommended that clubmakers consider investing in some type of motorized sanding equipment such as a belt sander to perform this task. A belt sander will not only do the job faster, but will do a better job of adequately abrading the shaft tip. The pros and cons of the various types of shaft tip abrading are discussed as follows:

1. Sandpaper

By far the least expensive but most time consuming method of shaft tip abrading involves hand sanding with strips of coarse sandpaper. 1" wide strips of a minimum of 80 grit, cloth-backed sandpaper can be used to sand the tip of the shaft, while the shaft is secured in a bench vise. 100 or 120 grit sandpaper is just not coarse enough to do the job when sanding by hand. Hand sanding is not a preferred method for preparing steel shafts, because the chrome plating on the shaft tip is very hard and difficult to abrade through. However, hand sanding is a satisfactory way to abrade graphite shafts, since the sandpaper will sufficiently cut through the shafts' urethane coating.

2. Hand Filing

Another manual procedure that has been used by clubmakers to abrade the tip of the shaft is hand filing. Filing is considered the least effective of all methods because with chrome plated steel shafts, it is very difficult to fully abrade the entire shaft tip area, and with graphite shafts, there is a risk of filing a notch or groove in the shaft that could later lead to shaft fracture.

3. Bench Grinder Stone

Many clubmakers will try to get "double duty" out of their motorized bench grinder by using the edge of the grinder stone to abrade the tip of the shaft. Again, because it is very difficult to achieve total abrasion of the tip of the shaft and because there is a risk of making

a potentially damaging notch or groove on both steel and graphite shafts, using a bench grinder stone is not considered a professional way to prepare the shaft tip for assembly.

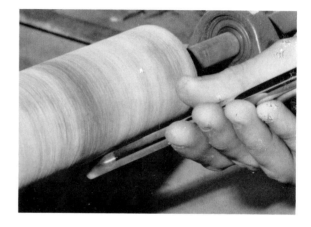

4. Woodhead Sanding Machine

Clubmaking shops that use a woodhead sanding machine for wooden head refinishing can also make use of this device for shaft tip abrasion as well. By attaching coarse (again, at least 80 grit) sandpaper to the machine, the correct level of abrasion can be achieved in a fast period of time. However, because the sanding would be performed by holding the shaft under the rotating drum (as pictured), it is difficult to see the part of the shaft being abraded. As a result, care must be taken not to sand too far up the tip of the shaft, thus leaving unsightly scratches exposed after the club is assembled.

5. Small Belt Sander

By far the best method for achieving professional quality shaft tip abrasion is to use a small belt sanding machine. The most popular belt sanding machines used by clubmakers are the 1" x 30", 1" x 42" or 2" x 48" size machines. By using a coarse or medium grit sanding belt (medium grit is acceptable because of the speed of the belt sanding machine), clubmakers can abrade shaft tips to the proper roughness and do so faster than with any other method. To avoid notching

or cutting a potentially damaging groove in the shaft, tip abrasion should always be performed on the flexible portion of the belt where there is no hard metal backing (platen) behind the abrasive belt.

Shaft Tip Crimping or Knurling

While adequate abrasion of the shaft tip is all that is required prior to epoxying the shaft into the clubhead, some clubmakers and manufacturers will also crimp the tip of shafts that are installed into metal woodheads and ironheads. Crimping involves slightly deforming the shaft tip for the purpose of creating a mechanical lock between the shaft and the clubhead. By slightly deforming the round shaft tip, such a procedure when completed is in essence, similar to inserting a square (crimped) shaft into a round hole (hosel). For example, when a taper tip iron shaft is installed into a tapered iron hosel, the tip of the shaft is designed so the shaft will not go all the way to the bottom of the bore simply under the force of normal hand insertion. To fully seat taper tip shafts, additional force is required to drive the shaft to the bottom of the bore. When this force fitting step is performed, the shaft tip actually forms a mechanical lock against the bottom diameter of the hosel that is tight enough that the shaft cannot be removed simply by hand twisting.

However, in the case of parallel shaft to parallel bore assembly, no such mechanical lock is designed to

assist in securing the shaft to the clubhead. Until the epoxy cures after insertion of the shaft, the clubhead could easily be pulled off the parallel tip shaft by hand. Therefore, in an effort to create a mechanical lock which will prevent the head from shifting or falling off the shaft until curing of the epoxy, some clubmakers choose to crimp the tips of steel shafts.

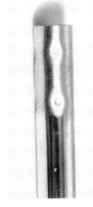

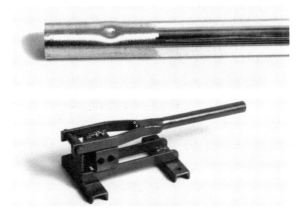

Although it is possible to deform the steel shaft tip by hand with a hammer and pin punch, crimping is usually performed with a special machine that is designed to squeeze small "dimples" into the sides of the shaft tip, thus deforming the tip in the process. Once the tip of the shaft has been crimped, it then must be driven into the hosel either with a driving plug or through the use of an air hammer. It is important for clubmakers to

understand that shaft crimping is not necessary for proper shaft installation. If the tip has been properly abraded and the shaft installed with the correct type of epoxy, the shaft-to-clubhead bond is considered adequate. The primary reason that shaft crimping is performed is so that manufacturers can save time by proceeding directly into the swingweighting and grip installation procedures without having to wait until the epoxy securing the shaft to the head has cured.

■ FERRULE INSTALLATION

If the hosel is produced with a rounded edge, the clubhead will not require the use of a ferrule. However, if the hosel is flat, with a square top edge shape, the clubhead has been designed to be assembled with a ferrule. The ferrule is simply a plastic trim piece that allows for a more aesthetically attractive transition from the hosel up to the shaft. When required on wooden or graphite woodheads, the ferrule provides a smooth transition for the string whipping to wind its way from the shaft down over the hosel. On metal woods or ironheads, the ferrule simply acts as a cosmetic trim piece for the golf club.

All ferrules must be installed after the shafts are tip trimmed but before they are installed into the clubhead. Clubmakers must understand that virtually all ferrules are designed oversize by nature. After shaft installation they must be filed or sanded down to meet the hosel and complete their assembly as part of the golf club. When selecting ferrules for golf club assembly, the requirement is to choose the type that is designed not only to fit the diameter of the shafts being used, but to suit the design of the clubhead as well. In clubmaking, the types of ferrules that will most often be encountered are:

1. Conventional Woodhead Ferrule

Available in a variety of sizes to fit the different shaft tip diameters that may be used, ferrules for conventional shaped woodheads (wooden, graphite, plastic woodheads) are intended to provide a smooth transition for the string whipping from the shaft down to the hosel. Therefore, conventional woodhead ferrules must be filed or sanded down in diameter along their entire length to provide this smooth taper over which the whipping will be wrapped.

2. Conventional Woodhead Ferrule with Shank

Similar to regular conventional woodhead ferrules that provide a foundation for the string whipping, shanked ferrules differ in that a small ledge is molded at the top (small end) of the ferrule to provide a starting point for the whipping. Because of this small ledge, all filing or sanding of shanked ferrules should be performed only at the bottom (large end) of the ferrule.

3. Metal Wood Ferrule

Metal wood ferrules are usually much shorter in length than their conventional wooden head counterparts, and should not be used on woodheads that require string whipping. Because no string whipping will be wrapped over, finishing of the metal wood ferrule is done strictly as a cosmetic operation, to sand or file the bottom diameter of the ferrule equal to the top of the hosel diameter and then return the ferrule to its original shine.

4. Ironhead/Putter Ferrule

Also installed for cosmetic purposes only, ferrules for ironheads and putters are never used in conjunction with string whipping. Therefore, ferrule dressing procedures are strictly performed to bring the bottom diameter of the ferrule equal to the top of the hosel diameter and to return the ferrule to its original shine.

Ferrule Installation Procedures

There are two primary methods of installing ferrules during the procedures of golf club assembly:

Methods of Ferrule Installation

Method #1

The ferrule is pushed only a short way on the tip of the shaft. During shaft installation the top of the hosel serves to drive the ferrule into its proper position as the shaft tip is pushed to the bottom of the bore.

Method #2.

A ferrule installing tool is used to push the ferrule into its permanent position on the shaft before the shaft is installed into the clubhead.

Method #1 is the recommended procedure to follow in clubmaking because it can take all possible variables of different hosel lengths and variations in bore depths within a set into account and puts the ferrules in exactly the proper position, snug against the top of the clubhead hosel. Too many times all of the careful calculations and calibration of ferrule setting tools go to waste when it is discovered that a clubhead's bore depth is slightly shorter than thought, thus leaving an unsightly gap between the ferrule and hosel.

The actual installation of the ferrule begins by sliding the ferrule over the shaft tip by hand, small end first. In the case of taper tip shafts, this is a very simple procedure since the bore of the ferrule is always larger than the tip end of the shaft. On taper tip shafts for woods, the ferrule will slide easily 2" or more up the shaft before it begins to become snug, and on taper tip iron shafts, the ferrule will glide up about 1" before stopping. From this point of snugness the procedure as described in Method #1 can be used to push the ferrule into its final position.

Installing ferrules on parallel tip shafts requires a little more work. Because the parallel tip shafts have one constant diameter from tip to first step down, the ferrule will be much more difficult to start over the tip and push up the shaft. To allow the insertion of the shaft into the hosel to drive the ferrule into position (Method #1) will require at least 1/2"-1" of the shaft tip to protrude out the bottom of the shaft before shaft installation. To install the parallel tip ferrule far enough onto the shaft to allow the top of the hosel to drive it up into place during shaft insertion, follow the steps detailed on page 138.

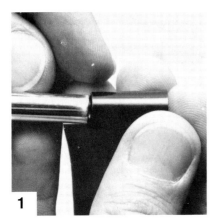

STEP 1: Twist the small end of the ferrule at least 1/8" onto the tip of the shaft by hand. Due to the tight nature of the fit, this will require some twisting force.

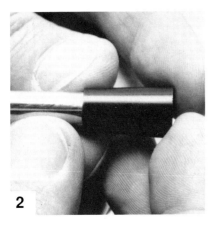

STEP 2: Straighten the ferrule so the bore of the ferrule is in the line with the tip of the shaft.

STEP 3: Place the butt of the shaft on the floor and use a rubber mallet to tap the ferrule about 1/4" further down onto the shaft. Stop and recheck the ferrule's alignment to the shaft, making sure it is not crooked. After re-aligning, use forceful blows with the rubber mallet to drive the ferrule all the way onto the shaft. Be sure to check the ferrule's alignment to the shaft after each blow.

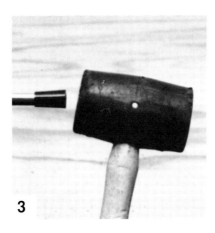

NOTE: The ferrule MUST be straight with respect to the shaft before and during the procedure of driving fully onto the shaft or the ferrule will be damaged and have to be replaced.

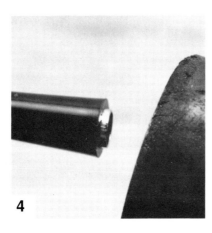

STEP 4: With the butt of the shaft still on the floor, hammer against the base of the ferrule until the tip of the shaft begins to penetrate into the soft face of the rubber mallet. This should leave the shaft tip protruding out about 1/8" to 1/4" from the bottom of the ferrule.

STEP 5: Make a wood block with two holes drilled through to match the various shaft tip diameters (3/8" hole for parallel iron shafts, 11/32" for parallel wood

shafts) and drive the ferrule @2" up the wood shaft and @1" up the iron shaft. The distance each ferrule needs to be driven up the shaft should only be far enough to allow Method #1 of ferrule installation during shaft insertion into the clubhead.

■ EPOXY BONDING THE SHAFT TO THE CLUBHEAD

Once the shafts have been properly prepared, the next procedure of shaft installation is to correctly choose, mix and apply the shafting epoxy.

Selecting the proper shafting epoxy is very important because it controls the bonding of the shaft to the clubhead. Granted, in the case of wooden woodheads with backscrews, irons that are to be pinned through the shaft, or force fit tapered hosel irons, the epoxy is not the only factor involved in securing the shaft to the head. But in the case of parallel shaft to parallel bore assembly, the most predominant form of shaft installation, unless crimping has been performed, the epoxy acts as the only means of securing the shaft and clubhead together.

While literally hundreds of different epoxies are available, clubmakers need to be aware of the requirements of a good shafting epoxy. To permanently secure shafts to clubheads, the epoxy should possess what is referred to as a high shear strength rating. Shear strength is defined as the amount of force required to twist or slide two bonded surfaces apart. Different from tensile strength and impact strength, shear strength most closely describes the type of bonding that takes place between the shaft and the clubhead. To be considered adequate for shaft installation, shafting epoxy must have a shear strength rating that is in excess of the force created between the head and the golf ball during the striking of the shot. At impact, tests have shown that as much as 2,000 lbs/sq. in. of force is exerted when the clubhead collides with the golf ball. Therefore, when selecting an epoxy for shaft installation, the shear strength rating must exceed at least 2,000 lbs/sq. in. Very few fast cure, or 5-minute epoxies that are available from local hardware stores possess a high shear strength rating, so it is much safer for clubmakers to source their shafting epoxy from a reputable clubmaking supplier. If you are unsure of the shear strength rating of the epoxy you are choosing to assemble golf clubs, be sure to ask the supplier for this information.

In addition to selecting an epoxy with adequate shear strength, it is absolutely necessary to become familiar with the mixing ratio of the shafting epoxy. Virtually all shafting epoxies are 2-part in nature, requiring a base and an activator to be combined before curing can commence. Depending upon the formulation of the epoxy, a variety of mixing ratios exist for combining the base and activator parts of epoxy, so it is very important to learn and follow the manufacturer's instructions for mixing. Some 2-part epoxies are mixed by weight and some are combined by volume, so it is a wise idea to test mix a batch and check it for hardness before ever using a new epoxy for clubmaking.

It is also vital to become familiar with both the "working life" and the "cure time" of the epoxy. An epoxy's working life is best defined as the length of time before the material's hardening process makes it too stiff to apply and use. An epoxy's working life becomes important when assembling large numbers of golf clubs at one time. If the number of clubs to be shafted will take longer

to assemble than what is the working time of the epoxy, less epoxy should be mixed at one time to avoid waste or an epoxy with a longer working life should be used. The cure time of an epoxy is the length of time required before the material has "cured" to its stated shear strength. While many varieties of epoxy do technically continue to harden for several days after the initial cure time has taken place, golf clubs should never be used until the proper minimum amount of cure time has passed.

Epoxy Application Methods

As with many procedures of clubmaking, there are several different acceptable methods for applying the epoxy to the shaft and the clubhead. Before applying the epoxy, always remember to first install any ferrules that may be required into place on the shaft. This will prevent the messy task of pulling the shaft and clubhead apart and trying to install a ferrule over uncured epoxy. The procedure you choose for epoxy application should be one that will enable you to properly coat all bonding surfaces in the shortest period of time. Some examples of acceptable epoxy application methods are:

1. Application of epoxy by mixing stick

The most thorough but slowest method of applying the epoxy to the shaft tip and inside the clubhead hosel is to use a 1/4" dowel or rod to smear the epoxy separately on the shaft tip and the inside of the hosel. While this method affords assurance that both surfaces are coated,

it does increase the time required to assemble sets of clubs.

2. Application of epoxy with the tip of the shaft

For speed, some clubmakers will dip a small portion of the shaft tip in the epoxy and then insert the shaft into the hosel with a rotating motion, thus relying on the shaft to do the job of coating the inside walls of the hosel. This method is completely acceptable providing the shaft is inserted slowly with a rotating motion.

Use of Bonding Additives with the Epoxy

To assist the bonding of the epoxy, some clubmakers introduce an additive (filler) such as silica sand to increase the bonding power of the epoxy. This can be done by pouring a small amount of sand in with the base and activator during the mixing of the epoxy, or by dipping the tip of the epoxied shaft tip into the sand just prior to insertion in the hosel. While not necessary given the availability of modern high strength epoxies, most clubmakers feel that the sand adds bonding strength to the epoxy which further ensures the permanent security of the shaft to the head. When choosing a sand, be sure to check the particle grit so it is fine enough to allow its positioning between the shaft tip and the inside walls of the hosel. Sand that is too coarse will simply be pushed to the bottom of the hosel by the shaft, thus negating its function in the operation. In addition, some grades of sand will crush into dust under the pressure of shaft insertion, rendering them less effective as a bonding additive.

■ SHAFT INSERTION INTO THE CLUBHEAD

The major goal when inserting the shaft into the hosel of the clubhead is to make sure that the shaft is properly seated to achieve the correct mounting that was set up as a result of the tip trimming. In the case of blind bore woodheads, short-bore metal woodheads, all ironheads and putters, this means that care must be taken to be sure the shaft has been installed all the way to the bottom of the bore. In the case of through-bore woods, the shaft must be installed so that it penetrates the proper amount through the bottom of the sole.

Parallel Tip Shaft Insertion

In the installation of parallel tip shafts into parallel bore clubheads, because both the bore of the clubhead and the tip section of the shaft are one constant diameter, inserting the shaft to achieve proper seating in the hosel is a very simple procedure. With the tip abraded and the shaft tip and inside hosel walls covered with a thin coating of epoxy, insert the shaft into the hosel and push it to the bottom of the bore, using a rotating motion. Rotating the shaft as it is pushed to the bottom of the bore will ensure that all surfaces of the hosel are coated with epoxy.

If the head requires a ferrule and the ferrule has not previously been pushed up the shaft into its final position before shaft installation, the shaft insertion procedure will require that the shaft be driven with force to bottom out in the hosel. The fastest way to drive the shaft into the hosel and with it, the ferrule up into its final position on the shaft, is to hold the shaft tight to the head while the butt of the shaft is driven firmly against a hard surface on the floor. Once the shaft is driven to the bottom of the bore, the ferrule will be automatically pushed up and into its final position. As a final check, hold the clubhead in one hand with the other hand on the shaft and tap the butt of the shaft one final time on the floor. This procedure will ensure that the shaft tip has reached its final position in the bottom of the bore. Photographs illustrating this

procedure can be found in Chapters 5-9.

Taper Tip Shaft Insertion

Proper seating and insertion of taper tip shafts into tapered hosels will require a little more care than for the previously described parallel tip method. For taper tip wood shaft assembly, first insert the shaft using a rotating motion. In most cases the shaft will glide down the hosel for only a few inches before it stops, due to the ferrule being stopped by the taper of the shaft. To push the shaft to the bottom of the bore will require forcefully driving the shaft into the hosel, thus pushing the ferrule up into position.

Seating the Shaft in the Hosel

If the shaft to hosel installation incorporates a ferrule in the assembly, force fitting techniques for shaft installation may be required due to the tightness of the ferrule on the shaft. Therefore, force fitting both parallel and taper tip shafts can be performed in the following ways.

1. Driving Plug

With the clubhead mounted in a bench vise protected by pads, a special tool called a driving plug is inserted into the butt of the shaft. The driving plug is hammered against the butt of the shaft, driving the shaft to the bottom of the hosel. In the process the ferrule will be pushed up to its permanent position on the shaft. Use of the driving plug method is very safe and effective, but it

is recommended primarily for use with irons, putters or blind bore type woods. A driving plug is not recommended for use with through-bore woods because there is a potential risk of driving the shaft too far through the head. For through-bore insertion, the hand driving method below is suggested.

2. Hand Driving

For purposes of speed, many clubmakers prefer to drive the shaft to the bottom of the bore by hand. After initial insertion of the shaft into the hosel, grasp the head in one hand, the shaft in the other hand, and while holding the shaft tight against the hosel, slam the butt of the shaft on a hard surface on the floor. Advantages to this method are that it is easy to "feel" when the shaft bottoms out in the hosel and, particularly with through-bore woods, it is possible to see when the shaft is about to penetrate through the sole.

NOTE: When using this method, do not begin tapping the butt of the shaft on the floor unless you have at least 1" of the iron shaft and 2" of the connectional wood shaft already inserted in the hosel. The motion of repeatedly slamming the butt of the shaft against the floor while holding the shaft tip in the hosel takes some practice to be able to keep the shaft in the hosel. Should the shaft tip come out of the hosel and be slammed back onto the floor before it is noticed, the shaft tip could possibly strike the hand holding the clubhead, thus causing a nasty cut.

Always keep the shaft and head tight together between impacts of the shaft butt on the floor.

In the case of through-bore wood assembly, after shaft insertion it is necessary to finish the job by tapping a wooden dowel plug into the tip of the shaft. Because the portion of the shaft tip that protrudes through the head will be filed or finished flush to the sole after the epoxy has cured, the plug will serve the purpose of filling the inside of the shaft. Specially-made tapered wood plugs are available from clubmaking component suppliers for the purpose.

■ CLEAN UP AND INSPECTION

After the shaft has been seated in the hosel, the final step of the installation involves cleaning up any excess epoxy and checking the mounting to assure shaft installation accuracy. The procedure of inserting the shaft will inevitably force excess epoxy between the bottom of the ferrule and the top of the hosel, or in the case of non-ferruled clubheads, at the top of the hosel itself. To create less work in the finishing of the ferrule or in the overall completion of the club, it is recommended that the clubmaker use a paper towel to immediately wipe the excess epoxy away right after the shaft has been seated in the bore of the hosel. On irons and metal woods, whether assembled with or without a ferrule, effort should be made to wipe off every bit of the epoxy. However, on string whipped woods, it is wise to leave just a little bit of the excess epoxy between the hosel and the ferrule. Often, the top of the hosel on string whipped woods is not perfectly square, so the epoxy can serve as a filler for any gap that may exist between ferrule and hosel. Finally, a quick inspection of the clubhead and shaft should be made to look for any smears of epoxy that may have accidently gotten on the head or shaft as a result of shaft installation.

Before setting the clubs aside for the epoxy to cure, take a final look at the shaft mounting in the head. During the course of clean up it is possible the handling

A Final Word About Shafts

Some Cardinal Rules About Shafts and Their Installation

1. ALWAYS calculate the required trimming and installation procedures BEFORE cutting the shafts.

2. NEVER be intimidated by the process of shaft trimming and installation; the concepts and procedures ARE logical once you learn how to use the shaft trimming charts.

3. KNOW and use comparable shaft patterns from the different shaft manufacturers whenever necessary.

4. STUDY as much as you can about shafts; the knowledge will pay off in club quality and increased club sales.

5. NEVER install tapered shafts in parallel bore clubheads.

6. NEVER worry about enlarging a hosel bore size to accommodate a different size shaft tip diameter. If proper reboring techniques are followed, no damage will occur to the head.

7. NEVER cut a graphite or composite shaft with a tube cutter.

8. KNOW and perform the proper degree of abrasion on shaft tips before assembly.

9. ALWAYS use only high shear strength epoxies for shaft installation.

10. ALWAYS check your work after completion.

11. When in doubt about how to properly trim a shaft, ALWAYS ask a reputable source before cutting. Suppliers will not offer free replacements for incorrectly cut shafts.

ALWAYS FOLLOW PROPER SAFETY PROCEDURES WHEN TRIMMING AND INSTALLING SHAFTS!!!

may have caused the shaft tip to withdraw slightly from the bottom of the bore. A final tap of the butt of the shaft on the floor will act as a check for proper seating of the shaft. For a professional job, when using shafts that either have a shaft label already installed, or have the manufacturer's silk-screen identification on the shaft, take the time to rotate the shaft so that these insignias always face up in the 12 o'clock position on the shaft.

Finally, when setting the club(s) aside to dry, never position the golf club with the shaft down and the head up. Positioning the club with the head pointing up will cause the epoxy inside the shaft tip to run down and create a potential rattle after the club is put into play. Hanging the clubs on horizontal racks or leaning them against a wall or bench with the head down on the floor are both acceptable methods for club positioning while curing the epoxy.

Shaft Glossary

Balance point - An expression of the weight distribution of the shaft whereby half of the shaft's mass is on the tip side of the balance point and the other half of the shafts mass is on the butt side of the balance point.

Bend point - One of the different ways to express the position of maximum bending in the shaft. Bend point is determined by applying equal amounts of force pushing in from the butt and the tip of the shaft. A shaft is usually one of three bend point types; a high bend point in which the tip section of the shaft is stiffer than the butt section, a low bend point in which the butt section is stiffer than the tip section, and a mid bend point in which the tip and butt sections are of equal flexibility.

Back stepping - A term describing the practice of trimming less from the tip than is required in the shaft installation process for the purpose of achieving a stiffness that is more flexible than what the shaft has been designed to be. Back stepping also refers to the assembly practice of choosing a longer than normal raw length taper tip shaft for the clubhead, again for the purpose of achieving a stiffness that is more flexible than what the shaft has been designed to be.

Bent Shaft - A specially formed metal shaft with a curve, or bend for use in putters.

Boron - A very high-strength element used in the manufacture of composite shafts to increase tip strength and improve resistance to torque. Boron is an element that does not occur freely in nature. To use it in shaft construction a chemical reaction must be created to deposit the boron on a filament. In the process, a tungsten wire is placed in an ionized chamber where the boron atoms are made to adhere to the tungsten. After the process is complete, it is the tungsten/boron filaments that are introduced into the shaft.

Butt - The large end of the shaft.

Butt diameter - The dimension of the large end of the shaft as measured from one outside wall of of the shaft to the other through the center of the shaft. Butt diameter is an important factor with regard to shaft stiffness and grip sizing.

Butt heavy - A type of shaft construction in which the butt section of the shaft is heavier than an equal length of the tip section. A butt heavy shaft shifts the balance point of the shaft closer to the butt.

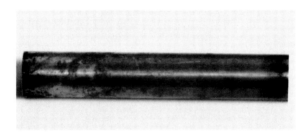

Butt Section

Butt section - The part of the shaft from the butt to the first step down from the butt.

Butt stiff - A shaft design construction in which the butt half of the shaft is made to be stiffer than the tip half of the shaft. Butt stiff can also be used as terminology to describe a low bend point shaft.

Composite - A term describing any combination of synthetic fiber type raw materials with binding resin used in the manufacture of shafts. Composite can also be used to describe any shaft that is made from a combination of synthetic fiber type materials.

Deflection - The amount of deviation between the shaft in its natural state and the shaft with a known mass is suspended from the tip. Deflection testing is one way to express the relative stiffness of a shaft.

Deflection board - A device for determining the relative stiffness of a shaft. The shaft is fixed in its natural state after which a known weight is suspended from the tip of the shaft. Deflection boards have a grid pattern behind the shaft to allow the measurement of the shaft's deflection and to allow recording the total curve as created by the tip weight.

Drawing - The process of steel or steel alloy shaft manufacture which successively reduces the tube diameter by stretching the tube through a series of forming dies. As the tubes are pulled through the successively smaller forming dies the tube reduces in diameter.

Filament winding - The process of composite shaft manufacture which incorporates winding a continuous strand of composite yarn around a forming mandrel.

Frequency - The number of oscillations (vibrations) of a shaft per unit of time, usually expressed in cycles per minute. The frequency of a shaft is derived from the mass of the shaft, the mass of the head, the length of the shaft, the elastic property of the material used in the shaft and a property which is defined by the cross section of the shaft and its ability to resist twisting.

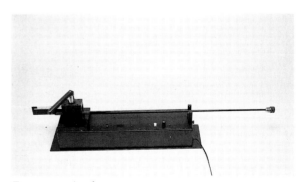

Frequency Analyzer

Frequency analyzer - A device that measures the vibrational frequency of the club or the shaft by securing the butt end of the shaft in a clamp and oscillating the tip. Pick off lights on the machine measure the number of oscillations over a period of time and express the measurement on a display on the machine, usually in cycles per minute.

Frequency matching - A method of assembling a set of clubs in which there is a constant relationship of stiffness between clubs as expressed by a constant incremental change of vibrational frequency between clubs. Two methods of frequency matching exist in the shaft industry: weight sorting such as with the True Temper Dynamic Gold and Gold Plus and electronic calibration as is used to match Brunswick's FM Precision steel and FibreMatch graphite shafts.

Frequency slope - The progression of frequency (flexibility) change from club to club within a set as plotted by series of points on a graph. If the line drawn on the graph through each club's point of frequency is steep, the increase in stiffness between each club is greater than if the slope line is flatter on the graph.

Graphite - A strong, lightweight synthetic fibrous material produced by carbonizing (high temperature heating) polyacrilenitrate (PAN) yarn under pressure.

Kick point - The other method of expressing a shaft's maximum point of bending. Kick point is measured by securing the butt and applying a known amount of force to the tip end only. When a line is drawn from tip to butt, the point of highest deviation from the line is considered the kick point. Kick point is also known as **flex point**.

Modulus - A measurement of a material's ability to resist stretching that is used to describe the strength of materials used in the manufacture of shafts. For example, fiberglass has a modulus rating of 17 million, steel 30 million and graphite as high as 55 million.

Nominal weight - Also known as raw weight, the nominal weight refers to the weight of a shaft as it is manufactured, before being trimmed for installation.

Overshaft Putter

Overshaft - The term given to any shaft that is manufactured for installation over a special hosel post. Once seen in ironhead design in the 1970s, overshafts are now almost exclusively used in the installation of some putter types and one major manufacturer's model of metal woods (Langert Company).

Parallel tip - A term describing one of the construction types of shafts in which the tip is made to be one constant diameter up to a certain point on the shaft. Typical parallel tip diameters are .335" and .320" for woods, and .370" and .395" for irons. In steel shafts, the tip diameter remains constant from the tip to the first step. In graphite shafts, the tip diameter remains constant from the tip up to a certain point on the shaft as designed by the manufacturer.

Pre-preg - The flat sheets of graphite/fiber material mixed with binding resins that are used in the sheet wrapping process of composite shaft manufacture.

Raw length - The length of a shaft as manufactured before trimming an installation.

Seamless - A term describing one type of steel or metal alloy shaft manufacture. As opposed to high frequency welded metal shafts, seamless shafts are not welded into a tube. These shafts are produced by piercing a hole

completely through a large diameter metal log (billet). After piercing, the billets are drawn through a series of operations to reduce the outside diameter and wall thickness to the required dimensions for shaft forming.

Sheet wrapping - A method of composite shaft manufacture which describes the successive wrapping of pre-preg sheets of graphite/fiber material around a forming mandrel to make the shaft.

Spine - The part of the shaft that exhibits the least resistance to bending. On steel shafts made through the high frequency welding process, the spine is the point where the ends of the steel used to form the tube are joined. On sheet-wrapped graphite shafts, the spine is the point where the beginning and ending edges of the graphite sheets lay on the shaft.

Step - Primarily on steel shafts, the radial protrusions formed on the shaft that allow the shaft to change in diameter.

Step length - The distance between any two steps measured from the start of one step to the start of the next step. Shafts with less than 2" step pattern are considered First Grade shafts while step patterns greater than 2" are considered Second Grade or Commercial Grade shafts because less step forming operations are required.

Step pattern - The configuration of steps in the shaft, expressed either as a constant or variable pattern. Constant step pattern shafts exhibit a similar spacing between steps while variable step patterns shafts exhibit a random or random repeating spacing between steps. Examples of shafts with a constant step pattern are Dynamic, Spectre or Microtaper. Examples of a few variable step pattern shafts are Matchflex, Shadow and Gold Plus.

Swaging - A process of reducing the steel or metal alloy shaft's diameter during its manufacture. Swaging describes the process of reducing the tip to a tapered configuration as well as the process of forming steps on a steel shaft.

Taper tip - A term describing one of the construction types of shafts in which the tip is made to gradually increase larger in diameter from the tip up to a specified point on the shaft. Taper tip steel shafts are made with a .0075"/ inch tapering rate on irons and .0132"/ inch on woods up to the beginning of the tip parallel section.

Tip - The small diameter end of the shaft. The tip is the portion of the shaft to be inserted into (or over) the hosel of the clubhead.

Tipping - A term describing the action of removing more than a standard amount from the tip of the shaft during installation to create a stiffer than normal flex in the shaft.

Tip diameter - The dimension of the small end of the shaft as measured from one outside wall of the shaft to the other through the center of the shaft. Tip diameter is an important factor with regard to shaft stiffness and clubhead hosel bore size.

Tip heavy - A type of shaft construction in which the tip section of the shaft is heavier than an equal length of the butt section. A tip heavy shaft shifts the balance point of the shaft closer to the tip. An example of a tip heavy shaft are the tip-reinforced version of certain shaft patterns manufactured exclusively for use in short bore metal woods.

Tip section - The portion of a steel shaft that extends from the tip of the shaft to the first step.

Tip stiff - A shaft design construction in which the tip half of the shaft is made to be stiffer than the butt half of the shaft. Tip stiff can also be used as terminology to describe a high bend point shaft.

Torque - The amount a shaft twists in relationship to the shaft's center of gravity upon a known amount of force (usually one foot-pound).

Unitized - A term describing a construction type of shafts in which one shaft can be used to build an entire set of irons and one shaft can be used to build an entire set of woods through successive trimming of the tip section.

Wall thickness - The thickness of the shaft walls, a major determinant of shaft strength and flex.

Yarn - Continuous thin strands of graphite/fiber material used in the manufacture of filament wound type composite shafts.

Shaft Specifications

ADVANCED COMPOSITE TECHNOLOGIES

Name	Flex	Tip Dia.	Butt Dia.	Raw Weight	Raw Length	Mfrs. Stated Torque
ACTivator Woods	L	.335"	.595"	2.54oz	44"	4.0°
	A	.335"	.600"	2.64oz	44"	3.9°
	R	.335"	.600"	3.17oz	45"	3.8°
	S	.335"	.600"	3.17oz	45"	3.7°
	X	.335"	.600"	3.17oz	45"	3.5°
TourStik Woods	R	.335"	.600"	3.24oz	45"	3.4°
	S	.335"	.600"	3.24oz	45"	3.2°
	X	.335"	.600"	3.24oz	45"	2.9°

ALDILA GRAPHITE SHAFTS

Name	Flex	Tip Dia.	Butt Dia.	Raw Weight	Raw Length	Mfrs. Stated Torque
HM-55 Woods	Regular	.335" T	.615"	3.77oz	44"	1.6°
	Firm	.335" T	.620"	3.77oz	44"	1.6°
	Strong	.335" T	.620"	3.77oz	44"	1.6°
HM-55 Irons	Regular	.370" T	.610"	3.35oz	39"	1.5°
	Firm	.370" T	.620"	3.46oz	39"	1.5°
	Strong	.370" T	.620"	3.60oz	39"	1.5°
HM-40 Woods	Light	.335" T	.615"	3.35oz	44"	2.2°
	Regular	.335" T	.615"	3.35oz	44"	2.2°
	Firm	.335" T	.615"	3.53oz	44"	2.2°
	Strong	.335" T	.615"	3.53oz	44"	2.2°
	Strong	.335" T	.630"	3.67oz	46"	2.2°
HM-40 Irons	Light	.370"	.610"	3.07oz	39"	2.0°
	Regular	.370"	.620"	3.21oz	39"	2.0°
	Firm	.370"	.625"	3.28oz	39"	2.0°
	Strong	.370"	.625"	3.32oz	39"	2.0°
HM-40 Low Flex -Woods	Light	.335"	.615"	2.86oz	44"	2.8°
	Regular	.335"	.615"	3.00oz	44"	2.8°
	Firm	.335"	.625"	3.07oz	44"	2.8°
	Strong	.335"	.625"	3.10oz	44"	2.8°

T - Taper tip

ALDILA GRAPHITE SHAFTS (cont'd.)

Name	Flex	Tip Dia.	Butt Dia.	Raw Weight	Raw Length	Mfrs. Stated Torque
HM-40 Low Flex -Irons	Light	.370"	.600"	2.75oz	41"	2.8°
	Regular	.370"	.600"	2.86oz	41"	2.8°
	Firm	.370"	.605"	3.03oz	41"	2.8°
	Strong	.370"	.605"	3.14oz	41"	2.8°
HM-30 Woods	Light	.335"T	.615"	2.68oz	44"	3.6°
	Regular	.335"T	.615"	2.79oz	44"	3.6°
	Firm	.335"T	.625"	3.14oz	44"	3.6°
	Strong	.335"T	.625"	3.28oz	44"	3.6°
HM-30 Irons	Light	.370"T	.610"	2.61oz	39"	3.6°
	Regular	.370"T	.610"	2.79oz	39"	3.6°
	Firm	.370"T	.620"	2.93oz	39"	3.6°
	Strong	.370"T	.620"	3.03oz	39"	3.6°
HM30 Superlite -Woods	Regular	.335"	.600"	2.12oz	44"	7.0°
HM-30 Superlite -Irons	Regular	.370"	.600"	2.37oz	39"	6.0°
HM-30 Ladies Superlite Woods	Light	.335"	.590"	2.05oz	44"	7.0°
HM-30 Ladies Superlite Irons	Light	.370"	.590"	2.22oz	39"	6.0°
Questar Woods	Light	.335"	.615"	2.86oz	44"	3.5°
	Regular	.335"	.620"	3.03oz	44"	3.5°
	Firm	.335"	.620"	3.10oz	44"	3.5°
	Firm	.335"	.620"	3.28oz	46"	3.5°
	Strong	.335"	.620"	3.21oz	44"	3.5°
Questar Irons	Light	.370"	.600"	2.75oz	41"	3.5°
	Regular	.370"	.600"	2.89oz	41"	3.5°
	Firm	.370"	.605"	3.03oz	41"	3.5°
	Strong	.370"	.605"	3.14oz	41"	3.5°
Low Torque Woods	Light	.335"/ .320"*	.615"	2.54oz	44"	5.0°
	Regular	.335"/ .320"*	.620"	2.72oz	44"	5.0°
	Regular	.335"	.625"	2.72oz	46"	5.0°
	Firm	.335"/ .320"*	.620"	2.82oz	44"	5.0°
	Strong	.335"/ .320"*	.620"	3.35oz	44"	5.0°

ALDILA GRAPHITE SHAFTS (cont'd.)

Name	Flex	Tip Dia.	Butt Dia.	Raw Weight	Raw Length	Mfrs. Stated Torque
Low Torque Irons	Light	.370"/ .355"*	.600"	2.61oz	39"	5.0°
	A/L	.370"	.600"	2.68oz	41"	5.0°
	Regular	.370"/ .355"*	.590"	2.82oz	39"	5.0°
	R/F	.370"	.595"	2.89oz	39"	5.0°
	R/F	.370"	.610"	2.96oz	41"	5.0°
	Firm	.370"/ .355"*	.600"	2.96oz	39"	5.0°
	Strong	.370"/ .355"*	.605"	3.10oz	39"	5.0°
Low Torque Woods	A/L	.335"	.590"	3.17oz	45"	5.0°
P711	R/F	.335"	.600"	3.35oz	45"	5.0°
Low Torque Irons	A/L	.370"	.585"	2.96oz	41"	5.0°
P711	R/F	.370"	.600"	3.10oz	41"	5.0°

* indicates available in both parallel and taper tip

ALDILA GRAPHITE PUTTER SHAFTS

Name	Tip Dia.	Butt Dia.	Raw Weight	Raw Length	Mfrs. Stated Torque
HM-30 overhosel	.299" I.D.	.585"	2.05oz	35"	3.1°
HM-40	.370"	.530"	2.68oz	36"	2.0°

ALLOY 2000 SHAFTS

Name	Flex	Tip Dia.	Butt Dia.	Raw Weight	Raw Length	Mfrs. Stated Torque
Alloy 2000 Woods	R	.335"	.600"	3.95oz	44"	2.5°
	S	.335"	.600"	3.99oz	44"	2.5°
	X	.335"	.600"	4.06oz	44"	2.5°

APOLLO PARALLEL TIP SHAFTS

Name	Code	Flex	Tip Dia.	Butt Dia.	Raw Weight	Raw Length
Masterflex Woods	1720	R	.335"	.600"	4.16oz	46"
(Variable Steps)	1722	S	.335"	.600"	4.46oz	46"
	1724	X	.335"	.600"	4.72oz	46"

APOLLO PARALLEL TIP SHAFTS (cont'd.)

Name	Code	Flex	Tip Dia.	Butt Dia.	Raw Weight	Raw Length
Masterflex Irons	1721	R	.370"	.600"	4.16oz	40"
(Variable Steps)	1723	S	.370"	.600"	4.46oz	40"
	1726	X	.370"	.600"	4.75oz	40"
AP44 Elite Woods	1890	R	.335"	.600"	4.37oz	45"
(1 7/8" Steps)	1892	S	.335"	.600"	4.37oz	45"
AP44 Elite Irons	1891	R	.370"	.600"	4.31oz	39"
(1 7/8" Steps)	1893	S	.370"	.600"	4.37oz	39"
AP44 Woods	1083	R/S	.335"	.600"	4.63oz	47"
(1 7/8" Steps)						
AP44 Irons	1085	R/S	.370"	.600"	4.56oz	41"
(1 7/8" Steps)	1084	R/S	.395" overfit	.600"	4.56oz	41"
Torsion Matched MK II	1588	R/S	.335"	.600"	4.38oz	47"
- Woods						
(Variable Steps)						
Torsion Matched MK II	1589	R/S	.370"	.600"	4.44oz	41"
- Irons						
(Variable Steps)						
Matchflex Woods	1760	AR	.335"	.600"	3.95oz	45"
(Variable Steps)	1762	R	.335"	.600"	4.10oz	45"
	1764	RS	.335"	.600"	4.25oz	45"
	1766	S	.335"	.600"	4.40oz	45"
Matchflex Irons	1761	AR	.370"	.600"	3.95oz	39"
(Variable Steps)	1763	R	.370"	.600"	4.10oz	39"
	1765	RS	.370"	.600"	4.25oz	39"
	1767	S	.370"	.600"	4.40oz	39"
Spectre Woods	1369	A/L	.335"	.580"	4.00oz	46"
(1 1/2" Steps)	1513	R/S	.335"	.600"	4.31oz	47"
Spectre Irons	1382	A/L	.370"	.580"	3.88oz	40"
(1 1/2" Steps)	1514	R/S	.370"	.600"	4.19oz	41"
Shadow Woods	1498	R/S	.335"	.600"	4.38oz	47"
(Variable Steps)						
Shadow Irons	1469	R/S	.370"	.600"	4.13oz	41"
(Variable Steps)						

APOLLO PARALLEL TIP SHAFTS (cont'd.)

Name	Code	Flex	Tip Dia.	Butt Dia.	Raw Weight	Raw Length
Lady Shadow Woods (Variable Steps)	1785	L	.335"	.580"	3.75oz	44°
Lady Shadow Irons (Variable Steps)	1786	L	.370"	.580"	3.63oz	38°
Senior Shadow Woods (Variable Steps)	1584	A	.335"	.580"	3.75oz	45°
Senior Shadow Irons (Variable Steps)	1585	A	.370"	.580"	3.63oz	39°
Acculite Woods (Variable Steps)	1700	R	.335"	.600"	3.56oz	45°
	1702	S	.335"	.600"	3.67oz	45°
Acculite Irons (Variable Steps)	1701	R	.370"	.600"	3.56oz	39°
	1703	S	.370"	.600"	3.67oz	39°
AP46 Woods (1 13/16" Steps)	1497	L	.335"	.560"	4.25oz	44°
	1153	R	.335"	.600"	4.38oz	44°
AP46 Irons (1 13/16" Steps)	1306	L	.370"	.560"	4.25oz	38°
	1305	R	.370"	.600"	4.38oz	39°

APOLLO REINFORCED TIP SHAFTS FOR METAL WOODS

Name	Code	Flex	Tip Dia.	Butt Dia.	Raw Weight	Raw Length
AP83 Woods (3" Steps)	1499	L	.335"	.560"	4.25oz	44°
	1075	R	.335"	.600"	4.38oz	44°
AP83 Irons (3" Steps)	1500	L	.370"	.560"	4.25oz	38°
	1077	R	.370"	.600"	4.38oz	39°
AP44 Woods (1 7/8" Steps)	1537	R/S	.335"	.600"	4.31oz	44°
Spectre Woods	TR 1522	R/S	.335"	.600"	4.25oz	44°

APOLLO TAPER TIP SHAFTS

Name	Code	Flex	Tip Dia.	Butt Dia.	Raw Weight	Raw Length
Masterflex Woods (Variable Steps)	1730	R	.294"	.600"	4.07oz	42 - 45°
	1732	S	.294"	.600"	4.36oz	42 - 45°
	1734	X	.294"	.600"	4.57oz	44 - 45°
	1735	X	.294"	.600"	4.48oz	42 - 43°

APOLLO TAPER TIP SHAFTS (cont'd.)

Name	Code	Flex	Tip Dia.	Butt Dia.	Raw Weight	Raw Length
Masterflex-Irons	1731	R	.355"	.600"	4.05oz	35 - 39"
(Variable Steps)	1733	S	.355"	.600"	4.35oz	35 - 39"
	1736	X	.355"	.600"	4.64oz	37 - 39"
	1737	X	.355"	.600"	4.59oz	35 - 36 1/2"
AP44-Woods	357	R	.277"	.600"	4.38oz	42 1/2 - 44 1/2"
(1 7/8" Steps)	510	S	.294"	.620"	4.50oz	43 1/2 - 44 1/2"
AP44-Irons	496	R	.355"	.580"	4.25oz	35 - 38 1/2"
(1 7/8" Steps)	361	S	.355"	.600"	4.38oz	35 - 39"
AP46-Woods	1269	R	.277"	.600"	4.38oz	44"
(1 13/16" Steps)						
AP46-Irons	1413	R	.355"	.600"	4.19oz	36-38"
(1 13/16" Steps)						

APOLLO PUTTER SHAFTS

Pattern	Code	Tip	Butt	Length
Straight Taper				
Plain and fluted	1211	.395"	.580"	35"
Plain and fluted	1393	.355"	.580"	35"
Plain	1450	.355"	.580"	35"
Step Formed				
3" step & flute	1390	Belled	.600"	35"
1 13/16" step AP46	1305	.370"	.600"	39"
1 13/16" step AP46	1306	.370"	.560"	39"
3" step AP83	1077	.370"	.600"	39"
1 1/4" step Hi-grip	1690	.370"	.600"	35"

APOLLO GRAPHITE SHAFTS

Name	Code	Flex	Tip	Butt	Weight	Length	Torque
G100-Woods	G100WL	L	.335"	.580"	2.68oz	45"	6.5°
	G100WR	R	.335"	.600"	2.82oz	45"	6.5°
	G100WS	S	.335"	.600"	2.93oz	45"	6.5°
G100-Irons	G100IL	L	.370"	.580"	2.43oz	39"	4.5°
	G100IR	R	.370"	.600"	2.57oz	39"	4.5°
	G100IS	S	.370"	.600"	2.75oz	39"	4.5°

APOLLO GRAPHITE SHAFTS (cont'd.)

Name	Code	Flex	Tip Dia.	Butt Dia.	Raw Weight	Raw Length	Mfrs. Stated Torque
HMF Lo Torque	HMFWR	R	.335"	.600"	2.89oz	45"	4.0°
-Woods	HMFWS	S	.335"	.600"	3.03oz	45"	4.0°
HMF Lo Torque	HMFIR	R	.370"	.600"	2.64oz	39"	3.5°
-Irons	HMFIS	S	.370"	.600"	2.82oz	39"	3.5°
Boron Tourline	BTWR	R	.335"	.620"	3.53oz	45"	3.5°
-Woods	BTWS	S	.335"	.620"	3.63oz	45"	3.5°
	BTWX	X	.335"	.620"	3.74oz	45"	3.5°
Boron Tourline	BTIR	R	.370"	.620"	3.21oz	39"	2.5°
-Irons	BTIS	S	.370"	.620"	3.32oz	39"	2.5°
	BTIX	X	.370"	.620"	3.49oz	39"	2.5°

BRUNSWICK SHAFTS

Name	Code	Flex	Tip Dia.	Butt Dia.	Raw Weight	Raw Length
Precision FM -Woods (Variable Steps)	WFM	3.5 - 8.0	.335"	.600"	variable	45"
Precision FM -Irons (Variable Steps)	IFM	3.5 - 8.0	370"	.600"	variable	variable
Precision FM Lite -Woods (Variable Steps)	WFML	3.5 - 4.0	.335"	.580"	variable	45"
		4.1 - 8.0	.335"	.600"	variable	45"
Precision FM Lite -Irons (Variable Steps)	IFML	3.5 - 4.0	.370"	.580"	variable	variable
		4.1 - 8.0	.370"	.600"	variable	variable
Precision Microtaper -Woods (3/4" Steps)	8656WAL	A/L	.335"	.560"	4.10oz	46"
	8676WRS	R/S	.335"	.600"	4.20oz	47"
Precision Microtaper -Irons (3/4" Steps)	8656IAL	A/L	.370"	.560"	4.10oz	40"
	8676IRS	R/S	.370"	.600"	4.20oz	41"
Precision Phoenix -Woods (1 1/2" Steps)	7556WAL	A/L	.335"	.580"	3.87oz	46"
	7576WRS	R/S	.335"	.600"	4.25oz	47"

BRUNSWICK PARALLEL TIP STEEL SHAFTS (cont'd.)

Name	Code	Flex	Tip Dia.	Butt Dia.	Raw Weight	Raw Length
Precision Phoenix	7556IAL	A/L	.370"	.580"	4.00oz	40"
-Irons	7576IRS	R/S	.370"	.600"	4.15oz	41"
(1 1/2" Steps)						
Precision Propel II	8056WAL	A/L	.335"	.560"	4.40oz	46"
-Woods	8076WRS	R/S	.335"	.600"	4.60oz	47"
(1 7/8" Steps)						
Precision Propel II	7856IAL	A/L	.370"	.560"	4.30oz	40"
-Irons	7876IRS	R/S	.370"	.600"	4.58oz	41"
(1 7/8" Steps)						
UCV-304 Woods	6169WR	R	.335"	.600"	3.60oz	44"
(Variable Steps)	6179WS	S	.335"	.600"	3.85oz	44"
UCV-304 Irons	6169IR	R	.370"	.600"	3.60oz	39"
(Variable Steps)	6179IS	S	.370"	.600"	3.80oz	39"
Super Champion	2823WL	L	.335"	.560"	4.20oz	43"
-Woods	2863WR	R	.335"	.600"	4.30oz	44"
(1 13/16" Steps)						
Super Champion	2823IL	L	.370"	.560"	4.30oz	38"
-Irons	2863IR	R	.370"	.600"	4.25oz	39"
(1 13/16" Steps)						
Champion Woods	2223WL	L	.335"	.560"	4.30oz	44"
(3" Steps)	2263WR	R	.335"	.600"	4.30oz	44"
Champion Irons	2223IL	L	.370"	.560"	4.30oz	38"
(3" Steps)	2263IR	R	.370"	.600"	4.30oz	39"

BRUNSWICK REINFORCED TIP SHAFTS FOR METAL WOODS

Name	Code	Flex	Tip Dia.	Butt Dia.	Raw Weight	Raw Length
Precision Microtaper	8956WAL	A/L	.335"	.560"	4.20oz	44"
(3/4" Steps)	8976WRS	R/S	.335"	.600"	4.30oz	45"
Precision Phoenix	7596WRS	R/S	.335"	.600"	4.25oz	44"
(1 1/2" Steps)						

BRUNSWICK TAPER TIP STEEL SHAFTS

Name	Code	Flex	Tip Dia.	Butt Dia.	Raw Weight	Raw Length
Precision FM Woods (Variable Steps)	WFM	3.5 - 8.0	.294"	.600"	variable	variable
Precision FM Irons (Variable Steps)	IFM	3.5 - 8.0	.294"	.600"	variable	variable
Precision FM Lite -Woods (Variable Steps)	WFML	3.5 - 4.0	.294"	.580"	variable	variable
		4.1 - 8.0	.294"	.600"	variable	variable
Precision FM Lite -Irons (Variable Steps)	IFML	3.5 - 4.0	.355"	.580"	variable	variable
		4.1 - 8.0	.355"	.600"	variable	variable
Precision Phoenix -Woods (1 1/2" Steps)	7268WR	R	.294"	.600"	3.90oz	42, 42 1/2, 43, 44"
	7278WS	S	.294"	.600"	4.02oz	42, 42 1/2, 43, 44"
Precision Phoenix -Irons (1 1/2" Steps)	7268IR	R	.355"	.600"	3.87oz	35 - 39"*
	7278IS	S	.355"	.600"	4.00oz	35 - 39"*
UCV-304 Woods (Variable Steps)	6529WL	L	.286"	.560"	3.60oz	41, 42, 43, 44"
	6569WR	R	.294"	.600"	3.64oz	42, 43, 44, 45"
	6579WS	S	.294"	.600"	3.88oz	42, 43, 44, 45"
UCV-304 Irons (Variable Steps)	6529IL	L	.355"	.540"	3.60oz	35, 36, 37, 38"
	6569IR	R	.355"	.580"	3.40oz	35 - 39"*
	6579IS	S	.355"	.600"	3.60oz	35 - 39"*
Super Champion -Woods (1 13/16" Steps)	2623WL	L	.294"	.560"	4.30oz	44"
	2663WR	R	.294"	.600"	4.30oz	44"
Super Champion -Irons (1 13/16" Steps)	2623IL	L	.355"	.560"	4.20oz	36, 38"
	2663IR	R	.355"	.600"	4.30oz	36, 38"

* available in 1/2" increments

BRUNSWICK PUTTER SHAFTS

Name	Code	Tip Dia.	Butt Dia.	Raw Length
Tapered, Flared Tip	9493P	.382" I.D.	.580"	35"
Microtaper, Par. Tip	9278P	.370"	.580"	35"
1 13/16" Steps	2663P	.355"	.600"	36"
Variable Steps	3863P	.355"	.600"	35"
Variable Steps	3893P	.370"	.600"	35"
Constant Taper	9093P	.355"	.580"	35"
Constant Taper	9063P	.370"	.580"	35"

BRUNSWICK GRAPHITE SHAFTS

Name	Code	Flex	Tip Dia.	Butt Dia.	Raw Weight	Raw Length
Fibrematch -Woods	WFMPC	3.5	.335"	.580"	2.90oz	45"
		4.5	.335"	.600"	3.15oz	45"
		5.5	.335"	.600"	3.20oz	45"
		6.5	.335"	.600"	3.20oz	45"
		7.0	.335"	.600"	3.20oz	45"
		7.5	.335"	.600"	3.20oz	45"
Fibrematch -Irons	IFMPC	3.5	.370"	.580"	2.93 oz	at #2-iron length
		4.5	.370"	.600"	3.06oz	at #2-iron length
		5.5	.370"	.600"	3.13oz	at #2-iron length
		6.5	.370"	.600"	3.13oz	at #2-iron length
		7.0	.370"	.600"	3.13oz	at #2-iron length
		7.5	.370"	.600"	3.13oz	at #2-iron length

CARBON FIBER PRODUCTS COMPOSITE SHAFTS

Name	Flex	Tip Dia.	Butt Dia.	Raw Weight	Raw Length	Mfrs. Stated Torque
CFP57 Woods	R	.335"	.590"	2.96oz	45"	2.5°
	S	.335"	.590"	2.96oz	45"	2.5°
	X	.335"	.590"	2.96oz	45"	2.5°
CFP57 Irons	R	.370"	.580"	2.82oz	42"	2.5°
	S	.370"	.580"	2.82oz	42"	2.5°
	X	.370"	.580"	2.82oz	42"	2.5°

CARBON FIBER PRODUCTS COMPOSITE SHAFTS (cont'd.)

Name	Flex	Tip Dia.	Butt Dia.	Raw Weight	Raw Length	Mfrs. Stated Torque
Novus II Woods	Super Flexible	.335"	.590"	3.39oz	46"	5.0°
	Very Flexible	.335"	.590"	3.39oz	46"	5.0°
	R	.335"	.590"	3.39oz	46"	5.0°
	S	.335"	.590"	3.39oz	46"	5.0°
	X	.335"	.590"	3.39oz	46"	5.0°
Novus II Irons	Super Flexible	.370"	.590"	2.96oz	42"	3.5°
	Very Flexible	.370"	.590"	2.96oz	42"	3.5°
	L	.370"	.590"	2.96oz	42"	3.5°
	R	.370"	.590"	2.96oz	42"	3.5°
	S	.370"	.590"	2.96oz	42"	3.5°
	X	.370"	.590"	2.96oz	42"	3.5°
Novus AC Woods	L	.335"	.590"	2.68oz	44"	6.5°
	R	.335"	.590"	2.68oz	44"	6.5°
	S	.335"	.590"	2.68oz	44"	6.5°
	X	.335"	.590"	2.68oz	44"	6.5°
Novus AC Irons	L	.370"	.590"	2.40oz	39"	5.5°
	R	.370"	.590"	2.40oz	39"	5.5°
	S	.370"	.590"	2.40oz	39"	5.5°
	X	.370"	.590"	2.40oz	39"	5.5°

CARBON FIBER PRODUCTS NOVUS PUTTER SHAFTS

Name	Tip Dia.	Butt Dia.	Raw Weight	Raw Length
Series A	.355 or .370"	.590"	2.64oz	36"
Series B	.370"	.600"	3.88oz	54"
Series C	.315" I.D.	.600"	3.74oz	52"

DYNACRAFT STEEL SHAFTS

Name	Code	Flex	Tip Dia.	Butt Dia.	Raw Weight	Raw Length
Dyna-Tech Standard -Woods (1 13/16" Steps)	USWRS	R/S	.335"	.600"	4.40oz	45"
Dyna-Tech Standard -Irons (1 13/16" Steps)	USIRS	R/S	.370"	.600"	4.40oz	40"
Dyna-Tech Classic -Woods (1 5/8" Steps)	UCWRS	R/S	.335"	.600"	4.40oz	45"
Dyna-Tech Classic -Irons (1 5/8" Steps)	UCIRS	R/S	.370"	.600"	4.40oz	40"

EASTON COMPOSITE SHAFTS

Name	Code	Flex	Tip Dia.	Butt Dia.	Raw Weight	Raw Length	Mfrs. Stated Torque
High Performance Series (Handicap of 15 and up)							
Women's Wood	HP-100L	L to R	.335"	.600"	2.68oz	44"	5.5°
Women's Iron	HP-100L	A to R	.370"	.600"	3.25oz	39"	3.0°
Men's Wood	HP-100M	A to S	.335"	.605"	2.68oz	44"	4.5°
Men's Iron	HP-100M	A to S	.370"	.605"	3.32oz	39"	3.0°
Maximum Performance Series (Handicap of 14 and under)							
Women's Wood	MP-200L	A to R	.335"	.600"	3.29oz	44"	4.5°
Men's Wood	MP-200M	R to X	.335"	.605"	3.29oz	44"	3.5°
Men's Wood	MP-300M	R to X	.335"	.605"	3.53oz	44"	3.0°
Men's Iron	MP-300M	R to X	.370"	.605"	3.67oz	39"	2.5°
Pro Wood	MP-300P	PRO-X	.335"	.605"	3.53oz	44"	2.5°

EASTON PUTTER SHAFTS

Category	Model	Tip Dia.	Butt Dia.	Raw Weight	Raw Length
In Hosel	IHP	.365"	.580"	2.65oz	42"
Over Hosel	OHP	.300" I.D.	.580"	2.30oz	42"
Extra-Long	XLP	.365"	.590"	5.65oz	52"

FENWICK WORLD CLASS PARALLEL TIP GRAPHITE SHAFTS

Name	Code	Flex	Tip Dia.	Butt Dia.	Raw Weight	Raw Length	Mfrs. Stated Torque
World Class 2 Woods	GS2P	F	.335"	.600"	3.28oz	45"	2.8°
3 Woods	GS3P	R	.335"	.600"	3.42oz	45"	2.8°
4 Woods	GS4P	S	.335"	.600"	3.46oz	45"	2.8°
5 Woods	GS5P	X	.335"	.600"	3.49oz	45"	2.8°
World Class 2 Irons	.237-.370	F	.370"	.600"	3.00oz	37"	2.8°
	.240-.370	F	.370"	.600"	3.21oz	40"	2.8°
World Class 3 Irons	.337-.370	R	.370"	.600"	3.00oz	37"	2.8°
	.340-.370	R	.370"	.600"	3.21oz	40"	2.8°
World Class 4 Irons	.437-.370	S	.370"	.600"	3.14oz	37"	2.8°
	.440-.370	S	.370"	.600"	3.31oz	40"	2.8°
World Class 5 Irons	.537-.370	X	.370"	.600"	3.16oz	37"	2.8°
	.540-.370	X	.370"	.600"	3.33oz	40"	2.8°

FENWICK WORLD CLASS TAPER TIP GRAPHITE SHAFTS

Name	Code	Flex	Tip Dia.	Butt Dia.	Raw Weight	Raw Length	Mfrs. Stated Torque
World Class 2 Woods	GS2	F	.300"	.600"	3.24oz	45"	2.8°
3 Woods	GS3	R	.300"	.600"	3.39oz	45"	2.8°
4 Woods	GS4	S	.300"	.600"	3.42oz	45"	2.8°
5 Woods	GS5	X	.300"	.600"	3.46oz	45"	2.8°
World Class 2 Irons	.237-.355	F	.355"	.600"	2.96oz	37"	2.8°
	.240-.355	F	.355"	.600"	3.17oz	40"	2.8°
World Class 3 Irons	.337-.355	R	.355"	.600"	2.96oz	37"	2.8°
	.340-.355	R	.355"	.600"	3.17oz	40"	2.8°
World Class 4 Irons	.437-.355	S	.355"	.600"	3.10oz	37"	2.8°
	.440-.355	S	.355"	.600"	3.28oz	40"	2.8°
World Class 5 Irons	.537-.355	X	.355"	.600"	3.12oz	37"	2.8°
	.540-.355	X	.355"	.600"	3.31oz	40"	2.8°

FIBER SPEED COMPOSITE SHAFTS

Name	Code	Flex	Tip Dia.	Butt Dia.	Raw Weight	Raw Length	Mfrs. Stated Torque
FS-100 Woods	FSW-100	Flexible	.335"	.620"	2.82oz	45"	
FS-200 Woods	FSW-200	Medium	.335"	.620"	3.14oz	45"	
FS-300 Woods	FSW-300	Firm	.335"	.620"	3.46oz	45"	

FIBER SPEED COMPOSITE SHAFTS

Name	Code	Flex	Tip Dia.	Butt Dia.	Raw Weight	Raw Length
TP-4000 Woods	TP-4000	Firm	.335"	.620"	3.03oz	45"
TP-4000-Plus Woods	TP-4000+	Firm	.335"	.620"	3.17oz	45"
FS-100 Irons	FSI-100	Flexible	.370"	.620"	3.03oz	40"
FS-200 Irons	FSI-200	Medium	.370"	.620"	3.03oz	40"
FS-300 Irons	FSI-300	Firm	.370"	.620"	3.03oz	40"
TP-4000 Irons	TP-4000	Firm	.370"	.620"	3.03oz	40"
Fiber Speed Putter	FSP		.355"*	.620"	2.65oz	37"

* Will fit taper hosel or trim to fit parallel hosel

GRAFALLOY GRAPHITE SHAFTS

Name	Flex	Tip Dia.	Butt Dia.	Raw Weight	Raw Length	Mfrs. Stated Torque
M14 Woods	L	.335"	.600"	3.17oz	45"	4.5°
	A	.335"	.600"	3.17oz	45"	4.5°
	R	.335"	.600"	3.17oz	45"	4.5°
	S	.335"	.600"	3.17oz	45"	4.5°
	X	.335"	.600"	3.17oz	45"	4.5°
I14 Irons	L	.370"	.600"	3.03oz	40"	3.0°
	A	.370"	.600"	3.03oz	40"	3.0°
	R	.370"	.600"	3.03oz	40"	3.0°
	S	.370"	.600"	3.03oz	40"	3.0°
	X	.370"	.600"	3.03oz	40"	3.0°
Lady Classic Woods	L	.335"	.580"	2.89oz	43"	4.5°
Lady Classic Irons	L	.370"	.580"	2.89oz	39"	3.0°
Senior Classic Woods	A	.335"	.600"	3.03oz	45"	3.75°
	R	.335"	.600"	3.03oz	45"	3.75°
	S	.335"	.600"	3.03oz	45"	3.75°

GRAFALLOY GRAPHITE SHAFTS

Name	Flex	Tip Dia.	Butt Dia.	Raw Weight	Raw Length	Mfrs. Stated Torque
M29 Woods	L	.335"	.600"	3.14oz	45"	4.8°
	A	.335"	.600"	3.14oz	45"	4.8°
	R	.335"	.600"	3.14oz	45"	4.8°
	S	.335"	.600"	3.14oz	45"	4.8°
	X	.335"	.600"	3.14oz	45"	4.8°
I29 Irons	L	.370"	.600"	3.03oz	40"	3.0°
	A	.370"	.600"	3.03oz	40"	3.0°
	R	.370"	.600"	3.03oz	40"	3.0°
	S	.370"	.600"	3.03oz	40"	3.0°
	X	.370"	.600"	3.03oz	40"	3.0°
M54 Woods	R	.335"	.600"	3.03oz	45"	3.3°
	S	.335"	.600"	3.03oz	45"	3.3°
	X	.335"	.600"	3.03oz	45"	3.3°
I54 Irons	R	.370"	.600"	3.03oz	40"	2.0°
	S	.370"	.600"	3.03oz	40"	2.0°
	X	.370"	.600"	3.03oz	40"	2.0°
M54 Lightweight -Woods	R	.335"	.600"	2.68oz	45"	2.8°
	S	.335"	.600"	2.68oz	45"	2.8°
	X	.335"	.600"	2.68oz	45"	2.8°
M60 Woods	L	.335"	.600"	3.35oz	45"	3.5°
	R	.335"	.600"	3.35oz	45"	3.5°
	S	.335"	.600"	3.35oz	45"	3.5°
	X	.335"	.600"	3.35oz	45"	3.5°
I60 Irons	L	.370"	.600"	3.17oz	40"	2.5°
	R	.370"	.600"	3.17oz	40"	2.5°
	S	.370"	.600"	3.17oz	40"	2.5°
	X	.370"	.600"	3.17oz	40"	2.5°
M66 Woods	R	.335"	.600"	3.17oz	45"	2.4°
	S	.335"	.600"	3.17oz	45"	2.4°
	X	.335"	.600"	3.17oz	45"	2.4°
M79 Woods	R	.335"	.600"	3.45oz	45"	2.5°
	S	.335"	.600"	3.45oz	45"	2.5°
	X	.335"	.600"	3.45oz	45"	2.5°

GRAFALLOY GRAPHITE SHAFTS (cont'd.)

Name	Flex	Tip Dia.	Butt Dia.	Raw Weight	Raw Length	Mfrs. Stated Torque
I79 Irons	R	.370"	.600"	3.39oz	40"	1.8°
	S	.370"	.600"	3.39oz	40"	1.8°
	X	.370"	.600"	3.39oz	40"	1.8°
I29 Iron	L	.350"	.600"	3.00oz	40"	3.0°
	R	.350"	.600"	3.00oz	40"	3.0°
	S	.350"	.600"	3.00oz	40"	3.0°
I54 Irons	R	.350"	.600"	3.00oz	40"	2.0°
	S	.350"	.600"	3.00oz	40"	2.0°
	X	.350"	.600"	3.00oz	40"	2.0°

KUNNAN GRAPHITE SHAFTS

Name	Flex	Tip Dia.	Butt Dia.	Raw Weight	Raw Length	Mfrs. Stated Torque
Autoclave Series 30 -Woods	A	.335"	.606"	3.14oz	44"	4.0°
	R	.335"	.606"	3.14oz	44"	4.0°
	S	.335"	.610"	3.28oz	44"	4.0°
Autoclave Series 30 -Irons	A	.370"	.606"	2.96oz	39"	3.5°
	R	.370"	.606"	2.96oz	39"	3.5°
	S	.370"	.610"	3.10oz	39"	3.5°
Autoclave Series 40 -Woods	R	.335"	.610"	3.21oz	44"	3.0°
	S	.335"	.610"	3.31oz	44"	3.0°
	X	.335"	.610"	3.42oz	44"	3.0°
Autoclave Series 40 -Irons	R	.370"	.610"	3.21oz	39"	2.5°
	S	.370"	.610"	3.31oz	39"	2.5°
	X	.370"	.610"	3.39oz	39"	2.5°
Autoclave Series 50 -Woods	R	.335"	.610"	2.89oz	44"	2.5°
	S	.335"	.614"	3.53oz	44"	1.9°
	X	.335"	.614"	3.53oz	44"	1.9°
	XX	.335"	.614"	3.88oz	44"	1.9°
COMP50 FCB Woods	R	.335"	.600"	3.19oz	44"	2.5°
	S	.335"	.610"	3.29oz	44"	2.5°
	X	.335"	.610"	3.40oz	44"	2.5°
COMP50 FCB Irons	R	.370"	.600"	3.12oz	39"	2.0°
	S	.370"	.610"	3.22oz	39"	2.0°
	X	.370"	.610"	3.35oz	39"	2.0°

KUNNAN GRAPHITE SHAFTS (cont'd.)

Name	Flex	Tip Dia.	Butt Dia.	Raw Weight	Raw Length	Mfrs. Stated Torque
1460 TFB Woods	R	.335"	.600"	2.97oz	44"	4.0°
	S	.335"	.610"	3.04oz	44"	4.0°
	X	.335"	.610"	3.12oz	44"	4.0°
1460 TFB Irons	R	.370"	.600"	2.90oz	39"	3.5°
	S	.370"	.610"	2.97oz	39"	3.5°
	X	.370"	.610"	3.04oz	39"	3.5°
1400 TFB Woods	L	.335"	.595"	2.90oz	44"	5.5°
	R	.335"	.602"	3.04oz	44"	5.5°
	S	.335"	.610"	3.26oz	44"	5.5°
	X	.335"	.610"	3.33oz	44"	5.5°
1400 TFB Irons	L	.370"	.600"	2.87oz	39"	4.5°
	R	.370"	.600"	3.01oz	39"	4.5°
	S	.370"	.600"	3.15oz	39"	4.5°
	X	.370"	.610"	3.26oz	39"	4.5°
1400 LFB Woods	A	.335"	.580"	2.97oz	44"	4.5°
1400 LFB Irons	A	.370"	.580"	2.62oz	44"	4.0°

SANDVIK TITANIUM PARALLEL TIP SHAFTS

Name	Code	Flex	Tip Dia.	Butt Dia.	Raw Weight	Raw Length	Mfrs. Stated Torque
Standard Woods	TIWL	L	.335"	.580"	3.14oz	45"	3.0°
	TIWA	A	.335"	.600"	3.25oz	45"	2.9°
	TIWR	R	.335"	.600"	3.53oz	45"	2.5°
	TIWS	S	.335"	.600"	3.70oz	45"	2.4°
	TIWX	X	.335"	.600"	3.74oz	45"	2.3°
Standard Irons	TI-L	L	.355/.370"*	.580"	3.30oz #1-iron	36 - 40"**	1.85 - 2.05°
	TI-A	A	.355/.370"*	.600"	3.47oz #1-iron	36 - 40"**	1.75 - 1.95°
	TI-R	R	.355/.370"*	.600"	3.66oz #1-iron	36 - 40"**	1.56 - 1.82°
	TI-S	S	.355/.370"*	.600"	3.66oz #1-iron	36 - 40"**	1.55 - 1.66°
	TI-X	X	.355/.370"*	.600"	3.66oz #1-iron	36 - 40"**	1.43 - 1.60°

* available in either .355 taper tip or .370 parallel tip   ** available in 1/2" increments

Name	Code	Flex	Tip Dia.	Butt Dia.	Raw Weight	Raw Length	Mfrs. Stated Torque
Low Flex Woods	TIWAR	A&R	.335"	.600"	3.54"	45"	2.5°
	TIWSX	S&X	.335"	.600"	3.72"	45"	2.4°

TRUE TEMPER PARALLEL TIP STEEL SHAFTS

Name	Code	Flex	Tip Dia.	Butt Dia.	Raw Weight	Raw Length
Dynamic Gold Woods	UDGWR	R-200	.335"	.600"	4.25oz	45"
(1 7/8" Steps)		R-300	.335"	.600"	4.31oz	45"
		R-400	.335"	.600"	4.37oz	45"
	UDGWS	S-200	.335"	.600"	4.31oz	45"
		S-300	.335"	.600"	4.37oz	45"
		S-400	.335"	.600"	4.43oz	45"
	UDGWX	X-100	.335"	.600"	4.38oz	45"
		X-200	.335"	.600"	4.44oz	45"
		X-300	.335"	.600"	4.50oz	45"
Dynamic Gold Irons	UDGIR	R-200	.370"	.600"	4.19oz	39"
(1 7/8" Steps)		R-300	.370"	.600"	4.25oz	39"
		R-400	.370"	.600"	4.31oz	39"
	UDGIS	S-200	.370"	.600"	4.31oz	39"
		S-300	.370"	.600"	4.37oz	39"
		S-400	.370"	.600"	4.43oz	39"
	UDGIX	X-100	.370"	.600"	4.38oz	39"
		X-200	.370"	.600"	4.44oz	39"
		X-300	.370"	.600"	4.50oz	39"
Dynamic Woods	UDWAL	A/L	.335"	.560"	4.37oz	46"
(1 7/8" Steps)	UDWR	R	.335"	.600"	4.31oz	45"
	UDWC	R/S	.335"	.600"	4.62oz	47"
	UDWS	S	.335"	.600"	4.38oz	45"
	UDWX	X	.335"	.600"	4.37oz	45"
Dynamic Irons	UDIAL	A/L	.370"	.560"	4.31oz	40"
(1 7/8" Steps)	UDIR	R	.370"	.600"	4.25oz	39"
	UDIC	R/S	.370"	.600"	4.56oz	41"
	UDICO	R/S	.395" Overfit	.600"	4.56oz	41"
	UDIS	S	.370"	.600"	4.37oz	39"
	UDIX	X	.370"	.600"	4.50oz	39"
Jet Step Woods (1" Steps)	UJWC	R/S	.335"	.600"	4.62oz	47"
Jet Step Irons (1" Steps)	UJIC	R/S	.370"	.600"	4.56oz	41"
	UJICO	R/S	.395" Overfit	.600"	4.56oz	41"

TRUE TEMPER PARALLEL TIP STEEL SHAFTS (cont'd.)

Name	Code	Flex	Tip Dia.	Butt Dia.	Raw Weight	Raw Length
Pro Fit Woods (1 1/2" Steps)	UPWC	R/S	.335"	.600"	4.62oz	47"
Pro Fit Irons (1 1/2" Steps)	UPIC	R/S	.370"	.600"	4.56oz	41"
	UPICO	R/S	.395" Overfit	.600"	4.56oz	41"
TT Lite Woods (1 1/2" Steps)	U2LWAL	A/L	.335"	.580"	4.00oz	46"
	UTTLWC	R/S	.335"	.600"	4.31oz	47"
TT Lite Irons (1 1/2" Steps)	U2LIAL	A/L	.370"	.580"	3.87oz	40"
	UTTLIC	R/S	.370"	.600"	4.19oz	41"
Gold Plus Woods (Variable Steps)	UGPWLH	L-200	.335"	.580"	3.31oz	44"
		L-300	.335"	.580"	3.37oz	44"
		L-400	.335"	.580"	3.44oz	44"
	UGPWRH	R-200	.335"	.610"	3.62oz	44"
		R-300	.335"	.610"	3.68oz	44"
		R-400	.335"	.610"	3.74oz	44"
	UGPWSH	S-200	.335"	.610"	3.72oz	44"
		S-300	.335"	.610"	3.78oz	44"
		S-400	.335"	.610"	3.84oz	44"
	UGPWXH	X-100	.335"	.620"	3.87oz	44"
		X-200	.335"	.620"	3.93oz	44"
		X-300	.335"	.620"	3.99oz	44"
Gold Plus Irons (Variable Steps)	UGPIL	L-200	.370"	.580"	3.31oz	39"
		L-300	.370"	.580"	3.37oz	39"
		L-400	.370"	.580"	3.44oz	39"
	UGPIR	R-200	.370"	.600"	3.56oz	39 1/2"
		R-300	.370"	.600"	3.62oz	39 1/2"
		R-400	.370"	.600"	3.68oz	39 1/2"
	UGPIS	S-200	.370"	.610"	3.69oz	39 1/2"
		S-300	.370"	.610"	3.75oz	39 1/2"
		S-400	.370"	.610"	3.81oz	39 1/2"
	UGPIX	X-100	.370"	.620"	3.87oz	39 1/2"
		X-200	.370"	.620"	3.93oz	39 1/2"
		X-300	.370"	.620"	3.99oz	39 1/2"
Flex Flow Woods (1 1/4" Steps with Recessed Section)	UTFFWL	L	.335"	.580"	3.74oz	41 1/2 - 44"*
	UTFFWA	A	.335"	.580"	3.74oz	41 1/2 - 44"*
	UTFFWR	R	.335"	.600"	3.74oz	41 1/2 - 44"*
	UTFFWS	S	.335"	.600"	3.88oz	41 1/2 - 44"*

TRUE TEMPER PARALLEL TIP STEEL SHAFTS (cont'd.)

Name	Code	Flex	Tip Dia.	Butt Dia.	Raw Weight	Raw Length
Flex Flow-Irons	UTFFIL	L	.370"	.580"	3.74oz	35 - 39"*
(1 1/4" Steps with	UTFFIA	A	.370"	.580"	3.74oz	35 - 39"*
Recessed Section)	UTFFIR	R	.370"	.600"	3.74oz	35 - 39"*
	UTFFIS	S	.370"	.600"	3.88oz	35 - 39"*
Comet-Woods	URWLM	L	.335"	.560"	4.25oz	44"
(1 13/16" Steps)	URWR	R	.335"	.600"	4.38oz	45"
Comet-Irons	URILM	L	.370"	.560"	4.25oz	39"
(1 13/16" Steps)	URIL	L	.320"	.560"	4.25oz	38"
	URIR	R	.370"	.600"	4.38oz	39"
Century-Woods	U3WL	L	.335"	.560"	4.25oz	44"
(3" Steps)	U3W	R	.335"	.600"	4.38oz	44"
Century-Irons	U3ILM	L	.370"	.560"	4.25oz	38"
(3" Steps)	U3IL	L	.320"	.560"	4.25oz	38"
	U3I	R	.370"	.600"	4.38oz	39"

* indicates available in 1/2" increments

TRUE TEMPER REINFORCED TIP STEEL SHAFTS FOR METAL WOODS

Name	Code	Flex	Tip Dia.	Butt Dia.	Raw Weight	Raw Length
Dynamic	UDWCH	R/S	.335"	.600"	4.25oz	45"
(1 7/8" Steps)						
TT Lite	UTTLWC	R/S	.335"	.600"	4.25oz	45"
(1 11/2" Steps)						
Flex Flow	UTFFWLH	L	.335"	.580"	3.74oz	40 1/2 - 43"*
(1 1/4" Steps with	UTFFWAH	A	.335"	.580"	3.74oz	40 1/2 - 43"*
Recessed Section)	UTFFWRH	R	.335"	.600"	3.74oz	40 1/2 - 43"*
	UTFFWSH	S	.335"	.600"	3.88oz	40 1/2 - 43"*

* indicates available in 1/2" increments

TRUE TEMPER TAPER TIP STEEL SHAFTS

Name	Code	Flex	Tip Dia.	Butt Dia.	Raw Weight	Raw Length
Dynamic Gold-Woods	DGWR	R-100	.277"	.600"	4.25oz	42 - 45"*
(1 7/8" Steps)		R-200	.277"	.600"	4.31oz	42 - 45"*
		R-300	.277"	.600"	4.37oz	42 - 45"*
		R-400	.277"	.600"	4.43oz	42 - 45"*
		R-500	.277"	.600"	4.50oz	42 - 45"*

TRUE TEMPER TAPER TIP STEEL SHAFTS (cont'd.)

Name	Code	Flex	Tip Dia.	Butt Dia.	Raw Weight	Raw Length
Dynamic Gold-Woods (1 7/8" Steps)	DGWS	S-100	.294"	.620"	4.25oz	42 - 45"*
		S-200	.294"	.620"	4.31oz	42 - 45"*
		S-300	.294"	.620"	4.37oz	42 - 45"*
		S-400	.294"	.620"	4.43oz	42 - 45"*
		S-500	.294"	.620"	4.50oz	42 - 45"*
	DGWX	X-100	.294"	.620"	4.38oz	42 - 45"*
		X-200	.294"	.620"	4.44oz	42 - 45"*
		X-300	.294"	.620"	4.50oz	42 - 45"*
		X-400	.294"	.620"	4.56oz	42 - 45"*
		X-500	.294"	.620"	4.63oz	42 - 45"*
Dynamic Gold-Irons (1 3/4" Steps)	DGIR	R-100	.355"	.580"	4.13oz	35 - 39"*
		R-200	.355"	.580"	4.19oz	35 - 39"*
		R-300	.355"	.580"	4.25oz	35 - 39"*
		R-400	.355"	.580"	4.31oz	35 - 39"*
		R-500	.355"	.580"	4.38oz	35 - 39"*
	DGIS	S-100	.355"	.600"	4.25oz	35 - 39"*
		S-200	.355"	.600"	4.31oz	35 - 39"*
		S-300	.355"	.600"	4.38oz	35 - 39"*
		S-400	.355"	.600"	4.44oz	35 - 39"*
		S-500	.355"	.600"	4.50oz	35 - 39"*
	DGIX	X-100	.355"	.600"	4.38oz	35 - 39"*
		X-200	.355"	.600"	4.44oz	35 - 39"*
		X-300	.355"	.600"	4.50oz	35 - 39"*
		X-400	.355"	.600"	4.56oz	35 - 39"*
		X-500	.355"	.600"	4.63oz	35 - 39"*
Dynamic-Woods (1 7/8" Steps)	DWA	A	.277"	.580"	4.25oz	42 - 45"*
	DWT	T	.277"	.600"	4.37oz	42 - 45"*
	DWS	S	.294"	.620"	4.37oz	42 - 45"*
	DWX	X	.294"	.620"	4.50oz	42 - 45"*
Dynamic-Irons (1 3/4" Steps)	DIA	A	.355"	.560"	4.25oz	35 - 39"*
	DIT	T	.355"	.580"	4.25oz	35 - 39"*
	DIS	S	.355"	.600"	4.37oz	35 - 39"*
	DIX	X	.355"	.600"	4.50oz	35 - 39"*

* indicates available in 1/2" increments

TRUE TEMPER TAPER TIP STEEL SHAFTS (cont'd.)

Name	Code	Flex	Tip Dia.	Butt Dia.	Raw Weight	Raw Length
Jet Step-Woods	JTWR	R	.277"	.600"	4.37oz	42 - 45"*
(1" Steps)	JTWS	S	.277"	.620"	4.37oz	42 - 45"*
Jet Step-Irons	JTIR	R	.355"	.580"	4.25oz	35 - 39"*
(1" Steps)	JTIS	S	.355"	.580"	4.25oz	35 - 39"*
Pro Fit-Woods	PFWL	L	.270"	.580"	4.10oz	42 - 44"*
(1 3/8" Steps)	PFWA	A	.277"	.580"	4.25oz	42 - 45"*
	PFWR	R	.277"	.600"	4.37oz	42 - 45"*
	PFWS	S	.286"	.620"	4.37oz	42 - 45"*
Pro Fit-Iron	PFIL	L	.300"	.580"	4.10oz	34 - 38"*
(1 3/8" Steps)	PFIA	A	.355"	.560"	4.25oz	35 - 39"*
	PFIR	R	.355"	.580"	4.25oz	35 - 39"*
	PFIS	S	.355"	.600"	4.37oz	35 - 39"*
TT Lite-Woods	2LWL	L	.294"	.580"	3.83oz @ 45"	42 - 45"*
(1 1/2" Steps)	2LWR	R	.294"	.620"	4.00oz @ 45"	42 - 45"*
	2LWS	S	.294"	.620"	4.15oz @ 45"	42 - 45"*
TT Lite-Irons	2LIL	L	.355"	.580"	3.67oz @ 38"	34 - 38"*
(1 1/2" Steps)	2LIR	R	.355"	.620"	3.87oz @ 39"	35 - 39"*
	2LIS	S	.355"	.620"	4.12oz @ 39"	35 - 39"*
Gold Plus-Woods	GPWR	R-200	.294"	.600"	3.24oz	42 - 44"*
(Variable Steps)		R-300	.294"	.600"	3.31oz	42 - 44"*
		R-400	.294"	.600"	3.36oz	42 - 44"*
	GPWS	S-200	.294"	.610"	3.34oz	42 - 44"*
		S-300	.294"	.610"	3.40oz	42 - 44"*
		S-400	.294"	.610"	3.46oz	42 - 44"*
	GPWX	X-100	.294"	.620"	3.87oz	42 -44"*
		X-200	.294"	.620"	3.93oz	42 - 44"*
		X-300	.294"	.620"	3.99oz	42 - 44"*
Gold Plus-Irons	GPIR	R-200	.355"	.600"	3.34oz	35 - 39 1/2"*
(Variable Steps)		R-300	.355"	.600"	3.40oz	35 - 39 1/2"*
		R-400	.355"	.600"	3.46oz	35 - 39 1/2"*
	GPIS	S-200	.355"	.610"	3.44oz	35 - 39 1/2"*
		S-300	.355"	.610"	3.50oz	35 - 39 1/2"*
		S-400	.355"	.610"	3.56oz	35 - 39 1/2"*
	GPIX	X-100	.355"	.620"	3.87oz	35 - 39 1/2"*
		X-200	.355"	.620"	3.93oz	35 - 39 1/2"*
		X-300	.355"	.620"	3.99oz	35 - 39 1/2"*

* indicates available in 1/2" increments

TRUE TEMPER TAPER TIP STEEL SHAFTS (cont'd.)

Name	Code	Flex	Tip Dia.	Butt Dia.	Raw Weight	Raw Length
Flex Flow Woods	TFFWL	L	.294"	.580"	3.74oz	41 1/2 - 44"*
(1 1/4" Steps with	TFFWA	A	.294"	.580"	3.74oz	41 1/2 - 44"*
Recessed Section)	TFFWR	R	.294"	.600"	3.74oz	41 1/2 - 44"*
	TFFWS	S	.294"	.600"	3.88oz	41 1/2 - 44"*
Flex Flow Irons	TFFIL	L	.355"	.580"	3.74oz	34 1/2 - 38 1/2"*
(1 1/4" Steps with	TFFIA	A	.355"	.580"	3.74oz	35 - 39"*
Recessed Section)	TFFIR	R	.355"	.600"	3.74oz	35 - 39"*
	TFFIS	S	.355"	.600"	3.88oz	35 - 39"*
Extra Lite Woods	SDLWL	L	.300"	.580"	3.30oz	42 + 43"
(Variable Steps)	SDLWR	R	.320"	.600"	3.30oz	42, 43, 44"
	SDLWS	S	.320"	.600"	3.40oz	42, 43, 44"
Extra Lite Irons	SDLIL	L	.355"	.580"	3.37oz	34 - 38"*
(Variable Steps)	SDLIR	R	.355"	.600"	3.40oz	35 - 39"*
	SDLIS	S	.355"	.600"	3.50oz	35 - 39"*

* available in 1/2" increments

TRUE TEMPER PUTTER SHAFTS

Name	Code	Tip Dia.	Butt Dia.	Raw Length
Straight Taper	YST	.355"	.580"	35"
Straight Taper, Fluted	YSTG	.355"	.580"	35"
Straight Taper, Fluted, Over Hosel	UYSTG	.395"	.580"	35"
Reinforced Tip, Flared	YHSF	.382" inside	.580"	35"
Straight Taper	UYST	.395"	.580"	35"
Flared Tip, Bright Chrome	YESTF	.282" inside	.580"	35"
Straight Taper, Bright Chrome	UYEST	.370"	.580"	35"

TRUE TEMPER PARALLEL TIP GRAPHITE SHAFTS

Name	Code	Flex	Tip Dia.	Butt Dia.	Raw Weight	Raw Length	Mfrs. Stated Torque
Black Gold Tour High Flex Woods	UBGTWSH	S-400	.335"	.600"	3.43oz	45"	2.0°
	UBGTWXH	X-100/ 400	.335"	.600"	3.50oz	45"	2.0°
Black Gold Tour Low Flex Woods	UBGTWSL	S-400	.335"	.600"	3.43oz	45"	2.0°
	UBGTWXL	X-100/ 400	.335"	.600"	3.50oz	45"	2.0°
Black Gold Woods	UCBHWL	L-2,3,400	.335"	.580"	2.89oz	44"	3.9°
	UCBHWR	R-2,3,400	.335"	.600"	3.17oz	45"	3.1°
	UCBHWS	S-2,3,400	.335"	.600"	3.21oz	45"	3.0°
	UCBHWX	X-1,2,300	.335"	.600"	3.31oz	45"	2.9°
Black Gold Irons	UCBHIL	L-2,3,400	.370"	.580"	2.96oz	38"	3.0°
	UCBHIR	R-2,3,400	.370"	.600"	3.17oz	40"	2.2°
	UCBHIS	S-2,3,400	.370"	.600"	3.28oz	40"	2.0°
	UCBHIX	X-1,2,300	.370"	.600"	3.28oz	40"	1.9°
Modulus EV40 Woods	UCMHWL	L	.335"	.580"	3.15oz	44"	4.1°
	UCMHWR	R	.335"	.600"	3.19oz	45"	3.3°
	UCMHWS	S	.335"	.600"	3.26oz	45"	3.2°
	UCMHWX	X	.335"	.600"	3.33oz	45"	3.1°
Modulus EV40 Irons	UCMHIL	L	.370"	.580"	3.22oz	38"	3.2°
	UCMHIR	R	.370"	.600"	3.29oz	40"	3.3°
	UCMHIS	S	.370"	.600"	3.36oz	40"	2.2°
	UCMHIX	X	.370"	.600"	3.43oz	40"	2.1°
Command Woods	UVWL	L	.335"	.580"	3.21oz	44"	4.4°
	UVWR	R	.335"	.600"	3.42oz	45"	4.0°
	UVWS	S	.335"	.600"	3.49oz	45"	3.9°
Command Irons	UVIL	L	.370"	.580"	3.07oz	38"	3.5°
	UVIR	R	.370"	.600"	3.42oz	39"	3.0°
	UVIS	S	.370"	.600"	3.49oz	39"	2.8°
EI-70 Woods	UEI7WL	L	.335"	.560"	2.61oz	44"	3.6°
	UEI7WR	R	.335"	.580"	2.72oz	45"	3.5°
	UEI7WS	S	.335"	.580"	2.75oz	45"	3.3°
EI-70 Irons	UEI7L	L	.370"	.560"	2.47oz	38"	2.9°
	UEI7R	R	.370"	.580"	2.72oz	40"	2.2°
	UEI7S	S	.370"	.580"	2.75oz	40"	2.2°

TRUE TEMPER TAPER TIP GRAPHITE SHAFTS

Name	Code	Flex	Tip Dia.	Butt Dia.	Raw Weight	Raw Length	Mfrs. Stated Torque
Black Gold Tour	TBGTWSH	S-400	.294"	.600"	3.43oz	45"	2.5°
High Flex-Woods	TBGTWXH	X-100/ 400	.294"	.600"	3.50oz	45"	2.5°
Black Gold Tour	TBGTWSL	S-400	.294"	.600"	3.43oz	45"	2.5°
Low Flex-Woods	TBGTWXL	X-100/ 400	.294"	.600"	3.50oz	45"	2.5°
Black Gold-Woods	TCBHWR	R-200,300,400	.294"	.600"	3.19oz	45"	3.0°
	TCBHWS	S-200,300,400	.294"	.600"	3.22oz	45"	3.8°
	TCBJWX	X-100,200,300	.294"	.600"	3.26oz	45"	3.5°
Black Gold-Irons	TCBHIR	R-200,300,400	.355"	.600"	3.29oz	40"	3.0°
	TCBHIS	S-200,300,400	.355"	.600"	3.36oz	40"	2.5°
	TCBHIX	X-100,200,300	.355"	.600"	3.43oz	40"	4.0°
EI-70 Woods	EI7WR	R	.294"	.580"	2.72oz	43 - 45"	3.8°
	EI7WS	S	.294"	.580"	2.75oz	43 - 45"	3.7°
EI-70 Irons	EI7IR	R	.355"	.580"	2.72oz	35 1/2 - 40"	2.2°
	EI7IS	S	.355"	.580"	2.75oz	35 1/2 - 40"	2.2°

UNIFIBER USA GRAPHITE SHAFTS

Name	Flex	Tip Dia.	Butt Dia.	Raw Weight	Raw Length	Mfrs. Stated Torque
MasterStroke-Woods	L	.335"	.600"	3.03oz	44"	4.5°
	R	.335"	.600"	3.14oz	44"	4.5°
	S	.335"	.600"	3.31oz	44"	4.5°
	X	.335"	.600"	3.42oz	44"	4.5°
MasterStroke-Irons	L	.370"	.600"	2.68oz	39"	4.0°
	A	.370"	.600"	2.75oz	39"	4.0°
	R	.370"	.600"	2.89oz	39"	4.0°
	S	.370"	.600"	2.93oz	39"	4.0°
	X	.370"	.600"	3.03oz	39"	4.0°
B7 Gold-Woods	L	.335"	.600"	2.96oz	44"	4.0°
	R	.335"	.600"	3.14oz	44"	4.0°
	S	.335"	.600"	3.31oz	44"	4.0°
	X	.335"	.600"	3.39oz	44"	4.0°
	XX	.335"	.600"	3.39oz	44"	4.0°

UNIFIBER USA GRAPHITE SHAFTS (cont'd.)

Name	Flex	Tip Dia.	Butt Dia.	Raw Weight	Raw Length	Mfrs. Stated Torque
B7 Gold Irons	L	.370"	.600"	2.96oz	39"	2.5°
	R	.370"	.600"	2.86oz	39"	2.5°
	S	.370"	.600"	3.07oz	44"	2.5°
	X	.370"	.600"	3.17oz	39"	2.5°
PowerStroke Woods	A	.335"	.600"	2.89oz	44"	3.5°
	R	.335"	.600"	3.10oz	44"	3.5°
	S	.335"	.600"	3.25oz	44"	3.5°
	XX	.335"	.600"	3.42oz	44"	3.5°
PowerStroke Irons	R	.370"	.600"	3.03oz	39"	2.5°
	S	.370"	.600"	3.21oz	39"	2.5°
	X	.370"	.600"	3.35oz	39"	2.5°
T50 Woods	R	.335"	.600"	3.14oz	44"	2.5°
	S	.335"	.606"	3.32oz	44"	2.5°
	X	.335"	.608"	3.39oz	44"	2.5°
	XX	.335"	.610"	3.42oz	44"	2.5°
ProStroke Woods	R	.335"	.600"	3.70oz	44"	2.0°
	S	.335"	.600"	3.70oz	44"	2.0°
	X	.335"	.600"	3.70oz	44"	2.0°
	XX	.335"	.600"	3.70oz	44"	2.0°
SilverStroke Woods	L	.335"	.600"	2.89oz	44"	2.5°
	R	.335"	.600"	3.03oz	44"	2.5°
	S	.335"	.600"	3.10oz	44"	2.5°
	X	.335"	.600"	3.17oz	44"	2.5°
	XX	.335"	.600"	3.28oz	44"	2.5°
UFX Woods	S	.335"	.620"	4.05oz	45"	1.9°
	X	.335"	.620"	4.05oz	45"	1.9°
	XX	.335"	.620"	4.05oz	45"	1.9°
Progressive Power -Irons	R, S, X	.370"	.600"	2.82oz	35"	2.5°
	R, S, X	.370"	.600"	3.00oz	37"	2.7°
	R, S, X	.370"	.600"	3.17oz	39"	2.9°

UNIFIBER USA GRAPHITE SHAFTS (cont'd.)

Name	Flex	Tip Dia.	Butt Dia.	Raw Weight	Raw Length	Mfrs. Stated Torque
MS II Irons	R, S, X	.370"	.615"	3.00oz	37"	2.7°
	R, S, X	.370"	.615"	3.17oz	39"	2.9°
Big Red Woods	R	.335"	.650"	4.94oz	60"	2.5° @44"
	S	.335"	.650"	5.08oz	60"	2.5° @44"
	X	.335"	.650"	5.22oz	60"	2.5° @44"
	XX	.335"	.650"	5.36oz	60"	2.5° @44"

SHAFT INDEX

Index for Shaft Trimming and Installation Charts
by Shaft Pattern or Model

Shaft Code	Shaft Name	Chart	Page
1726	Masterflex X	T	100
1891	AP44 Elite R	R	99
1893	AP44 Elite S	R	99
1085	AP44 R/S	P	98
1084	AP44 R/S Overfit	P	98
1589	Torsion Matched Mark II R/S	P	98
1761	Matchflex AR	R	99
1763	Matchflex R	R	99
1765	Matchflex RS	R	99
1767	Matchflex S	R	99
1382	Spectre A/L	Q	98
1514	Spectre R/S	P	98
1469	Shadow R/S	P	98
1786	Lady Shadow	R	99
1585	Senior Shadow	R	99
1701	Acculite R	U	101
1703	Acculite S	U	101
1306	AP46 L	R	99
1305	AP46 R	R	99
1500	AP83 L	R	99
1077	AP83 R	R	99

APOLLO IRONS - PARALLEL TIP GRAPHITE SHAFTS

Shaft Code	Shaft Name	Chart	Page
G100IL	G100 L	R	99
G100IR	G100 R	R	99
G100IS	G100 S	R	99
HMFIR	HMF Lo Torque R	R	99
HMFIS	HMF Lo Torque S	R	99
BTIR	Boron Tourline R	R	99
BTIS	Boron Tourline S	R	99
BTIX	Boron Tourline X	R	99

APOLLO WOODS - TAPER TIP STEEL SHAFTS

Shaft Code	Shaft Name	Chart	Page
1730	Masterflex R	L, M, N	94, 95
1732	Masterflex S	L, M, N	94, 95
1734	Masterflex X	L, M, N	94, 95
1735	Masteflex X	L, M, N	94, 95
357	AP44 R	L, M, N	94, 95
510	AP44 S	L, M, N	94, 95
1269	AP46 R	L, M, N	94, 95

APOLLO IRONS - TAPER TIP STEEL SHAFTS

Shaft Code	Shaft Name	Chart	Page
1731	Masterflex R	W, X	104-106
1733	Masterflex S	W, X	104-106
1736	Masterflex X	W, X	104-106
1737	Masterflex X	W, X	104-106

BRUNSWICK WOODS - PARALLEL TIP STEEL SHAFTS

WFM	Precision FM (all frequencies)	I	113, 114
WFML	Precision FM Lite (all frequencies)	I	113, 114
8656WAL	Precision Microtaper A/L	B	86
8676WRS	Precision Microtaper R/S	A	85
7556WAL	Precision Phoenix A/L	B	86
7576WRS	Precision Phoenix R/S	A	85
8056WAL	Precision Propel II A/L	B	86
8076WRS	Precision Propel II R/S	A	85
6169WR	UCV-304 R	E	88
6179WS	UCV-304 S	E	88
2823WL	Super Champion L	E	88
2863WR	Super Champion R	E	88
2223WL	Champion L	E	88
2263WR	Champion R	E	88

BRUNSWICK WOODS - REINFORCED TIP FOR METAL WOOD SHAFTS

8956WAL	Precision Microtaper A/L	D	87
8976WRS	Precision Microtaper R/S	C	87
7596WRS	Precision Phoenix R/S	C	87

BRUNSWICK WOODS - PARALLEL TIP GRAPHITE SHAFTS

WFMPC	Fibermatch (all frequencies)	KK	115

BRUNSWICK IRONS - PARALLEL TIP STEEL SHAFTS

IFM	Precision FM (all frequencies)	I	113, 114
IFML	Prcesion FM Lite (all frequencies)	I	113, 114
8656IAL	Precision Microtaper A/L	Q	98
8676IRS	Precision Microtaper R/S	P	98
7556IAL	Precision Phoenix A/L	Q	98
7576IRS	Precision Phoenix R/S	P	98
7856IAL	Precision Propel II A/L	Q	98
7876IRS	Precision Propel II R/S	P	98
6169IR	UCV-304 R	R	99
6179IS	UCV-304 S	R	99
2823IL	Super Champion L	R	99

Shaft Code	Shaft Name	Chart	Page
I2863IR	Super Champion R	R	99
2223IL	Champion L	R	99
2263IR	Champion R	R	99

BRUNSWICK IRONS - PARALLEL TIP GRAPHITE SHAFTS

FMPC	Fibermatch (all frequencies)	KK	115

BRUNSWICK WOODS - TAPER TIP STEEL SHAFTS

WFM	Precision FM (all frequencies)	JJ	114
WFML	Precision FM Lite (all frequencies)	JJ	114
7268WR	Precision Phoenix R	L, M, N	94, 95
7278WS	Precision Phoenix S	L, M, N	94, 95
6529WL	UCV-304 L	L, M, N	94, 95
6569WR	UCV-304 R	L, M, N	94, 95
6579WS	UCV-304 S	L, M, N	94, 95
2623WL	Super Champion L	L, M, N	94, 95
2663WR	Super Champion R	L, M, N	94, 95

BRUNSWICK IRONS - TAPER TIP STEEL SHAFTS

IFM	Precision FM (all frequencies)	JJ	114
IFML	Precision FM Lite (all frequencies)	JJ	114
7268I	Precision Phoenix R	W, X	104-106
7278I	Precision Phoenix S	W, X	104-106
6529I	UCV-304 L	W, X	104-106
6569IR	UCV-304 R	W, X	104-106
6579IS	UCV-304 S	W, X	104-106
2623IL	Super Champion L	W, X	104-106
2663IR	Super Champion R	W, X	104-106

CARBON FIBER PRODUCTS - PARALLEL TIP GRAPHITE SHAFTS

HMW series	Novus CFP57 woods all flexes	HH	111
HMI series	Novus CFP57 irons all flexes	HH	111
SMW series	Novus II woods all flexes	HH	111
SMI series	Novus II irons all flexes	HH	111
ACW series	Novus All Carbon woods all flexes	HH	111
ACI series	Novus All Carbon irons all flexes	HH	111

DYNACRAFT WOODS - PARALLEL TIP STEEL SHAFTS

USWRS	Dyna-Tech Standard R/S	F	89
UCWRS	Dyna-Tech Classic R/S	F	89

DYNACRAFT IRONS - PARALLEL TIP STEEL SHAFTS

Shaft Code	Shaft Name	Chart	Page
USIRS	Dyna-Tech Standard R/S	S	100
UCIRS	Dyna-Tech Classic R/S	S	100

EASTON COMPOSITES - PARALLEL TIP COMPOSITE SHAFTS

HP-100L	Women's HP-100 woods, irons	LL	116
HP-100M	Men's HP-100 woods, irons all flexes	LL	116
MP-200L	Women's MP-200L woods all flexes	LL	116
MP-200M	Men's MP-200 woods all flexes	LL	116
MP-300M	Men's MP-300 woods and irons	LL	116
MP-300P	Pro MP-300 X woods	LL	116

FENWICK - PARALLEL TIP GRAPHITE SHAFTS

World Class	all woods and irons and flexes	MM	116

FENWICK - TAPER TIP GRAPHITE SHAFTS

World Class	all woods and flexes	PP, O	96
World Class	all irons and flexes	MM	116

FIBER SPEED - PARALLEL TIP COMPOSITE SHAFTS

FS-100W	Fiber Speed flexible wood	NN	117
FS-100I	Fiber Speed flexible irons	NN	117
FS-200W	Fiber Speed medium wood	NN	117
FS-200I	Fiber Speed medium irons	NN	117
FS-300W	Fiber Speed firm wood	NN	117
FS-300I	Fiber Speed firm irons	NN	117
TP4000	TP4000 woods and irons	NN	117
TP4000-Plus	TP4000 woods	NN	117

GRAFALLOY - PARALLEL TIP GRAPHITE SHAFTS

Lady Classic	both woods and irons	OO	118
Senior Classic	all woods and irons all flexes	OO	118
M14	all woods and flexes	OO	118
I14	all irons and flexes	OO	118
M29	all woods and flexes	OO	118
I29	all iron and flexes	OO	118
M54	all woods and flexes	OO	118
I54	all irons and flexes	OO	118
M60	all woods and flexes	OO	118
I60	all irons and flexes	OO	118

Shaft Code	Shaft Name	Chart	Page
M66	all woods and flexes	OO	118
M79	all woods and flexes	OO	118
I79	all irons and flexes	OO	118

GRAFALLOY - TAPER TIP GRAPHITE SHAFTS

Shaft Code	Shaft Name	Chart	Page
I29	all irons and flexes	OO	118
I54	all irons and flexes	OO	118

KUNNAN - PARALLEL TIP GRAPHITE SHAFTS

Autoclave

Shaft Code	Shaft Name	Chart	Page
Series 30 Woods	all woods and flexes	PP	118
Series 30 Irons	all irons and flexes	PP	118
Series 40 Woods	all woods and flexes	PP	118
Series 40 Irons	all irons and flexes	PP	118
Series 50 Woods	all woods and flexes	PP	118
Comp50 FCB Woods	all woods and flexes	PP	118
Comp50 FCB Irons	all irons and flexes	PP	118
1460TFB Woods	all woods and flexes	PP	118
1460TFB Irons	all irons and flexes	PP	118
1400TFB Wood	all woods and flexes	PP	118
14000TFB Irons	all irons and flexes	PP	118
1400LFB Woods	all woods and flexes	PP	118
1400LFB Irons	all irons and flexes	PP	118

SANDVIK TITANIUM - PARALLEL TIP SHAFTS

Shaft Code	Shaft Name	Chart	Page
TIW	Standard Titanium woods, all flexes	QQ	119
TI	Standard Titanium irons, all flexes	QQ	119
TIWAR	Titanium Low Flex A/R	RR	120
TIWSX	Titanium Low Flex S/X	RR	120

TRUE TEMPER WOODS - PARALLEL TIP STEEL SHAFTS

Shaft Code	Shaft Name	Chart	Page
UDGWR	Dynamic Gold R	E	88
UDGWS	Dynamic Gold S	E	88
UDGWX	Dynamic Gold X	E	88
UDWAL	Dynamic A/L	B	86
UDWR	Dynamic R	E	88
UDWC	Dynamic R/S	A	85
UDWS	Dynamic S	E	88
UDWX	Dynamic X	E	88
UJWC	Jet Step R/S	A	85
UPWC	Pro Fit R/S	A	85
U2LWAL	TT Lite A/L	B	86

Shaft Code	Shaft Name	Chart	Page
UTTLWC	TT Lite R/S	A	85
UGPWLH	Gold Plus L	G	89
UGPWRH	Gold Plus R	G	89
UGPWSH	Gold Plus S	G	89
UGPWXH	Gold Plus X	G	89
UTFFWL	Flex Flow L	J	92
UTFFWA	Flex Flow A	J	92
UTFFWR	Flex Flow R	J	92
UTFFWS	Flex Flow S	J	92
URWLM	Comet L	E	88
URWR	Comet R	E	88
U3WL	Century L	E	88
U3W	Century R	E	88

TRUE TEMPER WOODS - REINFORCED TIP FOR METAL WOOD SHAFTS

Shaft Code	Shaft Name	Chart	Page
UDWCH	Dynamic R/S	C	87
UTTLWCH	TT Lite R/S	C	87
UTFFWLH	Flex Flow L	K	93
UTFFWAH	Flex Flex A	K	93
UTFFWRH	Flex Flow R	K	93
UTFFWSH	Flex Flow S	K	93

TRUE TEMPER WOODS- PARALLEL TIP GRAPHITE SHAFTS

Shaft Code	Shaft Name	Chart	Page
UBGTWSH	Black Gold Tour S High Flex	E	88
UBGTWXH	Black Gold Tour X High Flex	E	88
UBGTWSL	Black Gold Tour S Low Flex	E	88
UBGTWXL	Black Gold Tour X Low Flex	E	88
UCBHWL	Black Gold L	E	88
UCBHWR	Black Gold R	E	88
UCBHWS	Black Gold S	E	88
UCBHWX	Black Gold X	E	88
UCMHWL	Modulus EV40 L	E	88
UCMHWR	Modulus EV40 R	E	88
UCMHWS	Modulus EV40 S	E	88
UCMHWX	Modulus EV40 X	E	88
UVWL	Command L	E	88
UVWR	Command R	E	88
UVWS	Command S	E	88
UEI7WL	EI-70 L	E	88
UEI7WR	EI-70 R	E	88
UEI7WS	EI-70 S	E	88

TRUE TEMPER IRONS - PARALLEL TIP STEEL IRON SHAFTS

Shaft Code	Shaft Name	Chart	Page
UDGIR	Dynamic Gold R	R	99
UDGIS	Dynamic Gold S	R	99
UDGIX	Dynamic Gold X	R	99
UDIAL	Dynamic A/L	Q	98
UDIR	Dynamic R	R	99
UDIC	Dynamic R/S	P	98
UDICO	Dynamic R/S Overfit	P	98
UDIS	Dynamic S	R	99
UDIX	Dynamic X	R	99
UJIC	Jet Step R/S	P	98
UJICO	Jet Step R/S Overfit	P	98
UPIC	Pro Fit R/S	P	98
UPICO	Pro Fit R/S Overfit	P	98
U2LIAL	TT Lite A/L	Q	98
UTTLIC	TT Lite R/S	P	98
UGPIL	Gold Plus L	R	99
UGPIR	Gold Plus R	R	99
UGPIS	Gold Plus S	R	99
UTFFIL	Flex Flow L	V	102
UTFFIA	Flex Flow A	V	102
UTFFIR	Flex Flow R	V	102
UTFFIS	Flex Flow S	V	102
URIL	Comet L	R	99
URIR	Comet R	R	99
U3IL	Century L	R	99
U3I	Century R	R	99

TRUE TEMPER IRONS - PARALLEL TIP GRAPHITE SHAFTS

Shaft Code	Shaft Name	Chart	Page
UCBHIL	Black Gold L	R	99
UCBHIR	Black Gold R	R	99
UCBHIS	Black Gold S	R	99
UCBHIX	Black Gold X	R	99
UEI7L	EI-70 L	R	99
UEI7R	EI-70 R	R	99
UEI7S	EI-70 S	R	99
UCMHIL	Modulus EV40 L	R	99
UCMHIR	Modulus EV40 R	R	99
UCMHIS	Modulus EV40 S	R	99
UCMHIX	Modulus EV40 X	R	99
UVIL	Command L	R	99

Shaft Code	Shaft Name	Chart	Page
UVIR	Command R	R	99
UVIS	Command S	R	99

TRUE TEMPER WOODS - TAPER TIP STEEL SHAFTS

DGWR	Dynamic Gold R	L, M, N	94, 95
DGWS	Dynamic Gold S	L, M, N	94, 95
DGWX	Dynamic Gold X	L, M, N	94, 95
DWA	Dynamic A	L, M, N	94, 95
DWT	Dynamic R	L, M, N	94, 95
DWS	Dynamic S	L, M, N	94, 95
DWX	Dynamic X	L, M, N	94, 95
JTWR	Jet Step R	L, M, N	94, 95
JTWS	Jet Step S	L, M, N	94, 95
PFWL	Pro Fit L	L, M, N	94, 95
PFWA	Pro Fit A	L, M, N	94, 95
PFWR	Pro Fit R	L, M, N	94, 95
PFWS	Pro Fit S	L, M, N	94, 95
2LWL	TT Lite L	L, M, N	94, 95
2LWR	TT Lite R	L, M, N	94, 95
2LWS	TT Lite S	L, M, N	94, 95
GPWR	Gold Plus R	L, M, N	94, 95
GPWS	Gold Plus S	L, M, N	94, 95
GPWX	Gold Plus X	L, M, N	94, 95
TFFWL	Flex Flow L	L, M, N	94, 95
TFFWA	Flex Flow A	L, M, N	94, 95
TFFWR	Flex Flow R	L, M, N	94, 95
TFFWS	Flex Flow S	L, M, N	94, 95
SDLWL	Extra Lite L	L, M, N	94, 95
SDLWR	Extra Lite R	L, M, N	94, 95
SDLWS	Extra Lite S	L, M, N	94, 95

TRUE TEMPER WOODS - TAPER TIP GRAPHITE SHAFTS

TBGTWSH	Black Gold Tour S High Flex	SS	121
TBGTWXH	Black Gold Tour X High Flex	SS	121
TBGTWSL	Black Gold Tour S Low Flex	SS	121
TBGTWXL	Black Gold Tour X Low Flex	SS	121
TCBHWR	Black Gold R	SS	121
TCBHWS	Black Gold S	SS	121
TCBJWX	Black Gold X	SS	121
EI7WR	EI-70 R	SS	121
EI7WS	EI-70 S	SS	121

TRUE TEMPER IRONS - TAPER TIP STEEL SHAFTS

Shaft Code	Shaft Name	Chart	Page
DGIR	Dynamic Gold R	W, X	104-106
DGIS	Dynamic Gold S	W, X	104-106
DGIX	Dynamic Gold X	W, X	104-106
DIA	Dynamic A	W, X	104-106
DIT	Dynamic R	W, X	104-106
DIS	Dynamic S	W, X	104-106
DIX	Dynamic X	W, X	104-106
JTIR	Jet Step R	W, X	104-106
JTIS	Jet Step S	W, X	104-106
PFIL	Pro Fit L	W, X	104-106
PFIA	Pro Fit A	W, X	104-106
PFIR	Pro Fit R	W, X	104-106
PFIS	Pro Fit S	W, X	104-106
2LIL	TT Lite L	W, X	104-106
2LIR	TT Lite R	W, X	104-106
2LIS	TT Lite S	W, X	104-106
GPIR	Gold Plus R	W, X	104-106
GPIS	Gold Plus S	W, X	104-106
GPIX	Gold Plus X	W, X	104-106
TFFIL	Flex Flow L	W, X	104-106
TFFIA	Flex Flow A	W, X	104-106
TFFIR	Flex Flow R	W, X	104-106
TFFIS	Flex Flow S	W, X	104-106
SDLIL	Extra Lite L	W, X	104-106
SDLIR	Extra Lite R	W, X	104-106
SDLIS	Extra Lite S	W, X	104-106

TRUE TEMPER IRONS - TAPER TIP GRAPHITE SHAFTS

Shaft Code	Shaft Name	Chart	Page
TCBHIR	Black Gold R	SS	121
TCBHIS	Black Gold S	SS	121
TCBHIX	Black Gold X	SS	121
EI7IR	EI - 70 R	SS	121
EI7IS	EI - 70 S	SS	121

UNIFIBER USA GRAPHITE SHAFTS

Shaft Code	Shaft Name	Chart	Page
MasterStroke	all woods and irons and flexes	TT	122
B7 Gold	all woods and irons and flexes	TT	122
PowerStroke	all woods and irons and flexes	TT	122

Shaft Code	Shaft Name	Chart	Page
T50	all woods and flexes	TT	122
ProStroke	all woods and flexes	TT	122
SilverStroke	all woods and flexes	TT	122
UFX	all woods and flexes	TT	122
Progressive Power	all irons and flexes	TT	122
MS II	all irons and flexes	TT	122
Big Red	all woods and flexes	TT	122

CHAPTER 4 - The Role of the Grip in Clubmaking

A Technical Discussion of Grips
A Complete Guide to Grip Sizing
The Effect of the Grip on Golf Club Specifications
The Techniques of Grip Installation

The Golfer's Touch with the Club

If the shaft is the component that mystifies and intimidates clubmakers the most, then the grip has to stand out as the most overlooked component on the golf club. After all, since the 1950s and the introduction of the slip-on rubber grip, grip installation has essentially been reduced to the mere task of applying the 2-way tape, wetting the tape and grip core with solvent, and then sliding on the grip. While the procedures of installing a slip-on grip are easily mastered by beginning clubmakers, getting the grip onto the shaft is only a fraction of the grip knowledge that must be learned to become a competent clubmaker.

While slip-on rubber grips are by far the predominant type of grip in use today, there still do exist other grips that require entirely different skills for proper installation. Leather wrap-on grips, once the only type of grip, are still popular with a certain segment of players. While the old task of hand wrapping the underlisting has been replaced by the use slip-on underlistings, a definite skill

in professionally wrapping and finishing the leather strap over the underlisting still must be attained. Add to that the individual nuances of the variety of other grip styles and before long it becomes evident that there is more to grip installation than first meets the eye.

But learning to install all the different types of grips is still not the end of the knowledge required. All clubmakers will eventually be faced with installing each of the grip styles to custom fit sizes. The most requested customized feature in a set of golf clubs is an alteration of the size of the grip. While most golfers do not possess a great deal of awareness of golf club specifications such as face angle, lie, offset and the like, most are aware of the fact that grips can be installed to different sizes. While most clubmakers profess to know how to install oversized grips, an analysis of skills soon proves this is sorely not the case. In 1990, of the first 100 clubmakers who took the examination to attain the standard of Class A Clubmaker within the Professional Clubmakers' Society, by

far the most widely missed questions concerned the proper sizing of grips.

As the lists of the shaft manufacturers' available patterns in Chapter 3 reveals, shafts are produced in a variety of different butt diameters. Because of this, beginning clubmakers soon discover that three wraps of extra tape doesn't always result in a 1/32" oversize grip. Clubmakers must realize that accurately installing grips to specific sizes requires a full understanding of all the factors that can control the diameter of a grip - the shaft butt diameter, the amount of tape applied to the shaft, the inside core diameter of the grip, and even the resiliency or stretchability of the grip's material.

Not withstanding the installation procedures or sizing principles, real awareness of the importance of the grip lies in understanding how the grip can affect the specifications of the rest of the golf club. Grips of different weight materials, produced with different core sizes and installed to different sizes on the finished golf club can all be different in weight. Since the grip is an integral part of the weight and balance of the overall golf club, these weight differences in grips can have a profound effect on the swingweight and the total weight of a golf club. For example, just from a change in grip style and size, a golf club can experience a swingweight change of as much as 8 points and with it, a total weight modification of nearly 3/4 oz! Therefore, whether for installation and sizing purposes or for appreciating the relationship to club balance and weight, clubmakers must spend time developing a full understanding of grips.

A Technical Discussion of Grips

■ THE DIFFERENT TYPES OF GRIPS

Some 50 years ago, a discussion of the various types of grips would have begun and ended with the same word - leather. There were different colors of leather grips, different grades of leather grips, different shapes of leather grips, but still, all grips were made from leather! Just as the last 50 years have brought about a tremendous explosion of technological advances in the production of clubheads and shafts, so too has technology contributed to many changes in grip styles.

With the advent of vulcanizing a rubber grip directly onto the shaft followed by the invention of slip-on rubber grips in the early 1950s, the door was opened for a wide variety of different grip types and styles. Realizing that the grip is the golfer's contact with the club and capitalizing on the fact that each individual's perception of "feel" can be a little different, grip manufacturers today have responded with hundreds of types, styles and sizes of their products.

Composition Rubber Grips
The most commonly used grip in clubmaking today is the slip-on composition rubber grip. Available in a wide variety of rubber compounds, colors, styles and core sizes, composition rubber grips can be made from a

Slip-on Rubber Grip

variety of different rubber compounds or with rubber compounds that are blended with a filler material such as cork. By carefully selecting and blending different compounds of rubber, a grip manufacturer can vary the softness or texture of the grip, thus offering to golfers a difference in feel when holding onto the club. Rubber grips are produced through the compression, transfer and injection molding processes, after which they go through a series of sanding, painting and buffing steps to complete their manufacture. By virtue of the material, rubber composition grips have the ability to stretch larger in diameter when installed over successively larger shaft butt sizes, thus enabling clubmakers to achieve a very wide range of installed grip sizes. In addition, rubber grips can be molded into different shapes and different inside core configurations to further expand the differences in feel that can be offered to golfers.

Synthetic Grips
To offer a different feel and enhanced durability, slip-on grips may also be molded from non-rubber, synthetic materials. Two such examples are the Tacki-mac and Poulin Co. grips, produced from a thermoplastic

Tacki-Mac and Tac-Flo Grips

compound called Kraton, and the Tac-flo grips, molded from a silicone rubber compound called Silplus. By virtue of the material, Kraton and Silplus grips possess a tacky feel and are a favorite of golfers who fight excess hand perspiration or desire the almost sticky feel these

materials bring to a grip. Produced through the injection molding process, both are examples of the entry of new synthetic materials into golf.

An anomaly of the material, Kraton thermoplastic grips have a higher stiffness rating than rubber and as such, do not have the same ability to stretch, thus limiting their ability to conform over build-up tape to achieve an oversize condition. To achieve larger grip diameters, Kraton grip makers must produce grips that are specially made to a larger outside diameter.

Cord Grips
The golf industry's first alternative to leather grips, crude cord style grips were first introduced in the 1940s to offer golfers better traction when holding onto the club. Cord grips are characterized by an array of cloth or linen fibers

Cord and Half Cord Grips

that protrude through the surface of the rubber compound of the grip. Unlike rubber composition grips, cord style grips are only compression molded, starting with a process that actually "presses" the cotton fibers into the surface of the rubber grip. In a separate operation a "skim" layer of rubber is molded over the cord penetrated rubber. After this secondary molding the grip is carefully sanded to remove a portion of the "skim" layer, thus exposing the desired degree of cord fibers on the surface of the rubber. Because of the process and its higher percentage of rejects due to inconsistent cord penetration through the rubber, cord grips are more expensive than their all-rubber counterparts.

Early cord grips carried a very high percentage of fiber to rubber, with the surface consisting almost entirely of the cord material. As the modern trend has moved toward softer grips, cord grips have been redesigned so that today there are two basic styles available, the all velvet cord and the newer styles with cord protruding on only a portion of the grip's circumference. Today's all velvet cord models do have cord exposed over the entire circumference of the grip, but are still able to transmit a soft feel to the golfer through a high percentage of rubber material in contact with the golfer's hands. The other modern cord models, called the half cord and quarter cord styles, are manufactured with rubber only on the top half of the grip and cord fibers on the bottom half or bottom quarter of the grip.

Leather Wrap Grips

Still popular among traditional golfers as well as with players who live in warm or humid climates, wrapped leather grips have almost assumed a status today as the

Leather Wrap Grip

"Cadillac of grips," a reputation attributed to their high price when compared to the other styles of grips. A slip-on rubber foundation called an underlisting is first installed on the shaft butt to create the proper taper for the grip, over which the leather strap is wrapped. Improved tanning and finishing techniques have given the golf industry leather straps that are available in several colors, in varying degrees of tackiness, and pre-skived, or thinned on the edges for overlap wrapping purposes. Oversizing of leather wrap grips is performed by the use of build-up tape that is wrapped on the shaft butt before the underlisting is installed. The leather straps are produced from different grades of animal hide (usually cowhide), which then can be subjected to a variety of treatments to soften and add tackiness to their feel.

Leather Slip-on Grips

Conceived in an effort to eliminate the time-consuming

task of hand wrapping a leather strap over a separately installed underlisting, slip-on leather grips are produced with the strap pre-wrapped onto the underlisting. De-

Leather Slip-On Grip

signed to be installed in exactly the same manner as the rubber grips, slip-on leather grips have the disadvantage of not being able to stretch in diameter to accommodate either oversized installation or installation on larger butt diameter shafts. As a result, slip-on leather grips can only be effectively installed on shafts with a butt diameter equal to the core of the grip. This drawback means that for clubmakers to make full use of slip-on leather grip installation, a greater and more varied inventory of the grips will have to be kept on hand. In addition, slip-on leather grips are not pre-made with an end cap molded to the underlisting. Therefore an additional step of installing and shaping a plastic end cap must be added to the overall procedures of grip installation. Still, if skill is acquired in finishing the end cap, and if the grip is installed on matching shaft butt diameters (grip core size same as the shaft butt diameter), slip-on leather grips can present an attractive choice for golfers.

The Parts of a Grip

To acquire a full understanding of grips, it is necessary to become familiar with the different parts of the various types of grips. This discussion will cover the different parts by grip type.

■ RUBBER/SYNTHETIC SLIP-ON GRIPS

Mouth or Lip

The mouth, also referred to as the lip, of the slip-on rubber grip, is the small open end of the grip. All rubber

or synthetic slip-on grips are molded with a pre-finished lip, which means that today's slip-on grips do not require a plastic grip collar to be secured over the lip to finish the installation. Therefore, the lip, or final 1/2" of the grip, is made with a plain finish or a small engraved design to attractively accent the design.

Core

The inner bore of the grip is called the core. Each grip manufacturer can mold slip-on rubber and synthetic grips with different core sizes to match the various butt diameters of shafts that are available today. The four predominant shaft butt diameters in use are .560", .580",

Grip Core

.600" and .620". Grip makers can make these matching sizes for the core by substituting different diameter bars into their molding cavities. When the grip is molded, the material forms around the mandrel, thus creating the designated core size. The purpose of offering grips with different core sizes is to make the installed size of slip-on grips uniform from one shaft butt diameter to the next. For example, if the core size of a grip is equal to the shaft butt diameter, when the grip is installed with one layer of grip tape the result will be a standard size grip. Therefore, a men's 62 core size grip installed on a .620" shaft butt, a 60 core size installed on a .600" shaft butt and a 58 core size installed on a .580" shaft butt will all end up the same size.

Varigated Core

The surface of the core can assume a number of shapes so as to create a particular shape or feel for the grip.

Varigated Core

Predominantly, the core of a rubber slip-on grip is smooth from the mouth to the end cap. However, by creating a pattern on the core so that only a portion of the core will come in contact with the shaft butt, a feel much softer than normal can be created when the grip is installed. Such a varigated core design has given rise to a new generation of slip-on rubber grips known as "air cushioned" grips, a term derived from the grips' much softer feel in the hands.

Rib

Not to be confused with a varigated core, most slip-on grips are manufactured with a rib from the mouth to the end cap that is molded on the inside of the core. By making a visual inspection of the core of the grip, the rib can be seen as a flat section of rubber that runs lengthwise down the bottom side of the grip. This rib is created by using a core bar inside the molding cavity  that is machined with a narrow flat section. After molding, the flat side of the bar allows a small flat strip of rubber to be formed on the bottom side of the core. When the grip is installed on the shaft, the shaft pushes this strip of rubber outward, thus forming a slight protrusion or rib all along the bottom side of the grip. The purpose of the rib is to give golfers a way to develop grip "memory" and gain consistency in the way they apply their hands to the club. While ribbed grips are the dominant type of core construction, there also exists the non-ribbed, or round type of core design. For the round grip, a round core bar is inserted in the mold thus eliminating the strip of rubber in the core. After installation on the shaft, the result is a non-ribbed feel to the grip.

Grip Cap and Vent Hole

The butt end of the grip is called the grip cap. In the manufacture of slip-on grips, the grip cap may be molded as a part of the grip, or can be a separate disc made from a hard rubber or plastic material that is inserted into the base of each cavity before the molding of the whole grip. For inserted end caps, during the molding process the cap is joined with the body of the grip to become one unit. When the grip is installed on the shaft, the grip cap must be pushed snug against the shaft butt to ensure that the grip is completely on the shaft. To facilitate the sliding on of the grip, a vent hole is provided  in the middle of the cap as a release for air pressure that builds up inside of the shaft during installation.

Grip Core Size Codes

A letter and number, or number only code, is molded inside the lip of most manufacturers' slip-on grips to designate the core size, outside diameter size, or core shape of the grip. Such core codes are important for assuring the proper sizing of grips. The following chart offers a listing of the various code designations and their meaning.

GRIP CORE DESIGNATIONS

Code	Core Size	Diameter Outside	Inside Core	Code	Core Size	Diameter Outside	Inside Core
M58	.580"	Men's	Ribbed	L56R	.560"	Ladies	Round
M60	.600"	Men's	Ribbed	L58R	.580"	Ladies	Round
M62	.620"	Men's	Ribbed	L60R	.600"	Ladies	Round
58	.580	Men's	Ribbed	J50	.500"	Junior	Ribbed
60	.600"	Men's	Ribbed	J58	.580"	Junior	Ribbed
62	.620"	Men's	Ribbed	RM58	.580"	Men's Underlisting	Ribbed
M58R	.580"	Men's	Round	RM60	.600"	Men's Underlisting	Ribbed
M60R	.600"	Men's	Round	RM62	.620"	Men's Underlisting	Ribbed
M62R	.620"	Men's	Round	SM58	.580"	Men's Underlisting	Round
L56	.560"	Ladies	Ribbed	SM60	.600"	Men's Underlisting	Round
L58	.580"	Ladies	Ribbed	SM62	.620"	Men's Underlisting	Round
L60	.600"	Ladies	Ribbed	MKR	.700"	Men's Kinetic	Ribbed
56	.560"	Ladies	Ribbed				

■ SLIP-ON UNDERLISTINGS FOR LEATHER GRIPS

Slip-on rubber underlistings for leather wrapped grips are manufactured in conventional shapes for use on woods and irons, as well as in an assortment of special shapes for putters. Many of the parts of an underlisting are exactly the same as for slip-on rubber and synthetic grips, but because the underlisting's purpose is to serve as the foundation for a leather grip, there are a few features designed into them that stand as unique.

Mouth or Lip of Underlisting

The opening of the underlisting designed to slip over the butt end of the shaft is called the mouth, or the lip. Unlike conventional rubber grips the mouth of the underlisting is intentionally molded in a bell shape for ease in installation over the butt of the shaft. Since the underlisting is very thin, the mouth is flared to help prevent tearing during installation.

Bell and Bell Tab

The bell of the underlisting is the flared portion of the small end of the grip. This part of the grip is designed to aid in installation and prevent possible tearing of the rubber since the underlisting is much thinner than a conventional rubber grip. The bell is always intended to be cut away from the underlisting after it is installed on the shaft. Protruding from the bell of some underlistings is the bell tab, which indicates the underlisting's size and core code designation. Look on the previous chart of grip core designations for an explanation of the common codes that are seen on underlistings.

Core/Rib

As in the case of the slip-on rubber grips, the core is the inside bore of the underlisting. In the same light, the core of an underlisting can be molded in different diameters to match the various shafts sizes that will be encountered in assembly. Underlistings for regular grips are manufactured in .580", .600", .620" core sizes, both with and without an internal rib construction. However, unlike rubber grips, no underlistings are made with variagated core conformations.

Mold Release Holes

Along the back and sides of the underlisting can be seen a series of small recessions. These indentations are the release holes which come from protrusions in the mold during the manufacturing process. Of particular impor-

Mold Release Holes

tance are the holes located in a straight line directly on the bottom of the underlisting. Since underlistings have no design or insignia, this line of holes down the bottom side can be used to help clubmakers be sure of proper underlisting alignment during the installation procedure.

Leather Tab Recession

Some grip manufacturers' underlistings are formed with a recessed cavity just under the grip cap. This depression at the top of the underlisting is designed to receive the tab end of the leather strap to start the wrapping procedure. By providing a recess for the start of the leather wrap,

Leather Tab Recession

excessive "bunching" of the leather can be avoided just under the rubber end cap. Again, not every underlisting is made with such a leather tab recession.

Flashing

Since underlistings are always covered with a leather strap, the grip manufacturers do not bother to remove all of the thin portions of rubber that squeeze out between the halves of the grip mold during the molding process. Any excess flashing of rubber should be removed by the clubmaker before wrapping the leather to ensure consistent installation of the strap.

Grip Cap and Vent Hole

The grip cap and vent hole on the underlisting have the same function as on the conventional rubber grip, to serve as a cushion for the butt of the shaft and to allow air pressure to escape from the shaft during grip installation.

Paddle

Under the USGA Rules of Golf, a putter is the only golf club that can carry a non-round grip shape. Therefore, it is common for grip manufacturers to mold a distinctive shape onto the top of the underlisting for use with putters. This shape usually takes the form of

Paddle Putter Grip Underlisting

a narrow to wide flat surface and is referred to as the paddle of the grip.

Leather Straps

Clubmaking has come a long way since the time when leather grips were the only grip used in the assembly of a golf club. Forty years ago, companies had to cut, treat and shape each strip of leather in-house before it was ready for wrapping over the underlisting. Today, the industry's leather strap suppliers provide a finished piece ready for wrapping, a product that has been precisely made for the job complete with features to make the

Leather Strap

wrapping of leather more consistent and less time consuming. The parts of a leather strap that clubmakers should become familiar with are as follows:

Tab

The tab is the pre-cut, tapered end of the leather strap that is to be used to begin the wrapping procedure. The tab is designed to fit comfortably into the recessed cavity found under the end cap of many underlistings. The shape of the tab has also been designed to help prevent "bunching" of the leather when installed over underlistings that do not have a recessed area to start the grip.

Leather Tab

Skiving

In the days of hickory-shafted clubs, leather straps were butted edge to edge instead of overlapped, as is the customary form of installation today. To facilitate an overlap wrap, both edges of the leather strap are thinned down the entire length of the strap. These thinned sections are called the skiving of the strap and are provided to allow a smooth overlap wrapping of the

Skiving

leather down the length of the grip.

Tail

The square end of the leather strap opposite from the tab is the tail. Since leather grip makers wish to leave the decision of grip length and grip size to the clubmaker, it

Tail

is the job of the clubmaker to cut the tail of the strap and finish it for coverage with the grip collar.

A Complete Guide to Grip Sizing

■ GUIDELINES FOR STANDARD SIZE GRIP INSTALLATION

Because of the differences in player types, sizes and abilities, it is very common for a golfer to request a custom size grip. One of the most important skills for a clubmaker to acquire is to master the ability to install grips to different specified sizes. Given the assortment of shaft butt diameter sizes in use in clubmaking, along with the assortment of grip core sizes, it is vital that clubmakers fully understand all of the factors that control the size of the grip. A technical discussion of grip sizing must first begin with an understanding of just what the standards are for the size of a grip. Over the years, dimensions have been established in the golf industry for standard grip size diameters for men, women and junior golfers.

In clubmaking, the grip size is determined by recording its <u>outside diameter</u>, as measured at a series of precise locations along the length of the grip.

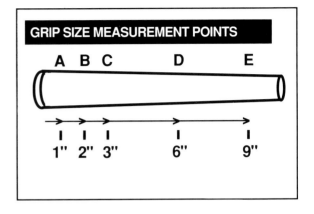

For precise measuring purposes it is possible to measure the outside diameter of a grip with a micrometer or calipers at the five points indicated in the above drawing. Care must be taken in recording these diameter measurements to always measure the grip from side to side and not from front to back. This is because many grips have a rib that protrudes from the back side of the grip enough to cause an incorrect reading of diameter. Once determined, each measurement can be compared to a series of accepted standards to determine the actual size of the grip. The drawing below indicates the exact size of a **men's standard grip** with diameter measurements taken at each of the five points along the grip's length.

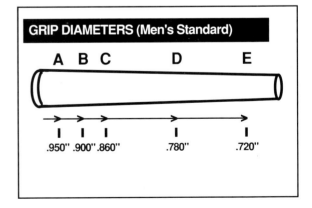

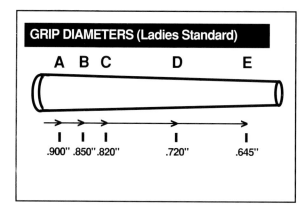

Above are the various diameters along the five measuring points that correspond to the golf industry's standard size for a ladies grip. Compare each of the measurements at identical points to those for the men's standard grip. Note at points A, B, and C, the ladies grip is between .040" to .050" smaller in diameter than the men's grip. Converting these decimal measurements to the closest common fraction (3/64"=0.046"), the following clubmaking principle can be established:

A Men's standard size grip is equivalent to a Ladies 3/64" oversize grip. Conversely, a Ladies standard size grip is equivalent to a Men's 3/64" undersize grip.

This statement will be important to remember as the discussion of grip sizing proceeds to cover the installation of oversize or undersize grips.

■ MEASURING GRIP SIZE IN THE SHOP

The previous drawings have been offered to explain the golf industry's standard sizes for men's and ladies grips. In your work as a clubmaker it is obvious that you cannot take the time to verify the size of each grip by recording five different diameter measurements. Therefore, to measure a grip to determine its size, it is an accepted clubmaking practice to record only the "B" diameter, 2" down from the edge of the grip cap.

Measuring the diameter of a grip at the B-position will require the use of a pre-made grip size gauge, calipers or a micrometer. Grip size gauges are available from several of the component supply companies and are very simple to learn to use. On one side of the gauge are formed rectangular openings that correspond to the B-position (2" down from grip cap) measurements for different grip sizes.

The rectangular openings on the gauge are designed to be slipped on the grip from the front (remember, always measure grip diameter with the gauge touching from side to side on the grip, to avoid the possible presence of a rib in the grip) and slid up toward the end cap until the gauge opening just begins to fit snug against the grip. Moving back and forth between the various gauge openings will finally result in finding the measurement that snugs against the sides of the grip at the B-position, thus enabling you to identify the grip's size.

Measuring grip diameter with a micrometer or calipers is more accurate than using a grip gauge. Measure the grip's diameter at the B-position, (2" down from the edge of the grip cap), taking the reading from side to side on the grip, not from front to back. Close the micrometer or calipers gently on the grip until the tool arms just touch against the sides of the grip. When the measuring tool touches both sides of the grip at precisely the 2" point, the actual diameter of the grip can be noted in a decimal inch reading. Below is a table of the decimal inch readings of the golf industry's most common grip sizes. To use the chart, compare the reading obtained at the B-position on any grip to the chart entries to determine the listed size.

Grip Size Diameter as measured 2" down from the edge of the grip cap

Decimal Reading 2" Down from Grip Cap	Grip Size	Decimal Reading 2" Down from Grip Cap	Grip Size
0.855"	Men's -3/64" Undersize (@ Ladies Standard)	0.915"	Men's +1/64" Oversize (@ Ladies +1/16" Oversize)
0.870"	Men's -1/32" Undersize (@ Ladies +1/64" Oversize)	0.930"	Men's +1/32" Oversize (@ Ladies +5/64" Oversize)
0.885"	Men's -1/64" Undersize (@ Ladies +1/32" Oversize)	0.945"	Men's +3/64" Oversize (@ Ladies +3/32" Oversize)
0.900"	Men's Standard (@ Ladies +3/64" Oversize)	0.960"	Men's +1/16" Oversize (@ Ladies +7/64" Oversize)
		1.025"	Men's +1/8" Oversize

All Ladies size descriptions are listed as @ (approximate) because the actual ladies decimal diameter sizes are .005" less than the above decimal inch measurements. However, the golf industry does not consider the .005" difference significant and therefore considers the above correlations between men's and ladies grip sizes as accurate.

In recalling the statement made earlier comparing men's and ladies standard grip sizes, notice on the chart that each men's size has an equivalent ladies size designation which in all cases are 3/64" apart. Later in the chapter when the matter of installing undersize grips is covered, this men's to ladies equivalency will become important.

■ CLUBMAKING GUIDELINES FOR OVERSIZE AND UNDERSIZE GRIPS

The clubmaking industry has a practice of referring to over- or undersized grips through the use of fractions. Many clubmakers are probably familiar with descriptions such as, "1/64th over," or "3/32nd over," or "1/64th under," just to name a few. What is expressed by this terminology is that the outside diameter of the grip is either larger or smaller than the standard size grip, by the amount of the fraction. Therefore, the term 1/64" over means the grip is 1/64" larger in diameter than **the standard size for that grip. Remember, the fractional amount refers to how much the grip is larger or smaller than the standard men's or ladies grip.**

Common Clubmaking Installed Grip Sizes

Installed Grip Size	Decimal Equivalent Inches Over/Under Standard
- 3/64" Undersize	0.045" smaller than standard
- 3/32" Undersize	0.030" smaller than standard
- 1/64" Undersize	0.015" smaller than standard
Standard Size	0
+ 1/64" Oversize	0.015" larger than standard
+ 3/32" Oversize	0.030" larger than standard
+ 3/64" Oversize	0.045" larger than standard
+ 1/16" Oversize	0.060" larger than standard
+ 1/8" Oversize	1.120" larger than standard

All decimal inch equivalents have been rounded for purposes of simplification. The golf industry does not consider decimal differences of 0.001 to 0.005" significant in establishing size designations.

When attempting to install over- or undersize grips it is necessary to get used to converting back and forth between decimal equivalents and fractions. This is because when describing grip core sizes or shaft butt diameters, the golf industry always uses decimal inch measurements, but when referring to over- or undersize grip dimensions, fractional equivalents are the norm. Today, the most common installed grip sizes and their decimal equivalents over or under the standard are listed at bottom left:

How Grip Oversizing/Undersizing Occurs

Before learning how to install grips to the various sizes, it is important to understand what makes the grip change in size. There are three major factors that control the size of the grip.

1. **The grip core size**
2. **The shaft butt diameter**
3. **The tape applied to the shaft for the purpose of increasing the butt diameter**

Previously in this discussion, the point was established if the grip's core size is the same as the shaft butt diameter, with one layer of 2-way grip installation tape, the grip will become standard in size.

Standard Grip Size Installation

Grip Core	Shaft Butt	Grip Size
M58	.580"	Men's Standard
M60	.600"	Men's Standard
M62	.620"	Men's Standard
L56	.560"	Ladies Standard
L58	.580"	Ladies Standard
L60	.600"	Ladies Standard

In all cases, one layer of 2-way grip tape is used in the installation.

From the previous chart it is important to realize that a standard size grip for men or women can be installed on virtually any shaft, providing the matching core size of grip is used. However, whenever the grip core size is not equal to the shaft butt diameter, a condition other than standard will result.

■ OVERSIZE/UNDERSIZE GRIPS
1. **The grip core size**
2. **The shaft butt diameter**

Installing a grip with a core size smaller than the shaft butt will create an oversized grip because the shaft acts to stretch the grip larger in diameter. How much the grip is stretched out larger than standard is determined by the difference in size between the grip core and the shaft butt.

- If the grip core size is smaller than the shaft butt diameter, the result will be an oversized grip.

- If the grip core size is larger than the shaft butt diameter, the grip will not necessarily become smaller than standard, but instead could come loose from the shaft.

For example, when an M58 grip is installed on a .600" shaft butt with the customary one layer of 2-way grip tape, the larger shaft butt will cause the grip to stretch larger by the size difference between the grip and the shaft, in this case by .020". The closest common fraction to .020" is 1/64" (0.015"). Therefore, if an M58 grip is installed on a .600" shaft butt with the customary single layer of 2-way grip tape, the grip will be +1/64" over Men's Standard Size.

- When the grip core size is smaller than the shaft butt diameter, oversizing will occur in the amount equal to the difference between the grip core and the shaft butt.

Oversize Grips
Grip core size smaller than shaft butt dia.
(With one layer of 2-way grip installation tape only)

Grip Core	Shaft Butt	Difference	Grip Size
M58	.600"	0.020"	+1/64" Over Men's Std[1]
M58	.620"	0.040"	+1/32" Over Men's Std[2]
M60	.620"	0.020"	+1/64" Over Men's Std[1]
L56	.580"	0.020"	+1/64" Over Ladies Std[1]
L56	.600"	0.040"	+1/32" Over Ladies Std[2]
L56	.620"	0.060"	+1/16" Over Ladies Std
L58	.600"	0.020"	+1/64" Over Ladies Std[1]
L58	.620"	0.040"	+1/32" Over Ladies Std[2]

The above table applies to underlisting installation as well. In all cases of slip-on grip installation, the one layer of 2-way grip tape is a constant.

[1]Even though 1/64"=0.0155", the golf industry refers to a grip diameter increase of 0.020" as being +1/64"
[2]Even though 1/32"=0.031", the golf industry refers to a grip diameter increase of 0.040" as being +1/32"

3. Build-up Tape

The above table lists all of the possible combinations for achieving an oversize grip simply by using a grip core size that is smaller than the shaft butt diameter. The third factor controlling the size of a grip is build-up tape. By wrapping layers of build-up tape on the shaft butt the clubmaker increases the diameter of the shaft, thereby causing the grip to stretch to larger diameters when it is installed.

The most commonly used tape for purposes of creating oversized grips is paper type masking tape. For purposes of gauging grip size accuracy, build-up masking tape should have a consistent strip thickness of .005". If so, each **single** layer of the tape wrapped **fully around the shaft** will have the effect of increasing the butt diameter by .010".

Grip Size Installation

This chart lists the combinations of grip core size, shaft butt diameters and build-up tape to achieve different oversize conditions.

Grip Core		Shaft Butt Diameter	Layers of Build-Up Tape Required to Achieve Stated Sizes				
			STD.	+1/64"	+1/32"	+1/16"	+1/8"
M58	+	.580"	0	1	3	6	12
M58	+	.600"	*	0	1	4	10
M58	+	.620"	n/p	*	0	2	8
M60	+	.580"	2	3	5	8	14
M60	+	.600"	0	1	3	6	12
M60	+	.620"	*	0	1	4	10
M62	+	.580"	4	5	7	10	16
M62	+	.600"	2	3	5	8	14
M62	+	.620"	0	1	3	6	12
L56	+	.560"	0	1	3	6	12
L56	+	.580"	*	0	1	4	10
L56	+	.600"	n/p	*	0	2	8
L58	+	.560"	2	3	5	8	14
L58	+	.580"	0	1	3	6	12
L58	+	.600"	*	0	1	4	10
L60	+	.560"	4	5	7	10	16
L60	+	.580"	2	3	5	8	14
L60	+	.600"	0	1	3	6	12

For all cases of grip installation in the above chart, it is assumed that one layer of 2-way grip installation tape will be added to the total number of build-up tape layers

* - Grip must be stretched @3/4" longer equally over its length to reduce its diameter and create this size.

n/p - Not possible to achieve this size with this grip core and shaft combination.

Calculating the effect of build-up tape in determining the size of a grip involves using the same principles described previously for grip core and shaft butt diameter size differences. Remember: by installing build-up tape you are simply increasing the butt diameter of the shaft. The difference between grip core size and the shaft butt plus build-up tape will reveal the amount of size change.

For example, a previous example illustrated when an M58 grip was installed on a .600" shaft, the installed grip was .020" larger than standard, and therefore was expressed as being a Men's +1/64" oversize grip. In the same example, if one layer of build-up tape is applied in addition to the customary single layer of 2-way grip tape, the shaft butt diameter will increase to .610". The difference between the M58 grip core and the shaft butt with build-up tape is now 0.030", which when converted to a fraction yields a grip that is +1/32" oversize (.031" = 1/32").

Remember: 2-way grip installation tape is never included in the calculation of the tape's effect on grip sizing. The golf industry agrees that the presence of the one layer of 2-way tape is a constant factor for all grips.

■ PUTTING IT ALL TOGETHER - CALCULATING THE INSTALLED GRIP SIZE

STEP 1: Note the customer's grip size request and determine the amount of oversizing that is required in decimal inches.

EXAMPLE #1: Men's +1/16" Oversize grip
  Step 1: Men's +1/16" Oversize = **.060"** larger than Men's Standard.

EXAMPLE #2: Men's +1/32" Oversize grip
  Step 1: +1/32" Men's Oversize = **.030"** larger than Men's Standard.

STEP 2: Check the grip core size and measure the butt diameter of the shaft.

EXAMPLE #1: Men's +1/16" Oversize grip
  Step 2: Grip = Men's M58, - Shaft = .600"

EXAMPLE #2: Men's +1/32" Oversize grip
  Step 2: Grip = Men's M60, - Shaft = .580"

STEP 3: Combine the core size and shaft butt to determine their relationship to standard grip size in decimal inches. Use no build-up tape in this calculation.

EXAMPLE #1: Men's +1/16" Oversize grip
  Step 3: M58 core + .600" shaft + one layer of 2-way tape = +.020" over Men's Standard.

EXAMPLE #2: Men's +1/32" Oversize grip
  Step 3: M60 core + .580" shaft + one layer 2-way tape = **-.020"**

(Remember, the grip is not undersized. In this case the shaft butt is going to have to be increased .020" just to achieve the Men's Standard.)

STEP 4: Compare the size of the grip as installed with one layer of 2-way tape (Step 3) to the final oversize condition required to determine the amount of necessary build-up tape.

EXAMPLE #1: Men's +1/16" Oversize Grip
  Step 4:
    Size increase required = +.060" (+1/16")
    Core + Shaft (Step 3)   +.020" (M58 + .600")
    Build-up tape required = +.040" (4 layers)

A +1/16" oversize grip is .060" larger than standard. Of that increase, .020" will be contributed by the M58 core stretching larger over the .600" shaft. So, .040" more diameter increase will be needed to achieve the +1/16" total, which equates to four layers of build-up tape, since each layer will add .010".

EXAMPLE #2:
  Step 4:
    Size increase required = +.030" (+1/32")
    Core + Shaft (Step 3)   -.020" (M60 + .580")
    Build-up tape required = +.050" (5 layers)

A +1/32" oversize grip is .030" larger than standard. Two layers of build up tape will be required to make the shaft butt equal to the grip core size. Three more layers of build-up tape will be needed to achieve the required 0.030" increase over standard grip size, thus making a total of five wraps of build-up tape required.

■ INSTALLING GRIPS TO SMALLER THAN STANDARD SIZES

The key to installing grips to smaller than standard sizes, or undersize conditions, is understanding the relationship between men's and ladies grip sizes. Earlier in the chapter the following chart was presented during the discussion on measuring grip sizes:

Grip Size Diameters
as measured 2" down
from the edge of the grip cap

Decimal Inch Measurement at the 2" Point	Grip Size
0.855"	Men's -3/64" Undersize (@ Ladies Standard)
0.870"	Men's -1/32" Undersize (@ Ladies +1/64" Oversize)
0.885"	Men's -1/64" Undersize (@ Ladies +1/32" Oversize)
0.900"	Men's Standard (@ Ladies +3/64" Oversize)
0.915"	Men's +1/64" Oversize (@ Ladies +1/16" Oversize)
0.930"	Men's +1/32" Oversize (@ Ladies +5/64" Oversize)
0.945"	Men's +3/64" Oversize (@ Ladies +3/32" Oversize)
0.960"	Men's +1/16" Oversize (@ Ladies +7/64" Oversize)
1.025"	Men's +1/8" Oversize

This chart establishes the point that there are equivalents for each of the various men's and ladies' sizes of installed grips. In other words, the same grip diameter may be expressed in ladies or men's grip size dimensions. For example, if you are asked to install a grip to a Men's -1/64" undersize condition, the best way to accomplish the task is to install a ladies grip to a +1/32" oversize dimension. Because of the difference between men's and ladies' grip sizes, a Ladies +1/32" oversize grip is equal to a Men's -1/64" undersize grip.

Study the chart of equivalent men's and ladies sizes and you will find it the fastest and most accurate way of satisfying that occasional request for undersize grips.

The second way to achieve an undersize grip is to stretch the grip longer on the shaft after installation.

For every 3/4" a grip is stretched longer over its entire length, its diameter will decrease by 1/64".

It is very important to understand that a slip-on rubber grip or underlisting is much thinner at the mouth end than it is at the butt end. Therefore, care must be taken to ensure that the stretching is performed over the entire length of the grip and not just over the bottom four inches. Failure to stretch the grip from the top, or thicker part of the grip, will result in a diameter that is incorrectly sized.

Stretching grips to achieve smaller sizes is only recommended for a decrease in size of the grip of 1/64". When a rubber grip is stretched more than 3/4" longer, the grip assumes a very unprofessional appearance; the grip's design becomes unsightly and the shaft butt begins to push the grip cap out in an undesirable manner. Following are the correct guidelines for installing grips to undersize dimensions.

Stretching the grip is acceptable for reducing the grip size by 1/64".

For a Men's or Ladies -1/64" undersize grip, install the men's or ladies grip to standard size, and stretch the grip 3/4" longer over its entire length, not just the bottom four inches of the grip.

For installation of -1/32" undersize or even smaller, learn and use the ladies to men's equivalent grip sizes.

Men's -1/32" undersize = Ladies +1/64" oversize; Men's -3/64" undersize = Ladies standard grip; These

will be the only other men's undersize grip conditions that you will likely face in your clubmaking.

■ SPECIAL CONDITIONS - UNDERSIZE LEATHER GRIP OR UNDERSIZE LADIES RUBBER GRIPS

As mentioned, installing Men's undersize grips is simply a matter of learning the ladies equivalent sizes. However, when faced with the task of installing undersize grips for ladies, or offering leather grips for ladies, special procedures must be followed.

Earlier in the chapter, both of these line drawings of grip dimensions were offered to explain the standard diameters for men's and ladies grips. Study both drawings and note the differences in diameter between the dimensions at Point A and Point B on the men's and ladies standard size grips. The difference for the men's and ladies grips at the 1" and 2" points down from the

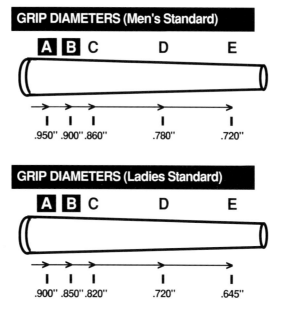

GRIP DIAMETERS (Men's Standard)

A B C   D   E

.950" .900" .860"   .780"   .720"

GRIP DIAMETERS (Ladies Standard)

A B C   D   E

.900" .850" .820"   .720"   .645"

grip cap is .050". As was stated before, .050" is roughly equivalent to a size decrease of 3/64". Therefore,

If 1" is cut off the end of a men's grip, the grip will be changed to a ladies standard size grip.

If 1" is cut off the end of a ladies grip, the result will be a grip that is 3/64" smaller than a standard ladies grip.

If a highly undersized ladies grip is desired, the task can be accomplished by cutting 1" off the end of the ladies grip and treating is as if it were now a 3/64" undersize ladies grip. The only drawback to this special procedure of installation is that the cut grip will now require the installation of a plastic end cap to replace the cut-off rubber grip cap.

Recently another alternative has been presented to allow creation of extremely undersized ladies rubber grips. Golf Pride Grip Co. now manufactures one of its junior grips in a .580" core size, so this grip can be used and even built up in size to fill the needs of the smaller-handed lady players.

Ladies Leather Grips

To create a ladies leather grip, cut 1" off the end of a men's underlisting and finish the end of the grip by installing a plastic end cap. Cutting 1" from the butt end of a men's underlisting will effectively make it a standard size ladies underlisting. Remember that the smallest core size for a men's underlisting is a 58 (.580"), so if the cut-off underlisting is to be installed on a traditional .560" ladies shaft, two layers of build-up tape will be required to properly secure the cut-off underlisting to the shaft and create the standard ladies size. After the underlisting has dried to the shaft, the leather strap can be wrapped followed by end cap assembly to complete the job.

The Effect of the Grip on Assembled Golf Club Specifications

■ GRIP WEIGHT & SWINGWEIGHT

While the major emphasis on the grip as a part of clubmaking is centered around sizing, it is also important to understand how the grip can affect other specifications of the assembled club. One of the most important tasks a clubmaker faces when assembling a set of golf clubs is establishing the swingweight of each club within the set.

Swingweight is defined as the relationship of the weight within a golf club as measured about a particular point of balance. Keeping that in mind, the recognized form of measuring swingweight in the golf industry is to determine this weight relationship on a swingweight scale with a 14" fulcrum or balance point. When a club is placed on a swingweight scale, the grip lies on the opposite side of the fulcrum point from the clubhead. Therefore, any weight changes that come about as a result of using different grips or from installing grips to different sizes will have the effect of changing the swingweight. As a result, the weight of the grip and any tape that is used for build-up purposes plays a very important role in establishing the club's final swingweight.

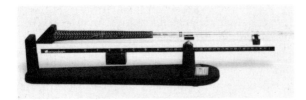

For purposes of illustration, the swingweight scale photo shows the normal position of a golf club on a 14" fulcrum type swingweight scale. With the club in level balance on the scale, it is possible to see that any addition or reduction of weight on the grip end will change the swingweight reading for the club. If we create an example of a standard condition of clubmaking, we can begin to explain the weight relationship that exists between each component part of the golf club.

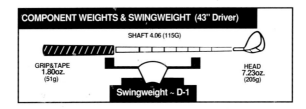

COMPONENT WEIGHTS & SWINGWEIGHT (43" Driver)

SHAFT 4.06 (115G)

GRIP & TAPE 1.80oz. (51g)

HEAD 7.23oz. (205g)

Swingweight ~ D-1

This drawing breaks down an example Driver of 43" playing length, Dynamic S shaft, and M60 core rubber grip with D-1 swingweight into each of the component weights of the grip, shaft and clubhead. In the example, the installed shaft weighs 4.06 oz (115g), the head has a weight of 7.23 oz (205g), and the grip **and the tape** used to install the grip weighs 1.80 oz (51g). This combination of component weights will result in a 43" golf club that has a swingweight reading of D-1 and a total weight of 13.1 oz (371g). In the example club on the scale, if the weight of the grip is reduced by 0.14 oz (4g) the swingweight will increase from D-1 to D-2, and conversely if the weight of the grip is increased by the same 0.14 oz (4g) amount, the swingweight will decrease from D-1 to D-0. Therefore, the following statement can be made describing the relationship of the weight of the grip to establishing the swingweight of a golf club:

For every 4 gram change in the weight of the grip, the swingweight of a golf club will change by 1 swingweight point.

The above weight relationship is a general guideline to follow when calculating the swingweight of a club before assembly. Refer to Chapter 10 for a complete discussion of pre-calculating golf club swingweight from known component part weights.

The Weight of Different Grips

Within the assortment of different grips that may be used in clubmaking there is also a range in the weight of the various types of grips. From rubber to leather to jumbo type grips, the weight of the grip alone can vary by up to 29 grams! With such a range representing a 7+ swingweight variance in the golf club, it is very important for

clubmakers to be aware of the weight of the grips used to make golf clubs.

The main reason for such a variance in grip weight is due to the design of the grip itself. While the majority of grips used in clubmaking are of the rubber slip-on type, models today can be made for ladies all the way up to the jumbo type grips. For example, a ladies Chamois grip with its varigated core and smaller outside diameter weighs just 40 grams while the greatly oversized Jumbo Victory weighs in at a hefty 69 grams. While most clubmakers will not be working with such a range for the same player type, there is still a distribution in weight among the most commonly used grips that must be understood and accounted for in the job of assembling golf clubs.

For example, Eaton Golf Pride manufactures its Men's Victory grip pattern in many different styles from standard rubber to all cord to half cord. Because each style of the Victory grip could be chosen for use by the same golfer, clubmakers must be aware of the fact that even within this one grip style, the grip weight can range from 47.5 grams to 51.5 grams.

The major reason that rubber grips do not weigh the same is due to the fact that grips are manufactured to different core sizes. To understand how such a condition exists, first remember that all men's grips or all ladies grips of a particular model have the same outside diameter. If the outside diameter of all men's grips, for example, is the same, when the core size is changed, the amount of rubber in the grip has to change. Therefore, when a popular rubber grip is produced in the M58, M60 and M62 core sizes, each of the grips will have a different weight. The M58 will have more rubber in the grip than the M60, and the M60 will have more rubber in the grip than the M62. Within the same rubber grip design, as the core size increases from 58 to 60 to 62, the grips become progressively lighter in weight.

The other reason that grips exhibit different weights is due to the actual methods used in their manufacture. Most of the golf industry's rubber slip-on grips are being converted over to injection molding as the primary method of production, a technique that does yield grips with a tight plus/minus weight tolerance. However some of the older grip models are still produced using the compression and transfer molding methods of manufacture. Therefore, when grip makers use three different molding methods to produce the same rubber grips, only an **average mean weight** can be stated for the standard weight of any grip.

What this means is that as a clubmaker, you may not know from one shipment to the next whether the grips you receive are produced by compression, transfer or injection molding. As a result, there could exist a difference in weight from high to low of as much as 3.5 grams for each of the core sizes of rubber slip-on grips you may use. Again, while most of the newer grip styles are being converted over to all injection molding, it is possible that a plus/minus weight tolerance of 3.5 grams could exist for each core size, which means that within the same grip model, a variation of 1 full swingweight point in the finished club could be seen.

To assist your understanding of grip weights, the following table lists many of the popular types of grips used in the golf industry today, along with their weights:

Grip Models and Their Weights

Grip Model	Manufacturer	Weight	Grip Model	Manufacturer	Weight
Men's Victory .580"	Eaton Golf Pride	51.5g	Men's Small	Tempo	45.0g
Men's Victory .600"	Eaton Golf Pride	49.5g	Men's Standard Half Cord	Tempo	54.0g
Men's Victory .620"	Eaton Golf Pride	47.5g	Men's Standard Full Cord	Tempo	56.0g
Half Cord Victory .580"	Eaton Golf Pride	51.5g	Men's Large	Tempo	53.0g
Half Cord Victory .600"	Eaton Golf Pride	50.0g	Jumbo Victory	Eaton Golf Pride	69.0g
Full Cord Victory .580"	Eaton Golf Pride	51.5g	Jumbo Chamois .600"	Avon	65.2g
Full Cord Victory .600"	Eaton Golf Pride	50.0g	Men's Arthritic .580"	Tacki Mac	78.0g
Men's Crown .580"	Eaton Golf Pride	51.5g	Ladies Victory	Eaton Golf Pride	47.5g
Men's Crown .600"	Eaton Golf Pride	51.0g	Ladies Crown	Eaton Golf Pride	44.5g
Crown Cord .600"	Eaton Golf Pride	52.5g	Ladies Air Cushion	Eaton Golf Pride	43.5g
Men's Eagle .580"	Eaton Golf Pride	49.0g	Ladies Sure Tac	Lamkin	44.0g
Classic Cord .580"	Eaton Golf Pride	53.5g	Ladies Chamois	Avon	40.0g
Men's Dimple .600"	Eaton Golf Pride	47.5g	Ladies Charger	Avon	51.9g
Men's Hi Tack .590"	Eaton Golf Pride	56.0g	Ladies Tacki Mac	Tacki Mac	45.5g
Men's Air Cushion	Eaton Golf Pride	45.0g	Ladies Standard	Tempo	44.0g
Dynacraft .580"	Eaton Golf Pride	51.5g	Ladies Small	Tempo	40.0g
Dynacraft .600"	Eaton Golf Pride	49.5g	Junior Victory .580"	Eaton Golf Pride	33.0g
Men's Sure Tac .580"	Lamkin	51.0g	Leather Slip On	Lamkin	55.5g*
Half Cord Sure Tac .580"	Lamkin	54.0g	Leather Wrap	Lamkin	60.0g**
Full Cord Sure Tac .580"	Lamkin	56.0g	Leather Wrap	Neumann	61.0g**
Men's Silouette .590"	Lamkin	55.5g	Underlisting RM58	Eaton Golf Pride	28.5g
Men's Chamois .580"	Avon	53.0g	Underlisting RM60	Eaton Golf Pride	27.5g
Men's Charger .580"	Avon	53.8g	Underlisting RM62	Eaton Golf Pride	26.5g
Std. Tacki-Mac .580"	Tacki Mac	52.0g	Leather Strap		26.5g
+1/32" Tacki Mac .580"	Tacki Mac	68.0g			
Soft Top .580"	Tacki Mac	47.5g			
Men's Standard	Tempo	49.0g			

*Weight including grip collar and end cap
**Weight including .600" round underlisting and grip collar

The weights listed are mean average weights and as such, could be subject to a weight tolerance range of ±3.5g. Therefore, it is recommended when pre-calculating swingweights that clubmakers always take individual weight readings of grips.

The Weight of Build-up Tape

In addition to the grip itself, the weight of any build-up tape used to create an oversize grip will also have an effect on the final swingweight of the golf club. It was mentioned earlier in this discussion that the most masking tape used for oversizing grips has a strip thickness of .005". Don't be confused - a strip thickness of .005" when wrapped around the shaft increases the shaft diameter by 0.010".

Build-up masking tape of this type can be purchased from suppliers in a variety of widths, with the most commonly used sizes being the 2" and the 3/4" width. When using the 2" wide rolls it is customary to apply each layer of tape lengthwise on the shaft butt, while when using the 3/4" rolls, it is the usual practice to spiral the tape around the shaft. Applying the 2" wide tape lengthwise is faster than spiral wrapping, so clubmakers who install a number of oversize grips will want to take note of this method in their shops.

Regardless of which tape width or wrapping method is used, the amount of weight that will be added to the butt end of the shaft will be the same.

Each single layer of build-up tape applied to the shaft will weigh 0.05oz and will decrease the swingweight of the club by 1/3 swingweight point.

Referring back to the D-1 swingweight Driver used in the previous example, if three layers of build-up tape had been applied to the shaft before installation of the grip, the club's final swingweight would have been D-0. This is because the three layers of build-up tape would have a total weight of .15oz (3 x .05oz) which when added to the grip end would decrease the club's swingweight by 1 point. Keeping in mind the effect of the weight of build-up tape, it is not hard to see how tape weight plus grip weight can together make a significant change in the swingweight of a golf club.

Effect of Different Grip Weights and Build-up Tape on Total Weight

In addition to affecting swingweight, the weight of the grip and any build-up tape that may be used can cause changes in the total weight of a golf club as well. The total weight of a golf club is simply the actual weight in ounces or grams of the assembled club. From Chapter 3, it was established that for a set of golf clubs, swingweight remains constant from club to club while the total weight increases progressively through the set.

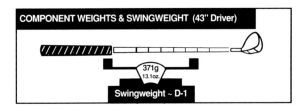

The drawing above is similar to the illustration used before to explain the relationship of the grip to swingweight. However, in this illustration that same example Driver has been depicted instead, on a total weight scale. As you can see, our D-1 swingweight example Driver with 51g grip, 115g shaft and 205g clubhead has a total weight reading of 371g (13.1oz).

When grips of different weight and with different amounts of build-up tape are used in the assembly of golf clubs, differences in each club's total weight will be noted that are often greater than just the weight of the grip and tape together. This is because when the weight of the grip and tape is changed, it is customary to not just accept the swingweight at the level to which it has been changed due to the different grip weight, but to re-establish the swingweight to its original desired level. Therefore, the change in grip weight is usually countered by an accompanying change in head weight to re-establish the swingweight.

As a result the club's total weight will not only reflect the amount of grip weight change but also any additional headweight changes that were necessary to restore the swingweight to its desired level. Had our example club been built with a 61 gram leather grip installed over five layers of build-up tape, the initial swingweight and total weight would be as illustrated below:

EXAMPLE: Substitute a 61g leather grip plus 7g of build-up tape (five layers).

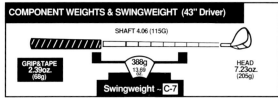

Under the effect of the leather grip with underlisting and five layers of build-up tape, this same 115g shaft and 205g clubhead will result in a Driver with an initial swingweight of C-7 and a total weight of 13.69oz. This is because the new grip with build-up tape is 17g heavier than the original grip. This total change of 17g is equivalent to slightly more than 4 swingweight points, and hence a change in the club's swingweight from D-1 down to C-7. At the same time, the total grip and tape weight increase of 17g (.59oz) when added to the original total weight of 13.1oz increases the club's total weight to 13.69oz.

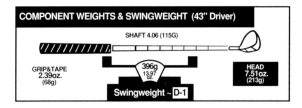

Finally, the drawing has been changed to illustrate how much weight has to be added to bring the club back to the customer's desired swingweight level of D-1. To increase the swingweight from C-7 to D-1 will require an addition of approximately .28oz (8g) to the head. Adding

this final amount of weight required for swingweight adjustment means that the final total weight of the assembled club will be 13.97oz.

Therefore, by simply building the Driver with an over-size leather grip instead of a standard size rubber grip, the golf club underwent a total weight increase of 25g (.87oz). In terms of total golf club weight, 7/8 of an ounce is significant, so you can see that the introduction of different grip styles and sizes in your clubmaking procedures can have a dramatic effect on not only swingweight but the total weight of a golf club as well.

Knowing before assembly what effect the grip and any build-up tape will have on the swingweight and total weight of each club is extremely important information for clubmakers to possess. For example, if you begin to build custom-made sets of golf clubs without paying attention to the grip and expect the clubs to always end up in the normal lower D-range of swingweight levels, you may be led to mistakenly believe that problems exist with the component suppliers' headweights.

By understanding that grips have a profound effect on swingweight and total weight, this information will enable you to always anticipate and make early allowances for what a club's initial swingweight and total weight will be before it is too late to solve the problem.

The Techniques of Grip Installation

■ TOOLS AND SUPPLIES REQUIRED

Chapter 2 includes a list of all the tools and supplies that are needed for full golf club assembly. Of the total list of items for clubmaking, the tools and supplies that will be needed for installing all types of grips are as follows:

TOOLS AND SUPPLIES FOR GRIP INSTALLATION

TOOLS

Item	Minimum Qty.	Use
Bench Vise[1]	1	Securing Club
Shaft Clamp[1]	1	Securing Club
Micrometer/Grip	1	Sizing Grips
Grip Collar Installer	1	Collar Installation
Razor Knife	1	Gen'l Installation
Knife Blades	6	Old Grip Removal
Medium File	1	Trim End Caps
Grip Remover[2]	1	Removing Grips
Remover Needles[2]	3	Removing Grips
Squeeze Bottle	1	Grip Solvent
Run-off Pan	1	Solvent Run-off

SUPPLIES

2-way Grip Tape[3]	2 rolls	Installation
Masking Tape[3]	2 rolls	Sizing
Grip Solvent	2 qts	Installation
Paper Towels	2 rolls	Clean up
.600" Grip Collars	3 doz	Leather Grips
.620" Grip Collars	3 doz	Leather Grips
.580" End Caps[4]	1 doz	Slip-on Leather
.600" End Caps[4]	1 doz	Slip-on Leather
.620" End Caps[4]	1 doz	Slip-on Leather
Contact Cement	1 pt	Collar Installation
Acetone	1 pt	Plastic Clean-ups

[1] Special lever action or air vises are available for larger shops engaged in higher volume grip installation
[2] Optional, should grip removal be a necessary part of shop services
[3] Either 2" or 3/4" wide versions may be used
[4] Optional, should slip-on leather grips be offered

The above list represents the tools and supply items required for installing all types of grips from rubber to leather to slip-on leather. Some of the items listed are optional or will only be needed if a very wide range of grips and services are offered.

Workbench Layout for Grip Installation
Most clubmakers find it is very efficient if a portion of their workbench is permanently set up as a gripping station. For small volume golf club assembly, it is fine to use the main bench vise as the grip installation station, but as volume increases it is a good idea to devote a small area on one end of your bench strictly for gripping.

A small to medium size workshop grip station area should be designed with a vise to secure the club and a paint roller pan or trough attached to the bench in the area where the grip end of the shaft will be positioned to catch any run-off of solvent. In addition, it is a good idea to plan a small storage or shelf area to keep all of the necessary grip supply items close at hand. Being organized and having everything necessary for grip installation within arm's reach will pay off in faster and more accurate work.

As your shop volume dictates, even more efficient methods for setting up a gripping station can be explored. When volume increases, the first logical expansion is to invest in a lever action vise. With such a tool, the action of securing the club is streamlined into one single clamping motion rather than wasting time attaching the shaft clamp and rotating the vise jaws closed.

Beyond a lever action vise, clubmakers can further speed up grip installation through the use of an air vise for holding the clubs. The method of choice for major manufacturers and large clubmaking shops, an air vise can be set up with a rubber shaft clamp attached to the vise jaws and activated with a foot switch. Such a production method is not totally out of the realm of possibility for many shops, for if you have a compressor, adding on the air vise and foot switch can be done for less than $200.

In addition, any streamlining of your grip station should include the use of tape dispensers for both the build-up tape and the 2-way grip tape. Standard tape dispensers for masking tape are inexpensive and can be purchased from office or shipping supply companies in your area. Special tape dispensers for rolls of 2-way grip tape are available from industrial supply firms and usually cost around $100. While somewhat expensive, these units are designed to automatically peel the backing off the 2-way tape and can prove to be a real timesaver for larger shops.

■ BASIC TECHNIQUES OF SLIP-ON GRIP INSTALLATION

While one of the most simple procedures of golf club assembly, installing slip-on grips does require a thorough understanding to ensure speed and accuracy. The following step-by-step procedures are offered to illustrate the proper small shop methods for installing all slip-on type grips, including rubber grips, synthetic grips and underlistings.

STEP 1: Secure the club in the vise
Secure the club by the shaft in the vise so that approxi-

1

mately 15" of the butt end of the shaft protrudes over the solvent catch pan. Position the club with the head toe up, with the face of the club set square.

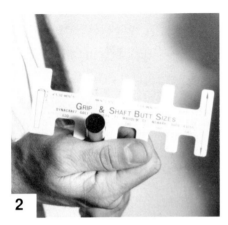

STEP 2: Calculate the amount of build-up tape required (if needed)
If build-up tape is required to establish the customer's desired grip size, calculate the number of wraps needed. Before starting the installation, organize all of the grips, tools, gauges and rolls of tape that are needed to make the total installation procedure as efficient as possible.

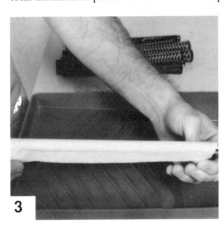

STEP 3: Apply build-up tape (if needed)
If build-up tape is needed to achieve the desired grip size, using the 2" wide type will be faster than using the 3/4"

wide roll. Tear off each strip no longer than 10-11" in length and start each layer by pressing one edge of the tape straight up and down on the shaft with approximately 1/2" left to extend past the shaft butt. Check to be sure the tape is straight up and down in line with the shaft. By keeping the length of each strip of tape shorter than the length of the grip you can avoid having the tape protrude below the mouth of the grip after installation, and eliminate an additional step of cutting back any excess tape after installation.

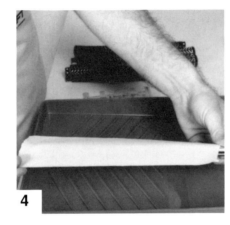

STEP 4: Wrap each layer of build-up tape around the shaft
After one edge of the tape is applied straight up and down the shaft, wrap the entire strip around the shaft, taking care to avoid wrinkling the tape. Using 2" wide tape, expect a small section of tape to overlap on itself. This small amount of overlap will not affect the size of the installed grip. However, if multiple layers of build-up tape are to be installed, it is a good idea to stagger the point each layer is started on the shaft to avoid placing the overlaps on top of each other.

STEP 5: Twist the end of the build-up tape and push into the end of the shaft
When installing each wrap of build-up tape, be sure at least 1/2" of each layer extends beyond the butt end of the shaft. After wrapping each layer around the shaft, twist the excess tape that extends over the shaft butt and push

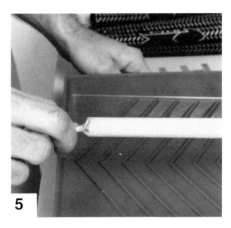

it into the end of the shaft. This will close off the end of the shaft and prevent dirt particles from getting into the shaft through the vent hole of the grip.

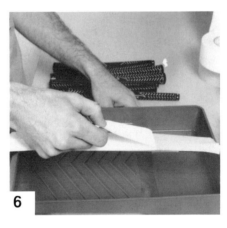

STEP 6: Apply the single layer of 2-way grip tape
2-way tape has adhesive on both surfaces and is used to secure the slip-on grip or underlisting to the shaft. Again, for the purpose of speed, use the 2" version of 2-way grip tape. Tear off a single 10" long strip of 2-way tape and remove the paper backing. Apply the tape length wise on the shaft (on top of the build-up tape, if build-up tape was required) with @ 1/2" of the end of the tape extended over the end of the shaft. Take care to prevent the tape from wrinkling when wrapping around the shaft. Twist the excess tape and push it into the end of the shaft.

STEP 7: Wet the inside of the grip with solvent
Hold one finger over the vent hole in the grip and squeeze a small amount of grip solvent into the grip core. Cover the mouth of the grip and shake the solvent around inside the grip. Make sure enough solvent is used to ensure a thorough wetting of the grip core.

STEP 8: Wet the 2-way tape with solvent
Hold the butt end of the grip over the 2-way tape and release your finger from the grip vent hole to wet the 2-way tape with the solvent that was used to wet the grip core. Be sure the entire surface of the tape is covered thoroughly with solvent. If the solvent inside the grip does not completely wet the tape, quickly use the grip solvent applicator bottle to squeeze more solvent on the

tape. Be sure to keep a run-off pan under the shaft butt to catch the excess solvent. Do not worry about the small black particles that stream over the tape from the grip. These are simply bits of rubber that have been washed out of the grip core and will not affect the installation of the grip.

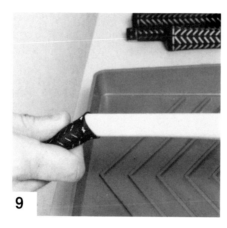

STEP 9: Start the mouth of the grip over the end of the shaft
With both hands placed near the mouth of the grip, start the grip over the bottom of the shaft butt and gently pull the grip up and over the shaft. Once the mouth is completely on the shaft, begin to push the grip onto the shaft.

STEP 10: Push the grip completely on the shaft
Waste no time in pushing the grip completely onto the shaft. Continue to push until you feel the end of the shaft butt against the grip cap. Take care to keep tape adhesive off your fingers to prevent soiling the grip.

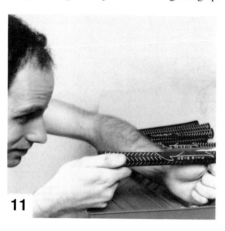

STEP 11: Align the grip
With the club positioned in the vise with the clubface square, look down the front of the grip to check alignment. Twist the grip so that any alignment insignia or design is perfectly in line with the top of the shaft.

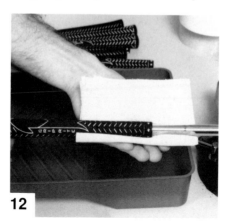

STEP 12: Clean off tape residue
Wipe all tape residue from the mouth of the grip with a paper towel. Take care when wiping to prevent smearing

the residue on the grip. Follow by wiping with a paper towel dampened in grip solvent to remove all traces of tape residue from the shaft and grip. Check all other surfaces of the grip for tape residue smears and remove with solvent.

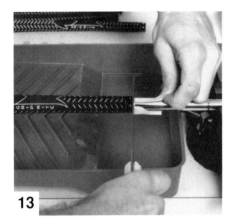

13

STEP 13: Cut off any excess tape protruding from the grip
If any build-up tape or 2-way grip tape protrudes from the mouth of the grip, use a razor knife to cut it away flush to the lip of the grip. Once more check for tape residue and clean as needed.

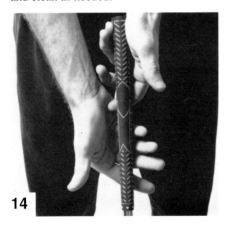

14

STEP 14: Perform final alignment check
Remove the club from the grip vise and position it on the floor in the playing position. While keeping the club in this position, check and final adjust the grip's alignment

insignia with the top of the shaft. For irons, position the clubface perfectly square to an imaginary target line while performing this check. For woods, allow the club to sit flat on its sole and assume its natural face angle while making final alignment adjustments. In other words, if the wood has a hook face angle, let the club sit flat to assume its closed face angle while adjusting the grip. **Do not artificially hold the face of a wood head square when adjusting the grip alignment.** The grip is considered to be aligned in standard form when the grip's alignment line or insignia is positioned directly in line with the top of the shaft while the club is placed in its standard playing position.

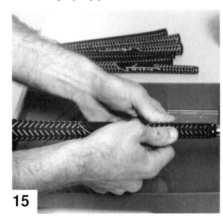

15

STEP 15: Stretch the grip to reduce its size (if needed)
If the size requirements call for the grip to be stretched longer to reduce its diameter, place the heel of both palms tight against the sides of the top of the grip and begin to slowly apply pressure against the grip as you push the grip down the shaft. Push the grip down the shaft until the desired decrease for grip diameter is achieved. Apply a strip of tape between the mouth of the grip and the shaft to hold the stretch in place until the tape adhesive dries. Stretching the grip 3/4" longer along its entire length will reduce its diameter by 1/64". Stretching a grip more than 3/4" is not recommended for its effect on grip appearance. After stretching make one final check for grip alignment before setting the grip aside to dry.

■ BASIC TECHNIQUES OF WRAPPED LEATHER GRIP INSTALLATION

While leather grips are not as popular among golfers as the slip-on rubber models, it is still important for clubmakers to develop the ability to properly wrap leather grips. The following step-by-step sequence covers all of the procedures of professionally installing and wrapping leather grips.

A key point about leather grip installation: When over-sized leather grips are desired, the layers of build-up tape are to be wrapped on the shaft **under** the underlisting. **Tape build-up for the purpose of oversizing should never be applied on top of the underlisting**.

Installing the plastic grip collar
Leather grips require the use of a plastic grip collar to finish off the mouth of the leather wrap. In the step-by-step procedures of club assembly to be covered in Chapters 5-9, it will always be recommended that the collar be installed up from the tip end of the shaft before the shaft is installed into the clubhead. Installing the collar before shaft installation will save time and reduce the chance of potentially damaging the collar from a butt installation.

A Word About Grip Collar Installation:
Grip collars are available in hard plastic form or in a soft, pliable form made from vinyl. Because the major golf club manufacturers never use vinyl collars, it is recommended for golf club assemblers to follow their lead and use only the hard plastic type. While stretchable collars are easier to install and finish, they do not have the same professional appearance as the rigid plastic collars.

Rigid plastic grip collars are sold in different sizes, to match the four different shaft butt diameters of .560", .580", .600" and .620". **For ease of installation and finishing, it is recommended to always select a grip collar that is one size larger than the shaft butt on the golf club.** For example, if the club to be leather gripped has a .580" shaft butt diameter, install the .600" size grip collar.

A. Installing the plastic grip collar from the butt end of the shaft

If the grip collar was not installed up from the tip before shaft installation, the only alternative will be to install it from the butt end. Available from golf component and repair companies is a small plastic tool called a grip collar starter tool. When working with .560", .580" or .600" shaft butt diameters, this tool will work well in allowing a butt installation of the collar. However, for .620" shafts this tool is difficult to use. This is because the base of the tool is not quite large enough in diameter to allow easy sliding of a collar on the largest of shaft butt diameters, the .620". For .620" shafts, the manual procedures of collar installation must be used as described in Step B.

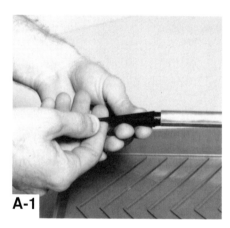

A-1

A. Installing the plastic grip collar from the butt end with the grip collar starter tool
A-1 - Insert tool in shaft butt

Secure the butt end of the shaft in the vise. Insert the large end of the collar starter into the shaft butt until the end of the shaft meets the lip on the collar starter tool.

A. Installing the plastic grip collar from the butt end with the grip collar starter tool
A-2 - Slide collar over the starter tool

Even when using the grip collar starter tool it is a good idea to use a plastic grip collar that is one collar size larger that the diameter of the shaft, e.g., a .600" collar on a

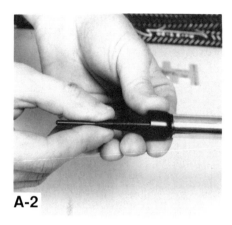

A-2

.580" shaft. Hold the collar tool tight into the end of the shaft and push the collar, rounded end first, over the tool onto the shaft. Push the collar down to the tip area of the shaft.

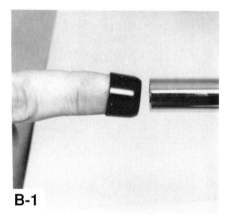

B-1

B. Installing the plastic grip collar from the butt end without the grip collar starter tool
B-1 - Place grip collar on your fingertip

Secure the butt end of the shaft in the vise. Place the grip collar over the tip of your index finger as pictured in Photo B-1. Note that the collar is positioned so the tip of the index finger is against one interior side of the grip collar

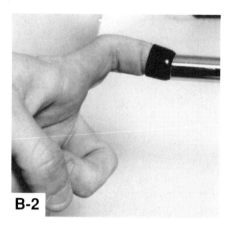

B-2

B. Installing the plastic grip collar from the butt end without the grip collar starter tool
B-2 - Start the collar over the end of the shaft

Start the lip of the collar just over the top edge of the shaft butt. Do not push the collar too far onto the shaft yet. Rather, just insert one edge of the lip of the collar about 1/32" onto the shaft.

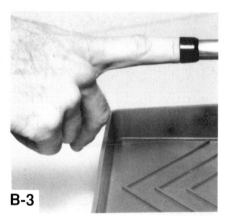

B-3

B. Installing the plastic grip collar from the butt end without the grip collar starter tool
B-3 - Pull collar over entire shaft butt

With your index finger in the collar, pull the collar across the end of the shaft, keeping the lip of the grip collar on the edge of the shaft butt. As you pull the collar across the shaft butt, begin to work the bottom lip of the collar over the bottom side of the shaft. Always keep your eyes focused sharply on the edge of the collar as you pull it on to look for the potential problem of the shaft cutting into and damaging the collar.

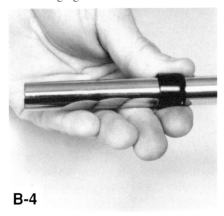

B-4

B. Installing the plastic grip collar from the butt end without the grip collar starter tool
B-4 - Push collar all the way onto shaft butt
If the entire lip of the collar has successfully made it over the entire shaft butt, remove your index finger from the collar and push it fully onto the shaft. If you have problems with the collar starting fully over the shaft, remember this tip: When starting the grip collar lip over one edge of the shaft butt, **do not** insert the collar too far onto the shaft.

■ INSTALLING THE WRAP-ON LEATHER GRIP

1

STEP 1: Install the slip-on underlisting
Use the same procedures to install the underlisting that were outlined for slip-on grip installation. Remember to always perform any wraps of build-up tape for grip oversizing **under** the underlisting.

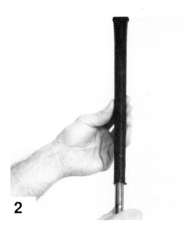

2

STEP 2: Line up the underlisting on the shaft
Leather grip underlistings do not have prominent alignment insignias as do slip-on rubber grips. To properly align underlistings, remove the club from the vise, turn it over with the bottom of the shaft pointing up, and use the four mold release holes found on the back side of the underlisting to line up the grip. Position these four small holes directly in a straight line with the very bottom of the shaft. Once the underlisting is lined up, clean up and set aside to dry for a minimum of two hours.

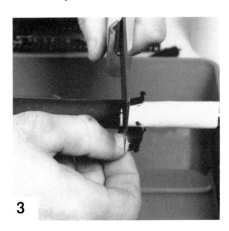

3

STEP 3: Cut the bell collar from the underlisting
Use a razor knife to cut the flared rubber bell from the base of the underlisting. Cut neatly all the way around the underlisting and discard this excess rubber piece.

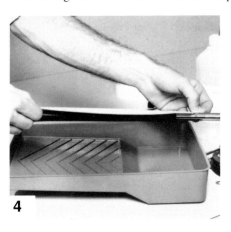

4

STEP 4: Apply 2-way grip tape to the body of the underlisting
Tear off a strip of the 2" wide, 2-way grip tape that is about 1" longer than the length of the underlisting. Remove the paper backing, start one end of the tape strip just under the grip cap and press **the center of the strip** down the underlisting, leaving both edges of the strip off the underlisting for now.

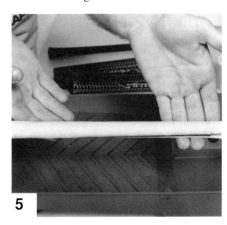

5

STEP 5: Pull both sides of the 2-way tape down and around the underlisting

Carefully pull the sides of the tape strip tightly around the underlisting, taking care to keep wrinkling at a minimum. Make sure that the 2-way tape wraps over the bare shaft at least 1" below the end of the underlisting. After wrapping the tape around the underlisting there will be a V-shaped area on the underlisting that is not covered by the tape. Do not waste time hand cutting a small piece of tape to fit into this area of the underlisting as it is customary to leave this small section uncovered.

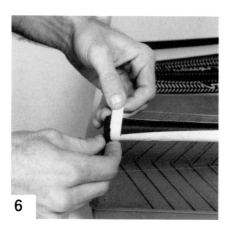

STEP 6: Insert a small piece of 2-way tape into the tab recess of the underlisting.   (If recess is present)
Tear off a strip of the 2" wide 2-way tape that is about 1" long by 2" wide. Fold this piece of tape over itself, half of its length, so the double thick portion is the same width as the tab recess on the underlisting. Press the double thick, folded portion of the tape into the tab recess of the underlisting. This step is necessary to ensure proper adhesion of the leather tab end to the underlisting and to make sure that the leather strap does not sink below the level of the outside edge of the grip cap. The depth of the tab as provided on Golf Pride brand underlistings is sometimes too deep for the thickness of the leather strap, and the double thickness of tape can help correct this problem.

STEP 7: Insert leather tab into the recess of the underlisting
Press the tapered (tab) end of the leather strap into the

recess of the underlisting against the 2-way tape. To prevent a gap between the grip cap and the leather strap, push the tab up against the grip cap.

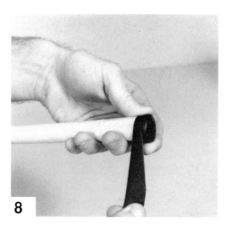

STEP 8: Wrap the leather strap tight against the base of the grip cap
While holding the leather tab in the recess, wrap the leather strap one full turn around the underlisting, making the sure the top edge of the strap stays tight against the bottom side of the grip end cap. **Do not** pull tight on the leather during this first wrap or gaps between the grip cap and leather strap will occur.

STEP 9: Complete the first wrap around and over the beginning of the leather strap
As the leather strap is wrapped completely around the underlisting, it must cover the beginning of the tab and tab recess end where the strap attaches to the grip.

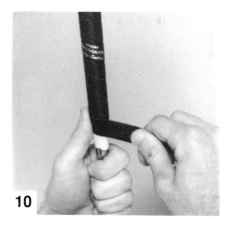

STEP 10: Continue wrapping the grip
Continue wrapping the leather around and around the underlisting, making sure the top of the strap covers approximately 1/16" to 1/8" of the bottom of the previous wrap. Pull tight on the **top half of the strap** as it is wrapped around the underlisting. This will secure the strap tight over the bottom of the previous wrap.

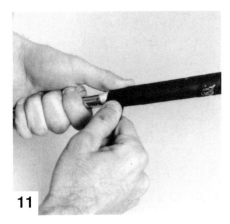

11

STEP 11: Pull tight on the leather over the end of the underlisting

When the leather strap approaches the end of the underlisting, begin pulling the strap very tight. The strap must be wrapped tight enough over the end of the underlisting so you can actually see the end of the underlisting show through the leather.

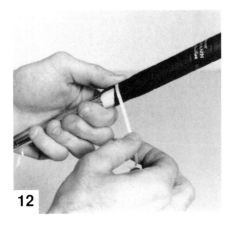

12

STEP 12: Secure leather strap with masking tape

Wrap the strap tight for at least 1" past the end of the underlisting. Use a strip of thin (1/8" or 1/2" wide) masking tape to secure the end of the leather strap. Place the tape @ 1/2" **below** the cut end of the underlisting.

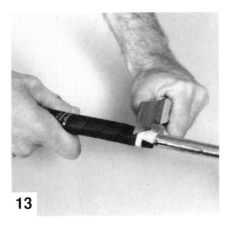

13

STEP 13: Cut the leather strap

Use a sharp knife to cut through the leather strap @ 1/2" below the end of the underlisting. Be sure to cut through or just below the masking tape to prevent the strap from coming loose. Cut completely around the shaft and discard the excess leather plus any tape that may be below the cut.

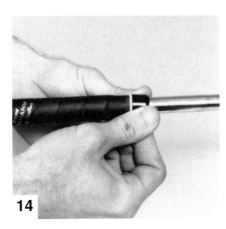

14

STEP 14: Test fit the grip collar

Slide the grip collar up and over the end of the leather grip to test its fit. The collar should fit snug over the end of the leather and butt up against the end of the cut underlisting that shows through the leather. If the collar fits over the end of the leather but stops short of the knob representing

the cut end of the underlisting, cut back more of the leather until the perfect fit is achieved. If the collar will not fit over the leather, use a razor blade to "shave" down the thickness of the leather grip until a snug fit is achieved.

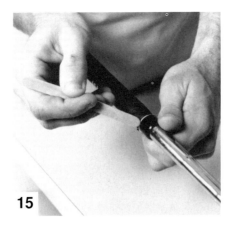

15

STEP 15: Secure the grip collar

After test fitting the grip collar, apply a thin coating of contact cement on the end of the leather grip. Slide and rotate the collar over the bottom of the leather, tight against the end of the underlisting. Wipe off any excess cement that oozes out, taking care not to smear the cement on the leather.

■ BASIC TECHNIQUES OF SLIP-ON LEATHER GRIP INSTALLATION

One of the more recent developments in grip manufacturing is the slip-on leather grip. These grips are produced with the leather strip already attached to a rubber underlisting that does not have an end cap molded to the underlisting. Therefore, after installation of the grip, an additional step of attaching a plastic end cap is required to finish the job.

One of the disadvantages of slip-on leather grips is that they cannot be effectively be installed on shafts with a greatly larger butt diameter than their inner core size. This is because the pre-attached leather strap will not allow stretching to an oversize consition. As a result it is recommended that slip-on leather grips only be installed on shafts of a .580" or .600" butt diameter.

Slip-on leather grips are made in round form for use on woods and irons as well as in a limited variety of shaped models for installation on putters. All types require the same basic step-by-step procedures which are outlined as follows:

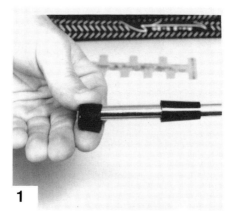

1

STEP 1: Install plastic grip collar (from tip end)
Slip-on leather grips also require the use of a grip collar to finish off the mouth of the leather wrap. In the step-by-step procedures of club assembly to be covered in Chapters 5-9, it will be recommended that the collar be installed from the tip end, before the shaft is installed into the clubhead. Installing the collar before shafting will save a lot of time and reduce the chance of potentially damaging the collar from a butt installation.

Remember:
Hard plastic grip collars are sold in different sizes, to match the four different shaft butt diameters of .560", .580", .600" and .620". <u>For ease of installation and finishing, it is recommended to always select a grip collar that is one size larger than the shaft butt on the golf club.</u> For example, if the club to be leather gripped has a .580" shaft butt diameter, select and use the .600" size grip collar.

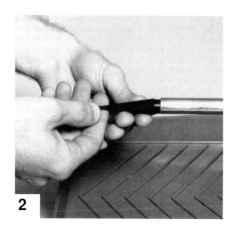

2

STEP 2: Install plastic grip collar (from butt end with collar starter tool)
If the grip collar was not installed from the tip before shaft installation, it must be installed from the butt end. There is available from golf component and repair companies a small tool called a grip collar starter tool that will help in this job. When working with both .580" or .600" shaft butt diameters, this tool will be very helpful. Install the tool in the butt end of the shaft as pictured and slide the collar over and onto the shaft, small end first.

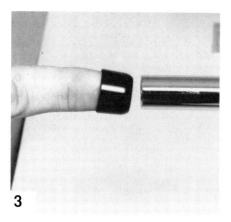

3

STEP 3: Install plastic grip collar (from butt end without collar starter tool)
{Place collar over fingertip.}
Secure the shaft in the vise in the same manner as for installing a slip-on grip. Place the grip collar over the tip of your index finger as pictured in PHOTO 3. Note that the collar is positioned so the tip of the index finger is against one interior side of the grip collar.

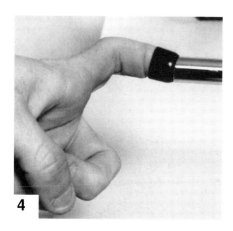

4

STEP 4: Install plastic grip collar (from butt end without collar starter tool)
{Start collar over shaft}
Start the lip of the collar just over the top edge of the shaft butt. Do not push the collar too far onto the shaft yet. Rather, just insert the top edge of the collar about 1/32" onto the shaft as pictured.

A Word About Grip Collar Installation:
Grip collars are available in hard plastic form or in a soft, pliable rubber form. Because professional golf club manufacturers never use the stretchable vinyl collars, it is recommended that golf club assemblers follow their lead and use only the hard plastic type. While stretchable collars are easier to install and finish, they are not considered as professional in appearance as the hard plastic type.

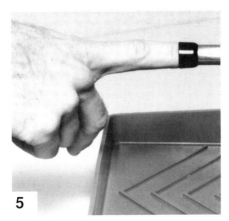

5

STEP 5: Install plastic grip collar (from butt end <u>without</u> collar starter tool)
{Pull collar over entire shaft butt}
Pull down against the top of the shaft with the index finger in the collar, keeping the top lip of the grip collar barely on the top edge of the shaft butt. As you pull down on the collar, begin to work the bottom lip of the collar over the bottom side of the shaft. Always keep your eyes focused sharply on the edges of the collar as you pull it on to look for the potential problem of the shaft cutting into and damaging the collar.

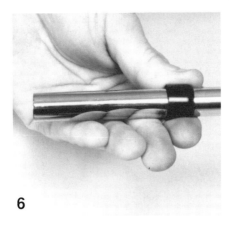

6

STEP 6: Install plastic grip collar (from butt end <u>without</u> collar starter tool)
{Push collar all the way onto shaft butt}

If the entire lip of the collar has successfully made it over the entire shaft butt, remove the index finger from the collar and push it fully onto the shaft. If you have problems with the collar starting fully over the shaft, remember this tip: When starting the grip collar lip over one edge of the shaft butt, **do not** insert the collar too far onto the shaft.

7

STEP 7: Apply 2-way tape to the shaft butt
With the club secured in the vise, apply a 10" long strip of 2" wide, 2-way grip tape, lengthwise up and down the shaft. Again, take care when securing the tape to the shaft to avoid wrinkling the tape. **Because a plastic end cap is going to be installed, <u>do not</u> allow an excess amount of the 2-way tape to extend over the end of the shaft.**

8

STEP 8: Apply solvent to the inside of the grip
Place your thumb over the large end of the grip and pour a small amount of grip solvent down the core. Take extreme care not to spill solvent on the leather while you slosh the solvent up and down the inside of the core.

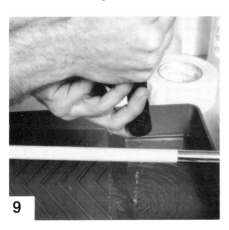

9

STEP 9: Drizzle the excess solvent from the grip core onto the 2-way tape
Hold the grip over the tape and slowly release your thumb from the grip, drizzling solvent over the entire tape surface.

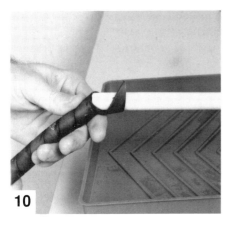

10

STEP 10: Install the grip
Using the same techniques for slip-on rubber grip installation, slide the grip over the butt of the shaft and push

into place. Push the grip onto the shaft until the shaft butt just begins to protrude out the end of the grip. Take care not to smear tape residue on any surface of the leather. Slip-on leather grips for woods and irons do not have a rib so no alignment will be necessary other than to see that the grip manufacturer's logo is facing up.

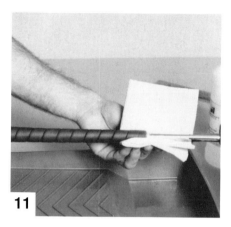

STEP 11: Wipe clean and set aside to dry

After installation, use a paper towel to carefully wipe away any tape residue from the mouth and the butt end of the grip. Again, take care not to smear tape residue on the leather. Check the butt end of the grip to make sure the shaft does not protrude more than 1/32" out of the end of the grip. After clean up and checking, set aside for several hours to dry.

STEP 12: Remove tape from end of shaft to prepare for end cap installation

Use a razor knife to cut away any excess tape from the inside of the butt end of the shaft.

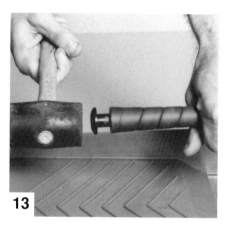

STEP 13: Insert end cap into the shaft butt

Select an end cap of the same butt diameter as the shaft. Insert the cap only into the shaft butt and tap all the way down into place with a mallet or hammer. No epoxy is used to install the cap.

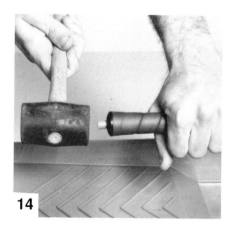

STEP 14: Tap the locking pin down the center of the end cap

Insert the plastic pin into the center of the end cap and push down until the pin stops. Use a pin punch and

hammer to drive the pin farther down into the end cap's center. As the pin is hammered down it will force the sides of the end cap against the inside of the shaft, thus locking it in place.

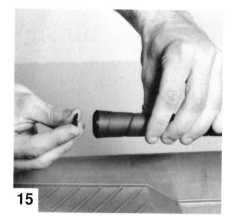

STEP 15: Epoxy or acetone the end cap cover on top of the end cap

The small, round plastic disc can be epoxied or melted with acetone to secure it to the end cap. If epoxy is used it is recommended to rough up the underside of the disc with sandpaper to aid the bonding of the epoxy.

STEP 16: Protect the top of the leather grip

Wrap a strip of 3/4" or 1" wide masking tape around the top of the leather grip, just under the end cap. The tape is used to protect the grip from scratches during the upcoming filing of the end cap.

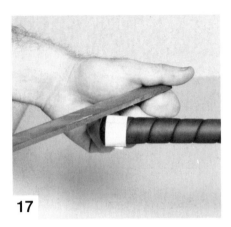

17

STEP 17: File the end cap flush to the top of the leather grip

Secure the grip in the bench vise between soft vise pads and begin filing the end cap to meet the top of the leather grip. Use a medium cut file for quick plastic removal. File, then rotate the grip, then file again until the end cap has been reduced in diameter to meet the grip. Take care not to scratch through the protective masking tape and damage the leather.

OPTIONAL STEP 17: Belt sand the end cap using a linen belt

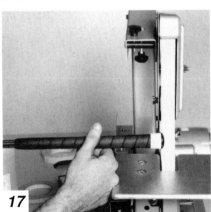

17

*If your shop has a 1" x 42" belt sander, use a linen belt to remove the excess plastic end cap material. This method of reducing the end cap to meet the leather grip is preferable to filing because it is much faster and will not damage the grip. Rotate the plastic cap **against** the direction of travel of the belt.*

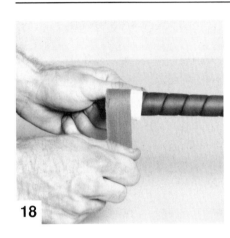

18

STEP 18: Lightly sand scratches from the end cap

Filing the end cap flush to the top of the leather grip will often leave scratches in the plastic. Use a strip of fine sandpaper to carefully remove these scratches.

NOTE: If the optional Step 17 with linen belt was used to dress the end cap, this sanding step will not be necessary.

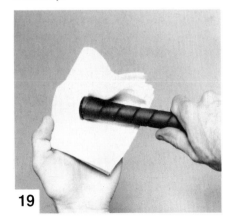

19

STEP 19: Restore end cap shine with acetone

The final step of dressing the end cap will be to wet a paper towel with acetone and wipe the edges of the plastic cap. In addition, wipe the top of the end cap with the acetone-wetted towel to restore its shine too.

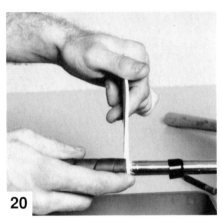

20

STEP 20: Secure end of leather with masking tape

Tape the end of the leather strip over the bottom of the underlisting and around the shaft just below the underlisting. Use a strip of thin (1/8" or 1/2" wide) masking tape to secure the end of the leather grip. **Be sure the end of the slip-on leather grip is past the underlisting and on the shaft**. If the leather is too short to extend below the underlisting, then cut off a portion of the underlisting.

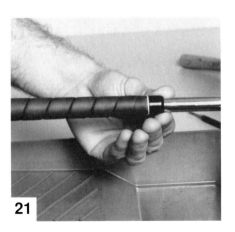

21

STEP 21: Test fit grip collar

Slide the grip collar up and over the end of the leather grip to test its fit. The collar should fit snug over the end of the leather and butt up against the raised portion of the leather grip that signifies the end of the cut underlisting. If the collar fits over the end of the leather but stops short of the knob representing the cut end of the underlisting, then cut back enough of the leather until a perfect fit of the collar is achieved. If the collar will not fit over the leather, use a razor blade to "shave" down the thickness of the end of the leather grip until a fit is achieved.

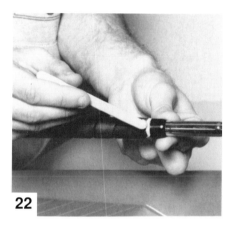

STEP 22: Secure the grip collar permanently with contact cement

After the fit of the grip collar is satisfactory, apply a very thin coating of contact cement on the end of the leather grip and slide the collar up into place. Wipe off any excess cement that oozes out, taking care not to smear the cement on the leather.

CHAPTER 5 - The Modern Assembly Procedures of Conventional Wooden Head Clubs

Step-by-Step Assembly of Woods from Finished or Unfinished Persimmon and Laminated Maple Heads

The Most Traditional Form of Clubmaking

Without a doubt, the oldest form of clubmaking involves the assembly of wooden head golf clubs. The mainstay of clubmaking for hundreds of years, in the 1980s the market share of wooden woods dropped from 100% to less than 20% by the end of the decade. While metal woods today do comprise the vast majority of "wood" making requests, clubmakers with a desire to offer their customers the most complete array of custom clubmaking options should take care not to forget or bypass the skills of wooden head clubmaking.

Despite the much publicized game improvement attributes of metal woods, there are a number of custom clubmaking options for golfers that can only be realistically attained through the use of wooden heads. By virtue of the repetitive manufacturing processes of investment casting and die casting, obtaining metal woodheads with such custom features as different face angles, different lie angles, different loft angles and many other important clubfitting options is not as easy as with wooden heads. While casting is ideal for repeating the same specifications head after head, it does not lend itself to the making of individually customized heads in small quantities. Instead, because wooden heads are made through a procedure that follows one production step at a time, clubmakers can list the most precise individual fitting specifications possible and order a small number of wooden heads through various component clubhead suppliers' custom woodhead programs.

When assembling wood clubs made with persimmon or laminated maple heads, the first decision the clubmaker must make is whether to build the clubs using heads in a finished or unfinished condition. While using pre-finished wooden heads eliminates the additional and often time-consuming steps of applying the urethane finish to the head, the clubmaker still must deal with several possible disadvantages. Using only pre-finished wooden heads will mean having a limited color selection to offer your customers. For example, if the model of choice is available from your supplier in black only while the customer wished to have a natural color finish on the woods, you could possibly lose the sale simply because you do not offer custom woodhead finish application as part of your service.

In addition to the potential disadvantage of limited color selection, working with pre-finished wooden heads means you must be very careful not to damage the existing finish during the assembly process. Your goal as a clubmaker is to offer the utmost in professional quality. Certain clubmaking procedures such as the installation of the backscrew are more difficult to perform on a pre-finished head than on an unfinished wood without causing damage to the head.

Not to "stack the deck" against using pre-finished wooden heads, there do exist a number of points that must be understood and accepted before choosing to assemble woods from unfinished heads. Currently, the average cost difference in the component clubhead industry between finished and unfinished wooden heads of the same model type is approximately $5.00. Therefore, to be cost effective in your shop you must have the ability to apply a finish for less than $5.00, taking materials and labor into account. If you can apply the finish economically, or equally important, if you feel that the reputation enhancing virtues of being able to offer any finish color outweigh the finishing cost disadvantages, then working with unfinished heads can offer even more opportunities to expand your ability to customize individual specifications of golf clubs.

Additionally, some clubmaking supply companies offer a limited choice of unfinished wooden heads produced without a face insert installed in the insert cavity. This extra custom option allows the clubmaker to not only customize the face insert type but also lets the clubmaker offer golfers the additional options of a custom loft angle and face screw/scoreline pattern.

Because advantages do exist for using either finished or unfinished wooden heads to build wood clubs, Chapter 5 will cover the full procedures of club assembly of both pre-finished and unfinished woodheads, including the step-by-step process for finish application on the unfinished heads. Each step in the procedures of assembly and finishing is explained in detailed text and is illustrated in photographs. While the assembly and finishing procedures show the use of persimmon woodheads, the steps outlined apply identically to all types of laminated maple heads as well as heads made from rarely seen hardwoods such as ash, dogwood or beech.

Persimmon/Laminated Maple Wood Assembly

Assembly Procedures of Pre-Finished Wooden Clubheads

1

STEP 1: Secure and organize each of the required components to anticipate any potential problems in assembly

Whether by laying all of the components out on your workbench or by making a mental note, be sure you have all the necessary components **and** supplies on hand to complete the assembly before you start the actual procedures of clubmaking. To avoid any potential swingweight problems that may be created by the customer's required custom fitting specifications, first note the desired length, shaft weight, grip size and swingweight in conjunction with the gram weight of the clubhead and calculate the anticipated swingweight of the club(s) **before** you begin work. By pre-calculating swingweight from the known assembly specifications, necessary adjustments can often be made before the assembly process begins, thus solving a potential problem before it occurs. See Chapter 10 for an explanation of how to calculate the swingweight of a golf club before it is assembled.

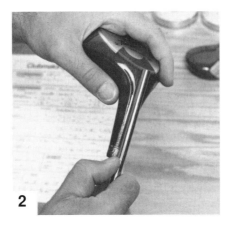

2

STEP 2: Test fit each shaft in the appropriate head
Test fit each shaft into its matching woodhead to check for proper fit. This step is performed to check the fit of the shaft into the bore of the head and to determine if any adjustments have to be made to the hosel bore diameter to assure the proper fit. Please note in cases of using some types of shafts that are to be pre-trimmed to the golf club's desired playing length **from the tip**, a test fit of the shaft into the head is a must to determine the necessary trimming (a description of changing or adjusting hosel bore sizes can be found in Chapter 10).

■ **NOTE:** On pre-whipped woodheads, the tension of the whipping over the ferrule can cause the inside diameter of the ferrule to be too small to allow the shaft to slide through. If the shaft does not slide easily through the ferrule on pre-whipped woodheads, ream out the ferrule with the appropriate size drill or reamer (.335" parallel bore = "R" drill bit).

3

STEP 3: Calculate proper tip trimming and mark each shaft for trimming (if tip trimming is necessary)
Either on paper or in your mind, first calculate the amount to tip trim from each of the shafts, if in fact the shafts being used call for tip trimming (while the majority of shafts will require tip trimming prior to installation, some by virtue of their design will not). Refer to the Shaft Trimming Index in Chapter 3 to find the correct chart of trimming procedures to follow for the shafts being used. Use a ruler and felt tip pen to mark the correct amount to trim from each shaft.

For the most accuracy in shaft flex feel, remember to take into acount the bottom of bore to heel dimension of the wooden head (through-bore vs. blind bore) and the required playing length of the golf club(s) before calculating the proper tip trimming for each shaft (see Chapter 3 for an explanation of how to adjust tip trimming based on the bottom of bore to heel dimension and playing length changes to assure consistent shaft installation).

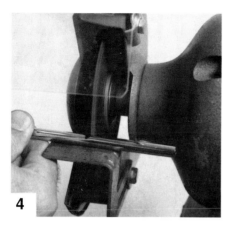

4

STEP 4: Tip trim all shafts

Use the method of shaft cutting that is best suited for the type of material from which the shafts are made. The use of a tube cutter or motorized abrasive cut-off wheel is recommended for steel and titanium (all metal types) and a grit edge saw or abrasive cut-off wheel is best for graphite and other fibrous composite shafts. Again, by intent of their design, some shafts will not require tip trimming before installation, so be sure to always check, then double check the proper trimming procedures for the shafts you are using.

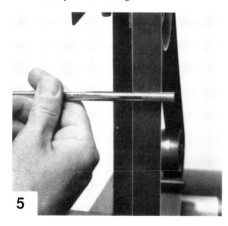

5

STEP 5: Abrade the tip of the shaft

With medium to coarse grit sandpaper, abrade the entire portion of the shaft tip that will not only be inserted in the

hosel, but under the ferrule as well (should a ferrule be required in the assembly). Abrading the shaft tip will allow the epoxy to assist in securing the shaft and ferrule, and greatly reduce the chance of the head and/or ferrule working loose at a later time. For assembling wooden heads, crimping or deforming the shaft to facilitate a mechanical lock of shaft to head is **not** recommended.

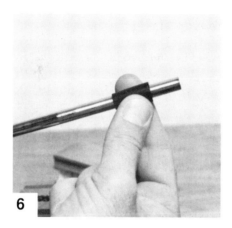

6

STEP 6: Install ferrule (and leather grip collar if required)

In virtually all cases of wooden head installation a ferrule will be required. The only exceptions will be if the head is made with a ferrule and whipping already in place, or in the rare case of a woodhead made with the top of the wooden hosel sanded into a thin taper to meet the shaft. **Follow the procedures illustrated in Chapter 3 to guide the installation of the ferrule.**

■ **NOTE:** It is not necessary to install and position the ferrule in its exact position on the shaft. The insertion of the shaft completely to the bottom of the hosel will push each ferrule up the shaft and into its proper location. **If a leather grip is called for in the assembly of the club, be sure to install the proper size plastic grip trim collar up from the tip end of the shaft at this time.**

STEP 7: Mix epoxy and apply to the shaft tip and inside of hosel

Always use a high shear strength, 2-part shafting epoxy

7

to secure the shaft to the head. Follow the epoxy supplier's mixing recommendations to ensure complete bonding strength of the epoxy. Using a 1/4" wood dowel rod or similar applicator, apply a thin, full coverage coating of the epoxy to the shaft tip and the inside of the hosel bore.

8

STEP 8: Install the shafts

One by one, insert each shaft into its proper clubhead. Rotate the shaft as it is inserted to ensure a complete coating of the epoxy between the shaft tip and the inside of the hosel. While it is not necessary since many shafting epoxies are manufactured with a form of filler within, Aluminum Oxide or Silica type sand may be used as an additional bonding aid without fear of damaging the hosel. If sand is used, dip only 1/4" of the tip of the shaft into the sand before inserting the shaft into the hosel. The use of sand can be a strength additive for tube type epoxies such as Conap which are made without a filler. Check to make sure that the manufacturer's silkscreen is properly aligned at the "12 o'clock" position at this time.

9

STEP 9: Properly seat the shafts into the hosel

For proper assembly, it is vital that each shaft be installed so that the shaft tip seats completely through the sole (in the case of through-bore type woodheads) or to the bottom of the bore (in the case of blind bore type woodheads). Note the following shaft seating procedures for each type of wooden head.

Through-Bore Woodhead - Whether pushing and rotating the shaft by hand or by tapping the butt of the shaft on the floor while holding the head secure to the shaft, drive the shaft into the hosel until the **entire circumference** of the tip penetrates through the sole.

Blind Bore Woodhead - Using either method described above, drive the shaft into the hosel until you feel it stop against the bottom of the bore (in most cases, hand pressure alone will be sufficient to properly seat the shaft in the hosel).

■ **NOTE: For through-bore woodheads**
The eventual sanding of the shaft tip flush to the sole of

a pre-finished through-bore type woodhead is **extremely** difficult to accomplish without damaging the finish on the sole of the head. Therefore, when installing a shaft into a pre-finished through-bore type woodhead, clubmakers may choose to minimize their chance for error by pre-sanding the shaft tip to the same angle as the sole of the woodhead before installation.

■ **NOTE: For pre-whipped woodheads**
Use extreme care when inserting shafts into pre-whipped woodheads. To prevent breaking off the ferrule be sure the shaft tip has been inserted past the bottom of the ferrule before tapping the shaft to the bottom of the bore. Should the ferrule break off during shaft installation, discard the whipping and ferrule and file the top of the hosel completely flat. When the top of the hosel is squared off, install a new ferrule on the shaft and epoxy the shaft in the hosel.

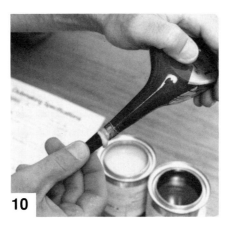

10

STEP 10: Work epoxy under the ferrule

After seating the shaft in the hosel, try to work some epoxy underneath the ferrule to protect it from working loose. Rotate and move the ferrule up and down against the the top of the hosel to draw epoxy under the ferrule. Finish by pushing the ferrule firm against the hosel to eliminate the possibility of a gap occuring between the top of the hosel and the ferrule. Wipe away any excess epoxy from the base of the ferrule. If the ferrule is very tight on the shaft after shaft installation such that no

epoxy can be worked underneath, do not worry about its working loose when the club is put into play.

11

STEP 11: Apply masking tape above ferrule

To prevent the ferrule from slipping up the shaft and creating a gap while the epoxy cures, wrap one layer of 1/2" or 1" wide masking tape around the shaft, butting one edge of the tape against the top of the ferrule. This tape will also protect the shaft from scratching when filing the ferrule.

12

STEP 12: Install plug in tip of shaft (for through-bore woodheads only)

If the woodheads being assembled are a through-bore design, a plug must be driven up steel shafts to fill in the opening of the shaft tip. You may choose to use either the special tapered wood plugs sold by component suppliers or a 1/4" or 5/16" wood dowels for this purpose. Most 1/4" dowels will fit a bit loose and may require epoxying, whereas the 5/16" variety must be sanded on the tip to allow driving up inside the tip of the shaft. Do not tap the wood plug up the tip of the shaft before installation of the shaft into the head. **Never** drive the tapered type of wood plugs or the 3/8" dowels their full length into the shaft tip or the plug will split. However, do be sure to drive the wood plug at least 1/2"-3/4" into the tip to adequately fill the shaft tip and ensure a tight fit. In the case of graphite or composite shafts installed into through-bore heads, use any type of epoxy to fill the tip of the shaft instead of a wood plug.

■ **NOTE**: Blind-bore woodheads never require a tip plug.

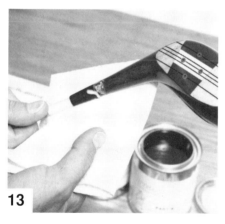
13

STEP 13: Clean up, check and set aside for the epoxy to cure
Before setting the club aside to dry, check the point between the top of the hosel and the bottom of the ferrule. Be sure any excess amounts of epoxy have been wiped away, but at the same time, do leave a small amount of epoxy on the line between the ferrule and the hosel. Because it is very common for the top of the hosel of a wooden head to not be perfectly square, the epoxy can serve as a filler to correct any small gap between hosel and ferrule. Check for epoxy smears on the head and

shaft and wipe clean with a rag dampened with grip solvent. Set the club aside horizontally on a rack or with the head down on the floor for the epoxy to cure. **Never** set clubs to dry with the head up and shaft down or epoxy could flow down the shaft, thus creating the potential for a rattle after the club is put into play.

14

STEP 14: Prepare for installation of backscrew by securing the woodhead in the bench vise
A backscrew, or shaft locking screw, is not required with graphite or composite shaft installation, but **for any type of metal shaft to wooden head assembly, the use of a backscrew is a must!!** The two major causes of wooden heads working loose from the shaft are the normal vibration of the wood hosel that naturally occurs from shot impact as well as the wood's swelling and shrinking from temperature changes that the club may be subjected to over the course of a season. Because these factors are normal and beyond the control of the clubmaker, you must afford yourself the protection against the head possibly coming off the shaft by installing a backscrew. To begin the backscrew installation procedure, secure the woodhead in the bench vise, toe down, with the head between soft vise pads. Place another pad under the toe of the head to prevent possible damage to the toe of the head when hammering down the screw.

STEP 15: Locate the point of backscrew entry on the back of the woodhead
By placing a straight rod on the back side of the shaft,

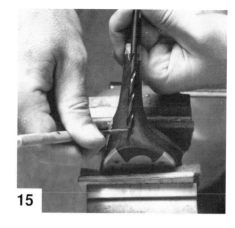
15

directly in line with the shaft, it is possible to locate exactly where the shaft lies inside the hosel. With the rod positioned on the top of the back side of the shaft (as pictured), make a small mark with an awl or scriber on the back of the head, directly in line with the shaft about 1/2" up from the back edge of the heel of the woodhead.

16

STEP 16: Place cellophane tape over the point of backscrew drilling
Drilling a hole through a pre-finished wood can tear the urethane coating and lead to an unprofessional looking clubmaking job. To ensure a clean, sharp-edged cut with the drill bit through the finish, apply two layers of cellophane tape on the back of the woodhead over the point of drill bit entry.

17

STEP 17: Properly line up the drill bit in relation to the shaft

Using the electric hand drill and a 1/8" high speed steel or cobalt bit, position the point of the bit on the mark, **perpendicular to the top of the shaft.** For accuracy of drilling, it is extremely important that the bit be perpendicular with the top of the shaft. Failure to do so can result in the bit glancing off or completely missing the shaft. Also check the angle of the bit with relation to the front of the hosel to avoid the potential problem of the bit coming through the front side of the hosel, thus ruining the head.

18

STEP 18: Drill to the top of the shaft

Once the bit is properly lined up, drill through the tape

and into the woodhead until you feel the bit touch the top surface of the shaft. Upon feeling contact with the top of the shaft, withdraw the drill bit from the hole. **Do not attempt to drill through the shaft!**

19

STEP 19: Punch a hole through the top of the shaft

Using an awl or a sharpened 1/8" pin punch, use a hammer to drive the tip of the punch/awl first through the top side of the shaft only. Do not attempt to pierce both sides of the shaft at this time. After piercing through the top of the shaft, wiggle the punch loose and remove it.

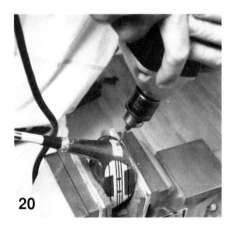

20

STEP 20: Drill through the punched hole and the bottom side of the shaft

Insert the electric drill with 1/8" bit into the backscrew

hole before activating the drill motor. Check once again for perpendicular bit to shaft alignment before drilling through the punched hole. Despite the punched hole, drilling through the top of the shaft will require some pressure to force the bit completely through. If after 5-10 seconds of drilling the bit has not penetrated the top of the shaft, stop and repeat STEP 19 to enlarge the punched hole diameter before drilling again. Because the hole through the top of the shaft will act as a bushing to hold the bit in the proper position, once the top of the shaft has been penetrated with the drill, continue drilling through the bottom side of the shaft. Again, firm pressure on the drill will be required to penetrate the bottom side of the shaft. Drill to a depth no more than 1 1/2" below the back surface of the head and then withdraw the bit. After drilling the hole, remove the club from the vise and dump any loose particles out the butt end of the shaft.

■ **NOTE:** After drilling through the top of the shaft, clubmakers may wish to withdraw the bit and repeat the punch then drill procedure to penetrate the bottom side of the shaft. While the procedure in STEP 20 is used by most experienced clubmakers, there is a slight chance the pressure required to help the drill penetrate the unpunched bottom of the shaft could result in a broken drill bit, or the mistake of driving the nose of the drill chuck into the back of the wood.

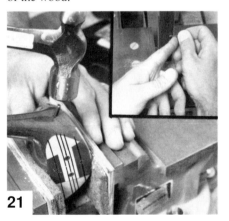

21

STEP 21: Install the backscrew

For a professional job, it is recommended to use a

"headless" type of backscrew. While some component companies do supply this type of screw, you may use a bench grinder or belt sander to grind the flared sides off the head of a #5x1 1/8" steel backscrew. When installing the screw do not rotate the screw into place. Tap it into the hole with a hammer, as if driving a nail.

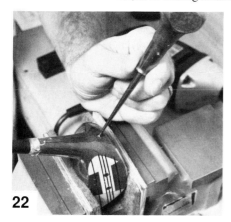

22

STEP 22: Tap the backscrew below the surface of the woodhead
After tapping the screw flush to the back surface of the head, use the sharpened 1/8" pin punch or awl to bury the head of the screw @ 1/8" below the surface of the head. Use a very light tapping force with the hammer to prevent driving the screw too deep into the head.

23

STEP 23: Fill the hole with an appropriate shade of fast dry epoxy

Mix a small amount of quick dry epoxy and tint it with an appropriate hue that will match or contrast nicely with the color of the woodhead finish. Color paste dispersions that are used to tint pour-in-place face insert epoxies work very well for coloring all quick dry epoxies. In lieu of the dispersion colors, a very small amount of enamel paint can be used. Use a toothpick to fill the backscrew hole, being sure to dab the epoxy slightly above the surface of the wood. Be as neat as possible with this step to prevent smearing epoxy on the head. Set aside to dry.

> **If you are assembling blind bore type wooden heads, go directly to STEP 27 from here. If the heads being assembled are of the through-bore variety, proceed on with STEP 24.**

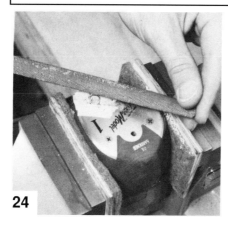

24

STEP 24: Grind or file the tip of the through-bore shaft
Break off the excess wood plug protruding from the shaft tip. With a medium cutting file or a belt sander with a medium to coarse abrasive belt, begin to grind off the shaft tip, removing material as close to the bottom of the wood as your skills will allow without gouging the sole. If you pre-ground the shaft tip to match the radius of the sole of the woodhead before shaft installation, you may skip this step and proceed to STEP 26.

STEP 25: Finish shaft tip area of through-bore

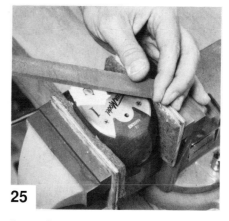

25

Depending upon your experience and preference, use a belt sander or fine cutting file with short accurate strokes to remove the final part of the shaft tip protruding from the sole. Placing tape around the area of the sole surrounding the shaft tip will help to protect the sole from file damage.

■ **NOTE:** When filing close to the head's finish, you can **scratch** the finish and still restore it with 400 grit sanding and Glanz Wach buffing; however, if you *gouge* through the finish completely, the mistake will show in the completed club.

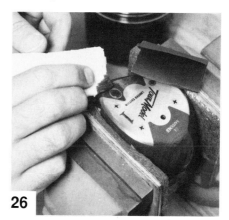

26

STEP 26: Restore finish luster to shaft tip area of through-bore head
After filing or belt sanding the shaft tip flush to the sole, sand the entire tip area with 320 grit or 400 grit wet/dry

sandpaper to remove any scratches. **Use no harsher grit than 320 or 400 to prevent sanding completely through the finish.** Use a matching stain to color the wood tip plug, then apply and rub with a dab of wood filler. 400 sand and steel wool rub not only the shaft tip area, but the entire woodhead to prepare it for a dip or spray coating of compatable polyurethane. Allow the stain and filler on the wood plug to dry for at least an hour before sanding and applying the touch-up polyurethane coating. For ease of application, a compatible aerosol type urethane finish may be used.

27

STEP 27: File the ferrule to prepare for the whipping

If you are skilled in the use of a belt sander with linen belt to turn down ferrules, then this method will be the fastest way to prepare the ferrule for whipping. If not, use a shaft clamp to secure the club in the vise as pictured. With a medium cut file, begin filing around the entire ferrule to reduce its diameter from top to bottom. Take extreme care to retain the perfect taper of the ferrule while filing. After the ferrule has been filed in an even taper from the shaft to the top of the hosel, use a strip of sandpaper to remove the file marks. If using a shanked type ferrule, no filing at the top of the ferrule will be necessary.

■ **NOTE:** For standard (non-shanked) ferrules, take care **not** to scratch the shaft too far (more than 1/8") above the top of the ferrule.

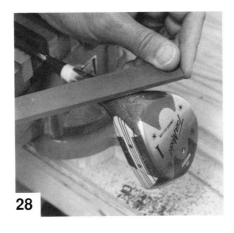

28

STEP 28: File and smooth the epoxy covering the backscrew

Begin removing the epoxy protruding over the backscrew hole with a fine cut file. Continue filing until the epoxy is just short of being flush to the back surface of the finished woodhead. Using very light strokes, keep filing until the first evidence of scratching of the surrounding finish is noticed. Switch to 320 or 400 grit sandpaper to dry sand the remaining epoxy flush to the back of the head. Remember, as long as very fine grit sandpaper is used, the entire finish surrounding the epoxy can be sanded and still be returned to its original luster with Glanz Wach buffing.

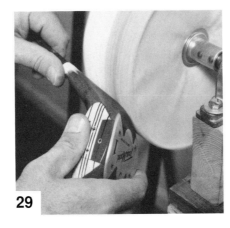

29

STEP 29: Buff the backscrew area to restore the shine of the finish

After 320 or 400 sanding, rub the entire area over and around the backscrew with 3/0 or 4/0 grade steel wool. Follow by buffing the entire backscrew area of the wood with machine driven, unstitched buffing wheels coated with Glanz Wach. Apply medium pressure with the buffing wheels first in one direction, then in a second direction that is 90° to the first. After buffing is completed, rub with a soft cloth and the epoxy covering and the surrounding finish will have the same shine as the rest of the head.

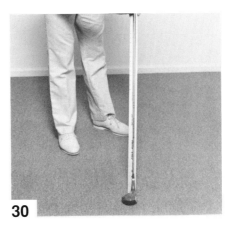

30

STEP 30: Measure and mark the shaft butt for the desired playing length

Place the club on the floor in the playing position, taking care not to rock the club either up on the toe or back on its heel. Slide a 48" clubmaker's ruler up behind the shaft, and carefully mark the desired playing length on the butt end of the shaft with a felt tip marker. Be sure to allow for the effect that the 1/8" thickness of the end of the grip will have on the club's playing length by marking the shafts 1/8" shorter than what is desired (e.g.- If a true 43" playing length is desired, the mark should be made at 42 7/8", for a 41 1/2" playing length, mark the shaft at 41 3/8", etc.).

■ **NOTE:** There are a limited number of shaft patterns

that will require no further butt trimming for playing length after installation, so be sure to re-check the trimming instructions for the shafts being used.

31

STEP 31: Cut the shaft to its desired playing length

Using the proper cutting procedure for the type of shaft being used, trim the shaft for its playing length. Always deburr and square off the shaft butt after trimming to remove sharp edges. If a graphite or composite type shaft has been installed, use an abrasive cut-off wheel or a grit edged hack saw blade to trim the shaft, **never** a tubing cutter.

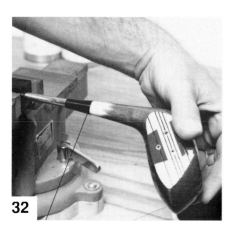

32

STEP 32: Install whipping

Whether with a whipping machine or by using hand winding procedures, install the string whipping and securely tie off to finish the job. The most simple method involves placing the club in the rubber shaft clamp and **loosely** securing it in the vise so that the head and shaft may still be rotated (a complete step-by-step sequence of hand tying the whipping is covered in Chapter 10).

33

STEP 33: Record the preliminary swingweight of the club

Place the club on a 14" fulcrum swingweight scale (Lorythmic or Prorythmic type) **without the grip installed** and record its swingweight. Do NOT push the butt of the ungripped club completely against the back of the scale. Because the grip cap provides the final 1/8" of club length, pull the shaft butt 1/8" away from the end of the scale before recording preliminary swingweight. This is important to achieve an accurate swingweight reading.

STEP 34: Subtract the swingweight equivalent of the grip from the ungripped club's preliminary swingweight to determine the <u>initial swingweight</u>

The swingweight of the ungripped club will read higher because the grip has not been installed. It will be heavier in the amount equal to the swingweight equivalent of the weight of the grip plus its installation and build-up tape.

Example:

Preliminary Swingweight (E-0)

– **Swingweight Equivalent of Grip (9SW)**

Initial Swingweight (D-1)

34

To determine what the club's **initial swingweight** will be once the grip is installed, subtract 9 swingweight points for a standard men's size rubber grip, 10 points for a cord or leather grip, and 1 additional swingweight point for every three layers of build-up tape that may be used (e.g.-An ungripped club with a swingweight of E-0, scheduled for installation with a Men's Victory grip with three layers of build-up tape will make the gripped club's **initial swingweight** D-0).

■ **NOTE: For alternative swingweight method**
Rather than use grip weight estimations to calculate the club's initial swingweight, clubmakers may wish to temporarily install a grip of the type to be used on the shaft butt. Keep a few grips in your shop (rubber, cord, 58 core, 60 core, etc.) that have been cut lengthwise with a knife or scissors to slide on the shaft for simulating the weight of the grip. This way when the club is placed on the swingweight scale, a very accurate estimation of the club's initial swingweight can be made. For oversize grips, allow 1 swingweight point for every three layers of build-up tape to be used.

Example:

Desired
Swingweight (D-3)

– Initial
Swingweight (D-1)
_____

Amount to Add (2SW)

35

STEP 35: Calculate the weight increase needed to establish the club's final desired swingweight
Subtract the initial swingweight from the customer's desired final swingweight to determine what amount of weight to add to the head (e.g. - Desired final swingweight of D-2 minus initial swingweight of D-0 = the amount of weight to add of 2 swingweight points).

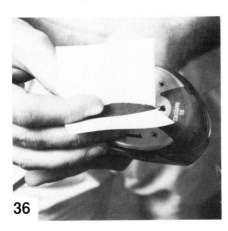

36

STEP 36: Increase swingweight to final level desired
Once the amount of weight increase is determined, use lead powder to establish the final swingweight of the club. Many wooden clubheads available for component clubmaking have set screw weight ports installed in the head for this purpose. The weight to be added may be

pre-weighed on a gram scale (allowing 1 swingweight point = @2 grams of lead powder as a formula) to save guess work. If a gram scale is not available in your shop, add the lead powder into the weight port by estimation, check the weight on the scale, then add or remove lead powder as needed to establish the final weight.

■ **NOTE: If the club's initial swingweight is too high,** the only professional method for removing weight from the head will be to remove the soleplate and take out some of the solid lead that is in place as a part of the head's manufactured weight. Pre-calculating swingweight before assembly is important because soleplate removal on a finished head is difficult to do without damaging the finish on the head.

37

STEP 37: If no weight port is present, add the weight down the shaft in the form of lead powder, held in place with a cork
An addition of 5 swingweight points (10 grams) or less down the shaft for the purpose of establishing final swingweight will not harm the playability of any club. Therefore, if no weight port is present, or if the capacity of the weight port is not sufficient for the final swingweight needs of the club, use lead powder to add the final amount down the shaft. Pour the amount needed into the shaft butt, tamp the head lightly to move the lead powder to the shaft tip and check the swingweight on the scale.

38

STEP 38: Secure the weight with a cork tamped down the shaft
When the proper swingweight is achieved, drop a small cork down the shaft to secure the weight. Use a 1/4" diameter steel ram rod to drive the cork completely down the shaft and in place on top of the lead powder. Because of the tightness of fit against the shaft walls, no epoxy is needed to secure the cork on top of the weight. Proper size corks for the job are available from the various component supply companies.

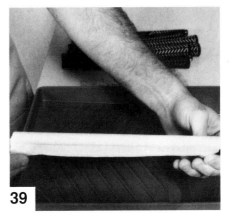

39

STEP 39: Apply grip tape (and leather grip collar if needed)
Secure the club in the bench vise with the head positioned

toe up and apply any required build-up tape and/or 2-way foundation tape. If a leather grip is to be installed it will require a plastic grip collar. If the collar has not already been put on during the installation of the shaft, slide it on over the shaft butt. Installing a grip collar from the butt end of the shaft requires a little practice but can easily be accomplished if the grip collar size used is one shaft size larger than the shaft butt. For example, use a .620" size grip collar on a .600" butt diameter shaft.

40

STEP 40: Install Grip and Final Check Swingweight
After wetting the 2-way grip tape and the inside of the grip with grip solvent, install and properly line up the grip. After installation, check to be sure the grip is completely seated against the shaft butt and clean up the tape residue that will be present at the mouth of the grip. Immediately put the club back on the swingweight scale to double check your work, now making sure the butt of the grip is pushed against the end of the scale. If the swingweight is incorrect, the grip adhesive from the tape should still be wet enough to allow you to pull off the grip and correct the problem. Once the swingweight is correct, install a protective plastic grip bag, held in place with a wrap of thin masking tape. Covering the grip not only adds a professional touch, but will protect the grip from soiling during the club's remaining time in your shop. **The complete step by step procedures for all**

types of grip installation and sizing are covered in Chapter 4.

41

STEP 41: Clean up, install the shaft label and check the club for proper final specifications
The club is now completed. Before the job is fully done, take time to inspect and clean up any soiling of the head, grip and shaft, and final check all specifications for accuracy. Finally, install plastic bags on the head and grip for protection and apply any necessary shaft labels in the proper place on the shaft. The golf industry's standard position for shaft labels is between the second and third step down below the mouth of the grip, with the label centered between steps, insignia facing forward.

Persimmon/Laminated Maple Wood Assembly

Procedures of Assembly for Unfinished Wooden Heads, Including Complete Finish Application Procedures

When assembling woods using unfinished wooden heads, all of the steps of assembly through the dressing of the ferrule that were just described in the assembly proce-

dures for pre-finished woodheads are to be duplicated, in the same order. After that, the assembly procedures will change to incorporate the necessary steps for the application of the finish. However, to make the unfinished wooden head assembly as clear and unconfused as possible, each of these steps of clubmaking leading up to finish application are illustrated again, this time using the unfinished wooden head as the example in the photographs.

The finishing procedures as outlined in this section of the chapter illustrate the use of an oil modified type polyurethane finish, applied in conjunction with water base stains and oil base fillers. Many different finishing systems do exist which are also acceptable for producing a quality finish. If you decide to use another type of finishing system, be sure to check with your supplier or finishing advisor to ensure proper application techniques, proper cure times, and inter-material compatibility.

1

STEP 1: Secure and organize each of the required components to anticipate any potential problems in assembly
Whether by laying all of the components out on your workbench or by making a mental note, be sure you have all the necessary components **and** supplies on hand to complete the assembly before you start the actual procedures of clubmaking. To avoid any potential swingweight problems that may be created by the customer's required

custom fitting specifications, first note the desired length, shaft weight, grip size and swingweight in conjunction with the gram weight of the clubhead and calculate the anticipated swingweight of the club(s) **before** you begin work. By pre-calculating swingweight from the known assembly specifications, necessary adjustments can often be made before the assembly process begins, thus solving a potential problem before it occurs. See Chapter 10 for an explanation of how to calculate the swingweight of a golf club before it is assembled.

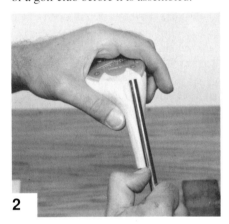

STEP 2: Test fit each shaft in the appropriate head

Test fit each shaft into its matching woodhead to check for proper fit. This step is performed to check the fit of the shaft into the bore of the head and to determine if any adjustments have to be made to the hosel bore diameter to assure the proper fit. Please note in cases of using some types of shafts that are to be pre-trimmed to the golf club's desired playing length **from the tip**, a test fit of the shaft into the head is a must to determine the necessary trimming (a description of changing or adjusting hosel bore sizes can be found in Chapter 10).

■ **NOTE:** On pre-whipped woodheads, the tension of the whipping over the ferrule can cause the inside diameter of the ferrule to be too small to allow the shaft to slide through. If the shaft does not slide easily through the ferrule on pre-whipped woodheads, ream out the ferrule with the appropriate size drill or reamer (.335" parallel bore = "R" drill bit).

STEP 3: Calculate proper tip trimming and mark each shaft for trimming (if tip trimming is necessary)

Either on paper or in your mind, first calculate the amount to tip trim from each of the shafts, if in fact the shafts being used call for tip trimming (while the majority of shafts will require tip trimming prior to installation, some by virtue of their design will not). Refer to the Shaft Trimming Index in Chapter 3 to find the correct chart of trimming procedures to follow for the shafts being used. Use a ruler and felt tip pen to mark the correct amount to trim from each shaft.

For the most accuracy in shaft flex feel, remember to take into account the bottom of bore to heel dimension of the wooden head (through-bore vs. blind bore) and the required playing length of the golf club(s) before calculating the proper tip trimming for each shaft (see Chapter 3 for an explanation of how to adjust tip trimming based on the bottom of bore to heel dimension and playing length changes to assure consistent shaft installation).

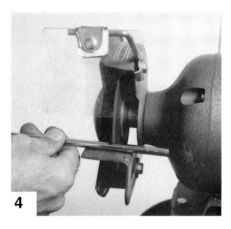

STEP 4: Tip trim all shafts

Use the method of shaft cutting that is best suited for the type of material from which the shafts are made. We recommend the use of a tube cutter or motorized abrasive cut-off wheel for steel and titanium (all metal types) and a grit edge saw or abrasive cut-off wheel for graphite and other fibrous composite shafts. Again, by intent of their design, some shafts will not require tip trimming before installation, so be sure to always check, then double check, the proper trimming procedures for the shafts you are using.

STEP 5: Abrade the tip of the shaft

With medium to coarse grit sandpaper, abrade the entire portion of the shaft tip that will not only be inserted in the hosel, but under the ferrule as well (should a ferrule be required in the assembly). Abrading the shaft tip will allow the epoxy to assist in securing the shaft and ferrule, and greatly reduce the chance of the head and/or ferrule working loose at a later time. For assembling wooden heads, crimping or deforming the shaft to facilitate a mechanical lock of shaft to head is **not** recommended.

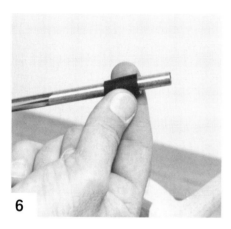

6

STEP 6: Install ferrule (and leather grip collar if required)

In virtually all cases of wooden head installation a ferrule will be required. The only exceptions will be if the head is made with a ferrule and whipping already in place, or in the rare case of a woodhead made with the top of the wooden hosel sanded into a thin taper to meet the shaft. **Follow the procedures illustrated in Chapter 3 to guide the installation of the ferrule.**

■ **NOTE**: It is not necessary to install and position the ferrule in its exact position on the shaft. The insertion of the shaft completely to the bottom of the hosel will push each ferrule up the shaft and into its proper location. **If a leather grip is called for in the assembly of the club, be sure to install the proper size plastic grip trim collar up from the tip end of the shaft at this time.**

STEP 7: Mix epoxy and apply both to the shaft tip and inside of hosel

Always use a high shear strength, 2-part shafting epoxy

7

to secure the shaft to the head. Follow the epoxy supplier's mixing recommendations to ensure complete bonding strength of the epoxy. Using a 1/4" wood dowel rod or similar applicator stick, apply a thin, full coverage coating of the epoxy to the shaft tip and the inside of the hosel bore.

8

STEP 8: Install the shafts

One by one, insert each shaft into its proper clubhead. Rotate the shaft as it is inserted to ensure a complete coating of the epoxy between the shaft tip and the inside of the hosel. While it is not necessary, since many shafting epoxies are manufactured with a form of filler within, sand may be used as an additional bonding aid without fear of damaging the hosel. If sand is used, dip

only 1/4" of the tip of the shaft into the sand before inserting the shaft into the hosel. The use of sand can be a strength additive for tube type epoxies such as Conap,which are made without a filler. Check to make sure the manufacturer's silkscreen is properly aligned at the "12 o'clock" position at this time.

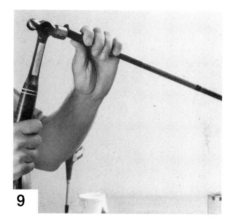

9

STEP 9: Properly seat the shafts into the hosel

For proper assembly, it is vital that each shaft be installed so that the shaft tip seats completely through the sole (in the case of through-bore type woodheads) or to the bottom of the bore (in the case of blind bore type woodheads). Note the following shaft seating procedures for each type of wooden head:

Through-Bore Woodhead - Whether pushing and rotating the shaft by hand or by tapping the butt of the shaft on the floor while holding the head secure to the shaft, drive the shaft into the hosel until the **entire circumference** of the tip penetrates through the sole.

Blind Bore Woodhead - Using either method described above, drive the shaft into the hosel until you feel it stop against the bottom of the bore (in most cases, hand pressure alone will be sufficient to properly seat the shaft in the hosel).

■ **NOTE: For pre-whipped woodheads**

Use extreme care when inserting shafts into pre-whipped woodheads. To prevent breaking off the ferrule be sure the shaft tip has been inserted past the bottom of the ferrule before tapping the shaft to the bottom of the bore. Should the ferrule break off during shaft installation, discard the whipping and ferrule and file the top of the hosel completely flat. When the top of the hosel is squared off, install a new ferrule on the shaft and epoxy the shaft in the hosel.

10

STEP 10: Work epoxy under the ferrule

After seating the shaft in the hosel, try to work some epoxy underneath the ferrule to protect it from working loose. Rotate and move the ferrule up and down against the the top of the hosel to draw epoxy under the ferrule. Finish by pushing the ferrule firm against the hosel to eliminate the possibility of a gap that occurs between the top of the hosel and the ferrule. Wipe away any excess epoxy from the base of the ferrule. If the ferrule is very tight on the shaft after shaft installation such that no epoxy can be worked under, do not worry about its working loose when the club is put into play.

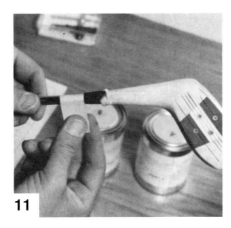

11

STEP 11: Apply masking tape above ferrule

To prevent the ferrule from slipping up the shaft and creating a gap while the epoxy cures, wrap one layer of 1/2" or 1" wide masking tape around the shaft, butting one edge of the tape against the top of the ferrule. This tape will also protect the shaft from scratching when filing the ferrule.

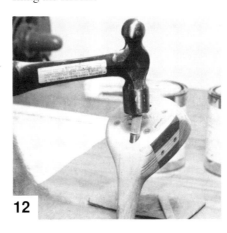

12

STEP 12: Install plug in tip of shaft (for through-bore woodheads only)

If the woodheads being assembled are a through-bore design, a plug must be driven up steel shafts to fill in the opening of the shaft tip. You may choose to use either the special tapered wood plugs sold by component suppliers or a 1/4" or 5/16" wood dowels for this purpose. 1/4"

dowels will fit a bit loose and may require epoxying, whereas the 5/16" variety must be sanded on the tip to allow driving up inside the tip of the shaft. Do not tap the wood plug up the tip of the shaft before installation of the shaft into the head. **Never** drive the tapered type of wood plugs or the 3/8" dowels their full length into the shaft tip or the plug will split. However, do be sure to drive the wood plug at least 1/2"-3/4" into the tip to adequately fill the shaft tip and ensure a tight fit. In the case of graphite or composite shafts installed into through-bore heads, use any type of epoxy to fill the tip of the shaft instead of a wood plug. **NOTE:** Blind bore woodheads never require a tip plug.

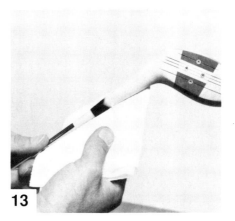

13

STEP 13: Clean up, check and set aside for the epoxy to cure

Before the setting the club aside to dry, check the point between the top of the hosel and the bottom of the ferrule. Be sure any excess amounts of epoxy have been wiped away, but at the same time, do leave a small amount of epoxy on the line between the ferrule and the hosel. Because it is very common for the top of the hosel of a wooden head to not be perfectly square, the epoxy can serve as a filler to correct any small gap between hosel and ferrule. Check for epoxy smears on the head and shaft and wipe clean with a rag dampened with grip solvent. Set the club aside horizontally on a rack or with the head down on the floor for the epoxy to cure. **Never** set clubs to dry with the head up and shaft down or epoxy could flow down the shaft, thus creating the potential for a rattle after the club is put into play.

14

STEP 14: Prepare for installation of backscrew by securing the woodhead in the bench vise

A backscrew, or shaft locking screw, is not required with graphite or composite shaft installation, but **for any type of metal shaft to wooden head assembly, the use of a backscrew is a must!!** The two major causes of wooden heads working loose from the shaft are the normal vibration of the wood hosel that naturally occurs from shot impact as well as the wood's swelling and shrinking from temperature changes that the club may be subjected to over the course of a season. Because these factors are normal and beyond the control of the clubmaker, you must afford yourself the protection against the head possibly coming off the shaft by installing a backscrew. To begin the backscrew installation procedure, secure the woodhead in the bench vise, toe down, with the head between soft vise pads. Place another pad under the toe of the head to prevent possible damage to the toe of the head when hammering down the screw.

STEP 15: Locate the point of backscrew entry on the back of the woodhead

By placing a straight rod on the back side of the shaft, directly in line with the shaft, it is possible to locate exactly where the shaft lies inside the hosel. With the rod positioned on the top of the back side of the shaft as

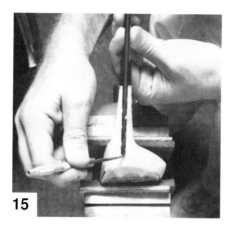

15

pictured, make a small mark with an awl or scriber on the back of the head, directly in line with the shaft about 1/2" up from the back edge of the heel of the woodhead.

16

STEP 16: Properly line up the drill bit in relation to the shaft

Using the electric hand drill and a 1/8" high speed steel or cobalt bit, position the point of the bit on the mark, **perpendicular to the top of the shaft.** For accuracy of drilling, it is extremely important that the bit be perpendicular with the top of the shaft. Failure to do so can result in the bit glancing off or completely missing the shaft. Also check the angle of the bit with relation to the front of the hosel to avoid the potential problem of the bit coming through the front side of the hosel, thus ruining the head.

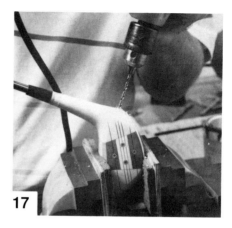

17

STEP 17: Drill to the top of the shaft

Once the bit is properly lined up, drill into the woodhead until you feel the bit touch the top surface of the shaft. Upon feeling contact with the top of the shaft, withdraw the drill bit from the hole. **Do not attempt to drill through the shaft!**

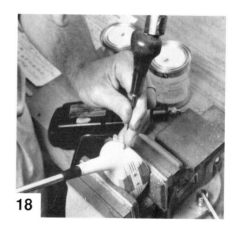

18

STEP 18: Punch a hole through the top of the shaft

Using an awl or a sharpened 1/8" pin punch, use a hammer to drive the tip of the punch/awl first through the top side of the shaft only. Do not attempt to pierce both sides of the shaft at this time. After piercing through the top of the shaft, wiggle the punch loose and remove it.

19

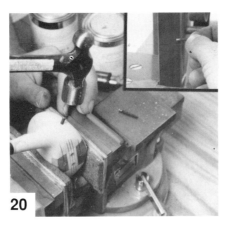

20

22

STEP 19: Drill through the punched hole and the bottom side of the shaft

Insert the electric drill with 1/8" bit into the backscrew hole before activating the drill motor. Check once again for perpendicular bit to shaft alignment before drilling through the punched hole. Despite the punched hole, drilling through the top of the shaft will require some pressure to force the bit completely through. If after 5-10 seconds of drilling the bit has not penetrated the top of the shaft, stop and repeat STEP 18 to enlarge the punched hole diameter before drilling again. Because the hole through the top of the shaft will act as a bushing to hold the bit in the proper position, once the top of the shaft has been penetrated with the drill, continue drilling through the bottom side of the shaft. Again, firm pressure on the drill will be required to penetrate the bottom side of the shaft. Drill to a depth no more than 1 1/2" below the back surface of the head and then withdraw the bit. After drilling the hole, remove the club from the vise and dump any loose particles out the butt end of the shaft.

■ **NOTE**: After drilling through the top of the shaft, clubmakers may wish to withdraw the bit and repeat the punch then drill procedure to penetrate the bottom side of the shaft. While the procedure in STEP 19 is used by most experienced clubmakers, there is a slight chance the pressure required to help the drill penetrate the unpunched bottom of the shaft could result in a broken drill bit, or the mistake of driving the nose of the drill chuck into the back of the wood.

STEP 20: Install the backscrew

For a professional job, it is recommended to use a "headless" type of backscrew. While some component companies do supply this type of screw, you may use a bench grinder or belt sander to grind the flared sides off the head of a #5x1 1/8" steel backscrew. When installing the screw do not rotate the screw into place. Tap it into the hole with a hammer, as if driving a nail.

21

STEP 21: Tap the backscrew below the surface of the woodhead

After tapping the screw flush to the back surface of the head, use the sharpened 1/8" pin punch or awl to bury the head of the screw @ 1/8" below the surface of the head. Use a very light tapping force with the hammer to prevent driving the screw too deep into the head.

STEP 22: Fill the hole with an appropriate shade of fast dry epoxy

Mix a small amount of quick dry epoxy and tint it with an appropriate hue that will match or contrast nicely with the expected color of the woodhead finish yet to be applied. Color paste dispersions that are used to tint pour-in-place face insert epoxies work very well for coloring all quick dry epoxies. In lieu of the dispersion colors, a very small amount of enamel paint can be used. Use a toothpick to fill the backscrew hole, being sure to dab the epoxy slightly above the surface of the wood. Be as neat as possible with this step to prevent smearing epoxy into the open pores of the wood. Set aside to dry. **If you are assembling blind bore type wooden heads, go directly to STEP 24 from here. If the heads being assembled are of the through-bore variety, proceed on with STEP 23.**

23

STEP 23: Grind or file the shaft tip of through-bore, flush to the bottom of the head

If the woodhead is a through-bore variety, break off the excess wood plug protruding from the shaft tip. With a file or belt sander, grind off the excess shaft tip, proceeding until the tip of the shaft is flush to the bottom of the wooden head. Even though the work is performed on an unfinished head, care should be taken not to gouge the sole with the file or belt sander.

24

STEP 24: File the ferrule to prepare for the whipping

If you are skilled in the use of a belt sander with linen belt to turn down ferrules, then this method will be the fastest way to prepare the ferrule for whipping. If not, use a shaft clamp to secure the club in the vise as pictured. With a medium cut file, begin filing around the entire ferrule to reduce its diameter from top to bottom. Take extreme care to retain the perfect taper of the ferrule while filing. After the ferrule has been filed in an even taper from the shaft to the top of the hosel, use a strip of sandpaper to remove the file marks. If using a shanked type ferrule, no filing at the top of the ferrule will be necessary.

■ **NOTE**: For standard (non-shanked) ferrules, take care **not** to scratch the shaft too far (more than 1/8") above the top of the ferrule.

25

STEP 25: Measure and mark the shaft for the desired playing length

Place the club on the floor in the playing position, taking care not to rock the club either up on the toe or back on its heel. Slide a 48" clubmaker's ruler up behind the shaft, and carefully mark the desired playing length on the butt end of the shaft with a felt tip marker. Be sure to allow for the effect that the 1/8" thickness of the end of the grip will have on the club's playing length by marking the shafts 1/8" shorter than what is desired (e.g.- If a true 43" playing length is desired, the mark should be made at 42 7/8", for a 41 1/2" playing length, mark the shaft at 41 3/8", etc.).

■ **NOTE**: There are a limited number of shaft patterns that will require no further butt trimming for playing length after installation, so be sure to re-check the trimming instructions for the shafts being used.

STEP 26: Cut the shaft to its desired playing length

Using the proper cutting procedure for the type of shaft being used, trim the shaft for its playing length. Always deburr and square off the shaft butt after trimming to

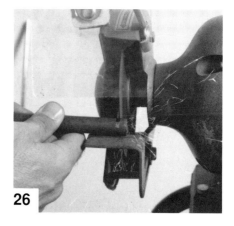

26

remove sharp edges. If a graphite or composite type shaft has been installed, use an abrasive cut-off wheel or a grit edged hack saw blade to trim the shaft, **never** a tubing cutter.

27

STEP 27: Record the preliminary swingweight of the club

Place the club on a 14" fulcrum swingweight scale (Lorythmic or Prorythmic type) **without the grip installed** and record its swingweight. Do NOT push the butt of the ungripped club completely against the back of the scale. Because the grip cap provides the final 1/8" of club length, pull the shaft butt 1/8" away from the end of the scale before recording preliminary swingweight. This is important to achieve an accurate swingweight reading.

Example:

**Preliminary
Swingweight (E-0)**

**– Swingweight
Equivalent of Grip (9SW)**

**Initial
Swingweight (D-1)**

28

STEP 28: Subtract the swingweight equivalent of the grip from the ungripped club's recorded swingweight to determine the <u>initial swingweight</u>

The swingweight of the ungripped club will read higher because the grip has not been installed. It will be heavier in the amount equal to the swingweight equivalent of the weight of the grip plus its installation and build-up tape. To determine what the club's **initial swingweight** will be once the grip is installed, subtract 9 swingweight points for a standard men's size rubber grip, 10 points for a cord or leather grip, and 1 additional swingweight point for every three layers of build-up tape that may be used (e.g.- An ungripped club with a swingweight of E-0, scheduled for installation with a Men's Victory grip with three layers of build-up tape will make the gripped club's **initial swingweight** D-0).

■ **NOTE:** Rather than use grip weight estimations to calculate the club's initial swingweight, clubmakers may wish to temporarily install a grip of the type to be used on the shaft butt. Keep a few grips in your shop (rubber, cord, 58 core, 60 core, etc.) that have been cut lengthwise with a knife or scissors to slide on the shaft for simulating

the weight of the grip. This way when the club is placed on the swingweight scale a very accurate estimation of the club's initial swingweight can be made.

29

STEP 29: Make necessary swingweight adjustments to the head, allowing for the weight of the finish and whipping

If the initial swingweight of the unfinished wooden club is **lower** than the desired final swingweight, following are your options for weight addition:

1. If the woodhead has a weight port, wait until the finish has been applied and all assembly procedures have been completed before establishing the final swingweight. At that time you will know precisely how much weight the finish, the whipping, and the grip have added to the club. Therefore, the weight added through the weight port will be the final clubmaking procedure for the club.

2. If the woodhead does **not** have a weight port, there are two swingweighting options:

> **a**. If the amount of weight to add is less than 5 swingweight points, after the finish and whipping have been applied add the required amount down the shaft in the form of lead powder held in place with a cork.

b. If the amount to add is more than 5 swingweight points, remove the soleplate NOW, before the finish is applied and make the addition under the plate. If weight is added under the soleplate, be sure to leave the swingweight @ 1.5 swingweight points UNDER the desired final swingweight to allow for the weight of the finish and whipping. See Chapter 10 for soleplate removal and weight addition procedures.

If the initial swingweight of the club is <u>higher</u> than the desired final level, remove the soleplate and drill out the necessary lead weight, being sure to leave the swingweight about 1.5 points below the desired final level to allow for the weight of the finish and whipping. Again, refer to the procedures outlined in Chapter 10 for soleplate removal and weight removal.

Final Sanding the Clubhead in Preparation for Finish Application

While unfinished wooden heads are sold and shipped "ready-to-finish," it will be necessary to fine sand the head once more, using 150-240 fine grit sandpaper. The final sanding will serve to give the head a fresh, unsoiled surface to assure consistent coloring and better finish adhesion. Sand the head on a woodhead sanding machine, leaving the face area to be final sanded by hand to avoid damaging the loft, roll and bulge specifications. The sanding procedure, in step-by-step form, is as follows:

30A

STEP 30A: Sand forward portion of toe area
Grasp the head firmly in both hands and begin sanding the front portion of the toe. Always keep the head moving when in contact with the sanding machine, moving back and forth across all surfaces of the toe. This will prevent flat spotting and assure consistent sanding contact with the head.

30B

STEP 30B: Sand back side of toe area
Switch the position of the head by holding the club with the shaft off your left hip, clubhead face pointing down. Begin sanding on the back side of the toe, sanding all the way completely around the back side of the head.

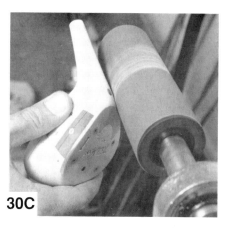

30C

STEP 30C: Sand the back of the head
Continue the sanding from the back of the club to the backscrew area on the back of the neck. Sand off any epoxy covering the backscrew hole and always keep the clubhead moving while in contact with the machine. Sand around the neck and just up to the edge of the heel side of the face.

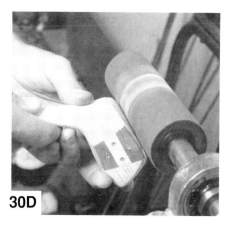

30D

STEP 30D: Sand soleplate and entire bottom surface
Shift the position of the club so that the sole is pointing up. Sand the entire sole area, taking care to move the club up and down against the sanding machine. The direction of the sanding scratches should be straight and consistent, moving from the toe down across the sole to the heel.

30E

STEP 30E: Sand leading edge of soleplate
Sand the leading edge of the sole plate by placing the toe end of the plate's leading edge on the sanding machine. Sand back and forth on the edge of the plate while keeping the leading edge always in contact with the sanding machine.

30F

STEP 30F: Sand the trailing edge of the plate
Shift the club's position so that you can perform the same sanding step to the back, or trailing edge of the soleplate. Again, always keep the head moving when in contact with the sanding machine.

30G

STEP 30G: Sand the base of the hosel
Hold the club with the shaft straight up, and place the back of the crotch area of the hosel against the sanding machine. Begin to spin the club against the sander, always keeping the base of the neck in contact with the sanding sleeve.

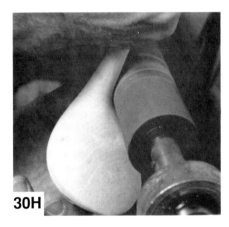

30H

STEP 30H: Sand the face side on the base of the hosel
As you spin the club around to sand the crotch, always keep the club moving when it is in contact with the sanding sleeve. Take care when sanding the base of the hosel near the face not to sand any portion of the face itself on the machine.

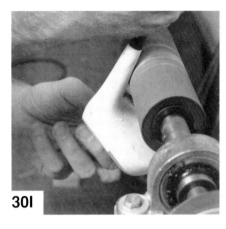

30I

STEP 30I: Sand up and around the neck
Move from the base of the hosel into sanding the entire circumference of the neck. Keep the club spinning around and around as you work your way up and then down the neck. **Always keep the club spinning as you sand the neck,** or flat spots may occur.

■ **NOTE:** Because sanding the neck on the machine requires practice before proficiency is developed, you may wish to place the club in the bench vise and hand sand with a strip of fine sandpaper as an alternative procedure.

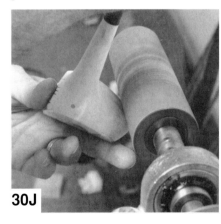

30J

STEP 30J: Begin sanding the top or crown
Begin sanding the top (crown) of the head by starting on the crown near the base of the hosel. Always move the

clubhead against the sanding sleeve in the direction of the grain (for persimmon especially), sanding across the head in a direction from face insert to back, never in a direction from the toe to the crotch.

30K

STEP 30K: Complete the crown sanding
Continue sanding from face to back as you work out toward the toe of the club. Sand right up to, but definitely not over, the edges of the face and the toe.

30L

STEP 30L: Lightly sand the edges of the toe and back of the head
Very lightly sand over and under the toe and back edges of the head. Use the lightest pressure possible in rounding these edges of the club and **always** keep the club

moving while in contact with the sanding machine. Again, until proficiency is developed on the machine, hand sanding of all edges may be performed. After this step the sanding is complete, so take time to check all surfaces for quality workmanship before proceeding to Step 31.

Before the unfinished wooden head can be colored with stain, the face and the insert must be protected from the stain by a polyurethane coating, or mask, as it is called. This step will dictate the exact outline of the face and keep stain from discoloring both the insert and the adjacent wood surfaces of the toe/heel, so **extreme care** must be taken to brush a perfect outline of the face. It is wise to use moisture cure type polyurethane or similar low viscosity finish for this step to prevent the masking from running down the scoring lines and on to the head. **If the face insert is made of paper fiber or phenolic fiber material the entire insert will have to be masked to protect it from permanent discoloration from the stain.** If the insert is made from plastic (Cycolac, ABS, etc.) or metal, it will not be susceptible to the stain, so only the wood portions of the toe and heel will have to be masked with the polyurethane. The entire face masking sequence is covered as follows:

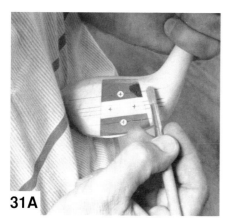

31A

STEP 31A: Mask top portion of heel
Hold the club close to your chest for stability and begin to brush the mask on the top edge of the heel. Keep all polyurethane edges sharp and clear, not jagged.

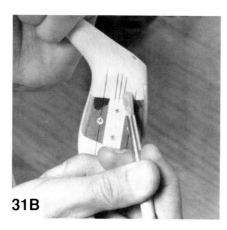

31B

STEP 31B: Round the corner and brush down to the bottom of the heel
Masking the corner of the heel is the most critical step in the procedure. Brush the urethane around the corner of the heel with one continuous motion. This will ensure a sharp line between face and head, thus eliminating an unsightly jagged look. The corner of the heel should be slightly rounded and not take on the appearance of a sharp angle. Finish the heel area by brushing down the edge of the heel to the edge of the face insert and over all of this portion of the wood's face surface.

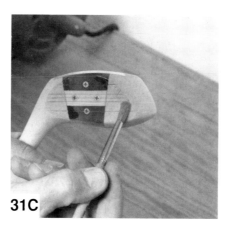

31C

STEP 31C: Mask bottom of toe area
Brush the polyurethane up from the bottom of the face insert, following the edge between the face and the front of the toe. Brush right up to the corner of the toe.

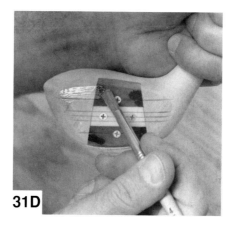

31D

STEP 31D: Mask top of toe area
Shift the position of the club against your chest so that you can begin to brush around the corner of the toe. Again, try to brush with a continuous motion of to ensure a smooth curve around the toe. Continue the masking along the line of the top edge of the toe to the top edge of the insert. Finish the toe area by covering all of the toe surface of the face with the masking.

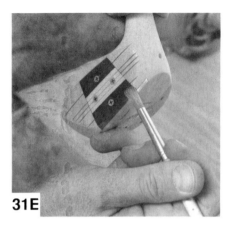

STEP 31E: Brush all insert surfaces if the face insert is made from paper fiber or phenolic fiber materials
The above mentioned inserts are susceptible to discoloring from the stain. If the club is made with one of these inserts, brush the entire face surface with the masking.

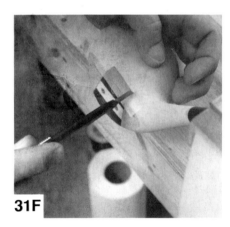

STEP 31F: Tape mask the top of the insert
If the insert is fiber or phenolic, use permanent adhesive cellophane tape to cover the top of the insert. Place a strip of the tape perfectly against the back edge of the insert, then use a razor knife (blade) to cut the tape precisely down the sides of the insert. Press the tape down firmly to prevent stain from bleeding underneath.

■ **NOTE:** Before proceeding, inspect for and sand off

any urethane that may be on the parts of the head to be stained.

STEP 32: Apply water base stain of choice
The polyurethane mask does not have to dry before applying the stain. For best coloring results, it is recommended to use water base type stains. Water base stains are available in a variety of colors from many component suppliers. Either by dipping or brushing, quickly apply the stain color of choice to the entire head. When dipping, completely immerse the head, making sure the stain travels far enough up the neck to be covered later by the whipping.

STEP 33: Wipe off excess stain
To ensure consistent color penetration and prevent a

"splotching" of the color, immediately after staining wipe the entire head dry with a paper towel, taking care not to wipe across or touch the wet polyurethane mask on the face.

STEP 34: Blow down scoring lines to remove excess stain
Hold the club over the stain container and blow down the scoring lines to remove excess stain. Quickly wipe away the excess stain that travels out the lines with a paper towel. This step is performed to prevent this trapped stain from dribbling out and "splotching" the head while the club is drying. Set the club aside to dry for a minimum of 4-6 hours at room temperature (70° F), or for 1-2 hours at 100°F.

STEP 35: Apply paste wood filler

After the stain has dried, for open grain hardwoods such as persimmon, a paste filler must be applied to close the pores and protect the wood against moisture. For laminated maple woodheads, while it will enrich the color, a filler is not absolutely necessary. Fillers, like stains, are made in a variety of colors. However, for shop economy it is recommended to restrict filler usage to deep black or less intense black filler for the black clubheads and natural filler for all other stain colors. Thoroughly mix the filler (again, available from component suppliers) and apply to the head by brushing or by dabbing on and rubbing in with a cloth.

STEP 36: Wipe all filler off the woodhead

After allowing 10-15 minutes after application for the filler to sit, or "flash" on the head, use terrycloth or burlap rags to wipe all of the filler off the head. The main purpose of the filler is to fill the pores of the wood, **not** to remain on the surface, so it is <u>very</u> important to wipe all traces of excess filler from the woodhead. After wiping, allow a minimum of 8 hours for the filler to dry at room temperature (70°F) or 4-6 hours at a force drying temperature of 100°F.

■ **NOTE:** If the woodhead is being finished in a stain color (with grain exposed, not to be color coted or painted in black or another opaque finish) proceed directly to STEP 50.

TIP: A second application of filler should be applied to fully seal the pores of persimmon heads that have never yet been finished.

The following steps are to be followed in sequence if the woodhead is finished using an opaque color cote (paint) such as black. A color cote is thought of in the same way as a paint, since its purpose is to completely hide the grain of the woodhead, thus leaving a plain opaque surface. An assortment of color cotes are available from the golf industry's finish suppliers, most of which are designed to be applied only through the use of a spray gun and compressor. However, a limited selection of color cote colors are available in aerosol spray can form from component supply companies. Unless your shop is equipped with professional air spray equipment, color cote use should be restricted to the varieties available in aerosol form.

STEP 37: Buff the soleplate to prepare for color cote application

Use a fine grade of steel wool (3/0 or 4/0) to clean the soleplate and backweight (if present). While hand buffing can be performed, it is recommended to use a steel wool sleeve attached to the motorized woodhead sanding machine for a faster and better job. Buff in an up and down direction until all traces of grime from the filler have been removed from the plate and backweight. Do <u>not</u> steel wool any of the stained portions of the head.

STEP 38: Solvent wipe all wood surfaces

No matter how much care may have been taken to wipe off all traces of excess filler, a thin film of the material will still be present on the woodhead's surface. To remove this film and assure good adhesion between head and color cote, wipe **all** surfaces of the head with a rag **dampened** (not soaked) in acetone or a grip solvent such as perchlorethylene or naphtha (it is recommended to wear non-porous gloves to prevent repeated skin contact with these solvents).

STEP 39: Acetone wipe the top of plastic and metal face inserts

For plastic-type (Cycolac, ABS, etc.) and metal inserts, **wet** a towel with acetone and quickly wipe across the top of the insert to restore its clean appearance.

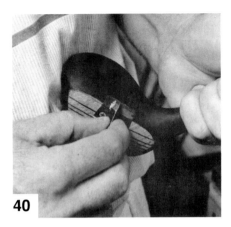

40

STEP 40: Detail the top of fiber or phenolic inserts
If the woodhead has one of these types of inserts, a scraping technique for restoring a fresh look is recommended. Use a razor blade or scraper (a scraper may be created by running the back of a knife blade against the face of a grinder stone) to remove grime from the top of the insert and expose a fresh, clean surface. Finish with a quick wipe with a solvent dampened towel.

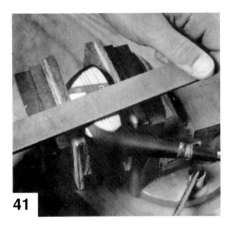

41

STEP 41: Detail and clean up the face
Secure the head in a vise between soft vise pads. Gently use a fine cut file to remove all the grime from the entire face and restore a fresh look to the wood and insert surfaces. Take care when filing in the corner of the heel area not to destroy the perfect line between stain and clean face area. Follow by carefully sanding with fine

grit sandpaper to remove all evidence of file scratches. If further removal of scratches is required, use the scraper. Wipe or blow all dust from the face.

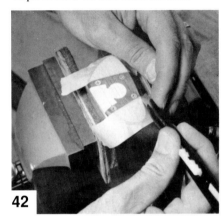

42

STEP 42: Tape mask the face (Heel area)
Use strips of 1" wide masking tape to cover the toe and heel areas of the face. Working under an overhead shop light will allow you to see the outline of the face through the tape to enable you to cut the outline of the face areas. Use a razor blade or razor knife to cut a perfect outline, thus defining the face for painting. Extreme care should be taken to acquire the skill to cut a perfect curve around the corner of the heel

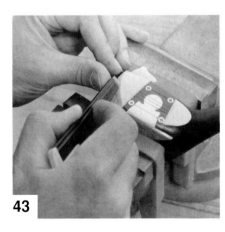

43

STEP 43: Tape mask the face (Toe area)
Use the razor blade to also cut a perfect outline around the

toe of the head. Again, care should be taken to accurately cut the curve around the tip of the toe.

44

STEP 44: Tape mask the soleplate
With the head secured sole up in the vise, apply masking tape over the sole. Masking tape is preferred over clear cellophane tape because it has less of a tendency to leave a tape residue on the soleplate when removed. Use a sharp razor blade or razor knife to cut a perfect outline between all edges of the soleplate and the head. When finished, peel the excess tape away, leaving all parts of the soleplate covered with tape. Press any tape wrinkles flat.

45

STEP 45: Tape mask all other metal surfaces
If the woodhead has a backweight or other exposed metal

parts, these too must be perfectly masked over with tape, using the same razor blade cutting techniques. Cover the metal part with tape, leaving exposed all wood areas to be painted.

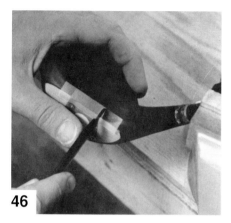

46

STEP 46: Tape mask top of face insert
Reposition the head in the vise with the crown of the club pointing up. Use either masking tape, or for this case, cellophane tape, to cover the top of the face insert. Use a razor blade or razor knife to perfectly cut on the line between the insert and surrounding wood area. Cellophane tape is preferable to masking tape in this case because it is much easier to see where to cut the tape mask. In addition, celophane tape has a very straight edge which makes it very easy to apply accurately along the straight back line of the insert.

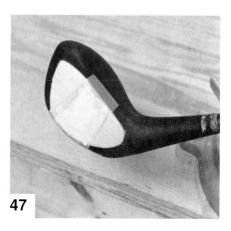

47

STEP 47: Tape mask the rest of the face insert
Finish tape masking by applying masking tape to the center of the insert and any other areas of the face previously left exposed. Do not forget to cover the very bottom edges of the insert that may be exposed on the bottom of the face.

48

STEP 48: Spray color cote over entire head
Thoroughly shake the aerosol color cote to mix all of the components within the spray can. Gently tack rag the head to remove dust. Hold the spray nozzle about 12" away from the head and spray a light but full coverage coating over the entire head. **Remember:** Spray light but spray to fully cover the grain of the wood. **The proper look of the surface right after spraying should be fully covered and somewhat "mottled," not glass smooth and glossy.** Allow 8 hours for drying at room temperature (70°F) or 4 hours if force dried at 100°F.

49

STEP 49: Remove tape masking
After the color cote has fully dried, carefully peel off the tape masking. Be careful not to touch or handle the color coted surface during this procedure as skin oils that can affect finish adhesion may be left from the hands.

OPTIONAL METHOD FOR TAPE MASKING/ COLOR COTE APPLICATION
In this optional method, instead of first detailing and cleaning the face of the club and then covering the entire face with a tape mask, start by performing STEPS 37-40 and then follow with STEPS 44-46. After completing STEP 46 proceed directly to application of the spray color cote. After the color cote has dried, all the tape will be peeled off, leaving the soleplate, metal surfaces and top of the insert completely clean. Secure the head in the vise by the shaft, NOT between vise pads, held in a shaft clamp positioned close to the top of the ferrule. Remove the color cote from the face and then complete the full detailing clean up of the face **as covered in STEP 41. Paint that has been sprayed on the face will come off very easily following this detailing step with the file or scraper.** In review, the two different methods for tape masking and color cote application are contrasted in the following chart:

Order of Sequence	Optional Method 1	Optional Method 2
1.	Step 37	Step 37
2.	Step 38	Step 38
3.	Step 39	Step 39
4.	Step 40	Step 40
5.	Step 41	Step 44
6.	Step 42	Step 45
7.	Step 43	Step 46
8.	Step 44	Step 48
9.	Step 45	Step 41
10.	Step 46	------
11.	Step 47	------
12.	Step 48	------
13.	Step 49	------

If you are finishing a stained only type of head, you will be proceeding with STEP 50 after having completed STEP 36. If the head is being finished with a color cote, proceed from STEP 49 to STEP 54.

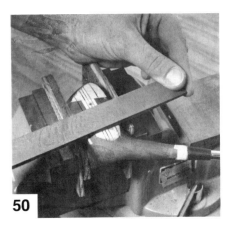

50

STEP 50: Detail and clean up face of stained clubhead

In the procedures for finishing wooden heads with a stained, non-color coted (non-painted) finish, refer back to STEP 36 to note that the last assembly step was to rub off the filler and set the club aside to dry. The next step after filler drying will be to detail and clean up the face and face insert areas of the stained clubhead to prepare it for primer sealer and polyurethane application. To detail the face, secure the head in the vise between soft vise pads and begin filing the wood portions of the face with a fine cut file. **Take extreme care when filing around the heel corner of the face to retain its perfect curved outline**. Continue filing all of the grime from the face without changing the face curvature specifications for bulge and roll.

STEP 51A: Remove scratches from the face area of the stained woodhead - scraping method

After detailing and cleaning the outline of the face with a fine file, there may be scratches on the face that were left as a result of the filing. There are two basic procedures for removing file scratches; scraping and

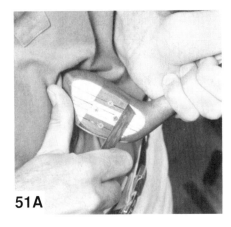

51A

sanding. The face scraping technique requires the use of a metal blade that has a sharp or burred edge suitable for "shaving" a very thin portion of material off the face and face insert. Specially-made scrapers are available from some suppliers. If you do not have one of these tools, a burr edge created on the back of a small knife will work well. By running the back of a knife across a bench grinder stone, a burr for scraping can be created on one of the edges. Scrape across the face from heel to toe to "freshen up" the look of the face.

51B

STEP 51B: Remove scratches from the face area of the stained woodhead - sanding method

The other method for smoothing out the face and removing file scratches before finish application in-

volves carefully sanding across the face with fine grit (150-180 grit) sandpaper. Secure the head in the vise and sand across the face from toe to heel, taking care not to sand any of the stained parts of the head.

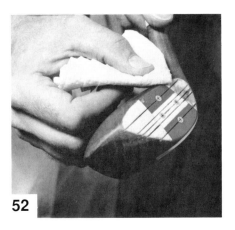

52

STEP 52: Clean up the top of the insert with acetone

If the face insert is a cycolac or plastic type, a simple wipe with a rag dampened with acetone is all that is needed to clean up and shine the top of the insert. Do not rub the stained areas surrounding the top of the insert with the acetone or some fading of the stain can result. If the insert is made from fiber or phenolic resin, minor scraping with a razor blade (See Step 41) before acetone wiping will often be necessary to remove all the dirt.

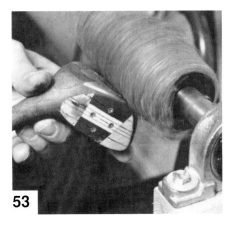

53

STEP 53: Steel wool buff the soleplate
Clean the grime and dirt off the soleplate by buffing with fine grade (3/0 or 4/0) steel wool. **Do not buff any stained portions of the head with the steel wool or fading of the stain will result.**

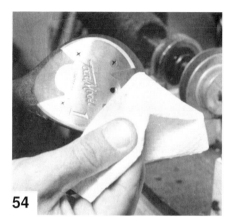

54

STEP 54: Solvent wipe the soleplate and all metal surfaces
Wipe the soleplate and any other metal surfaces (backweight, e.g.) with an acetone dampened cloth. This is a step performed to remove the last possible traces of dirt and oxidation of the metal to ensure the best possible adhesion between primer coat and metal surfaces. For color coted woodheads, this will be the next step after completing STEP 49.

Caution: Acetone will remove color cote so be **very** careful not to touch any color coted surface with the solvent. Note that the technique pictured involves drawing the cloth tightly over the finger to allow the fingernail covered by the cloth to touch just up to the edges between metal and wood.

■ **NOTE**: After solvent wiping, wait no longer than 20 minutes before applying the primer sealer to avoid oxidation of the metal surfaces.

STEP 55: Spray primer sealer over entire head
While not absolutely necessary with the new oil modi-

55

fied polyurethanes, it is a good idea to use the primer sealer as a base coating to give better adhesion of the polyurethane coats to all of the surfaces, both wood and metal, of the head. Primer sealer, which is designed primarily as a base for moisture cure polyurethanes, is compatible with the oil modified polyurethane and can be purchased in aerosol form. Very lightly tack rag the head to remove dust. Hold the spray nozzle at least 12" away from the clubhead and spray a light, but full coverage coat over the **entire head**.

TIP: Spray light but spray to fully to cover the woodhead. **The proper look of the surface after spraying should be somewhat "mottled," not glassy smooth and glossy.** Allow 4 hours for drying at room temperature (70°F) or 1 hour if force dried at 100°F.

56

STEP 56: Polyurethane coat #1 application: Dip clubhead and begin polyurethane run-off
Gently tack rag the head to remove dust and attach a drip catcher to the shaft just above the ferrule to keep excess polyurethane from running down the shaft during drying. Rubber drip catchers can be purchased from golf finishing suppliers or a doubled over strip of paper towel can be taped to the shaft to do the job too. Dip the head into the can of polyurethane so that the material covers well up the hosel. Remove the head from the can toe down so the stream of polyurethane begins to run off the tip of the toe back into the can.

57

STEP 57: Polyurethane coat #1 application: Allow the polyurethane to complete its run-off
When the run-off changes from a stream to a drip, turn the head over and hold it over the can with the toe up, the face turned slightly open, and the shaft pointing at a 45° angle to the floor. To keep the scoring lines from filling up with the polyurethane, briskly blow down the face scoring lines from toe to heel. Excess material will run off into the can, thus making it easier to perform the job of paint filling the lines later. After changing the position of the head, the dripping should come off the head near the back of the ferrule.

58

STEP 58: Polyurethane coat #1 application: Position the club for drying

Once the dripping of the finish off the heel has slowed considerably, put the club aside to continue the setting up of the polyurethane on the head's surface. Position the club in a drying rack so that the toe is still up, face is still slightly open, and the shaft is angled down to the floor. The club must stay in this position until the polyurethane has ceased flowing, or moving on the head. To hang the club in a horizontal position too soon before the finish settles will result in unsightly drips.

■ **NOTE:** When using the oil modified polyurethane, allow coat #1 to dry 2 hours at room temperature. Do not force dry coat #1 at high temperatures.

59

STEP 59: Polyurethane coat #2 application

After 2 hours of room temperature drying for coat #1, repeat STEPS 56, 57 and 58 for applying the second polyurethane coat. Perform **no** hand sanding or steel wooling between coats #1 and #2.

■ **NOTE:** Allow coat #2 to dry 8 hours at room temperature (70°F) or force dry for 6 hours at 100°F.

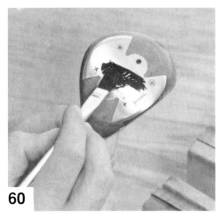

60

STEP 60: Paint filling scorelines and soleplate stampings: Apply paint

After proper drying of polyurethane coats #1 and #2, brush the chosen colors of fast dry latex type paint over the scoring lines and soleplate stampings. Do not waste time trying to be neat. The goal is to fill the lines and stampings with paint so be sure to brush a liberal amount of paint over the lines or stampings to be filled.

61

STEP 61: Paint filling scorelines and soleplate stampings: Wipe off paint

Wipe immediately with a dry paper towel to remove the excess surface paint. Do not be concerned if paint smears are left around the face or soleplate as these smears will all be removed in the process of completing the upcoming steps. Follow the drying time as recommended by the type of paint being used. As a protection, it is recommended to force dry all paint filling at high temperatures.

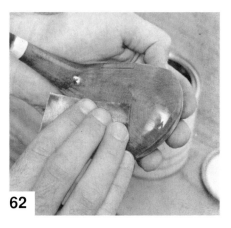

62

STEP 62: Fine sand the woodhead with finishing sandpaper

After proper drying of the face line and soleplate paint, hand sand the entire head with 400 grit sandpaper to level the polyurethane finish and provide adequate adhesion for the succeeding coats of polyurethane. Use light to medium pressure to avoid sanding through the finish. Do not try to sand the entire finish perfectly level, since the thickness of the coating at this time is not strong enough to withstand heavy sanding pressure. **Caution:** Do **not** sand any edges of the woodhead.

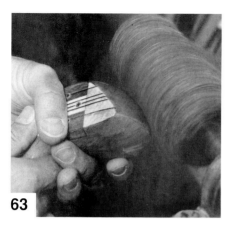

63

STEP 63: Steel wool the clubhead
Follow the 400 sanding procedure by steel wooling the head to smooth out scratches left by the 400 grit sandpaper. While steel wooling can be performed by hand rubbing, it is recommended to do the job by machine, as pictured. Use 3/0 or 4/0 grade steel wool under medium pressure and **do not** buff any of the edges of the head.

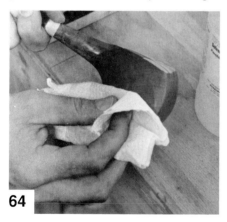

64

STEP 64: Degrease the woodhead
Because there is a small amount of oil naturally present in steel wool, and because the head has undoubtedly been handled during the sanding/steel wooling operations, it is recommended to wipe the head with a cloth **lightly dampened** in naphtha or perchlorethylene (grip solvents). After wiping allow at least 5-10 minutes for the

solvent to evaporate completely from the surface. **Caution: Do not** use acetone as a degreasing solvent as it will dissolve the finish.

65

STEP 65: Apply decals (if required)
If decals are required, it is recommended to use only the water transfer types. To loosen the decal from its paper backing, blot it on top of a wetted paper towel, printed side up. **Do not immerse decals under water as this can wash away much of the decal's adhesive.**

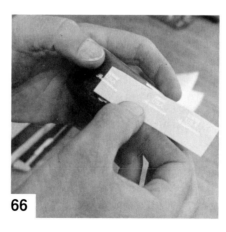

66

STEP 66: Slide decal onto woodhead surface
When the decal has released from the paper, slide it on the head into its proper position and check for correct positioning and alignment.

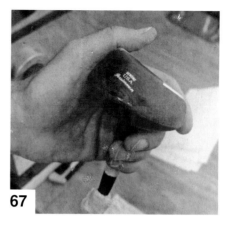

67

STEP 67: Blot decal dry
Carefully press the decal flat with a dry facial tissue, working from one side of the decal to the other. Gently wipe away any excess water moisture and set aside to dry for at least 10 minutes.

68

STEP 68: Application of polyurethane coats #3, #4
Since the head was sanded and steel wooled before decal application, no further abrasion is needed before proceeding directly into the application of the third polyurethane coat. **Use the same procedures for third and fourth coat application and drying that are described in STEPS 56, 57, 58.**

69

STEP 69: Fifth and sixth polyurethane applications
Prepare the head for its final two polyurethane coats by hand sanding, steel wooling and degreasing as described in STEPS 62, 63, 64. Follow with the same dipping and drying procedures as described in STEPS 56, 57, 58.

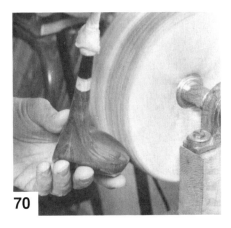
70

STEP 70: Inspection and touch-up (if necessary)
After the sixth and final coat of the polyurethane has dried, inspect the club for finish errors such as sags, runs or drips. If such mistakes are found, hand sand the defect completely flat with 400 grit sandpaper. Follow the corrective sanding by steel wooling to smooth out the scratches from the sandpaper. If you wish to dip a coat of polyurethane over the entire head to finish the touch-up,

be sure to hand sand and steel wool all surfaces before dipping. The other option for completing the correction is to Glanz Wach buff the affected area to return its luster and shine. Final inspection and touch-up steps must include the removal of the dipping collar and cleaning off any excess polyurethane that may have run down the shaft.

71

STEP 71: Final sand the ferrule to prepare for whipping
Secure the head in the vise as pictured and gently sand the base of the ferrule and top of the hosel to remove any build-up of polyurethane. The ferrule must be perfectly smooth and properly tapered from the shaft to the hosel to allow the string whipping to be installed smoothly.

72

STEP 72: Install whipping
Whether by machine or by hand wrapping procedures, install the string whipping and securely tie off to finish the job (a complete step-by-step sequence of hand tying the whipping is covered in Chapter 10).

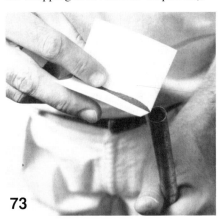
73

STEP 73: Make final swingweight adjustments (if necessary)
Place the club on the swingweight scale to perform a final check. If the head has a weight port and the swingweight is below the desired level, make the final additions through the port. If the head does not have a weight port and the swingweight is below the desired level, make the final additions by placing lead powder down the base of the shaft, to be held in place by a small cork. As any weight adjustments will be made without the grip installed, remember to allow 9 points for a rubber grip, 10 for a cord type grip and 1 point more for every three layers of build-up tape installed on the shaft. Or, a cut grip of the same type may be temporarily installed on the shaft butt for the purpose of obtaining the swingweight. **Remember**: In assembling woods from unfinished wooden heads, it was advised in the beginning of the procedures to perform major weight adjustments under the soleplate. Therefore, any final swingweight adjustments should be very small, with usually no more than 1-2 swingweight points that would have to be added down the shaft. **Any addition of 5 swingweight points (10 grams) or less down the shaft will not harm the playability of any club.**

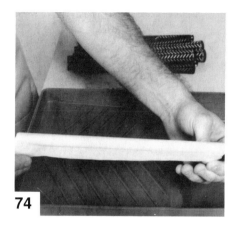

74

STEP 74: Apply grip tape (grip collar if needed)
Secure the club in the bench vise as pictured and apply the required build-up tape and/or 2-way foundation tape. If the grip to be installed requires a plastic grip collar that has not already been put on at the time of the installation of the shaft, slide it on now over the shaft butt.

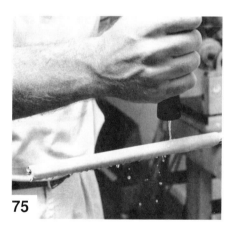

75

STEP 75: Install grip and final check swingweight
Install and properly line up the grip. After installation, clean up any tape residue present at the mouth of the grip. Immediately put the club back on the swingweight scale to double check your work, making sure the butt of the grip is pushed against the end of the scale. If the swingweight is off, the grip adhesive from the tape should still be wet enough to allow you to pull off the grip

and correct the problem. Once the swingweight is correct, install a protective plastic grip bag, held in place with a wrap of thin masking tape. Covering the grip not only adds a professional touch, but will protect the grip from soiling during the club's remaining time in your shop.

76

STEP 76: Clean up, install the shaft label and check the club for proper specifications
Before the job of assembly is fully done, take time to inspect and clean up any soiling of the head, grip and shaft and recheck all specifications for accuracy. Finally, install a plastic head bag for protection and apply any necessary shaft labels in the proper place on the shaft. The golf industry's standard position for shaft labels is between the second and third step downs below the mouth of the grip, with the label centered between steps, insignia facing up.

CHAPTER 6 - The Modern Assembly Procedures of Graphite & Composite Woodheads

Step-by-Step Assembly of Woods from Pre-Finished Graphite and Composite Woodheads

A Product of Modern Technology

The newest entries among the variety of component clubheads available for golf club assembly are woodheads produced from graphite and other moldable composite materials. Having made their debut in golf during the early 1980s, two different types of graphite woodheads currently exist in the golf industry - those injection molded from short fiber graphite and resin and those compression molded from long fiber graphite. In Chapter 2 a brief description was offered of the manufacturing differences between the two types of graphite woodheads. In the discussion the point was established that from a **playability standpoint,** there is no difference between compression and injection-molded graphite heads. While the compression-molded graphite heads do possess greater strength, this physical characteristic has little to do with playability or clubhead activity.

Recently, another form of space age, high-tech material has also entered the golf equipment industry. In the late 1980s woodheads produced from high-strength composites such as thermoplastics and fiber-reinforced plastics have become a small but growing part of clubmaking.

A product of high-tech research in the '80s, these modern composites are usually produced through injection molding and bring to the clubhead design field a high strength to weight ratio in woodhead design. Whether such modern composite materials represent the future of clubhead design remains to be seen at this time, however, with the capability just being realized of how to combine manufacturing processes to engineer better weight distribution, clubmakers may soon begin to see more and more clubheads produced from such light yet strong plastic composites.

From the standpoint of clubmaking and assembly, the procedures for building both injection and compression-molded graphite woodheads as well as high-strength composite woodheads are virtually identical to those used to build clubs from finished wooden heads. Because graphite woodheads are rarely available in unfinished form, the procedures for assembly that follow will be restricted to the steps required to complete the club using pre-finished composite heads only.

Assembly with Graphite/ Composite Woodheads

Procedures of assembly for building golf clubs from finished graphite and composite woodheads

1

STEP 1: Secure and organize each of the required components to anticipate any potential problems in assembly

Be sure you have all the necessary components **and** supplies on hand to complete the assembly before you start the actual procedures of clubmaking. In particular, to avoid any potential swingweight problems that may be created by the customer's required custom fitting specifications, first note the desired length, shaft weight, grip size and swingweight in conjunction with the gram weight of the clubhead to calculate the anticipated swingweight of the club(s) **before** you begin work. By pre-calculating swingweight from the known assembly specifications, necessary adjustments can often be made before the assembly process begins, thus solving a potential problem before it occurs. See Chapter 10 for an explanation of how to calculate the swingweight of a golf club before it is assembled.

STEP 2: Test fit each shaft in the appropriate head
Test fit each shaft into its matching woodhead to check for proper fit. This step is performed to check the fit of the shaft into the bore of the head and to determine if any adjustments have to be made to the hosel bore diameter to assure the proper fit. Please note in cases of using the types of shafts that are to be trimmed to the golf club's desired playing length **all from the tip**, a test fit of the shaft into the head is a must to determine the necessary trimming.

■ **NOTE:** On pre-whipped woodheads, the tension of the whipping over the ferrule can cause the inside diameter of the ferrule to be too small to allow the shaft to slide through. If the shaft does not slide easily through the ferrule on pre-whipped woodheads, ream out the ferrule with the appropriate size drill or reamer (.335" parallel bore = "R" size drill bit).

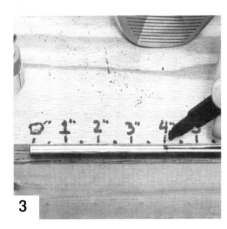

STEP 3: Calculate proper tip trimming and mark each shaft for trimming (if tip trimming is necessary)
First calculate the amount to tip trim from each of the shafts, if in fact the shafts being used call for tip trimming. While the majority of shafts will require tip trimming prior to installation, some by virtue of their design will not. Refer to the Shaft Trimming Index in Chapter 3 to find the correct chart of trimming procedures to follow for the shafts being used. For shaft trimming purposes, virtually all graphite and composite woodheads are a blind bore design. Once you have determined the proper shaft trimming, use a ruler and felt tip pen to mark the correct amount to trim on each shaft. **For the most accuracy in shaft flex feel, remember to take into account the required playing length of the golf club(s) before calculating the proper tip trimming for each shaft** (see Chapter 3 for an explanation of how to adjust tip trimming based on playing length changes to assure consistent shaft installation).

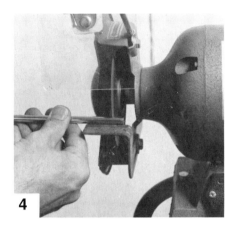

STEP 4: Tip trim all shafts
Use the method of shaft cutting that is best suited for the type of material from which the shafts are made. We recommend the use of a tube cutter or motorized abrasive cut-off wheel for steel and titanium (all metal types) and a grit edge saw or abrasive cut-off wheel for graphite and other fibrous composite shafts. Again, by intent of their design, some shafts will not require tip trimming before installation, so be sure to always check, then double check the proper trimming procedures for the shafts you are using.

STEP 5: Abrade the tip of the shaft
With medium to coarse grit sandpaper, abrade the entire portion of the shaft tip that will not only be inserted in the

hosel, but under the ferrule as well, should a ferrule be required in the assembly. Abrading the shaft tip will allow the epoxy to assist in securing the shaft and ferrule, and greatly reduce the chance of the head and/or ferrule working loose at a later time. For assembling composite heads, crimping or deforming the shaft to facilitate a mechanical lock of shaft to head is **not** recommended.

6

STEP 6: Install ferrule (and leather grip collar if required)

In virtually all cases of graphite and composite head installation a ferrule will be required. The only exceptions will be if the head is made with the ferrule and whipping already in place, or in the rare case of a woodhead made with the top of the hosel manufactured to a thin taper to meet the shaft. Follow the procedures illustrated in Chapter 3 to guide the installation of the ferrule.

■ **NOTE**: It is not necessary to install and position the ferrule in its exact position on the shaft. The insertion of the shaft completely to the bottom of the hosel will push each ferrule up the shaft and into its proper location. **If a leather grip is called for in the assembly of the club, be sure to install the proper size plastic grip trim collar up <u>from the tip end of the shaft</u> at this time.**

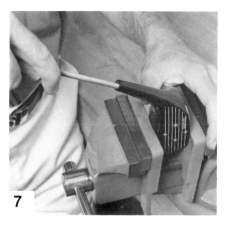

7

STEP 7: Scratch or abrade the inside of the hosel

The inside of the hosel of most graphite and composite woodheads is usually a smooth surface which can make it more difficult for the epoxy to permanently bond the shaft to the head. To add greater holding power to the epoxy, use a rat-tail or round file to thoroughly scratch up the inside walls of the hosel.

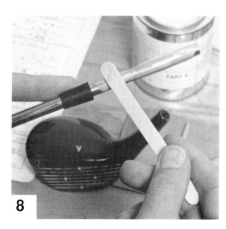

8

STEP 8: Mix epoxy and apply to the shaft tip and inside of hosel

Always use high shear strength, 2-part shafting epoxy to secure the shaft to the head. Follow the epoxy supplier's mixing recommendations to ensure the complete bonding strength of the epoxy is achieved. Use a 1/4" wood dowel rod or similar applicator to apply a thin

but full coverage coating of epoxy to the shaft tip and the inside of the hosel bore.

9

STEP 9: Install the shafts

One by one, insert each shaft into its proper clubhead. Rotate the shaft as it is inserted to ensure a complete coating of the epoxy between the shaft tip and the inside of the hosel. While it is not necessary, Aluminum Oxide or Silica type sand may be used as an additional bonding aid without fear of damaging the hosel. If sand is used, dip only 1/4" of the tip of the shaft into the sand before inserting the shaft into the hosel. As the shaft slides down the hosel the sand will spread and/or crush between the shaft tip and the hosel wall, thus acting as a bonding "filler" to the epoxy. The use of sand can be a strength additive for tube type epoxies such as the Conap brand which are made without a filler. Check to make sure that the shaft manufacturer's silkscreen is properly aligned in the "12 o'clock" position at this time.

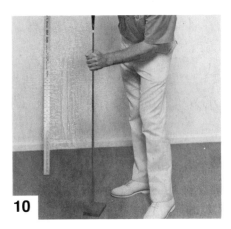

10

STEP 10: Properly seat the shafts into the hosel

For proper assembly, it is vital that each shaft be installed so that the shaft tip seats completely to the bottom of the bore. Whether pushing and rotating the shaft by hand, or by tapping the butt of the shaft on the floor while holding the head secure to the shaft, drive the shaft into the hosel until you feel it stop against the bottom of the bore.

■ **NOTE:** Use extreme care when inserting shafts into pre-whipped clubheads. To prevent breaking off the ferrule be sure the shaft tip has been inserted past the bottom of the ferrule before tapping the shaft to the bottom of the bore. Should the ferrule break off during shaft installation, discard the whipping and ferrule and file the top of the hosel completely flat. When the top of the hosel is squared off, install a new ferrule on the shaft and epoxy the shaft in the hosel.

11

STEP 11: Work epoxy under the ferrule

If the head is not pre-whipped, try to work some epoxy underneath the ferrule to protect it from working loose. Rotate and move the ferrule up and down against the the top of the hosel to draw epoxy under the ferrule. Finish by pushing the ferrule firm against the hosel to eliminate the possibility of a gap occurring between the top of the hosel and the ferrule. Wipe away any excess epoxy from the base of the ferrule. If the ferrule is very tight on the shaft after shaft installation such that no epoxy can be worked underneath, do not worry about its working loose when the club is put into play.

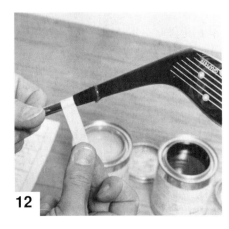

12

STEP 12: Apply masking tape above ferrule

To prevent the ferrule from slipping up the shaft and creating a gap while the epoxy cures, wrap one layer of 1/2" or 1" wide masking tape around the shaft, butting one edge of the tape against the top of the ferrule. This tape will also protect the shaft from scratching when filing the ferrule.

STEP 13: Clean up, check and set aside for the epoxy to cure

Before setting the club aside to dry, check the point between the top of the hosel and the bottom of the ferrule. Be sure any excess amounts of epoxy have been wiped away, but at the same time, do leave a small amount of epoxy on the line between the ferrule and the hosel.

13

Because it is very common for the top of the hosel of a woodhead to not be perfectly square, the epoxy can serve as a filler to correct any small gap between hosel and ferrule. Check for epoxy smears on the head and shaft and wipe clean with a rag dampened with grip solvent. Set the club aside horizontally on a rack or with the head down on the floor for the epoxy to cure. **Never** set clubs to dry with the head up and shaft down or epoxy could flow down the shaft, thus creating the potential for a rattle after the club is put into play.

14

STEP 14: Prepare for installation of backscrew by securing the woodhead in the bench vise

A backscrew, or shaft locking screw, is not required with graphite or composite shaft installation, but **for any type** of metal shaft to graphite or composite head assembly, **the use of a backscrew is a must!!** The two major causes of composite heads working loose from the shaft are the normal vibration of the hosel that naturally occurs from shot impact as well as the effect of temperature changes on the shaft to head epoxy bond. Because these factors are normal and beyond the control of the clubmaker, you must afford yourself the protection against the head possibly coming off the shaft by installing a backscrew. To begin the backscrew installation procedure, secure the head toe down in the bench vise, with the head between soft vise pads. Place another pad under the toe of the head to prevent possible damage to the toe of the head when tapping down the screw.

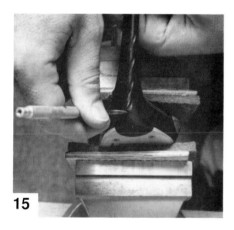

15

STEP 15: Locate the point of backscrew entry on the back of the woodhead

By placing a straight rod on the back side of the shaft, directly in line with the shaft, it is possible to locate exactly where the shaft lies inside the hosel. With the rod positioned on the top of the back side of the shaft as pictured, make a small mark with an awl or scriber on the back of the head, directly in line with the shaft, about 1/2" up from the back edge of the heel of the woodhead.

STEP 16: Place cellophane tape over the point of backscrew drilling

Drilling a hole through a finished graphite or composite woodhead can tear the polyurethane coating and lead to an unprofessional looking job. To ensure a clean, sharp-edged cut through the finish with the drill bit, apply two layers of cellophane tape on the back of the head over the point of drill bit entry.

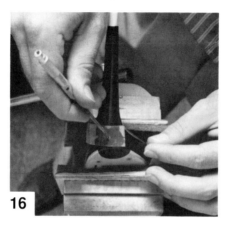

16

■ **NOTE:** Many modern graphite and composite woodheads are manufactured with a satin or matte finish. While not as susceptible to finish tearing as the gloss finished heads, it is still recommended to apply cellophane tape to the back of the hosel before drilling for the backscrew.

17

STEP 17: Line up the drill bit in relation to the shaft

Using an electric hand drill and a 1/8" high speed or cobalt bit, position the point of the bit on the mark, **perpendicular to the top of the shaft.** For accuracy of drilling, it is extremely important that the bit be perpendicular with the top surface of the shaft. Failure to do so can result in the bit glancing off or completely missing the shaft. Also check the angle of the bit in relation to the front of the hosel to avoid the potential problem of the bit to coming through the front side of the hosel, thus ruining the head.

18

STEP 18: Drill to the top of the shaft

Once the bit is properly lined up, drill through the tape and into the woodhead until you feel the bit touch the top surface of the shaft. Upon feeling contact with the top of the shaft, withdraw the drill bit from the hole. **Do not attempt to drill through the shaft!**

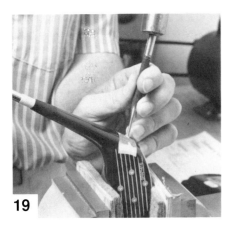

19

STEP 19: Punch a hole through the top of the shaft
Using an awl or a sharpened 1/8" pin punch, use a hammer to drive the tip of the punch/awl through the top side of the shaft only. **Do not attempt to pierce both sides of the shaft at this time.** After piercing through the top of the shaft, wiggle the punch loose and remove it.

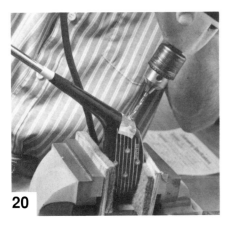

20

STEP 20: Drill through the punched hole and the bottom side of the shaft
Insert the electric drill with 1/8" bit into the backscrew hole before activating the drill motor. Check once again for perpendicular bit to shaft alignment before drilling through the punched hole. Despite the punched hole, drilling through the top of the shaft will require some pressure to force the bit completely through. If after 5-

10 seconds of drilling the bit has not penetrated the top of the shaft, stop and repeat STEP 19 to enlarge the punched hole diameter before drilling again. Because the hole through the top of the shaft will act as a bushing to hold the bit in the proper position, once the top of the shaft has been penetrated with the drill, continue drilling through the bottom side of the shaft. Again, firm pressure on the drill will be required to penetrate the bottom side of the shaft. Drill to a depth no more than 1 1/2" below the back surface of the head and then withdraw the bit. After drilling the hole, remove the club from the vise and dump any loose particles out the butt end of the shaft.

■ **NOTE**: After drilling through the top of the shaft, clubmakers may wish to withdraw the bit and repeat the punch then drill procedure to penetrate the bottom side of the shaft. While the procedure in STEP 20 is used by most experienced clubmakers, there is a slight chance the pressure required to help the drill penetrate the unpunched bottom of the shaft could result in a broken drill bit, or worse, driving the nose of the drill chuck into the back of the wood.

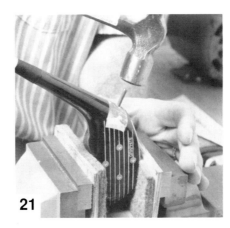

21

STEP 21: Install the backscrew
For a professional job, it is recommended to use a "headless" type of backscrew. While some component companies do supply this type of screw, you may use a bench grinder or belt sander to grind the flared sides off the head of a normal #5x1 1/8" steel backscrew. When

installing the screw do not rotate the screw into place. Tap it into the hole with a hammer, as if driving a nail.

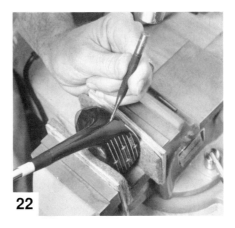

22

STEP 22: Tap the backscrew below the surface of the woodhead
After tapping the screw flush to the back surface of the head, use the sharpened 1/8" pin punch or awl to bury the head of the screw @ 1/8" below the surface of the head. Use a very light tapping force with the hammer to prevent driving the screw too deep into the head.

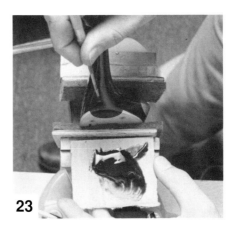

23

STEP 23: Fill the hole with black colored epoxy
Almost all graphite woodheads are finished in black or

gray. To match the epoxy covering to the head, mix a small amount of quick dry epoxy and color it with a black color paste dispersion. Color paste dispersions are used to tint pour-in-place face insert epoxies and are available from golf repair suppliers. In lieu of the dispersion colors, a very small amount of enamel paint can be used to color the epoxy. Use a toothpick to carefully fill the backscrew hole, being sure to dab the epoxy above the surface of the head. Be as neat as possible with this step to prevent smearing epoxy on the head. Set aside to dry.

STEP 24: File the ferrule to prepare for the whipping
If you are skilled in the use of a belt sander with linen belt to turn down ferrules, this method will be the fastest way to prepare the ferrule for whipping. If not, use a shaft clamp to secure the club in the vise as pictured. With a medium cut file, begin filing around the entire ferrule to reduce its diameter from top to bottom. Take extreme care to retain the perfect taper of the ferrule while filing. After the ferrule has been filed in an even taper from the shaft to the top of the hosel, use a strip of sandpaper to remove the file marks. If using a shanked type ferrule, no filing at the top of the ferrule will be necessary.

■ **NOTE**: For standard (non-shanked) ferrules, take care **not** to scratch the shaft too far (more than 1/8") above the top of the ferrule. Of course, in the case of pre-whipped woodheads, no ferrule filing or preparation will be necessary.

STEP 25: File and smooth the epoxy covering the backscrew
Begin removing the epoxy protruding over the backscrew hole with a fine cut file. Continue filing until the epoxy is just short of being flush to the back surface of the finished woodhead. Using very light strokes, keep filing until the first evidence of scratching of the surrounding finish is noticed. Switch to 320 or 400 grit sandpaper to dry sand the remaining epoxy flush to the back of the head. Remember, as long as very fine finishing sandpaper is used, the entire finish surrounding the epoxy can be sanded and still be returned to its original luster with Glanz Wach buffing.

STEP 26: Buff the backscrew area to restore the shine of the finish

After 320 or 400 sanding, rub the entire area over and around the backscrew with 3/0 or 4/0 grade steel wool. Follow by buffing the entire backscrew area of the wood with machine driven, unstitched buffing wheels coated with Glanz Wach. Apply medium pressure with the buffing wheels first in one direction, then in a second direction that is 90° to the first. After buffing is completed, rub with a soft cloth and the epoxy covering and the surrounding finish will have the same shine as the rest of the head.

STEP 27: Measure and mark the shaft for the desired playing length
Place the club on the floor in the playing position, taking care not to rock the club either up on the toe or back on its heel. Slide a 48" clubmaker's ruler up behind the shaft, and carefully mark the desired playing length on the butt end of the shaft with a felt tip marker. Be sure to allow for the effect that the 1/8" thickness of the end of the grip will have on the club's playing length by marking the shafts 1/8" shorter than what is desired (e.g.- If a true 43" playing length is desired, the mark should be made at 42 7/8", for a 41 1/2" playing length, mark the shaft at 41 3/8", etc.).

■ **NOTE**: There are a limited number of shaft patterns that will require no further butt trimming for playing length after installation, so be sure to recheck the trimming instructions for the shafts being used.

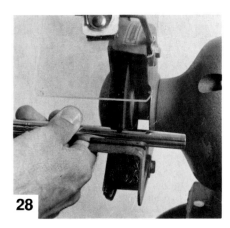

STEP 28: Cut the shaft to its desired playing length
Using the proper cutting procedure for the type of shaft being used, trim the shaft for its playing length. Always deburr and square off the shaft butt after trimming to remove sharp edges. If a graphite or composite type shaft has been installed, use an abrasive cut-off wheel or a grit edged hack saw blade to trim the shaft, **never** a tubing cutter.

STEP 29: Install whipping
Whether with a whipping machine or by using hand winding procedures, install the string whipping and securely tie off to finish the job. The most simple method involves placing the club in the rubber shaft clamp and **loosely** securing it in the vise so that the head and shaft

may still be rotated (a complete step-by-step sequence of hand tying the whipping is covered in Chapter 10).

STEP 30: Record the preliminary swingweight of the club
Place the club on a 14" fulcrum swingweight scale (Lorythmic or Prorythmic type) **without the grip installed** and record its swingweight. Do **not** push the butt of the ungripped club completely against the back of the scale. Because the grip cap provides the final 1/8" of club length pull the shaft butt 1/8" away from the end of the scale before recording preliminary swingweight. This is important to achieve an accurate swingweight reading.

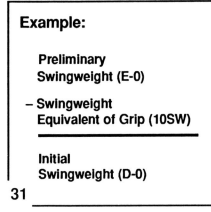

> **Example:**
>
> Preliminary
> Swingweight (E-0)
>
> − Swingweight
>   Equivalent of Grip (10SW)
>   _____
>
> Initial
> Swingweight (D-0)

STEP 31: Subtract the swingweight equivalent of the grip from the ungripped club's preliminary swingweight to determine the initial swingweight

The swingweight of the ungripped club will read higher because the grip has not been installed. It will be heavier in the amount equal to the swingweight equivalent of the weight of the grip plus its installation and build-up tape. To determine what the club's **initial swingweight** will be once the grip is installed, subtract 9 swingweight points for a standard men's size rubber grip, 10 points for a cord or leather grip, and 1 additional swingweight point for every three layers of build-up tape that may be used (e.g.- An ungripped club with a swingweight of E-0, scheduled for installation with a Men's Victory grip with three layers of build-up tape will make the gripped club's **initial swingweight** D-0).

■ **NOTE: For alternative swingweight method**
Rather than use grip weight estimations to calculate the club's initial swingweight, clubmakers may wish to temporarily install a grip of the type to be used on the shaft butt. Keep a few grips in your shop (rubber, cord, 58 core, 60 core, etc.) that have been cut lengthwise with a knife or scissors to slide on the shaft for simulating the weight of the grip. This way when you place the club on the swingweight scale you will get a very accurate estimation of what the club's initial swingweight will be. For oversize grips, allow 1 swingweight point for every three layers of build-up tape to be used.

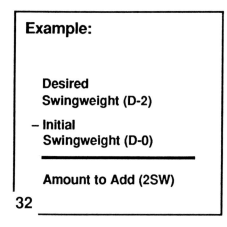

> **Example:**
>
> Desired
> Swingweight (D-2)
>
> − Initial
>   Swingweight (D-0)
>   _____
>
> Amount to Add (2SW)

STEP 32: Calculate the weight increase needed to establish the club's final desired swingweight

Subtract the initial swingweight from the customer's desired final swingweight to determine what amount of weight to add to the head (e.g. - Desired final swingweight of D-2 minus initial swingweight of D-0 = the amount of weight to add is 2 swingweight points).

33

STEP 33: Increase swingweight to final level desired
Once the amount of weight increase is determined, use lead powder to establish the final swingweight of the club. Many graphite and composite clubheads available for component clubmaking have set screw weight ports installed in the head for this purpose. The weight to be added may be pre-weighed on a gram scale (allowing 1 swingweight point = @2 grams of lead powder as a formula) to save guess work. If a gram scale is not available in your shop, add the lead powder into the weight port by estimation, check the weight on the scale, then add or remove lead powder as needed to establish the final weight.

■ **NOTE:** If the club's initial swingweight is too high, the only professional method for removing weight from the head will be to remove the soleplate and take out some of the weight that may be in place as a part of the head's manufactured weight. Pre-calculating swingweight before assembly is important because soleplate removal on a finished head is difficult to do without damaging the finish on the head.

34

STEP 34: If no weight port is present, add the weight down the shaft in the form of lead powder, held in place with a cork
If no weight port is present, or if the capacity of the weight port is not sufficient for the final swingweight needs of the club, use lead powder to add the final amount down the shaft. Pour the amount needed into the shaft butt, tamp the head lightly to move the lead powder to the shaft tip and check the swingweight on the scale.

Remember: An addition of 5 swingweight points (10 grams) or less down the shaft for the purpose of establishing final swingweight will not harm the playability of any club.

■ **NOTE:** Final swingweighting with graphite-shafted composite woods by adding lead powder down the shaft is NOT recommended due to the very small inside diameter of all graphite shafts. As a result, when assembling graphite-shafted composite woods without a weight port, it is very important to pre-calculate final swingweight needs before assembly. In such cases, it is better to epoxy a specially-made graphite shaft tip weight (sold by many component suppliers) up the graphite shaft tip before the shaft is installed into the head.

STEP 35: Secure the weight with a cork tamped down the shaft
When the proper swingweight is achieved, drop a small

35

cork down the shaft to secure the weight. Use a 1/4" diameter steel ram rod to drive the cork completely down the shaft and in place on top of the lead powder. Because of the tightness of the cork against the shaft walls, no epoxy is needed to secure the cork on top of the weight. Proper size corks for the job are available from the various component supply companies.

36

STEP 36: Apply grip tape (and leather grip collar if needed)
Clamp the shaft to secure the club in the bench vise with the head positioned toe up and apply the required build-up tape and/or 2-way foundation tape. If a leather grip is to be installed it will require a plastic grip collar. If the

collar has not already been put on during the installation of the shaft, slide it on over the shaft butt. Installing a grip collar from the butt end of the shaft requires a little practice but can easily be accomplished if the grip collar size used is one shaft size larger than the shaft butt. For example, use a .620" size grip collar on a .600" butt diameter shaft, a .600" collar on a .580" shaft, etc.

STEP 37: Install grip and final check swingweight

After wetting the 2-way grip tape and the inside of the grip with grip solvent, install and properly line up the grip. After installation, check to be sure the grip is completely seated against the shaft butt and clean up any tape residue that is present at the mouth of the grip. Immediately put the club back on the swingweight scale to double check your work, making sure the butt of the grip is pushed against the end of the scale. If the swingweight is off by more than 1/2 point, the grip adhesive from the tape should still be wet enough to allow you to pull off the grip and correct the problem. Once the swingweight is correct, install a protective plastic grip bag, held in place with a wrap of thin masking tape. Covering the grip not only adds a professional touch, but will protect the grip from soiling during the club's remaining time in your shop. **The complete step-by-step procedures for all types of grip installation and sizing are covered in Chapter 4.**

STEP 38: Clean up, install the shaft label and check the club for proper final specifications

The club is now completed. Before the job is fully done, take time to inspect and clean up any soiling of the head, grip and shaft, and final check all length, swingweight and grip specifications for accuracy. Finally, install plastic bags on the head and grip for protection and apply any necessary shaft labels in the proper place on the shaft. The golf industry's standard position for shaft labels is between the second and third step down below the mouth of the grip, with the label centered between steps, insignia facing forward.

CHAPTER 7 - The Modern Assembly Procedures of Metal Woodheads

Step-by-Step Assembly of Metal Woods from Finished Stainless Steel and Aluminum Woodheads

The Golf Industry's Most Popular "Wood"

From the beginning of the 1980s, the stainless steel metal wood has risen from a modest introduction to the point where today it now commands an incredible 80% of the total woodhead market. Never before in golf has a clubhead design experienced such a rapid evolution from its origin to becoming the most popular type of wood in golf. With true research now showing that metal woods do not possess such a dramatic advantage in game improvement benefits over conventional woodheads, nonetheless stainless steel woods do "own" the market in the minds and golf bags of golfers today. In fact, the metal wood is now so well known and accepted that virtually all touring professionals carry at least one metal wood in their golf bags.

For the clubmaker, the advent of metal woods has afforded a tremendous opportunity. Not only do the stainless heads prove to be very sellable and popular with many golfers, but they are extremely easy to assemble too. Whether stainless or aluminum, all component metal woods are sold in finished form, so there will never

be a situation in which the clubmaker is required to apply a finish to the head. In addition, stainless metal woods do not require the use of a back screw to secure the shaft in place, and because virtually all are produced with a .335" parallel bore hosel, only parallel tip shaft installation procedures will be required.

However, there are a few points of difference that must be kept in mind regarding the assembly of metal woods. While almost all shaft installation will be with parallel tip shafts, in many cases different trimming procedures will have to be followed to take the metal wood's comparatively much shorter bore depth into account. For metal woods, most conventional parallel tip steel and graphite shafts *will* withstand the increased stress imparted on the tip by the short, rigid hosel. All of this information relating to shaft installation for metal woods has been provided in Chapter 3, so for purposes of explanation, Chapter 7 will deal only with the actual step-by-step procedures of assembling woods from finished component metal woodheads.

Metal Wood Assembly

STEP 1: Secure and organize each of the required components to anticipate any potential problems in assembly

Whether by laying all of the components out on your workbench or by making a mental note, be sure you have all the necessary components **and** supplies on hand to complete the assembly before you start the actual procedures of clubmaking. To avoid any potential swingweight problems that may be created by the customer's required custom fitting specifications, first note the desired length, shaft weight, grip size and swingweight in conjunction with the gram weight of the clubhead to calculate the anticipated swingweight of the club(s) **before** you begin work. By pre-calculating swingweight from the known assembly specifications, necessary adjustments can often be made before the assembly process begins, thus solving a potential problem before it occurs. See Chapter 10 for an explanation of how to calculate the anticipated swingweight of a golf club before it is assembled.

STEP 2: Test fit each shaft in the appropriate head

Test fit each shaft into its matching metal woodhead to check for proper fit. This step is performed to check the fit of the shaft into the bore of the head and to determine if any adjustments have to be made to the hosel bore diameter to assure the proper fit. Please note in cases of using some types of shafts that are to be pre-trimmed to the golf club's desired playing length **from the tip**, a test fit of the shaft into the head is a must to determine the necessary trimming (a description of changing or adjusting hosel bore sizes can be found in Chapter 10).

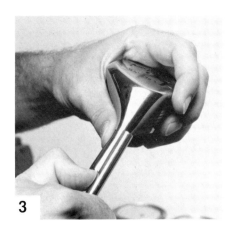

STEP 3: Check bore depth and bottom of bore to heel dimension of the metal woodhead

Many metal woodheads, particularly stainless steel heads, are designed with a short hosel and short bore depth which keeps the shaft tip from penetrating into the open cavity of the head. However, within the clubhead industry, there are differences in the hosel length and bore depth from one metal wood design to the other that must be taken into account before calculating the proper shaft trimming procedures. Therefore, as a first step in calculating the proper trimming for the shafts to be used, measure the length of the hosel and subtract the bore depth to determine the bottom of bore to heel dimension.

■ **NOTE**: The metal wood shaft trimming column in each trimming chart in Chapter 3 is based on a golf industry standard metal wood design with a bottom of bore to back edge of heel dimension of 1 1/2". If the bottom of bore to heel dimension differs from this 1 1/2" standard on the metal woods you are assembling, that difference should be taken into account in calculating the proper trimming. Guidelines for making such allowances can be found on Pages 80-81 in Chapter 3.

STEP 4: Calculate proper tip trimming and mark each shaft for trimming (if tip trimming is necessary)

Either on paper or in your mind, use the bottom of bore to heel dimension determined in Step 2 along with the proper shaft trimming chart in Chapter 3 to calculate the

amount to tip trim from each of the shafts, if in fact the shaft pattern being used calls for tip trimming. Once you have determined the proper trimming, use a ruler and felt tip pen to mark the correct amount to trim from the tip of each shaft. While the majority of shafts do require tip trimming prior to installation, some by virtue of their design will not.

For the most accuracy in shaft flex feel, remember to also take into account the required playing length of the golf club(s) before calculating the proper tip trimming for each shaft (see Pages 83-84 in Chapter 3 for an explanation of how to adjust tip trimming based on playing length changes to assure consistent shaft installation).

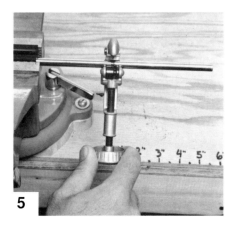

STEP 5: Tip trim all shafts

Use the method of shaft cutting that is best suited for the type of material from which the shafts are made. We recommend the use of a tube cutter or motorized abrasive cut-off wheel for steel and titanium (all metal types) and a grit edge saw or abrasive cut-off wheel for graphite and other composite shafts. Again, by intent of their design, some shafts will not require tip trimming before installation, so be sure to always check, then double check the proper trimming procedures for the shafts you are using.

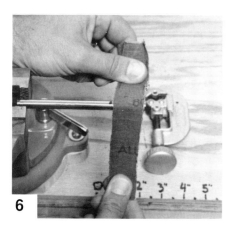

STEP 6: Abrade the tip of the shaft

With medium to coarse grit sandpaper, abrade the entire portion of the shaft tip that will not only be inserted in the hosel, but under the ferrule as well, should a ferrule be required in the assembly. Abrading the shaft tip will allow the epoxy to assist in securing the shaft and ferrule, and greatly reduce the chance of the head and/or ferrule working loose at a later time. For assembling metal woodheads, a crimping or deforming of the shaft to facilitate a mechanical lock of shaft to head can be done, but is **not** required.

STEP 7: Install the ferrule (and leather grip collar if required)

If a ferrule is required in the assembly of the metal wood, select the proper type and size ferrule and follow the procedures illustrated in Chapter 3 to guide the installation of the ferrule. When installing graphite shafts, it is advisable to use specially made beveled ferrules.

■ **NOTE**: It is not necessary to install and position the ferrule in its exact position on the shaft. The insertion of the shaft completely to the bottom of the hosel will push each ferrule up the shaft and into its proper location. **If a leather grip is called for in the assembly of the club, be sure to install the proper size plastic grip trim collar up <u>from the tip end of the shaft</u> at this time.**

STEP 8: Bevel top inside edge of the hosel (for graphite/composite shaft installation)

A beveling of the top inside edge of the hosel bore must be performed to relieve the stress a metal wood hosel can place on the tip of graphite/composite shafts. If the head(s) being assembled are not pre-beveled by the manufacturer, use a 20° countersink or rotary file fixed in your electric hand drill to bevel the top inside edge of the hosel. Be sure the beveling is @ 1/8" deep into the hosel. Remove any burrs from the hosel after beveling.

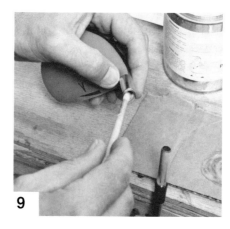

STEP 9: Mix epoxy and apply to the shaft tip and inside of hosel

Always use a high shear strength, 2-part shafting epoxy to secure the shaft to the head. Follow the epoxy supplier's mixing recommendations to ensure the proper bonding strength of the epoxy is achieved. Use a 1/4" wood dowel rod or similar applicator to apply a thin but full coverage coating of epoxy to the shaft tip and the inside of the hosel bore.

STEP 10: Install the shafts

One by one, insert each shaft into its proper clubhead. Rotate the shaft as it is inserted to ensure a complete coating of the epoxy between the shaft tip and the inside of the hosel. While it is not necessary since many shafting epoxies are manufactured with a form of filler within, Aluminum Oxide or Silica type sand may be used as an additional bonding aid without fear of damaging the hosel. If a sand is used, dip only 1/4" of the tip of the shaft into the sand before inserting the shaft into the hosel. As the shaft slides down the hosel the sand will spread and/or crush between the shaft tip and the hosel wall, thus acting as a bonding "filler" to the epoxy. The use of sand can be a strength additive for tube type epoxies such as Conap, which are made without a filler.

■ **NOTE: For graphite shaft installation**
When installing graphite shafts, be sure a ring of epoxy occupies the space between the shaft and the beveled edge of the hosel. This will form the required epoxy "cushion" between shaft and hosel to relieve stress on the shaft tip.

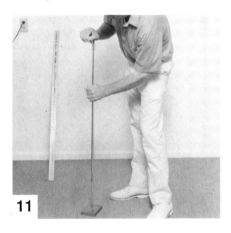

STEP 11: Properly seat the shafts into the hosel
For proper assembly, it is vital that each shaft be installed so that the shaft tip seats completely to the bottom of the bore. Whether pushing and rotating the shaft by hand or by tapping the butt of the shaft on the floor while holding the head secure to the shaft, drive the shaft into the hosel until you feel it stop against the bottom of the bore.

STEP 12: Work epoxy under the ferrule
After seating the shaft in the hosel, try to work some epoxy underneath the ferrule to protect it from working loose. Rotate and move the ferrule up and down against

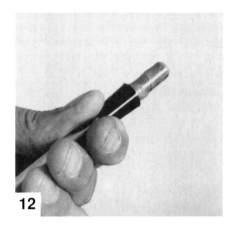

the the top of the hosel to draw epoxy under the ferrule. Finish by pushing the ferrule firm against the hosel to eliminate the possibility of a gap occurring between the top of the hosel and the ferrule. Wipe away any excess epoxy from the base of the ferrule. If the ferrule is very tight on the shaft after shaft installation such that no epoxy can be worked underneath, do not worry about its working loose when the club is put into play.

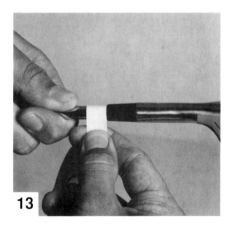

STEP 13: Apply masking tape above ferrule
If the ferrule is loose on the shaft, wrap one layer of 1/2" or 1" wide masking tape around the shaft, against the top of the ferrule, to prevent the ferrule from slipping up the shaft and creating a gap while the epoxy cures. The tape will also protect the shaft from scratching when filing the ferrule.

STEP 14: Clean up, check and set aside for the epoxy to cure
Before the setting the club aside to dry, once more check the line between the top of the hosel and the bottom of the ferrule to be sure all excess epoxy has been wiped away. Check for epoxy smears on the head and shaft and wipe clean with a rag dampened with grip solvent. Set the club aside to cure either horizontally on a rack or with the head down on the floor. **Never** set clubs to dry with the head up and shaft down or epoxy could flow down the shaft, thus creating the potential for a rattle after the club is put into play. For assembly of a typical metal woodhead, proceed to STEP 16 after the epoxy has cured.

Special Assembly Procedures for Metal Woodheads with Imitation Plastic Whipping Covers

Certain models of metal woodheads are designed to assume the "look" of a conventional wood, complete with false soleplate, false face insert and a long plastic ferrule that simulates string whipping. Because this type of metal woodhead requires slightly different assembly procedures, the following steps are offered to guide your clubmaking.

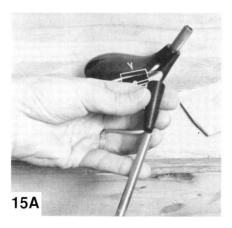

15A

STEP 15A: Install whipping cover on shaft

After abrading the shaft tip, insert the whipping cover on the tip end of the shaft. Slide the cover up the shaft, past the abraded surface of the shaft.

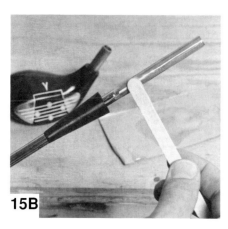

15B

STEP 15B: Apply epoxy to shaft tip and inside the hosel

Use an acceptable grade of shafting epoxy and apply a liberal amount to the shaft tip and inside of hosel.

STEP 15C: Install shaft and slide whipping cover down on the hosel

Using the same procedures outlined in STEPS 10 and 11, install the shaft. After seating the shaft to the base of the

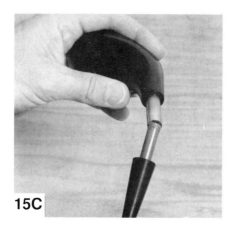

15C

hosel bore, slide the whipping cover down against the base of the hosel. After rechecking to make sure the shaft tip is still bottomed out in the hosel, use a paper towel to wipe all the excess epoxy away. Set the club aside to dry.

Continued Steps for Assembly of Metal Woodheads

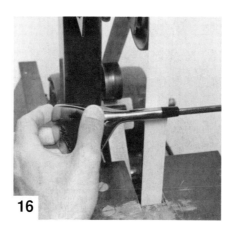

16

STEP 16: Method A: Dress ferrule with belt sander (if ferrule is present, sand ferrule with linen belt)

If you are skilled in the use of a 1"x42" belt sander with linen belt to turn down ferrules, then this method will be

the fastest way to finish off the metal wood ferrule. To accurately use a belt sander to turn ferrules, it will be helpful to devise a holding fixture for the clubs. With the linen belt mounted on the belt sander, rotate the ferrule *against* the direction of travel of the belt. Do not turn down the top of the ferrule. Always keep the club rotating while in contact with the belt or the plastic will friction burn. Turn the ferrule down until its base is flush to the top of the hosel.

■ **NOTE:** If the metal woodhead has an imitation whipping cover, no dressing of the ferrule usually will be necessary.

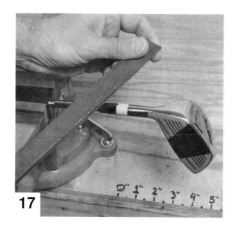

17

STEP 17: Method B: Dress ferrule with file (if ferrule is present, file the ferrule)

To dress the ferrule with a file, secure the club in the vise as pictured and place a strip of masking tape around the top of the hosel for protection from filing scratches. With a medium cut file, file completely around the bottom of the ferrule to reduce its diameter flush to the top of the hosel. On metal woods do not file the top of the ferrule flush to the shaft. However, if the metal wood is intended to be string whipped for cosmetic reasons, the top of the ferrule must be filed flush to the shaft to allow a smooth transition of the whipping from shaft to hosel. Take extreme care not to scratch the top of the metal wood hosel or the shaft above the top of the ferrule.

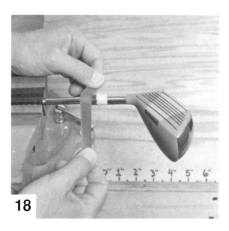

STEP 18: Method B: Dress ferrule with file (if ferrule is present, sand scratches from ferrule]
If the ferrule was turned on a belt sander with linen belt, it will not have any scratches and can be shined with the acetone to complete the job (STEP 19). However, if the ferrule was filed to reduce its diameter, use a thin strip of fine sandpaper (150 grit) to sand out the file scratches.

STEP 19: Methods A & B: Dress ferrule (if ferrule is present, acetone ferrule to restore shine)
Spin the ferrule against a paper towel thoroughly wetted with acetone to restore the original shine of the plastic. Remember, most metal wood ferrules are to be left exposed, so a high quality shine must be achieved.

■ **NOTE:** If the metal wood requires string whipping to be installed over the ferrule, STEPS 19-20 are not necessary)

STEP 20: Methods A & B: Dress ferrule (if ferrule is present, buff ferrule to deep shine with Glanz Wach, if desired)
Sometimes the acetone wipe will leave the ferrule with a shine that is slightly less than perfect. If desired, you may buff the ferrule on unstitched buffing wheels that have been coated with Glanz Wach to bring out a deep gloss finish. **Remember:** This step is entirely optional and is not a must to perform.

STEP 21: Measure and mark the shaft for the desired playing length

Place the club on the floor in the playing position, taking care not to rock the club either up on the toe or back on its heel. Slide a 48" clubmaker's ruler up behind the shaft, and carefully mark the desired playing length on the butt end of the shaft with a felt tip marker. Be sure to allow for the effect that the 1/8" thickness of the end of the grip will have on the club's playing length by marking the shafts 1/8" shorter than what is desired (e.g.- If a true 43" playing length is desired, the mark should be made at 42 7/8", for a 41 1/2" playing length, mark the shaft at 41 3/8", etc.).

■ **NOTE**: There are a limited number of all tip trim shafts that require no further butt trimming for playing length after installation. If you are working with such a shaft, proceed to STEP 23.

STEP 22: Cut the shaft to its desired playing length
Using the proper cutting procedure for the type of shaft being used, trim the shaft for its playing length. Always deburr and square off the shaft butt after trimming to remove sharp edges. If a graphite or composite type shaft has been installed, use an abrasive cut-off wheel or a grit edged hack saw blade to trim the shaft, **never** a tubing cutter.

23

STEP 23: Record the preliminary swingweight of the club

Place the club on a 14" fulcrum swingweight scale (Lorythmic or Prorythmic type) **without the grip installed** and record its swingweight. Do **not** push the butt of the un-gripped club completely against the back of the scale. Because the grip cap provides the final 1/8" of club length, pull the shaft butt 1/8" away from the end of the scale before recording preliminary swingweight. This is important to achieve an accurate swingweight reading.

◼ **NOTE:** See Chapter 10 for procedures for swingweighting golf clubs with graphite shafts that do not have a weight port. Final swingweighting graphite-shafted metal woods by adding lead powder down the shaft is not recommended due to the very small inside diameter of all graphite shafts. As a result, when assembling graphite-shafted metal woods without a weight port, it will be very important to pre-calculate the final swingweight needs before assembly. In such cases, it will be better to epoxy a specially-made graphite shaft tip weight (sold by many component suppliers) up the graphite shaft before the shaft is installed into the head.

STEP 24: Subtract the swingweight equivalent of the grip from the ungripped club's preliminary swingweight to determine the _initial swingweight_

The swingweight of the ungripped club will read higher because the grip has not been installed. It will be heavier in the amount equal to the swingweight equivalent of the weight of the grip plus its installation and build-up tape. To determine what the club's **initial swingweight** will be once the grip is installed, subtract 9 swingweight points for a standard men's size rubber grip, 10 points for a cord or leather grip, and 1 additional swingweight point for every three layers of build-up tape that may be used (e.g.- An ungripped club with a swingweight of E-0, scheduled for installation with a Men's Victory grip with three layers of build-up tape will make the gripped club's **initial swingweight** D-0).

◼ **NOTE: For alternative swingweight method**
Rather than use grip weight estimations to calculate the club's initial swingweight, clubmakers may wish to temporarily install a grip of the type eventually to be used. Keep a few grips in your shop (rubber, cord, 58 core, 60 core, etc.) that have been cut lengthwise with a knife or scissors to slide on the shaft for simulating the weight of the grip. By using cut grips mounted temporarily on the shaft you will get an accurate estimation of what the club's initial swingweight will be when you place the club on the swingweight scale . For oversize grips, subtract 1 more swingweight point for every three layers of build-up tape to be used.

STEP 25: Calculate the weight increase needed to establish the club's final desired swingweight

Subtract the initial swingweight from the customer's desired final swingweight to determine what amount of weight to add to the head (e.g. - Desired final swingweight of D-2 minus initial swingweight of D-0 = the amount of weight to add is 2 swingweight points).

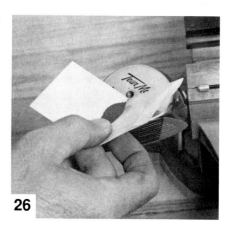

26

STEP 26: Increase swingweight to final level desired
Once the amount of weight increase is determined, use lead powder to establish the final swingweight of the club. Many metal woodheads available for component clubmaking have set screw weight ports installed in the head for this purpose. The weight to be added may be pre-weighed on a gram scale (allowing 1 swingweight point = @2 grams of lead powder as a formula) to save guess work. If a gram scale is not available in your shop, add the lead powder into the weight port by estimation, check the weight on the scale, then add or remove lead powder as needed to establish the final weight.

Example:

Preliminary Swingweight (E-0)

− **Swingweight Equivalent of Grip (10SW)**

Initial Swingweight (D-0)

24

Example:

Desired Swingweight (D-2)

− **Initial Swingweight (D-0)**

Amount to Add (2SW)

25

STEP 27: If no weight port is present, add the weight down the shaft in the form of lead powder, held in place with a cork. Remember: An addition of 5 swingweight points (10 grams) or less down the shaft for the purpose of establishing final swingweight will not harm the playability of any club. Therefore, if no weight port is present, or if the capacity of the weight port is not sufficient for the final swingweight needs of the club, use lead powder to add the final amount down the shaft. Pour the amount needed into the shaft butt, tamp the head lightly to move the lead powder to the shaft tip and check the swingweight on the scale. Do NOT use this method for metal woods being assembled with graphite shafts.

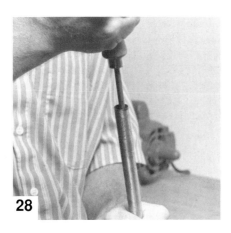

STEP 28: Secure the weight with a cork tamped down the shaft

When the proper swingweight is achieved, drop a small cork down the shaft to secure the weight. Use a 1/4" diameter steel ram rod to drive the cork completely down the shaft and in place on top of the lead powder. Because of the tightness of fit against the shaft walls, no epoxy is needed to secure the cork on top of the weight. Proper size corks for the job are available from the various component supply companies.

STEP 29: Apply grip tape (and leather grip collar if needed)

Secure the club in the bench vise with the head positioned toe up and apply any required build-up tape and/or 2-way foundation tape. If a leather grip is to be installed it will require a plastic grip collar. If the collar has not already been put on during the installation of the shaft, slide it on over the shaft butt. Installing a grip collar from the butt end of the shaft requires a little practice but can easily be accomplished if the grip collar size used is one shaft size larger than the shaft butt. For example, use a .620" size grip collar on a .600" butt diameter shaft, a .600" collar on a .580" shaft, etc.

STEP 30: Install grip and final check swingweight

After wetting the 2-way grip tape and the inside of the

grip with grip solvent, install and properly line up the grip. After installation, check to be sure the grip is completely seated against the shaft butt and clean up the tape residue that will be present at the mouth of the grip. Immediately put the club back on the swingweight scale to double check your work, now making sure the butt of the grip is pushed against the end of the scale. If the swingweight is incorrect, the grip adhesive from the tape should still be wet enough to allow you to pull off the grip and correct the problem. Once the swingweight is correct, install a protective plastic grip bag, held in place with a wrap of thin masking tape. Covering the grip not only adds a professional touch, but will protect the grip from soiling during the club's remaining time in your shop.

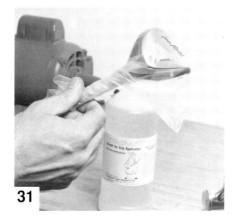

STEP 31: Clean up, install the shaft label and check the club for proper final specifications

The metal wood is now completed. Before the job is fully done, take time to inspect and clean up any soiling of the head, grip and shaft, and final check all specifications for accuracy. Finally, install plastic bags on the head and grip for protection and apply any necessary shaft labels in the proper place on the shaft. The golf industry's standard position for shaft labels is between the second and third step down below the mouth of the grip, with the label centered between steps, insignia facing forward.

CHAPTER 8 - The Modern Assembly Procedures of Irons and Wedges

Step-by-Step Procedures of Assembly for Building Clubs from Component Ironheads and Wedges

Simple Procedures Yet Many Options for Customizing

On the surface, building clubs from component ironheads and wedges would seem to be a very simple task. A head, a shaft, a grip … epoxy the shaft, install the grip … no finishing, no sanding, no whipping. Yet while iron and wedge assembly is simple and uncomplicated, there is still a requirement for a full understanding of all the technical principles of clubmaking, particularly shaft trimming and installation.

No part of golf club assembly requires a greater awareness of the principles of accurate shaft trimming and installation than do irons. With wooden heads, although there are through-bore, blind bore and short-bore types of hosel designs, little variation exists within each type of hosel design. Through-bore and blind bore woodhead designs are almost always so consistent from one manufacturer to another that clubmakers can usually count on a precise 1/2" difference in tip trimming between the two types of designs. And, even in the design of metal woods, the vast majority of stainless steel heads are all cast with the industry's standard bottom of bore to heel dimension of 1 1/2". Therefore, with such consistency

between woodhead types, it is routine for clubmakers to get accustomed to following similar shaft trimming procedures for each of the various types of woods.

To contrast, in the case of ironheads so much variation exists between manufacturers in the design of ironhead hosel length, bore depth and the resulting bottom of bore to heel dimension, that clubmakers cannot take anything for granted when it comes to properly installing shafts. It is now a recognized fact that the golf industry's standard dimension for the bottom of bore to heel of an ironhead is 1". Therefore, it is upon that measurement that the golf industry's standard shaft trimming charts are based. When the measurement from the bottom of bore to the back edge of the heel deviates from the 1" standard, it is important to adjust the trimming of shafts accordingly to be able to achieve standard shaft mounting from one set design to the other.

When the bottom of bore to back edge of heel dimension of an ironhead is greater than 1", the increase over the standard is to be added to the amount to tip trim for each club. Additionally, when the bottom of bore to back edge of heel dimension of an ironhead is less than 1", the decrease from the standard is to be subtracted from the amount to tip trim for each club.

Because so many ironhead designs do deviate from the bottom of bore to heel standard of 1", it is wise for clubmakers to get into the habit of measuring hosels and bore depths early in the assembly process so that the necessary trimming adjustments will ensure a perfect job of shaft installation. For a complete discussion of shaft trimming for irons and wedges, refer to Pages 83-84 in Chapter 3.

While there is no difference in the assembly procedures of the investment cast vs. forged, or the stainless steel vs. carbon steel types of ironheads, there are differences in ironhead design types that clubmakers must be aware of with regard to achieving certain custom fitting specifications. As with woodhead assembly, it is always wise to weigh the components and pre-calculate swingweight before beginning the building procedures for irons. In so doing, you will be able to determine if the combination of ironhead weights and overall specifications will result in swingweights that are within normal ranges. Should the combination of head weights and specifications point toward a swingweight that is too light, you will be able to decide before assembly which option for swingweight adjustment should be followed.

Very few models of ironheads are produced with weight ports. For one, the methods of designing weight ports for ironheads are very limited. In the case of medallion/lead disc type weighting, all too often the frequent failure of the medallion bond to the head coupled with the increased cost such a weighting system brings to the head often make the use of such a design hardly efficient or worthwhile. Even if an ironhead does have a weight port, there are times the capacity of the port might not meet the swingweight increase need.

When this occurs, or in the case of the majority of ironheads without a weight port, weighting down the tip of the shaft becomes the only alternative means of achieving the club's final swingweight. Attaching lead tape to the back of each head may be thought of as an option for weight addition, but no customer will want to pay for **new** clubs with lead tape applied. Therefore, clubmakers are advised to use a practical approach to clubmaking and remember the **5 Swingweight Point Rule** - 5 points or less placed down the shaft is **OK**; more than 5 points is **NOT** recommended.

While the situation does not present itself too often, when the swingweight of the assembled irons is too high (such as the case when overlength clubs are built), decreasing the head weight of the irons can be very difficult. This is where a sound awareness of the production differences in ironhead types can help. If a chrome plated, forged carbon steel ironhead is reground to decrease the weight, a new chrome plating job will have to be performed. But, grind a little off a stainless steel ironhead and the club can usually be buffed back to normal without fear of rusting. Therefore, if you foresee conditions of building overlength irons or are called upon to deliver clubs built to lower

than normal swingweights, choosing stainless steel ironheads can allow you to perform custom weight changes to fill the order correctly.

The most popular alterations performed by clubmakers on iron clubs is that of changing the lie and/or loft angle of the heads. Forged carbon steel heads require little force to bend, but carry the possibility of fracturing the chrome plating. On the other hand, investment cast stainless ironheads run the gamut in bendability; some stainless steels are very bendable while others are very hard, and difficult to alter through bending. Therefore, knowledge and experience in bending all types of ironheads will serve you well whenever loft and lie alterations are called for in the assembly.

So while iron assembly might present itself to beginning clubmakers as a very easy way to get into the business of assembling golf clubs, it does in fact require its own extensive level of training and awareness. The following step-by-step sequence deals with the procedures necessary to ensure a professional job of assembling iron clubs from component parts. However, because custom alterations are also an important aspect of iron assembly, several of these procedures are covered in step-by-step form in Chapter 10.

Iron and Wedge Assembly

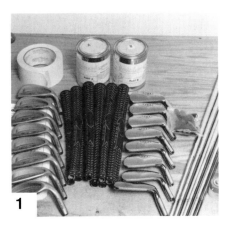

1

STEP 1: Secure and organize each of the required components to anticipate any potential problems in assembly

Be sure you have all the necessary components **and** supplies on hand to complete the assembly before you start the actual procedures of clubmaking. To avoid any potential swingweight problems that may be created by the customer's required custom fitting specifications, first note the desired length, shaft weight, grip size and swingweight in conjunction with the gram weight of the ironhead to calculate the anticipated swingweight of the club(s) **before** you begin work. By pre-calculating swingweight from the known assembly specifications, necessary adjustments can often be made before the assembly process begins, thus solving a potential problem before it occurs. In addition, because alterations of loft and lie are very common in the total job of building iron clubs for your customers, it may be wise to perform these changes before the assembly process begins. See Chapter 10 for how to estimate swingweight before assembly and how to alter loft and lie.

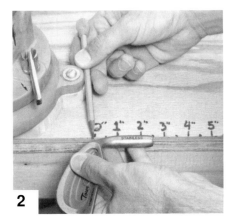

2

STEP 2: Measure hosel length as the first step toward determining bottom of bore to heel dimension

Measure the total length of the hosel from the back edge of the heel to the top of the hosel. If the ironhead design does not have a well defined heel, an estimation will have to be made. Such approximations can easily be made within +/- 1/8".

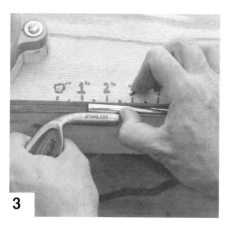

3

STEP 3: Measure bore depth as the second step toward determining bottom of bore to heel dimension
Measure the bore depth of the ironhead, either by inserting a shaft and recording its penetration or by using a depth gauge. Subtract the bore depth from the hosel length to determine the bottom of bore to heel dimension. Compare this measurement to the golf industry's standard of 1" to determine if the shaft tip trimming amounts for each head need to be adjusted.

■ **NOTE**: The charts for shaft trimming in Chapter 3 are based on a golf industry standard ironhead design with a bottom of bore to back of heel dimension of 1". When the bottom of bore to back edge of heel dimension of an ironhead is greater than 1", the increase over the standard is to be added to the amount to tip trim for each club. Additionally, when the bottom of bore to back edge of heel dimension of an ironhead is less than 1", the decrease from the standard is to be subtracted from the amount to tip trim for each club.

STEP 4: Calculate proper tip trimming and mark each shaft for trimming (if tip trimming is necessary)
Either on paper or in your mind, use the bottom of bore to heel dimension determined in STEPS 2 and 3 along with the proper shaft trimming chart in Chapter 3 to calculate the amount to tip trim from each of the shafts. Once you have determined the proper trimming, use a

ruler and felt tip pen to mark the correct amount to trim from the tip of each shaft. While the majority of shafts do require tip trimming prior to installation, some by virtue of their design will not.

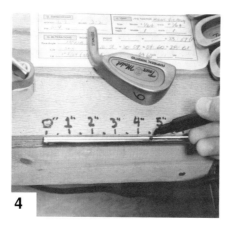

4

For the most accuracy in shaft flex feel, remember to also take into account the required playing length of the golf club(s) before calculating the proper tip trimming for each shaft (see Pages 126-129 in Chapter 3 for an explanation of how to adjust tip trimming based on playing length changes to assure consistent shaft installation).

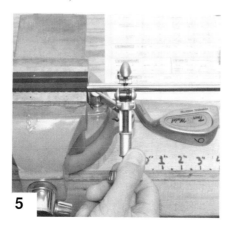

5

STEP 5: Tip trim all shafts
Use the method of shaft cutting that is best suited for the type of material from which the shafts are made. We

recommend the use of a tube cutter or motorized abrasive cut-off wheel for steel and titanium (all metal types) and a grit edge saw or abrasive cut-off wheel for graphite and other composite shafts. Again, by intent of their design, some shafts will not require tip trimming before installation, so be sure to always check, then double check the proper trimming procedures for the shafts you are using. To keep each shaft matched to the ironhead into which it will be installed, mark the ironhead number on the butt end of each shaft after it has been trimmed.

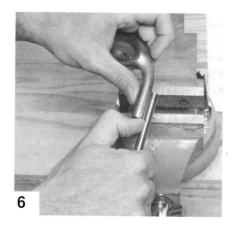

6

STEP 6: Test fit the shafts
After trimming, test fit each shaft into its proper head to check for proper fit and mounting. In the case of parallel shaft to parallel bore assembly this will be very easy to do as the shafts will slide easily to the base of the bore. For taper tip shafts a proper test fit will see the shaft stop approximately 1/4" short of touching the bottom of the bore. Because most shaft tip and iron hosel bore diameters are produced to a size tolerance of +/- .002" there *will* often be cases when the shaft tip does not slide easily into the hosel. **If this occurs and you are <u>sure</u> the reason is because of the size tolerances, then removing an extra .001" to .002"" from the shaft tip diameter to make it fit is acceptable. The tip of iron shafts have wall thicknesses of at least .035" which will allow <u>very slight</u> reductions in their diameters without fear of damaging the shaft.** Test fitting shafts is also performed to determine how far up the shaft to abrade the tip for

epoxying purposes. If there are any adjustments that have to be made to the shaft to assure proper mounting, perform them now.

7

STEP 7: Rebore hosel (if necessary)

If any tipping has to be performed on taper tip shafts to achieve the desired mounting, the hosel will have to be rebored for the shaft to fit. In addition, should a parallel tip shaft not seat properly, unless the fit is very close the hosel should be rebored (see exception in STEP 6). Complete step-by-step procedures for reboring irons are included in Chapter 10.

8

STEP 8: Bevel top inside edge of the hosel (for graphite/composite shaft installation only)

A beveling of the top inside edge of the hosel bore must be performed to relieve the stress an iron hosel can place on the tip of graphite/composite shafts. If the head(s) being assembled are not pre-beveled by the manufacturer, use a 20° countersink or rotary file fixed in your electric hand drill to bevel the top inside edge of the hosel. Be sure the beveling is @1/8" deep into the hosel. Remove any burrs after beveling.

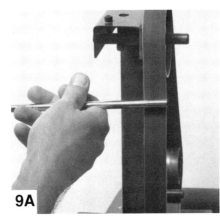

9A

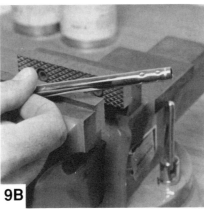

9B

STEP 9: Prepare the tip of the shaft by abrading (photo 9A) or crimping (photo 9B)

Abrade the entire portion of the shaft tip that will not only be inserted in the hosel, but the portion that will be under the ferrule, should a ferrule be required. **Take extreme care** when abrading the shaft tip not to sand too far up the shaft, thus leaving scratches that would show above the

top of the hosel or ferrule. Crimping, or deforming the shaft tip, is a step used by many large shops to ensure a mechanical lock between the shaft and the head. While not necessary, crimping is an acceptable method of tip preparation for iron assembly.

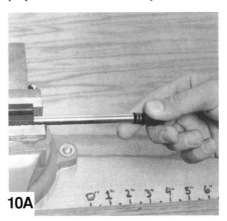

10A

STEP 10A: Install ferrule (and grip collar if required)

If the ironhead or wedge is designed with a squared off hosel, it is intended to be assembled with a ferrule. If the top of the iron hosel is rounded or tapered, it is designed to be assembled without a ferrule. If the ironhead does call for a ferrule, begin the ferrule installation procedure by twisting the small end of the ferrule onto the shaft tip.

■ **NOTE**: It is not necessary to install and position the ferrule in the exact position on the shaft that it will assume after assembly. The installation of the shaft into the hosel will serve the purpose of pushing the ferrule into its final location up the shaft. However, for safety be sure to have at least 1" of the shaft tip penetrating from the bottom of the ferrule before driving the shaft to the bottom of the bore. **Also, if a leather grip is to be installed later in the assembly procedure, it is a wise idea to install the plastic grip collar from the tip end at this time.**

STEP 10B: Install ferrule - Tap ferrule on the shaft

Once the ferrule is lined up with the shaft, use a rubber mallet to drive the ferrule up the shaft. Begin tapping gently at first to keep the ferrule straight to the shaft, and

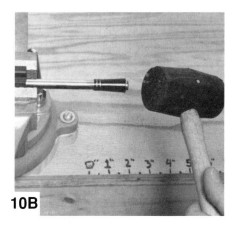

10B

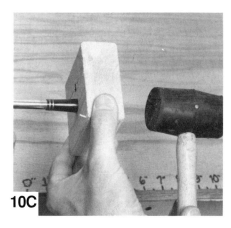

10C

then increase the force of the blows. Hammer with the mallet until the tip of the shaft protrudes from the base of the ferrule.

STEP 10C: Install ferrule - Drive the ferrule at least 1" up the shaft

While specially made ferrule installing tools are available, all that is needed to drive the ferrule farther up the shaft is a wood block with a 3/8" diameter hole. Insert the block on to the shaft tip that is protruding from the base of the ferrule and hammer it against the ferrule, thus applying the force to drive the ferrule up the shaft.

11

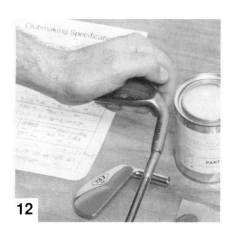

12

STEP 11: Mix epoxy and apply to the shaft tip and inside of hosel

Always use a high shear strength 2-part shafting epoxy to secure the shaft to the head. Follow the epoxy supplier's mixing recommendations to be certain the complete bonding strength of the epoxy is achieved. Use a 1/4" wood dowel rod or similar applicator to apply a thin but full coverage coating of epoxy to the shaft tip and the inside of the hosel bore.

STEP 12: Install the shafts

One by one, insert each shaft into its proper ironhead. Rotate the shaft as it is inserted to ensure a complete coating of the epoxy between the shaft tip and the inside of the hosel. While it is not necessary, sand may be used

as an additional bonding aid without fear of damaging the hosel. If a sand is used, dip only 1/4" of the tip of the shaft into the sand before inserting the shaft into the hosel. As the shaft slides down the hosel the sand will spread and/ or crush between the shaft tip and the hosel wall, thus acting as a bonding "filler" to the epoxy. The use of sand can be a slight strength additive for tube type epoxies such as Conap, which are made without a filler.

■ **NOTE: For graphite shaft installation**

When installing graphite shafts, be sure a ring of epoxy occupies the space between the shaft and the beveled edge of the hosel. This will form the required epoxy "cushion" between shaft and hosel to relieve stress on the shaft tip.

13

STEP 13: Seat the shaft into the hosel (parallel tip shafts)

For **parallel tip shaft** assembly, driving the shaft tip to the bottom of the hosel will be a very easy procedure. With at least 1" of the shaft tip in the hosel, grasp the head in one hand with the other hand placed on the shaft, approximately 12" down from the top of the hosel. Holding the shaft tightly into the head, drive the butt of the shaft against a hard surface (such as a cement floor). Note the difference in the feel of the shaft movement when the shaft tip reaches the bottom of the bore. When this point is reached, the shaft is considered to be properly seated in the hosel.

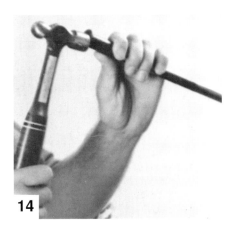

14

STEP 14: Seat the shaft into the hosel (taper tip shafts)

For **taper tip shaft** assembly, driving the shaft to the bottom of the bore will require some force, due to the nature of the mechanical lock of the force fit assembly. The same hand driving procedure outlined in STEP 13 can be used to seat the shaft into the hosel. In addition, a driving plug can be used to drive taper tip shafts into the hosel. If the driving plug method is used, first secure the ironhead in the vise between soft metal (brass, aluminum) vise pads. With @1" of the shaft inserted in the hosel, place the driving plug in the butt end of the shaft and begin striking the plug against the shaft butt with a hammer. Feeling the shaft bottom out will be difficult, so after 4-5 strong blows with the hammer, remove the club and drive the shaft butt 1-2 more times against a hard surface, trying to feel if the shaft is moving down any farther in the hosel. If the feel of the driving against the floor is very rigid, the shaft will be considered to be properly seated.

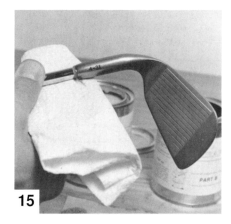

15

STEP 15: Clean up, check and set aside to dry

Wipe away any excess epoxy that has accumulated at the top of the hosel or between the hosel and the bottom of the ferrule (if a ferrule has been installed). Check for any epoxy smears on the head or shaft and wipe clean. For graphite shaft installation, be sure to leave a small ring of epoxy around the top of the hosel for cushioning purposes.

16

STEP 16: Additional clean-up step for ironheads with a ferrule

Normal wiping with a paper towel may not remove the excess epoxy at the base of the ferrule. To eliminate the possibility of a thin ring of the epoxy setting up between the ferrule and the hosel, use a paper towel backed by one

of your finger nails to actually "dig" epoxy out from under the edge of the ferrule. Clean with a rag dampened with grip solvent. Set the club aside to cure either horizontally on a rack or with the head down on the floor. **Never** set clubs to dry with the head up and shaft down or epoxy could flow down the shaft, thus creating the potential for a rattle after the club is put into play.

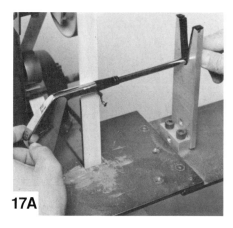

17A

STEP 17A: Dress down the ferrule - Belt sanding procedure

Using a 1"x42" belt sander with linen belt will be the fastest way to dress down the ferrule. Replace the abrasive belt on the sander with a linen cloth belt, specially made for sanding plastic. To keep the club steady while in contact with the belt, it is recommended to fashion a holding fixture to attach to the machine, as pictured. Begin rotating the bottom of the ferrule in a direction that is **against** the direction of travel of the belt. **Always** keep the ferrule moving while in contact with the cloth belt to avoid "burning" the ferrule. Do not attempt to dress down the top of the ferrule flush to the shaft. On iron clubs, it is customary to only sand the bottom of the ferrule flush to the top of the hosel.

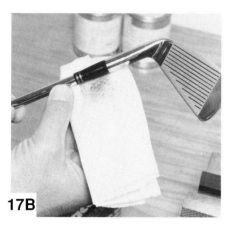

17B

17C

STEP 17B: Dress down the ferrule - Belt sanding procedure
Acetone the ferrule
After reducing the ferrule to meet the top of the hosel, wipe it with a paper towel wetted with acetone to restore the shine. For the deepest shine, use full circular rotations of the ferrule against the acetone soaked towel.

STEP 17C: Dress down the ferrule - Belt sanding procedure
Buff ferrule with Glanz Wach
If desired, the ferrule can be buffed to an even greater shine using unstitched buffing wheels coated with Glanz Wach. For best results, spin the ferrule against the direction of travel of the buffing wheels.

18A

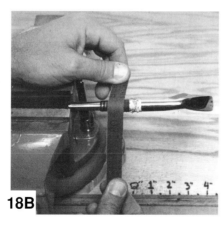

18B

STEP 18A: Dress down the ferrule - Filing procedure
File base of ferrule flush to the hosel
Secure the club in the vise as pictured and place a strip of masking tape around the top of the hosel for protection from the filing. With a medium cut file, begin filing around the bottom of the ferrule only to reduce its diameter to match the top of the hosel. It is not customary to file the top of an iron ferrule flush to the shaft, so do no filing at the top of the ferrule. Take extreme care not to scratch either the iron hosel or the shaft above the top of the ferrule.

STEP 18B: Dress down the ferrule - Filing procedure
Sand ferrule to remove scratches
To remove the scratches left from the file, use a 1" strip of medium to coarse sandpaper and sand all the way around the ferrule.

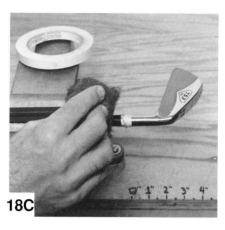

18C

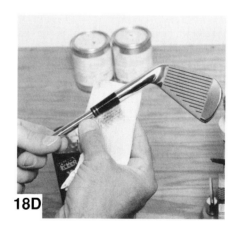

18D

STEP 18C: Dress down the ferrule - Filing procedure
Steel wool the ferrule
Rub the ferrule vigorously with fine steel wool (3/0 or 4/0 grade) until the surface is smooth with only a few minor scratches.

STEP 18D: Dress down the ferrule - Filing procedure
Wipe with acetone
Wipe the ferrule with a paper towel wetted with acetone to restore the shine. For best results use full circular rotations of the ferrule against the acetone soaked towel.

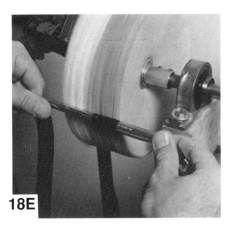

18E

STEP 18E: Dress down the ferrule - Filing procedure Buff ferrule with Glanz Wach

The ferrule may be buffed to an even greater shine with unstitched buffing wheels coated with Glanz Wach. Use a rotating motion of the ferrule against the direction of travel of the buffing wheels.

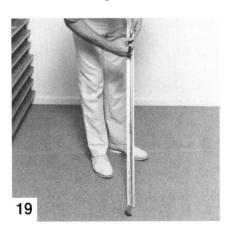

19

STEP 19: Measure and mark the shaft for the desired playing length

Place the club in the playing position touching the floor in the center of the sole. Take care not to rock the club either up on the toe or back on its heel. Slide a 48" clubmaker's ruler up behind the shaft, and carefully mark the desired playing length on the butt end of the shaft with a felt tip marker. Be sure to allow for the effect that the 1/8" thickness of the end of the grip will have on the

club's playing length by marking the shafts 1/8" shorter than what is desired (e.g.- If a true 39" playing length is desired, mark the shaft at 38 7/8", for a 37 1/2" playing length, mark the shaft at 37 3/8", etc.).

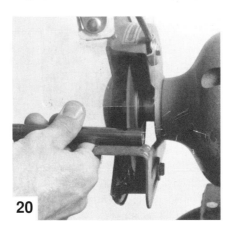

20

STEP 20: Cut the shaft to its desired playing length

Using the proper cutting procedure for the type of shaft being used, trim the shaft for its playing length. Always deburr and square off the shaft butt after trimming to remove sharp edges. If a graphite or composite type shaft has been installed, use an abrasive cut-off wheel or a grit edged hack saw blade to trim the shaft, **never** a tubing cutter.

■ **NOTE**: There are a limited number of all tip trim shafts that require no further butt trimming for playing length after installation. If you are working with such a shaft, proceed to STEP 21.

STEP 21: Record the preliminary swingweight of the club

Place the club on a 14" fulcrum swingweight scale (Lorythmic or Prorythmic type) **without the grip installed** and record its swingweight. Do **not** push the butt of the ungripped club completely against the back of the scale. Because the grip cap provides the final 1/8" of club length pull the shaft butt 1/8" away from the end of the scale before recording preliminary swingweight. This is important to achieve an accurate swingweight reading.

21

■ **NOTE:** It is not recommended to swingweight graphite shafted clubs with lead powder down the shaft. See Chapter 10 for procedures for swingweighting golf clubs with graphite shafts that do not have weight ports in the head.

Example:

Preliminary Swingweight (E-0)

– Swingweight Equivalent of Grip (10SW)

Initial Swingweight (D-0)

22

STEP 22: Subtract the swingweight equivalent of the grip from the un-gripped club's preliminary swingweight to determine the <u>initial swingweight</u>

The swingweight of the un-gripped club will read higher because the grip has not been installed. It will be heavier in the amount equal to the swingweight equivalent of the weight of the grip plus its installation and build-up tape. To determine what the club's **initial swingweight** will be once the grip is installed, subtract 9 swingweight points for a standard men's size rubber grip, 10 points for a cord or leather grip, and 1 additional swingweight point for every three layers of build-up tape that may be used (e.g.- An ungripped club with a swingweight of E-0, scheduled for installation with a Men's Victory grip with three layers of build-up tape will make the gripped club's **initial swingweight** D-0).

■ **NOTE: For alternative swingweight method**
Rather than use grip weight estimations to calculate the club's initial swingweight, clubmakers may wish to temporarily install a grip of the type eventually to be used. Keep a few grips in your shop (rubber, cord, 58 core, 60 core, etc.) that have been cut lengthwise with a knife or scissors to slide on the shaft for simulating the weight of the grip. By using cut grips mounted temporarily on the shaft you will get an accurate estimation of what the club's initial swingweight will be when you place the club on the swingweight scale. For oversize grips, subtract 1 more swingweight point for every three layers of build-up tape to be used.

Example:

Desired
Swingweight (D-2)

− **Initial**
Swingweight (D-0)

──────────────────

Amount to Add (2SW)

23

STEP 23: Calculate the weight increase needed to establish the club's desired final swingweight
Subtract the initial swingweight from the customer's desired final swingweight to determine what amount of weight to add to the head (e.g. - Desired final swingweight of D-2 minus initial swingweight of D-0 = the amount of weight to add is 2 swingweight points).

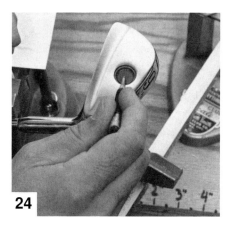
24

STEP 24: Increase swingweight to desired final level (for ironheads with weight port, add the weight)
Once the amount of increase is determined, establish the final swingweight of the club. Very few ironheads or wedges are designed with a weight port. If one is provided, by all means use this as the primary way to add weight. The weight to be added may be pre-weighed on a gram scale (allowing 1 swingweight point = 2 grams of lead powder or lead discs as a formula) to save guess work. If no gram scale is available in your shop, add the lead powder or lead discs by estimation, check the weight on the scale, then add or remove as needed to establish the final weight. If lead discs are being used, epoxy the discs into the cavity.

25

STEP 25: Increase swingweight to desired final level (for ironheads with weight port, epoxy the medallions in place
Most ironhead weight ports accept 1/2" diameter lead discs, to be covered with a medallion. After epoxying the lead weights in place, cover the rim of the cavity with epoxy and press the medallion in place. If the back side of the medallion is not roughed up to aid in epoxy adhesion, take time to abrade the back of the medallion with sandpaper. The proper positioning of medallions on ironheads is to place them so that any artwork can be read when the shaft is pointing down (as when in the golf bag).

■ **NOTE:** If the swingweight is too high, there are very few options for removing the weight. If the heads are chrome plated, no weight may be removed or else the heads will have to be replated. If the heads are made from stainless steel and are satin or high polish finished, weight can be removed by grinding the toe and/or sole areas on a belt sander followed by buffing to restore the head's original finish. Because such steps require skill and are time consuming, pre-calculating swingweight before assembly is an important task to do.

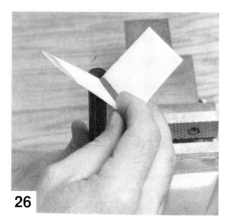
26

STEP 26: Increase swingweight to desired final level (for ironheads without a weight port, add the weight down the shaft in the form of lead powder)
An addition of 5 swingweight points (10 grams) or less down the shaft will not harm the playability of any

golf club. Keeping this point in mind, if no weight port is present, or if the capacity of the weight port is not sufficient for the final needs of the club, add the final amount down the shaft, using lead powder only. Again, a gram scale can be used to pre-weigh the amount of powder necessary to achieve the final swingweight, or you can add the weight down the shaft by estimation, followed by a check reading on the swingweight scale.

> **Be sure to follow "The 5-point rule;" 5 swingweight points or less down the hosel, OK. More than 5, NO!**

■ **NOTE:** Final swingweighting graphite-shafted irons by adding lead powder down the shaft is NOT recommended due to the very small inside diameter of all graphite shafts. As a result, when assembling graphite-shafted irons without a weight port, it will be very important to pre-calculate the final swingweight needs before assembly. In such cases, it is recommended to epoxy a specially-made graphite shaft tip weight (sold by many component suppliers) up the shaft tip before the shaft is installed into the head.

27

STEP 27: Increase swingweight to desired final level (for ironheads without weight port, secure lead powder with a cork)
When the proper swingweight is achieved, drop a cork down the shaft, small end first, to secure the weight. Using a 1/4" diameter steel ram rod attached to a file

handle, tamp the cork down against the weight to secure it. Finish by checking the swingweight on the scale. Remember, the grip has not been installed, so the swingweight should read higher than the desired final level by the amount equivalent to the weight of the grip and its build-up tape.

28

STEP 28: Apply grip tape (and leather grip collar if needed)
Secure the club in the bench vise with the head positioned toe up and apply any required build-up tape and/or 2-way foundation tape. If a leather grip is to be installed it will require a plastic grip collar. If the collar has not already been put on during the installation of the shaft, slide it on over the shaft butt. Installing a grip collar from the butt end of the shaft requires a little practice but can easily be accomplished if the grip collar size used is one shaft size larger than the shaft butt. For example, use a .620" size grip collar on a .600" butt diameter shaft, a .600" collar on a .580" shaft, etc.

STEP 29: Install grip and final check swingweight
After wetting the 2-way grip tape and the inside of the grip with grip solvent, install and properly line up the grip. After installation, check to be sure the grip is completely seated against the shaft butt and clean up the tape residue that will be present at the mouth of the grip. Immediately put the club back on the swingweight scale to double check your work, now making sure the butt of

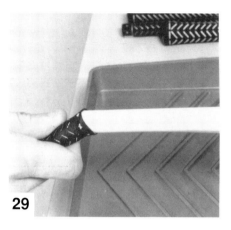

29

the grip is pushed against the end of the scale. If the swingweight is incorrect, the grip adhesive from the tape should still be wet enough to allow you to pull off the grip and correct the problem. **The complete step-by-step procedures for all types of grip installation and sizing are covered in Chapter 4.**

30

STEP 30: Final check swingweight
After installing the grip, place the club on the swingweight scale to perform a final check of the weight. Once the grip is lined up properly, install a protective plastic grip bag held in place with a wrap of thin masking tape. Covering the grip not only adds a professional touch, but will protect the grip from soiling during the club's remaining time in your shop.

STEP 31: Clean up, install the shaft label and check the club for proper specifications

The club is now completed. Before the job is fully done, inspect the club one last time to clean up any soiling of the head, grip and shaft and check all specifications for accuracy. Finally, install a plastic head bag for protection and apply any necessary shaft labels in the proper place on the shaft. The golf industry standard position for shaft labels is between the second and third step down below the mouth of the grip, with the label centered between steps, insignia facing up.

CHAPTER 9 - The Modern Assembly Procedures of Putters

Step-by-Step Procedures of Assembly for Building Putters

Though Easy To Assemble, a Club Not To Be Taken For Granted

An analysis of golfers' scoring tendencies will often reveal that 40 to 50% of all the shots in an average round are made on the green. Yet one club that is almost entirely overlooked from a clubmaking standpoint is the putter.

Because of their potential for greater sales and profit dollars, full sets of woods and irons must be thought of as a clubmaker's first priority offerings. While it is nice to ring up sales of four woods, or nine irons, putters can also represent a nice, solid, consistent addition to your profits. Even though players invest in just one set of woods and irons at a time, due to the nature of golfers it is likely they will be candidates for buying more than one putter! The sheer importance of putting within the the game coupled with its elusiveness of success mean that many golfers will buy three or four new putters each season, as if looking for that "magic" club that will instantly allow them to make those nerve-wracking 5-footers. The sheer fact that putters are sold as a single club and therefore represent a low cost makes the customer's decision to purchase more impulsive than a full set of woods or irons.

Yet from a clubmaking standpoint, most clubmakers overlook many of the technical factors that go into the building of this single club.

"How much is there to building a putter? A head, a shaft, a grip; slap them together and you have a putter," is often the thought that goes with making a putter.

While the mechanics of putter assembly are simple, an emphasis must still be placed on proper clubmaking procedures. For example, few clubmakers ever pay attention to swingweight when assembling putters. But if you consider the difference between a putter that "feels good" and one that doesn't, swingweight can play an important role. Currently, most manufacturers design putter headweights that when built to industry standards of length (35" for men, 34" for ladies) and grip size will be in the range of D-3 for men and C-7 for ladies. Keeping these standards in mind will help you to build

putters of higher quality than clubs that are just "slapped together."

The wide variety of putter head designs available today requires that clubmakers also possess a sound technical background in putter head design. Clubmakers will need to be aware of the differences in blade, mallet, flange, cavity back, heel/toe weighted and long pendulum style putter heads and their tendencies on the various types of putting surfaces to be able to properly advise golfers of the right model.

Another important putter assembly consideration concerns the custom putter alterations you can offer. Many clubmakers are aware that golfers may need to have the lie and, in some cases, the loft of their putters customized to meet their individual game requirements. Putter heads are fashioned from a wide variety of materials and produced through a host of different manufacturing methods. Because of the variety of materials available on the market, not all putters are able to be bent for lie and loft changes. Putter heads that are produced through forging will, of course, be bendable. Heads that are made by investment casting also will be bendable, with the degree of alterability dependent on the hardness of the stainless used. And, owing to the soft nature of the material, brass or aluminum putter heads will also be very easy to alter. But there do exist a large number of die cast zinc putter heads, which due to the brittle nature of the metal will usually not allow the head to be bent. Therefore, it is absolutely necessary for clubmakers to train themselves to be able to recognize the material and manufacturing differences between putter heads before attempting loft and lie alterations.

Unlike any other golf club, putters can be assembled with a tremendous assortment of grip styles and shapes. Over the last decade, changes within the rules of the game have resulted in a number of the clubmaking industry's popular grip styles to be deemed non-conforming. From standard slip-on rubber models to leather wraps to custom-shaped leather grips, clubmakers need to apprise themselves of the legality of, and become aware of, the tremendous variety of grip styles their customers may request. While clubmaking suppliers are able to provide a selection of different shapes and styles of rubber grips and leather underlistings, many golfers will want a "special grip shape" that sometimes has to be custom made.

■ SHAFT SELECTION FOR PUTTERS

A variety of specially-made shafts are now produced by the various shaft manufacturers for use in putters. From straight taper, non-stepped patterns to fluted shafts to flared tip to bent shaft models, the choice of what shaft to use in what type of putter can be somewhat confusing. While the differences from one putter shaft to another are primarily cosmetic and do not involve flex or bend point, the most obvious factor to consider when selecting a shaft for a putter is to match the tip diameter of the shaft to the bore diameter of the hosel.

Specially-made putter shafts are currently available in .370" parallel, .300" and .355" taper tip or .386" flared tip

design. While it is best to perform putter assembly with a shaft made expressly for a putter, it is acceptable to use a standard iron shaft should one of the putter shafts not be available. For example, a golfer may request a more flexible putter shaft for use on fast greens. Because putter shafts are not made in different flexes, fulfilling such a request will require the use of a softer flex version of a standard iron shaft. When trimming a standard iron shaft for use in a putter, the proper procedure for installation will be to mount the shaft with its first step down placement identical to that for a #9-iron.

■ **REMEMBER**: In Chapter 3 (pages 122-123) it was stated the standard dimension for bottom of bore to heel measurement of putters is substantially different than for ironheads. While the golf shaft manufacturers' standard tables for iron shaft trimming is based on ironheads with a 1" bottom of bore to back edge of heel dimension, for inside the hosel type putters the dimension is 2 1/2" from the bottom of the bore to the SOLE and for over the hosel type putters, 2 1/4" from the bottom of the bore to the SOLE. Please note that it is the custom for this tip trimming standard to extend to the sole for putters while for ironheads the dimension is from the bottom of the hosel bore to the back edge of the heel.

Therefore, for the installation of shafts made expressly for use in putters, 0" tip trimming will be required when the shaft is installed into putter heads with the respective 2 1/2" and 2 1/4" bottom of bore to sole dimensions. For putter heads with a bottom of bore to sole dimension that is greater than 2 1/2" (for shaft inside hosel type putters) or 2 1/4" (for shaft over the hosel type putters), the amount to tip trim from the putter shaft will be the putter's measured bottom of bore to sole dimension minus the 2 1/2" or 2 1/4" standards for the type of putter being assembled.

Before selecting a shaft for overshaft hosel putters, always check the diameter of the hosel post over which the shaft will be installed. If the diameter of the hosel post is @.320" it has been designed for use with a .370" parallel tip shaft. Most overshaft hosel putter heads

today require a .370" putter shaft or a conventional .370" parallel tip iron shaft to fit **over** the hosel post. For purposes of determining the bottom of bore to heel dimension to establish the proper tip trimming of the shaft, consider the lip at the base of the hosel post to be the bottom of the bore. Measuring from this lip or edge to the heel of the putter will give you the bottom of bore to heel dimension to reference to the shaft trimming charts.

Putters can demand a lot more in the utilization of clubmaking skills than what first meets the eye. While some custom putter options such as loft/lie alteration may require advanced clubmaking skills, the following step-by-step outline covers the basic procedures that must be followed to ensure a professional job of putter assembly. For instruction on some of the aspects of customizing putters, see Chapter 10.

Putter Assembly

1

STEP 1: Secure and organize each of the required components to anticipate any potential problems in assembly

Be sure you have all the necessary components **and** supplies on hand to complete the assembly before you start the actual procedures of building the putter. Should swingweight be a major concern, weigh the clubhead and use the information in Chapter 10 to pre-calculate the swingweight. Note the desired length, shaft weight, grip size and swingweight in conjunction with the gram weight of the putter head to calculate the anticipated swingweight of the club(s) **before** you begin work. By virtue of their design, conventional putter heads can range in weight from 280 to 330 grams, so if swingweight is a concern be sure to note the head's weight before you order. In addition, because alterations of lie or loft can be very common in the total job of building putters for your customers, it may be wise to perform these changes before the assembly process begins. See Chapter 10 to learn how to estimate swingweight before assembly and altering loft and lie.

■ **NOTE:** Putter heads designed for extra long assembly (50" pendulum type putters) are usually produced to be much higher in headweight than conventional putters. Because such a heavy headweight (350 grams and higher) is conceived for the pendulum style of putting, clubmakers will not be able to follow standard swingweight principles.

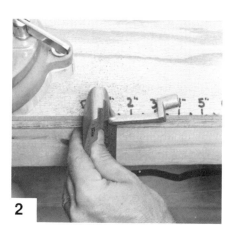

STEP 2: Measure hosel length as a first step toward determining bottom of bore to heel dimension
Measure the total length of the hosel from the back edge of the heel to the top of the hosel. This will be a little more difficult on putter heads than on ironheads because of the wide variety of hosel designs that are seen on putter heads today. **On shaft over hosel type putters, do not measure hosel length. For these types of putter heads, the distance from the lip at the bottom of the hosel post to the sole is considered to be the actual bottom of bore to sole dimension.**

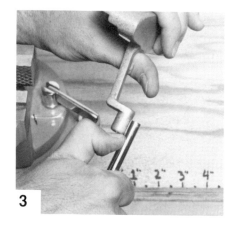

STEP 3: Measure bore depth as the second step toward determining bottom of bore to sole dimension
Measure the depth of the bore, either with a depth gauge or by inserting the shaft and checking its depth of penetration. Subtract the bore depth from the hosel length to determine the bottom of bore to sole dimension It is this measurement that must be compared to the golf industry's putter head standard of 2 1/2" (shaft inside hosel type putters) and 2 1/4" (shaft over the hosel type putters) and then to the shaft trimming charts to determine the amount to tip if an actual putter shaft is being used in the putter assembly.

■ **NOTE:** If the shaft being used is an standard iron shaft, clubmakers are advised to trim the shaft for an R-flex with the same tip trimming that would be performed for a conventional #9 iron. After such tip trimming and installation, trimming for the desired playing length would be perfomed from the butt end of the shaft.

STEP 4: Calculate proper tip trimming and mark the shaft for trimming (if tip trimming is necessary)

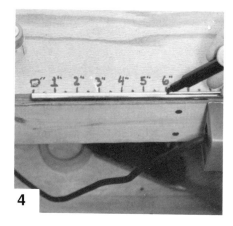

Once the proper trimming has been determined, use a ruler and felt tip pen to mark the correct amount to trim from the tip of the shaft.

■ **NOTE:** In cases of extraordinary bottom of bore to sole dimension or longer conventional putter playing lengths (not including the 50" type pendulum putters), the question of whether additional tip trimming should be performed is a decision of the clubmaker. Due to the very low clubhead speed at which the putter is swung, the changes in putter shaft flex feel caused by length or hosel anomalies are far less likely to be felt by the golfer.

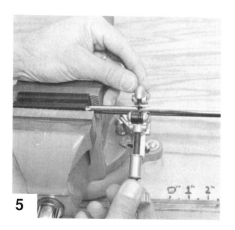

STEP 5: Trim the Shaft
If tip trimming is necessary, use the proper means of

cutting for the type of shaft being installed, tube cutter or abrasive wheel for steel, abrasive wheel or hacksaw for graphite. If the shaft is intended for over the hosel installation, it is highly recommended to use only the abrasive cut-off wheel to ensure a clean, straight cut. A tubing cutter will pinch the shaft and reduce the tip diameter enough that the shaft will not slide over the hosel post.

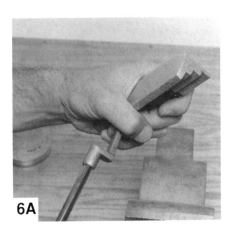

6A

STEP 6A: Test fit the shaft (shaft inside hosel designs)
After any necessary tip trimming, test fit the shaft into the putter to check for proper fit and mounting. For parallel shaft to parallel bore assembly this will be very easy as the shaft should slide easily to the base of the bore. Because shaft tip and iron hosel bore diameters are produced to a size tolerance of +/-.002" there will occasionally be times when the shaft tip does not slide easily into the hosel. **If this occurs and you are <u>sure</u> the reason is because of the size tolerances, then removing an extra .001" to .002" from the shaft tip diameter to make it fit will be OK. Most putter and iron shafts possess tip wall thicknesses of at least .035" - .050" which will allow <u>slight</u> reductions in tip diameter without fear of damaging the shaft. However, if the shaft does not fit after light sanding correct the fit by enlarging the hosel bore.** Test fitting shafts is also performed to determine how far up the shaft to abrade the

tip for epoxying purposes. If there are any adjustments that have to be made to the shaft or hosel to assure proper mounting, perform them now.

■ **NOTE:** Due to the lower clubhead speed of putter use, beveling the hosel for graphite shaft installation is not necessary.

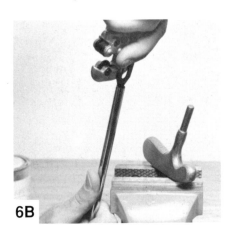

6B

STEP 6B: Test fit the shaft (shaft over hosel designs)
The procedure of tip trimming will leave burrs inside the shaft tip that may prevent the shaft from sliding over the hosel post of the putter head. The flaring tool on a tube cutter is a good tool to use to remove the inner burrs. Rotate the flaring tool around the inside tip of the shaft to remove these burrs (again, if the shaft has not been cut square, belt sanding or filing the tip will be necessary to ensure the shaft tip fits free of gaps, flush against the bottom of the hosel).

STEP 7A: Prepare the tip of the shaft for installation (shaft inside hosel designs)
For putter shafts installed inside the hosel, sand or abrade the entire portion of the shaft tip that will not only be inserted in the hosel, but the portion that will be under the ferrule, should a ferrule be required. **Take extreme care** when abrading the shaft tip not to sand too far up the shaft, thus leaving scratches that would show above the top of the hosel or ferrule. Crimping is not generally recom-

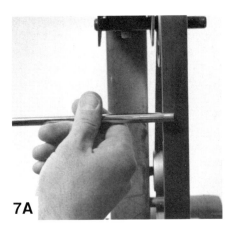

7A

mended except for shaft installation into the investment cast type stainless steel putter heads. Sometimes the force that is required to drive a crimped shaft to the bottom of a die cast or sand cast type putter head could break the hosel.

STEP 7B: Prepare the hosel post of the putter head for shaft installation (shaft over hosel designs)
On the overshaft type of shaft to putter head installation, abrade the hosel post of the head to ensure adequate epoxy adhesion, **not the shaft tip**. The same procedures of sanding can be used on the hosel, with care taken not to scratch the portions of the head below the lip of the hosel. Note that most overshaft hosel posts are made with grooves to collect epoxy and thus further ensure proper epoxy adhesion.

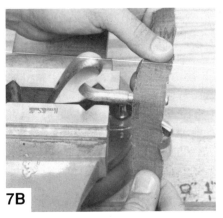

7B

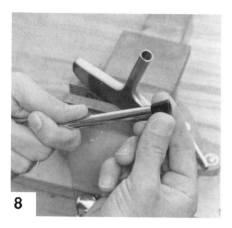

STEP 8: Install ferrule (grip collar if needed)
If the hosel of the putter is squared off at the top, it is intended to be assembled with a ferrule. If the design being built does call for a ferrule, use the procedures covered in Chapter 3 to guide your installation.

■ **NOTE:** It is not necessary to install and position the ferrule in its exact position on the shaft that it will assume after assembly. The installation of the shaft into the hosel will serve the purpose of pushing each ferrule into its final location up the shaft. **Also, if a leather grip is to be installed on the putter, it is a wise idea to install the plastic grip collar from the tip end at this time.**

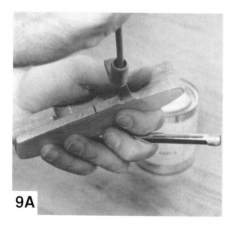

STEP 9A: Mix epoxy and apply to shaft tip and inside

of hosel (shaft inside hosel designs)
Always use high shear strength 2-part shafting epoxy to secure the shaft to the head. Follow the epoxy supplier's mixing directions to be sure the complete bonding strength of the epoxy is achieved. Use a 1/4" wood dowel rod or similar applicator to apply a thin but full coverage coating of epoxy to the shaft tip and the inside of the hosel bore.

STEP 9B: Install shafts (shaft inside hosel designs)
Insert the shaft into the hosel with a rotating motion to ensure a coating of all bonding surfaces. Again, sand is not necessary, but can be used as a bonding filler when assembling putters. If the sand is used, just dip the very tip of the shaft into the sand before inserting the shaft into the hosel. Wipe away the excess epoxy from the top of the hosel with a paper towel.

STEP 10A: Apply epoxy to inside of shaft and outside of the hosel post (shaft over hosel designs)
Use high shear strength grade shafting epoxy and apply a thin, but full coverage coating to the inside of the shaft tip as well as the outside of the abraded hosel post.

STEP 10B: Install shafts (shaft over hosel designs)
Use the same rotating motion to insert the shaft over the hosel post of the putter head. Wipe away the excess epoxy from the base of the shaft with a paper towel.

STEP 11A: Properly seat the shaft into the hosel (parallel tip shafts)
For **parallel tip shaft** inside the hosel assembly, driving the shaft tip to the bottom of the hosel will be a very easy

procedure. With at least 1/4" of the shaft tip inserted into the hosel, grasp the head in one hand with the other hand placed on the shaft, approximately 12" down from the top of the hosel. Keeping the shaft tight to the head, tap the butt of the shaft against a hard surface (such as a cement floor). Note the feeling of resistance when the shaft tip reaches the bottom of the bore. When this point is reached, the shaft is considered to be properly seated in the hosel. If there is no ferrule installed, the shaft does not need to be tapped on the floor, as there will be no resistance encountered in pushing the shaft tip to the bottom of the bore.

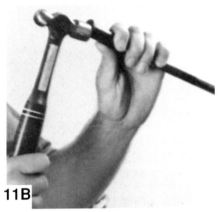

STEP 11B: Properly seat the shaft into the hosel (taper tip shafts)

For **taper tip shaft** assembly, driving the shaft to the bottom of the bore will require some force, due to the nature of the mechanical lock of the force fit assembly. The same hand driving procedure outlined in STEP 11A can be used to seat the shaft into the hosel. In addition, a driving plug can be used to drive taper tip shafts into the hosel. If the driving plug method is used, first secure the ironhead in the vise between soft metal (brass, aluminum) vise pads. With @1" of the shaft inserted in the hosel, place the driving plug in the butt end of the shaft and begin striking the plug against the shaft butt with a hammer. Feeling the shaft bottom out will be difficult, so after 4-5 strong blows with the hammer, remove the club and drive the shaft butt 1-2 more times against a hard surface, trying to feel if the shaft is moving down any

farther in the hosel. If the feel of the driving against the floor is very rigid, the shaft will be considered to be properly seated.

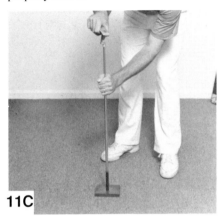

STEP 11C: Properly seat the shaft over the hosel (shaft over hosel designs)

For shaft over the hosel type putters, the shaft will almost always slide all the way to the lip at the base of the hosel post. However, if the shaft or hosel post diameters are close to being outside their +/- size tolerances, a slight driving force may have to be applied. In these rare cases, use the same shaft tapping procedure as outlined in STEP 11A.

STEP 12: Clean up, check and set aside to dry

Wipe away any excess epoxy that has accumulated at the

top of the hosel or between the hosel and the bottom of the ferrule (if a ferrule has been installed). Check for any epoxy smears on the head or shaft and wipe clean. After inspection, set the club aside for the epoxy to cure. **Never** set clubs aside to dry with the head up and shaft down.

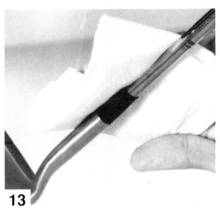

STEP 13: Additional clean-up step for putters with a ferrule

Normal wiping with a paper towel may not remove the excess epoxy at the base of the ferrule. To eliminate the possibility of a thin ring of the epoxy setting up between the ferrule and the hosel, use a paper towel backed by one of your finger nails to actually "dig" epoxy out from under the edge of the ferrule. Clean with a rag dampened with grip solvent. Set the club aside to cure either horizontally on a rack or with the head down on the floor. **Never** set clubs to dry with the head up and shaft down or epoxy could flow down the shaft, thus creating the potential for a rattle after the club is put into play.

STEP 14: Dress down the ferrule (if ferrule is present)

If you are skilled in the use of a 1"x42" belt sander with linen belt to turn down ferrules, use this method to dress down the ferrule. If not, use a shaft clamp to secure the club in the vise as pictured and place a strip of masking tape around the bottom of the hosel for protection from filing. With a medium cut file, begin filing only around the bottom of the ferrule, reducing its diameter to match the top of the hosel. It is not customary to file the top of a putter ferrule flush to the shaft, so do not file the top of

14

the ferrule. Take extreme care not to scratch the hosel when filing (because the procedures for ferrule filing are identical to those used for ironheads, refer to Chapter 8 for a complete discussion of the procedures to be used).

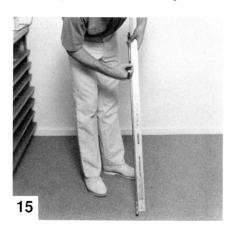

15

STEP 15: Measure and mark the desired playing length
Place the putter on the floor in the playing position, taking care not to rock the club either up on the toe or back on its heel. Slide a 48" ruler up behind the shaft, and carefully mark the desired playing length with a felt tip marker on the butt end of the shaft. The heel design of many putters may not allow sliding the ruler right up against the back of the shaft. In these cases, holding the ruler to the side of the shaft will be the measuring method

to use. Be sure to allow for the effect that the 1/8" thickness of the end of the grip will have on the club's playing length by marking the shafts 1/8" shorter than what is desired (e.g.- If a true 35" putter length is desired, the mark should be made at 34 7/8", for a 35 1/2" putter length, mark the shaft at 35 3/8", etc.).

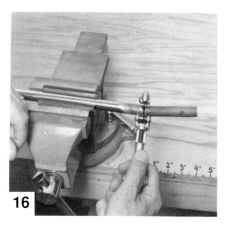

16

STEP 16: Cut the shaft to its desired playing length
Using the proper cutting procedure for the type of shaft being used, trim the shaft from the butt end for its playing length. Always deburr and square off the shaft butt after trimming to remove sharp edges. If a graphite or composite type shaft has been installed, use an abrasive cut-off wheel or a grit edged hack saw blade to trim the shaft, **never** a tubing cutter.

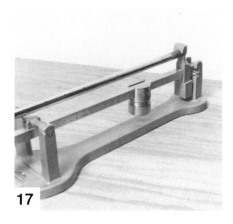

17

STEP 17: Record preliminary swingweight
Swingweight is often ignored when assembling putters. For a club that is used so often during a round of golf, time should be allowed to check and establish a playable swingweight. Follow the same procedures established in checking the preliminary swingweight of all other clubs by placing the club on a 14" fulcrum (Lorythmic or Prorythmic type) swingweight scale.

■ **REMEMBER:** Do **not** butt the ungripped shaft completely against the back of the scale. Since the grip cap will provide the final 1/8" of club length, pull the butt 1/8" away from the end of the scale before recording swingweight.

Example:

Preliminary
Swingweight (E-0)

– Swingweight
Equivalent of Grip (10SW)
_____

Initial
Swingweight (D-0)

18

STEP 18: Subtract the swingweight equivalent of the grip from the ungripped putter's preliminary swingweight to determine the <u>initial swingweight</u>
The swingweight of the ungripped putter will be higher than with the grip installed, by the amount equivalent to the weight of the grip and its foundation tape. To determine what the club's swingweight will be once the grip is installed, subtract 10 swingweight points for a standard men's size rubber putter grip, 11 points for a paddle style leather grip and @ 15 points for an extra large putter grip such as the Tiger Shark model. (e.g.-An ungripped club with a swingweight of E-0, scheduled for installation with most Men's rubber putter grips will make the gripped clubs initial swingweight D-0).

■ **NOTE: For alternative swingweight method**
Rather than use grip weight estimations to calculate the club's initial swingweight, clubmakers may wish to temporarily install a putter grip of the type eventually to be used. Keep a few grips in your shop (Paddle, Grip Rite, etc.) that have been cut lengthwise with a knife or scissors to slide on the shaft for simulating the weight of the grip. By using cut grips mounted temporarily on the shaft, you will get an accurate estimation of what the club's initial swingweight will be when you place the club on the swingweight scale. Subtract 1 more swingweight point for every three layers of build-up tape to be used.

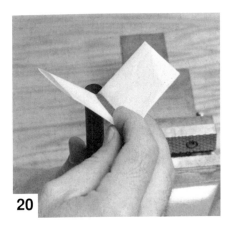

20

Example:

**Desired
Swingweight (D-2)**

**– Initial
Swingweight (D-0)**

Amount to Add (2SW)

19

STEP 19: Calculate the swingweight increase needed to establish the final desired swingweight
Once the club's initial swingweight has been determined (STEPS 17 and 18) subtract that swingweight from the customer's desired final swingweight to determine what amount of weight to add to the head (e.g.-Initial swingweight of D-0; desired swingweight of D-3; amount to add=3 swingweight points).

STEP 20: Increase swingweight to final level
If no weight port is present, which is the case with most putter heads, or if the capacity of the weight port is not sufficient for the final needs of the club, add the final amount down the shaft, using lead powder only. When the proper level is achieved, tamp a cork down the shaft

to secure the weight. For woods and irons, it was recommended not to add more than 5 swingweight points down the shaft. However, this rule is not quite as critical to follow when building putters. Because the vertical position of the center of gravity is not quite as important with respect to playability in putters, additions of up to 8 points down the shaft will be OK. However, if the headweight is so low as to require 10 or more points down the shaft, this addition can have the effect of moving the CG (sweet spot) too close to the heel of the putter, thus confusing the golfer when he/she lines up and strokes the putt. Still, if the golfer accepts this and simply lines up and plays the ball in back of the altered sweet spot, no unfavorable playability results will take place. **This is the only deviation in the 5-Swingweight Point Rule that is acceptable in clubmaking.**

■ **NOTE:** Because adding weight to putters is similar to adding weight to ironheads, a complete discussion of the precise steps involved in adding weight to putters can be found in Chapter 8, STEPS 24-27.

STEP 21: Apply grip tape (and leather grip collar if needed)
Secure the putter in the bench vise with the head positioned toe up and apply any required build-up tape and the 2-way foundation tape. If a leather grip is to be installed it will require a plastic grip collar. If the collar has not already been put on during the installation of the

21

shaft, slide it on over the shaft butt. Installing a grip collar from the butt end of the shaft requires a little practice but can easily be accomplished if the grip collar size used is one shaft size larger than the shaft butt. For example, use a .620" size grip collar on a .600" butt diameter shaft, a .600" collar on a .580" shaft, etc. A complete step-by-step procedure for grip collar and leather grip installation can be found in Chapter 4.

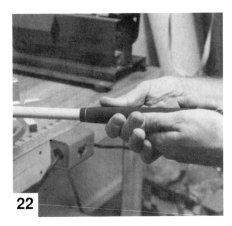

22

STEP 22: Install grip and final check swingweight
After wetting the 2-way grip tape and the inside of the grip with grip solvent, install and properly line up the grip. After installation, check to be sure the grip is completely seated against the shaft butt and clean up the tape residue that will be present at the mouth of the grip.

Because most putter grips have a very distinctive alignment aid, take time to carefully line up the grip. Immediately put the club back on the swingweight scale to double check your work, now making sure the butt of the grip is pushed against the end of the scale. If the swingweight is incorrect, the grip adhesive from the tape should still be wet enough to allow you to pull off the grip and correct the problem. Once the grip is lined up properly, install a protective plastic grip bag held in place with a wrap of thin masking tape. Covering the grip not only adds a professional touch, but will protect the grip from soiling during the club's remaining time in your shop. **The complete step-by-step procedures for all types of grip installation and sizing are covered in Chapter 4.**

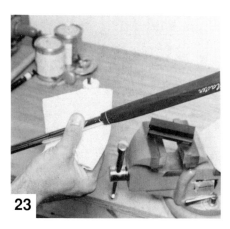

23

STEP 23: Clean up, install the shaft label and check the club for proper specifications
The club is now completed. Before the job is fully done, inspect the putter one last time to clean up any soiling of the head, grip and shaft and check all specifications for accuracy. Finally, install a plastic head bag for protection and apply any necessary shaft labels in the proper place on the shaft. The golf industry standard position for shaft labels is between the second and third step down below the mouth of the grip, with the label centered between steps, insignia facing up.

CHAPTER 10 - Common Custom Clubmaking Alterations & Procedures

Woodhead Loft Alteration
Calculating Swingweight From Known Component Parts
Woodhead Face Angle and Lie Alterations
Woodhead Soleplate Removal and Swingweight Alteration
Woodhead Weight Port Installation
Installation of String Whipping
Ironhead Loft and Lie Alterations
The Relationship of Swingweight and Balance Point
Changing Bore Diameter and Hosel Beveling

When Standard Procedures and Specifications Are Not Enough

The previous chapters of *The Modern Guide to Golf Clubmaking* have carefully outlined all of the procedures of standard golf club assembly. While most clubmakers will devote the majority of their time to the practice of building standard sets of golf clubs, the real advantage to learning the skills of clubmaking is to be able to assemble and offer sets of clubs built to the individual golfer's custom specifications.

In today's market, the major golf club manufacturers are not organized and designed to be able to satisfy golfers' requests for golf clubs that have been tailored to meet the unique and various needs of their games. Virtually all major manufacturers have set up their production lines to supply sets made only to standard specifications. To offer sets of clubs made to custom specifications would require the major manufacturers to deviate too much

from their large scale, mass-production assembly lines and would cause the price of their golf clubs to rise even higher. As a result, small clubmaking firms and individual golf club builders are in the best position to meet the ever-growing call for custom-made clubs. Their ability to deal with sets of clubs on a set-by-set basis affords them the time necessary to make the various alterations that can satisfy the discerning player and garner more sales.

The skills required to perform alterations to component heads require some practice to master, but when learned, will open the door to expanding any clubmaker's business. In this chapter are outlined many of the most commonly requested custom alterations for both wood and ironheads, each illustrated in comprehensive step-by-step form in the following pages.

Woodhead Loft Alteration

Offering custom changes of the loft angle of woodheads is the most significant way to change the shot trajectory, and potentially the distance any golfer can achieve with his/her clubs. Of the four most common material types of woodheads, persimmon, laminated maple, stainless steel and graphite, only the stainless steel metal woods cannot be altered for loft. Because the face of investment cast woodheads is very thin, material cannot be removed to make a change in the loft. Should custom loft angle changes be necessary in a metal wood, the clubmaker must purchase a head with the desired loft engineered into the face.

When altering the loft of persimmon and laminated maple woodheads, it is much easier and far more cost effective to perform the change on unfinished heads. However, because most custom wooden and graphite wood clubs are assembled from pre-finished heads, should clubmakers wish to change the loft angle, it will be necessary for clubmakers to learn how to execute the loft change and then restore the finish. Therefore, the following section illustrating the procedures of altering wooden and graphite woodhead loft will cover the skills necessary for working on both unfinished and finished heads. **In all cases, it is not recommended to alter the loft through material removal from the face more than 2° stronger or weaker.**

■ CHANGING LOFT ANGLE ON PRE-FINISHED WOODEN AND GRAPHITE WOODHEADS

■ **NOTE:** The procedures for altering loft and restoring the head finish are virtually the same for all types of wooden and graphite woodheads. For ease of explanation, the procedures that follow have been illustrated using a persimmon woodhead.

1

STEP 1: Measure the existing loft angle of the woodhead
The loft of a woodhead is defined as the angle between the sole and the face, as measured between the center of

the sole and a point on the face referenced at half the vertical face height. To measure loft, place one arm of a standard protractor flat across the center of the sole and adjust the protractor scale so that it makes contact with the face at precisely half the vertical face height. The loft angle is read in degrees as compared to the 90° mark on the protractor scale.

■ **NOTE:** For woodheads with a 4-way radius sole, position the protractor arm so that it touches the center of the sole.

STEP 2: Measure existing horizontal face bulge and vertical face roll
When changing woodhead loft, it is important to retain the head's original face curvatures, the horizontal bulge and the vertical roll. Recording an accurate measurement will enable you to retain both of the face curvatures during the loft changing procedure. Bulge and roll are expressed in inches of radius and are measured through the use of specially-made face radius gauges.

2A

STEP 2A: Measure horizontal bulge
Three different face radius gauges are offered by most clubmaking suppliers. The gauge with 8", 10", 12" and 14" radii cut into the sides is the most commonly used tool for measuring roll and bulge. First use the 8/10/12/14 face radius gauge to check for the horizontal curvature, bulge. Hold the club at eye level as pictured and

position the gauge across the face from toe to heel. Move the gauge up and down the face, alternating each radius on the gauge to the horizontal curvature of the wood's face until you discover which radius most closely matches the bulge. Note this reading.

2B

STEP 2B: Measure vertical roll
Using the same procedure, compare the various gauge radii to the up and down face curvature of the woodhead. Note the radius that most closely matches the vertical roll of the woodhead.

■ **NOTE:** The most common specifications for roll and bulge are listed below, with each standard dimension listed in inches of radius:

Clubhead	1	3	4	5	7
Roll	10/12"	12"	12"	14"	14"
Bulge	8/10"	10"	10"	12"	12"

STEP 3: Secure woodhead in vise
Secure the woodhead in the bench vise with the face up between urethane or wood/felt vise pads. Make sure that the clubface protrudes above the top of the vise jaws to

3

prevent the file from contacting the vise during the filing procedures.

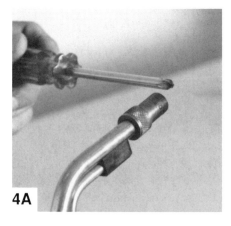

4A

STEP 4A: Prepare to remove insert screws (if present) Method #1 - Heat transfer by screwdriver

Increasing or decreasing the loft of a wooden or graphite woodhead involves filing top or bottom of the face. If face insert screws are present on the woodhead, filing the face will greatly reduce the diameter of one or more of the screws, thus creating an undesirable look on the club. Therefore, before changing loft it will be necessary to remove each of the face insert screws. Most face insert screws are epoxied in place, so they must be heated to loosen the epoxy bond before any attempt is made to turn them out with a screwdriver. There are two very common

methods for applying heat to the screw. Method #1 is to heat an **old** screwdriver red hot with a propane torch and insert it in the head of each screw for the purpose of transferring heat through the body of the screw to break the epoxy bond. Depending upon the amount of epoxy used to secure the screws, as many as 4-5 applications of heat may be required for each screw.

■ **NOTE: Always** use an **old** screwdriver for this purpose. After heating then rotate the screws out with a new screwdriver.

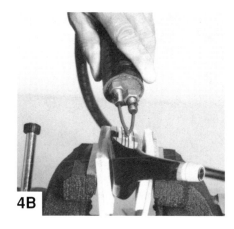

4B

STEP 4B: Prepare to remove insert screws (if present) Method #2 - Heat transfer by electric screw heater

The fastest method for heating the insert screws is to use an electric screw heater. For the screw heater's electrodes to make contact with the screw, it is recommended to file the finish off the top of the screw, thus exposing bare metal to the electrodes. Touching the electrode tips to the head of the screw will very quickly heat each screw and loosen the epoxy. With most woodheads, no longer than 3-4 seconds of heating will be required.

■ **NOTE:** Care must be taken not to leave the electrodes on the screw head too long or heat damage to the insert surrounding the screw will result. With Cycolac or plastic face inserts, it is common for a small part of the insert surrounding the screw to soften from the heat applied. As long as care is taken to avoid overheating, the

insert will not be damaged permanently and normal filing upon reinstallation of the screws will smooth out the softened areas of the insert.

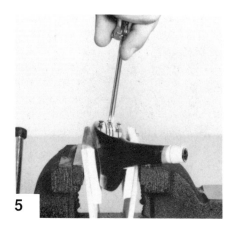

5

STEP 5: Remove the insert screws

After heating all of the insert screws, select the proper screwdriver and rotate each screw out . You may discard these screws as it will be much easier to install new ones after the loft change has been made. Note the drawings below that illustrate the difference between a Reed/Prince and a Phillips style screw head. Before rotating the screws out of the insert, be sure to check and use the proper screwdriver to match the screw head.

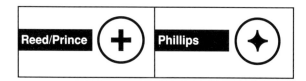

STEP 6A: File face to change loft - increasing loft

Increasing the loft of a woodhead requires filing material from the top three quarters of the face for the purpose of changing the degree reading of loft higher in number. In other words, an example of increasing loft would be to change a Driver from 11° to 13°. Use a medium cutting file for fast material removal and begin filing from three quarters of the way down the insert, up to the top of the insert. Use a radiusing motion when filing, taking care to retain the head's original bulge and roll specifications

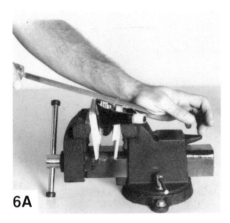

6A

while the loft is being increased. Using a radiusing motion with the file while you increase loft will help in the task of retaining face curvatures.

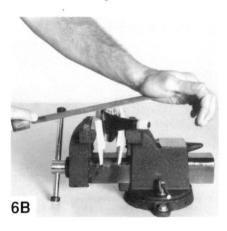

6B

STEP 6B: Filing to change loft - decreasing loft

Decreasing the loft of a woodhead requires filing material from the bottom three quarters of the face to change the degree reading of loft lower in number. In other words, an example of decreasing loft would be to change a Driver from 11° to 9°. Use a medium cut file for fast material removal and begin filing from three quarters of the way up the insert down to the very bottom of the insert. File across the face from toe to heel using a radiusing motion with the file, taking care to retain the head's original bulge and roll specifications while the

loft is being decreased. Using a radiusing motion with the file will help in the task of retaining face curvatures.

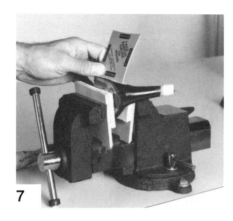

7

STEP 7: Check loft, bulge and roll periodically during the filing procedure

After you have removed what you judge to be a moderate amount from the proper portion of the face, stop and perform loft, bulge and roll specification checks. Reaching the final loft usually consists of repeated steps of filing, checking, filing, etc., until the final desired specs are achieved.

■ **NOTE:** If you have never performed a loft change, be sure to practice on older woodheads before attempting the procedure on a new clubhead.

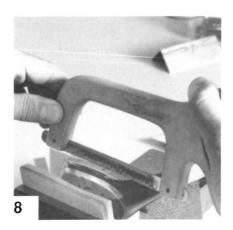

8

STEP 8: Recut the score lines

Changing loft will usually remove enough material from the face that the scoring lines will have to be recut to achieve their original depth. Use a specially-made scoring saw or hacksaw that has a blade without what is called **set** on the cutting teeth. **Set** is defined as a flaring out of the teeth of the blade which makes the actual width of the cut wider than the thickness of the blade, and is not desired on scoring saws for woodheads. Face scoring saws without set are available from various clubmaking supply companies.

9

STEP 9: Recountersink the insert screw holes

Filing to change loft will also reduce the diameter of the countersinking for the insert screws. If the face insert is made of a hard material such as fiber, metal or phenolic resin, use a standard countersink in an electric drill to restore the screw's original countersinking. If the insert material is made from plastic or epoxy resin, it is recommended to do the job holding the countersink between the fingers and simply rotating it in the hole. This will prevent the mistake of countersinking the hole too large.

STEP 10: Install <u>new</u> insert screws

Most face insert screws are a #4 size brass screw that is 5/8" or 1/2" long. When installed, new screws will protrude slightly up from the surface of the face. Filing performed after installation will reduce the screws flush to the surface of the insert. For appearance sake, rotate

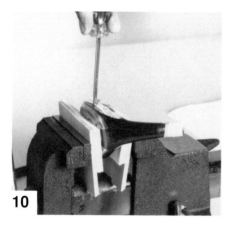

10

the screws down with the cross slots of each screw head identically aligned to each other. A dab of epoxy placed on the tip of each screw before installation will ensure that the screws will not come loose at a later date.

■ **NOTE:** Brass insert screws are fragile and must **not** be over-rotated too tight or the head will break off. During installation, if the screw begins to exhibit even a slight amount of resistance, remove it and redrill the hole to relieve the pressure. For a #4 brass screw, the pilot drill size of choice is 3/32".

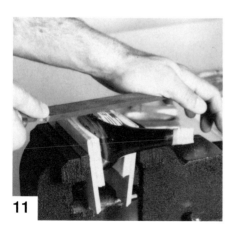

11

STEP 11: Fine file the insert screws flush to the face
Use a fine cutting file to remove the protruding screw

head, thus bringing the level of the new screws flush to the face. Again, use a radiusing motion with the file, moving in a direction across the face. This procedure should remove the scratches left on the insert from the medium file that was used to change the loft.

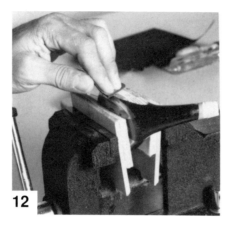

12

STEP 12: Sand out scratches with sandpaper
Finish the job by sanding across the entire face and face insert with 100 or 120 grit equivalent sandpaper. This step is performed to further remove scratches left by filing. Finish by brushing all dust and material shavings off the face.

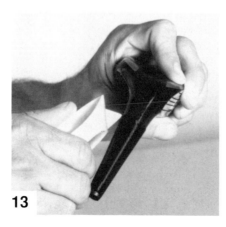

13

STEP 13: Remove whipping (if present)
Loft changes are recommended to be performed before

the woodhead is assembled, in which case there will usually not be whipping already present on the hosel. However, if the woodhead is pre-whipped, or if the loft change is being made after the club was whipped, the whipping should be removed before finish coat application. This will prevent the polyurethane from accumulating in between the strands of whipping.

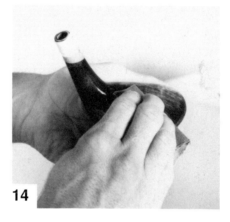

14

STEP 14: 400 sand entire head
Prepare the head for the urethane application by sanding the **entire head** with 400 grit finishing sandpaper.

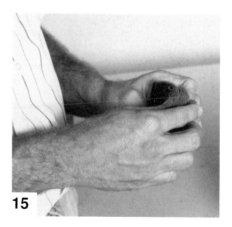

15

STEP 15: Steel wool buff the finished portion of the head
Blend out the fine scratches of the 400 sandpaper on the

head by steel wool buffing the finished portion of the head only. **DO NOT steel wool the unfinished face of wooden heads or the wood may become darkened.**

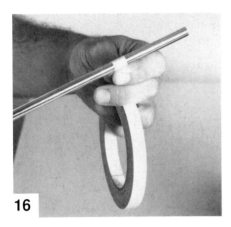

16

STEP 16: Insert a shaft into the hosel for purposes of holding the club during the finish application procedures

If the loft changes are being made on the component woodhead **before** the club is assembled, you will need to insert a shaft into the head for purpose of holding the head during the dipping (or spraying) and drying procedures. If the shaft fits loosely in the hosel, wrap a layer of masking tape around the shaft tip to allow it to fit tight in the hosel.

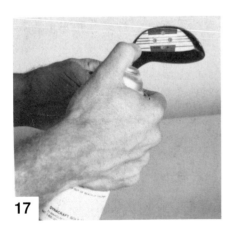

17

STEP 17: Apply primer sealer to the face

If the loft change is being performed on a pre-finished head, you will now have a woodhead with its full finish on all surfaces except the face. Use aerosol primer sealer to spray a medium thick coating over the face only. Do not worry if any of the primer sealer is oversprayed on the rest of the head. After application, set the club aside to dry for 1 hour.

18

STEP 18: Dip entire head in polyurethane

Attach a drip catcher or small rolled piece of paper towel above the ferrule to deflect the excess polyurethane from running down the shaft. Using the same techniques outlined in Chapter 5 (STEPS 56-59), dip the first of two finish coats over the entire head. If using the oil-modified polyurethane, set the club aside to dry for 2 hours. If using a moisture cure type polyurethane, set the club aside to dry for at least 24 hours at room temperature (more than 70° F) or 12 hours if force dried at 100°F.

STEP 19: Dip second coat of polyurethane

If using the oil modified polyurethane, do not sand the head but proceed right after the 2 hour dry period into dipping coat #2. If using the moisture cure polyurethane, 400 sand and steel wool the head before dipping coat #2.

19

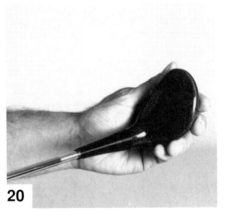

20

STEP 20: Proceed with assembly procedures

After the second polyurethane coat the loft change procedure is complete. Therefore, if the loft was changed on the woodhead before assembly, you may proceed into the actual assembly procedures as outlined for finished heads in Chapter 5. If the alteration for loft was performed on a fully built club, the procedure is completed by smoothing the hosel and installing the whipping.

■ CHANGING LOFT ANGLE ON UNFINISHED WOODHEADS

The initial procedures for altering the loft on unfinished woodheads are exactly the same as outlined for the pre-finished heads. Follow STEPS 1-11 for changing loft that were outlined previously in this section and then finish the head using the steps illustrated in Chapter 5 for finish application.

Calculating Swingweight From Known Component Parts

There is nothing more frustrating than to spend the time required to assemble a set of clubs only to discover the swingweight is much higher or lower than what is desired in the finished clubs. Because building golf clubs to precise swingweights is a prerequisite of quality clubmaking, it is very important for clubmakers to gain the ability to accurately predict the swingweight of any club before it is assembled. The following information will allow you to apply and compare known specifications of components to closely estimate the initial swingweight of the golf clubs.

■ FACTORS CONTROLLING SWINGWEIGHT

There are now recognized five distinct factors in clubmaking that combine to determine the swingweight of a golf club:
1. **The Weight of the Clubhead**
2. **The Length of the Club**
3. **The Weight of the Grip and Grip Tape**
4. **The Weight of the Shaft**
5. **The Balance Point of the Shaft**

1. The Weight of the Clubhead

One of the most difficult tasks for a clubhead designer is not to invent a design that is playable, but to decide what the finished weights of each of the clubheads should be. Knowing that clubmakers are called upon to build golf clubs to a variety of different swingweights, the clubhead designer must choose a series of finished clubhead weights that will satisfy the greatest majority of clubmaking circumstances. Despite the fact clubmakers are called upon to build sets of golf clubs to lengths that are longer or shorter than standard, with grips that are installed to a variety of different sizes, swingweights that

range from C-0 to E-0, all with a variety of different weight shafts, the clubhead designer just cannot create one series of clubhead weights that will satisfy all of the clubmakers' needs. Instead, he has to recognize that even though custom building is popular, the majority of clubs built from component parts are going to be assembled to standard lengths with standard size grips, and assembled with standard weight or medium lightweight steel shafts.

With this in mind, component clubhead designers will ordinarily select a series of headweights which will result in finished clubs with an initial swingweight of approximately C-9 to D-0, when the heads are built into golf clubs at standard lengths with standard size grips and standard weight shafts. Experienced component clubhead designers try to keep finished headweights at a level that will leave the initial swingweight of the assembled club slightly lower than the golf industry's standard final swingweight range of D-1 to D-2. This is because adding weight to a clubhead is always easier than having to remove weight. Therefore, when a designer issues instructions for the production of a set of clubheads, taking the head manufacturer's plus or minus finished weight tolerances into account, the clubheads will still result in initial swingweights that are equal to or slightly below the industry's standard ranges of swingweight.

With the recent growth in popularity of graphite shafts, the business of designing clubheads that will satisfy all of the swingweight needs of clubmakers has been complicated even further. Due to the very light nature of graphite shafts when compared to the weight of the most popular steel shafts, standard weight clubheads will simply not allow the clubmaker to achieve standard ranges of swingweight, unless the heads have been produced with an adequate weight cavity for making final swingweight adjustments. Despite the fact that more and more heads with weight ports are becoming available, and the fact that special "graphite weighted" clubheads are available for clubmakers, this still does not take into account what could happen to swingweight should the clubmaker choose to also build the set to a

custom length or with an oversize grip.

In the field of clubhead design, finished clubhead weights are always expressed in grams. Following is an example of just how an average set of clubheads might be designed for headweight:

Example Chart of Finished Clubhead Weights	
Clubhead	**Finished Weight (in Grams)**
1w	198g[1]
2w	203g
3w	208g
4w	213g
5w	218g
7w	228g
1i	230g
2i	237g
3i	244g
4i	251g
5i	258g
6i	265g
7i	272g
8i	279g
9i	286g
Pitching wedge	293g
Sand wedge	305g
Utility (60°) wedge	298g

[1]All head weights to be produced to a weight tolerance of +2g and -4g.

Because clubmakers are familiar with the approximation that 2 grams of headweight is equivalent to 1 swingweight point, the manufacturer's ± tolerance in headweight can also be expressed as +1 swingweight point and -2 swingweight points. For clarification it must be stated that serious clubmakers know from testing that 2 grams does not precisely equal 1 swingweight point in all clubs. Because of the accepted presence of progressive length changes within sets of golf clubs, the longer the club, the less actual weight is required to achieve 1 swingweight point and the shorter the club and the more actual weight is required to equal 1 swingweight point. Precisely speaking, for a golf club of 38.75" in playing length, 2 grams = 1 swingweight point. For clubs longer than 38.75", a little less than 2 grams = 1 swingweight point and for clubs shorter than 38.75", a little more than 2 grams = 1 swingweight point. Still, for purposes of calculating swingweight before assembly, an assumption of 2 grams = 1 swingweight point will be made. Hence the first precept for calculating swingweight before assembly can be made:

For every increase in headweight of 2g, the swingweight will increase by 1 point, and for every decrease in headweight of 2g, the swingweight will decrease by 1 point.

2. The Length of the Club

Clubhead weight has no relevance to swingweight unless it is accompanied by a specification for club length. In clubmaking it is currently an accepted practice for the clubs within a set of woods and irons to change in length by 1/2" increments. This progression of length is one of the factors that accounts for the fact that the various clubs within the set will hit shots that achieve different distances.

At the same time, it is also an accepted practice in clubmaking to build each of the clubs except the pitching wedge and sand wedge to the same identical swingweight. Since lengths progressively change within a set while remaining constant in swingweight, the weight of each head has to change from club to club. To further express this weight to length relationship, if a set of clubs were made to identical lengths with identical swingweights, the head weights for each club would have to be the same. In 1988, the Tommy Armour Golf Company introduced such a model, the EQL, in which the woods were all built to the length of a #5-wood and the irons all built to the length of a #6-iron. As could be deduced from this reasoning, to achieve a constant swingweight at such common lengths, the EQL woodheads were all made to

one identical weight and the EQL irons to another.

Following is a chart which illustrates the relationship that headweight and playing length have on the swingweight of a golf club:

Effect of Club Length on Swingweight					
Club	Head Weight	Shaft Weight	Swingweight at		
			38 1/2"	39"	39 1/2"
2i	236g	4.37oz	C-7	D-0	D-3
2i	236g	4.00oz	C-5.5	C-8.5	D-1.5
2i	236g	3.00oz	B-9	C-2	C-5

The above examples illustrate the effect of club length on swingweight, given the same headweight and shaft weight. As depicted in the chart, for every change in length of 1/2", the swingweight will change by 3 swingweight points. This is because as length is changed while all other factors remain constant, the mass of the head and all other weight forward of the swingweight scale's fulcrum point is changed with respect to the position of the scale's fulcrum point. As a result, the next assumption that can be made to assist in calculating swingweight is:

For every increase in length of 1/2", swingweight will increase by 3 points, and for every decrease in length of 1/2", the swingweight will decrease by 3 points.

3. The Weight of the Grip and Grip Tape

Another clubmaking factor that controls the swingweight of a golf club is the weight of the grip, along with the weight of any build-up tape used to increase its size. In Chapter 4, it was revealed that the different styles of grips range widely in weight as a result of their material composition and core size. For example, charts published in Chapter 4 illustrate that the difference in weight between a Jumbo Victory grip made by Eaton Golf Pride and a conventional M62 core size men's rubber grip is

1/2oz (14g). Add to that the fact that clubmakers are often called upon to install grips to oversized dimensions through the application of multiple layers of build-up tape on the shaft butt and it is possible to see that the weight of the grip can vary quite dramatically.

From a swingweight standpoint, 4 grams of weight on the grip end of the scale is roughly equivalent to 1 swingweight point. However, because the grip is on the opposite end of the scale than the head, the effect of a weight difference in the grip is opposite to that of the head. Therefore, the third assumption that can be expressed to assist in the calculation of swingweight before assembly is:

For every 4 grams the weight of the grip is increased, the swingweight of the golf club will decrease by 1 swingweight point. For every 4 grams the weight of the grip is decreased, the swingweight of the golf club will increase by 1 point.

4. The Weight of the Shaft

The list of finished clubhead weights presented earlier in this discussion, along with club length and grip weight would also be meaningless with regard to calculating the swingweight of a golf club unless the weight of the shaft is included.

Often overlooked by clubmakers in their calculation of swingweight, yet another very important factor in dictating the swingweight of a golf club is the weight of the shaft. As mentioned in Chapter 3, there can now be described four basic shaft types (weight classifications) that are created in the shaft manufacturing industry. Those four types of shafts and their approximate accepted weight ranges are listed as follows:

Shaft Type	Weight Range
Standard Weight	4.25 - 4.62oz (120g - 132g)
Medium Light Weight	3.80 - 4.24oz (109g - 120g)
Very Light Weight[1]	3.4 - 3.79oz (99g - 109g)
Ultra Light Weight[2]	2.0 - 3.6oz (57g - 99g)

[1]Very light weight shafts are most often steel with a few graphite/composite patterns.

[2]Ultra light weight shafts are virtually all graphite/composite patterns.

As many clubmakers have realized after assembling clubs with very light shafts, shaft weight plays a very important role in establishing a club's swingweight. Referring to the following chart, if a club is assembled using each of the four shaft types, the swingweight will be greatly affected.

Effect of Shaft Weight on Swingweight

Club	Head Weight	Shaft Weight	Swingweight at Standard Length[1]
2i	236g	4.37oz	D-0
2i	236g	4.00oz	C-8.5
2i	236g	3.75oz	C-7
2i	236g	3.00oz	C-2

[1]Standard length defined as 39" for the #2 iron

From the above chart it can be seen that given the same headweight and length, different weight shafts will create golf clubs that result in different swingweights. In most cases as shaft weight decreases, so will the club's swingweight. Explained earlier in Chapter 3, this is because on a Lorythmic swingweight scale with 14" fulcrum, almost two-thirds of the shaft lies in front of the fulcrum point. Therefore, all weight lying forward of the fulcrum will be counted as headweight and all weight lying in back of the scale's fulcrum will be counted as grip weight. When a change is made from a heavy to a light shaft, more weight loss is experienced in front of the fulcrum due to the fact that two-thirds of the shaft was lying in front of the fulcrum. Therefore, it can be seen that a decrease in shaft weight will create almost the same effect on swingweight as will a decrease in headweight. Hence, as shaft weight decreases, so does the swingweight.

In the task of calculating swingweight before assembly, it will be necessary for you to know the approximate weight of the shaft being used. This information can be found in the charts of shaft patterns found between pages 145-171 in Chapter 3. Establishing a correlation between the amount of shaft weight change and swingweight is very difficult because the weight of most shafts may or may not be distributed evenly over the entire shaft length. Unlike headweight or grip weight, where the component is on one end or the other of the swingweight scale, a change in shaft weight is reflected over the entire length of the shaft. Therefore, some weight change occurs on both sides of the swingweight scale's fulcrum point. As a result it is difficult to say with any precise level of accuracy that a change of x-number of grams of shaft weight is exactly equivalent to y-swingweight points. Despite this fact, the following point can be made to help clubmakers incorporate shaft weight within their calculation of swingweight:

In general, for a shaft weight change of 9 grams, the swingweight will change by 1 point. In other words, an increase in shaft weight of 9g will increase the swingweight by 1 point, and a decrease in shaft weight of 9g will lower the swingweight by 1 point.

5. The Balance Point of the Shaft

Recent developments in shaft design have enabled shaft manufacturers to create shafts that vary in the distribution of the shaft's weight over its length. Prior to this development in shaft design, virtually all shafts were produced with an even distribution of weight. For example, the original Dynamic shaft from True Temper was produced such that the balance point of the raw uncut shaft was located in the exact center of the shaft. In other words, if the Dynamic shaft were to be cut in half, both the tip and the butt halves would weigh the same; if it was cut into thirds, each of the three equal length sections would weigh the same, and so on. The accepted manner of manufacturing shafts for decades, such shafts were said to possess standard weight distribution and were characterized as having a center-located balance point.

With such standard weight distribution shafts, it could always be said that as shaft weight decreased so too would the swingweight of golf clubs built with the lighter shafts. Hence if a clubmaker was faced with building a set of clubs with a very light weight shaft with a center-located balance point, he would automatically know that the initial swingweight of the set would be lower than a set built with a standard weight shaft.

With the advent of shafts such as True Temper's Gold Plus, clubmakers could no longer assume that swingweight would decrease as shaft weight decreased. One of the unique design features of the Gold Plus is its "tip heavy" design. Said by the company to be a feature contributing to better accuracy, "tip heavy" means that the shaft has been designed with a balance point located on the tip side of shaft center. In turn, a balance point located on the tip side of shaft center indicates that the tip half of the shaft has been intentionally designed to weigh more than the butt half.

With more weight in the tip half of the shaft than the butt, when a club with such a shaft is placed on the swingweight scale more of the shaft's weight will count as headweight, and will in turn have the effect of keeping the swingweight higher than what might ordinarily be thought for such a lighter overall weight shaft.

Again, the five factors that control the swingweight of any golf club are Headweight, Club Length, Grip Weight, Shaft Weight and Shaft Weight Distribution (Balance Point). For easy reference, the following table is offered to further explain the effect each of these factors will have on swingweight :

Table 10A
Effect of Headweight, Shaft Weight, Club Length and Grip Weight On Swingweight

Swingweight Change	Increase Factor by	FACTOR	Decrease Factor by	Swingweight Change
+ 1	2 grams	Headweight	2 grams	- 1
+ 3	1/2 inch	Club Length	1/2 inch	- 3
- 1	4 grams	Grip Weight	4 grams	+ 1
+ 1*	9 grams	Shaft Weight	9 grams	- 1*

* The shaft swingweight equivalent of shaft weight is for estimation purposes only. Unlike the other three factors, as shaft weight changes, its effect on swingweight changes at a disproportionate rate. However, for estimation purposes only, the above shaft weight to swingweight equivalent is acceptable.

Table 10B
Swingweight As Determined From Standard Component Specifications for Headweight, Shaft Weight, Club Length and Grip Weight

Club	Headweight	Raw Shaft Weight	Grip Weight	Club Length	Swingweight
1 wood	198 grams	125 grams[1]	52 grams[2]	43"	D-0
3 wood	208 grams	125 grams	52 grams	42"	D-0
4 wood	213 grams	125 grams	52 grams	41 1/2"	D-0
5 wood	218 grams	125 grams	52 grams	41"	D-0
7 wood	228 grams	125 grams	52 grams	40"	D-0
1 iron	230 grams	125 grams[1]	52 grams	39 1/2"	D-0
2 iron	237 grams	125 grams	52 grams	39"	D-0
3 iron	244 grams	125 grams	52 grams	38 1/2"	D-0
4 iron	251 grams	125 grams	52 grams	38"	D-0
5 iron	258 grams	125 grams	52 grams	37 1/2"	D-0
6 iron	265 grams	125 grams	52 grams	37"	D-0
7 iron	272 grams	125 grams	52 grams	36 1/2"	D-0
8 iron	279 grams	125 grams	52 grams	36"	D-0
9 iron	286 grams	125 grams	52 grams	35 1/2"	D-0
PW[3]	293 grams	125 grams	52 grams	35 1/2"	D-3
SW[3]	305 grams	125 grams	52 grams	35 1/2"	D-6

[1] Raw shaft weight is based on a 45" UDWS (parallel tip Dynamic S-flex for woods) and a 39" UDIS (parallel tip Dynamic S-flex for irons). Under proper trimming and installation, each shaft's weight will drop slightly through the set.

[2] Grip weight is based on an average weight of an M58 Men's Victory rubber grip. Despite the fact the UDWC and UDIC both posses a .600" butt diameter, most clubmakers purchase M58 grips. Therefore, the table for comparison will be compiled based on an M58 rubber grip.

[3] Traditionally, the pitching wedge and sand wedge are designed to be played at slightly to significantly higher swingweights than the #1-9 irons.

PRE-CALCULATING SWINGWEIGHT - A STANDARD FROM WHICH TO BEGIN

In clubmaking there are literally thousands of possible combinations of headweight, shaft weight, club length and grip weight that can be used to build golf clubs. To be able to estimate the swingweight resulting from a particular combination of components, it is necessary for clubmakers to have a standard combination of these factors from which to perform calculations for estimating swingweight. Regardless of whether you are building clubs to standard specifications, it is highly recommended to begin pre-calculating swingweight by weighing the clubheads, shafts and grips and compare them to the requested club length **before** beginning the assembly procedures.

Table 10B lists headweight, shaft weight, club length and grip weight for an example set of golf clubs to use as an initial guide for pre-calculating swingweight.

This table is offered to illustrate a standard for pre-calculating swingweight from known component weights and specifications. In other words, **Table 10B will become the constant against which you can use the information contained in Table 10A to determine the swingweight for any club you intend to assemble.** Here's how it works. Using the #2-ironhead as an example, Table B illustrates that a #2-iron with a headweight of 236 grams, when assembled with a shaft of 125 grams to a length of 39" and installed with a 52 gram grip will result in an initial swingweight of D-0. If ANY of the four factors are different than these standard measurements, the swingweight will change. How much will the change be? Refer back to Table A to determine the amount of change. Following the example, if the headweight of the #2-iron was 232 grams, but the shaft weight, grip weight and length were all the same as stated, the swingweight would be C-8 instead of D-0. Why? Because as Table A notes, the 4 gram decrease in headweight represents a 2 swingweight point decrease from the D-0 standard.

But why take the time to pre-weigh the components

before beginning the assembly? Shouldn't a clubmaker be able to order clubheads, shafts and grips and assume that if they are assembled to standard length they will result in standard swingweights?

Each of the component parts that make up a golf club are produced to specific weights. By contacting the clubhead supplier it is possible to find out what the gram weights of all their models may be. In addition, by referencing the information contained within books such as *The Modern Guide to Golf Clubmaking*, you can discover the stated weights for each of the various manufacturers' shafts and grips. Yet, even though such dimensions are accessible, it is very important to realize that each of the component parts of a golf club are produced with plus/minus tolerances for weight. For example, the highest quality clubheads in the golf industry are produced to specific weights with a tolerance of ±3 grams or + 2 grams/ - 4 grams. Comparing such normal plus/minus weight tolerances to the information in Table A, you will find that represents a ±1.5 swingweight variation for each head. In other words, going back to Table B for reference, if each of the clubheads were produced with a weight tolerance of ±3 grams, the swingweight could come out anywhere between C-8.5 and D-1.5.

While shafts are made to a variety of plus/minus weight tolerances depending on the particular pattern, a usual tolerance for the most popular shafts is ±5 grams. Compare that to the table and you can see that represents a swingweight tolerance of approximately ±1/2 point. Adding that to the plus/minus tolerance of the clubheads, we now can have clubs built with standard components that vary from C-8 to D-2.

Finally, grips also have a weight tolerance which generally averages ±3.5 grams for any rubber or cord style model. Since 4 grams of grip weight is equivalent to 1 swingweight point, we can add that tolerance to the cumulative clubhead and shaft tolerances and see that our standard club can now range in swingweight from C-7 to D-3. Add to that any mistakes that the club-

maker could make in trimming the shafts to playing length and this range of standard swingweight resulting from supposedly standard components becomes even larger.

This range in initial swingweight from C-7 to D-3 can occur from a combination of all of the components **that are each within their stated tolerance for weight!** Understand that **weight tolerances of ±3 grams for clubheads, ±5 grams for shafts and ±3.5 grams for grips are all considered to be representative of high quality manufacture within the golf industry.** Every single major golf club manufacturing company, no matter how large or how small, works within tolerances such as these. As a clubmaker you too will have to work within these tolerances. To buy components for clubmaking and expect that the swingweights for each club in the set will be exactly the same is not realistic. Getting into the habit of pre-calculating swingweight before assembly will be important and very helpful to the efficiency of your clubmaking.

To help understand how to pre-calculate swingweight of any golf club before it is assembled, use Tables A and B to understand the following examples.

EXAMPLE 1: Assemble a #3-iron with a UDIR shaft and an M60 Rubber grip to a length of 39". After weighing each of the components you record the following information:

Clubhead	Shaft	Grip	Length
245g	120g	46g	39"

STEP 1: Compare each factor to Table B to determine the deviation from standard.

Clubhead	Shaft	Grip	Length
+ 2g	- 5g	- 6g	+ 1/2"

STEP 2: Use Table A to determine each factor's deviation in swingweight points.

Clubhead	Shaft	Grip	Length
+ 1.0 sw	- 0.5 sw	+ 1.5 sw	+ 3.0 sw

STEP 3: Combine the swingweight equivalent changes and compare that to the D-0 swingweight standard from Table B.

Clubhead	+ 1.0 sw
Shaft	- 0.5 sw
Grip	+ 1.5 sw
Length	+ 3.0 sw
Net Change	**+ 5.0 sw over D-0 standard = D-5**

EXAMPLE 2: Assemble a #1-wood with a U2LWS shaft and an M62 Rubber grip to a length of 42 1/2". After weighing each of the components you record the following information:

Clubhead	Shaft	Grip	Length
195g	115g	48g	42 1/2"

STEP 1: Compare each factor to Table B to determine the deviation from standard.

Clubhead	Shaft	Grip	Length
- 3g	- 10g	- 4g	- 1/2"

STEP 2: Use Table A to determine each factor's deviation in swingweight points.

Clubhead	Shaft	Grip	Length
- 1.5 sw	- 1.0 sw	+ 1.0 sw	- 3.0 sw

STEP 3: Combine the swingweight equivalent changes and compare that to the D-0 standard from Table B.

Clubhead	- 1.5 sw
Shaft	- 1.0 sw
Grip	+ 1.0 sw
Length	- 3.0 sw
Net Change	**- 4.5 sw under D-0 standard = C-5.5**

EXAMPLE 3: Assemble a #5-iron with a UCV-304 R flex shaft and an M58 rubber grip to 37 3/4" length. After weighing each of the components you record the following information:

Clubhead	Shaft	Grip	Length
260g	96g	54g	37 3/4"

STEP 1: Compare each factor to Table B to determine the deviation.

Clubhead	Shaft	Grip	Length
+ 3g	- 29g	+ 2g	+ 1/4"

STEP 2: Use Table A to determine each factor's deviation in swingweight points.

Clubhead	Shaft	Grip	Length
+ 1.5 sw	- 3.2 sw	- 0.5 sw	+ 1.5 sw

STEP 3: Combine the swingweight equivalent changes and compare that to the D-0 standard from Table B.

Clubhead	+ 1.5 sw
Shaft	- 3.2 sw
Grip	- 0.5 sw
Length	+ 1.5 sw
Net Change	**- 0.7 sw under D-0 standard = C-9.3**

By following the previous examples, it is easy to see how to weigh heads, shafts and grips and compare them to club length to estimate swingweight. Obviously, to determine clubhead, shaft and grip weights you will need to have a gram weight scale. While at first this may seem to be an unnecessary expense for your shop, after understanding the value of being able to pre-calculate swingweight to predict any potential problems, the expense will be worthwhile.

Again, be aware that the described method for estimating swingweight prior to assembly is an approximation at best. Under real circumstances of clubmaking such factors as the headweight to swingweight and shaft weight to swingweight relationships are not perfectly proportional for all conditions. In addition, because the effect of shaft balance point depends upon the particular type of shaft trimming employed as well as other clubmaking factors, its effect on swingweight is not included in the numerical examples. To include the effect of shaft balance point in any pre-calculation of swingweight will require the clubmaker to know each particular shaft example as expressed in this discussion.

Woodhead Face Angle and Lie Alterations

The most professional way of offering assembled wooden clubs with custom changes in face angle and/or lie angle is to have the heads custom bored to the desired degree of face angle or lie change. However, many component clubhead suppliers do not offer this service, and for those that do, the delay in delivery of custom-bored woodheads is usually 8 weeks or more.

Yet even if every clubhead supplier did offer custom boring, golf industry statistics now indicate that stainless steel metal woods hold more than 80% of the total market share of woods. Because the face angle and lie of metal woods is not achieved through boring, but is rather cast as a part of the mold, it is not possible to change face angle or lie angle on a metal wood through custom boring.

Does that mean a golfer in search of a metal wood with a custom lie or face angle is out of luck? Fortunately some clubhead suppliers do cast a limited selection of metal woods with a different lie or face angle. While this is a great benefit to clubmakers, the custom face angle and lie options are not extensive and will not cover all custom fitting needs of golfers. So again, are golfers in need of a custom lie or face angle on metal woods left with no option?

In the early years of the metal woods' popularity, it was thought that altering the face angle or lie angle through bending the hosel was not possible. Virtually all stainless woods have been produced from 17-4 type stainless steel, a grade which after conventional heat treating was considered impossible to bend. Recently, techniques for changing these specifications on 17-4 stainless metal woods through bending have been developed which now allow clubmakers to offer a wide variety of customization on stainless woods.

The other woodhead type, graphite, brings an entirely different set of custom lie and face angle circumstances from the wooden or metal head types. While injection and compression-molded graphite woodheads are shaped like conventional wooden heads, their face angle and lie specifications are not achieved through boring, but rather through molding. Therefore when a mold for any type of graphite woodhead is constructed, its lie and face angle are virtually set as a permanent part of the mold. Since custom boring is not an option for changing the face angle or lie, the options for customizing graphite heads are limited.

■ WOODEN AND GRAPHITE WOODHEADS

There are a number of methods that have been employed by clubmakers over the years to change the existing face angle or lie of a persimmon, laminated maple or graphite woodhead. One method of changing face angle involves filing the face of the club, taking more material off either the toe or heel areas to change the direction that the face points with regard to the ground line. This method requires removing a substantial amount of material from the face to affect any real change in face angle and usually leaves the club's face insert noticeably thinner on one side, depending upon which side of the face has been filed. Because this method of altering face angle is time-consuming, cannot realistically achieve a change greater than 1°, plus leaves the club looking odd, face filing is **not** recommended as a procedure to use to change face angle.

While virtually unknown to modern clubmakers, another old-time method for changing the face angle of a wooden or graphite woodhead has been to sand or grind off a portion of the sole. By removing a portion of the sole located on the heel side near the face, the head could be made to sit more closed, and vice versa, by removing a portion of the sole located on the heel side near the back, the head could be made to sit more open. A method that sounds good at first, the problems involved with removing the soleplate, sanding, rerouting the soleplate cavity to fit the plate and refinishing the head far outweigh the possible benefits. As a result sanding the sole of a wooden or graphite woodhead should **never** be employed as a method of changing face angle.

Trying to redrill a hosel to create a different face angle or a more upright or flat lie angle also is not a viable option for altering lie. Though many clubmakers like to think they can professionally redrill or ream a hosel bore with accuracy, often the successes are outweighed by the failures of cracking the hosel, breaking the neck, or just the inability to make a change of much more than 1°.

When custom boring of the hosel is not an option, the very best method for changing the face angle or lie of a wooden or graphite woodhead involves making a very slight bend in the shaft right at the point between the base of the ferrule and the top of the hosel. This "trick of the trade" is old in its origin, having been used by manufacturers for years to correct errors that were made in the boring process during the head's manufacture.

Before describing the process it is very important for clubmakers to understand that making a small bend in the shaft for the purpose of changing face angle and/or lie by 2-3° will not harm the playability of the club or the shaft in any way.

Therefore, if purchasing custom bored woods is not convenient, bending the shaft at the top of the hosel is the method of choice. Shaft bending allows the most dramatic change in face angle or lie measurement, is very quick to perform and does not subject the woodhead to an involved series of touch-up steps to restore the finish.

■ METAL WOODS

To change the face angle and/or lie of a metal wood, a clubmaker must possess a keen eye and be well versed in both shaft bending and hosel bending to be able to satisfy all custom requests. If you do not own a hosel bending fixture or machine, you will still be able to perform limited face angle/lie alterations, although not within as wide of a range as would be possible with the use of a bending machine.

Face filing or sole grinding as possible methods for face angle alteration are simply not possible on stainless metal woods. Not only is the 17-4 stainless steel very hard to file or grind, stainless woods are customarily produced with a very thin face and sole wall that will not withstand material removal for the purpose of making custom face angle changes. In the case of aluminum metal woods, while face filing and/or sole grinding are feasible due to these heads' softer metal and much greater face thickness, filing/grinding is just not a realistic method for making a change.

Shaft Bending

Changing the face angle/lie of metal woods by bending the shaft just above the hosel is entirely acceptable, although there will be a limit of how much change can be made. Unlike the conventional hosel shape of a wooden or graphite woodhead, most metal woods are designed with a straight, "pencil" shaped hosel. With such a hosel configuration, no more than a 1° to 1.5° face angle/lie change through shaft bending will be possible or else the shaft will appear bent to the golfer when the club is placed in the playing position.

It is important to note that the goal of shaft bending is to change the face angle/lie while still giving the club the appearance that the shaft is **not** bent. The tapered outside shape of a wooden or graphite woodhead combined with the presence of string whipping has a much greater optical ability to "hide" a bend in the shaft than does the thin pencil hosel of a metal wood. However, if the metal wood does happen to have a tapered outside shape, it will accommodate slightly more of a face angle/lie change through shaft bending than will the pencil hosel varieties of metal woods.

Hosel Bending

The most modern method of altering the face angle and lie of stainless metal woods is through the actual bending of the hosel, following the same manner in which irons are adjusted for loft and lie. Specially-designed holding fixtures to accommodate metal woodheads are now available for use with both electric and manual bending machines to secure the heads for bending. These fixtures plus the skill of the clubmaker with the bending bar are now making it possible to bend the hosel of stainless steel woods and customize the face angle and lie of the heads.

There are a number of points for the clubmaker to consider before attempting to bend stainless metal woods. First is the hardness/bendability of the steel. Since most metal woods are investment cast from 17-4 stainless steel, and since 17-4 stainless is the hardest of all steel alloys from which clubheads are made, bending the hosel of a metal wood will require some experience. Therefore, clubmakers **must** take time to practice the techniques for bending hard steel clubheads before offering the service to golfers.

Next, the clubmaker must decide whether to use a manual or an electric bending machine. Since metal woodhead holding fixtures are available for both types of machines, the clubmaker must look at several factors before making a decision. Electric bending machines will cost from $3,000-$4,000 as compared the the $400-$1,000 range for a manual machine. Electric machines, while taking the physical effort of bending out of the hands of the clubmaker, are slower than manual machines and can still break the hosel if care is care is not taken in controlling the application of force.

Because of the tremendous force required to bend the hosel of a stainless metal wood, both types of machines can leave pressure marks on the clubhead. Because such marks are unsightly to the consumer, the clubmaker must be prepared to make padding modifications to the holding fixture of the machine in an effort to keep pressure marks at a minimum.

In the end, the decision of what type of machine to employ can be summarized. If you have hosel bending experience and need to save every minute of your time, use the manual machine. If you have limited experience in bending, are not quite as judicious with your time, are able to charge accordingly for your services and have the funds to invest, the electric machine may represent the best decision.

Finally, in offering the service of metal wood hosel bending, it is a wise choice to limit your bending to stainless metal woods. Because of material differences and their reaction to bending pressure it will be best to avoid bending cobalt steel, beryllium copper, titanium, aluminum or other exotic alloy heads. In addition, do not attempt to bend metal woods designed with a hosel shape similar to that of a wooden or graphite woodhead. Most bending bars are not shaped to conform to the tapered shape of a conventionally shaped hosel. As a result the bar can slip under application of pressure, preventing the bend and usually producing a mar on the hosel at the same time. Finally, metal woods designed with a plastic imitation whipping ferrule to cover the hosel are far easier to adjust for face angle or lie by bending the shaft rather than by bending the hosel.

Techniques of Shaft Bending to Alter Face Angle/Lie Angle

The main goal of bending the shaft to change the face angle and/or lie is such that after completion, the shaft must not appear to be bent when the club is placed in the playing position. For wooden and graphite woodheads (or some metal woods with a conventional

shaped hosel), this is relatively easy to accomplish. All of these woodhead types usually require a ferrule in the assembly process. When the shaft is bent at the point between the bottom of the ferrule and the top of the hosel, a change in the face angle or lie of 2-3° will usually not be apparent to the golfer. With this type of clubhead design, the tapered ferrule and string whipping combine to create an optical illusion that can actually hide the bend.

Because so many stainless steel metal woods are produced with a pencil shaped hosel, clubmakers are going to be very limited in the degree of change that can be made on these types of woods. With no ferrule or whipping present, a change of 2° **will** be noticed in the form of a bend in the shaft, so clubmakers must understand that with metal woods, the amount of face angle change is limited. Unlike face angle, a shaft bend to alter lie is made in a vertical plane with respect to the golfer's vision. Therefore, while a 2° lie bend is noticeable when viewed from the target line, to the golfer looking down the shaft, it is not as apparent.

When performing a shaft bend to change face angle or lie, it is best to make the alteration after the shafting epoxy has cured and the ferrule has been filed to its final shape. If a small gap occurs between the ferrule and the top of the hosel as a result of the bend, the separation can be repaired before proceeding with the rest of the assembly steps. Should the bend be made after the wood is fully completed and a ferrule to head separation occurs, the whipping will have to be removed to repair the gap, and much more time will be lost.

Clubmakers must also understand that not all golf shafts can be bent. Obviously, the graphite and other composite type shafts cannot be bent. In addition, shafts made from **very light weight steel alloys** will not easily stretch and deform enough to bend. This means that some shaft patterns such as True Temper's Extralite as well as Brunswick's UCV-304, Brunslite and Vanadium Sonic cannot be bent with any consis-

tent degree of success. Because steel alloys can vary in malleability, there is no hard and fast rule governing what shafts can and cannot be successfully bent. As a guideline, all standard weight and all medium lightweight steel shafts can easily be bent to accommodate 2-3° of face angle or lie change.

The following step-by-step illustrated procedures show how to bend the shaft to change face angle and/or lie.

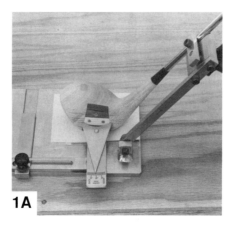

1A

STEP 1A: Measure existing face angle and decide on direction to bend as well as the amount of change to be made

Whether working with a wooden, graphite or metal woodhead, the best time to make a shaft bend to change face angle or lie is after shaft installation and the filing of the ferrule are complete. After these steps in the assembly process are complete (see Chapter 5 for a description of the assembly steps through ferrule filing) measure the face angle and/or the lie angle of the woodhead, depending which specification(s) you are going to alter. Accurate measurement will require the use of a golf club specifications measuring gauge, different models of which are available from component supply companies. To measure face angle, place the shafted woodhead in the machine's holding fixture and position the club with the center of the sole in contact with the base of the machine. Use the machine's face angle indicator to center against the insert and read the face angle in degrees open, closed or square (0°). After measuring the face angle, note your customer's request or your recommendation to determine the direction and the amount of change to make.

1B

STEP 1B: Measuring lie angle

To measure the lie angle of the woodhead, use the same specifications measuring device used to measure the face angle. Secure the shaft in the machine's holding clamp and gradually lower the clubhead down to touch the baseplate of the machine at a point directly in the center of the sole. Once the clubhead has been properly positioned, the lie angle may be read in degrees by using a protractor that is placed on the shaft or the machine's holding arm. After measuring the lie, note your customer's request or your recommendation to determine the direction and the amount of change to make.

STEP 2A: Position club in shaft bending block (to change face angle more open)

Bending the shaft at the point between the base of the ferrule and the top of the hosel will require the use of a specially-made shaft bending block. Very simple to make, the block can be fashioned from hardwood with a 1" x 1" notch cut into one side. All edges of the notch should be grooved with a half-round file and covered with small strips of leather for padding. To change the

2A

face angle more open, position the club in the block with the face pointing up, with the line between hosel and ferrule placed on the front lower edge of the notch as pictured.

2B

STEP 2B: Position club in shaft bending block (to change face angle more closed)

To bend the face angle more closed than its current specification, position the club in the notch of the block with the face pointing down with the line between hosel and ferrule placed on the front lower edge of the notch as pictured.

STEP 2C: Position club in shaft bending block (to change lie angle more upright)

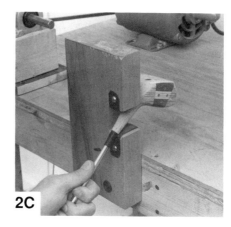

2C

To bend the lie angle more upright than its current specification, place the club in the notch of the block with the toe of the head pointing down to the floor, with the line between hosel and ferrule placed on the front lower edge of the notch as pictured.

2D

STEP 2D: Position club in shaft bending block (to change lie angle flatter)

To bend the lie more flat than its current specification, place the wood in the block with the toe pointing up, with the line between hosel and ferrule placed on the front lower edge of the notch as pictured.

■ **NOTE:** Be sure to understand what is expressed by the terms "more open, more closed, more upright and more flat" than the club's current specifications. For example, if you wish to change the face angle of a wood from 3° closed to 1° closed, the bend will make the club "more open" than its current specification, despite the fact the club will still have a closed face angle. And likewise for lie, if you wish to change the lie of a wood from 3° flat to 1° flat the bend will make the club "more upright" than its current specification, despite the fact the club will still have a flat lie angle.

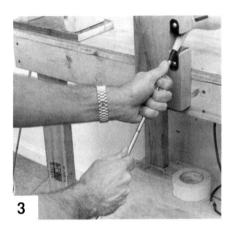

STEP 3: Position the hands on the shaft to prepare for bending

Place both hands on the shaft as pictured to prepare for making the bend. The weak hand should be just below the ferrule, while your strength hand should be positioned approximately 8-12" down from the ferrule on the shaft.

STEP 4: Push down on the shaft using a bouncing motion

Regardless of the alteration desired, the shaft should always be bent downward to take advantage of the design of the bending block. Remember that the specification change is dictated by the position of the head in the bending block; toe up = lie more flat, toe down = lie more upright, face up = face angle more open, face down = face angle more closed. To make the bend, exert a firm bouncing action on the shaft, pushing down, then letting the shaft spring back up, and then

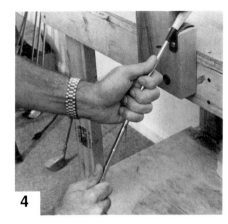

pushing back down again. This type of bouncing action of the hands on the shaft will allow you to vary the pressure necessary to create the desired degree of bend in the shaft. A 2-3° bend should only require about two or three light bouncing motions **down** on the shaft.

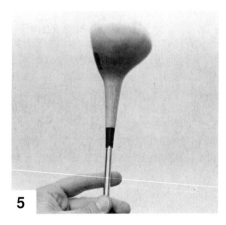

STEP 5: Check the appearance of the bend

After bouncing the shaft two or three times down against the bending block, withdraw the club and place it on the floor in the playing position. Look carefully down the shaft to the hosel to see if the shaft appears to be bent. If it appears bent, the shaft must be changed back to the point where there is no outright appearance

of a bend. To do this, simply place the club back in the bending block, with the head positioned opposite to the original way it was placed in the block. Then make the readjustment bend by lightly bouncing **down** on the shaft.

STEP 6: Measure the degree of change

After the appearance of the club has been adjusted, place the club in the measuring gauge to check the amount of change that has been made. If further adjustments are necessary, make them now, using the same bending procedures outlined before.

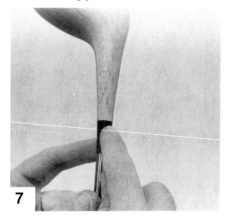

STEP 7: Check for gaps around the base of the ferrule

After completing all of the necessary bending alterations, check to see if a gap has been opened up between the ferrule and the top of the hosel. If a gap exists, also check to see if the ferrule has come loose. If the ferrule is tight and yet a gap has opened, simply dab some quick set epoxy into the gap and sand off when dry. However, if the entire ferrule is loose, work some of the epoxy under the ferrule through twisting and rotating the ferrule against the epoxy.

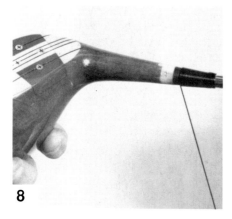

STEP 8: Install whipping
After completing the bend and any required touch-ups, install the whipping. If no whipping is required, the alteration is complete.

Important information about shaft bending: Bending the shaft to change face angle or lie is a procedure that requires "touch" on the part of the clubmaker. If the bend is too severe and results in a wrinkle or a knurl of the shaft, **the shaft must be replaced.** Therefore, it is highly recommended that clubmakers practice on old golf clubs before attempting the procedure on a new club.

The amount of change that may be made before the club takes on the appearance of being bent will be different from one club to another. How much a shaft can be bent before it appears to be crooked is dependent upon several different clubhead design factors. Still, with experience, clubmakers will soon find that shaft

bending to change face angle is a very easy procedure that can result in effective changes of 2-3°.

Soleplate Removal and Changing Swingweight

In the assembly procedures for building woods from **unfinished** persimmon or laminated maple woodheads without a weight port, it was stated if the amount of swingweight increase needed is more than 5 swingweight points, the weight should be added under the soleplate instead of down the shaft. While clubmakers would think this amount of weight addition might not occur very often, with the popularity of graphite and other very light shafts, there may be several occasions when the wood being built will require more than 5 points to bring it up to the desired final swingweight.

In clubmaking, there will also be times when the customer desires custom alterations in playing length. Because most clubhead weights are set up for assembly to standard club lengths, weight may have to be removed from (longer lengths) or added to (shorter lengths) the woodhead to be able to achieve a standard swingweight.

Therefore, if you assemble golf clubs from unfinished wooden heads, it will be important to learn how to properly remove the soleplate and make the necessary changes in swingweight. If you have decided to remove the soleplate to make swingweight changes, be sure that the shaft has been installed, cut to the desired playing length and the grip has been installed before proceeding with the swingweight adjustment. This will assure more accuracy in your work. The following steps detail the procedures for properly removing the soleplate and making weight changes on unfinished persimmon or laminated maple woodheads:

STEP 1: Record the swingweight of the club and determine the amount of weight to add/remove

With the unfinished woodhead shafted, cut to length and gripped, record the swingweight. Note the customer's desired final swingweight and determine how many swingweight points to be added or removed. Remember to allow for the additional weight increase that will come from the application of the head's finish and whipping, usually 1.5 swingweight points.

STEP 2: Secure the woodhead in the vise
Secure the woodhead in the bench vise between protective vise pads. Position the club sole up, with the bottom of the head at least 1/4" above the level of the vise jaws to allow the later use of a tool to pry the plate off the bottom of the head.

3

STEP 3: Clean out the screwheads (if necessary)
It is not likely that an unfinished woodhead will have any dirt or residue in the screwheads. However, it is a good idea to use a scriber or dental pick to check and remove any material that may prevent the screwdriver from seating properly in the screw slots.

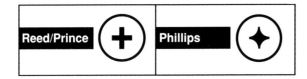

STEP 4: Determine the type of screwdriver to use
For proper screw removal it is important to use the right type of screwdriver to match the screwhead. Soleplate screws on woodheads are either the Phillips type or the Reed/Prince type. Inspect the heads of the screws on the woodhead and compare what you see to the diagrams on this page before selecting which screwdriver to use.

STEP 5A: Heat the screwheads to loosen the epoxy bond (heated screwdriver method)
Part 1 - Heat screwdriver tip
The soleplate screws in virtually all component woodheads are epoxied in place as a normal step in the manufacturing process. To loosen the epoxy bond it is

5A

necessary to apply heat to the head of the screw. If you do not have an electric screw heater in your shop, the most economical way to apply heat to the screwhead is through the use of an old Phillips or Reed/Prince screwdriver. Heat the tip of an old screwdriver in the point of the flame until it is red hot. Be sure to use an old screwdriver as the heating will remove the temper from the tip and make it unusable for removing screws.

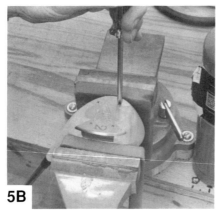

5B

STEP 5B: Heat the screwheads to loosen the epoxy bond (heated screwdriver method)
Part 2 - Place heated screwdriver on the screw
When the screwdriver is red hot insert it into the

screwhead. To loosen the epoxy using this method will require several applications of the heat, so it is recommended to repeat this step 4-5 times for each screw.

5C

STEP 5C: Heat the screwheads to loosen the epoxy bond. (electric screw heater method)
Part 1 - Place electrode tips on screw
An electric screw heater transfers heat through two electrode tips to the head of the screw. Some minor wiggling of the electrodes will be necessary to start the current, but after the tips begin to heat up, only about 7-10 seconds of heating will be required to loosen the epoxy holding each screw.

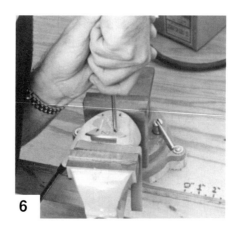

6

STEP 6: Seat screwdriver into the screwhead and check for screw tightness before removing

Regardless which method of screw heating was employed, after heating the last screw, place the proper type of screwdriver into the screwhead and push down into the screw with a moderate amount of force. With the first application of rotating pressure, look for any movement of the screwhead. If the screwhead begins to turn, increase the force of rotation with the screwdriver and slowly begin to turn the screw out. If the screw does not move, or offers resistance, remove the screwdriver and apply more heat. **Never** force the screw with more pressure. The slots of brass screws do not require much force before they can become stripped.

7

STEP 7: Heat soleplate to release the epoxy bond (propane torch method)

In addition to the screws, clubhead manufacturers also use epoxy to secure the soleplate in its recessed cavity. Never assume that the heating of the screwheads will transfer enough heat to also loosen the soleplate. If you do not have an electric screw heater, turn down the flame on your propane torch and move the tip of the flame around the center of the soleplate. **Avoid scorching the wood by keeping the flame away from the edges of the plate**. Normally, 10 seconds of heating followed by 15-20 seconds to allow the heat to soften the epoxy should be enough to loosen the soleplate.

8

STEP 8: Heat soleplate to release the epoxy bond (electric screw heater method)

To use the electric screw heater to loosen the epoxy bond holding the soleplate, place the electrode tips in the countersunk recess of each screw hole. Five seconds of heating in each hole should be sufficient to break the epoxy bond.

9

STEP 9: Remove the soleplate

To pry off the soleplate insert use the hammer to tap a strong but thin blade between the head and the plate. With each tap from the hammer the plate should begin to rise off the bottom of the head. **If the plate has not begun to release after 3-4 taps, remove the knife and apply more heat to the plate.** If the plate has not

begun to move up and out of its cavity, continued hammering will only serve to damage the head. After releasing the plate from its cavity, gently begin to pry the plate up until it is off the head.

■ **NOTE:** Depending upon the amount of heat applied, the soleplate will likely be hot so take care to avoid burning your fingers!

10

STEP 10: Record the swingweight of the club without the soleplate

From STEP 1 you will have determined how many swingweight points need to be added or removed from the head for the final swingweight, minus the 1.5 points for the weight of the finish and whipping yet to come. To prevent the needless task of repeatedly attaching and removing the soleplate to take swingweight readings during the weight addition or removal process, it is best to perform the weight change without ever having to reinstall the soleplate until the job is done. First record and note the swingweight of the club without the soleplate. Then from STEP 1 note the number of swingweight points that have to be added or removed to achieve the desired weight. Perform the addition or removal of the necessary **weight difference** and when you reinstall the plate, the final swingweight will be correct. For example, if the club's initial swingweight before removal of the soleplate was C-5 and the customer desires D-2, you would have to add

5.5 swingweight points. That 5.5 points plus the 1.5 points for the weight of the finish and whipping yet to come results in the final D-2 swingweight. After removal of the soleplate, record the swingweight reading. For example, if the club weighed B-5 without the soleplate, all you have to do is increase the weight to C-0.5 without the plate. After installation of the soleplate, application of the finish and the whipping, the club should then achieve the final D-2 swingweight.

11A

STEP 11A: Remove the necessary weight (if weight needs to be removed)

If weight needs to be removed, weigh the club without the soleplate and determine the amount of weight to remove. For weight reductions, look for the existing lead cavity under the plate and begin to drill out some of the lead. Estimate the depth and diameter to drill to achieve the necessary swingweight reduction. After drilling, check the weight of the club **without the soleplate** on your swingweight scale. If you have not achieved the necessary reduction, drill again and recheck until you have removed the proper amount of weight.

STEP 11B: Add the necessary weight (if weight needs to be added)
Part 1 - Locate the point of drilling

For weight additions, you will likely have to drill a new hole into the wood and add the weight in the form of solid lead. First inspect the area under the soleplate to

11B

determine where to drill. Weight additions should be performed as close to the center line of the head as possible so as not to adversely affect the head's center of gravity.

11C

STEP 11C: Add the necessary weight (if weight needs to be added)
Part 2 - Drill the hole for the lead

Use the following chart to determine the diameter and depth of hole to drill in the wood under the plate.

Hole Diameter	Hole Depth	Swingweight Change
1/4"	1/4"	1 sw
1/4"	1/2"	2 sw
1/4"	1"	4 sw
3/8"	1/2"	4.5 sw
3/8"	1"	9 sw
1/2"	1/2"	7 sw
1/2"	3/4"	10.5 sw
1/2"	1"	14 sw

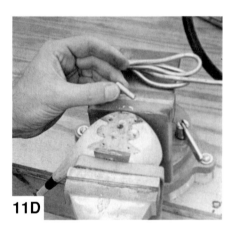

11D

STEP 11D: Add the necessary weight (if weight needs to be added) - Solid lead rod method
Part 1: Cut the lead rod

Depending on your preference, lead weight additions to the woodhead can be made by using lead rod that is snipped to desired length (weight) or through melting lead into the hole. For clubmaking, lead rod is most frequently sold in 1/4" diameter size, so if your hole size is 1/4" this will be the fastest method of lead installation to use. If the weight hole size is larger than 1/4", melt the lead into the hole to add the weight. Wire cutting tools or pliers will easily cut the lead rod, so first cut a length of rod that will correspond to the depth of the hole.

11E

STEP 11E: Add the necessary weight (if weight needs to be added) - Solid lead rod method
Part 2: Tap the lead rod into the hole
After cutting the lead rod, tap it into the hole with a small ball peen hammer. When the lead reaches the bottom of the hole, check to see that the top of the rod length is flush to the bottom surface of the wood. No epoxy need be used to secure the lead rod.

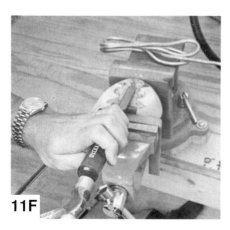

11F

STEP 11F: Add the necessary weight (if weight needs to be added) - Solid lead rod method
Part 3: Shear off the excess lead
If any of the lead rod protrudes from the hole, use a chisel to shear it off flush to the surrounding wood surface.

11G

STEP 11G: Add the necessary weight (if weight needs to be added) - Solid lead rod method
Part 4: Peen the lead to lock in place
Once the top of the lead rod is flush, lock it in the hole by driving a screwdriver point into the top of the lead. This peening action of the screwdriver on the lead will spread out the lead, thus securing it in the hole.

11H

STEP 11H: Add the necessary weight (if weight needs to be added - Melted lead method
Part 1: Melt the lead into the hole
Solid lead may be purchased from component suppliers in sheet, rod or ingot form. With the woodhead secured sole up and level in your bench vise, begin to melt lead into the hole. One way of melting the lead

into the hole is to cut sections of lead to place in an iron ladle and apply flame heat to the bottom of the ladle with a propane torch. In addition, electric ladles are also available to melt the lead. Or, you may also unwind several inches of lead rod and point the propane torch flame at the tip of the rod while holding the lead over the hole. After installation, allow 10-15 seconds for the molten lead to solidify.

11I

STEP 11I: Add the necessary weight (if weight needs to be added - Melted lead method
Part 2: Peen the lead to secure it
Once the lead has hardened, scrape, file or chisel off any excess lead from the top of the hole. Place the tip of a screwdriver on top of the lead and tap with a hammer to spread and peen the lead into the hole, thus securing it in place.

STEP 12: Temporarily install the soleplate and final check the swingweight
After checking to make sure the lead is flush with the surface of the wood, temporarily attach the soleplate. Do not turn the screws in place, rather, simply place them loosely in the screw holes. Place the club on the swingweight scale to check the accuracy of your work. If weight still needs to be added or removed to achieve the desired weight, take off the plate and complete the job. When swingweighting unfinished wooden heads, be sure to leave the swingweight 1.5 points under the

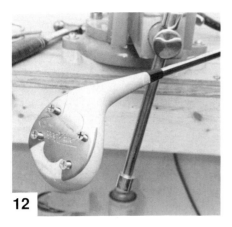

12

14

16

final desired weight to allow for the weight of the finish and whipping yet to come.

13

STEP 13: Apply epoxy to the sole plate cavity of the woodhead

The soleplate needs to be installed with epoxy to permanently secure it to the head. Place the head back in the bench vise between soft vise pads, with the sole pointing up. Using the same high shear strength epoxy used to install shafts, mix a small amount and brush a thin coating over the entire surface of the bottom of the woodhead.

STEP 14: Press down the soleplate

Press the soleplate down firmly into its cavity. The fit

will be tight, so **light tapping** with a hammer may be necessary to push the plate completely down. Expect some epoxy to ooze out from under the plate.

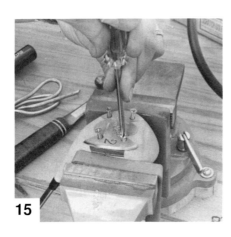

15

STEP 15: Install new screws

Even if the screws were not damaged during removal, it is a good idea to re-install the soleplate. Most woodheads will require a brass screw of #7 x 3/4" or #8 x 5/8" size, the most common being the #8 x 5/8" variety. Insert the new screws into the holes in the plate and begin to turn them down into place.

STEP 16: Tighten the screws and set the club aside to cure the epoxy

As the screws are tightened into the countersunk portion of the holes, care should be taken not to overtighten and shear off the heads. New screws will protrude from the plate after tightening, so do not expect the screws to fit flush to the surface of the plate. As the plate is squeezed into its cavity from the tightening of the screws, more epoxy will be forced out between the plate and head. Because the unfinished head will be final sanded before finishing, it is best to wipe away some but not all of this excess epoxy. Should there be any slight gaps present between plate and head, the epoxy will act as a filler, thus keeping moisture from getting into the head. However, do check and remove any epoxy that may be inside the screwhead slots.

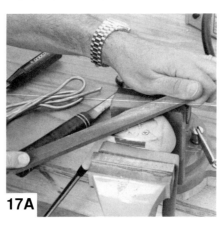

17A

STEP 17A: File or belt sand the screwheads flush to the soleplate - Filing method

After the epoxy has cured, the protruding screwheads must be sanded down flush, to the surface of the soleplate. If you do not have a small belt sander in your shop, secure the woodhead in the vise and file down the screwheads. If a medium cut file is used to speed up the process, take care not to gouge the soleplate, then finish the job with a fine cut file.

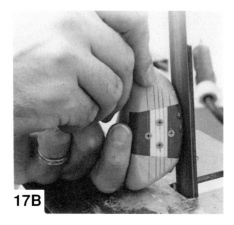
17B

STEP 17B: File or belt sand the screwheads flush to the soleplate - Belt sanding method
Part 1 - Sand off the top of the screws

The fastest way to grind the heads of the screws down to the surface of the plate is with a belt sander. Fix a medium or fine grit belt on your sander and position the head with the toe down against the work table and the soleplate against the sanding belt. Press each screwhead against the hard-backed portion of the belt sander (where the belt travels over the steel platen) and sand until the screwheads are flush to the plate.

■ **NOTE:** Always keep the surface of the soleplate parallel to the surface of the belt to prevent gouging the plate with the edge of the belt.

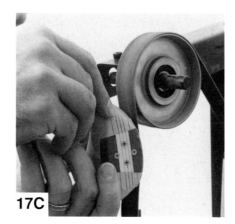
17C

STEP 17C: File or belt sand the screwheads flush to the soleplate
Belt sanding method
Part 2 - Smooth the scratches left by the belt

On most small belt sanders there will be a 6-9" section of the belt behind which there is no metal backing. Move the woodhead up to sand the entire bottom of the plate on this area of the sander. Press the head gently into the belt and the belt will deflect to conform to the exact radius of the sole, thus affording a good method for finishing off the job.

■ **NOTE:** Do not press into the belt too hard or the sander may remove wood just above and just below the soleplate.

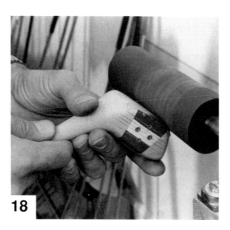
18

STEP 18: Sand soleplate on the woodhead sander

To finish the job, sand the bottom of the soleplate on a woodhead sanding machine. Use fine grit (150 to 200 grit) sandpaper to smooth out any harsh scratches left from the belt sander or the file, depending upon which method of screwhead removal was used.

■ **NOTE:** After sanding the soleplate, the job of swingweight alteration is complete and the head may be final sanded as described in Chapter 5 to prepare it for the application of finish and completion of the total assembly procedures.

Woodhead Weight Port Installation

In the task of assembling woods from component parts, it is extremely helpful for achieving accurate swingweights if a weight port is present in the head. With the tremendous variety of shaft weights, grip weights and overall custom assembly specifications that a clubmaker can encounter, having the ability to make swingweight changes through a weight port can become a real time saver. Therefore, if the woodheads do not have a weight port, it might be a wise choice to install one before the head is assembled.

For a weight port to truly be effective, the weight cavity should have the capability of receiving 8 or more swingweight points of weight (@ 15+ grams). Since small diameter set screw (1/4" or less) openings are preferred by head manufacturers, to be able to hold such an amount of weight the cavity inside the head must be larger in diameter than the set screw hole installed in the head itself.

If the head is not manufactured with a large weight port cavity beneath a small set screw opening, the only way this can be accomplished is on a head with a soleplate. Such a procedure involves removing the soleplate to drill the larger hole, then reinstalling the plate to establish the smaller weight port access hole. Therefore, the first weight port installation procedure that will be outlined in this section will be for woodheads with a soleplate. Before turning to the procedures for weight port installation into a woodhead with a soleplate, refer to the previous section in this chapter for the step-by-step procedures of removing soleplates.

Metal Wood Weight Ports
As of the early 1990s the types of woodheads with a soleplate (graphite and wood) make up little more than 20% of the total woodhead market today. Since stainless steel metal woods make up 80% of the 1990s woodhead market, it is very important for clubmakers to have weight ports on metal woods to satisfy custom swingweighting needs.

While many stainless woodheads are produced with a weight port, there still may be times when clubmakers encounter metal heads that do not. Faced with a need to swingweight stainless woods, many clubmakers wonder whether it is possible to install a set screw type weight port in a stainless metal wood.

Because metal woods do not have a removable soleplate, it is not possible to install a weight port with a large weight port cavity beneath a small set screw opening. However, it is possible to install a weight port of limited capacity, with a cavity that would be equal in diameter to the set screw opening created in the sole.

While installing such a weight port in a stainless wood is possible, it does bring with it some limitations of which clubmakers must be aware:

1. The weight capacity of a clubmaker installed weight port will not be as great as for a weight port that was engineered during the manufacture of a metal wood.

2. A much greater potential exists for the set screw to come loose in a metal wood weight port installed by a clubmaker than with a weight port that was created during the manufacture of the metal wood. A foundry created weight port has a greater thickness of the area where the set screw penetrates through the sole. This added sole thickness affords more holding power to

prevent the set screw from coming loose. When a clubmaker drills and taps threads through a metal wood sole for a set screw, the screw only has the thickness of the sole (@0.080") to provide holding threads for the screw. Even if the set screw is epoxied in place, there is still a chance the screw will come loose during the course of play.

3. On foundry engineered metal wood weight ports, the weight cavity is often an enclosed chamber welded to the underside of the sole during manufacture. This chamber keeps the granulated lead powder from interspersing with the foam that fills the interior of the head, thus preventing the possibility of a rattle inside the head. Installing a set screw weight port into a stainless woodhead by drilling and tapping through the sole leaves the clubmaker with no alternative but to pour the lead powder into a cavity made in the foam. While not a great problem, this does create the possibility for the lead powder over the course of play with the wood to dislodge some of the foam and cause a rattle.

Before beginning the weight port installation procedures, it is important to understand it is best to install the port before installation of the shaft.

■ PROCEDURES FOR WEIGHT PORT INSTALLATION INTO A WOODHEAD WITH A SOLEPLATE (GRAPHITE AND WOODEN WOODHEADS)

STEP 1: Remove the soleplate and choose the location of the weight port cavity
Follow the procedures illustrated in this chapter for removing the soleplate. Inspect the surface under the soleplate of the woodhead for a suitable location for the weight port cavity. If possible, try to locate the cavity in the back center of the head, directly in line with the center of the face insert. Take care to stay well away from screw holes as well as away from the back of the face insert to avoid running into the insert screws. If locating the port cavity in the center of the sole is not

possible, choose an area just above the center line toward the toe of the wood. Also, note the location of the stampings on the soleplate to prevent having to drill the set screw hole through any identifying logo.

STEP 2: Drill the weight cavity in the woodhead
An adequate size for a weight port cavity is 1/2" diameter by 1/2 - 3/4" deep. Make sure the location you have picked will allow such a hole size before you begin drilling. With the head secured in the vise between pads, carefully drill to the desired depth. After drilling, clean out all of the wood chips before proceeding.

3

STEP 3: Find location of set screw on the soleplate
Temporarily tap the soleplate back into its cavity on the woodhead and find the point on the plate that is directly over the weight port cavity. Use a scriber or a center punch to make a mark on the soleplate for drilling. **Always** double check the location for the set screw hole to make sure the hole is centered over the cavity. Do not reinstall the soleplate yet.

4

STEP 4: Drill the set screw hole
Installing the set screw is a two part procedure involving drilling a hole through the plate followed by tapping the threads for the screw. The most common set screw for use on wooden or graphite heads is a 10/32 size hex head screw. This size screw will require a #21 size bit to drill the hole. If you are installing a set screw of a different size be sure to check the proper pilot drill size before proceeding. To ensure proper threading take care to keep the drill bit perpendicular to the soleplate when drilling.

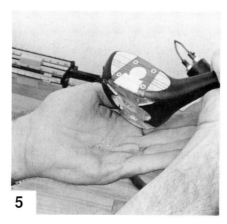

5

STEP 5: Dump out metal fragments from drilling
Pry off the soleplate, remove the head from the vise and empty out any metal fragments from the drilling that may have fallen into the weight cavity. Failure to do so could result in rattles after the plate has been re-epoxied on the head.

6

STEP 6: Insert and align the screw tap into the hole
For accurate threading of the set screw hole the tap must be perpendicular to the pilot hole. Put the 10/32 tap (or proper size if using a different size screw) into the tap wrench and place it directly on top of and into the hole. Take time to again check the alignment of the tap before proceeding.

7

STEP 7: Push and rotate the tap into the hole
Push the tap firmly into the hole and begin rotating in a clockwise direction. Continue to push down on the tap during rotation until you begin to feel the tap begin to cut threads. Once the tap has made 2-3 turns of actual cutting, you may let up on the downward pressure. While cutting threads, **always** keep the tap lined up perpendicular to the surface of the soleplate. Rocking the tap back and forth while cutting threads will result in a sloppy job and threads that will not hold the screw tight in the hole.

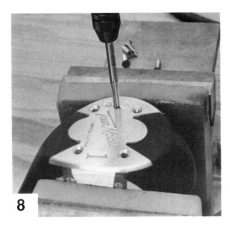

STEP 8: Reverse the tap out of the hole
Once the threads are cut all the way through the plate, reverse the tap out of the hole. Take care while removing the tap not to rock it back and forth.

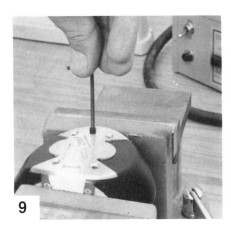

STEP 9: Test install the set screw
Place the set screw on the hex head wrench and rotate it into the hole. Turn the screw down until it is flush to the surface of the soleplate to check the fit. If the screw begins to bind very tightly, remove it and retap the threads.

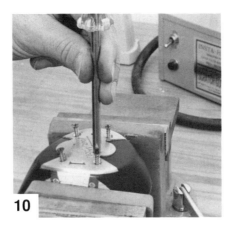

STEP 10: Reinstall the soleplate with epoxy
Refer to the section on soleplate removal in this chapter for the complete procedure of reinstalling the soleplate.

■ **NOTE:** When installing the soleplate, use very little epoxy to prevent the adhesive from oozing into the weight port cavity.

Installing String Whipping On Woodheads

One of the simplest procedures of assembly to experienced clubmakers is the installation of string whipping. However, all experienced clubmakers will undoubtedly recall that learning the procedure took some practice to get over the feeling of having "10 left thumbs." For a complete discussion, the procedures for installing string whipping that follow cover the installation of whipping both by hand and by machine.

STEP 1: Check the ferrule and the hosel for a smooth tapered surface
For the whipping to be installed perfectly, the ferrule must be correctly filed and sanded to a perfect taper and the hosel of **the woodhead must be free of "bumps"** and irregularities. Perform a visual inspection of the

neck and correct any deficiencies that are present by filing and/or light sanding.

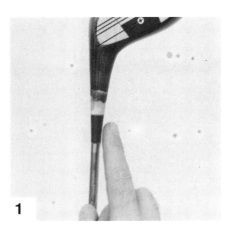

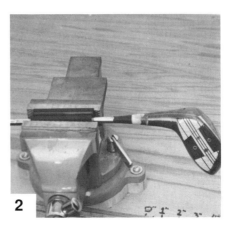

STEP 2: Place the club in the bench vise
Slip the rubber shaft clamp on the shaft, about 2-3" above the top of the ferrule. Tighten the club in the bench vise enough to prevent the clamp from slipping out of the vise yet still loose enough to allow the shaft to rotate freely inside the clamp. Position the head with the back of the hosel pointing up as pictured.

STEP 3: Attach the whipping
Lay the end of the whipping over the top of the shaft,

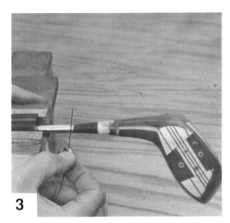

at least 1/8" above the top of the ferrule. If the ferrule is a shanked type, the whipping will be laid over the **top** of the ferrule against the lip of the ferrule.

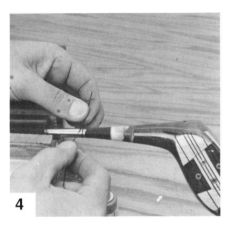

STEP 4: Begin wrapping whipping

Wrap the end of the whipping around the shaft and back on top of the shaft. Note in the picture that the end of the whipping is on the clubhead side of the continuous strand of the whipping.

STEP 5: Cinch the top of the whipping

Pull the whipping **tight** over the end strand to cinch it in place.

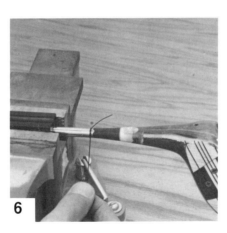

STEP 6: Prepare for continuous wrapping of the whipping

Let go of the end of the whipping but retain a **light** pressure on the string that is cinching over the end of the strand. The tension holding the string over the end of the whipping should be tight enough to keep the strand in place, but light enough to prevent pulling the whipping off the shaft. This step may require practice to prevent pulling the whipping off the shaft. Never tie a knot in the whipping to hold it in place.

■ **NOTE:** This step is much easier to accomplish using the larger .022" diameter twisted braided nylon type of string whipping.

STEP 7: Begin wrapping the whipping

Move your free hand to the woodhead and begin to rotate the head, all the while retaining the same light tension on the whipping with the other hand. In most cases, the head should be rotated in a counter clockwise direction to wrap the whipping over the end strand. After 2-3 wraps, increase the tension on the string.

STEP 8: Cut the end strand of the whipping

After 6-8 wraps over the end of the string, cut away the excess end of the string as close to the last wrap of the whipping as possible. Place a razor blade or X-acto type knife on top of the end strand and press down to make the cut. Do not press too hard or the ferrule underneath the whipping could be damaged. Always use a sharp blade for this step.

STEP 9: Continue to wrap the whipping down the hosel

After cutting away the excess string, shift the free hand back to the head and continue rotating the head to apply the whipping, this time pulling tight on the whipping as you rotate the head. Pull the whipping slightly back against the previous strand to eliminate the possibility of leaving any gaps between strands.

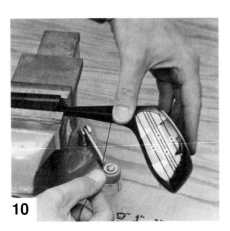

STEP 10: Prepare for tying off the whipping

As the whipping approaches the base of the hosel, lay your thumb on the side of the hosel, with one side of the thumb right against the outline of the heel corner of the face. The opposite side of the thumb will represent the point where the whipping should stop on the hosel.

STEP 11: Insert a whipping loop

A free loop of whipping or a loop puller tool is required to pull the whipping back under itself and complete the knotting. Place the loop on the back of the hosel, under the last wrap of the whipping. Keep tension on the whipping to hold the loop in place.

STEP 12: Wrap over the loop

Wrap 6-8 more turns of whipping over the top of the loop. Be aware that 3-4 wraps is not enough to hold the whipping while 10 or more will leave an unprofessional appearance.

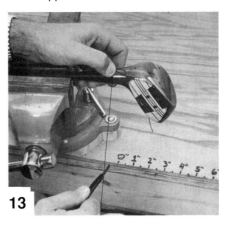

STEP 13: Cut the whipping

Hold the whipping and the loop with your thumb to keep it in place. With your free hand cut the whipping from the spool, leaving 3-4" of whipping to be inserted through the loop.

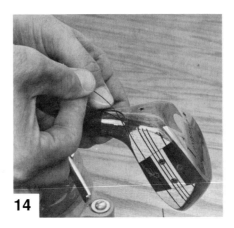

STEP 14: Insert the end of the whipping through the loop

Feed the cut end of the whipping through the loop. It does not matter whether the cut end is placed through the loop from the bottom or the top. Make sure the thumb on the opposite hand is still holding the whipping to keep it from unraveling.

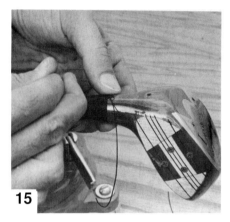

STEP 15: Pull the loop under the whipping
Keep the thumb tight on top of the whipping to prevent it from slipping. With one quick motion, pull the loop under the final strands of the whipping. With the loop will come the end of the whipping. Continue to keep the thumb in place and pull the whipping tight. When complete the underlap of string should be on the back of the hosel, not on the sides. If the underlap has slipped to one side, you can **carefully** pull it completely around the hosel until it comes back into the desired position.

STEP 16: Cut the whipping
After hand tightening of the whipping, about 3" of the strand will protrude. Use a sharp razor blade or knife to cut off the "tail" of the whipping. Take care not to cut any of the overlapping strands when removing the "tail."

STEP 17: Tap the tail down to secure in place
After cutting, use a file handle or small ball peen hammer to tap the overlapped portion of the tail of the whipping. This step will help to prevent the whipping from coming loose. Never dab polyurethane or nail polish on top of the underlap portion of the whipping as a method of holding.

■ INSTALLING WHIPPING BY MACHINE

After installing whipping a number of times by hand, clubmakers will soon discover the timesaving benefit of investing in a small whipping machine. Relatively inexpensive (less than $100), a motor powered whipping machine can pay for itself in a short time through increased efficiency in the shop.

To properly use a whipping machine, follow the same procedures outlined before for manual whipping, substituting the machine as the means of rotating the golf club. The method of starting the whipping thread by machine will be exactly the same as described in STEPS 3-8 of the hand procedures. For the first 6-8 wraps of the whipping do not activate the machine. To do so will cause the whipping to come off the shaft and ferrule. Instead, even though the club is being held in the machine, rotate the first 6-8 turns of the clubhead by hand. Only after the whipping is tight can the machine be activated to turn the head.

Once the whipping has been wrapped down the hosel to the point that you are ready to tie off, stop the machine's rotation and use the same procedures for tying off that are described in STEPS 10-17 of the hand procedure.

Ironhead Loft and Lie Alterations

The single most common clubmaking alteration performed by clubmakers on ironheads is the changing of the loft and/or the lie angles. Because lie angle is a prime determinant of shot accuracy, golfers will try to improve their games by asking clubmakers or club repairmen to customize the lie angle on their irons. Loft is also a major factor in clubfitting because it has a profound effect on a golfer's shot distance and trajectory. Because more and more players have become aware of the fact that improperly fitted loft or lie angles can affect the success they achieve with their equipment, clubmakers should develop the ability to perform these alterations.

Changing the loft and lie of an ironhead involves bending the hosel. Therefore, the most important point in bending loft and lie is the head itself; in other words how easy will the iron be to bend, and how much can it be bent? In the design of ironheads there are three factors that control the bendability of an ironhead - the hardness of the metal in the finished ironhead, the length of the hosel and the thickness of the base of the hosel.

METAL HARDNESS

As outlined in Chapter 2, ironheads are produced from a variety of different steels as well as a number of other non-ferrous metals. Despite the fact that some ironheads are manufactured through the forging process, some by die casting and many more by investment casting, the main factor that controls the bendability of an iron is its hardness or malleability. An ironhead's hardness is determined by the metal used to create the iron combined with any heat treatment process that may or may not be applied to the head after forming. Hardness can be measured in a number of different ways, but the most common reference is a procedure called the Rockwell hardness test.

To test a clubhead's Rockwell measurement, a special device is used to press a small metal ball into different surfaces of the head. The force required to depress the metal ball to a specified depth is recorded by the machine and referenced to a letter and number scale whose comparative readings are much the same as those on a golf club swingweight scale; the lower the letter and number, the softer and more bendable will be the iron. For example, most forged carbon steel ironheads have a Rockwell hardness reading around B-75. Ironheads that are investment cast from 4-31 type stainless steel which has been subjected to a standard heat treatment will exhibit a Rockwell reading around C-20. Finally, ironheads that are cast from 17-4 stainless followed by heat treating will have a Rockwell reading of around C-35, indicating that this type of steel is ranked among the hardest of all materials used in the manufacture of ironheads. As a general rule of thumb, the higher the Rockwell hardness reading, the more difficult the head will be to bend.

One of the most common misconceptions about bending the loft and lie on ironheads concerns the difference in bendability between forged and investment cast heads. All too many clubmakers mistakenly cling to the belief that all investment cast clubheads either cannot be bent or will be so difficult to bend so as to prevent changing loft and lie. The reason this misconception exists is because the majority of all investment casting is done using harder grades of stainless steel. Because the predominant types of stainless steel used to make clubheads are harder than the carbon steel most commonly used in the forging process, the mistaken assumption has come about that cast clubs cannot be bent.

In truth, the processes of casting or forging have virtually nothing to do with the ability of an ironhead to be altered for loft and lie. Some types of stainless steel that are used in investment casting ironheads are in fact, softer and more bendable than some carbon steels used in forging. In addition, a variety of heat treatment/hardening procedures are available to ironhead makers, another factor that has a tremendous effect on bendability. Therefore, as a first step to determining the bendability of any ironhead, it is advised to check with your clubhead supplier for advice on comparative hardness of the clubheads.

IRONHEAD DESIGN

The other factors that control the bendability of ironheads are found in the actual shape and style design characteristics of the head. The shorter the hosel, the more difficult the clubhead will be to bend. In the late 1980s, Callaway Golf Company introduced the concept of a very short hosel on its S2H2 ironhead design. This "no hosel" design leaves virtually no hosel for the loft and lie machine's bending bar to hold on to. As a result, unless the clubhead design has enough hosel length for the bar to grasp, or until bending bars are redesigned to apply the bending force from **inside** the hosel, very short hosel ironhead designs will be virtually impossible to alter for loft and lie.

Another clubhead design factor that controls the degree of bendability concerns the thickness of the area at the base of the hosel. When properly performed, the alteration of an ironhead's loft or lie should elicit a bend in the clubhead just below the base of the hosel, in the area of the head referred to as the crotch. The thinner crotch, the more bendable will be the iron because there will be less metal to resist the bend.

As a rule most ironhead designs with offset will possess a much thinner crotch than the more traditional muscleback, non-offset design heads. This is not intentional, but is rather a characteristic of the design requirements necessary to incorporate offset into the clubhead. To create offset on an ironhead, the design must incorporate a curve of the metal that connects the hosel to the blade. As a result, heavily offset ironheads will usually have a thin crotch area.

On the other hand, in the design of a non-offset ironhead, the hosel flows directly down into the topline and leading edge of the blade. This feature usually creates a design characteristic of a thicker crotch and with it, more resistance to bending. If the hardness ratings of an offset and a non-offset iron design are identical, then the offset design will be easier to bend by virtue of the thinner crotch area. Therefore, when evaluating the bendability of an ironhead for loft and lie alteration purposes, check not only the hardness of the metal, but the design of the base of the ironhead's hosel as well.

DEGREE OF BENDABILITY

A product of the hardness of an ironhead is the degree to which the head can be bent. While the softer the metal, the more the ironhead can be bent, as a general rule, it is not recommended that clubmakers perform a change in loft or lie of more than 3°. As students of clubhead design principles are aware, the proper bending of lie will not change any other design characteristic of the head. But when loft is changed by bending, the specifications of sole angle and the hosel offset of the ironhead will both be altered. Depending on the ironhead's original specifications, a loft change of 3° could change the sole angle and offset to a point that may adversely affect the playability of the head.

Limiting the amount of change of the lie angle is not as

critical as it is for the loft. Unlike loft, when lie is changed no other critical design specification is altered. However, when lie is altered by more than 3° the hosel begins to take on a less desirable curved appearance, a point that could affect a golfer's aesthetic perception of the iron. Bending chrome-plated ironheads by more than 2° is also not recommended due the possible result of cracking the chrome plating on the head. The brighteners that are often incorporated within the electroplating chemistry to assure a brilliance of shine usually have the effect of increasing the brittleness of the plating. Hence when a chrome plated head is bent, the stretching of the metal can cause the chrome to give way and peel off the head in the area of the bend. When such a situation occurs, there is no alternative but to have the head replated.

As was stated, the hardness of an ironhead will be the chief factor in determining how far the head can be bent. Forged carbon steel heads or 18-8 type stainless heads in the Rockwell B-75 to B-90 measurement range can easily be bent 3° or more as individual needs dictate. With practice, 4-31 type stainless heads can be bent 2°, but the method of bending should be altered by the clubmaker to achieve this amount of change (methods of bending will be covered later in this section). Ironheads cast from 17-4 or heads hardened to the higher C-ranges on the Rockwell scale will be very difficult to bend more than 2°.

Fortunately, the vast majority of ironheads available to component clubmakers are produced from carbon steels or stainless steels that are changeable by 2-3°. Still, it must be stressed that clubhead design variations and assorted heat treating methods may create differences in hardness for the same type of metal. In other words, it is often not possible to approach all 4-31 stainless heads with the assumption they will all bend the same. Therefore, because of these small but important differences, it is very important for clubmakers offering loft and lie alterations to acquire experience and develop a precise sense of "feel" in bending ironheads.

■ PROCEDURES OF IRONHEAD LIE AND LOFT ALTERATION

The actual procedure for altering the loft and lie of an ironhead consists of three parts:

1. **Measuring the ironhead's loft and lie**
2. **Bending the ironhead**
3. **Remeasuring the ironhead to check the bend**

1. Measuring Ironhead Lie and Loft

Before any alteration is made, it is necessary to accurately measure the ironhead's existing specifications for lie and loft as a base for comparison. To record the lie and loft specifications, it is necessary to have a specially made gauge for securing the head in what will be referred to as the "playing position." Most loft and lie bending machines that incorporate measuring with bending are not accurate and should not be used for measurement purposes. As of this edition of *The Modern Guide to Golf Clubmaking*, the only loft and lie machine that can accurately record loft and lie specifications while the clubhead is being held in the position for bending is the Steel Club Angle Machine, manufactured by Centre Golf of Centerville, Ohio. If this particular machine is not being used, the only way that lie and loft can be accurately recorded is by using a separate gauge that will hold the clubhead in the playing position to allow the measurement of loft and lie.

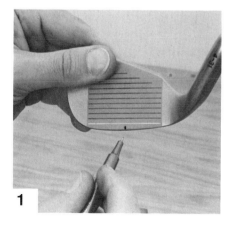

STEP 1: Mark the leading edge of the ironhead at a point one-half the scoring line width

For accurate measurement the head will have to be positioned in the measuring gauge with the sole of the ironhead touching the base plate of the gauge at a point just below one-half of the scoring line width. Measure the length of the bottom score line of the ironhead and make a small pencil mark on the leading edge of the head at precisely the point that is one-half the width of the score line.

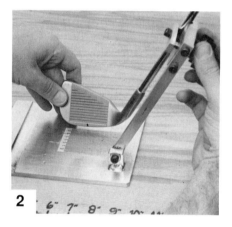

STEP 2: Insert a shaft tip into the hosel and fixture the head in the gauge

Lie and loft measurements can easily be made on the component head before it is assembled. To perform the measurements, insert a cut-off shaft tip section into the hosel and place the club in the machine's holding fixture.

STEP 3: Position the ironhead on the gauge

Carefully lower the ironhead down so the mark representing one-half of the scoring line width makes contact with the base of the machine. Square the blade so that the face isn't open or closed. Alignment lines may be provided on the base of the gauge to assist in squaring the face. It is extremely important that the head be positioned accurately in the gauge to ensure the accuracy of measuring the lie and loft! Small mistakes in positioning can cause as much as a 1-2° error, so if

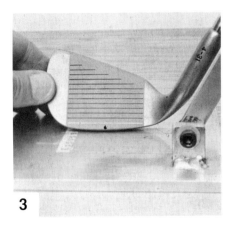

3

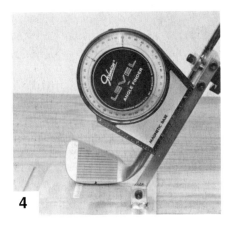

4

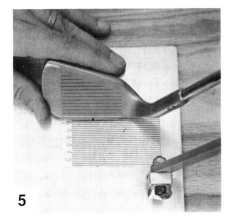

5

you are not proficient in measuring loft and lie, be sure to gain instruction and practice before relying on your measurements.

STEP 4: Measure the lie angle
The lie is defined as the angle in degrees between the center of the bore and the sole line. After correctly positioning the head in the measuring device, a magnetic protractor can be placed on the arm of the holding device or the shaft to read the lie angle directly in degrees. While placing the protractor on the machine or shaft, take care not to move the head.

STEP 5: Measure the loft
Loft is defined as the angle in degrees between the

center of the bore and the face plane. With the clubhead correctly positioned in the measuring gauge, place the protractor flat on the plane of the face, taking care not to shift the head open or closed. If you use a magnetic protractor be sure to place the vertical side (the side without the magnet) flat on the face to be able to read loft directly. If you place the horizontal side (with the magnet) on the face you will have to subtract the reading obtained from 90° to record the real loft.

2. Bending the Ironhead
The prime requirements for successfully bending loft and lie are a good bending machine, a bending bar that will securely grasp the hosel of the ironhead and a good working knowledge of ironhead materials to know what technique for bending should be used to make the change. Within the clubmaking industry quite a number of loft and lie bending machines are currently available. In making your choice, be sure to select a machine that can hold all types of ironhead designs without making indentations on the heads from the clamping fixture. Because the bending bar is the tool used to apply force to the hosel to make the bend, it too should be able to hold the hosel securely without leaving marks on the hosel.

Electric motor powered bending machines are available in addition to manual machines. While an electric bending machine takes the physical effort out of the

job, they are expensive and do take longer to perform the alterations. Whether the decrease of physical effort is worth the increase in cost and time is a choice that clubmakers must make for themselves.

For bending clubheads manually, it is important for clubmakers to realize that two different techniques for physically applying the force for bending should be used, one for the softer metal heads and another for the harder metal heads. Because utilizing two different techniques is very important, both will be described within the following procedures for bending:

> **Example:**
>
> **Measured Lie**
> **– Desired Lie**
> **Amount of Change**
>
> **Measured Loft**
> **– Desired Loft**
> **Amount of Change**

1

STEP 1: Note the amount of change to be made for both lie and loft
With the measurements for both the lie and loft recorded, compare them to the desired specifications to determine the amount of bending change that must be made.

STEP 2: Secure the ironhead in the clamping fixture of the machine
Follow the instructions of the bending machine manufacturer to properly secure the head. Before inserting the head into any machine it is a good idea to apply strips of lead tape on the topline and around the hosel or any other area of the head that will receive direct clamping pressure from the machine. This will help

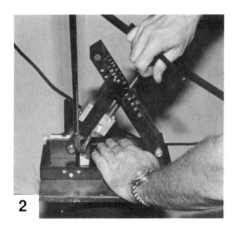

2

keep the heads looking new and as free of marks as possible after the bend has been made.

STEP 3A: Technique for bending soft metal ironheads

When a bend is made on a soft metal ironhead, you will actually be able to feel the hosel stretch and move as force is applied with the bending bar. To make a bend on a soft metal head, attach the bending bar low on the hosel and start the bend with a moderate amount of pressure on the bar, steadily increasing the force until you begin to feel the movement of the hosel. At the point you begin to feel the hosel move, immediately decrease the force applied to the bending bar. Another way to describe the application of force to the bar for softer metal heads is shown through Graph 3A.

The line on the graph represents a slowly increasing level of pressure on the bending bar that increases with force applied, peaks when the bending of the hosel is felt and then decreases after the bend is complete. For a better understanding of the manner in which the bending force should be applied to a soft metal head, contrast this description with the Graph 3B, describing the proper force technique for hard metal heads.

STEP 3B: Technique for bending hard metal ironheads

Unlike soft metal heads, the actual bend on a hard metal head cannot usually be felt as it can with soft metal clubheads. Therefore, if the soft metal bending technique is used to alter the lie and loft of a hard metal head, clubmakers could make the mistake of increasing the force more and more, all the time waiting to feel the bend until the head actually breaks. Instead, the method to use for bending hard metal heads is to apply a series of short, hard jolts of force with the bending bar to the hosel to literally "shock" the head into bending. Obviously this will require some practice, because the bend is rarely felt on harder metal heads when it occurs. The best way to describe the application of force to the bar for harder metal heads is through Graph 3B.

The line on the graph represents a series of sharp jolts on the bending bar that quickly rise in force, peak and then fall in force. For better understanding of the type of bending pressure that should be applied to a hard metal head, contrast this description with the graph provided previously to describe the proper force technique for soft metal heads.

STEP 4: Position the bending bar on the hosel, first for altering lie

If a change of the lie is required, perform this alteration first. To properly bend the lie angle without affecting the loft, position the bar directly on the side of the hosel with the bar directly in line with the sole. The bend for lie and loft alteration should be made low on the hosel.

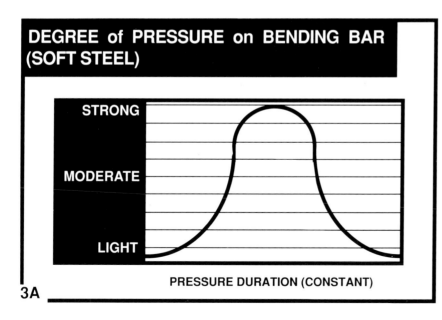

3A

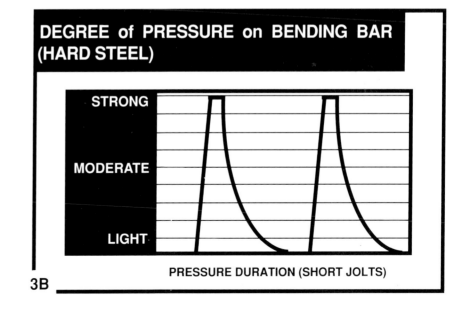

3B

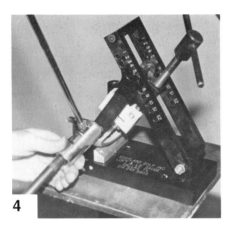

4

5A

Therefore, attach the bar as low as possible on the hosel.

STEP 5: Determine which direction to move the bar to change lie

If the clubhead must be bent more upright (Photo 5A) the bar will be pulled upward, moving in a direction that is **directly in line with the shaft.** If a flatter lie is called for, the bar should be pushed down (Photo 5B), also **in line with the shaft**. Imagine that the shaft and the bending bar form two legs of a right triangle. For accurate lie bending move the bar so that this imaginary triangle moves in the same plane, up for a more upright lie and down for a flatter lie.

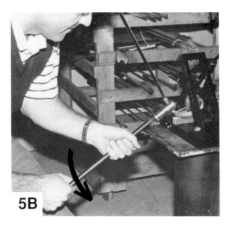

5B

STEP 6: Shift the position of the bar to alter the loft

Once the lie angle bend has been successfully made, shift the bending bar around into position for altering loft. The proper bar position for bending loft is to clamp the bar low on the hosel with the shaft of the bending bar perpendicular to the face/leading edge.

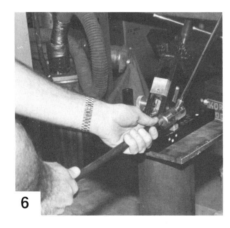

6

7A

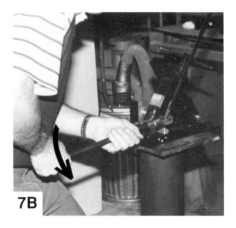

7B

STEP 7: Determine which direction to move the bar to change loft

If you wish to decrease the loft angle, thus making the clubhead "stronger" (Photo 7A), the bar will be pulled straight up. If an increase in loft is called for, thus making the head "weaker," the bar should be pushed straight down (Photo 7B).

STEP 8: Use the proper force technique for bending loft

Review the methods for bending soft and hard metal ironheads that were described previously in this section. Use the same techniques as necessary to perform the actual loft bend. Remember: soft metal, steadily

**Refer to Graphs 3A
and 3B
on Page 315**

8

9

increasing force; hard metal, a series of firm jolts.

3. Remeasuring the Ironhead to Check the Bend

STEP 1: Check the bends that have been made and readjust (if necessary)
After performing the required bend(s), remove the clubhead from the loft and lie machine and remeasure the specifications (again, if the machine being used is the Steel Club Angle Machine, the actual loft and lie can be read while the head is fixtured in the machine). If the head needs further bending to achieve the desired lie or loft angles, reinstall it into the machine and make the necessary adjustments.

■ LOFT AND LIE ALTERATION - A FINAL WORD

In trying to instruct clubmakers in an area that is dependent on the development of a certain degree of "feel," words cannot totally describe what has to happen to achieve success. The bending of loft and lie is very much this way, because so much of any clubmaker's success and skill in bending is dependent on experience and a keen sense of feel.

The most important points to note from the previous procedures for bending are the two different techniques for applying the bending force to the ironhead. It is strongly advised that all clubmakers practice, practice and practice again before ever attempting to alter the loft and lie on a new set of irons. In addition, the best techniques for actually bending ironheads are a total waste if the clubmaker cannot accurately measure the loft and lie specifications of each head. In this area too, practice and become confident with being able to measure these specs accurately. To achieve skill in this area, it is recommended to have an experienced clubmaker measure a practice set of heads and write down the loft and lie angles for your reference. During your practice, if you can measure the heads and come up with the same readings, you can be reasonably assured that your techniques are sufficient for achieving accurate measurements.

The Relationship of Swingweight and Balance Point

While swingweight is by far the most popular method of establishing a form of club to club matching, what is actually being measured and expressed is often confusing to clubmakers and golfers alike. Because clubmakers for decades have agreed that some form of club to club matching was needed to assure a consistency of some type of feel within a set of golf clubs, through the work of Robert Adams of Massachusetts and later,

Kenneth Smith of Kansas City, the golf industry has adopted the use of the current 14" fulcrum (Lorythmic/Prorythmic) swingweight scale and its letter/number designations.

But what does it all mean, and more important, what is being expressed within any particular measurement? At best swingweight is defined as an expression of the weight distribution in a golf club about a fixed point, with the said fixed point being the fulcrum point of the swingweight scale. Under recent study, the swingweight scale does more than measure the clubhead's mass compared to the weight of the rest of the golf club. Any golf club can be moved back and forth across one's finger until it achieves a point at which the golf club remains steady in a horizontal position. Such a position indicates that there is an equal amount of weight lying on either side of the point of balance.

To better describe this position and express the weight distribution of the golf club requires the introduction of a fixed point of reference. Such a fixed point is required because balance point can change from club to club. Since it is the balance point that needs to be compared from club to club, there needs to be a fixed point from which comparisons can be made. In the golf industry, the fixed point of 14" measured down from the grip is designated as the fulcrum point, or point of reference.

Referring back to the golf club that is balancing on your finger, if you move the golf club so that your finger is located 14" down from the butt end of the club, you will first notice that the club no longer balances. In order for the club to become balanced on your finger at this 14" point, weight will have to be moved toward the butt end of the golf club. As such mass gets closer to the butt end of the golf club, once again a point of balance can be achieved with the club resting horizontally on your finger.

Such mass that is shifted away from the fulcrum point can be used to describe what is called in physical terms, a moment. The distance from the center of gravity of the sliding weight to the fulcrum of the scale times the mass of the slide weight will yield a measurement that can be expressed in inch/ounces. And on a swing-weight scale such a relationship can be computed to establish the statement that 1 swingweight point is equivalent to 1.75 inch/ounces. Expressed differently to illustrate how weight in one part of a golf club can affect the swingweight scale, 1 ounce of weight that is 1.75" from the fulcrum point would have the same effect on the scale as 1 gram of weight being 49.61" from the fulcrum point.

In the section of this chapter dealing with pre-calculating swingweight it was approximated that 1 swing-weight point was equivalent to 2 grams of headweight. Using close calculations that incorporate balance point it becomes apparent that the approximation of 2 g=1 sw point is true for only one playing length, that being a 38.75" golf club. Due to the effect of weight in relationship to the fulcrum point of the scale, less than 2 grams is required to make 1 swingweight point when clubs are longer than 38.75" and more than 2 grams is required to make 1 swingweight point when clubs are shorter than 38.75".

But headweight is only one source of the mass that must all be combined on a scale to build a golf club and be accountable in the calculation of swingweight. In addition to the headweight, factors such as the grip weight, shaft weight, grip tape, epoxy, ferrule, backscrew and whipping all must be included before swingweight can accurately be understood. Clubmakers may decry the effect that components other than the head, grip and shaft will have on swingweight. While each "small" component on its own may be relatively insignificant in its effect on swingweight, combined as they often are on a golf club, they may account for a significant amount of weight.

Average Mass of Minor Components for Clubmaking

2" Double Sided Grip Tape (10" strip)	2.8g	0.10 oz
2" Build up Tape (10" strip)	1.4g	0.05 oz
Epoxy	3+ g[1]	0.11+ oz
Ferrule	1 - 3g	0.03 - 0.12 oz
Backscrew	1.5g	0.05 oz
Whipping	1.5g	0.05 oz

[1]Epoxy weight is equal to the minimum required to adequately bond the shaft to the head. Overuse of epoxy (as is often the habit of clubmakers) will significantly affect the weight.

Using the balance point determination, swingweight can be calculated by using the following formula:

Swingweight = Static Weight x Balance point of the club down from the butt minus 14" (or)
[Inch/Ounces] = [Ounces] x [Inches]

The swingweight formulation is derived from the summation of all the distances from the balance point of each component from the scale fulcrum point, then multiplied by the mass of each component. Therefore, by understanding balance point relationships, swingweight can be estimated prior to the assembly of the golf club. To make the calculations as accurate as possible the 1/8" thickness of the rubber grip cap must be allowed when determining the balance point location of the shaft.

To determine the balance points of the various component parts, set up a piece of angle iron on a level surface. Balance each component on top of the edge of the angle iron and mark each component's point of balance. Use a ruler to record the balance point dimension for each part of the golf club. The distance of each component's balance point to the 14" fulcrum point of the swing-weight scale must then be determined. For example, the grip has a balance point 5" down from the butt end.

This balance point is therefore 9" from the fulcrum point of the scale (14" - 5" = 9"). After determining all balance point data and the weight of each component part, the swingweight of the golf club can be calculated. To illustrate how all the balance points of the all the components used to make a golf club can be applied to estimate swingweight, study the following example:

Q: A 200 gram metal wood Driver with square hosel and a 1.5" bottom of bore to back edge of heel is to be built with an Aldila HM-40 R-flex shaft and M60 rubber Victory grip. The Driver will be built to 43" playing length and the grip will be installed to +1/32" oversize condition (for reference, two strips of build-up tape plus one strip of 2-way grip tape will be used to achieve the grip size). What will be the swingweight of this golf club with no extra headweight added?

A: Calculate the balance point and weight of each component part used in the assembly.

Component	Weight	Balance Point From 14" Fulcrum
Head	200g / 7.05 oz	29"
Shaft (cut)	86.7g / 3.06 oz	4 1/2" (Bal Pt is 18 3/8" from butt)[1]
Grip	50.8g / 1.79 oz	10 1/2" (Bal Pt is 3 1/2" from butt)
2" 2-way grip tape	2.8g / 0.10 oz	9" (Bal Pt is 5" from butt)
2" Build up tape (2)	2.8g / 0.10 oz	9" (Bal Pt is 5" from butt)
Ferrule	2.0g / 0.07 oz	25 3/4"
Epoxy	3.0g / 0.11 oz	27"

[1] 1/8" is added to the cut shaft balance point to allow for the thickness of the grip cap.

To calculate swingweight multiply each component's mass in ounces times each component's distance from its balance point to the scale fulcrum point and apply to the following formula:

Head + Shaft + Ferrule + Epoxy - Grip/Grip Tape = swingweight calculation in inch/ounces

Head	(7.05)	x	(29)	= 204.45
Shaft	(3.06)	x	(4.5)	= 13.78
Ferrule	(0.07)	x	(25.75)	= 1.80
Epoxy	(0.11)	x	(27)	= 2.97
Total				223.00
Grip	(1.79)	x	(10.5)	= 18.80
Grip Tape	(0.10)	x	(9)	= 0.90
Build-up Tape	(0.10)	x	(9)	= 0.90
Total				20.60

223.00 - 20.60 = 202.40 inch/ounces

From previous inch/ounce balance point research done in clubmaking it has been determined that a D-0 equivalent is 213.50 inch/ounces (see *Golf Club Design, Fitting, Alteration and Repair* by Ralph Maltby, ©GolfWorks 1982). By comparing the calculations used in the example to the D-0 inch/ounce equivalent, the following conclusions can be made.

Example:
213.50 in/oz - 202.40 in/oz = 11.10 in/oz
1.75 in/oz = 1 swingweight point
11.10 in/oz = 6.34 swingweight points less than D-0

Hence the club will have a swingweight of C-3.66.

To calculate precisely how much weight will be required to increase the swingweight of the golf club to D-0, first understand that we are working within the scope of all golf club component balance points. Since the weight that must be added to increase the swingweight will be introduced into the clubhead, the calculation must incorporate the clubhead's balance point. Therefore, the distance of the clubhead's balance point to the swingweight scale fulcrum (29") must be divided by the inch/ounces required to achieve D-0 (11.10 in/oz) to reveal the ounces that must be added to the head

to make the D-0 swingweight.

29" balance point of clubhead ÷ 11.10 in/oz = 0.383 oz (10.85 grams)

Since we discovered that the example Driver needed 6.34 swingweight points to achieve D-0 (D-0 - C-3.66 = 6.34 points) you can now see that indeed 2 grams does not equal 1 swingweight point for this golf club.

At best a somewhat complicated look at the overall picture, using balance points of each golf club component is one way to accurately predict swingweight and in the process, take each of the variables concerned into account. This information is offered not in the expectation that you will adopt this procedure in your workshop, but strictly for information sake. In the world of clubmaking, the goal of pre-calculating swingweight before assembly is not so much to gauge exactly what the swingweight will be as much as it is to gain an idea of whether you will encounter swingweight problems during the assembly. Still this data concerning the relationship of golf club balance points is presented for your use as you see fit and to add to your clubmaking knowledge.

Changing Bore Diameter and Hosel Beveling

Once a procedure that was frequently performed in clubmaking, today thanks to the ever increasing popularity of parallel tip diameter shafts and parallel bore clubheads, changing the hosel bore diameter is a procedure that is not as frequently required in the workshop. When component clubheads first became available to clubmakers, most woodheads were manufactured with a .277" tapered bore and most ironheads with a .355" tapered bore. Manufacturers chose this selection of bore diameter for two major reasons. First, taper tip shafts were the predominant shafts of choice in the industry and second, should a larger shaft diameter need to be used, it was considered a simple procedure to simply enlarge the bore to match the shaft

tip diameter.

Today, .335" parallel tip diameter wood shafts and .370" parallel tip diameter iron shafts account for well over half of the shaft sales in the entire golf industry. With such acceptance, virtually all new shaft designs are introduced in parallel tip form. Even the older shaft designs once made only in taper tip version are being made in parallel tip form. As a result there is virtually no shaft design in all of the golf industry that cannot be purchased in parallel tip form.

With the increase in popularity of parallel tip diameter shaft designs, so too have many of the clubhead manufacturers changed their standard bore diameters from tapered to parallel. In turn this has eliminated many of the small problems that occurred in trying to force fit taper tip shafts into tapered bore hosels. As a result, most clubmakers today do not have to perform full bore diameter changes to accommodate shaft installation.

Still, there are situations in assembling golf clubs that will require clubmakers to alter the bore diameter of the clubheads with which they work. For one, some component companies still make their head designs with tapered bore diameters in an effort to offer a full selection of shaft installation possibilities to clubmakers. Should a clubmaker purchase a clubhead with a tapered bore and wish to install a larger tapered shaft or a parallel tip diameter shaft, the clubhead bore will have to be altered to fit the shaft.

Most frequently though, clubmakers today will have to use the techniques of bore alteration to correct for slight errors in shaft manufacture or to accommodate the installation of one of the modern composite shafts into a wooden or composite woodhead. Both the tip diameter of all shafts as well as the bore diameter of all clubheads are subject to plus/minus tolerances in their manufacture. Steel shafts are produced to a ±0.002" tip diameter, composite shafts to a ±0.004" tip diameter and investment cast clubheads to a ±0.0015" bore diameter. Because it is a fact that clubmakers will encounter shafts that are on the plus side of their tolerance and hosel bores that are on the minus side of their tolerance, it is also a fact that not all shafts will slide easily to the bottom of the clubhead's bore.

When a shaft will not fit easily into the hosel, the clubmaker will have to increase the bore diameter to meet the diameter of the shaft. While there are some circumstances in which the shaft tip can be sanded ever so slightly smaller to accommodate the fit, as a general rule clubmakers should be instructed to always change the bore and never sand down the shaft tip. Gauging the amount of shaft tip reduction through sanding is virtually impossible to control. Removing too much of the shaft tip's diameter can result in a broken shaft when the club is put into play. In contrast, clubhead hosels are manufactured with enough thickness to easily withstand major changes in bore diameter.

Another problem that is often encountered in clubmaking concerns the installation of modern graphite/composite shafts into wooden and graphite/composite woodheads. Wooden and graphite/composite woodheads are designed with much longer hosels than are today's metal woods or irons. Along with the longer hosel, they are also manufactured with much deeper bore depth than are the metal clubheads. Such a deep bore design means that the hosel of a wooden or graphite/composite woodhead will sleeve a much greater length of the shaft's tip section than will the metal wood or iron.

Because the parallel portion of the tip of a graphite/composite shaft varies in length from one shaft design to another, it is quite common for the depth of the bore to be greater than the length of the parallel portion of the shaft tip. When this happens, the shaft cannot be inserted to bottom out in the clubhead bore. Clubmakers who are not aware of this possibility all too often learn of the problem when the customer returns the club in two pieces, the result of the neck fracturing because it is not fully seated into the hosel.

The procedures for changing bore diameter on clubheads will be divided into two parts, one outlining the steps for wooden and graphite/composite type woodheads and the other to illustrate the techniques for metal clubheads (woods and irons). The difference in material hardness between the clubhead types dictates that different procedures be used to alter the bore diameter. In the procedures reference will be made to two types of drilling techniques, step drilling and drilling to the bottom.

Step drilling will always mean the first bit will be drilled to the full bottom of the bore, the second bit will be drilled to two-thirds of the depth of the bore and the last bit will be drilled to one-third of the bore depth. Drilling to the bottom of the bore will reference drilling the single listed bit or all the bits listed completely to the bottom of the bore.

In the illustrated procedures to follow, bore changing procedures will show the change to a parallel bore, .335" for woods and .370" for irons. For bore changes other than parallel refer to the following chart to determine the proper drill bit diameters and drilling techniques to use:

Bore Changing Procedures

Current Bore	Desired Bore	Bit(s) to Use [In order]	Technique
.277"	.294"	19/64"; 5/16"; 21/64" or .294" tapered reamer	Step drill Drill to bottom
.277"	.335" Steel	19/64"; 5/16"; 21/64"; "R"	Drill to bottom
.277"	.335" Graphite	19/64"; 5/16"; 21/64"; "R" 11/32"	Drill to bottom with first four bits; then step drill the 11/32"
.294"	.335" Steel	5/16"; 21/64"; "R"	Drill to bottom
.294"	.335" Graphite	5/16"; 21/64"; "R"; 11/32"	Drill to bottom with first four bits; then step drill the 11/32"
.335"	.335" Steel	"R"	Drill to bottom
.335"	.335" Graphite	"R"; 11/32"	Drill to bottom with "R"; then step drill the 11/32"

Special Notes:
1. The "R" drill bit is a special letter size bit that is available from machine tool supply companies or from selected clubmaking suppliers. Having a .339" diameter, the "R" bit is the only correct drill bit to use for .335" parallel tip shafts.
2. In the chart, reference is made for changing a bore to a .335" Steel or a .335" Graphite bore. Use the .335" Steel bore procedure when installing any steel shaft of .335" tip diameter or any .335" steel shaft that will not fit due to the ± tolerance problem that was mentioned before.
3. Use the .335" Graphite procedure when install a .335" parallel tip graphite shaft to ensure that the shaft completely bottoms out in the hosel bore.

■ CHANGING BORE DIAMETER WOODEN AND GRAPHITE/ COMPOSITE WOODHEADS

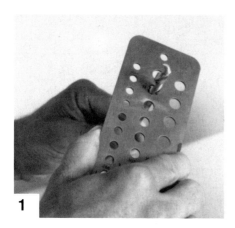

1

STEP 1: Determine the drill bit(s) to use

The goal of accurate bore alteration is to change the bore diameter without affecting the face angle or lie. To accurately change bore diameter will require the proper selection of drill bit(s), with the major point being not to enlarge the bore by too much, too soon. Use the previous chart to select the correct drill bits and drilling procedure for the bore you need. Always use multiple drills to increase a bore size from .277" to .335" or from .294" to .335". Enlarging the hosel a little bit at a time instead of using the "R" bit in a single drilling operation will ensure that the face angle and lie are not changed.

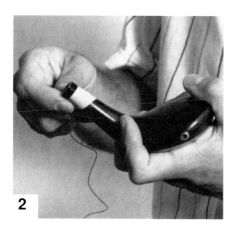

2

STEP 2: Wrap hosel for protection

The bore thickness at the top of a wooden or graphite hosel is thin and will often crack during the drilling procedures. To prevent any cracks from extending down the hosel, or in fact, to prevent a section of the hosel from completely breaking away, it is wise to wrap the hosel with tape and whipping. Cut off a 2-3' long piece of string whipping and wrap it around the top one-third of the hosel. Without tying it off, wrap over the whipping with tape to hold it in place.

■ **NOTE:** Do not be alarmed when the top 1/2" or so of the hosel develops a crack from the bore drilling. This is customary, will not harm the head and will in fact be repaired sufficiently when the shaft is installed with epoxy.

3-1

STEP 3: Drill the hosel - Hand drill method
Part 1 - Secure the head in the vise

Two methods are widely used to drill the hosel. For shops that do not have the luxury of having extra electric motors, using a variable speed, electric hand drill will perform the job properly. To start the hand drill method, secure the woodhead in the bench vise between pads with the hosel pointing up.

STEP 3: Drill the hosel - Hand drill method
Part 2 - Drill with the first bit

Select the first drill bit needed and secure it in the

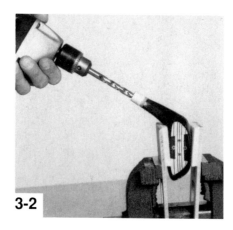

3-2

electric hand drill. Start the bit rotating and drill to the required depth. Always start the drill rotating before entering the hosel to keep cracking and chipping of the hosel at a minimum. Once the bit begins to move down the hosel, increase the speed of bit rotation and push the drill to the bottom of the bore. Do not worry about over-deepening the bore as it is very easy to feel when the bit reaches the bottom. Keep the bit rotating as the bit is withdrawn.

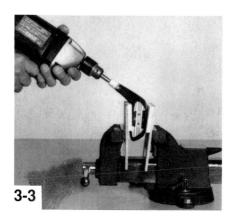

3-3

STEP 3: Drill the hosel - Hand drill method
Part 3 - Drill with the remaining bits

If successive bits are needed to achieve the desired bore, change to the next size required and complete the drilling. Always be careful when step drilling to be sure the correct depth is achieved. Remember - for three step drills, the first one goes all the way to the bottom of the bore, the second one down two-thirds of the bore depth and the last one down one-third of the bore depth. For accurate step drilling, use drill stops on the bits or wrap a piece of tape around the bit at the point of correct penetration.

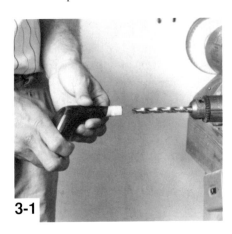

3-1

STEP 3 - Drill the hosel - Electric motor method
Part 1 - Secure the first bit and position the head for drilling
Larger shops are advised to use a bench mounted 1725 rpm, 1/3 hp electric motor with a drill chuck attached to the motor shaft to perform the drilling operations. When setting up a motor for such jobs, be sure the correct rotation of the shaft is achieved (counterclockwise as you **face** the motor shaft). Select the first drill bit required and secure it in the electric motor's drill chuck. Grasp the woodhead with both hands as pictured. Keep the hands away from the bottom of the woodhead. Should the drill bit unexpectedly penetrate through the bottom of the head this will prevent injury.

STEP 3 - Drill the hosel - Electric motor method
Part 2 - Drill with the first bit
Switch on the motor before you begin drilling. Grasp the head very firm and push it slowly onto the drill bit. Electric motor mounted drill bits tend to "grab" as they drill and you will feel as if the head is being pulled by

3-2

the bit toward the motor. Therefore, hang onto the head firmly when the hosel is pushed on to the bit. Continue drilling to the bottom of the bore and withdraw the head while the motor remains on.

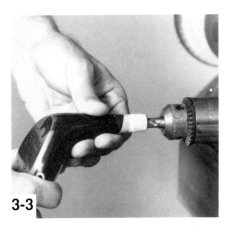

3-3

STEP 3 - Drill the hosel - Electric motor method
Part 3 - Drill with the remaining bits
If successive bits are needed to achieve the desired bore, change to the next size required and complete the drilling. Always be careful when step drilling to be sure the correct depth is achieved. Remember - for three step drills, the first one goes all the way to the bottom of the bore, the second one down two-thirds of the bore depth and the last one down one-third of the bore depth. For accurate step drilling, use drill stops on

the bits or wrap a piece of tape around the bit at the point of correct penetration.

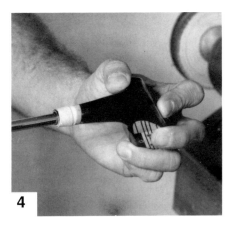

4

STEP 4 - Dump out particles and check bore size
After completing all steps of drilling, dump out all particles from the hosel bore. Select the shaft to be installed and insert into the bore to check the bore size. If the shaft does not fit, redrill as necessary. If after several attempts the shaft still does not fit, there is a chance you may have to drill with the next larger size drill bit. When drilling softer materials like wood or graphite, the speed of drilling can create enough heat that the hosel is actually pushed outward from the bit instead of actually drilled. In particular this can happen if the drill bits being used are dull and worn. When the bore is correct, remove the tape and whipping from the hosel.

■ CHANGING BORE DIAMETER METAL WOODHEADS, IRON-HEADS AND PUTTERHEADS

An important point to note when changing the bore size of metal clubheads is to **never** use the electric motor method that was described for use with wooden and composite woodheads. The motor speed is far too fast for drilling metal hosels and failure to heed this warning can result in serious injury. The rule of thumb is to use the hand drill or a drill press only for metal clubheads.

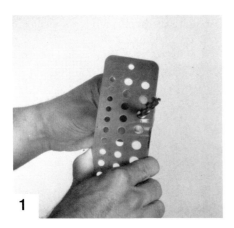

1

STEP 1: Determine the drill bit(s) to use

The goal of accurate bore alteration is to change only the bore diameter without affecting the straightness of the bore. To accurately change bore diameter will require the proper selection of drill bit(s), with the major point being not to enlarge the bore by too much, too soon. Use the previous chart to select the correct drill bits and drilling procedure for the bore you need. Always use multiple drills to increase a bore size from .277" to .335" or from .294" to .335". Boring a little bit at a time instead of using only the "R" bit will ensure that the bore remains straight.

2-1

STEP 2: Drill the hosel - Hand drill method
Part 1 - Secure the head in the vise

Two methods are widely used to drill the hosel. For shops that do not have the luxury of having a drill press and hosel boring vise, a variable speed, electric hand drill with reversing capability will perform the job properly. To start the hand drill method, secure the head in the bench vise between pads (soft pads for woods and brass or aluminum pads for irons and putters) with the hosel pointing up.

2-2

STEP 2: Drill the hosel - Hand drill method
Part 2 - Drill with the first bit

Select the first drill bit needed and secure it in the electric hand drill. Squeeze cutting oil inside the hosel and on the drill bit to facilitate drilling the metal and to keep the bit temperatures low. Start the bit rotating with medium slow speed and drill to the required depth. Always start the drill rotating before entering the hosel. Once the bit begins to drill down the hosel, increase the speed of bit rotation and push the drill to the bottom of the bore. If the bit binds up during drilling, stop, reverse out the bit and start over. Do not be discouraged when the drill bit binds as this is a common occurrence. Once the bottom of the bore is reached, reverse the rotation of the bit with the drill as it is withdrawn.

STEP 2: Drill the hosel - Hand drill method
Part 3 - Drill with the remaining bits

If successive bits are needed to achieve the desired

2-3

bore, change to the next size required and complete the drilling. Because metal woods, irons and putters are all classified as short bore depth clubheads, there will probably never be a situation in which you have to step drill the hosel. Therefore, successive drilling of metal hosels will always be made to the bottom of the bore. In all cases if the bit begins to smoke, apply more cutting oil.

2-1

STEP 2 - Drill the hosel - Drill press method
Part 1 - Secure the first bit and position the head for drilling

Larger shops will be advised to use a drill press with a hosel boring vise to perform the drilling operations. When selecting a drill press for such jobs, be sure the motor is at least 1/3 to 1/2 hp and the press has the capability of achieving a slower rotation speed of @350-700 rpm. Select the first drill bit required and secure it in the drill chuck. Tighten the head in the boring vise and mount the vise on the drill press work table. Position the vise and the hosel directly under the drill bit. Check position by rotating the drill spindle up and down to make sure the bit is centered in the bore. Secure the boring vise on the work table with at least two C-clamps.

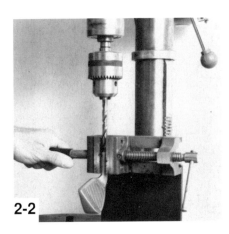

2-2

STEP 2: Drill the hosel
Drill press method
Part 2 - Drill with the first bit
Squeeze cutting oil inside the hosel and on the drill bit. Start the bit rotating at medium-slow speed and begin drilling to the required depth. Always start the drill rotating before entering the hosel. If the bit binds up during drilling, stop the press, reverse out the bit by hand and start over. Once the bottom of the bore is reached, reverse the spindle travel and withdraw the bit.

STEP 2 - Drill the hosel
Drill press method
Part 3 - Drill with the remaining bits
If successive bits are needed to achieve the desired bore, change to the next size required and complete the drilling. Each time a bit is changed take care to realign

2-3

the bit with the bore. Because metal woods, irons and putters are all classified as short bore depth clubheads, there will probably never be a situation in which you have to step drill the hosel. Therefore, successive drilling of metal hosels will always be made to the bottom of the bore. In all cases if the bit begins to smoke, apply more cutting oil.

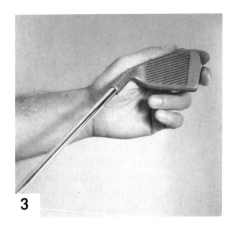

3

STEP 3 - Dump out particles and check bore size
After completing all steps of drilling, remove the head from the vise and dump out all particles from the hosel bore. Select the shaft to be installed and insert into the bore to check the bore size. If the shaft does not fit, redrill as necessary. If after several attempts the shaft still does not fit, switch to a fresh drill bit as drilling

metal hosels can quickly wear out high-speed steel drill bits.

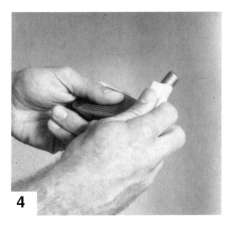

4

STEP 4 - Clean the bore
Because of the use of cutting oil, the hosel bore will have to be flushed out and cleaned with acetone or a suitable solvent before proceeding with shaft installation. Failure to properly clean will result in epoxy failure.

■ BEVELING HOSELS FOR GRAPHITE SHAFT INSTALLATION

Whenever a graphite/composite shaft is installed into a metal clubhead, the top of the hosel must be beveled. Fiber material shafts can be susceptible to fracture if a cushion of epoxy is not created at the top of the hosel to help absorb the shock of impact. During impact, metal hosels do not yield or absorb the shock of impact as do wooden and graphite hosels. This coupled with a sharp edge on the top of the hosel can create enough stress to break the shaft.

If any clubhead being built with a graphite/composite shaft is not properly beveled during its manufacture, the clubmaker will have to perform this step before shaft installation. Before the procedures for hosel beveling are illustrated, be sure to note that hosel beveling need only be performed on metal woodheads and ironheads. Wooden or graphite woodheads as well as putters do not need to be beveled as these clubhead types do not impart the same severe degree of stress on the shaft as do the metal clubheads.

If a clubhead is beveled properly, it will not need a beveled ferrule to ensure shaft integrity. While many shaft manufacturers advise the use of beveled ferrules, their use alone will not prevent shaft fracture. The key point to preventing composite shaft fracture is, and will remain, proper beveling of the hosel.

1-1

STEP 1: Bevel the hosel - Hand drill method
Part 1 - Secure the head in the vise
Two methods are widely used to bevel the hosel. For shops that do not have the luxury of having extra electric motors, use a variable speed, electric hand drill to perform the job. To start the hand drill method, secure the woodhead in the bench vise between pads with the hosel facing you.

STEP 1: Bevel the hosel - Hand drill method
Part 2 - Begin beveling
Select a 20° high speed steel rotary file and secure it in the electric hand drill. Start the bit rotating and push into the hosel firmly with the cutter. Once the bit begins to cut the top inside edges of the hosel increase the speed of bit rotation and push the drill to bevel at least 1/16" to 1/8" down the hosel.

1-2

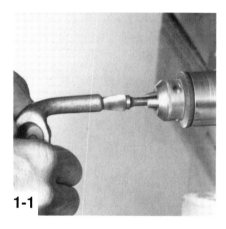

1-1

STEP 1 - Bevel the hosel - Electric motor method
Part 1 - Secure the first bit and position the head for drilling
Larger shops will be advised to use a bench mounted 1,725 rpm, 1/3 hp electric motor with a drill chuck attached to the motor shaft to perform the beveling operations. An electric motor is completely safe for beveling hosels because unlike a drill bit, the cutter does not have a chance of binding up inside the hosel. When setting up a motor for such jobs, be sure the correct rotation of the shaft is achieved (counterclockwise as you **face** the motor shaft). Select the 20° cutting bit and secure it in the electric motor's drill chuck. Grasp the clubhead with both hands as pictured.

1-2

STEP 1 - Bevel the hosel
Electric motor method
Part 2 - Begin beveling
Switch on the motor, grasp the head very firm and push it slowly on to the beveling cutter. Hang on to the head firmly when the hosel is pushed on to the cutter. Cut the bevel to a depth of 1/16" to 1/8" down the bore.

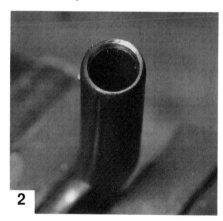

2

STEP 2 - Dump out particles and check beveling depth
After completing the beveling, dump out any particles that may be in the hosel bore. Inspect the bevel with a shaft inserted into the bore to make sure an adequate ring of space exists between the inner edge of the hosel and the outside of the shaft. To assure the proper cushion of epoxy after shaft installation, the bevel should be at least 1/16" to 1/8" deep inside the hosel.

Index

Shaft Index

Index for Shaft Trimming and Installation Charts by Shaft Pattern or Model

Shaft Code	Shaft Name	Chart	Page
ADVANCED COMPOSITE TECHNOLOGIES - PARALLEL TIP GRAPHITE SHAFTS			
ACTivator	all woods and flexes	Y	106
TourStik	all woods and flexes	Y	106
ALDILA - PARALLEL TIP GRAPHITE SHAFTS			
HM-55	all woods and irons and flexes	Z	107
HM-40	all woods and flexes	Z	107
HM-40	all irons and flexes	BB	108
HM-40 Low Flex	all woods and flexes	AA	108
HM-40 Low Flex	all irons and flexes	CC	109
HM-30	all woods and iron and flexes	Z	107
HM-30 Ladies Superlite	all woods and irons and flexes	Z	107
HM-30 Superlite	all woods and irons and flexes	Z	107
Questar	all woods and flexes	AA	108
Questar	all irons and flexes	CC	109

Shaft Code	Shaft Name	Chart	Page
Low Torque	all woods (individual flexes)	AA	108
Low Torque	all irons (individual flexes)	CC	109
Low Torque 45" AL	Combination A&L woods	FF	110
Low Torque 45" RF	Combination R&S woods	FF	110
Low Torque 41" AL	Combination A&L irons	EE	110
Low Torque 41" RS	Combination R&S irons	EE	110
Low Torque 39" AL	Combination A&L irons	DD	109
Low Torque 39" RS	Combination R&S irons	DD	109
Receptor	all woods	Z	107
Alda VIII	all woods	Z	107
GLT	all woods	Z	107
ALDILA - TAPER TIP GRAPHITE SHAFTS			
Low Torque Woods	all flexes	GG, O	111, 96
Low Torque Irons	all flexes	GG	111
ALLOY 2000 - PARALLEL TIP GRAPHITE SHAFTS			
Alloy 2000 Woods	all flexes	EE	110
APOLLO WOODS - PARALLEL TIP STEEL SHAFTS			
1720	Masterflex R	H	90
1722	Masterflex S	H	90
1724	Masterflex X	H	90
1890	AP44 Elite R	E	88
1892	AP44 Elite S	E	88
1083	AP44 R/S	A	85
1588	Torsion Matched Mark II R/S	A	85
1760	Matchflex AR	E	88
1762	Matchflex R	E	88
1764	Matchflex RS	E	88
1766	Matchflex S	E	88
1369	Spectre A/L	B	86
1513	Spectre R/S	A	85
1498	Shadow R/S	A	85
1785	Lady Shadow	E	88
1584	Senior Shadow	E	88
1700	Acculite R	I	91
1702	Acculite S	I	91
1497	AP46 L	E	88
1153	AP46 R	E	88
1499	AP83 L	E	88
1075	AP83 R	E	88

Shaft Code	Shaft Name	Chart	Page
7596WRS	Precision Phoenix R/S	C	87

BRUNSWICK WOODS - PARALLEL TIP GRAPHITE SHAFTS

WFMPC	Fibermatch (all frequencies)	KK	115

BRUNSWICK IRONS - PARALLEL TIP STEEL SHAFTS

IFM	Precision FM (all frequencies)	I	113, 114
IFML	Prcesion FM Lite (all frequencies)	I	113, 114
8656IAL	Precision Microtaper A/L	Q	98
8676IRS	Precision Microtaper R/S	P	98
7556IAL	Precision Phoenix A/L	Q	98
7576IRS	Precision Phoenix R/S	P	98
7856IAL	Precision Propel II A/L	Q	98
7876IRS	Precision Propel II R/S	P	98
6169IR	UCV-304 R	R	99
6179IS	UCV-304 S	R	99
2823IL	Super Champion L	R	99
I2863IR	Super Champion R	R	99
2223IL	Champion L	R	99
2263IR	Champion R	R	99

BRUNSWICK IRONS - PARALLEL TIP GRAPHITE SHAFTS

FMPC	Fibermatch (all frequencies)	KK	115

BRUNSWICK WOODS - TAPER TIP STEEL SHAFTS

WFM	Precision FM (all frequencies)	JJ	114
WFML	Precision FM Lite (all frequencies)	JJ	114
7268WR	Precision Phoenix R	L, M, N	94, 95
7278WS	Precision Phoenix S	L, M, N	94, 95
6529WL	UCV-304 L	L, M, N	94, 95
6569WR	UCV-304 R	L, M, N	94, 95
6579WS	UCV-304 S	L, M, N	94, 95
2623WL	Super Champion L	L, M, N	94, 95
2663WR	Super Champion R	L, M, N	94, 95

BRUNSWICK IRONS - TAPER TIP STEEL SHAFTS

IFM	Precision FM (all frequencies)	JJ	114
IFML	Precision FM Lite (all frequencies)	JJ	114
7268I	Precision Phoenix R	W, X	104-106
7278I	Precision Phoenix S	W, X	104-106
6529I	UCV-304 L	W, X	104-106

Shaft Code	Shaft Name	Chart	Page
6569IR	UCV-304 R	W, X	104-106
6579IS	UCV-304 S	W, X	104-106
2623IL	Super Champion L	W, X	104-106
2663IR	Super Champion R	W, X	104-106

CARBON FIBER PRODUCTS - PARALLEL TIP GRAPHITE SHAFTS

HMW series	Novus CFP57 woods all flexes	HH	111
HMI series	Novus CFP57 irons all flexes	HH	111
SMW series	Novus II woods all flexes	HH	111
SMI series	Novus II irons all flexes	HH	111
ACW series	Novus All Carbon woods all flexes	HH	111
ACI series	Novus All Carbon irons all flexes	HH	111

DYNACRAFT WOODS - PARALLEL TIP STEEL SHAFTS

USWRS	Dyna-Tech Standard R/S	F	89
UCWRS	Dyna-Tech Classic R/S	F	89

DYNACRAFT IRONS - PARALLEL TIP STEEL SHAFTS

USIRS	Dyna-Tech Standard R/S	S	100
UCIRS	Dyna-Tech Classic R/S	S	100

EASTON COMPOSITES - PARALLEL TIP COMPOSITE SHAFTS

HP-100L	Women's HP-100 woods, irons	LL	116
HP-100M	Men's HP-100 woods, irons all flexes	LL	116
MP-200L	Women's MP-200L woods all flexes	LL	116
MP-200M	Men's MP-200 woods all flexes	LL	116
MP-300M	Men's MP-300 woods and irons	LL	116
MP-300P	Pro MP-300 X woods	LL	116

FENWICK - PARALLEL TIP GRAPHITE SHAFTS

World Class	all woods and irons and flexes	MM	116

FENWICK - TAPER TIP GRAPHITE SHAFTS

World Class	all woods and flexes	PP, O	96
World Class	all irons and flexes	MM	116

FIBER SPEED - PARALLEL TIP COMPOSITE SHAFTS

FS-100W	Fiber Speed flexible wood	NN	117
FS-100I	Fiber Speed flexible irons	NN	117
FS-200W	Fiber Speed medium wood	NN	117
FS-200I	Fiber Speed medium irons	NN	117
FS-300W	Fiber Speed firm wood	NN	117

Shaft Code	Shaft Name	Chart	Page
UBGTWXL	Black Gold Tour X Low Flex	E	88
UCBHWL	Black Gold L	E	88
UCBHWR	Black Gold R	E	88
UCBHWS	Black Gold S	E	88
UCBHWX	Black Gold X	E	88
UCMHWL	Modulus EV40 L	E	88
UCMHWR	Modulus EV40 R	E	88
UCMHWS	Modulus EV40 S	E	88
UCMHWX	Modulus EV40 X	E	88
UVWL	Command L	E	88
UVWR	Command R	E	88
UVWS	Command S	E	88
UEI7WL	EI-70 L	E	88
UEI7WR	EI-70 R	E	88
UEI7WS	EI-70 S	E	88

TRUE TEMPER IRONS - PARALLEL TIP STEEL IRON SHAFTS

Shaft Code	Shaft Name	Chart	Page
UDGIR	Dynamic Gold R	R	99
UDGIS	Dynamic Gold S	R	99
UDGIX	Dynamic Gold X	R	99
UDIAL	Dynamic A/L	Q	98
UDIR	Dynamic R	R	99
UDIC	Dynamic R/S	P	98
UDICO	Dynamic R/S Overfit	P	98
UDIS	Dynamic S	R	99
UDIX	Dynamic X	R	99
UJIC	Jet Step R/S	P	98
UJICO	Jet Step R/S Overfit	P	98
UPIC	Pro Fit R/S	P	98
UPICO	Pro Fit R/S Overfit	P	98
U2LIAL	TT Lite A/L	Q	98
UTTLIC	TT Lite R/S	P	98
UGPIL	Gold Plus L	R	99
UGPIR	Gold Plus R	R	99
UGPIS	Gold Plus S	R	99
UTFFIL	Flex Flow L	V	102
UTFFIA	Flex Flow A	V	102
UTFFIR	Flex Flow R	V	102
UTFFIS	Flex Flow S	V	102
URIL	Comet L	R	99
URIR	Comet R	R	99
U3IL	Century L	R	99

Shaft Code	Shaft Name	Chart	Page
U3I	Century R	R	99

TRUE TEMPER IRONS - PARALLEL TIP GRAPHITE SHAFTS

Shaft Code	Shaft Name	Chart	Page
UCBHIL	Black Gold L	R	99
UCBHIR	Black Gold R	R	99
UCBHIS	Black Gold S	R	99
UCBHIX	Black Gold X	R	99
UEI7L	EI-70 L	R	99
UEI7R	EI-70 R	R	99
UEI7S	EI-70 S	R	99
UCMHIL	Modulus EV40 L	R	99
UCMHIR	Modulus EV40 R	R	99
UCMHIS	Modulus EV40 S	R	99
UCMHIX	Modulus EV40 X	R	99
UVIL	Command L	R	99
UVIR	Command R	R	99
UVIS	Command S	R	99

TRUE TEMPER WOODS - TAPER TIP STEEL SHAFTS

Shaft Code	Shaft Name	Chart	Page
DGWR	Dynamic Gold R	L, M, N	94, 95
DGWS	Dynamic Gold S	L, M, N	94, 95
DGWX	Dynamic Gold X	L, M, N	94, 95
DWA	Dynamic A	L, M, N	94, 95
DWT	Dynamic R	L, M, N	94, 95
DWS	Dynamic S	L, M, N	94, 95
DWX	Dynamic X	L, M, N	94, 95
JTWR	Jet Step R	L, M, N	94, 95
JTWS	Jet Step S	L, M, N	94, 95
PFWL	Pro Fit L	L, M, N	94, 95
PFWA	Pro Fit A	L, M, N	94, 95
PFWR	Pro Fit R	L, M, N	94, 95
PFWS	Pro Fit S	L, M, N	94, 95
2LWL	TT Lite L	L, M, N	94, 95
2LWR	TT Lite R	L, M, N	94, 95
2LWS	TT Lite S	L, M, N	94, 95
GPWR	Gold Plus R	L, M, N	94, 95
GPWS	Gold Plus S	L, M, N	94, 95
GPWX	Gold Plus X	L, M, N	94, 95
TFFWL	Flex Flow L	L, M, N	94, 95
TFFWA	Flex Flow A	L, M, N	94, 95
TFFWR	Flex Flow R	L, M, N	94, 95
TFFWS	Flex Flow S	L, M, N	94, 95

STANDARD LENGTH SPECIFICATIONS

Club	Men's Traditional Standard	Men's Modern Standard*	Ladies Standard	Petite Ladies Standard
1-wood	43"	43"	42"	41 1/2"
2-wood	42 1/2"	42 1/2"	41 1/2"	41"
3-wood	42"	42"	41"	40 1/2"
4-wood	41 1/2"	41 1/2"	40 1/2"	40"
5-wood	41"	41"	40"	39 1/2"
6-wood	40 1/2"	40 1/2"	39 1/2"	39"
7-wood	40"	40"	39"	38 1/2"
1-iron	39"	39 1/2"	38 1/2"	38"
2-iron	38 1/2"	39"	38"	37 1/2"
3-iron	38"	38 1/2"	37 1/2"	37"
4-iron	37 1/2"	38"	37"	36 1/2"
5-iron	37"	37 1/2"	36 1/2"	36"
6-iron	36 1/2"	37"	36"	35 1/2"
7-iron	36"	36 1/2"	35 1/2"	35"
8-iron	35 1/2"	36"	35"	34 1/2"
9-iron	35"	35 1/2"	34 1/2"	34"
PW	35"	35 1/2"	34 1/2"	34"
SW	35"	35 1/2"	34 1/2"	34"
UW	35"	35 1/2"	34 1/2"	34"

* Men's Modern Standard is the recognized standard length among clubmakers today.

The above standard length tables are provided for your reference only. Golf club manufacturers are not bound by such measurements for the production of clubs and are free to establish their own standards.

STANDARD LOFT SPECIFICATIONS

Club	MEN'S			LADIES		
	Weak	Standard	Strong	Weak	Standard	Strong
1-wood	12°	11°	10°	13°	12°	11°
2-wood	14°	13°	12°	15°	14°	13°
3-wood	17°	16°	15°	18°	17°	16°
4-wood	20°	19°	18°	21°	20°	19°
5-wood	23°	22°	21°	24°	23°	22°
6-wood	26°	25°	24°	27°	26°	25°
7-wood	29°	28°	27°	30°	29°	28°
1-iron	18°	17°	16°	—	—	—
2-iron	21°	20°	19°	22°	21°	20°
3-iron	25°	24°	23°	26°	25°	24°
4-iron	29°	28°	27°	30°	29°	28°
5-iron	33°	32°	31°	34°	33°	32°
6-iron	37°	36°	35°	38°	37°	36°
7-iron	41°	40°	39°	42°	41°	40°
8-iron	45°	44°	43°	46°	45°	44°
9-iron	49°	48°	47°	50°	49°	48°
PW	53°	52°	51°	54°	53°	52°
SW	57°	56°	55°	58°	57°	56°
UW	61°	60°	59°	62°	61°	60°

The above table of standard loft specifications is considered to be golf industry standards for reference only. Golf club manufacturers are not bound by such measurements for the production of their clubs or heads and are free to establish their own standard specifications.

STANDARD LIE SPECIFICATIONS

Club	MEN'S			LADIES		
	Flat	Standard	Upright	Flat	Standard	Upright
1-wood	53°	55°	57°	51°	53°	55°
2-wood	53.5°	55.5°	57.5°	51.5°	53.5°	55.5°
3-wood	54°	56°	58°	52°	54°	56°
4-wood	54.5°	56.5°	58.5°	52.5°	54.5°	56.5°
5-wood	55°	57°	59°	53°	55°	57°
6-wood	55.5°	57.5°	59.5°	53.5°	55.5°	57.5°
7-wood	56°	58°	60°	54°	56°	58°
1-iron	54°	56°	58°	—	—	—
2-iron	55°	57°	59°	53°	55°	57°
3-iron	56°	58°	60°	54°	56°	58°
4-iron	57°	59°	61°	55°	57°	59°
5-iron	58°	60°	62°	56°	58°	60°
6-iron	59°	61°	63°	57°	59°	61°
7-iron	60°	62°	64°	58°	60°	62°
8-iron	61°	63°	65°	59°	61°	63°
9-iron	62°	64°	66°	60°	62°	64°
PW	62°	64°	66°	60°	62°	64°
SW	62°	64°	66°	60°	62°	64°
UW	62°	64°	66°	60°	62°	64°

The above table of standard lie specifications is considered to be golf industry standards for reference only. Golf club manufacturers are not bound by such measurements for the production of their clubs or heads and are free to establish their own standard specifications.

STANDARD HEADWEIGHT SPECIFICATIONS

Club	Standard	For 1/2" Longer	For 1/2" Shorter
1-wood	198g	191g	205g
2-wood	203g	196g	210g
3-wood	208g	201g	215g
4-wood	213g	206g	220g
5-wood	218g	211g	225g
6-wood	223g	216g	230g
7-wood	228g	221g	235g
1-iron	230g	223g	237g
2-iron	237g	230g	244g
3-iron	244g	237g	251g
4-iron	251g	244g	258g
5-iron	258g	251g	265g
6-iron	265g	258g	272g
7-iron	272g	265g	279g
8-iron	279g	272g	286g
9-iron	286g	279g	293g
PW	293g	286g	300g
SW	305g	298g	312g
UW	298g	291g	305g

The above table of standard headweight specifications is considered to be golf industry standards for reference only. Golf club manufacturers are not bound by such measurements for the production of their clubs or heads and are free to establish their own standard specifications.